Praise for *No I in Team*

"*No I in Team* pulls back the curtain on the inner workings of Canadian party politics, revealing how loyalty, message discipline, and branding shape the lives of parliamentarians. This is a timely and provocative account of how political parties manage their members – and what happens when those members push back."

Stephen Azzi, Professor of Political Management, Carleton University

"Alex Marland, Jared Wesley, and Mireille Lalancette document in *No I in Team* the ongoing creep of party discipline into the actions of Canadian elected representatives, with a keen focus on the range of forces that incentivize conformity. It will be essential reading for those interested in how Canadian political parties and representatives operate, especially in the digital era with an ever-expanding range of communication tools and strategies."

Kelly Blidook, Associate Professor of Political Science, Memorial University of Newfoundland

"*No I in Team* exposes the costs of 'unity' in Canadian politics. Taking readers well beyond the concept of party discipline, Alex Marland, Jared Wesley, and Mireille Lalancette explain why some politicians break ranks, or make the painful decision to switch teams – even when it means the end of their political career. This book is essential reading for anyone interested in loyalty, dissent, and betrayal in political parties and legislative politics."

Rob Currie-Wood, Assistant Professor of Political Science, Mount Royal University and author of *Renegotiating the Bargain: The Formation of Power-Sharing Arrangements within Canadian Political Parties*

"In an environment of heightened partisan pressures and social media scrutiny, *No I in Team* attempts to account for why certain politicians step outside of the bounds of party discipline, resigning their seats, occasionally sitting as independents, or going so far as crossing the floor. In essence, it argues that in order to understand the inner workings of party loyalty in Canada, one needs also to understand what leads some elected officials to abandon their parties."

Joanna Everitt, Professor of Political Science, University of New Brunswick (Saint John) and former President, Canadian Political Science Association

"*No I in Team* pulls back the curtain on one of the most hidden dimensions of Canadian politics: party loyalty. Drawing on extensive research and written in an accessible style, the authors reveal how the unwritten 'loyalty agreement' between party leaders and MPs has undergone profound changes over several decades. To confront the rise of hyperpartisanship and centralized party control, the book offers a practical roadmap for strengthening political parties and parliaments that will interest a wide audience. *No I in Team* is essential reading for anyone seeking to understand how Canadian politics *really* works and how it can be improved – beyond the headlines and behind closed caucus doors."

Tracey Raney, Professor of Politics & Public Administration, Toronto Metropolitan University

"In *No I in Team*, Alex Marland, Jared Wesley, and Mireille Lalancette take on a serious problem of Canadian democracy, the suffocating hyper-loyalty of Canadian legislators to their parties. Their imaginative approach focuses on elected members' *disloyalty*: members who speak out or vote against their parties and those who leave their caucuses to sit as independents or cross the floor. Their engagingly presented analysis of their original, extraordinarily rich data set is insightful and nuanced. With its recommendations for loosening the reins on Canadian legislators, this is a must-read for anyone concerned about the health of Parliament and the provincial assemblies. Do you want to understand party loyalty in Canada? Read this terrific analysis of legislators who were *disloyal* to their parties ... and typically suffered the consequences."

Graham White, Professor Emeritus of Political Science, University of Toronto

"Powerful bonds of loyalty and discipline tie Canadian elected officials to their political parties. *No I in Team* offers a rich exploration of how politicians internalize, reinforce, challenge, and sometimes reject their roles as loyal partisans. Through the stories of team players, mavericks, and party leavers, the book brings these dynamics to life, offering insight into why some politicians remain devoted to their party while others break away. The book is essential reading for anyone seeking to understand this dynamic that shapes Canadian political life."

Lisa Young, Professor of Political Science, University of Calgary

NO I IN TEAM

Party Loyalty in Canadian Politics

Why are Canadian politicians so loyal to their parties? Why do so few parliamentarians rebel as mavericks or switch sides? And can anything loosen the grip that party leaders have on elected representatives?

No I in Team: Party Loyalty in Canadian Politics by Alex Marland, Jared J. Wesley, and Mireille Lalancette provides the first in-depth examination of the forces shaping party loyalty in Canadian politics, revealing how members of Parliament and provincial legislators are conditioned to prioritize partisan interests over constituents and independent judgment. The authors show how institutional rules, political pressure, social dynamics, and digital technologies reinforce a system demanding unwavering loyalty. Drawing on extensive interviews with politicians and senior staff, plus analyses of thousands of news stories spanning four decades, this book traces how party discipline evolved into message discipline, where control over speech is as strict as control over votes.

As political parties consolidate power and dissenting voices grow rarer, *No I in Team* raises urgent questions about the state of democratic representation in Canada – one of the world's most stable democracies – where elected officials increasingly act as partisans rather than delegates of their communities or trustees of the broader public good.

ALEX MARLAND is a professor of politics and the Jarislowsky Chair in Trust and Political Leadership at Acadia University.

JARED J. WESLEY is associate dean of graduate studies, a professor of political science, and a member of the Black Faculty Collective at the University of Alberta.

MIREILLE LALANCETTE is a professor of political communication at Université du Québec à Trois-Rivières.

No I in Team

Party Loyalty in Canadian Politics

ALEX MARLAND, JARED J. WESLEY,
AND MIREILLE LALANCETTE

UNIVERSITY OF TORONTO PRESS
Toronto Buffalo London

ISBN 978-1-4875-6720-0 (cloth)   ISBN 978-1-4875-6723-1 (EPUB)
ISBN 978-1-4875-6721-7 (paper)   ISBN 978-1-4875-6722-4 (PDF)

Library and Archives Canada Cataloguing in Publication

Title: No I in team : party loyalty in Canadian politics / Alex Marland, Jared J. Wesley,
    and Mireille Lalancette.
Names: Marland, Alex, 1973–, author | Wesley, Jared J., 1980–, author | Lalancette,
    Mireille, 1974–, author.
Description: Includes bibliographical references and index.
Identifiers: Canadiana (print) 20250229781 | Canadiana (ebook) 2025022979X |
    ISBN 9781487567200 (cloth) | ISBN 9781487567217 (paper) |
    ISBN 9781487567231 (EPUB) | ISBN 9781487567224 (PDF)
Subjects: LCSH: Party discipline – Canada. | LCSH: Political parties – Canada. |
    LCSH: Politicians – Canada. | LCSH: Loyalty – Political aspects – Canada.
Classification: LCC JL195 .M36 2025 | DDC 324.271 – dc23

Cover design: John Beadle

We wish to acknowledge the land on which the University of Toronto Press
operates. This land is the traditional territory of the Wendat, the Anishnaabeg, the
Haudenosaunee, the Métis, and the Mississaugas of the Credit First Nation.

This book has been published with the help of a grant from the Federation for the
Humanities and Social Sciences, through the Awards to Scholarly Publications Program,
using funds provided by the Social Sciences and Humanities Research Council of Canada.

University of Toronto Press acknowledges the financial assistance to its publishing
program of the Canada Council for the Arts and the Ontario Arts Council, an agency of
the Government of Ontario.

Canada Council   Conseil des Arts
for the Arts   du Canada

ONTARIO ARTS COUNCIL
CONSEIL DES ARTS DE L'ONTARIO
an Ontario government agency
un organisme du gouvernement de l'Ontario

Funded by the   Financé par le
Government   gouvernement
of Canada   du Canada

Canada

Contents

Figures, Tables, and Boxes

Figures

Tables

Boxes

Preface: The Persistence of Party Loyalty

No I in Team examines party loyalty among Canadian parliamentarians up to the end of Justin Trudeau's tenure as prime minister in 2025. A series of dramatic events unfolded as the book was going to print. Many of these developments can be better understood through the enduring insights presented in the chapters ahead, and through our argument that institutional, political, social, and technological forces interact to infuse parliamentarians with party loyalty, conditioning most to become dutiful team players.

As we discuss in chapter 3, party leaders have many levers with which to command the allegiance of their parliamentary caucus, but that power is not absolute. Case in point: the Liberal Party became so closely tied to Trudeau that even as his and the party's approval ratings collapsed heading into an election year, most Liberals balked at the betrayal of calling for him to step down. It was not until Chrystia Freeland – deputy prime minister, finance minister, and longtime Trudeau loyalist – posted her resignation from cabinet on social media in December 2024 that regional caucuses were finally galvanized to demand a change in leadership. The prime minister's reluctant retirement announcement in the new year demonstrated the limits of a leader's control over their party, even one built around a cult of personality.

The fortunes of Canadian political parties rise and fall with the popularity of their leaders. With their chief stepping aside, the Liberals saw a surge in support, propelled by the leadership campaign of Mark Carney, who became Canada's twenty-fourth prime minister in March 2025. The norms of party unity and primacy of message discipline persisted during and following the transition of power. Despite years of the Liberal government advocating that the consumer carbon price was vital for addressing climate change, not a single Liberal minister or MP

publicly objected when Carney swiftly repealed it. By theatrically signing a decision note in front of the media to cancel the carbon tax, he
echoed the performative authority of a US president issuing an executive order, reflecting a display of personal power that embodies the
presidentialization of the parliamentary system.[1] Buoyed by a resur-
gence in public approval, several Liberal ministers and backbenchers
who had implied their frustrations with Trudeau by announcing they
would not seek re-election abruptly reversed course and decided to
run again. The ensuing election campaign focused on the main party
leaders and treated local candidates as brand ambassadors tasked with
repeating party messaging.[2] The Liberals completed their improbable
comeback just three seats shy of a majority, a result that included Tati-
ana Auguste's one-vote victory in Terrebonne, Quebec, which is des-
tined to be cited in future campaigns as proof that every vote counts.
However, the broader reality is that party affiliation and leadership
support play a far greater role in electoral success than individual candidate appeal. As we note, parliamentarians interested in re-election are
strongly motivated to stay aligned with the party leadership to secure
re-nomination, as their chances of returning to office drop significantly
if they run as Independents or with another party.

Between elections, party leaders exercise reward power that incentivizes parliamentarians to fall in line. Prime Minister Carney's new cabinet featured a blend of full ministers and secretaries of state. One of the
latter was Buckley Belanger, a Saskatchewan MP we mention in chapter 7 – one of the many federal and provincial politicians with atypi-
cal career paths we profile. Among those dropped from cabinet was
Nathaniel Erskine-Smith, the Ontario maverick we highlight in chapter
5 for his readiness to publicly scrutinize his own party's government, a
form of principled dissent that is increasingly rare in Canadian politics.[3]
As we detail, the political influence of ministers and government-side
backbenchers contends with strong centralizing pressures, most notably the concentration of authority in the Prime Minister's Office (PMO)
and premiers' offices. While centripetal forces ebb and flow – for example, Carney's decision to exclude staff from caucus meetings signalled a
willingness to give backbenchers a voice[4] – the broader trend continues
to point towards increasing top-down coordination and control.

Meanwhile, despite failing to win the election, Conservatives largely
supported leader Pierre Poilievre, in contrast with the internal dissent
often faced by leaders who fall short of expectations, as discussed in
chapter 6. His appointment of seventy-four MPs as shadow ministers
was a striking example of how the tools of office are used to encourage

conformity. Nevertheless, Conservative MPs once again adopted the provisions of the *Reform Act* (discussed in chapter 4), which empowered them to initiate a leadership review if desired and to collectively decide on the expulsion or readmission of fellow members. For its part, the New Democratic Party failed to secure official party status in the House of Commons, and, unlike the Liberals, for the first time voted to adopt the Act's provisions about caucus membership.[5] Throughout the book, we show that faltering parties often become fertile ground for internal turmoil, which can lead to parliamentarians sitting as Independents, forming a splinter group of dissidents, or joining another caucus. When CTV asked if he had spoken with anyone about crossing the floor to push his government into majority territory, Carney point-blank answered "No."[6] This was predicable because encouraging a legislator to switch parties is controversial, raises ethical questions, and is potentially illegal if inducements are offered. Moreover, as we explain in chapter 8, national party leaders are typically left out of negotiations around party switching until their agents feel that an agreement is close. Brokering a deal for a parliamentarian to change parties is a highly secretive affair due to the considerable ramifications for political power, reputations, and morale.

One lesson from this book is that Canadian parliamentary politics is as much about human resources management as it is about leadership or communications. News stories frequently emerge about power struggles and personality clashes among partisans. For instance, as we went to press, the Conservative leader in British Columbia accused some former caucus members of blackmailing their ex-colleagues by threatening to release phone recordings and text messages.[7] *No I in Team* provides both context and theoretical tools for understanding internal party conflicts such as this. More importantly, it sheds light on the powerful forces that condition the seemingly unremarkable and non-newsworthy behaviour of hundreds of sitting members of the House of Commons and provincial legislatures, within a political system where adherence to the whims of the party, the leader, and senior political staff is deeply normalized. We demystify why team players who toe the party line typically attract little attention or critique, while acts of individualism are discouraged and, when they do occur, are often dramatized as self-centred behaviours at odds with Canadian political culture.

For better or for worse, party loyalty is a defining feature of Canada's parliamentary institutions and those elected to serve within them. As the political landscape continues to evolve, the stories within these pages will provide both context and caution, demonstrating that respectful advocacy is possible within a party-centric system, while also cautioning that putting the party first can undermine democratic representation and good governance.

Acknowledgments

Many people and organizations made this book possible. It began as research to investigate the reasons why Canadian parliamentarians cross the floor, which received financial support from the Social Sciences and Humanities Research Council of Canada (SSHRC), Insight Grant no. 435-2018-0404. The more that we explored that phenomenon, the more we realized that to understand floor crossers we needed to understand the universe of all types of parliamentarians. The project expanded into a much deeper undertaking about party loyalty than we originally envisioned.

We want to recognize the many politicians and political staff who took the time to speak with us (listed in appendix 2). This research would not be possible without their support; thank you. We are grateful that the Samara Centre for Democracy provided us with transcripts of its interviews with former members of parliament. We wish to acknowledge other organizations that curated similar data: the Library of Parliament, CBC Radio, the Canada West Foundation, and the Churchill Society for the Advancement of Parliamentary Democracy, notably Vice-Chair Corinne Murray. The Royal Society of Canada (Atlantic) sponsored a public discussion about party discipline that we held at Memorial University. We'd like to thank Adam Scotti for permission to reproduce his photo in chapter 3.

More than two-dozen students contributed valuable research assistance across Memorial University, Université du Québec à Trois-Rivières, the University of Alberta, and Acadia University. We are especially grateful for Gala Palavicini's meticulous attention to detail. She compiled information about the Library of Parliament's Oral History Project, prepared briefing notes about party switchers, gathered literature, liaised with legislative libraries, and formatted the manuscript, along with a range of additional research tasks, including the challenging work of identifying party switchers across Canada. We also appreciate research support from Naslati Assany, Anol Azad, Alex Ballos, Alexandre Brouillard, Gillian Brown, Nick Carlson, Adrian Castro, Keith Chipare, Megan Dibartolo, Al Hassania Khouiyi, Olivia Labelle, Hannah Loder, Victoria Matejka, Charlotte Moase, Benjamin Moncrieff, Nonso Morah, Rissa Reist, Colleen McCool, Duke Nguyen, Mitchell Pawluk, Jordan Plunkett, Lex Pytlarz, Jessica Rakotoarisoa, Devin Shaw, Esther Uhlman, and Jim Youk. In addition to the SSHRC Insight Grant, funding for research assistants was supported by Canada Summer Jobs wage subsidies through Employment and Social Development Canada, student employment programs at Memorial University, and the Jarislowsky Chair in Trust and Leadership at Acadia University.

Along the way several scholars kindly commented on our draft work presented at academic conferences, including Jim Bickerton, Ian Brodie, Keith Brownsey, Marcus Closen, Erin Crandall, Charlie Feldman, J.P. Lewis, and Tracey Raney. We thank Jean-François Godbout, Matthew Kerby, and Feodor Snagovsky for their assistance with data, and Anna Esselment, Thierry Giasson, and Tamara Small for sharing ideas for reform. We would like to express our gratitude to the University of Toronto Press, including Dan Quinlan, Mary Lui, and Melissa MacAulay. We were fortunate to receive invaluable feedback on an initial draft of the manuscript from two anonymous external referees, as well as insightful comments from Graham White. Together, they provided over 250 suggestions (!) that greatly enhanced its accuracy and helped us incorporate additional examples.

Although the widespread disruption caused by the COVID-19 global pandemic is now behind us, readers should be aware that our research came to an abrupt halt in 2020. This setback forced us to postpone interviews, delay access to books and files in our university offices and libraries, rely on limited student research assistance, and push back other data collection and dissemination efforts. The disruption led to us expanding our study period to 2021, which ultimately proved fortuitous given the considerable tests of party loyalty during the pandemic.

Throughout this journey, we have been fortunate to receive unwavering encouragement from our families and colleagues. We are deeply grateful to them, and especially to Karly, Jamie, and Éric, whose loyalty and support have been invaluable.

Abbreviations

AI	artificial intelligence
BC	British Columbia
CAQ	Coalition Avenir Québec
CBC	Canadian Broadcasting Corporation
CCF	Cooperative Commonwealth Federation
DRC	Democratic Representative Caucus (Ottawa)
EDA	electoral district association
GST	Goods and Services Tax
MHA	member of the House of Assembly (Newfoundland & Labrador)
MLA	member of the Legislative Assembly (Maritimes, Prairies, British Columbia)
MNA	member of the National Assembly (Quebec)
MP	member of Parliament
MPP	member of provincial Parliament (Ontario)
NDA	non-disclosure agreement
NDP	New Democratic Party
PDA	Progressive Democratic Alliance (British Columbia)
PC	Progressive Conservative
PCO	Privy Council Office (Ottawa)
PEI	Prince Edward Island
PMB	private members' bill
PMO	Prime Minister's Office (Ottawa)
PQ	Parti Québécois (Quebec)
SMP	single member plurality electoral system
UCP	United Conservative Party (Alberta)

NO I IN TEAM

1 Party Loyalty in Canada

In *The Candidate: Fear and Loathing on the Campaign Trail*, Noah Richler shares his experience as a New Democratic Party (NDP) candidate in Toronto–St. Paul's during the 2015 Canadian federal election. When he expresses interest in running, party officials ask him to complete a "prospective candidate information package" and disclose anything about himself that might be controversial so that party staff can assess his suitability.[1] As part of the vetting process, they create a fake social media account to scrutinize his online history.[2] Once he is approved to be the party's candidate, Richler is instructed to support the party's election platform, avoid talking about policy minutia, and stick to a message guide with key lines that were tested in focus groups.[3] When the leader visits during the campaign, local candidates are told to applaud and nod supportively as part of the visual backdrop, and not to talk to journalists. Suddenly, national party personnel swoop in when some of Richler's old online posts become a news story. An apology is drafted for him, the posts are taken down, and he is told to stay out of public view, including feigning ill for an all-candidates' debate. When he pushes back on the apology's wording, a communications staffer asserts that her role is "to protect the brand and the leader," a *modus operandi* echoed by the party's director of organization.[4] That he ends up with less than 15 per cent of the vote is less surprising to Richler than learning how vigilant party operatives in Canada are in ensuring that party representatives stay in lockstep. Had he been elected, the real shock would likely have been discovering how campaign discipline extends to the management of parliamentarians.

Party politics in Canada was once far less rigid. Not long ago, before the rise of social media and the fragmentation of the news media, charismatic personalities in cabinets, shadow cabinets, and on the back benches commanded public attention. These colourful figures made bold statements, stirred controversy, and became influential, particularly within their own regions. Federal and provincial politics continue to feature outspoken politicians who serve as voices of conviction, some with large online followings, alongside unruly actors and renegades. At times, caucus unrest even escalates into fierce power struggles that can destabilize leadership, resembling a defenestration movement. However, a troubling norm has emerged in Canadian politics: the widespread acceptance among members of a parliamentary caucus, particularly those in the governing party, that they must exhibit unwavering loyalty to the leader and the party. Elected representatives in the House of Commons and provincial legislatures are increasingly expected to act as compliant party spokespeople, repeating a scripted message, while steering clear of public disagreement, individuality, or any behaviour that could be seen as disloyal or unbecoming of a team player. Politics is simultaneously more sanitized and more polarized.

For Canada's political parties, especially those in power, presenting a unified front has become paramount. This imperative increases the influence of party leaders and their entourage, who encourage party candidates, members of Parliament (MPs), and provincial legislators to adhere to approved messages. While experiences differ, politicians have more independence than they realize,[5] and few political careers flame out due to a single errant remark.[6] Nonetheless, institutional, political, social, and technological pressures generally compel them to show commitment to the party and its leader by voting and speaking in harmony. This conformity can hinder their ability to effectively represent their constituents, particularly when party interests conflict with local concerns or their personal judgment.

The primacy of party has characterized Canadian legislatures for decades, especially on the government benches. That age-old concern has a new foe that imbues all parties whose leaders are motivated to preside over a unified group. In this book, we contend that party message discipline has become an inescapable yet insidious force that is deepening the problem of caucus members yielding to the party leadership. Unified messaging is good for political parties, but there is a price to pay for democracy: unwavering unity comes at a cost of the people's elected representatives insufficiently scrutinizing or challenging the actions of party leaders, cabinet ministers, and senior political staff, and of parliamentarians relinquishing the ability to voice their convictions and advocate for their constituents. We contend that the evolving communications landscape has heightened the inclination of party leaders and their agents to manage the message and, consequently, to insist on steadfast public support from their parliamentary caucus. This elite behaviour is a function of people entering into a franchising relationship with a political party, like how the local operator of a restaurant or gas station benefits from a turnkey setup, a trade name, marketing, and increased sales, but who is contractually obliged to abide by decisions made in corporate headquarters and who is subject to branding uniformity that sometimes clashes with local market sensibilities.[7] This party-centric mentality has led to meeker contrarians within party caucuses, with harmful consequences for democratic representation, including constituents' concerns not being expressed, extreme partisanship, and transferring power from elected representatives to political staff in the leader's office.

Undoubtedly, there are many advantages of belonging to a unified political party. Canadian parliamentarians (i.e., members of Parliament and provincial legislators)[8] bind together because of their joint convictions and impulse to advance policy or to stymie its backsliding. In election campaigns, partisans can access resources and benefit from rules that improve their chances of getting (re-)elected; in the legislature, they are part of an organized group that promotes change to policy or procedure, and if their party forms government they might sit in cabinet to shape the direction of the country, their province, and their community. Political parties simplify and provide clear choices, structure competition, and aggregate public needs and wants into refined policy proposals. They enable large assemblies to function efficiently, to identify who is in charge, and to establish who should be accountable. They also serve as a means for advancing one's career.

However, the trade-offs of party membership can negatively impact public perceptions of democratic representation. In parliamentary systems, elected officials are prone to behave as party ambassadors, particularly when their party is well-resourced and well-organized.[9] A group orthodoxy that dissent must be expressed *in camera* means that representatives who forcefully advocate for their constituents internally are publicly indistinguishable from compliant partisans. Loyalty to the leader fuels opinions that party interests prevail over constituent interests and that politics is a closed shop reserved for staunch partisans. As a result, rank-and-file politicians are becoming indistinguishable and dispensable in a political system that places them on the front lines of democracy to champion constituent interests and hold the government to account. Furthermore, their deference to authority enables political power to accrue in the leader's office. The problem is acute in Canada, where open disagreement with leaders is uncommon and can be treated as insubordination. In short, no matter if Canadian parliamentarians are passionate, indifferent, or frustrated about an issue – and despite their claims of prioritizing people – they usually end up putting their party first. Why?

No I in Team channels a common saying in workplaces, team sports, and party politics, according to which members of an organized group should place the greater good ahead of personal gain. In *The Prince: The Turbulent Reign of Justin Trudeau*, journalist Stephen Maher writes that "every backroom veteran will tell you that 'politics is a team sport.' It regularly requires the subordination of individual desires to a broader group, reaching decisions through a frustrating process in which partisan considerations must be balanced."[10] In this sense, a close-knit team refers to a cohesive parliamentary party (i.e., the caucus) and its staff, distinct from the broader "party," which also encompasses the wider, non-parliamentary apparatus of the party executive, electoral district associations (EDAs), donors, and party members who are focused on election readiness.[11] This idea that political parties function as teams is apt given that both count on social cohesion, assign roles, resist internal disruptions, and are hostile to opponents as they strive to achieve a common task.[12] The psychology is militaresque: there is strategic planning, a shared vision, morale-building, role clarity, cohesion, lines of communication, emotions management, momentum, and leadership.[13] Prioritizing the party team is deeply ingrained in Canadian political culture, a concept that can be perplexing to those outside of the political bubble.

In this team-first culture, the candidness of nonconformists can be a welcome tonic for journalists and citizens who have become acclimatized to parliamentarians acting as party mouthpieces. Message discipline creates a vicious circle: norms of team solidarity make political candour and bold remarks more compelling, causing even subtle deviations from the party line to be seen as acts of defiance. Flashes of individuality run up against an array of forces that pressure parliamentarians to conform to group consensus and align with the party leader's views. The resulting chill among members of a party caucus to either fall in line or leave undermines the very principles of democracy. If parliamentarians cannot speak out without fear of reprisal, they are unlikely to ask difficult questions, present policy alternatives, or voice concerns that could upset their party's leader and their colleagues, particularly if their party is in government. Overly rigid party messaging can also make populists, who reject conventional norms and project authenticity, appear more attractive.[14]

Part of our objective in this book is to answer a straightforward question that has become an enduring puzzle: why are so many Canadian politicians so loyal to their political party? The motivations and implications of party loyalty among members of the House of Commons and provincial legislatures are not well understood. We lack a clear understanding of what differentiates the mass of team players from the small number of agitators who push the terms of the party franchising contract. If party lines are cut, those rogue actors sit as an Independent, commit the treachery of switching parties, or fade away by resigning their seat or not seeking re-election. For those left behind, party cohesion intensifies as dissenters and troublemakers are siphoned away.[15] Thus, if we want to understand loyalty in parliamentary parties, we must also consider the varying degrees of disloyalty.

Canada is an ideal case for examining party loyalty in a parliamentary system. Caucus unity within Canadian parties is robust and has been growing,[16] fuelled by the need for message discipline to counter the bedlam of social media.[17] In addition to the national stage, there are provincial political arenas that share much in common even when the party systems differ, providing fertile ground for study.[18] At any given moment, over a thousand parliamentarians are actively serving in those eleven assemblies, and most of them faithfully abide by their party franchising agreement. In all cases, compared to their predecessors, elected officials face heightened partisan pressures due to immense demands to operate as a unified team, a situation made more intense by the influence of social media.

Several theories rationalize why elected officials in Western liberal democracies are loyal to political parties.[19] The conditional party government theory holds that the homogeneity of group members in a party caucus contributes to unity, including how much parliamentarians share an ideology and the relative similarity of constituencies they represent.[20] Thus, leaders of like-minded caucuses have a greater ability to advance a political agenda, particularly if they are united against common foes.[21] Conversely, when a parliamentarian prioritizes their own ideology over their political reputation, they are more likely to reject the group.[22] A related theory submits that party unity responds to how unified other parties are. The strategic party government model contends that political parties' activities are geared towards winning elections and that fear of losing causes partisans to unite when an opposing party is doing so.[23] As we will explain, the parliamentary system's design entices a governing party to project unity, which is mimicked by political parties aspiring to form government.

More ominously, the cartel theory treats parties as organizations that change rules and use state resources to increase their power, exclude new entrants, and advance their own interests.[24] Governing parties do this more often than many people realize. For instance, after the 2018

Ontario election, the Liberals fell just one seat short of achieving official party status at Queen's Park. In response, the Progressive Conservative (PC) government used the pretext of some of its own members crossing the floor as justification for raising the minimum seat threshold for official status, thereby denying their rivals access to essential parliamentary resources.[25] Established parties also collectively support systemic norms that treat Independents as anomalies and outcasts. Cartel behaviour is reflected in the "iron law of oligarchy," a viewpoint that political parties are elite structures that impose discipline on subordinates who must follow rules, and that suspicious members have limited opportunities to push back against dubious policies.[26] We contend that whether a parliamentary party behaves as a cartel, a homogenous group, or a caucus of strategic actors, communications pressures are a formidable factor in the cultivation of loyalty to the party and its leader.

Then there is personal allegiance to a leader and the leader's entourage. Loyalty in this context involves taking action to support the inner circle and to protect them from harms; in exchange, individuals in positions of authority convey gratitude by providing benefits.[27] To keep the caucus united, leaders and their surrogates deploy rewards and punishments that incentivize members' behaviour and condition loyalty, a practice that is most fruitful if their party controls the most seats and has greater access to private goods and policy tools. In the US Congress, for instance, legislators in a majority party who go along with the leader on important votes are rewarded with appointments to plum committees.[28] But following a leader can present a moral conundrum. Leaders who demand loyalty to the party can create ethical dilemmas for people who prioritize service to country and community, who believe in upholding the rule of law and preserving the independence of political institutions, who hold incompatible values or opinions, and who resist rhetoric, misinformation, and immorality. Disloyalty can have dire consequences. People at the top of the political hierarchy can derail and even destroy the career of someone whose actions prevent the leader and the leader's agents from getting their way. Some might say that this power over elected officials produces a team of acolytes.

Social pressure is a further factor that influences party loyalty among parliamentarians. One theory is that members of a parliamentary caucus buckle to the conformity demands of fellow partisans, regardless of any potential disciplinary actions from the leadership.[29] This is because when a party is a key part of their political identity, politicians have an innate desire to go along with group culture in order to reap the benefits of membership and avoid the social repercussions of disloyalty.[30] Canadian parliamentarians are immersed in social norms that reinforce a partisan identity and promote uniformity, whether by advocating for a policy that benefits the party or remaining silent during a caucus meeting.[31] In short, a member of a caucus who causes trouble will feel the wrath of their partisan colleagues, which is a powerful force to keep them in line.

As for the contextual dimension, we argue that the many institutional, political, and social forces that condition loyalty among Canada's parliamentarians have been fortified by advancements in communications technology (table 1.1). Previous generations of parliamentarians lacked handheld devices, social media platforms, and even basic computer literacy, which now allow them to blast opinions across cyberspace in real time. Nor did they have to be nearly as concerned with someone surreptitiously recording them or digging up and weaponizing information about them. Getting their views out required a keen sense of publicity by jockeying for interviews with journalists, writing letters to the editor, calling into open-line radio shows, and placing ads in community newspapers. They could also go unseen for weeks at a time. Their commentary was less frequent and more time-consuming, and what they had to say was often filtered by media gatekeepers and confined to their area of the country. While party leaders preferred, as they do now, that caucus members keep disagreement private, in the past there was much more tolerance, even admiration, towards those who attracted media attention for opining. As far as caucus unity was concerned, the priority of the party leadership was usually about getting everyone to vote as one on major bills and motions.

The digital communications landscape has transformed party discipline from a focus on voting in legislatures into a relentless drive for message consistency. It is axiomatic that internet-based communications are unparalleled in speed, breadth, volume, and audience engagement. They enable selective exposure that reinforces audiences' pre-existing beliefs, such as via the niche online platforms that cater to narrow interests or the social media algorithms that amplify extreme viewpoints to motivate user engagement. Furthermore, internet communications empower both politicians and citizens as content generators without reporters, editors, or producers controlling what information is disseminated or how it is framed. So, while politicians can broadcast their unfettered messages, they are also subject to instant criticism and rebuke in an unmediated digital town square that chastises, catastrophizes, and polarizes to the point that a leader can feel compelled to weigh in.[32]

As a consequence, partisans now believe that everyone associated with the party, and even politics as a vocation, suffers when a

Table 1.1. Forces Behind Canadian Parliamentarians' Party Loyalty

Forces	Themes	Examples
Institutional	Leader-focused systems	centralization, coercive power, entourages, party discipline, reward power
	Legal frameworks	election rules, party financing, standing orders
	Governance structures	amateurism/turnover, caucus unity, confidence convention, electoral system, legislative practices, war rooms
	Party rules and frameworks	candidate selection, caucus engagement, culture, election platforms, party constitutions
Political	Leadership and ambition	election-driven mentality, leader's image, leadership style, motivations, status positions
	Marketing and communications	branding, crisis communications, denigration of defectors, fundraising, hyper-partisanship, permanent campaigning, rhetoric
	Networks and unity	caucus, constituents, mentors, party executives, party members, volunteers
	Policy positioning	ideology, priorities, strategy, values
Social	Class and world view	belief system, lived experience, organizational culture, social activities
	Group dynamics	groupthink, intra-party relationships, peer pressure, scolding of individualism, team culture
	Relationships	colleagues, family, friendships, disagreements, personalities, social compatibility
	Shared identity and belonging	common goals, in-/out-groups, partisanship, role satisfaction, social acceptance
Technological	Media and messaging	24/7 news, mediatization, message coordination, social media
	Public opinion research and data mining	data-driven strategies, focus groups, media monitoring, polling, relationship management databases
	Digital communications	AI, the Cloud, digital disruption, echo chambers, online journalism, smartphones, technological adoption

low-ranking politician speaks off the cuff, especially if the move plays into the hands of a rival party.[33] Error-free communications is of great importance to leaders who want to avoid being plunged into damage control over the online behaviour of party candidates and caucus members, which can begin with as small of an act as a hastily deleted social media post,[34] the nuances of a single word riling the online commentariat,[35] a typo generating widespread mocking,[36] and liking the wrong online content.[37] The leader's circle has profited from the need for top-down coordination to combat competing narratives from a growing array of digital platforms. It is textbook media management for a wayward partisan to quickly backtrack, say they misspoke, take down the online post, and become inaccessible.[38]

Today's politicians learn brutal lessons about how frank conversations can turn into an online spectacle. Consider Arielle Kayabaga, elected in 2021 as the MP for London West. Following a Liberal caucus meeting (a confidential gathering of all sitting parliamentarians belonging to the same party), Kayabaga divulged to journalists that, like many Canadians in their early thirties, she lacked the financial means to purchase a house. Her comment was promptly trumpeted by the Conservative Party as evidence of the Liberal government's failed housing policy (figure 1.1). In another case, a recording of a parliamentary secretary's telephone conversation with a constituent was leaked to the media, in which the MP expressed critical views about the government, leading to a *CBC News* headline of "Key Liberal MP Rips His Government's Policy."[39] The harsh treatment of loose lips deters many parliamentarians from speaking candidly with people outside the team circle of trust and results in elected representatives who are short on public personality as they and their staff find refuge in recycling party-approved messages. A corollary of stark partisanship within and outside Canadian legislatures is a citizenry that believes MPs follow the views of their leader, which contributes to public distrust in government, legislatures, and the Prime Minister's Office.[40]

In this book, we chronicle the intensification of public loyalty among Canadian politicians and the decline of a party leader's office accepting spirited conduct by caucus members. We focus on the 1980 to 2021 period, which is bookended by election years that saw voters return Trudeau Liberals to office amid tumultuous political circumstances that tested the limits of party loyalty. The first campaign took place amid divisive negotiations to amend Canada's constitution and quell a national unity crisis; the other occurred amid global upheaval wrought by the COVID-19 pandemic. In this time frame, party systems across the country morphed from being relatively aligned at the federal and provincial levels and dominated by big-tent parties of the centre to becoming increasingly separate and polarized political worlds.[41]

Party loyalty already ran deep among Canadian parliamentarians in the 1980s. Back then, it was well established that they were afterthoughts in public policy decision-making and that they voted foremost with their party.[42] Party leaders and their advisors were considered to

Conservative Party ✓
CPC_HQ

After 8 years of Trudeau, even a Liberal MP can't afford a home.

EVEN TRUDEAU'S OWN MP
CAN'T AFFORD A HOME

"I'm 32 years old, I'm a member of Parliament.
I haven't been able to purchase a home."

- Liberal MP, Arielle Kayabaga

SOURCE: CTV NEWS, SEPTEMBER 12, 2023

Figure 1.1. Partisan Pouncing on a Backbencher's Public Comments

Source: Conservative Party of Canada, "After 8 Years of Trudeau," X (post), 13 September 2023a, https://x.com/CPC_HQ/status/1702066897502527932.

have the most political power in Canadian politics,[43] and critics warned about the presidentialization of the parliamentary system resulting from concentrated power and the marginalization of Parliament.[44] Communication with political audiences centred on political operatives employing publicity techniques to earn news coverage or purchasing advertising in wide-reaching print, radio, and television outlets.[45] The resulting narratives were painted with very broad strokes, designed to appeal to audiences across the country,[46] and leaders of brokerage parties struggled to keep regional factions unified.[47] Prime ministers shared the spotlight with powerful ministers whose vibrant personalities were the face of the federal government in their region and beyond during a political era marked by constitutional bargaining, patronage, and pork-barrel politics.[48] Research about Canadian parliamentarians and caucus cohesion emphasized that party discipline is a function of institutional incentives and corrective action.[49]

Since the late twentieth century, several interrelated phenomena have intensified partisan rhetoric, further dividing politicians into opposing teams. The news media has endured an identity crisis as many local newspapers changed from daily to weekly, went digital, merged, or shuttered operations, resulting in local news deserts; as 24/7 television cable networks proliferated, developed digital newsrooms, and then saw audiences decline as people gravitated towards international streaming; and as public trust in news organizations and journalists plummeted.[50] The splintering of information across numerous online platforms, which can sort people into echo chambers that affirm their existing beliefs, has weakened the traditional media's role as a unifying force in nation- and province-building.[51] Alongside the never-ending news cycle, the permanent campaign became entrenched, whereby partisans are driven to leverage all available resources to win communications skirmishes as though the election campaign never stopped.[52] Innovative tactics of the 1990s, such as establishing a campaign war room where staff systematically archive information on opponents and swiftly deploy it to discredit them, have since become routine political strategy, extending well beyond election periods.[53] The fierce one-upmanship driven by opposition research, issues management, and rapid response messaging is now practised daily by well-resourced parties, often bypassing the mainstream media altogether. All of it poses a substantial challenge to the capacity of democratic processes to generate consensus.

Another factor was the demise of the Progressive Conservative Party as a moderating element in Canadian federal politics in the early 2000s and the rise of new conservative parties in some provinces.[54] Rather than relying on brokerage politics, where parties aggregate diverse interests, seek compromise amid regional tensions, and present themselves as moderate, catch-all organizations, political operatives now use marketing data to pinpoint specific segments of the electorate. They rally these groups into a minimum winning coalition and engage in narrowcasting microtargeted messages that tend to deepen societal divides rather than bridge them.[55] Parliamentarians and their staff are enlisted to promote messages crafted by the leader's inner circle.[56] The effects of party message discipline are of heightened importance as populists respond to the public appetite for authenticity and anti-elitism, which includes aggressively targeting critics and stirring cynicism in institutions.[57] The resulting dynamics pose dire problems for democratic discourse ranging from information silos to rage-farming that inflame polarization and simultaneously augment the strategic appeal of a coordinated response.[58]

Team Players, Party Mavericks, Party Leavers, and Party Switchers

In the current political marketplace, party leaders dominate the public conversation. Ministers of the Crown are so cautious and have such low visibility that many Canadians are unable to name or recognize them, and there is little incentive for citizens to get to know their local representatives, who often fade into the background as stand-ins of the leader and the party brand.[59] Instead of presidentialization, scholars now talk about democratic backsliding whereby norms and rules are ignored by an executive branch that systematically undermines checks on its power by the legislative branch, a parliamentary party caucus that accepts these transgressions as a reasonable function of political power, and a general public that accepts misdeeds as long as they get the public policy they want.[60] As a result, the power gap between leaders and strategic advisors has been widening over elected officials who are lower on the partisan hierarchy. The party dominant culture has endured despite the evolving composition of parliamentary caucuses, which has seen an influx of women parliamentarians (rising from fourteen MPs in 1980 to 103 in 2021) and, at a slower pace, more racialized members (a "breakthrough" of thirteen MPs elected in 1993 escalated to fifty-three in 2021).[61] This infusion of diversity has done little to stem the prevalence of a team doctrine.

To understand the complexity of loyalty in Canadian party caucuses, we draw on a robust set of data to create a detailed portrait of four broad archetypes of parliamentarians who respond in different ways to both internal and external pressures to support their party (table 1.2). The most common partisans are *team players* who have the most hardwired loyalty to a political party and its leader. They generally accept codes of behaviour that dampen agitation, condition compliance, and define representation. This includes parliamentarians who internalize their frustrations by passively exhibiting loyalty through optimism that circumstances will get better, as well as team players who occasionally

Table 1.2. Archetypes of Party Loyalty in Canadian Parliamentary Legislatures

Type of Partisan	Description
1. Team Player	Parliamentarians elected with a party and who normally toe the party line, including those who prioritize constituency casework, internal advocates who build relationships, and hyper-partisans.
2. Party Maverick	Parliamentarians elected with a party who repeatedly rebuff norms of party loyalty, yet who remain in the party.
3. Party Leaver	Parliamentarians who cease being a member of a parliamentary caucus, whether voluntarily or involuntarily.
Quitter	Parliamentarians who decide to quit a party caucus and sit as an Independent.
Expelled Member	Parliamentarians who are expelled from a party caucus and sit as an Independent.
4. Party Switcher	Parliamentarians elected with a party and who, while elected, join a different party's caucus.
Floor Crosser	Parliamentarians who leave a party caucus to immediately join another party.
Two-Stepper	Parliamentarians who have an interregnum before joining another caucus, normally by sitting as an Independent.
Party Hopper	Parliamentarians who change party caucuses more than once.
Boomerang Partisan	Parliamentarians who leave a party caucus and later rejoin it.
Party Entrepreneur	Parliamentarians who leave a party caucus to create a new party.

Notes: We focus on parliamentarians who change their party affiliation while holding a seat. We do not include politicians who change affiliation while out of office, those who switch after a legislature is dissolved for a general election, or parliamentarians who change parties when moving between provincial and federal politics.

present alternate views, which they usually express in a constructive, respectful manner. A pertinacious breed of team player is the hyper-partisan whose behaviour can be vicious (chapter 4).

Next on this loyalty scale are the *party mavericks* who have a knack for controversy yet remain in the party fold. Outspoken politicians who deftly brush aside strict party discipline are portrayed as insurgents who call out poor decisions and as ideologues who put everything on the line. Mavericks can be framed in the news media as folk heroes for speaking truth to power, as martyrs for pursuing the common good, and as rebels for challenging officialdom, in contrast with the mass of team players who are portrayed as trained seals or party robots for expressing loyalty to their party at all costs.[62] Mavericks are committed to their party, yet the leader's willingness to grant them leeway and keep them within the fold can be perplexing. If a maverick pushes too far in challenging group norms, their membership in the caucus is effectively over, whether by their own choice or not. We discuss them in chapter 5.

Then there are *party leavers* who sit as Independents after severing their partisan ties by disconnecting, turning their criticism inward, going rogue, or engaging in other forms of untenable conduct. Voluntarily leaving a caucus is one of the most powerful ways that a parliamentarian can diminish a leader's power, sharply contrasting with the syndicate of team players and party mavericks who would rather bow out of politics entirely than quit the squad. Conversely, those who are expelled for unacceptable behaviour set a powerful example for the rest of the caucus, illustrating the parameters of caucus membership and the primacy of the leader. Party leavers are the subject of chapter 6. Some of them never return to a party, few can get re-elected on their own name, and they all experience challenges in a political system that treats Independents as outcasts. Others eventually end up with a different party.

Party switchers, the topic of chapter 7, commit the ultimate betrayal by joining another party's caucus by crossing the floor directly, or after an interlude as an Independent or resigning their seat to contest a by-election under another party banner.[63] Switching parties is a rare political event that attracts a surge of attention and can have immense consequences, particularly for a politician who experiences harsh treatment amid allegations of being a career-minded turncoat seeking better opportunities. Whereas ambition is the main impetus for American legislators choosing to switch political parties,[64] we believe that a Canadian partisan's evaluation of the leader is at the core of whether they voluntarily remain or flee, which can manifest as frustrations over policies, re-election, or role. As we shall demonstrate, Canadian party leaders have extensive control over ambition being realized and are usually at the centre of personal, ideological, or policy differences. Understanding the complexities of leaving and changing political parties allows us to create a more nuanced portrait of the pressures that drive party loyalty among parliamentarians.

Using these archetypes as guides to organize the book, we strive to address some nagging questions about partisanship among Canadian politicians. Later in this opening chapter we will summarize our research questions and our data. We will also provide an overview of our prescriptions for reform which, while falling short of putting an "I" in team, would enhance the collegiality of party politics. But first we make some observations about studying party allegiance.

Partisanship in Canadian Legislatures

Anchoring our knowledge about team culture in party politics is scholarship about voters. Political behaviour studies have consistently shown that people develop psychological connections to political parties based on their own social characteristics.[65] Many people identify with a single political party, even if they intermittently vote for a different one; the rest have allegiances that fluctuate depending on circumstances,[66] although occasionally seismic changes in party affiliation erupt when a mass of voters lose trust in government and mainstream political parties.[67] A well of interconnected variables inform political attachments: people's social background, their beliefs and values, how they feel about parties, their economic views, and their opinions on issues, as well as their evaluation of party leaders.[68] These political attitudes and policy stances are often shaped by life experiences, social class, or geography.[69]

Among these values, those associated with ideology tend to receive the lion's share of attention. Like most Western democracies, observers often view Canadian party politics in left/right terms.[70] For decades, the New Democrats have occupied the political left, and the (Progressive) Conservatives the political right, while the Liberals have straddled the centre.[71] Federally, parties at either pole attract some of the most durable partisans,[72] whereas the Liberal Party's more amorphous ideology appeals to floating voters.[73] It is a similar story in the provinces, albeit with different party constellations, except in Quebec where an ideological axis has turned on federalism versus nationalism. At both levels, would-be candidates are drawn to the ideological and policy positions of the party, and members look for candidates and leaders that espouse similar values to their own.[74]

Whether as brokerage or catch-all organizations, the most successful parties have erected "big tents" to appeal to the mass of median voters who are the key to winning elections.[75] Parties often struggle to maintain ideological unity under these broad tarps, particularly when it comes to caucus cohesion. Within the New Democratic Party, hardline socialists are frequently at odds with moderate social democrats about the depth and pace of reforms; left-leaning Liberals who focus on social justice can have different priorities than blue Liberals who are concerned foremost about economic matters; and Conservatives face tensions over the role of the state among their libertarian, social conservative, and red tory wings. Ideological cohesion is burdensome for other parties, too, given that all party leaders stir dissent when they impose policy priorities and electoral strategies on their caucus. This is why Canadian parties avoid taking firm positions on divisive issues: for fear of offending one or another segment of their caucus.[76] It is also why party leaders employ disciplinary measures to keep members onside (see chapter 3), a practice that has become paramount with the rise of internet communications.

The entwinement of discipline and partisanship has entered a new phase. As communications technology has evolved, politicians have heightened their focus on winning partisan battles over public policy, government, and popularity. Their rhetoric can be strategically differentiated by demonizing opponents in a relentless ideological battle of one-upmanship that gets amplified through message repetition by multiple actors across multiple platforms. In the United States, over-exuberant party loyalty has transformed into the disease of hyper-partisanship. The dislike, even hatred, of another party and its leader can motivate hyper-partisans to promote negative depictions of their opponents and to employ uncivil tactics that compromise thoughtful deliberation about policy options and which impair good governance.[77] The extremes of partisanship result in "mutual incomprehension and mutual revulsion" towards rivals, which is anathema to working together to solve public problems.[78]

The anti-democratic ethos of partisans who rationalize destructive strategies and tactics to crush opponents is alarming. Fortunately, this type of hyper-polarization in Canadian party politics today is less dire than the situation south of the 49th parallel. There are many reasons for the drift between the two countries' politics, starting with diverging political cultures that saw one forged out of armed rebellion to authority and the parliamentary system, while the other provided safe harbour to British loyalists and the accommodation of French systems in Quebec.[79] Yet there is historical precedent in Canada: politics in the late nineteenth century featured the reckless partisanship of newspapers blithely making accusations about opponents; fraudulent practices such as falsification of lists of electors and influence peddling; and campaign activities aimed at entertaining rather than informing.[80] Consider also the Conservatives' impersonation of political figures on the radio in 1935, which amounted to character assassination of Prime Minister

Mackenzie King;[81] the polarizing upheaval of the 1960s, egged on by the personal animosity between leaders John Diefenbaker and Lester Pearson;[82] the harsh 1993 PC television ads mocking Liberal leader Jean Chrétien's partial facial paralysis;[83] and the Liberals posting a digital ad in 2006 fearmongering that a Conservative government would deploy armed soldiers in Canadian cities[84] – just a few among many such examples. Aligning into a political camp where members hold similar views and fundamentally differ from those in another faction is not a new phenomenon, just as political posturing, brinksmanship, and name-calling are not new either. Some believe this sort of chicanery lies at the heart of modern democracy.[85] While political disagreement is necessary, even valuable, in pluralistic democracies like Canada, it becomes problematic when these tensions escalate into rage, distrust, resentment, and mutual disdain between party supporters.[86] At that point, the pursuit of the common good for society is seriously undermined.

In Canada, polarization revolves around the widening chasm between political parties on the left and right, each pushing distinct ideological messages.[87] The conflict is contributing to a dour public mood about politics and political institutions. Recent evidence indicates that partisanship in Canada has edged higher since the 1980s[88] and that many Canadians would never consider voting for a party that they disdain.[89] A 2023 EKOS survey showed that Canadians are more anxious about growing ideological polarization and about the decline of democratic institutions than they are about many public policy issues,[90] while a 2024 Angus Reid poll found that more than a third of Canadians felt politically orphaned because federal parties are too extreme.[91] In Alberta, a highly polarized province, followers of the two leading parties are so divided that most are uncomfortable with someone from the opposite party marrying into their family.[92] Nonetheless, among many Canadians, partisanship is a form of identity that colours how they view politics.[93] Its excesses are a threat to political stability and public confidence in institutions.

Partisanship has become a normal function of parliamentary politics, and it is endemic when a legislative assembly has many members. It operates along a spectrum, from politically acceptable to democratically dangerous. At one end, *ad hominem* attacks are distasteful for all but rabid partisans. While the leader of the Official Opposition calling the prime minister a "wacko" during Question Period may be unparliamentary behaviour,[94] and it may be distasteful when a parliamentarian berates a retiring opponent rather than saluting their contribution to public life,[95] such antics do not pose a threat to our democratic institutions. In fact, by some measures incivility in parliamentary debate has been improving. In the nineteenth century, intoxicated MPs hurled objects to interrupt speakers,[96] while a study of heckling in the House of Commons found that interruptions have been declining since 1979, likely a result of the introduction of television cameras and changes to the Standing Orders brought about by the McGrath Committee (see chapter 2).[97] Indeed, Hansard records are replete with a troubling history of personal attacks that would be shocking by today's standards. "We'll stick a doughnut on the member's nose, and stuff a few in his mouth too," is one of countless barbs levelled during parliamentary debates, in this case by an Ontario Progressive Conservative member of provincial Parliament (MPP) in 1975.[98]

At the opposite pole, hyper-partisanship discourages moderate partisans from engaging in pluralistic debate and relationship-building that contributes to strong policy and good governance if they fear staunch supporters in their own party turning on them. This is what concerns us: the primacy of partisanship leads too many politicians and their supporters to echo variations of a scripted message track that ridicules and demonizes opponents, which hinders efforts to build consensus across party lines. It is one thing to be theatrical against an opponent in the heat of the moment; it is another to habitually commend and defend one's political team, to slag adversaries, and for a win-at-all-costs mentality to equate compromise with losing. Allegations of incivility, hyper-partisanship, and polarization are widespread, with claims that governing parties use polemical messaging to depict opponents as untrustworthy dissidents, positioning the government as a safe and competent alternative.[99] Critics argue that Question Period has devolved into an adversarial theatre of accusations and spin, designed to refine lines of attack,[100] while excessive partisanship is undermining the effectiveness of parliamentary committees.[101] In the extreme, hyper-partisanship and polarization have been linked to democratic backsliding,[102] and they contribute to an unwelcoming and inhospitable workplace.[103] Consider the retirement announcement of Pam Damoff, a Liberal MP in Ontario, who in 2024 posted on Facebook that she had enough:

> The hyper-partisan nature of politics today is not the environment I see myself serving in.... The tone and tenor of public discourse has deteriorated significantly, and I fear the loss of trust in public institutions we are seeing that is driven by misinformation and lies being spread by politicians and on social media. Unfortunately, the toxic drive for social media likes and clips among elected officials has hindered constructive conversations, exacerbated differences between us, and diminished our capacity to show empathy towards each other. The threats and misogyny I have

experienced as a Member of Parliament are such that I often fear going out in public, and that is not a sustainable or healthy way to live.[104]

The more that a group of partisans treats their opponents as enemies who must be stopped at all costs, the likelier they are to shut down opportunities for those opponents to contribute to debate and discourse.[105] Hyper-partisans are also disposed to close ranks around their leadership, forgiving if not encouraging anti-democratic behaviour, which can include rationalizing political violence.[106] In this polarizing environment, only the purest of partisans are deemed trustworthy and are rewarded for their loyalty.

Unity in Parliamentary Parties

The psychology and structures that lead to such varied degrees of partisan identity and loyalty among parliamentarians are poorly understood in Canada. Comprehending group solidarity requires delving into a web of consensus-building, social bonding, moral convictions, political coalitions, and communications,[107] including facets that some partisans are unwilling to disclose because doing so would expose uncomfortable truths. Researchers studying party loyalty must contend with the catch-22 that for staunch partisans, sharing frank opinions and insider information with outsiders is, in their world, an act of disloyalty. Consequently, existing scholarship emphasizes parliamentarians' voting records[108] and, to a lesser extent, the reasons for switching political parties[109] and not seeking re-election,[110] as well as touching on factors contributing to cohesion in party caucuses.[111] Internationally, studies attribute loyalty to the length of time that a parliamentarian was a party member before entering Parliament.[112] In Canada, researchers have pointed to the importance of tighter procedural rules (commonly known as Standing Orders),[113] leaders' willingness to dispense and withhold rewards,[114] the conformity required of brokerage politics,[115] and an evolution in political communications that both compels and enables the leadership circle to coordinate message consistency.[116]

Research is needed about the pressure points of loyalty on the mass of parliamentarians who are not part of cabinet and are officially known as private members. Those with the least authority and seniority are assigned seats away from the front rows of the assembly, hence the popular term "backbencher," which denotes obscurity and limited influence, irrespective of their competencies. Most rookie parliamentarians start out as backbenchers, and their orientation to the job reinforces their subordination to the party leadership. In the governing party's caucus, backbenchers are normally brought into public policy discussions so far down the decision-making pipeline that there is little to no opportunity for debate. It is sometimes too late to flag local implementation challenges, let alone go in a different direction. In urgent situations, they are not involved at all.[117] What is more, they are tasked with persuading constituents about the merits of a policy that, having been thrust upon them, they may not fully comprehend or endorse.[118] A backbencher in the governing party who votes against the government invites various degrees of punishment because dissent is equated as registering that they do not support the cabinet to govern.

Parliamentary democracies like Canada are rooted in the dual principles of cabinet solidarity (ministers speaking frankly in private meetings and supporting government decisions in public) and ministerial responsibility (individual accountability for decisions by ministers or those reporting to them). A minister's public comments represent the government's official position. This principle of collective responsibility within the executive is meant to be balanced by the autonomy of other parliamentarians, who are free to question and seek information independently. The system of responsible government relies on all other members of the legislature, regardless of party, holding the cabinet to account. Under this system, the government must resign if a majority of elected members disagree with it on an important issue. The confidence convention – the principle that the government must have the support of a majority of members of the legislature – ensures that the cabinet can only advance major initiatives that are backed by at least half of the voting members. This places a considerable onus on backbenchers in the governing party to be onside with the government.

What constitutes a matter of confidence can be ambiguous, particularly when a governing party has only a minority of seats, yet mostly concerns one of three areas: any item that the government declares a test of confidence; motions to endorse a key component of the government's policy agenda such as a throne speech, budget, or major legislation; and opposition motions or amendments that are worded to denote a loss of confidence in the government.[119] Members of cabinet are almost always drawn from the governing party's caucus, which promotes stability on the government side of the House out of fear of losing power by way of a confidence vote and by encouraging ambitious members to toe the line if they wish to benefit from the perks of office.[120] Furthermore, incumbents seeking to continue their parliamentary career must align with their party and its leader, or risk forfeiting the opportunity to run for re-election as the party's candidate. The threat of not securing the party nomination is a key institutional mechanism that reinforces a norm of unity within parliamentary caucuses.

Thus, a system designed to ensure that the appointed executive acts in line with the preferences of the elected legislature is susceptible to imbalance, where the authority of party leaders – especially premiers and prime ministers – can overshadow efforts to counterbalance their control over the roster of team players. This is why, in our concluding chapter, we urge reforms that limit the abuse of the confidence convention as a bludgeon for brinksmanship.

Make no mistake: party loyalty is strong in the House of Commons. One study of recorded division votes in the 1990s found Canada to have among the highest incidences of party unity in parliamentary votes among eleven countries, with MPs voting with their party 98.3 per cent of the time.[121] Vote cohesion tightened as internet-based communications became the norm. Consider the 40th Parliament (2008 to 2011), when Prime Minister Stephen Harper led a minority Conservative government that was lampooned for its control freakery. Group loyalty was evident among all recognized parties in the House of Commons: over one-third of members (35 per cent) voted with their party on every single bill and motion, and nearly half (47 per cent) of MPs did so 99 per cent of the time.[122] The most rebellious was MP Keith Martin who sided with the Liberal party on 91 per cent of the votes. This is partly explained by a pliable partisan identity, given that he was first elected with Reform, then with the Canadian Alliance, and then left to sit as an Independent before being elected as a Liberal in 2004 – a multipartisan career path that we shall delve into later. During the 42nd Parliament (2015 to 2019), members of Parliament demonstrated less rigidity when Prime Minister Justin Trudeau headed a majority government, yet on average they voted with their party 99.6 per cent of the time, four in five MPs voted differently than their party on five or fewer occasions, and nearly 13 per cent voted exclusively with their party.[123] The most disloyal MP was Nathaniel Erskine-Smith, a parliamentary purist who nevertheless voted in alignment with the Liberals 96.6 per cent of the time. Comparable levels of solidarity are believed to exist in Canadian provincial legislatures, although to our knowledge there has not been a recent study of division votes in the provinces.[124]

Division voting records are a useful proxy for party loyalty, but numbers do not tell the whole story. In fact, these statistics exaggerate the extent of party cohesion.[125] Dissent in legislatures is higher than the figures suggest given that loyalty scores are inflated by procedural votes, such as government-side backbenchers voting against a series of frivolous and obstructionist motions by the opposition. Data on division votes do not capture degrees of fidelity, meaning that we cannot differentiate between passionate supporters of a bill, loyalists who habitually vote the party line, or firebrands who begrudgingly end up voting with the party. Resulting loyalty scores struggle with outliers, such as inflating the proportion of dissenting votes by members who serve less than a full term or under-representing a single dissenting vote by a long-time partisan whose disagreement on a key issue generates a torrent of controversy, or even rare cases of a parliamentarian accidentally voting the wrong way. Furthermore, in Canada disagreement with one's party is normally expressed by being intentionally absent for a recorded vote or by defying the party line on a lower-stakes matter that never makes it to a vote.[126] As well, cabinets are sometimes on the losing side of motions, especially when the governing party has a minority of seats.[127] That said, the prevailing norm in Canada is for elected partisans to vote with their party, particularly when the leader maintains tight control, which is even more pronounced during periods of minority governance.[128] While proximity to an election often intensifies partisanship, electoral pressure itself does not necessarily lead to higher levels of party loyalty in legislative voting.[129] Why is defying the party line so uncommon?

Quantitative data confirm that Canada's elected representatives used to have more freedom from political parties. In *Lost on Division: Party Unity in the Canadian Parliament*, Jean-François Godbout looked at how Canadian MPs voted in the House of Commons from 1867 to 2011. He determined that changes to the Standing Orders gradually reduced the ability of backbenchers to scrutinize and delay bills, increased the government's ability to control the agenda, and caused opposition leaders to be more selective about who gets to speak. Orchestrated by party leaders and their inner circles, and acquiesced to by private members, reforms between 1906 and 1913 limited the time available for discussion, including the rule of closure that enables a majority of members to agree to conclude debate.[130] As we explain in chapter 2, by the time of World War II, MPs were increasingly reluctant to speak out in a system designed to minimize individual influence, reward fidelity, and punish nonconformity.[131] As time passed, fewer and fewer partisans openly challenged authority, yet the uncertainty of whether backbenchers would fall in line kept leaders on their toes.[132] Nowadays, the mantra of supporting the party and its leader is an inviolable ethos.[133] Yet for some parliamentarians, the demands of party loyalty become overwhelming, leading them to break away.

Whether a Canadian parliamentarian's departure from a party caucus signals or results from a changing party system, it can lead to negative publicity that tarnishes the party's popularity, emboldens other caucus members to follow suit, and, in some cases, culminates in the leader's resignation. Ethical concerns emerge when a parliamentarian switches parties, especially if a floor crosser is immediately appointed to a ministerial position. This was evident in 2005, when Conservative MP Belinda Stronach made a bold move into Liberal Prime Minister Paul Martin's cabinet, followed by outgoing Liberal Minister David Emerson brashly joining Conservative Prime Minister Harper's cabinet after the 2006 federal election. The federal ethics commissioner eventually ruled that offering a cabinet post to a member of a different party does not constitute a special inducement unless it is done to secure the MP's support for a crucial vote.[134] While most partisans never leave their party, even in the face of immense frustration, the constraints felt by many team players often result in representation that, though reasonable and uncontroversial, can also be underwhelming, uninspiring, and easily overlooked.

Representation and Teamwork

As we have noted, political parties are essential to large-scale democracies and, by and large, are a force for good. They organize a cacophony of personalities, priorities, and perspectives. Large assemblies function in a more orderly manner when elected officials work together in groups and assign roles; and stable governments can be formed, operate competently, and be held accountable when a group of compatible politicians who support one another is in charge. Elections are smoother when politicians have institutional supports and electors can easily process information. Without parties to broker consensus in a large assembly, the public and legislative agenda would be chaotic, as parliamentarians would be incentivized to pursue narrower sets of interests without much thought to competing viewpoints or the broader public good. Electors would lack a coherent set of policy proposals and a clear choice of who they want to be the head of government. It is less clear whether parties are indispensable in a small assembly, such as Prince Edward Island (PEI), and whether a consensus model of government might work.[135]

Assessing the representational style of parliamentarians usually begins with the classic views of eighteenth-century British MP Edmund Burke who, in a seminal essay, suggests that they either behave as a trustee who follows personal convictions and judgments or as a delegate who prioritizes constituent interests even if that clashes with personal principles. The trustee encourages a deliberative approach to governance, where diverse perspectives can be considered and integrated into policy decisions, even when those policies are not universally popular. Conversely, the delegate ensures that a wide array of specific, often competing interests are directly represented in the political process. The former ensures a measured approach to accommodating interests; the latter ensures that the legislature reflects, if not responds to, the diverse needs of the electorate. Theorists later added a middle-ground category of a politico who floats between the two roles in response to circumstances.[136] The politico role enables a more nuanced and comprehensive approach to governance and complex policy landscapes, where decisions are made based on a blend of public opinion, ethical considerations, and informed judgment. This delegate–trustee balance is crucial for addressing complex, long-term challenges that demand foresight and expertise beyond the immediate pressures of electoral politics, party loyalty, or the perspectives of a few at the top of the party hierarchy. Parliamentarians who are free to draw on their knowledge, lived experiences, and personal convictions can offer more creative and effective solutions to public issues. However, scholars have identified another orientation: the loyal partisan, who prioritizes maintaining good standing with the party over nurturing relationships with constituents.[137] More harshly, team players are labelled as party hacks whose fierce partisanship contributes to growing public distrust.[138]

Politicians have varied motives for acting as trustees, delegates, politicos, or loyal partisans. A dominant motivational taxonomy is the policy, office, and votes model advanced by Wolfgang Müller and Kaare Strøm in *Policy, Office, or Votes? How Political Parties in Western Europe Make Hard Decisions*.[139] Grounded in a rational choice approach that applies economic principles to political behaviour,[140] this framework assumes that politicians are logical actors who strategically align their actions to implement preferred laws, move up the political ladder, and secure electoral victories. The policy/office/votes model suggests that elected officials are foremost interested in directing government action, having access to the spoils of office, or obtaining as much support as possible to be re-elected. Being a member of a political party may help the politician achieve these ends. There are numerous other classifications of motivations and representation styles, such as the theory that loyalty in a parliamentary caucus arises from shared ideological principles and behaviours shaped by party leadership through tools of advancement, discipline, and socialization.[141] Our focus, however, is on understanding these and other factors – particularly communications – that condition so many parliamentarians, especially those without a front-bench seat, to prioritize party interests and, by extension, self-interest.

Whereas policy-seeking motives and the defence of constituent interests tend to be viewed as matters of conviction, in contrast vote- and office-seeking behaviours are often framed in terms of career objectives.

One classic American typology of political ambition is instructive in this respect.[142] "Discrete" ambition entails a legislator's desire to be in office for a defined period before voluntarily withdrawing from the political arena. Those politicians feel less impetus to support their party if they are dissatisfied with the job and/or if they have career alternatives. If they are nearing the end of their elected career, some have little to lose by defying edicts from the leadership, while others might redouble their partisanship because they want to boost their prospects for a government appointment. "Static" ambition concerns legislators who are satisfied securing the same role for a prolonged period. They prioritize constituency casework because they want to help people in their community as well as improve their chances of re-election.[143] Their work in the legislature is often unremarkable. The most active politicians have "progressive" ambition to secure a higher-ranking role. These position-seekers develop policy expertise as they introduce a bill, irrespective of whether it will pass, so that they may speak to it and attract media attention that, they hope, will increase their chances of promotion. This can include chairing a prominent committee as a route to exerting policy influence. Finally, "intra-institutional" ambition refers to politicians who aspire to a leadership position, such as House leader or party leader, or who wish to jump from subnational to national politics. These politicians are better at forging consensus and mobilizing support within their party to advance policy.

By definition, if Canadian parliamentarians were more selfish, they would be less team-oriented, and so it follows that their policy motives dominate over personal ambition (chapter 8). Canadian election candidates are eager to advocate specific issues, to improve life in their communities, to further their political values, and to achieve better political representation.[144] Once elected, they are loyal to their party because of ideological congruence and because they want to fulfil their policy objectives.[145] However, many fail to have much influence over the government. Constituency demands can dominate their time, with some prioritizing local events in their riding over duties in the legislature.[146] They can be sidelined as frontline salespeople who are tasked with persuading audiences about the wisdom of decisions made by the leadership. Their minimalist contribution to policy soon has them asking if they truly represent what matters to people in their electoral district.[147] In the concluding chapter, we suggest reforms that would help parliamentarians better balance their representational styles and responsibilities.

Each backbencher holds the government accountable in their own way, but siding with a political team is usually the simplest and most prudent route. In part, the tendency to go along to get along is rooted in the most basic elements of human behaviour. Human beings have an innate desire to form social bonds, to belong to groups, and to maintain those relationships.[148] The shared sense of identity can be gratifying. People are content and proud when a group accepts them: they value their peers' approval, and they become unhappy if they are ostracized.[149] In fact, many humans are so keen for social acceptance and so fearful of being left out that they will yield their own opinion to go along with others, even if doing so runs counter to observable facts.[150] For many people, the pull to be part of a group is a potent force that can lead them to behave in surprising ways.

Throughout society, and especially in politics, organized groups evoke clichés that they are stronger together. The emotive word "team" elicits a collaborative outfit working as one to achieve shared goals that would be unattainable as individuals or as smaller clusters working at cross-purposes. Teamwork inspires a community spirit among supporters who identify with a brand, who follow a leader, and who connect through a shared history, accomplishments, failures, and foes. Successful habits developed through competition are valued, including dependability, discipline, a strong work ethic, and a drive to prevail. Achieving goals boosts morale and cohesion. Paradoxically, so does losing: group failure can strengthen collective identity when members sense that their loss would have been greater had they gone it alone.[151] More ominously, the duty to support teammates can twist ethical norms when it involves disparaging opponents and shunning colleagues whose actions endanger the group.

Since at least the 1930s, parliamentarians and political staff in Canada have evoked the language of "team play" to describe the sunny disposition of a cohesive caucus.[152] Team is now an embedded fixture of party nomenclature. The analogy extends to the electoral arena, where campaign slates equate the party leader to the team leader, with accompanying taglines emblazoned on party merchandise and candidates' campaign signs. Party websites feature a team section that houses information about caucus members or, during a campaign, their candidates (figure 1.2). The jargon is often used when announcing a cabinet, parliamentary secretaries, or a shadow cabinet, framing these individuals as a cohesive group. The importance of teamwork is further emphasized visually at media events, where supportive figures stand behind a leader, serving as props to reinforce a collective image. Party loyalists such as Sheila Copps, the Chrétien-era deputy prime minister, avow the team concept. "Like sport, party politics is based on teamwork. You rise and fall together," she has opined.[153] "When any player signs onto a team, they cannot individually change the lineup or the game plan. So, too, party politics involves commitment, in this case to the [party's] team." In Canadian party politics, team engenders a sense of fellowship, duty, and continuity that boosts collective action, minimizes spontaneity, and instils a respect for a unified chain of command. It is also a euphemism to justify group compliance.[154]

Public attitudes towards party politics are so jaded that leaders have added incentive to substitute the word "party" with a call for people to join their team or movement, which reflects that many politically minded people are choosing to work outside of conventional institutions. Partisans go further amongst themselves by equating the party

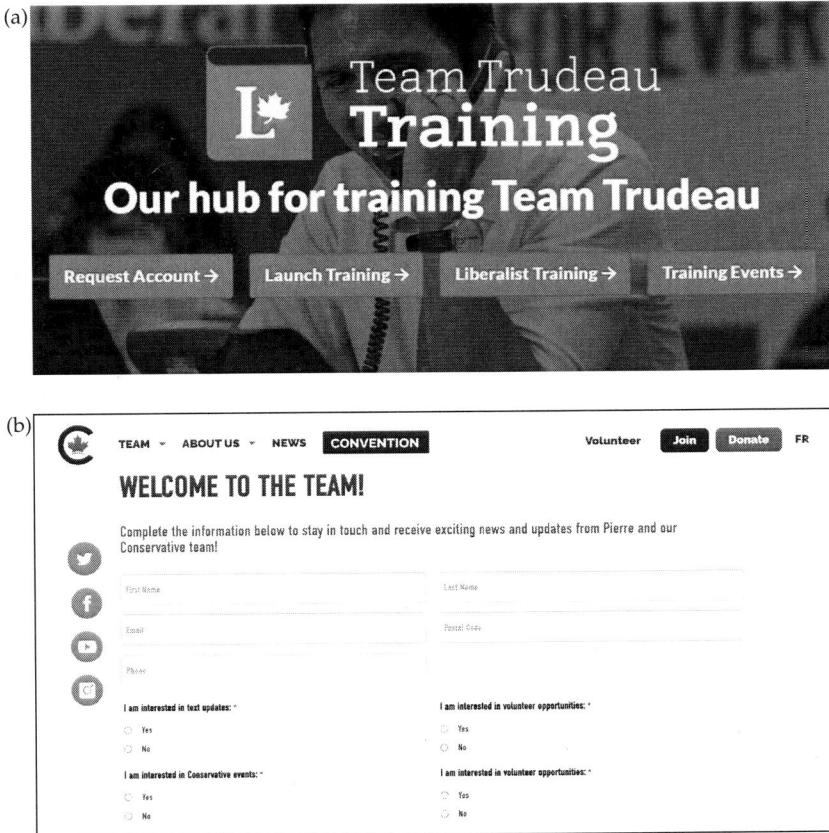

Figure 1.2. Team Nomenclature in Canadian Party Politics: (a) Election Training, Liberal Party; (b) Database Marketing Recruitment, Conservative Party; (c) Campaign Volunteers, NDP; (d) Caucus Members, CAQ

Sources: Coalition Avenir Québec, "Votre équipe"; Conservative Party of Canada, "Welcome to the Team!"; Liberal Party of Canada, "Team Trudeau Training"; New Democratic Party of Canada, "Team Jagmeet – Équipe Jagmeet."

(c)

(d)

Figure 1.2. Continued

to a family. For example, fresh off a landslide election victory in 2022, Quebec Premier François Legault cautioned the Coalition Avenir Québec (CAQ) caucus that they can say anything to each other in private, after which they must be *un bloc uni, impossible à traverser* (an impenetrable unified bloc) and that he would not tolerate *la chicane dans la famille* (bickering in the family).[155] The jargon is also used as a rallying cry when a leader attempts to manage dissent. "We're one family, one team – sure, families disagree sometimes, but most importantly we all keep together," said Ontario Premier Doug Ford about some PC caucus members disagreeing with him.[156] The emotive word equates a caucus to a nurturing social unit where everyone looks after one another, is bonded for life, follows the same rules,[157] and ought to defer to the head of the family, who is typically a male authority figure.

Research Method

Understanding the dynamics of such a regimented, partisan, and deferential political environment is the main objective of this book. Our study aims to provide deeper context and insight into party loyalty, complementing quantitative studies that analyse parliamentarians' voting patterns. These national studies paint a limited picture of the *who*, *when*, and *where* of partisanship and tell us little about the *what*, *why*, and *how* of party loyalty in party leaders' offices or subnational settings. There is a need for qualitative research about the internal operations of parliamentary parties whose private affairs are hidden behind a cloud of secrecy.[158]

Our investigation sets out to address our overarching research question: why are most Canadian parliamentarians so loyal to their party? As a subset to this, we want to understand the institutional, political, social, and technological forces fuelling expectations that everyone in Canadian party politics must be a team player. This involves looking into the psychology of group loyalty and team constructs, and what workplace relations can inform us about behaviour in partisan groups. We are curious about the ways that loyalty is conditioned among election candidates, rookie parliamentarians, and party veterans and, relatedly, what levers of power a leader has available to command loyalty, and why party loyalty is more impenetrable in some provinces than in others. Our approach to explaining why Canadian parliamentarians are so loyal includes assessing the reasons why most are abiding members of a caucus whereas others challenge party norms and a small number leave.

Some related questions arise. We are especially inquisitive about why party discipline has expanded to become message discipline. This requires awareness of why leaders, their agents, and most partisans believe that a unified caucus is crucial, and why so many partisans support a system of rewards and punishments that is imposed by the party leadership. The answer requires unpacking how parliamentarians relinquished power to political parties, what role leaders and their staff play in extolling loyalty and unity, and how the news media conditions party cohesion. Furthermore, we need to consider how internet and social media communications have altered party discipline, and the strategy behind message consistency, as well as how hyper-partisanship and polarization contribute to party loyalty. Changes in ethical and moral norms have also affected leaders' tolerances of controversial behaviour. A related avenue of inquiry is gaining insight into how it is that certain partisans who disrupt norms of party loyalty are tolerated, even celebrated, while others are shunned. We are only beginning to comprehend how leaders and their surrogates manage caucuses and deal with troublemakers, and we know little about the rabble-rousers who complete a long career with the same party while others are dismissed from the caucus, leave in a huff, or find opportunity with another party.

A further area of study is addressing an information deficit about what happens in the lead-up to a parliamentarian becoming an Independent or joining another party. The circumstances that cause a partisan to change their affiliation in Canada are murky. We want to understand the motivations for leaving and switching, what goes through a parliamentarian's mind when they realize that their party affiliation is untenable, and what types of conversations occur when they explore leaving their party. We lack knowledge about the decision to banish a partisan from a caucus, and why some parliamentarians cross the floor to an opponent whereas others sit as an Independent. Little is known about extraordinary party desertions, such as splinter groups forming or people changing parties multiple times, although the stories are so rich that they could be the basis of their own books. In considering these different pathways, we want to touch on life as an Independent relative to the opportunities and consequences resulting from a changed party affiliation.

We will make a case that most Canadian parliamentarians are unflappably loyal to their party because of a complex mix of institutional, political, social, and technological forces. We contend that party discipline has become message discipline because of the strategic value to the party and its leader of harmonizing disparate voices, communicating cohesive information, and avoiding the crisis communications that can result from a parliamentarian expressing an independent opinion. We will demonstrate that some parliamentarians who disrupt norms of party loyalty remain because they embody party values, have a loyal following, and back off when they need to. We will explain that, normally, a series of concerns arise in the lead-up to a parliamentarian becoming an Independent or joining another party, and that, unlike in the notorious cases of Stronach and Emerson, party leaders rarely offer inducements during the negotiations about bringing someone into their caucus. Finally, we will show that the outcomes for most parliamentarians who reject their party is condemnation, attacks on their character, and difficulty getting re-elected, but also personal fulfilment at having left an untenable situation and, for some, the delight of being free of party control. Along the way, we will describe the anatomy of a caucus departure, from the early beginnings, when an elected official senses that something is wrong, through to the spectacular news coverage when they quit and/or commit the treachery of joining another party. This portrait of the Canadian parliamentary world illuminates the unseen reasons why so many elected representatives are so loyal to their party.

As mentioned, studying the inner workings of party loyalty among politicians presents a research conundrum given that a condition of membership in a party caucus is keeping internal matters confidential, especially in an era of message discipline. Partisans are the only ones who know what happens behind closed doors. However, they may have a history of embellishing, being deceptive, or even fabricating information.[159] They can be paranoid, especially if they are still in office. They avoid writing things down for fear that it could be used against them and develop an invisible wall to keep outsiders at bay. Political parties sometimes guard against risks by directing their caucus not to participate in academic research about internal party matters,[160] and partisans who nevertheless agree to talk with a researcher will self-censor if they fear retribution. The trepidations are understandable, given stories like the snafu of a former Speaker's recollections being played by the Canadian Broadcasting Corporation (CBC) instead of being deposited under embargo with the National Archives,[161] or MPs being conned by opponents who dispatched workers to gather information under the ruse of conducting research interviews.[162] A growing platoon of staff gatekeepers add another layer: they worry about their boss's remarks ending up on social media and so they scrutinize a researcher's online profile when an interview request is placed.[163] Even anonymous sources might require that turns of phrase be reworded.[164]

A pivotal moment that is difficult to study occurs when partisans cast out one of their own members or when a partisan shrugs off loyalty by joining another caucus. Parliamentarians' career decisions are highly individualistic and idiosyncratic,[165] and they are zealous about spinning their reasons for a change in party affiliation. In an ordinary workplace, there are different perspectives about the causes of a job departure,[166] with workers who voluntarily leave due to external factors being more willing to disclose their reasons compared with those who resign because of internal factors.[167] In politics, parliamentarians in compromising situations come up with all sorts of angles to rationalize their behaviour. Many defend their rejection of a party norm by claiming to put constituents first, to want to spend more time with their family, or to battle poor health.[168] Politicians can leak or fabricate information to contrive a version of events that journalists have no reason to question or ability to verify, and media accounts can offer a completely different reason than a politician does.[169] Party leaders likewise apply a strategic spin to personnel change, and sometimes they work with a departing colleague to manage the fallout.[170] It is even fuzzier when a parliamentarian does not condemn their former colleagues, is unable to present a reason for moving, or obscures irritations that would paint them as a sore loser.[171] Covering up true intentions is also a feature of ministerial exits from cabinet.[172]

To make matters more complicated, the reasons behind a decision to change parties are subject to reinterpretation and distortion. Pauline Jewett, one of the few female MPs elected in 1963, was shunned when Prime Minister Pearson proclaimed that his cabinet already had a woman.[173] After losing her seat in 1965, and failing again in the 1968 election, she became a vice-president of the Liberal party, but her animosity with new leader Pierre Trudeau contributed to members replacing her in 1970.[174] Conditions were ripe for Jewett gravitating to another party: she was ambitious, she lacked a lifetime attachment to the Liberals, she had endured isolation on Parliament Hill, she felt ignominy at being shut out by the party establishment, she was frustrated with centralizing power, she disagreed with the party's direction under a leader she did not like, she craved electoral success, and she was concerned that Liberal candidates were backed by American financiers.[175] In 1972, Jewett announced that she would seek the New Democratic Party nomination because she was concerned about the Trudeau government's loose political financing rules, its economic policies, and inaction on American business ownership.[176] News reports mentioned that her trepidations in the Liberal party had begun when the government deployed the *War Measures Act* during the 1970 October crisis, an account that she repeated several years later.[177] Jewett went on to serve as an NDP MP from 1979 to 1988, and died in 1992. In her final public interview she stated that the reason she left the Liberals was the *War Measures Act*,[178] and multiple sources, including recent news reports, publications, Wikipedia, and even the Pauline Jewett Institute, have erroneously claimed that she became a national figure for quitting the Liberal party in 1970 over it.[179] Evidently, multiple sources of data are needed to uncover why some politicians change party allegiances and most do not. For each case, there are multiple sources with multiple tales (each a data point) and events are subject to historical revisionism. Thus, not only can it be impossible to be ascertain facts, but sometimes more than one thing can be true. Multiple sources of information are therefore needed.

Understanding parliamentarians' motivations for challenging political party norms and identifying patterns requires "a full situational analysis" because even the politicians themselves might not be aware of the causal factors or the circumstances.[180] Given that so much information about politicians' partisanship is secret, spin, or conjecture, we embark on mixed method research to triangulate what goes on behind closed doors and to draw out parliamentarians' private ruminations. Our goal is not to establish the facts about any one departure event; rather, it is to uncover patterns and trends in how departures come to pass and, in turn, improve our understanding about party loyalty in general. Investigating why some partisans' loyalty is impenetrable whereas others quit, are expelled, and/or change parties requires an awareness of motivations and pathways across many parties, jurisdictions, and time horizons. As noted, we concentrate on Canadian politicians elected to federal and provincial legislatures from 1980 to 2021, a time frame marked by the dealignment and realignment of many party systems, profound changes in information communications technology, and the emergence of permanent campaigning.

We avail of a trove of data to learn about Canadian partisans' motives and justifications, characteristics, circumstances, and aspirations. Our focus is on MPs and provincial parliamentarians whose political behaviour has challenged or defies norms of team loyalty. We spend little time on the politicians banished from a caucus for ethical, moral, or legal misconduct and who become pariahs to all parties. We set aside the Senate of Canada, whose members do not contest elections; we omit municipalities and land claim–based assemblies because few of them have political parties; and we exclude the three territories given that Nunavut and Northwest Territories do not have parties, though we do consider Northern MPs and take note of a couple of unusual cases involving members of the Legislative Assembly (MLAs) in Yukon. We also avoid focusing on parliamentarians who carve career paths in different parties across the federal/provincial divide, centring our analysis on those who defect and stay at one level, particularly those who do so while in office.

We began our investigation by scouring political science journals and books about party loyalty and Canadian parliamentary politics. Research assistants combed dozens of biographies and autobiographies about former Canadian politicians. We also considered scholarship in media studies, social psychology, marketing, and workplace relations.

Next, we created a party defector database of parliamentarians who exited a party caucus in Canada from 1980 to 2021 and who continued sitting either as an Independent and/or joined a different caucus during that Parliament. We identified 349 cases involving 333 politicians – 93 members of Parliament and 240 provincial parliamentarians who sat after departing their caucus voluntarily or through expulsion between 1 January 1980 and 31 December 2021, some of whom did so more than once. We documented names, year of exit, year of defection (if applicable), years in office, province, gender, age, and the political parties involved. We cross-referenced our list with an existing database of Canadian party switchers.[181] A team of research assistants compiled information about each case by consulting news stories, interview transcripts, reports from election authorities, Statistics Canada data, and parliamentary websites including the Library of Parliament's database of MPs.[182] They coded each case according to a host of characteristics, including the demographics of the person who left caucus; the reported motivations, circumstances, and parties involved; and the subsequent career path of the party switcher. Inter-coder reliability testing resulted in over 80 per cent agreement across all coding choices, after which a researcher adjudicated the remainder. We draw upon our party defector database to provide quantitative evidence behind the trends and patterns observed in our analysis, including comparisons of defections across time, regions, and jurisdictions. The database has been deposited with the open-access University of Alberta Dataverse, available through Borealis.

These data were augmented by a synthesis of exactly 3,300 news stories into 333 briefing notes about the controversial behaviour of every party leaver we identified from 1980 to 2021. We also prepared separate briefing notes for a selection of team players, mavericks, and party leaders. We developed lists of federal and provincial politicians in each province known to have an independence streak by drawing on our regional expertise, by inviting suggestions from legislative librarians and some academic experts in each region, and by conducting online searches. Research assistants collected English and French news reports about those politicians using the subscription news databases Eureka, Factiva, and ProQuest, along with Google searches. They also used more than two dozen search terms such as "maverick" and "rebel" (and their French equivalents) to identify additional uninhibited parliamentarians in Canadian news stories during this time frame.[183] Each of the briefing notes began with a précis of a pivotal breach in the politician's party loyalty, followed by a summary of the reported reasons, key quotes from political actors at the time, a timeline, and the applicable news sources. We used the briefing notes to inform our party defector database, shared them with people we planned to interview, and utilized them to review a broad range of case studies. Additionally, they informed our discourse analysis of media framing. We consulted them to identify commonalities, extract key themes, and highlight anomalies and noteworthy examples. We read the original news stories when we investigated a case more deeply, meaning that we reviewed hundreds of news reports and aggregated information from thousands more. We supplemented this with our own daily news monitoring of current events beyond 2021. The summaries revealed facts and perspectives that are not easily found elsewhere. However, compiling data from electronic sources has its limitations, primarily in under-representing minor shifts in political affiliation in smaller provinces.[184] The briefing notes have likewise been deposited in the University of Alberta Dataverse.

Next, we conducted in-depth interviews with Canadian politicians and political staff, prioritizing those with experiences during our 1980 to 2021 study period. Former parliamentarians are more willing to speak frankly about sensitive matters than sitting members are, although we were turned down by some past floor crossers who were not ready to share their stories, including one high-profile figure who feared legal action. The period of our study presented its own limitations because many of those involved in tests of loyalty decades ago are now deceased, do not have publicly available contact information, or are otherwise unreachable. When designing our sample, we prioritized those involved in a party switch and employed a combination of purposive and convenience sampling to collect a range of perspectives across regions, political parties, time periods, and gender. Near the end of our study, we administered unstructured conversations with a variety of partisans who we selected using convenience sampling. Information about our recruitment methods and our interview script is in appendix 1. All told, we interviewed ninety people across Canada between 2018 and 2024, encompassing seventeen former party leaders (many of whom changed political parties themselves); eighteen parliamentarians who sat with one political party; thirty politicians whose final stopping point was as an Independent at the time of the interview; twelve partisans who switched political parties; and thirteen political staffers (appendix 2).[185] Of these, eighteen conversations were conducted in French. We analysed the interview transcripts with both deductive and inductive approaches. We sought nuanced insights that could be categorized based on frameworks identified during our literature review, such as the policy/office/votes model. We also developed structures by analysing news stories, such as the stages involved in negotiating a party switch. We supplement these frameworks with a narrative analysis to discover new angles and to emphasize the experiences of politicians and political staff in their own words.

Additionally, we incorporate six supplementary sources of qualitative secondary data to further inform our findings.[186] We inspected transcripts of wide-ranging, deep conversation interviews conducted as part of the Library of Parliament's Oral History Project with a dozen MPs who served in the mid- to late twentieth century and who changed parties, among them Pauline Jewett, Hazen Argue (the former CCF, NDP, and Liberal MP), David Kilgour (a former PC, Independent, and Liberal MP) and John Reid (a former Liberal-Labour and Liberal MP). We commissioned a transcript of a panel discussion about party discipline that we organized with some parliamentarians who left their parties, including former federal ministers Jane Philpott and Jody Wilson-Raybould, which was held at Memorial University in February 2020. We listened intently to fifteen long-format interviews conducted in 2022 and 2023 by CBC radio's *The House*, featuring a diverse group of sitting MPs as part of its "Backbenchers' Backyards" series. We examined transcripts of the Canada West Foundation's webinars with some former premiers and provincial ministers about life in a government caucus, which aired in January 2024. Finally, we examined the transcript of a recorded panel discussion of three parliamentarians, including Independent MPP Bobby Ann Brady, on the topic of party politics and Independents. This panel was hosted in January 2024 by the Churchill Society for the Advancement of Parliamentary Democracy in Toronto.

A further source of interview data was supplied by the Samara Centre for Democracy, which interviewed ninety-one MPs who retired between 2008 and 2021. Most of these MPs would be considered team players. Using MAXQDA qualitative data analysis software, we analysed the English-language transcripts using an inductive, three-stage coding process to identify common themes.[187] This involved two independent coders reading through each interview in its entirety, identifying passages that pertained to party loyalty and disloyalty (open coding). In their second pass through the transcripts, they tagged specific snippets of text as belonging to a series of themes, including maverick-like behaviour, loyalty, party discipline, and becoming an Independent (axial coding). A final round of selective coding involved the lead researcher reviewing the transcripts for accuracy in tagging. Using this as a coding frame, the French-language transcripts were reviewed using keyword searches for similar themes. A previous analysis of a smaller corpus of the Samara Centre transcripts found considerable evidence that former MPs "highly value loyalty to and within their party caucus team."[188]

Finally, distinct from our briefing notes, we created a separate news stories database concerning party switchers from 1980 to 2021 that informed our analysis of media frames. In media studies, "framing" involves political actors highlighting a fragment of information to define a problem, establish a cause, evoke a moral dimension, and recommend a solution.[189] For example, Conservatives attempted to frame Emerson's floor crossing as providing a new government with ministerial experience and a foothold in Vancouver, and as reflecting the nobility of a faithful public servant who prioritized public service over partisanship.[190] We learnt from the briefing notes that exiting a party typically attracts a burst of attention that soon dies out. So, we searched the Canadian Newsstand (English) and Eureka (French) subscription news databases using the name of a party leaver and the date of the departure to compile media articles, op-ed columns, editorials, and opinion letters published from the day of the defection up to fourteen days after the event. After we removed duplicates, we ended up with 2,850 stories. A further 450 stories were later identified during the briefing notes phase of our study.

The media stories of each switcher were coded using the qualitative analysis software NVivo. We created a coding grid to identify the absence/presence of various themes in each news story, such as the motivations for switching, fallout discussions, framing (e.g., events, switching, gender), and adjectives describing the switch. The coding was conducted by a research assistant. A pretest of the coding grid using 10 per cent of the articles reached 92 per cent inter-coder reliability. After the discrepancies in our coding were resolved, we reached 100 per cent reliability for the entire corpus. Frames were identified through an exploratory inductive analysis of a sample of content in the news stories database,[191] which involved reading each news item to identify the different narratives about the types of defections and reasons to leave one's party, enabling us to inductively identify patterns and the different tales being told.

Outline of the Book

We begin with party message discipline. Chapter 2 describes how political parties have accumulated power, which has deepened with their use of public opinion research and brand management. Parties assert their control from the moment that they recruit election candidates. They demand such strict adherence to message discipline that parliamentarians become brand ambassadors, which can flounder when the communications orthodoxy emboldens the public's preference for candid politicians who seem authentic. Next, we establish the broader authority of party leaders and political staff over Canadian parliamentarians. Chapter 3 outlines how a leader and the leader's agents manage caucuses by reaching out to them, by rewarding supporters, and by reining in dissidents. Backbenchers counteract that power when many of them rebel.

We then delve into the main types of partisans featured in the loyalty scale presented in table 1.2. In chapter 4, about team players, we discuss the socio-psychological connections to a party identity that inhibit dissent or facilitate loyalty. Implicitly, this chapter describes the normal path in Canadian party politics – that of party loyalists whose values, voting, and communications all align with the group. We differentiate low-profile backbenchers from hyper-partisans and relationship-builders. Some team players do clap back, and leaders must contend with moments of friction with even the most devout partisans.

One step along the party loyalty spectrum are the party mavericks who stay with a party but test their colleagues' tolerance for acrimony. In chapter 5 we discuss tempestuous partisans who develop reputations for being outspoken but who, despite their bluster, can carve out long political careers within their respective parties and outlast a carousel of leaders. We discuss the moniker of a maverick, a label applied to politicians whose individualism and authenticity are publicly revered, and who are difficult for the party leadership to manage. We compare the antics of party mavericks, both past and present, showing how the activism of independent-minded parliamentarians has evolved. This is illustrated through a brief case study of two contrasting examples of caucus management in 2002 and 2023. We also comment on how frustrations in a caucus can boil over into rebellion.

Parliamentarians who shed their party affiliation without assuming another are party leavers. In chapter 6, we discuss the deteriorating relationships that lead to a turning point that results in a parliamentarian quitting the caucus or being kicked out of it. While most cases of voluntary and involuntary departures are isolated individualistic events, sometimes extraordinary situations arise involving mass resignations, splinter groups, coalition governments, or a party disbanding. We untangle the murky grounds for expulsion and the process of expelling partisans. We explain that many ex-partisans embrace freedom as an Independent, at least until they are confronted with the difficulty of being re-elected as one.

Some politicians who leave a political party join a rival group. Chapter 7 differentiates the main types of party switchers as those who "two-step" (becoming an Independent before changing teams) and those who cross the floor directly. We delve into extraordinary defections: party hoppers, boomerang partisans, leaders who switch parties, mass defections, party rebranding and mergers, and party entrepreneurs who start their own organizations. Chapter 8 gets into motivations and private negotiations. While media narratives often attribute party exits to policy disputes and career ambition, we suggest that most Canadian parliamentarians who switch parties do so driven by ideological conviction or personal differences with the leader. We organize behind-the-scenes discussions along the four stages of discussion, bargaining, agreement, and framing. This chapter presents the dramatic days and hours before a caucus member switches parties and sets in motion a grand unveilling that is often timed to embarrass the leader of the vacated party.

In chapter 9, we document the aftermath of a parliamentarian leaving a party. We identify three main frames in news stories about defections: power dynamics between the leader and the leaver, political ambition, and loyalty to constituents. We synthesize the benefits and the considerable toll of leaving a party, which include personal, social, and political costs. We discuss the changing relationships that a party switch brings, the public reaction, and the career implications, which are reasons why so many partisan parliamentarians dismiss switching as non-viable.

We conclude in chapter 10 by discussing strategies to enhance the role of team members in parliamentary politics. We summarize our findings and outline potential areas for reform, including proposals for empowering parliamentarians through new, non-partisan training; restrictions on the presence and role of senior political staff in caucus business; and adjustments to election laws and rules of procedure, including limits on the use of confidence as tool of party discipline. We call for new rules prohibiting floor crossing, instead requiring would-be party switchers to spend time as an Independent or stand for re-election before they can be permitted to take up another party's banner. Combined, these measures would help build public trust in Canadian democracy by restoring the role of parliamentarians as trustees of the public good and as delegates of their constituents, and by counteracting the considerable pressures that incentivize them to become mouthpieces for their respective parties.

We will show that personalities and egos in parliamentary caucuses are held together by a glue of institutional, social, political, and technological dynamics. We will explain how efforts to stamp out individualism reflect a normative dimension that Canadian political parties ought to be stable and unified, which, in the current environment, reflects a credo of message discipline.[192] The insights in *No I in Team* provide fresh perspectives on how loyalty, representation, and communications intersect within political parties and their parliamentary caucuses.

2 Party Message Discipline

In 2006, Prime Minister Harper informed the Conservative national caucus of pending cutbacks to government programs. He warned his MPs to say nothing about it. "There will be impacts in some of your ridings," he remarked, according to a former member of that caucus.[1] "They will affect people, and you may be tempted to talk about them. But don't. Anyone who has anything to say about this will soon find out they have a very short political career." Scenarios like this are baked into parliamentary politics, pitting elected representatives in dilemmas of balancing loyalty to their party and how to best represent constituent interests. Unity of message is now paramount.

For decades, party affiliation and loyalty have imbued Canada's legislatures, accompanied by critiques of party higher-ups going too far in their management of how backbenchers vote and, more recently, what they say in public forums. The complaints have been accelerated by electronic communications that enable central agents to circulate messaging to parliamentarians and monitor what is said. Message discipline – the act of sticking to consistent talking points that mimic the leader and which are peddled by communications staff – has sharpened hyper-partisan discourse, which draws deeper divisions between political parties, increases in-group affinities, and enhances out-group animosities. How does the changing media environment inform the desire to control the message? What are the key components of message discipline? How do regimented communications foster party loyalty – and how can partisans carve a niche within those constraints? To answer these questions and to understand party loyalty in Canada, we need some awareness of the evolution of political parties as conduits for parliamentary representation and as engineers of interest aggregation. In this chapter, we summarize the accrual of power in political parties and the communications pressures that drive message discipline.

Accrual of Power by Political Parties

Throughout Canadian history, parliamentarians have gradually ceded power to party leaders and their proxies. Political parties were still forming at Confederation in 1867, and they are not mentioned in the *British North America Act*. In the late nineteenth century, Canadian political parties were such insular, informal configurations that some election candidates did not commit to one, and elected officials were not hardbound to voting as a cohesive group. Members of Parliament traded their votes on bills and motions in exchange for government spoils, such as jobs for supporters and infrastructure for their electoral district. Following an election, as back-room negotiations to secure Independents' support were in motion, the party press would claim that these parliamentarians were allies of their party.[2] Once these "loose fish" chose a side, their loyalty had to be maintained.[3] Bargaining power tilted in their favour, partly because the Standing Orders enabled an individual MP to prolong debate by speaking at length, which resulted in government bills being held up and even occasionally defeated without being deemed a test of confidence.[4] As well, the feebleness of political parties complicated government accountability due to limited structure in legislative proceedings, resulting in grandstanding and deadlocking.[5]

Political parties soon gained steam. The introduction of secret ballot voting in 1878 curbed the ability of an election candidate's supporters to intimidate voters and for the winner to declare allegiance to a party only after the broader election results were known. The gradual expansion of the right to vote caused parties to expand their reach into society. Combined, these factors contributed to a pronounced drop in the number of Independents elected.[6] In the early twentieth century, extra-parliamentary party organizations within emerging Conservative and Liberal traditions became structured operations with permanent staff who provided centralized supports,[7] while backbenchers saw their input diminish on election policy.[8] As federal elections shifted away from staggered voting days, these old-line parties became more cohesive and integral to running nationwide campaigns. Most operated provincial-level wings as well, contesting provincial elections with the same resources and personnel. The advent of radio elevated the presence of the leader as a spokesperson for the entire party, reducing the influence of local newspaper owners as regional chieftains, while the adoption of the merit principle in government hiring hampered the ability of individual parliamentarians to distribute the public goods that could attract local support.[9]

As political parties congealed into powerful organizations, some politicians spurned the scourge of partisanship by underscoring their independence, such as Mary Ellen Smith, the first woman elected to the British Columbia (BC) legislature. In 1918 she campaigned in a by-election as an Independent "free woman," a term used in liberal circles to tout virtue, reform, and policies that were ignored by men in the two-party system.[10] Smith was re-elected as a Liberal and became the first woman in Canada to serve as a cabinet minister, but resigned soon thereafter because she could not abide by the constraints of cabinet solidarity that prevented her from publicly critiquing government policy. The rise of the progressive movement became the most important driver of party politics in the inter-war period. This is ironic, given that many progressive activists like Smith viewed partisanship as a capitalist tool to oppress the masses. They sought to replace elite-based party politics with a corporatist form of representation based on competing class groups. Progressives aligned as farmer and labour parties to contest elections, sometimes with great success, as with the United Farmers forming provincial governments in Ontario, Manitoba, and Alberta. Once in power, however, these progressive groups adopted party discipline and hierarchical organizational structures.[11] A loose coalition of provincial groups, the Progressives won enough seats in the 1921 federal election to become the second-largest contingent in the House of Commons.[12] They implemented measures to prioritize constituency representation, including a requirement that their election candidates sign a formal resignation letter, which was held by their local nominating committee.[13] The letter provided the local party executive with the ability to remove a Progressive MP who did not actively communicate with constituents or follow through on localized platform commitments. The old-line parties adapted. They expanded their extra-parliamentary organizations, built local constituency associations, and sold party memberships. Without the shackles of party discipline, the Progressives became divided on policy, which led to threats of resignations, floor crossing, and an existential crisis.[14]

As the progressive movement waned, many of its proponents moved into old-line or newly formed parties, further embedding party organizations as the foundation of elections. Over time, parliamentarians ceded authority to the broader Conservative and Liberal party membership who selected leaders and weighed in on policy at party conventions.[15] The entrenchment of third parties like the Cooperative Commonwealth Federation (CCF) and Social Credit reduced the incentives for backbenchers to seek more opportunity within the two dominant parties because they had other options.[16] What happened next is consistent with the "organization pressure theory" that parliamentary caucuses congealed in response to the growing clout of more active extra-parliamentary party organizations.[17]

In Parliament, the formal recognition of parties took shape through a series of measures, including seemingly minor steps such as assigning different rooms for caucus meetings to each parliamentary group.[18] The Standing Orders were modified to grant the government more control over the parliamentary agenda through the power to introduce closure and restrict the number of amendments, and by reducing time for private members' business.[19] Introduced in 1913, closure in particular tipped the scale in favour of the governing party – "the moment when the government won almost total control over the legislative process," as Godbout put it.[20] The result was more government business on the daily agenda, fewer opportunities for backbenchers to intercede, and fewer topics of debate.[21] This had a centralizing effect: the cabinet now had more control over the legislative agenda and leaders' offices needed to coordinate limited speaking time.[22] Party whips were tasked with presenting the Speaker with an ordered list of MPs who should be invited to speak. By the mid-twentieth century, these and other changes to the rules of Parliament left little time for private members' business. The pendulum swung briefly when several changes, notably in 1955 and 1962, provided backbenchers with more opportunities to introduce bills and motions,[23] but it drifted back in 1968 when time allocation – whereby the government sets a timetable to limit debate on each stage of a bill – was introduced to further limit debate. In chapter 10, we urge scholars to examine similar trends at the provincial level and encourage lawmakers to revisit these earlier reforms as a means of restoring parliamentarians' authority as trustees and delegates, and empowering Independents.

This reduction of time and autonomy in the House of Commons for individual members of Parliament contributed to centralizing power in the hands of party leaders.[24] Partisanship was in full force when the government-side MPs who thumped on their desks in approval of the cabinet were derided as trained seals by the opposition beginning in 1951[25] and as pundits lampooned backbenchers as "a faceless swarm" who voted with their party and avoided saying anything offensive.[26] However, the uproar over the Louis St. Laurent government's use of closure in 1957 to conclude heated debate over its plans to fund a trans-Canada natural gas pipeline thrust into the spotlight the perils of the appointed executive disrespecting the elected legislature.[27]

As the size of government grew and the number of parliamentarians increased to reflect population growth, parliamentary parties gained greater formal recognition, leading to a reduction in backbenchers' independence. Partisanship coursed through debates and votes at the same time as members began being identified by their political party in *Hansard*.[28] In 1963, political parties were officially recognized as entities in the House of Commons, provided they had at least a dozen MPs.[29] Party status accorded exclusivity to partisans in larger parliamentary groups to respond to ministerial statements, to ask most of the questions during Question Period, to determine the order of speaking, to appoint members of parliamentary committees, and to receive research budgets.[30] This meant that MPs depended on the parliamentary party hierarchy, including the whips, to authorize a meaningful role in Parliament. It also accorded Independents and members of small parties fewer resources and speaking opportunities. Even then, most backbenchers had little to no role in Question Period and their speeches were often delivered to a nearly empty chamber. "What am I here for? To be affable under all circumstances?" wondered an MP in 1969.[31]

Backbenchers turned to other settings on Parliament Hill to exert influence. Caucus meetings became a more important link with the leader and their inner circle, while regional caucus meetings provided a party's MPs from a defined geographical area with an intimate forum to vocalize and mobilize.[32] Standing parliamentary committees of the House of Commons were institutionalized in 1968 as forums to monitor departmental activity. For many MPs in recognized parties, this review work offered a chance to perform a meaningful role as legislators, and they lobbied the party whip to secure appointments to committees of interest (chapter 3).

Nevertheless, the accrual of power from individual parliamentarians accelerated as broadcast television trained the public eye on leaders, as the media was supported by a growing nationwide polling industry, and as political parties employed professional news-management strategies.[33] Outspoken MPs were further marginalized with the televising of House of Commons proceedings in 1977 that introduced structure and controls, such as microphones to limit speaking time, and which increased the ability of party officials and other observers to scrutinize their actions.[34] As attention shifted outside the legislature, political parties gained further ground over parliamentarians. Until the early 1970s, federal ballots listed a candidate's name, civic address, and occupation – rather than their party affiliation – requiring voters to have at least a basic familiarity with the individuals running to represent them. In 1970, the *Canada Elections Act* deemed that only the party's official nominee could publicly identify with a party, assigned the leader responsibility for approving nominees, and, as of the 1972 election, replaced the candidate's occupation with a party (if any) on the ballot.[35] Ever since, Canadians who know what party they support have been able to send a representative to Ottawa without a need to even recognize the name of who they are voting for, which has amplified the importance of party in vote decisions.[36] A similar setup exists in the provinces, where party labels appeared on ballots at vastly different times, including 1944 in Alberta, 1967 in New Brunswick and PEI, 1970 in Manitoba and in Nova Scotia, 1991 in Newfoundland and Labrador, and 2007 in Ontario.[37] Moreover, the practice of authorizing party leaders to decide who may seek (re-)election under the party banner further tilted the balance of power in their favour.

The requirement that the leader sign candidate nomination papers created a serious threat to troublesome caucus members, who henceforth faced the prospect that party resources would be redirected to other districts or, far worse, that they would be barred from running with the party again. The lack of standardized, transparent nomination rules persists across most parties, adding to the leader's advantage and which ought to be reformed (chapter 10). Parliamentarians interested in seeking re-election had tangible reasons to avoid conflict with the leader, as they do in other countries where leaders influence candidate selection.[38] As one Liberal MP put it in 1971, "The whole party is changing. It's becoming much more centralized. Much more directed to the leadership. Members of Parliament are basically elected as party supporters, not as individuals."[39] Rugged individualism began to fade.

MPs reclaimed some ground in the mid-1980s with reforms resulting from the Special Committee on Reform of the House of Commons (known as the McGrath Report after its chair, Newfoundland MP James McGrath). It sought, in part, to address the dominance of parties in the legislature. Backbenchers, the Committee reported, were "often obliged to submerge their personal beliefs in those of the party and vote accordingly in the House of Commons. The member that disagrees consistently with the party is often dismissed as a maverick."[40] Instead, the Committee argued that parliamentarians should be empowered to serve as both trustees and delegates, not merely partisans. It emphasized that MPs ought to have a greater role in shaping legislation and enjoy "a reasonable measure of freedom from party discipline."[41] Some in the media agreed, with the *Globe and Mail* calling for parties not to "trumpet signs of disagreement in the ranks of the other parties as evidence that those parties are falling apart"[42] – something that the media itself often does. The McGrath Report led to the Brian Mulroney government endorsing a suite of reforms, including the Speaker being elected in a secret ballot vote, an expanded committee system, and bills or motions advanced by private members becoming votable instead of for debate only.[43] Crucially, the government did not meaningfully address other concerns raised by the McGrath Committee, including the overuse of confidence measures and whipped votes.[44]

Centralization of power within political parties continued through other means. Rule changes reduced the amount of time allotted for MPs to introduce their own bills.[45] The formalization of election promises was an additional constraint because partisans are bound to publicly support the policies in their party's platform. For much of the early twentieth century, a party's election pledges were scattered across a hodge-podge of parliamentary debates, leader's stump speeches, news stories, and ephemera such as brochures and newspaper advertisements.[46] Local candidates sometimes made promises that did not align with one another or the position of the leader. The era of programmatic parties arrived in 1993 when the Liberal Party of Canada unveiled a corporate-style booklet that itemized and costed the promises in its campaign platform, which became an accountability instrument and publicity tool.[47] Prime Minister Chrétien cited that platform as why all Liberal MPs were obliged to vote a certain way, such as in favour of tougher sentences for hate crimes against members of the LGBTQ2+ community: "You are a member of a team. You cannot have the ticket of being a Liberal but after that you're not supporting the party.... [The campaign pledge] was written on page 86 of the red book. I don't need to read that to everybody. I said, 'You campaigned on it.'"[48] The influence of the caucus and individual representatives was further diluted as the party leaders' staff drove platform development based on public opinion research and input from party officials, in contrast with a fading practice of party delegates and caucus members setting election policy at party conventions.[49]

Throughout their collective evolution – from cadres of parliamentarians to mass parties with larger membership bases to today's electoral-professional parties waging permanent campaigns[50] – party leaders have found ways to consolidate power over parliamentarians. Take for example Premier Ford who, while running to become leader of the PC Party of Ontario, pledged to "never muzzle members of our caucus."[51] Yet there are limits, especially once a party forms government. Outspoken maverick Randy Hillier discovered as much in 2019 when he was suspended from the Ontario PC caucus for a controversial exchange with the parent of an autistic child. What got him expelled was his ensuing public retort that the premier's staff were vindictive because he had brushed off their edicts to cheer the premier in Question Period and share government posts online.[52] In a letter, the caucus chair admonished the garrulous backbencher for escalating the feud and for having a chronic disinterest in being "a team player."[53] That messaging was repeated by caucus members, who observed that there are consequences for not behaving as part of a united team.[54] Premier Ford echoed these sentiments following a pair of expulsions involving PC MPPs who refused to follow the government's COVID-19 public health restrictions,[55] and did so again when he turfed a backbencher after she posted a video of her meeting with an anti-Islam activist.[56] It is common for caucus evictions to be the climax of many internal disagreements – leaders want to grow their caucus, not shrink it, and they can stir caucus backlash if they overplay their authority. A leader's power is finite and vulnerable if caucus members are unhappy which, paradoxically, incentivizes leaders and their staff to urge everyone to fall in line. Changes in communication technologies have accelerated this inclination.

Political Communications

Journalists have long acted as intermediaries between politicians and their audiences, continually filtering, shaping, and prioritizing what they believe Canadians need to know about public affairs. Politicians quickly learn that the fourth estate is rarely a neutral or dispassionate participant in the production of news.

In a process known as mediatization, the press participates in the construction of political reality by framing and packaging information, and by prioritizing which issues warrant public attention.[57] It applies game and war frames to reportage that emphasizes conflict over consensus, assigns winners and losers, and uses hostile language that pits opponents against one another.[58] Discord within a political party is newsworthy, even more so if that party controls the government. Instead of being framed as healthy democratic discourse, mild disagreement between a parliamentarian and the official party line can be depicted as animosity, and one or two voices of dissent within a parliamentary caucus can be presented as the pretext to full-on mutiny.[59] The propensity of the news media to dramatize and editorialize, such as by portraying leaders as willing to do anything to win or by treating party volunteers as affiliates whose words or actions reflect party values,[60] contributes to cynicism about politicians and political institutions.[61] Politicians sustain the media's interest in political battles by criticizing and denigrating members of other political parties – and sometimes their own wayward colleagues. As a result, the media environment for most parliamentarians becomes fraught with risk if they stray from approved messaging.

Digital disruption adds to this peril. Until recently, politicians could count on community newspapers as a mediated forum to raise awareness of local issues, and much of the attentive public tuned in together to watch one of a few television news programs. As more Canadians turn towards foreign-owned social media, streaming platforms, and international news sources for information, the advertising revenues that sustain mainstream community news production, particularly print, suffer. Local reporting about legislatures and civic affairs has correspondingly declined,[62] creating information vacuums that are susceptible to the spread of distortions and lies. When politicians canvass for votes or interact with constituents, they are startled by how many people do not talk about local matters, assert falsehoods and conspiracy theories, or have tuned out of news entirely.[63]

A further concern is that hyper-partisan communication feeds the forces of affective polarization that have gradually sorted Canadians into ideological camps over the past two decades.[64] Increasing numbers of Canadians are exposed to information that reinforces their interests and biases, whether it is shared online by friends or recommended by platforms that track their online behaviour and suggest tailored content. In political circles, these filter bubbles run deep, reflecting growing pressure on partisans to publicly support their own team and to criticize other parties. Seemingly petty tests of party loyalty are common. Even something as simple as liking a social media post from a member of an opposing caucus can prompt someone in the leader's office to advise a parliamentarian or political staffer to retract the action.

All too often, politicians witness the strategic adoption of policy stances designed to start a conflict, deepen divisions, and provoke debates that put opponents on the defensive while becoming fodder for party fundraising appeals.[65] Erin O'Toole, former leader of the Conservative Party, has warned that parliamentarians are chasing "algorithms down a sinkhole of diversion and division," where "performance politics is fuelling polarization [and] virtue signalling is replacing discussion."[66] He criticized MPs for using the House of Commons to "generate clips," referring to instances where MPs stage performances in the chamber to create social media content. This includes provocative exchanges at otherwise mundane parliamentary committee meetings[67] or the opposition leader directing questions to the prime minister even when the PM is absent.[68] Some MPs feign indignation for the video clips, which causes ministers to attempt to stymie the digital theatrics, such as by responding in the other official language.[69] The content is ushered into an unruly online public sphere where politicians are subjected to abuse from trolls who criticize them relentlessly, which aggravates feelings of a hostile political environment, particularly for women and other politically marginalized groups.[70] Looming large is the disruption that generative artificial intelligence (AI) is starting to unleash on politics, including the role of automated bots in manipulating online discourse,[71] and its ability to speed up message creation and distort reality.[72] If history is any guide, AI will likely give further reason for political parties to encroach upon local candidates and representatives.

The proliferation of public opinion research is another factor in the diminishing influence of parliamentarians, especially backbenchers. Parliamentarians were once relied upon by the party leader's office as crucial intermediaries for understanding their constituents' concerns. Their local interactions provided them with a unique insight into the public's mood. They and their local supporters maintained their own membership lists and records, rudimentary as they may have been, and were responsible for what they needed to know to be a successful representative and candidate for office. Some politicians organized their own constituency-level opinion polls, whether by telephone or on-the-spot interviews outside grocery stores, churches, or major events.[73] Political parties counted on certain parliamentarians, their staff, and local party presidents to report on developments in geographic areas that were key to the party's success. Regional ministers were party chieftains, and caucus meetings were important sounding boards, filtering local perspectives into party decision-making.

Parliamentarians still act as interlocutors with the leader's office; however, their monopoly on local market intelligence faded away as public opinion survey research became more affordable in the late twentieth century. Computer-assisted telephone interviewing, reduced overhead, and falling long-distance fees led to lower costs, enhanced precision, and faster results.[74] The arrival of online panels and interactive voice response systems increased the ability of political parties to fund large-scale tracking surveys as well as narrowly focused surveys, effectively cutting parliamentarians out of the political marketing process altogether.[75] Public opinion polls have become so ubiquitous that the media regularly reports on the latest horse race numbers, focusing on which party is leading and which leader is most popular, thus emphasizing macro-level factors that influence voter behaviour.

At the same time, political financing practices have become more centrally coordinated with technology. By the late twentieth century, political parties were building comprehensive databases of supporters, drawing on data from government sources like lists of electors, poll-by-poll vote results, donor records, and census data. Additionally, they purchased demographic maps and customer lists from private companies, enabling them to construct consumer behaviour profiles and tailor their outreach efforts more effectively.[76] The compilation of individualized data served multiple purposes: identifying supporters for microtargeting with persuasive messages, encouraging attendance at rallies, urging canvassing efforts, mobilizing voters on Election Day, and prompting donations.[77]

These databases became the engines behind customer relationship management software, enabling parties to send regular appeals through email, social media, and text messages, after which they can analyze the success rate of different messaging and refine their strategies. The ability to track which issues and messaging are resonating with specific segments of the electorate informs highly targeted communications that galvanizes partisans to act.[78] As the internet became more widespread, the search for supporters spread to data mining and digital interactions through party websites, social media, e-petitions, robocalls, and canvassing efforts that uploaded information to the Cloud.[79] Many parliamentarians across the country grew to rely on their party's digital infrastructure for data capture and storage.

Coinciding with these technological developments were the rule changes that motivated electronic fundraising drives. At the federal level, donation limits were drastically reduced in 2004, and a per-vote subsidy was introduced. This was followed by the prohibition of corporate and union donations in 2007, a further reduction in the individual contribution limits, and the eventual elimination of the per-vote subsidy in 2015.[80] Provincially, fundraising rules vary, with many provinces still permitting traditional fundraising from individuals and organizations with deep pockets. Whatever the political financing regime, all major political parties now use data-driven, targeted tactics to supplement traditional fundraising.

As a result of these changes, in many circumstances the direction of information flow has reversed, from bottom-up to top-down. Particularly at the federal level, some parties have turned their franchising approach up a notch by compelling parliamentarians and their local supporters to feed national voter databases with local information.[81] For some, centralization of database marketing is part of their role as brand ambassadors, with those who are more reliant on the party for funding being more likely to emphasize the party's brand in their communications, rather than focusing on themselves. The constant updating of party databases allows central party organizers to directly engage with a mass of supporters and to run statistical analysis. This reduces the perceived value of a parliamentarian's role in speaking for their constituents because party operatives can generate a data report and dismiss a backbencher's interpretation of local issues or trends as being too narrow or impressionistic. Caucus meetings used to be an exclusive forum for leaders to learn about public opinion; increasingly, they are opportunities for party pollsters to present the latest market research and for staff to recommend messaging strategies.[82] Rural parliamentarians in particular worry that influential staff working in office towers in the capital rely on numerical analyses and make assumptions about life in rural areas without ever visiting these communities.[83] This said, the raft of data is a double-edged sword. Leaders must now contend with metrics that constantly rate their performance in the public's eyes, which can create anxiety in the caucus – members who Chrétien once dubbed "nervous Nellies."[84]

Another way that backbenchers, even ministers, have been sidelined is through political strategists' focus on minimizing the risk of lower ranking affiliates tarnishing the party's brand. As we have mentioned, individual parliamentarians can stir trouble with as little as an erratic social media post whereby they are accused of improper, but not illegal, conduct that is buoyed by news coverage, rumours, and misinformation that feed criticism and public outrage.[85] Claims of inappropriateness must be quickly assessed by the leader's circle to determine the relative harm and what, if any, rapid response is warranted. The fastest way to defuse a crisis is often to conclude the story arc by accepting responsibility and, when appropriate, delivering a sincere apology.[86] Nevertheless, some politicians are unwilling to admit fault; as one Conservative MP conceded, her social media post claiming that the rising cost of living was causing some parents to traffic their children was "inartfully worded."[87] Whatever the pathway, controversies that are swiftly dealt with to the apparent satisfaction of critics deny opponents an opportunity to prolong the uproar. A preferable situation, of course, is to take steps to prevent a communications crisis from occurring in the first place.

Senior partisans and their staff emphasize the importance of politicians being consistent in everything they say. Party leaders learn that it is vital for caucus members to avoid spontaneity, especially when interacting with journalists. Former federal NDP leader Tom Mulcair believes that repetition is crucial for maintaining control over messaging. "Message discipline is essential in party politics. If you leave the media a crack at the base of a window big enough to stick a crowbar in, they will," he told us.[88] "Repeating the same line over and again without saying anything drives people crazy, but it works. If you are good at it, you'll avoid problems." Applying a slant and reiterating a key message irrespective of the question is a timeworn component of spin that politicians employ to manage the media.[89] The repetition of interconnected, simple messages that communicate consistent principles and values across all platforms has an even deeper purpose: fostering loyalty to a brand.

Branding is a marketing strategy that recognizes that many human judgments are based on emotions, identity, and habits, and that memorable visuals convey information faster and more powerfully than the written word.[90] At its core, a party's brand is the identity that the public attaches to it. Managers wrap unique selling propositions into a brand that is strategically different from what competitors are offering, aligning all communications touchpoints so that every interaction with an organization is reasonably consistent. Consistency extracts value: brands are shaped by the sum of all communications impressions, from advertising and publicity to personal experiences and long-standing loyalties. Logos, symbols, slogans, attributes, and promises that reinforce each other increase the chances of audiences noticing a singular overarching message and remembering it, which is smart strategy in a fragmented information landscape where people are exposed to vastly different communications channels, form impressions based on limited information, and typically do not conduct a detailed review of options.[91] Repeating simple messages responds to humans speeding up decision-making by drawing on stored knowledge to rapidly process new stimuli and recalling messages that they have been exposed to multiple times.[92] A cabaret of mixed messages and complexity generates confusion, whereas harmonizing communications saves time and money, and fosters goodwill among customers and workers.

A powerful facet of branding is its strategic objective to nurture an emotional connection and loyalty, both within the organization and with external supporters. Marketers seek to ignite positive perceptions which, in addition to solidifying market share, can lead to consumers trusting a brand enough to pay a premium above its real value.[93] For brand enthusiasts, the brand becomes part of their identity, to the point that lifestyle groups emerge,[94] and they remain loyal even if the brand fails to live up to expectations or is outperformed by competitors.[95] The challenge for marketers is thus to translate consumer awareness of a brand into preference and then insistence.[96] Political strategists adopt many of the same approaches to instil loyalty to and throughout the party.

Political operatives approach the electoral battleground as a competition to win over electors who have a weak commitment to parties, who pay limited attention to politics, and who experience information overload. These strategists, as with journalists, understand that most people are uninterested in a lengthy policy proposal or participating in the evaluation of an obscure government program. Complex issues are compressed into themes that are packaged in a straightforward, pithy manner, often accompanied by buzzwords. They isolate sub-messages designed to resonate with slivers of the electorate who are reached through coded language and narrow forms of electronic communication, such as email blasts and social media advertising.[97] The strategic objective is to nurture a relationship with a swath of supporters who will be loyal, recruit others, forgive mistakes, and be impervious to opponents' critiques and appeals.

A well-structured political brand brings clarity to a turbulent communications ecosystem. Soon after Justin Trudeau became Liberal leader in 2013, the party implored local adherence to its brand standards to prevent actions that could harm the image of the party or its leader.[98] Manuals advised Liberal candidates, MPs, electoral district associations, and staff to standardize all contact – "everything from party colours, logos and websites to the way we interact on the phone, on the doorstep and on social media."[99] The manuals stressed that consistent branding generates recognition and referrals, provides clear direction for volunteers, enhances voter understanding, and strengthens emotional connections. For all electoral-professional parties, brand-reputation management extends beyond managing candidates and parliamentarians: it includes dealing with controversial comments of a riding association president[100] and distancing the party from irate constituents who livestream their visit to the legislature.[101] A culture of brand image obsession sees the leader's office seeking to influence every point of interaction.

Evolving Attitudes

The primacy of franchisor brands in Canadian politics – the party, the party leader, the government – has contoured and limited what franchisees can say and do. In the 1980s, parliamentarians had more licence to express their genuine opinion, which was considered part of the fabric of democratic representation. Backbenchers could raise doubts, or even be inimical, about party policy. A glib comment in a community hall might have been reported in a local newspaper without attracting broader attention. More ominously, the principle of presumption of innocence, coupled with their elite status, meant that parliamentarians formally charged with a criminal offence merely withdrew from an active role in the caucus. Those who sat as Independents could be reinstated if the criminal charges were dropped or they were acquitted in court.[102]

This changed. By the twenty-first century, party leaders preferred to permanently sever connections with politicians who commit intolerable actions. Partisans now instinctively disassociate from candidates and caucus members who exhibit prejudice[103] and, as we will explain, aspiring candidates are dropped if their murky past is likely to be a problem. With some exceptions, a parliamentarian facing allegations of workplace harassment is sidelined while an investigation is underway and is unlikely to return,[104] while those charged with a crime usually resign or are expelled.[105] There are exceptions, such as when a premier has few qualified people to replace a cabinet minister[106] or a bad actor has their own independent base of support.[107] As well, there is a double standard for leaders, some of whom run governments despite revelations about their past that would have hobbled the career of a lower-ranking politician. Abuses of power are usually a ticket out of cabinet and out of the party, however.

The hypersensitivities to bad conduct reflect the so-called cancel culture that weaves throughout the modern political and media ecosystem. The impulse to vanquish opponents from the public sphere has expanded inward as organizations seek to purify their own teams as part of what some call the culture wars.[108] The digital political landscape is filled with potential hazards: reposting information can get a parliamentarian in trouble because of the original author's shady background,[109] and word choices during a parliamentary committee meeting can touch off social media backlash.[110] Doorbell camera footage can cost you a seat at the cabinet table,[111] as can odious remarks in a secretly recorded conversation.[112] All of this drives or amplifies headlines, travelling between mainstream media and the digital marketplace. As mentioned, one containment tactic is to coordinate an apology, which can satisfy the leader,[113] but sometimes apologies and reparations are not warranted nor viable.

On the other hand, there can be public empathy for a politician who is forthcoming about their frailties and/or owns up to their mistakes. Political parties attempt to control the frame about certain types of missteps by having a politician reveal an indiscretion or conviction from long ago, express regret, or say that they learnt from the experience and that the poor behaviour does not reflect who they are today.[114] Someone struggling with a relatable human frailty, such as mental health, drug addictions, or alcoholism, can open up publicly to share their story.[115] While attitudes vary, as morality standards evolve so does the political response.

In the legislature, attitudes evolve with each cohort and with more diverse membership. Certain types of social groups are more welcoming of diverse voices than others: those that emphasize the achievement of shared goals, for example, give greater space to members from under-represented social categories than do groups that emphasize coordinated behaviour and norms.[116] Women, Indigenous Peoples, racialized Canadians, members of the LGBTQ2+ community, younger people, immigrants, and others are, in theory, more likely to be uncomfortable with the procedural rules, parliamentary traditions, and cultures of a political system they did not design and within which they are outnumbered by older, white, Christian, heterosexual men.[117] "It was a male place to be. Some want to treat it like a hockey game. They openly talked about offense and defense. I couldn't really relate to that," a female politician told us.[118]

In the early 1990s, author Sherrill MacLaren argued in *Invisible Power: The Women who Run Canada* that women tend to see themselves as part of a team when joining male-dominated boardrooms and clubs, including staying silent when they disagree. She makes the case that loyalty is paramount within Canadian circles of power, accompanied by a strong code of message discipline, humility, and teamwork.[119] A generation later, legislatures are populated by more women who are motivated to challenge the status quo. Case in point: Catherine Dorion, who as a thirty-seven-year-old rookie member of the National Assembly (MNA) was admonished for defying a formal dress code by wearing a hooded sweatshirt in the chamber of the Quebec National Assembly.[120] To her, denying elected officials the ability to express their individuality through clothing is a control mechanism that transcends physical presentation; it promotes mental and verbal uniforms devoid of personality. As she explained to us, "politicians are expected to all speak the same way.... There is a code for politicians, and you are asked to assert your personality by moving a millimetre to the left or right, but nothing more. If you decide not to match this code, you can express yourself through your clothes, your way of speaking, your way of defending causes, or your means of expression."[121] In Dorion's experience, the political system reduces politicians to a clique of scripted zombies.[122] Her approach diverges from that of veteran parliamentarians, particularly white men, who support requirements to wear conventional business attire out of a need to "respect the institution."[123]

Well beyond dress codes, many women have pushed the norms of accessibility around parliamentary careers and motherhood.[124] Others pose questions internally about the quality of the parliamentary workplace, such as overnight filibusters that present health hazards and intrude on family life.[125] The resistance is consistent with broader social trends such as women being more likely than men to share their concerns in an effort to improve a situation,[126] and today's workers being less loyal to employers and having different expectations than previous generations.[127] Indigenous and racialized women contend with even greater barriers, including microaggressions that make them feel out of place in parliamentary settings, such as security guards on Parliament Hill treating them as intruders.[128] Upon joining the Liberal Party, Jody Wilson-Raybould was befuddled by the combative style of party politics:

> I was immediately struck by the mentality of being on a team or in a club that spent a lot of time talking and strategizing about how to beat others and win. In the Indigenous world of politics, we would certainly foster and encourage team building, but the dialogue was always focused on how to build momentum to achieve a social outcome, to address wrongs, and to better the lives of people. Moreover, everyone was a part of the team, not just those in your party. The team was the collective.[129]

In her experience, political parties wield almost complete control and sway over parliamentarians.[130] Ultimately, in partisan environments conformity is more common than resistance. Newly elected representatives who arrive sporting tattoos, piercings, and combat boots, and who speak with colloquialisms, gradually adopt the conventional persona of a button-down politician,[131] or they leave politics altogether.

Authenticity

The party-first culture creates a fertile market for politicians who say what is on their mind and wear what they want without worrying about the consequences. In party politics, parliamentarians can carry more clout if they project an image of being sincere and true to oneself, within reason. Honesty, openness, and reliability are often considered markers of authenticity, contrasted with the caginess, conformity, and opportunism associated with most forms of party politics.[132] The exuberant loyalty that many partisans express in their communications and, to a lesser extent, how they vote can come across as the antithesis of authenticity.

Authentic politicians resist being defined by their party or the political establishment. They express what is seen as their real opinions and make decisions based on their own values as opposed to personal gain, political advantage, or unwavering partisanship.[133] They can be portrayed as speaking truth to power. A set of behaviours contribute to an authentic aura: consistency, whereby a politician advocates in similar ways for specific values, ideologies, or causes over time; intimacy, through which they connect on a personal level with audiences; ordinariness, insofar as their image is more like a regular person than a professional politician; and immediacy, in that they make spontaneous, unvarnished comments.[134] Displaying empathy and interest in others gives them a human touch. A crucial element is being a formidable communicator who uses a vocabulary that is accessible and intelligible – as opposed to one that is filled with jargon and spin – or what Francophones call *langue de bois*. News reports might remark on their unconventional appearance or mannerisms, and highlight features deemed to denote an anti-authority personality, such as a cowboy hat, a motorcycle, or piercings.[135] An air of authenticity is also communicated through unorthodox actions, such as planting flowers in potholes to draw attention to the need for road repairs.[136]

An example of an authentic politician is Ron MacKinley, who served as an MLA in Prince Edward Island from 1985 to 2015 and, at one point, was the only Liberal in the legislature. He was so deeply in tune with his rural constituents that his party affiliation seemed incidental. MacKinley had a dishevelled appearance and mannerisms, including chomping an unlit cigar.[137] He excelled at retail politics by visiting coffeehouses to chat with locals and spending his evenings on the telephone, as well as stopping into small shops to create the impression of being everywhere in his riding – what a former rural MP told us includes "eat and greet" (restaurants where you eat little to save your appetite for others) and "snack and chat" (buying confectionary in convenience stores and gas stations).[138] MacKinley had a strong grasp of issues and a retinue of informants who used him as a conduit. He begrudgingly conformed to the legislature's dress code by donning a slip-on tie and got in trouble with the Speaker for using unparliamentary language until he learnt to level cleverly worded accusations. Like other party loyalists of his ilk, the party higher-ups accepted that he sometimes did the opposite of what they instructed him to do and that his constituents admired him for it.

Authenticity like this carries more weight in a political climate of distrust. Trust in political parties, the mass media, first ministers, and legislators is considerably lower than trust in non-partisan institutions involved in public administration and justice,[139] while trust in government is particularly low among Canadians on the political right and those without post-secondary education.[140] Backbenchers may not have much influence over public policy, but they can control being trustworthy, honest, and respectful.[141] Those who do so can benefit from an enlarged public profile and from the virtue signalling that equates defying the party line with trustworthiness.[142] In Britain, citizens have a strong preference for MPs who voice dissent, and these sentiments are believed to increase when public confidence in political parties is low.[143] In Canada, for reasons outlined throughout this book, parliamentarians have less disposition to rebel. Those who project unbridled authenticity face a conundrum of being themselves within the limits of what their party will support and condone. For some, a political party embodies their core values, enabling them to passionately advocate for policies with genuine conviction. Take, for example, soft nationalists in the Bloc Québécois or the Parti Québécois, who promote Quebec-centric views and are content with the measured pace at which their leaders advance efforts toward sovereignty-association with Canada. For others, particularly those in big-tent parties, there is a constant need to compromise. This suits most team players just fine, but some parliamentarians struggle. They wrestle with the hypocrisy of their party claiming to value their perspectives while showing little interest in actually listening to their opinions. They might ask themselves, "What's the point of finding your voice, if it is muzzled because the simple truth of your message makes others uncomfortable?"[144] These tensions make nonconformists who remain within the party ranks uncommon and even more remarkable, especially considering that political parties have been taking steps to weed out individualists from the earliest stages of candidate recruitment, discussed next.

Becoming a Parliamentarian

The road to a seat in a Canadian legislature normally goes through a political party. During election campaigns, the crucial factors determining the election of local candidates are opinions about party leaders and their parties, not about the candidates themselves. Many Canadians are aware of the local front-runner(s), particularly when a party is strong in their electoral district.[145] Nevertheless, in federal elections the candidate is a decisive factor for only about 5 per cent of voters and affects the election outcome in roughly 10 per cent of electoral districts.[146] Put another way, nationally, about 95 per cent of voters prioritize the party, the party leader, and factors other than the local candidate, and about 90 per cent of federal seats are won by parties irrespective of candidate considerations. Even when electors prioritize a candidate over the leader, as they are more likely to do in provincial elections where the electoral districts are usually much smaller, macro-level factors may be present in their decision-making, including strategic and bandwagon voting.[147] The most significant candidate effects are found among voters leaning towards a party[148] and who believe the local race is competitive.[149] Incumbents attract the largest personal share of the vote at roughly 10 per cent – meaning that most rookie candidates matter relatively little to the outcome.[150] The electoral importance of political parties is reflected in the sobering statistic that 99.8 per cent of people elected to the House of Commons and provincial legislatures are partisans, almost exclusively with major parties.[151] The small number of Independents who are elected are three times more likely to be sitting parliamentarians who left their party and seek re-election as an Independent. In Canada, it is exceedingly rare for someone to be elected as a first-time parliamentarian without a party label on the ballot.

Despite the daunting statistics, some parliamentarians convince themselves that they can be re-elected based on their own reputation. Certainly, there are those who have a loyal following, and a popular local representative can eek out victory in a marginal seat. For many other partisans, their political career comes to an abrupt halt when the electoral tide goes out. "I sacrificed my family, and I went to every event there was, and I did everything possible. And nobody cares," lamented a former MLA to us.[152] The reality in party systems across Canada is that mediocre representatives in safe seats are often re-elected, while exceptional performers in swing ridings can face defeat.[153]

For most aspiring parliamentarians, a political party is the gateway to standing as a candidate for elected office. An assortment of local partisans can stoke their interest and encourage them to run, as can a well of non-partisan actors such as community leaders, co-workers, friends, and family.[154] Ambition is a common trait among those who want to get elected, whether they are confident extroverts, self-centred battlers, or insincere opportunists.[155] Naturally, some are more motivated than others to run a winning campaign.

Parliamentarians were initially drawn to partisan politics for many reasons.[156] Our interviews reveal their passion to make a difference in their community or society in general, and a desire to join a network of like-minded people to drive change. In the first category fall people like Donna Kennedy-Glans, a PC MLA from Alberta who shared with us that her career abroad led her to realize "we weren't doing better at home and I felt like we could."[157] Among those looking for a team to pursue reform, count Jim Melenchuk from Saskatchewan, who joined the provincial Liberals because "their policies made sense to me."[158] These public interest, ideological, and network motivations align well with the sort of policy-seeking behaviours we discuss in chapters 1 and 8.

Candidate recruitment is particularly effective when it targets politically interested younger people who possess a strong sense of self-importance,[159] especially if they share similar socio-demographic characteristics with the president of the party's local EDA (a group of local party supporters who are involved with grass-roots election readiness).[160] A degree of courage is needed, especially for those who feel that they are political outsiders; ultimately, candidates need to take the initiative themselves.[161] As a result, many people do not follow through with their interest in running, including persons with disabilities who lack formal support mechanisms,[162] and an untold number withdraw because the party discourages or disqualifies them. As we shall explain, nowadays most Canadians who step up to seek a party's nomination as its election candidate undergo considerable scrutiny by party operatives who are tasked with rejecting applicants deemed to be too risky.

In parliamentary democracies, party leaders have considerable control over candidate selection.[163] Across Canada – whether due to laws, party constitutions, or convention – they, or potentially their delegate, must sign off on candidates before those partisans can be listed on an election ballot or, in many cases, raise or spend campaign funds. The party's leadership can exploit an incumbent's desire to be renominated by requiring that they meet quotas for signing up recurring donors, knocking on doors, placing phone calls, and recruiting new party members.[164] The numbers are tracked in a central database.

Central party operatives used to get involved only when there was a weak local presence or a desire to install a preferred nominee.[165] Local quarrels sometimes arose (and still do) when a leader intervened to ensure that women and racialized candidates were recruited, to ward off special interest groups from mobilizing to nominate a single-issue candidate, or to appoint a star recruit.[166] Central party officials began taking on a bigger role in the 1980s when public outrage about politicians' sordid behaviour spurred leaders to clamp down on who could run for the nomination.[167] This central involvement expanded as candidates became susceptible to journalists, opponents, and agitators scouring online sources for salacious information about a nominee's life and opinions.[168] Worldwide, employers are turning to online sleuthing to assess whether a job applicant would be a good fit and to identify those who could cause reputational problems.[169] Likewise, Canadian political parties rigorously vet prospective candidates. The process resembles a job application, focusing on the applicant's positive attributes while also serving as a trust assessment. The real mission is for the vetters to identify anything that could embarrass the party or its leader and derail the campaign.

Political parties require that aspiring candidates complete a nomination form of perhaps thirty to fifty pages of questions. Typically, the forms include a confidentiality clause declaring the application process a secret, which might extend to signing a non-disclosure agreement (NDA).[170] Applicants must consent to a criminal record check and a credit check, and declare that they agree to abide by the party's constitution.[171] They might need to provide proof of credentials, such as school transcripts, and write answers to probing personal questions, as well as turn over social media passwords to strangers. Requiring that they affirm support for the party's principles and values helps to steer away people who have incompatible political beliefs and becomes a form of contract. Invasive interviews can follow, along with reference checks, which some vetters supplement by purposely speaking with people who do not like the applicant.[172] As well, in between elections, some political staffers archive screenshots of criticisms levelled on social media by potential candidates.[173] This internal scrutiny is likely to intensify in the wake of revelations of foreign actors infiltrating Canadian party politics through the candidate nomination process.[174]

If anything untoward is identified, a review committee may deliberate on whether to recommend to the leader that an applicant be rejected.[175] Party officials may disagree on the basis for disavowal, such as when there are differences of opinion along gender lines or if someone has personal connections to the candidate.[176] According to a former Liberal MP who handled complaints from rejected contestants, the internal appeals process is murky and unfair because the party wants to control who is nominated.[177] Indeed, we were told about the subjectivity of vetting and how it can be a mechanism to weed out candidates that the party or the leadership do not want. As one senior staffer explained to us, "Parties don't want troublemakers. They don't have a problem with independent thinking, but what they want to know is: are you part of the team or not?"[178] Another was more direct: "If you're friends with the president of a local EDA you can ensure that the desired result is achieved."[179] Decisions to disqualify can lead to the rejected applicant levelling allegations, about which party officials say little to minimize a public airing of internal matters and to avoid being sued for defamation.[180] As we explain in chapter 6, a similar pattern occurs when someone is evicted from caucus, except that the party lays out its complaints.

After being cleared to run, an aspiring candidate is either acclaimed as the party's nominee or must compete for the nomination. A nomination contest is the only time that they will run on their own name. The process can feature opaque rules, obscure timelines, idiosyncratic processes, party interference, manipulated membership lists, secretive vetting discussions, information voids, and parachuted candidates.[181] The party may rig the competition to favour a preferred contestant by selectively informing them about the call for nominations, abruptly closing the nomination period, and restricting access to the candidate application portal.[182] In a rural riding, polling stations can be set up in areas where the favoured person is popular.[183] Local party executives allege that the central interference is undemocratic; some resign in protest. For their part, incumbents are keenly aware that the party leader and their inner circle possess the authority to block or revoke their renomination, which can inhibit them from carrying out the most basic of account- ability functions. This control over the nomination process was cited by several Liberal MPs as the reason many caucus members were reluctant to sign a letter to Justin Trudeau requesting a national caucus meeting to discuss the party's and his declining public approval ratings.[184]

A party's candidates – as Noah Richler discovered with the NDP – encounter a centralized campaign environment, where they are treated as franchisees of a broader organizational network.[185] This offers advantages, like the cost efficiency of using party templates when buy- ing campaign advertisements at a discounted rate, which is especially helpful when a local campaign is under-resourced or in the event of a snap election.[186] Tapping into the experience of local partisans experi- enced in campaign work and having access to scripted lines instead of researching policy to develop positions are among other advantages of party infrastructure. The central party has considerable leeway to flex its might if its leader is popular or it is the primary source of cam- paign money.[187] Candidates are generally willing to support whatever the leader announces, given that they were drawn to a party that aligns their policy preferences and political values.[188]

Party candidates are urged to exercise caution because opponents are watching. "Remember that anything you say can be used against you by those opposed to our party's success and their allies in the media. Message discipline doesn't work if it's only part time," wrote Jason Kenney, the leader of the United Conservative Party (UCP) of Alberta in an internal memo to nominees.[189] At training sessions, candidates are informed that few of them will be elected on their own recognizance and are told to avoid being baited into philosophical discussions on the campaign trail. They are warned that opponents will weaponize clips of a candidate who opines and are told stories about how stupidity costs elections.[190] Amid this ominous backdrop they are instructed to draw upon a catalogue of the party's policy stances and messaging.[191] Parties that release their platform early in the official campaign, even beforehand, give candidates the confidence to know what to say and to communicate its messaging.

The treatment of candidates as frontline employees leaves little room for them to make policy contributions or to opine in public.[192] Those who are a source of negative publicity are contacted by a war room staffer to "walk back" comments and discuss issuing a statement that the opinions were "ill-considered," under threat of being dropped from the party ticket.[193] A candidate might be required to submit a monetary deposit, which is refunded at the end of the campaign, provided they stay out of trouble. Consequently, many are inclined to emulate the leader, to use party templates, and to repackage central messaging for local audiences instead of forging a distinct persona.[194] They mostly stick to emphasizing their personal experiences and roots in the community, such as conveying trustworthiness by showcasing their family or displaying connectedness by championing localized issues.[195]

That said, candidates have more room to diverge from their party than they are told. They can question aspects of the platform, formulate their own positions, or deviate from branded templates.[196] A measure of autonomy is particularly viable for incumbents in safe seats and those who do not rely on the party for campaign funds,[197] as well as for candidates with specialized expertise or those who want to comment on localized matters that attract broader attention. Candidates can also clap back against central party operatives' passion about database marketing, particularly in rural ridings where personal connections are so important.[198]

Following a successful election, a novice parliamentarian hopes to offer diverse perspectives that the government or party might otherwise be unaware of.[199] Instead, they find themselves being more deeply embedded into a political team as they get ready to be sworn in and start their new career. In Ottawa and many provincial capitals, parliamentary staff offer a few days of formal orientation, after which elected officials can turn to the whip's office or an incumbent for assistance, instilling a bond of in-group mentorship if not dependence.[200] The training largely concerns human resources onboarding, and newbies can feel that they lack sufficient supports to prepare them for what's next.[201] In practice, then, they learn on the job. Instead of being taught about their roles as trustees of the public good and delegates of their constituents, or familiarizing themselves with the Standing Orders, rookies are primarily oriented to uphold the norms of party loyalty. They are instructed to raise counterviews in private and to treat caucus meetings as strictly confidential matters. They can be shocked by the limits on what they can say in public, such as a staffer in an opposition leader's office advising a backbencher that the role of the opposition is to always criticize the government and never offer a solution.[202] The party leviathan may extend to requiring a portion of candidates' spending refunds, provided by the elections agency,[203] as well as expectations that parliamentarians continue collecting data on constituents and fundraising – activities that could increase their chances of promotion.[204] Early on, some are told to stop talking about campaign promises in case the pledges cannot be delivered.[205]

An "us" versus "them" mentality is foisted upon new parliamentarians by a political system rooted in conflict, with symbols that reflect a tradition of hostility and origins of brutality.[206] In most legislatures, members of the government and opposition benches face each other in an adversarial debate format, separated by the length of two swords plus an inch, and each party designates a whip to keep everyone in line. The combativeness is egged on by political banter and news reports that embellish slivers of political division, and which evoke the language of violence and war.[207] These embedded arrangements motivate elected representatives to entrench with a party and its customs. For some parliamentarians, the setup can be uncomfortable from the moment they set foot in the legislature, and they feel that they do not belong. Adapting to colonialist structures can be especially challenging for Indigenous Peoples who prefer a consensus approach.[208]

Rookies are kept busy learning on the job, and many serve only one term. Canada's legislatures must grapple with amateurism due to mass turnover and due to new entrants' limited political experience.[209] In Ottawa, approximately 30 per cent of MPs typically do not return after an election because they retired or are defeated,[210] a figure that we suspect is reasonably constant in the provinces and higher in elections when the tide turns on the governing party. The large number of parliamentarians trying to navigate the system gives a considerable edge to the party leadership. It is the seasoned partisans who understand how the system operates, who can challenge the leader's staff, and who are skilled at negotiating multi-partisan agreements.[211] Whereas some parliamentarians get caught up chasing advancement, sponsored travel, and other opportunities, others eventually realize that loyalty does not require saying yes to everything and does not necessarily translate into political influence.[212] Of course, experiences vary, as do federal and provincial dynamics.

Their limited role in law-making allows backbenchers and their staff to spend more time on constituency casework. They field constituents' enquiries, act as ombudspersons with government, and attend community events throughout their electoral district.[213] Paying close attention to constituents does not ensure re-election; some parliamentarians may still lose elections despite their diligent efforts to address local concerns,[214] and some find that listening to people's problems takes such a toll on their own mental health that they step away from politics.[215] While representatives have more freedom to speak plainly on doorsteps, at community festivals, or at funerals, they must still exercise caution in these settings due to the danger that a private conversation could be recorded and leaked.[216]

Parliamentarians must even be cautious about their own database technologies. Constituency offices keep files on individuals who reach out for assistance, and campaign workers closely affiliated with a parliamentarian regularly update voter information files. In some parties, elected officials, their staff, and volunteers relinquish their exclusive control over local data by uploading information about identified supporters to a centralized party database. The central repository enables the party to solicit local donations and collect information independently of the parliamentarian,[217] allowing the leader's staff to access extensive local data.[218] Additionally, if a parliamentarian leaves the party, their access to these files can be swiftly revoked, resulting in disputes over ownership of constituent information.[219] The whip's office may confiscate files stored on an office computer,[220] or a defector could be accused of violating privacy by misappropriating proprietary data.[221] This practice is the subject of one of our proposed reforms (chapter 10).

Brand Ambassadors

Under their franchising relationship, Canadian parliamentarians act as brand envoys who balance the roles of legislating, constituency casework, and promoting their party.[222] The franchisor (mostly the leader's office) sets the parameters of what party spokespeople and backbenchers ought to be communicating to support a unified agenda. Accordingly, leaders and ministers are trained to repackage scripted responses to hypothetical questions, and backbenchers are told to repeat the party line, to apply a local twist on messages, or to avoid comment.

Branding influences how members of a party caucus communicate, particularly in terms of reaching broader audiences. An organized, well-resourced leader's office supplies parliamentarians and their staff with a stream of simple messages that are bundled within a strategic theme. Parliamentarians receive talking points and canned speeches, and are directed to refer media enquiries to a designated spokesperson.[223] They are told to "stay in their own lane" and to avoid any "daylight" between them.[224] In the legislature, they repeat catchphrases designed to frame their party, policies, and opponents to maximum rhetorical advantage.[225] Outside the legislature, party messaging infuses what they say to journalists, how they interact with constituents, and the memes that they post online.[226] If they veer off-script, the party leadership can dismiss them as unimportant.[227] A secret recording illustrates that caucus meetings are seen as the only space for disagreement. "It is a big courage to tell you that was not appropriate stuff by my government, and I acknowledge that," confided a Saskatchewan Party MLA to a constituent who recorded their conversation in 2024. "You gotta toe the leader's line, actually. That's the policy you have, to toe that. But you are given 100 per cent the right, on that [caucus] table inside, to disagreement.... [Publicly], I'm not going to come out and say that [the government was wrong]."[228] For every instance of a politician publicly challenging the leader's authority, there are countless behind-the-scenes episodes where partisans privately question the leadership and pursue their own agendas, all while outwardly adhering to a centrally crafted message.

The primacy of unified communications can help political parties reach and sustain consensus on sensitive topics. In 2021, the federal Conservative caucus agreed that party unity is more important than being divided over a government bill to criminalize conversion therapy, such as counselling, that attempts to change someone's gender identity or sexual orientation. The caucus was previously split on the matter.[229] Keen to avoid a political feud bursting into the open, a Conservative MP called for unanimous consent to expedite the passage of the bill, which was approved without a single dissenting voice. Transgender politics re-emerged a few years later about schools informing parents when their child asks a teacher to be addressed using a different gender pronoun. Conservative MPs received a memo from the leader's office that began, "This messaging is for reactive use only. Please do not talk to media or post on social media about this issue."[230] The memo stated that communications with constituents should follow talking points and be guided by leader Pierre Poilievre's previous public statements, and that caucus was the appropriate forum to air disagreement.[231] In an email, MPs were asked to inform the leader's office about all media requests and were provided with four key messages.[232] The caucus fell in line. One Conservative MP told a journalist that he would echo whatever policy the leader crafted,[233] even cancelling a scheduled media appearance after the internal talking points were leaked.[234] Subsequent news reports revealed that some of them were unsettled by the message control coming from Poilievre's office. "Everybody is being watched. What we say, what we do, who we talk to. We're told not to fraternize with MPs from the other parties," one Conservative remarked.[235] Another added, "If you repeat the slogans, you get rewarded. You are celebrated in front of the entire caucus for being a good cheerleader. And you get more speaking time in the House and during Question Period."

In 2024, the New Democrats used similar message management tactics when their leader Jagmeet Singh suddenly ended the party's confidence and supply agreement with the Liberal government. His office sent an email to NDP MPs instructing them to refrain from speaking with journalists, direct all media inquiries to the communications team, and amplify the leader's message by availing of pre-prepared materials, including a social media kit.[236] In situations like this, backbenchers understand that defying central guidance could jeopardize their standing in the party.

Coordinated communications make strategic sense for political parties, but certain elements of a branding doctrine are harmful to democracy and undercut local representation. Branding can instil a culture of risk aversion and secrecy, and when message discipline descends into spin, it suppresses scrutiny and deflects probing questions from journalists and critics alike. Simple messages become problematic when politicians use them to obscure facts, dismiss nuance, and obstruct meaningful dialogue, relying instead on recycled talking points aimed at persuasion rather than genuine information. Politicians can become deeply entrenched in a culture of relentless message repetition, convinced of the rhetorical advantage it offers. As a Liberal minister put it in a candid video that was hastily deleted, "we've learned in the House of Commons, if you repeat it, if you say it louder, if that is your talking point, people will totally believe it."[237] However, when what they say is unoriginal, parliamentarians have more difficulty getting noticed. In 1969, Pierre Trudeau famously claimed that opposition members become "nobodies" once they leave Parliament Hill.[238] Half a century later, the put-down could apply to many government frontbenchers as well: 60 per cent of Canadians were unable to name a single member of the federal cabinet during Justin Trudeau's eighth year in power.[239] In another survey, almost everyone (98 per cent) recognized his photo, yet sizeable majorities failed to identify his most prominent cabinet ministers when shown their images.[240]

Another concern is that brand management can promote the use of divisive, disparaging messaging and provide cover for hyper-partisan tactics. Party strategists employ demarketing and debranding to create harmful impressions about political choices and policies with an intent to cause people to lose confidence in an opponent and consider alternatives.[241] Branding can also backfire: when negativity engulfs a party brand, it drags down the electoral prospects of its candidates,[242] sometimes triggering cascading consequences for partisans in other jurisdictions.[243] Message discipline has its drawbacks.

Summary

Message discipline is a key factor in both party unity and strategic success in politics. When effectively directed and cohesive, party communications can bridge social and ideological divides. However, political parties can also become abettors of polarization if divisiveness becomes part of the party line. The rise of political parties as central forces in modern parliaments, alongside the influence of the media and the proliferation of information technologies, has created a political landscape where partisans either reinforce or undermine the leader's messages. To maintain a cohesive party brand, aspiring candidates' pasts are scrutinized to weed out controversial figures, and nominated candidates are expected to adhere to party values and repeat authorized statements. These control mechanisms minimize the possibility of a crisis arising when a rogue partisan expresses an opinion contrary to the party's official position. Tolerance for off-brand remarks, personal flaws, or poor judgment fluctuates over time, aligning with shifting moral, ethical, and political norms. Orientation for newly elected parliamentarians does little to dispel the idea that staying on message is a priority. The question of who dictates message discipline is the focus of the next few chapters.

3 Caucus Management

Morose supporters of Paul Martin Sr. griped when Pierre Trudeau won the Liberal leadership in 1968. Their candidate had been a Liberal MP for over three decades, was an experienced senior cabinet minister and had just suffered his third failed attempt to become leader. By comparison, Trudeau was a political neophyte who had only been a party member for a few years. Undeterred, Martin Sr. rallied his entourage, including his dejected son (a future prime minister himself), saying, "We will have none of that. He is now our leader, and we will be loyal to our leader."[1]

The head of a party sits at the apex of its brand. Leaders are the party's primary symbol and chief spokesperson and are supported by a crew of political staff and designated caucus members who act as their agents. Together they have considerable clout and command loyalty, particularly after a successful election campaign which emboldens supporters and quells doubters.[2] Yet even a popular leader who delivers an excellent election result must contend with a larger caucus that has more demands, more personalities, and greater expectations, and their power diminishes with negative news coverage, dips in public opinion polls, and as talk of change grows.[3] Do party leaders and their staff really wield as much authority as some observers suggest? What levers do they have to encourage caucus unity and loyalty? This chapter demonstrates that leaders and their staff brandish considerable power and influence to manage the party's parliamentary caucus, particularly in a communications-driven political landscape.

The Power of Political Leaders

Within organized groups, humans are inclined to follow the requests of a leader who reflects their ideals and social identity.[4] Sometimes a leader's authority is exerted through harder means, like inducement or coercion; other times, they use softer and subtler methods of influence by drawing on status or charm. Power bases arise from the ability to distribute resources and benefits (reward power) or dispense punishments (coercive power), from holding a position of official authority to instruct behaviour (legitimate power), from having admirable personal traits such as charisma that enable persuasion (referent power), and from specific knowledge and competencies (expert power).[5] When assessing a political leader's power, we must recognize that supporters emphasize the central coordination necessary to organize, manage, and advance an agenda, whereas opponents denounce centralization as oppressive and anti-democratic, potentially labelling the leader as authoritarian. Control is pejorative in a democratic system, without regard to its gradients, purposes, or necessity.

In parliamentary politics, power is concentrated in party leaders, provided they are backed by their caucus. Party leaders command loyalty, respect, and deference by virtue of holding the title, particularly among their staunchest supporters. What they say attracts attention. They inspire and motivate followers and cultivate a leader-centric culture by defining values, norms, and identities.[6] Many party leaders and their inner circle control vast amounts of information about the organization and its competitors, from internal polling to voter databases, helping them construct reality for their followers. Heads of government, ministers, and senior political staff can initiate and steer policy negotiations and exert control over a legislative agenda, including the timing. They dispense promotions and appointments, as well as authorize punishments, which engenders sycophancy and tempers agitation. A leader is not necessarily beholden to a caucus, especially if they were chosen by the entire party membership and have a broad base of support; however, if there is sufficient caucus unrest, they may be pressed to resign. While circumstances vary, party leaders usually have vastly more power, influence, and control than anyone else in their party, especially if they head a government.

In Canadian politics, party leaders are so omnipresent that the political fortunes of the party and its leader are entwined, with much at stake for their supporters. Upon winning a leadership contest, they immediately call for competing camps within the party to unite behind them, and usually make it clear that they are in charge. Sometimes this means inviting rivals into cabinet or critic roles; as we will discuss, the failure to do so can be the pretext for maverick behaviour and defection. Between elections, leaders can breezily disregard policies passed by party delegates, a stark contrast to a generation ago when party presidents were influential figures and policy conventions carried substantial weight. In elections, campaigns have turned on leader personalities since at least the 1980s.[7] Leaders are central in campaign advertising[8] and their debates are pivotal,[9] to the point that their last name becomes a marketing vessel and part of political vernacular, such as the Harper government, the Layton NDP, or Team Trudeau.[10] It follows that a leader's reputation influences their party's,[11] that higher levels of media exposure are correlated with a greater likelihood of prioritizing leaders at the ballot box,[12] and that electoral landslides are attributed to mass appeal of the leader of the winning party.[13] Some leaders are more powerful than others, of course. Nevertheless, many parliamentarians equate loyalty to the leader with loyalty to the party.[14]

The leader with the greatest authority is the one leading a government. As mentioned, the parliamentary system is thought to have become presidentialized and the power of the executive has been aggrandized. In the 1960s and 1970s, the size of the Prime Minister's Office (PMO) expanded along with its bureaucratic equivalent, the Privy Council Office (PCO). Pierre Trudeau filled the PMO with partisans, dispensing with the practice of recruiting staff from the public service to become partisan advisors.[15] Senior political staff gained more influence, ministers became more scripted, and decision-making was siphoned from the cabinet to the PMO.[16] The geographic powerbase of regional ministers whose personalities loomed over the party apparatus and who forcefully lobbied for their region's interests eroded as leaders and strategists turned to pollsters for information about the public mood.[17] Ever since, prime ministers and their staff have been accused of commanding more power, even if they initially pledge to devolve it.[18] Their influence is so extensive that an international study found that Canadian prime ministers in office between 1980 and 2000 were perceived to have wielded more authority than their counterparts in any other established parliamentary democracy.[19]

Consider that Justin Trudeau, who as an opposition leader moved to dominate his caucus by introducing policies without consultation,[20] said during the 2015 federal election campaign that he liked the "symmetry" of being the one to unwind the PMO control that emerged under his father.[21] The pledge was a refreshing anecdote to the control freakery that characterized the Harper PMO. Yet soon after becoming prime minister, Trudeau told the caucus that his chief of staff and principal secretary constituted his inner circle and that they would communicate on his behalf.[22] Ministerial staff were tightly vetted by the PMO, which gradually installed its own staff in ministers' offices,[23] while the public disclosure of mandate letters affirmed that ministers take orders from the top, while playing a pivotal role in central coordination and locking in the government's agenda.[24] Trudeau dispensed with the title of regional minister, other than a Quebec lieutenant, which augmented his status atop the pinnacle of government and diminished theirs. His official photographer and the party made copious use of social media to post backstage moments that highlight the primacy of the leader and his celebrity, in a narrative where ministers are, at best, supporting actors.[25] Liberal MPs regularly fell in line with their leader on policy matters.[26] Trudeau also remade the extra-parliamentary party in his image by overseeing the rewriting of its constitution to reassign powers from the party apparatus to the leader.[27]

Nevertheless, a party leader faces many constraints. A prime minister or premier can only advance so many files, and must trust ministers, the party whip, and a retinue of competent staff to deftly advance policy.[28] Heads of government have limited time to accomplish goals, especially where the legislature is concerned (in Ottawa more so than in the provinces), and must make strategic choices to advance a policy agenda.[29] Public opinion polls, civil unrest, finite resources, institutions and agreements, economic forces, natural disasters, other leaders, and various other factors limit what is possible. Above all, a leader's authority and tenure are in danger of unravelling if caucus members publicly disagree – a concern that is top of mind for party loyalists. "The worst thing that we can do is have a divided caucus or one that's talking about a lack of confidence in the leader," remarked a seasoned Liberal MP as the Trudeau government's popularity sagged.[30] Prime ministers and premiers must be mindful of the adage that the Official Opposition may sit across from them in the legislature, but the real opposition is seated in the back benches behind them.[31]

The Power of Political Staff

Leaders and their front bench are supported by a crew of unelected partisans who manage growing volumes of speedy exchanges. Political staff are like air traffic controllers in that they operate in a control centre using communications technology to provide advice, share information, coordinate activities, and avoid collisions, as well as practice damage control.[32] Partisans who work for politicians have long played a pivotal role in politics as interlocutors, especially where interparty affairs are concerned. As the volume and intensity of communications grow, more staff are needed to be directly involved in various aspects of political work and to perform an essential coordination role. A side effect is that staff have absorbed power from elected officials.

Partisans are recruited to fill senior political roles on the basis of their political acumen and loyalty, although some are hired due to their personal connections and are appointed on an impermanent basis without competition, formal qualifications, or job security, which instils its own form of loyalty.[33] We distinguish the ones who work for politicians in the upper levels of the organizational hierarchy, particularly in the leader's office, as senior political staff.[34] Those with the most responsibility hold strategic and tactical roles, principally in the Prime Minister's Office or a premier's office. They act as the leader's coteries; participate in high-level policy discussions; triage and manage communications; coordinate legislative activities; and engage with the party whip on discipline and human resources management, among other managerial functions. The most senior staff participate in discussions about who should be in cabinet.[35] A smaller troupe performs comparable tasks in an opposition leader's office. Utter loyalty to their political masters has long been viewed as the most important qualification of staff working with the leader and senior ministers.[36] It is also paramount in entry-level roles. One parliamentarian told us of how aspiring office assistants are asked to complete an application form that includes the following question: "Of the adjectives in the following list, which do you feel is most important for working in a political environment: honest, hard-working, punctual, loyal, diligent?"[37] Loyalty is a key factor in hiring decisions, while its absence can be grounds for termination.

Staff loyalty is imperative because politicians must trust the people involved in political decisions.[38] Leaders lean on their close confidants to provide credible information and strategic counsel, to broker disputes, to leverage networks, and to coordinate policy.[39] Senior personnel counsel about appointments and policy, discuss legislative proceedings, liaise with other politicians and their staff, provide institutional memory, and offer strategic guidance.[40] They engage in general planning and coordination, communications, policy research and analysis, and Question Period preparation, as well as buffer lobbyists, stakeholder groups, and constituents. Staff collaborate on issues management, such as working with ministers and other politicians to manage a problem before it escalates into a crisis or coordinating the response when an unexpected event knocks the leader off-message. Their expertise reflects the preferences and needs of their political boss, be it specialized knowledge, a knack for generating good press, or experience with managing noncompliance.[41] The most trusted personnel act as sentinels and sounding boards for sensitive political bargaining, including when a parliamentarian is contemplating crossing the floor (see chapter 7). They often wield far more policy sway than an individual backbencher does, as a former senior staffer explained to us: "Most MPs are accomplished people who have taken on a job that has the least amount of autonomy, power, and influence than they've had in their professional careers. That's a big adjustment for people who think they're going to be able to immediately make a difference. You have infinitely more power as a junior staffer in a leader's office than you do as an elected official. You have so much more ability to change things. You have more influence as a city councillor than you do as an MP. People chafe at that."[42] Some parliamentarians bristle at staff in their twenties with limited life experience instructing them what to do, and can view them as messengers rather than respected team members.[43] To some extent, the frustration that parliamentarians feel towards the leader's staff reflects their exasperation with their own perceived lack of influence, despite being the ones who were elected.

Political staff may be unaware of how intimidating their proximity to the leader can be to others. Unlike the 1980s when PM Brian Mulroney fielded questions solo at national caucus meetings and went out of his way to connect with MPs, or even when Prime Minister Harper was accompanied only by his chief of staff, a crew from the leader's office is now embedded in many caucus gatherings. They make presentations, take notes, and observe and absorb. Staff from Justin Trudeau's PMO routinely attended caucus meetings, along with personnel from the whip's office and House leader's office, and a staffer from the caucus chair's office.[44] PM Carney pledged to end the practice. Because these agents have the leader's ear, backbenchers want to put their best foot forward in these closed-door sessions that are intended to be part sounding board for the leader, part cathartic enclave for parliamentarians.

The presence of watchful staff contributes to national caucus meetings becoming "a perfunctory operation of a gabfest," as one former MP put it to us, where virulent debate is replaced with the respectful decorum of everyone on good behaviour and backbenchers getting up to the microphone to say wonderful things as though they are auditioning for a promotion.[45] "When you have staff in the meeting, you know you're going to get knifed in the back when you stand up," added another former Liberal MP, who believes that Trudeau inoculated himself with staff from hearing "the hard truths" that only backbenchers can deliver.[46] The first time that Trudeau held a caucus meeting without staff present occurred nearly seven years after forming government in response to a request from backbenchers who wanted the freedom to raise concerns about his aides.[47] Protected from the possibility of staff animus, backbenchers complained that senior staff were unresponsive to policy feedback, sometimes ignored them, and blocked access to the prime minister. After the snub, chief of staff Katie Telford observed that staff need to take notes in caucus so that they can champion backbenchers' causes with policymakers.[48] While the presence of senior staff is now essential, due to its detrimental effects, we believe caucus members should insist that staff be required leave for at least part of the meeting (chapter 10).

A combination of factors has tilted power in favour of the leader's staff, often at the expense of the party's parliamentarians. This growing influence stems from the complexities of larger, more interconnected governments, the importance of central coordination, advancements in communications technologies, the rise of permanent campaigning, and the pervasive impact of social media.[49] While their numbers in government fluctuate,[50] a higher proportion of political staff are involved with communications management than in the past. In the mid-twentieth century, press officers were added in the government ranks when television became popular,[51] and earlier this century an influx of communications personnel coincided with the expansion of online platforms.[52] Communications has become the largest department in the PMO, making up more than a quarter of its staff, who work in areas such as advertising, digital content, media relations, speechwriting, leader's tour planning, photography, and videography.[53] Others deal with issues management, field correspondence, and choreograph responses during political chaos.[54] Similar roles are present in most premiers' offices.[55]

The emergence of the smartphone made political staffers even more indispensable to leaders. The ubiquitous device is invaluable in most workplaces and is regularly checked while multitasking.[56] The normalcy of such connectivity, convenience, and productivity makes it easy to overlook that cell phones arrived in Canada in the mid-1980s as cumbersome, temperamental, expensive voice-only gadgets. In the early 2000s, wireless phones with Web browsers, email, and texting capabilities emerged, with political staff and journalists among the early adopters. But internet access was still clunky: less than two-thirds of Canadian households had at least one regular internet user, and roughly a third had high-speed access.[57] In 2004, BlackBerry phones altered media relations in the federal election campaign because email portability meant that party war rooms could quickly supply journalists travelling on a leader's tour with rapid response messaging and could spin what an opponent said before a story was filed.[58] The release of the first iPhone in 2007 integrated the capabilities of a tablet into a mobile phone, which popularized user-friendly touch screens and apps during a period of improving bandwidth, coverage, and affordability. In 2010, Prime Minister Harper was regularly depicted talking on a

Figure 3.1. PMO and PCO Staff Working on Smartphones (2020)
January 2020: Katie Telford (PMO Chief of Staff; seated), Brian Clow (PMO
senior advisor; back left), Maxime Dea (PMO issues management), David
Morrison (PCO advisor), and Patrick Travers (PMO senior advisor; back right)
on standby in the Prime Minister's Office building, Ottawa.

Source and photo credit: Scotti, "A Photographic Year in Review." Used with permission.

landline telephone;[59] now, ministers have abandoned desk phones and
are turning to video calls.[60] Staff are glued to their smartphones, which
they use to manage a raft of email, direct messages, and texts. The technology enables them to accompany their political bosses, multitask
during meetings, and remain connected during the frequent pauses
when they are on standby (figure 3.1).[61]

A related dimension is political staff establishing a public profile on
social media. Until recently, staff have veered away from the limelight,
in deference to the elected officials they serve.[62] Jean Pelletier – the long-
time chief of staff to Chrétien, known for his discretion, loyalty, and
smile that masked an authoritative demeanour – insisted that political staff should not be in the media.[63] Little was publicly known about

Table 3.1. Social Media Followers of Governing Party Parliamentarians and PMO Staff (2023)

Liberal Ministers, MPs, and PMO Staff	Followers*
Prime Minister Justin Trudeau	6,170,570
Deputy PM and Minister of Finance Chrystia Freeland	599,620
Other cabinet ministers	88,920
PMO Chief of Staff Katie Telford	79,250
Former ministers in the back benches	78,550
PMO Lead Photographer Adam Scotti	64,220
Remaining government-side backbenchers	23,430

*Combined followers on Facebook, Instagram, LinkedIn, and X/Twitter platforms in October 2023. Average follower counts for other cabinet ministers, Liberal MPs who had previously served in the Trudeau cabinet, and all remaining Liberal MPs except the Speaker. Rounded to the nearest 10.

Harper's final chief of staff.[64] Then the swearing in of the Trudeau government in 2015 ushered in a new class of partisans who churn out rhetoric on their social channels during an election campaign and whose banter can persist after being employed as a staffer.[65] Staff who amass larger online followings than backbenchers position themselves as political insiders with the power to influence decision-makers and amplify messages they helped create (table 3.1). The adage that perception is reality applies: the number of social media followers has become a new form of currency for political influence, augmenting the power of senior political staff and enhancing their visibility.

The use of social media by political staff can be hard-hitting, even nefarious. Justin Trudeau's principal secretary fiercely defended his boss online and slammed critics in the digital public square,[66] and a senior advisor in the Trudeau PMO got into a vulgar online exchange that Conservative staff called out for its unprofessionalism.[67] An influential political strategist within the Poilievre camp was quick to disparage the leader's predecessor, Erin O'Toole, for posting well wishes to a Liberal minister of defence following her announcement that she would not seek re-election.[68] Meanwhile, in Alberta, issues management staff in Premier Kenney's office used the online workspace platform Slack to notify ministerial staff about abrasive social media remarks, urging a response, and encouraging other staff to like or repost it.[69] In the extreme, a small number of acolytes ruthlessly troll, discredit, and dehumanize political enemies as part of a campaign to silence critics, stir mistrust, and generate media stories that frame debates and are used for fundraising.[70] Whether staff lambaste opponents online or simply repost information, their public advocacy contributes to polarized discourse and intensifies both real and perceived power dynamics among parliamentarians, heightening concerns about staff influence and the hazards of crossing them. This matters because the leader's staff play such an important role in caucus management.

Managing Disloyalty

In organizational behaviour, the disruption of group norms is viewed as counterproductive, antisocial, and dysfunctional[71] which can have corrosive effects on cohesion, image, and morale.[72] Individualists reject a consensus of opinions and beliefs, and they undermine a group's resolve to define and achieve goals through coordinated action.[73] Some loyal members distance themselves from subversives, while others rally behind the leader, covertly or openly chastising nay-sayers and treating them as pariahs.[74] However, black sheep are not always bad actors. Disruptors can channel group principles from which the team has strayed or call attention to group values that have become harmful.[75] In a team-oriented workplace, nonconformists must be managed when their behaviour either exposes or creates internal divisions, causing discomfort for some while being endorsed by others. The main problem with disagreement is when actions or attitudes are damaging, and colleagues are treated poorly. The team leader might tolerate an outburst from an egotistical nonconformist but is compelled to intervene when contrarianism puts collegiality in jeopardy.

Managing disloyalty in a party caucus has two poles. At one end, the leader ignores individualism because interfering would be more damaging to group harmony than quietly shunning a troublemaker and allowing the furore to subside. A case in point is the absence of overt discipline for the Quebec Liberal MP who held a news conference to criticize the government's messaging on COVID-19.[76] Though we cannot be certain, it is likely the prime minister turned a blind eye because that backbencher was expressing what other caucus members were too hesitant to say, and taking action against him could have deepened internal divisions. At the other pole, a leader becomes outraged by toxic dissidence, which culminates in the agitator leaving in a spectacular break-up. Banishment for illegal behaviour or bigotry is even swifter. We deal with that in chapter 6. Ruling with an iron fist is only feasible if the leader is confident of caucus support for administering punishment. In between, leaders accept, even embrace, selfless and collegial disagreement that yields constructive outcomes. This is why leaders sometimes appear to do nothing in response to a parliamentarian's provocative behaviour and how contrarians can be a positive force – or a source of political entropy.

Disagreements and disciplinary actions grab headlines, but the ongoing effort by the leader's office and its agents to maintain caucus harmony goes unnoticed. Backbenchers can feel like they are part of an out-group within their own caucus, particularly that of a governing party. An in-group of title holders can be distant – for example, ministers might plunk down their briefing books in a caucus meeting and pay little attention.[77] Fuelling this dynamic is that ministers cannot discuss some government measures before they are publicly announced because of cabinet confidence along with a host of reasons, such as national security, market implications, and regulatory constraints. Backbenchers get flustered when their input is repeatedly invited after policy has already been formulated, in rushed circumstances or in a cursory manner, if at all. They can find out about policy in news stories, causing them to feel detached from the leadership.[78] Caucus chairs can make no headway when they relay that backbenchers want changes to a bill and parliamentarians can feel slighted if they are not informed in advance of funding decisions for their riding.[79] As one MP complained, "We pretend like we are involved in big decisions of the government when in fact we aren't."[80]

A system that treats backbenchers like an afterthought requires constant effort by the leadership to nurture caucus loyalty.[81] With experience, a leader can realize that decisions made by cabinet or an inner group of confidants without consulting the full caucus are often the wrong decisions.[82] The Harper government chose to delay and ultimately amend its electoral reform legislation based on caucus feedback, for example.[83] To include backbenchers, some heads of government open up internal avenues for input. Pierre Trudeau's ministers were required to consult caucus about draft bills and motions,[84] as were Harper's,[85] which kept backbenchers informed and gave them an opportunity to flag problems. Mirroring the cabinet committee process, some premiers have established a parallel caucus committee to permit their backbenchers the opportunity to review government policies prior to formal adoption. Many caucus members welcome the process, although inclusivity can only go so far because of the need to preserve cabinet secrecy and ministerial responsibility.[86]

We heard repeatedly from all types of interview participants that leaders need to connect on a personal level with members of their caucus. Parliamentarians who like and respect the leader are far more content and do not want to disappoint. Loyalty, affection, and friendship develop for someone who recruited them for a successful run, makes time to listen, and generally inspires. Leaders build goodwill by visiting backbenchers in their constituencies, holding caucus meetings outside the capital city, and assigning caucus chairs to build camaraderie. Caucuses participate in social gatherings such as meals and cocktail parties and attend getaway retreats featuring guest speakers and team-building activities, such as paintball games.[87] The leader's spouse might coordinate socials with other spouses and get them involved in community work. Outreach to spouses helps politicians manage their work-life balance and engenders feelings of a political family. It can be an early warning sign of a member's apathy if their spouse does not participate.[88]

Direct conversation with caucus members is a priority for many party leaders, whether by addressing a disagreement with a backbencher as soon as possible or permitting open discussions in caucus meetings.[89] A simple gesture by the leader or senior officeholder – such as reaching out to talk with a member of caucus – has remarkable impact. Whether chatting informally with parliamentarians in small groups, addressing their concerns, understanding their perspectives, or trying to relate on a personal level, these interactions build trust and demonstrate genuine interest. We were told that table talk over a meal can provide both participants with useful information, and that a leader explaining why something can or cannot be acted upon can open up common ground and "help build the team."[90] People appreciate it when a leader arrives early for Question Period and lingers afterwards to chat.[91] As premier of British Columbia, Christy Clark would try to make members of her caucus feel valued by talking with them during their House duty assignments: "It's so easy to just go in there and saddle up to somebody for fifteen to twenty minutes or half an hour and just talk about whatever. That was for me the most effective use of my time with caucus that there is because it's face time. You're one-on-one. Everybody just wants to talk, and they're sitting in the chamber beside the premier and everybody can see it happening.... I loved getting to know what was going on with them and their families.... I felt like my caucus was my family."[92]

Some leaders are deft caucus managers. The storied attentiveness of Mulroney stands out in this regard – he was constantly phoning backbenchers, giving them things to do, praising them locally, inviting them over for dinner, and sending congratulatory messages to their family members.[93] He listened to them at caucus meetings, took notes and directed ministers and staff to follow up on the concerns. Affections ran so deep that most of them were intensely loyal when his government's popularity plunged; even some of those who left the party during policy disputes did not have personal qualms with him or his leadership.[94] Jean Charest was a member of that caucus, went on to lead the PC Party, and was Liberal premier of Quebec for nearly a decade. Charest told us that it is essential for a leader to pay attention to the caucus: "Listening to caucus is absolutely vital. It is a condition of survival for a leader. The ability of a party leader and a head of government to function, to be able to make decisions, to execute decisions and to implement them depends on caucus support. There is a direct link between the two."[95] Another leader known for caucus outreach was Jack Layton, who died in 2011, just four months after leading the federal New Democratic Party to its only stint as Official Opposition. Many NDP MPs had strong feelings for him:

> "It was Jack Layton who encouraged me to run. I had always been a New Democrat, but I had retired.... With Jack, I had confidence.... Jack had an extraordinary radiance and presence.... He was very open to ideas, he was very attentive."[96]
> "You don't say no to Jack.... He killed you with kindness. That's his passion, his love. It just seeped out of all his pores, and you just wanted to help out however you could."[97]
> "If he were still there, I would still be there. I can affirm this without any doubt.... My Jack was a gentleman."[98]

Yet even an adored leader must contend with internal critics and foes. Initially, lifelong New Democrats were suspicious when the then Toronto city councillor defeated several party stalwarts to become the leader, and dogmatists got into profanity-laced arguments with Layton as he moved the party towards the political centre.[99] Most of them warmed to his charm and accorded respect as the party gained seats in each successive election. Another leader who listens and asks questions is Alberta Premier Danielle Smith, who spends extra time in caucus meetings, holds monthly phone calls with UCP riding association presidents, and actively mingles with people at events.[100] Such interactions must be perceived as genuine and backed up by tough decisions. If not, a leader who listens to caucus can be critiqued for being weak and pandering instead of barrelling forward and inspiring them.[101]

Other leaders do not make a special effort to connect with backbenchers. A federal opposition leader may meet for fifteen to twenty minutes with an MP[102] – a stark contrast to the mere five minute meeting granted by Prime Minister Justin Trudeau many weeks after a request was made, as arranged by his staff.[103] When backbenchers became frustrated about Trudeau's inaccessibility, the PMO created a caucus liaison officer position,[104] but then he showed no interest in assembling the national caucus following general election victories.[105] As well, the move to a hybrid Parliament has reduced opportunities for MPs to engage directly with ministers.[106] Within such constraints, backbenchers who want more influence can try to claim it by demanding the decentralization of policy decisions and greater leadership accountability.[107] Leaders who fail to cultivate intra-party support, who reject elite culture, and who were unfamiliar with the political arena before becoming leader have the most difficulty dealing with the many personalities angling to get what they want.[108] Much depends on the leader's popularity: there are few internal rumblings in a party when a leader is seen as its ticket to victory.

Staff play an important role in caucus outreach. A staffer with a knack for diplomacy can be the right tonic for an angry parliamentarian. Leaders direct their staff to go for coffee with an upset caucus member;[109] likewise, senior staff encourage a leader to reach out to someone who seems unhappy, a tactic that one staffer dubs "charm and disarm."[110] "It's about soft hands to get people onside without them feeling manipulated or coerced," another told us.[111] When a senior staffer suddenly shows interest in a caucus member and their well-being, and praises them for their hard work, the staffer's motive may well be to shore up support and loyalty. Some junior staff in the leader's office keep meticulous records of when backbenchers are consulted. All of them are on the alert for potential nonconformity if their outreach to a backbencher is rebuffed.

Keeping differences of opinion within the family is about more than unity: the hazard of losing someone to an opponent or, worse, broader mutiny compels a leader to ensure that the caucus is reasonably satisfied. In addition to working out disagreements internally through negotiation and compromise, the leadership is equipped with the tools of reward power and coercive power to encourage compliance and constructive behaviour. As we will explain, these tools disarm individualism and contribute to a "web of authority" that conditions the caucus to align with the party's identity and support the leader's direction.[112]

Rewards for Loyalty and Consequences for Disloyalty

The party leader, senior staff, party whip, and caucus chair are keen to dissuade individualism and incentivize compliance. They leverage institutional rules to influence behaviour and demand loyalty in exchange for opportunities. This management strategy includes stoking parliamentarians' progressive ambition with the allure of promotion and pairing it with the implicit threat of demotion.[113]

Rewards for caucus members who show loyalty to their party and the leader's inner circle span from positive reinforcement to privileged access to the corridors of power (box 3.1), which can boost a group's *esprit de corps* and forge cohesive legislative voting.[114] A backbencher might be told, "You're doing a great job, we're going to make you the caucus chair," and, upon becoming caucus chair, be told, "My God, you're doing a wonderful job. We're going to make you a parliamentary secretary. You're this close to cabinet, you're the next one."[115] Many of them feed off the encouragement and believe that their loyalty will be recognized, especially when they observe that those who make waves are demoted or passed over. The belief of a former MP that "the path to career advancement is to keep your nose clean, your head down, vote as you're told, clap on demand, and good things will happen to you" is widely shared in Canadian parliamentary caucuses.[116] This *quid*

Box 3.1. Potential Rewards for Party Loyalty

- accomplishment of shared policy objectives
- appointments with prestige, power, profile, and resources (e.g., various ranks in cabinet, parliamentary secretary, committee chair, ministerial critic)
- approval of requests to go to constituency while legislature is sitting
- being treated with respect as part of a team
- better seat in the legislative chamber
- colleagues who attend fundraising events
- election affiliation and supports
- invitations to social events
- media opportunities
- moral and personal support
- more speaking time in the legislature
- opportunity to serve on preferred parliamentary committee
- participation in announcements
- political allies and lifelong friendships
- positive reinforcement from peers
- possibility of working with a minister on a file of interest
- post-parliamentary appointment
- travel junkets

pro quo aligns with the cynical observation of former federal Liberal leader Michael Ignatieff, who remarked that "politics is a team sport that rewards loyalty and punishes cleverness."[117] Many backbenchers naively believe that their loyalty to the team and its leader is reciprocal. They underestimate the vagaries of plums being dispensed and withdrawn at the pleasure of those at the top of the hierarchy, of which there are considerably more when a party controls the resources of government.

Prime ministers and premiers use their reward power to incentivize agreement. A common tactic is to grow the size of cabinet and create a suite of positions with limited responsibility, which can placate the backstabbing that arises from backbenchers jockeying for status who complain about their colleagues getting more media attention and more speaking opportunities.[118] Cabinet is the ultimate sustainer of loyalty and solidarity, for reasons that extend beyond self-importance, power, money, or the principle of collective responsibility, because being a minister awakens parliamentarians to the necessity of party unity to get things done. Louise Harel, a former Parti Québécois MNA, told us how her views about party discipline changed when she joined the cabinet: "I sat as a backbencher when I was first elected in 1981. For a few years I called the party line a dictatorship. Then I became minister for the status of women. At that point, I realized that progress on the role of women and women's cause for equality would not have moved forward so quickly without the party line."[119]

While cabinet is the most craved prize, it is the slew of lower-profile inducements that bolster caucus discipline. In Ottawa, since 1959 a consolation for government-side MPs with bruised egos has been appointment as a parliamentary secretary to assist a minister.[120] Parliamentary secretaries act as ministerial stand-ins by being designated to speak during Question Period, go on political talk shows, and make lower-profile announcements. Although not part of the cabinet, they take an oath of secrecy and loyalty and are privy to confidential information that the minister chooses to share. A blatant example of how reward power buys solidarity occurred in 2006 when a Conservative MP who was vocal about opposing floor crossing – including when she vowed to advance anti-crossing legislation in the wake of David Emerson's move from the Liberal to Conservative cabinet – fell silent after she was appointed his parliamentary secretary.[121] Backbenchers might think that this role brings them closer to a cabinet post when in fact, at the federal level at least, time on the opposition benches is a better route because it affords the experience that appeals to a first minister.[122]

The trend towards incorporating a greater share of the caucus into the governing apparatus has been termed "executive creep," reflecting its negative impact on responsible government.[123] The expansion of cabinet and the corresponding growth in the number of parliamentary secretaries are commonly viewed as strategies to secure caucus loyalty, as is the practice of appointing junior ministers and ministerial assistants. Leaders can also create titles, such as a special advisor or a community liaison, and invite backbenchers to write policy reports.[124] A caucus member who says something critical can find that they are offered a specific role that will keep them busy and onside.[125] In the provinces, executive creep may lead to every member of the governing caucus holding a title that symbolizes their alignment with the government, which can easily be revoked for acts of disloyalty or incompetence.[126]

Parliamentarians who accept appointments gain influence but lose freedoms. For example, we learnt of a backbencher who, after being appointed to a Treasury Board subcommittee, received a curt phone call from the PMO chief of staff saying that as a member of the Privy Council (albeit not in cabinet) he would now be expected to vote accordingly.[127] A counterview is that party discipline can be so rigid and the consultation process so haphazard that assigning backbenchers responsibility acknowledges their desire to contribute. As one staffer observed to us, "you need to give MPs opportunities. There's no reason why a smart, hardworking MP cannot play a bigger role than just vote as they are told and deal with immigration and tax inquiries in their constituency office. You try to give them that sense of being valued and part of the team so that when something shocking happens it's not a big slap in the face."[128] The bottom line is that responsible government relies on members of a parliamentary legislature holding the government accountable for its actions. This accountability is undermined when so many parliamentarians, whether directly or indirectly, consider themselves part of the government.

Though less of a career coup, parliamentary committees are where many parliamentarians believe they have the best opportunity to make meaningful contributions to public policy and legislation.[129] These supposedly arms-length bodies reduce internal agitation among members and contribute to caucus unity, serving as a rich source of perspectives for the minister's office.[130] In theory, parliamentary committees ought to act as a formidable check on government; in practice, they can be a forum for partisan theatre, in part because party whips assign membership and the minister's office has a heavy hand in their operations.[131] Some backbenchers manoeuvre for preferred appointments that match their policy interests and for committees that travel to interesting places, and for the prestige and pay bump of being chair or vice-chair, whereas other committees are a political graveyard.[132]

In the United States, a coveted committee assignment is a formidable factor in whether legislators would cross the floor to achieve a higher profile.[133] In contrast, some Canadian parliamentarians view being a committee chair as a career impediment because espousing neutrality in the role means sacrificing the boisterous partisanship that gets noticed and is rewarded with more substantial promotion.[134] Furthermore, members of tightly run parties lack the independence needed to flex their political muscles, particularly if the governing party has a majority of seats on the committee. "If you tell all of your members to vote down every amendment that comes forward on Bill XYZ, every amendment is going to be voted down. If you say we don't want any studies conducted on the oil sands, there won't be a study on the oil sands," explains a former government House leader.[135] Parliamentary committees in the provinces can likewise be held back from reaching their potential as checks on the government.[136] In fact, some provinces rely on a committee of the whole (the entire membership of the assembly except the Speaker) and make limited use of a standing committee system.

Another plum is being tapped as caucus chair or, in a large caucus, as chair of a sub-caucus such as a regional caucus or the women's caucus.[137] These inward-facing roles carry little public status but do provide access to the leader and the leader's inner circle who need to listen to what is on the mind of a subset of the caucus. Frank conversations with higher-ups can both empower these chairs and afford an opportunity to form connections with powerful people. A further loyalty reward is being appointed to the executive of a parliamentary association, which is normally conditional on a formal affiliation with the party that recommended the appointment.[138] Being selected to travel with the association is an escape from the narrowness of domestic partisan affairs when it involves visiting international destinations, meeting parliamentarians from other jurisdictions, and debating issues without the authority to make decisions.[139] In Ottawa, this travel typically requires permission from the whip's office; in the provinces, there are fewer opportunities for politicians to go abroad.

Opposition caucuses have far less responsibility and their leaders have fewer resources. Members of non-governing parties can have spectacular policy conflicts with a leader who has limited reward power to rein them in.[140] Without control over state spending, opposition leaders cannot engage in the pork-barrel politics that government leaders do to satisfy caucus members, though in minority government situations they can band together to collectively pass amendments to spending allocations or vote down an appropriation act that issues funding. They promote loyal followers to front-bench positions, such as ministerial critic or deputy leader, that bring influence and profile, and to several posts out of the spotlight, such as deputy opposition whip and caucus chair. Compared with a seat in cabinet, these roles have limited visibility and responsibility and rarely accord extra pay. Staff can dangle the prospect of asking a question during Question Period or going on a televised political panel, but the lack of opportunity for impact in an opposition caucus renders some backbenchers unmotivated.[141] A former Quebec NDP MP reflects on the strings being pulled by the leader's office and the caucus: "To have an impact as an MP, your party must give you opportunities. And put you in the spotlight. That's just it. The rest will follow. The party, unfortunately, must agree with the member on the issue being put forward. Because if it goes against the values of the party, you know what happens next."[142] Without relying on reward power, deference to authority, or employing referent power to charm supporters into action, the main alternative for a leader to encourage loyal behaviour is the intimidation or pressure that accompanies the use of coercive threats.

A thriving democracy depends on robust debate over policy options. Within political parties, diverging viewpoints are constructive when respectful communication helps to sort out disagreements and clarify roles.[143] As discussed, in Canada, disagreement within party caucuses largely plays out in secret, as members are reminded that they were elected under the party banner and campaigned in support of the party's policy platform. Canadian parliamentarians' public displays of unity and loyalty are evident in them routinely toeing the party line during legislative debates and voting on bills. The expectation that partisans vote together unless given permission for a free vote can involve formal instructions. In Ottawa, each party whip's office circulates voting recommendations as MPs enter the chamber to vote or staff lay the guidelines on each MP's desk. A Conservative describes how vote sheets look for that caucus: "Generally, there are three columns. In the left column is the bill or motion number. The middle column is a brief description. The right column is the whip's recommended position, usually expressed as support or oppose. Sometimes it states support level one, which is a free vote; support level two, where members are encouraged to vote the party line; or support level three, a whipped vote."[144] Guidelines about how to vote alleviate decision-making fatigue. Inevitably, an irreconcilable difference between the leader and a caucus member arises. When parliamentarians dig in, they set off predicaments that pit loyalties against personal convictions and constituency interests.

Looming large is the parliamentary duty of an elected representative to express and champion causes. If mishandled, an internal dispute can escalate to splintering the caucus itself.

Leaders who tolerate caucus members shooting from the lip often find that support for the party drops.[145] Furthermore, disruptors and self-aggrandizers can become tiresome, and walk a thin line. As one former MP observed, "a maverick becomes a rebel, a heretic, a thing to flout. It is a great way of attracting a great deal of attention, at least for a short while."[146] The consequences of unchecked dissent can be stark, as demonstrated by NDP MLA Jim Walding, who was excluded from Manitoba cabinets in the 1970s and 1980s. A vocal critic of NDP Premier Howard Pawley and his government's policies, Walding's grievances contributed to internal conflict. As Speaker, his decisions caused problems for his party.[147] Eventually, as a backbencher, he cast the decisive vote in favour of an opposition motion to amend the budget, leading to the government's collapse and the New Democrats' defeat in the ensuing election. It was a harsh lesson that a government can lose power if it fails to neutralize a contrarian in its ranks.

Backbenchers who disregard group norms can expect some form of disciplinary action. The severity of response increases with the perceived slight,[148] although those closely connected to the leader have more leeway than those on the periphery of power, and unwritten codes of conduct are always shifting. They can learn that independently questioning witnesses at a parliamentary committee instead of rehashing supplied questions will get them rotated off, that if they vote differently at committee they will not be permitted to travel with it, and that paranoia in a leader's office about something they said can result in lost speaking privileges in the legislature.[149] Troublemakers are marginalized, kept away from media opportunities, seated on the back benches away from a camera view – for extra punishment, next to someone they dislike – and are assigned low-profile duties, such as membership on a lightweight committee (box 3.2).[150] Those badged as unhelpful miss out on opportunities, as a former Quebec NDP MP explains:

> Are you doing what you are told to do?... You do it. Period. If you don't, they list you as lazy, not supporting the party, not part of the gang, unwilling to do anything for the rest of us. It's an unwritten law. And as a consequence, when it's Question Period, they cut you off from questions. You make proposals, they refuse them, even if the issues are current, even if it affects your region. Then the more it goes on, the more they squash you. So that you just end up with the shit. No more visibility; it's like you don't exist anymore.[151]

Box 3.2. Potential Punishments for Party Disloyalty

- becoming frozen out of conversations
- being required to publicly backtrack
- demotion or loss of role
- denial of opportunities for legislative activities
- directives to stop posting on social media
- fewer allowable days to tend to constituency matters
- getting passed over for promotion
- losing permission to be absent from the legislature
- party supporting another nominee or withholding campaign resources
- private and/or public scoldings
- receiving orders to disappear from public view
- reduced speaking time in the legislature
- refusal of leader to sign nomination papers
- routine requests being denied
- seat at the back of the chamber
- shortened or cancelled parliamentary travel
- social ostracization by colleagues
- staff not prioritizing requests
- threat of being expelled from caucus

The exercise of coercive power causes backbenchers to believe that higher-ups, particularly the leader's staff, keep tabs on them and continuously rate their performance. Wanting to be seen as a team player, they evade the defiance of declining requests by citing a prior commitment or a lack of time. For many with ambition, it is better to clam up because of the perception of career consequences. In the words of one MP, "Everybody knows that if you do anything to agitate ... then you're at risk. Your committee memberships are gone, your prospects of promotion are finished."[152]

Small perks like larger legislative office space can be revoked, as one former caucus chair discovered after backing the wrong side in a leadership review.[153] The whip can withhold granting permission to be absent from the legislature while it is sitting, which can be a sore point for a parliamentarian in a swing riding who is eager to attend community events in their electoral district. Troublemakers run the risk of receiving fewer campaign resources and, in the extreme, warnings that they will not be renominated as the party's candidate and will be booted from the party. One of the most powerful sanctions is organic: caucus members, whose loyalty is offended by acts of disloyalty, may instinctively distance themselves from a rebel, particularly if they feel frustrated by their own supporters branding them as partisan sycophants in contrast to their more audacious colleague. They can urge compliance when a teammate breaks rank, and both they and disciplinarians make veiled threats of "unspecified consequences."[154] While this social pressure may be effective, the leader's office must keep a watchful eye that the shunning does not lead to alienation.

Leaders depend on their political lieutenants to shore up support and act as sentinels. Capable staff can anticipate a problem and flag which members of the caucus are likely to cause a stir about a policy or procedure. For the most part, they employ the soft power diplomacy of brokering concerns and acting as intermediaries. Skilled staff are excellent listeners, and make backbenchers feel valued. At the same time, some of them are unambiguous about the boss's wishes and take a hard line with troublemakers. There is no point in sugar-coating a leader's decision, as a senior staffer explained to us: "You will never keep everyone happy in a caucus. Treat people with respect, be honest, be up front. A lot of responsibility involves meeting with them for coffee. Tell them, 'You're not going to be happy with X decision, but let's discuss another priority that you have.' You have to have honest dialogue. You can't blow sunshine up someone's ass. You might as well rip the Band-Aid off."[155] Conversely, inattentive staff in the leader's office can inflame tensions by ignoring caucus members, who then test the limits of loyalty.

The Limits of Loyalty

When managing caucus disruptions, party leaders must be careful because their actions can backfire and weaken their grip on a leadership position that ambitious caucus members may covet. A heavy-handed use of coercive power to moderate dissent must be reserved for egregious situations, as inclusion is usually a better route to cohesion than admonishment is.[156] In fact, punishment can stoke sympathy for an outspoken member, motivate other members to stake a united stand, cause someone to leave the caucus, or, in the extreme, ignite a cascade of resignations.[157]

Party loyalists have various ways to sabotage their allegiance to a leader. Leaders must tread carefully, as parliamentarians who leak information or speak to the media anonymously can gain the upper hand. A backbencher who is left out of cabinet can vent that the latest shuffle will undermine caucus morale[158] or can complain that loyalty to the leadership team is fragile because they treat parliamentarians as disposable.[159] A leader can brush aside one or two of these anonymous sources, but a chorus of malcontents chirping in the media about the leader can grow into a crescendo of discord. These frustrated members can mobilize to oust the leader by leaking insider information and subverting the unity that a leader needs to move forward. The leader's obligation to assuring caucus confidentiality typically prevents them from discussing internal matters publicly, leaving them vulnerable and at a disadvantage.[160] A leader who connects on a personal level with the caucus enjoys more goodwill to stave off such unruliness.

Resigning from an appointed role can be a bold act of disagreement, especially when a minister levels criticism at the leader and signals their intent to remain in the caucus. Some ministers step down over a policy dispute, because of internal conflict, or possibly to avoid the embarrassment of being fired.[161] A new normal for a resentful minister is to post online a biting letter of resignation filled with accusations that frames the reasons for the departure and admonishes the leader.[162] Shadow ministers can do the same with far less effect. Choosing an adversarial route under the guise of what's best for the party and/or public is the antithesis of quietly stepping down for personal reasons and can critically weaken a head of government's ability to lead.[163] In this regard, Finance Minister Chrystia Freeland's decision to release her resignation letter on the very day she was set to deliver the Fall 2024 economic statement sent shockwaves across the country, ultimately delivering a fatal blow to Prime Minister Trudeau's political career.

For backbenchers, an open expression of disappointment in the party's position or raising inconvenient questions can be a normal function of representation, provided such moments are rare, and at the risk of being branded a rogue or a radical.[164] News of caucus discord is seized upon by opponents, bolstering the narrative that unity is essential for stability and success, thereby perpetuating the cycle of silence. To wit, amid rising inflation, in 2023 a band of Liberal MPs in the Atlantic region called on the Liberal government to revise its carbon tax policy. Ken McDonald, a Liberal from Newfoundland and Labrador, voted for a Conservative motion to abandon the policy even though it was a signature piece of his party's election platform, and despite pleas from the chief government whip and a PMO Atlantic desk staffer. Afterward, McDonald calmly explained on CBC's *Power & Politics* that the rising cost of home heating oil was having severe economic repercussions on low-income constituents in his riding. There was no news of him being punished for his insubordination, perhaps because he did not grandstand and had made a point for the Atlantic caucus. The Conservatives pounced on the disagreement with alarmist memes such as "LIBERAL MP BREAKS RANKS WITH TRUDEAU" and some Conservative MPs approached him to cross the floor.[165] Within a month, the government backtracked by pausing its carbon price on heating oil in Atlantic Canada. It was a different story a few months later when McDonald called for a leadership review; such an open challenge of a leader's competency can result in a caucus member being expelled.[166] This time, the defiance was met by a brigade of Liberal MPs affirming their approval of the prime minister.[167] Lacking broader support, McDonald was subject to standard caucus management: within twenty-four hours he issued a written statement to retract his remark and pledge loyalty to the leader, and then vanished from public sight.[168] He later announced that he would not seek re-election, and generally fell into line. The episode validated that there is strength in numbers, that individualism is punished in party politics, and that it is far easier for the leader's office to extinguish a solitary voice. However, it also shows that a single backbencher can succeed in changing government policy, though often at a personal cost.

It is particularly difficult for the leader's office to exercise coercive power when dealing with multiple actors. Backbenchers can publicly object to a policy that will affect their community,[169] or a coalition can form within a caucus to campaign for change that culminates in a group of them voting in favour of a motion from an opposing party.[170] They can find refuge in signing a group letter calling upon their party's government to stop dragging its heels on implementing a campaign promise or addressing a crisis,[171] or they can vote as a bloc in defiance of the party line, as with the ten Liberal MPs in 1995 who opposed the government's proposed long-gun registry which prompted Prime Minister Chrétien to threaten their renomination.[172] When several team players are unnerved by a policy or inaction, the usual strong-arm tactics pack less punch.

A rare case of many backbenchers defying their government's wishes on a major bill occurred in 2017 when the House of Commons voted in favour of a private member's bill (PMB) that originated in the Senate. Bill S-201, the *Genetic Non-Discrimination Act*, proposed to prevent employers and insurance companies from requiring that Canadians take genetic tests. The measure was part of the 2015 Liberal Party platform and enjoyed broad approval in Parliament. Despite passing the committee stage with minor changes and support across party lines, the Liberal government attempted to introduce amendments to prevent sanctions against insurance companies.[173] Prime Minister Trudeau added that he considered the bill unconstitutional as it infringed on provincial jurisdiction, and he abstained. The amendments were swiftly defeated, and the bill passed, with only four Liberal backbenchers siding with the cabinet and the Bloc Québécois.[174] The remainder of the Liberal caucus voted with the Conservatives and New Democrats in support of the new law. The Supreme Court of Canada later ruled that the act was indeed constitutional,[175] raising the spectre that the split in the governing caucus had resulted from insurance companies exacting lobbying pressure. Moments like this, when a back-bench coalition rebuffs their leader, provoke discussion about the struggle for power and influence in legislatures.[176]

More ominous for a leader is when a group of caucus members plot how to achieve change at the top. Leaders can stare down those demanding their resignation and find that nobody is prepared to follow through on threats to leave, as with former prime minister John Turner who, as opposition leader, quashed an aborted coup by calling the bluff of MPs who signed a letter saying they wanted him out.[177] But few heads of government survive when an ensemble of ministers resign in protest, such as the seven ministers who stepped down from Prime Minister Mackenzie Bowell's government in 1896 (which he infamously decried as "a nest of traitors")[178] and the five ministers who quit on Manitoba Premier Greg Selinger in 2014 (which the media dubbed "the gang of five").[179] Alternatively, the abrupt resignation of a key minister can galvanize a critical mass of caucus members to call for leadership change, as occurred after Freeland quit cabinet. A single backbencher leaving the parliamentary caucus can also hobble a leader, particularly if others seem poised to follow suit. In Alberta, ten Progressive Conservative MLAs reportedly deliberated over dinner whether they should leave the caucus after one of their colleagues did so out of disdain for Premier Alison Redford, who was mired in negative headlines about her lavish spending. News of the backbenchers' scheming added to the mayhem, which culminated in the premier resigning.[180] As we shall explain in chapter 6, disunity can erupt into mass resignations from caucus as well.

Another rebellion that took down an Alberta premier occurred during the COVID-19 pandemic. Within a year of leading the United Conservative Party from opposition to a resounding election victory, Alberta Premier Jason Kenney presided over a party that became deeply divided on government interventionism. He tolerated two of the party's MLAs joining a national anti-lockdown coalition, until he declared that any caucus members not following public health rules would be expelled.[181] An ideological schism erupted when sixteen UCP MLAs, including the Speaker, signed a letter opposing the government's public health restrictions.[182] In a bit of irony, details of an emergency meeting about preventing leaks were leaked, at which the caucus voted to expel two MLAs who issued a public letter urging the premier to resign.[183] Kenney battled many instances of subversiveness, including a backbencher posting a Facebook video accusing the premier of promoting a culture of fear; another tweeting that the leader should step down; and multiple backbenchers openly criticizing his leadership.[184] The uprising included the unusual sight of a government-side backbencher remaining in the caucus after chiding the government in a member's statement and during Question Period.[185] All of this unruliness stood in stark contrast to the premier's reputation as a controlling political operative whose staff were ruthless with his political enemies.[186] After conceding to the demands of UCP electoral district associations for a leadership review vote, Kenny received a tepid endorsement from party members and announced that he would step down.

Even heads of government with strong public approval ratings can endure political regicide. After leading the Liberals to a third consecutive majority government in 2000, and with the opposition parties in disarray, Prime Minister Chrétien was labelled a "friendly dictator" due to his folksy image juxtaposed against the power concentrated in his office.[187] Change came from within. He was sabotaged by MPs who supported his finance minister, Paul Martin, who took public swipes that the prime minister could do little about. Less than two years after the resounding election victory, the caucus unrest climaxed in Chrétien firing Martin and subsequently announcing his plan to step down as leader. As prime minister, Martin rewarded many of the MPs who undermined his predecessor by appointing them to cabinet. These occasional bouts of leadership turnover are a stark reminder that a leader's considerable power puts them in jeopardy of being dethroned, and that there are limits to loyalty.

Summary

The extent to which parliamentarians hold sway with the party leader and central operatives has real-world implications for representation and governance in political milieux that are pulled apart by hyperpartisan factionalism. Leaders and their agents, particularly when their party controls the government, have a mighty yet tenuous hold over backbenchers through a mix of incentives and penalties, all shaped by institutional, political, social, and technological forces. The integration of smartphones into day-to-day political work is one of the ways that changes in communications technology have both empowered staff and made them a constant presence in the lives of parliamentarians.

Part of their work is helping to keep the caucus happy, including by reaching out for direct conversation. Rewards ranging from resources and promotions to social invitations and a better seat in the legislature are used to nurture loyalty and group cohesion. Caucus members who defy authority and resist the team mantra are subject to punishments such as a demotion, their requests not being prioritized, or being scolded. As we will show in the next chapter, most parliamentarians in Canada dare not criticize their leader or their party in public. They prefer to be viewed as team players.

4 Team Players

After the Coalition Avenir Québec (CAQ) secured a landslide victory in the 2018 Quebec election, two of the party's MNAs had markedly different reactions to being passed over for cabinet positions. Rookie Ian Lafrenière took it in stride by declaring himself a *joueur d'équipe*: "I am a team player; I will collaborate with everyone when asked. I will help the team, I am a team man," he said.[1] Soon afterwards he was appointed as a parliamentary assistant, and within two years he became a minister. On the other hand, Claire Samson, who had been the CAQ culture critic, walked out of the audience at the cabinet swearing-in ceremony and declared to the media that she would ponder her political future.[2] A few years later, she was expelled from the caucus for donating $100 to another party.[3] Samson chastised a political system gone amuck. She labelled backbenchers as *plantes vertes* (green plants) who stand at media events as background décor behind the leader.[4] She decried that partisans are told what to say in the legislature and how to vote on bills and she alleged that political staff reduce politics to pantomime by training parliamentarians to be theatre actors who rehearse lines for journalists and memorize questions to be put to ministers at parliamentary committees. These types of complaints only surface when a partisan is no longer committed to the team code of party politics.

Party culture shapes most of Canada's parliamentarians into team players. They dutifully parrot the party line, are fanatical supporters of the leader in public, and reserve blunt opinions for private conversation. They conform to diktats from the leadership and admonish colleagues who buck that orthodoxy. Outside their electoral district, and even within it, they are rarely a household name. Why do so many politicians become deeply attached to one political party? Why do they so often relinquish their autonomy to party interests? What is the psychology behind the team paradigm in politics? And, as one study asked, "Can Canadian legislatures promote a culture of looser discipline when members themselves see it, in some contexts, as a virtue?"[5] To answer these questions, we need to examine why people belong to groups at all. In this chapter, we consider social identity literature and institutional incentives in party politics to shed light on the deep-seated nature of partisanship among team players and to flesh out the factors that condition party loyalty.

Party Loyalty

An organized group is bound together to the extent that its members identify with it.[6] Social units bring together like-minded individuals who share an affinity, who interact, who have reasonably common goals, and who follow norms that both limit and guide actions.[7] Before choosing to join a group, some people collect and consider information about available options, and then select one that aligns with their identity and which they estimate will provide the maximum personal benefit at the lowest cost.[8] Others join without much thought. Upon joining, a member finds a place within the organizational hierarchy: social structures grant more status to certain members, and there is only so much power to go around as the group competes with others for resources.[9] Membership can lead individuals to adjust their sense of self, or possibly the group might pivot to accommodate them, or both may happen. Members implicitly agree to a bargain of supporting a set of expected behaviours and mindsets in return for the advantages of belonging.

Groups and organizations want their members to be loyal in part because of moral undertones that can drive virtuous and ethical behaviour.[10] Ardent supporters are valuable assets who make individual sacrifices, put in the work to advance the collective interest, and want to belong.[11] Typically, group members are loyal even when they are uncomfortable with a course of action because they want to contribute to a positive social identity and achieve shared objectives. They are willing to trade their independence in exchange for a sense of increased social power and standing, and they believe that they will accomplish more as part of a collective effort.[12] Joiners are susceptible to going along with others because of a host of cognitive biases, from bandwagon pressures to false consensus. They become immersed in a team culture as they interact with like-minded colleagues, as individualists are scolded for straying from group norms, and as colleagues become a source of emotional support.[13] Additional factors in group cohesion include the frequency of interactions, whether members are attracted to the group's purpose and its image, and uniformity of opinion.[14] In short, devotees become wrapped in a shared identity and mission.

However, loyalty to a group can erode members' individuality and judgment. Group members are depersonalized through a team-first mentality, resulting in some of them putting the welfare and agendas of other people and social units ahead of their own.[15] Groupthink can foster a false sense of social reality, which leaders can exploit to their advantage and to the detriment of their followers,[16] and free-riders who refuse to leave the group can become a drain.[17] The wicked side of loyalty becomes acute when psychological connections and a competitive drive to prevail fuels immoral behaviour.[18] A siege mentality takes hold when a group perceives a threat and the superiority of an in-group is exalted as opponents are vilified and prevented from accessing resources.[19] More concerning, prejudice can erupt as members of other groups are scapegoated and become a target of aggression.[20] The anti-democratic nature of these factional tendencies place the interests of insular groups ahead of the common good,[21] and the divisions can manifest into personal agendas as members conflate their personal and social identities.[22] In the extreme, their judgment can be infused by a sense that their opponents are no longer adversaries to be defeated but enemies to be vanquished.[23]

Unsurprisingly, constructive loyalty is a strategic priority for organizations. Employers nurture allegiance among workers to improve productivity and to forego the time, upheaval, and financial costs of losing employees, as well as to guard against a competitor poaching them.[24] Employers build commitment by onboarding workers who embrace the organization's traditions, who embody its values, and who communicate its identity.[25] They enhance retention by promoting top performers to higher ranks and offering challenging roles for people who thrive on complexity.[26] To them, loyalty drives results.

From a worker's perspective, loyalty to an employer requires good financial compensation, meaningful roles, training opportunities, a positive workplace, and support for their lives outside of work hours.[27] For workers to feel valued and included, and for superiors to be aware of ways to improve policies, leaders and managers need to promote a culture where subordinates can practise upwards communication.[28] Employees stick with an organization when they develop job satisfaction, when their initial expectations align with the role, and when they do not perceive viable alternatives.[29] Those with access to resources and who enjoy a modicum of autonomy are more likely to stay,[30] while those holding senior positions feel greater commitment.[31] Job embeddedness arises when there is social compatibility, whereby an employee's work aligns with their affinity towards colleagues, there is a fit with their personal values and goals, and they feel that leaving their occupation would mean sacrificing friendships and opportunities.[32] Conversely, employees remain in unhealthy workplaces when they are financially dependent on the job, when it has a psychological hold on them, and/ or when they discount alternatives, including an aversion to change.[33] Ultimately, people are loyal to a group and its leader as long as they feel that the advantages of staying outweigh the disadvantages of leaving.[34]

The human aspects of loyalty within a parliamentary party are similar those found in other types of organizations. We have established that organized groups feature loyal members who are committed to a common cause. In politics, some team players begin as rank-and-file, card-carrying adherents with an integrationist character that is ripe for immersion in a group's political identity.[35] They work their way up a scale of party loyalty, graduating from supporters to registered members to holding a role in their electoral district association. They display their partisanship by wearing party colours and branded merchandise. While there are exceptions, these partisans are prone to be more committed at each stage, becoming closer with members of their in-group and more antagonistic towards adversaries in other parties.[36] If they become election candidates and parliamentarians, they find that being part of a political party incurs transactional costs and a loss of individual freedoms.[37] In those roles they learn to follow well-worn mantras, such as "We are all links in a chain," "We are stronger together," "There is no 'I' in 'team,'" and many other sayings that urge cooperation and compromise. Their deepening commitment to a partisan identity results in behavioural change and making compromises. For most of them, membership in a political party is a good thing.

As with voters, some politicians form a lifelong connection to a party beginning at a young age when they are exposed to influences from their family, friends, social networks, and community. Since the mid-twentieth century, American studies have affirmed that most voters prioritize one party over another, often because of sociological influences.[38] The most enthusiastic supporters volunteer, particularly around election time,[39] and constitute members of fan communities who participate in cheerleading rituals.[40] These militants allocate considerable time to meetings, communications, and election readiness, and regularly give money to the party.[41] The socialization of politicians receives less study, though there are indications that those who are involved in lower-level party activities prior to being elected are more likely to vote the party line than are parliamentarians who recently joined the party.[42] In other words, people who are immersed into a party before their election are more likely to adopt a team-oriented mindset once they join a parliamentary caucus.

In Canada, extensive research about electors has affirmed that party affinity results from ideological alignment, demographics, and socioeconomic status, including social class, religion, education, and career pathways.[43] Lifelong partisans are deeply ingrained with touchpoints from a young age, which become part of who they are and shape their perception of reality. Loyalty runs deep when a partisan's parent(s) engage(s) them in election campaigning.[44] In our interviews, many politicians shared their experiences of political awakening: how they became involved with their party during childhood or adolescence, often through family connections or university clubs. They spoke of being inspired by the leader of the time and felt a connection with the party's values. We heard about how role models invited them to participate, and how it was thrilling to get involved with a party on the rise. Carolyn Parrish, a four-time Liberal MP whose brash style got her expelled from the caucus, is among those who shared memories of a formative period when their party identification took shape: "What you learn at home and in school informs your opinions. My parents were Liberal party supporters. Mom helped Liberal candidates. We didn't put a sign on our lawn because dad was a policeman. In grade 11, my history teacher was a fan of Red Kelly, the hockey player, and got us delivering pamphlets for Kelly's campaign to be a Liberal MP. Once you get to the stage of making a decision about a party, you decide this suits me."[45] Others told us that they grew up in partisan families but never paid much attention to party politics until adulthood, or signed up to run with a political party to which they had little attachment. For them, a party identity forms soon after joining. New entrants can quickly immerse themselves in party culture by developing friendships and loudly criticising opponents.

The most common reason for joining a political party in Canada is to express support for its policy positions.[46] While militants are the lifeblood of a political party's operations, their numbers have been dwindling since the 1990s. Party memberships have declined to about 8 per cent of Canadians, of which many are inactive,[47] and members are more reluctant to volunteer compared with the past.[48] Nevertheless, before they sought election, many Canadian parliamentarians belonged to their party for some time and were fairly active, including as donors. Socialization is more pronounced with male parliamentarians, who tend to have been party members for longer than women and who have spent more time working with their local EDA.[49]

It comes as no surprise that politicians are drawn to a party whose political values closely resonate with their own. This can include solidary obligations that meld communities of interest, which historically has included religious groups, union workers, and farmers, to name some. A contemporary political cause is climate change, which is a calling for Green Party candidates who see hyper-partisanship as a serious impediment to addressing a global crisis.[50] Partisans told us that it is fulfilling to work with like-minded people in politics. They are attracted to a group whose members they admire, respect, and trust, which nurtures a sense of belonging, extended community, and fellowship. When they and their colleagues support one another and accomplish shared objectives, it seems far more viable to advance change as part of a political group than without one.

The staunchest partisans are true believers when the party is an opposition rump, its election prospects look dire, and other supporters are abandoning it. They might be unwavering in their support of the leader even if they privately have doubts. They are suspect of new recruits who join when the party becomes popular, whom they view as opportunists or tourists. Unflappable team players, such as Anne McLellan, can be a regional beacon in a barren political landscape. Dubbed "Landslide Annie" for winning her Alberta riding by one vote in the 1993 federal election, which increased to twelve votes after a judicial recount, the Liberal MP was re-elected three times despite the province being a hotbed for conservative parties, each time prevailing by 3.5 per cent or less, until a close loss in 2006. McLellan's political identity meant that she would never consider another party. She grew up in a Liberal family in Nova Scotia. As a teenager, she was drawn to the values espoused by Pierre Trudeau and, when she moved to Alberta, she became deeply engaged with the Liberal party but learnt not to talk openly about her involvement. Being a minister in the Chrétien and Martin governments enabled her to do things to improve society, and sitting on the opposition benches held no appeal. Her sense of loyalty to a party, its values, and its people is typical of team players in Canadian legislatures: "Your team only succeeds if you have each other's backs. If you find fault with fellow team members and you undercut them, the team won't get ahead, and it will go through a rough period. Teams are groups of people who share the same end goal and people have to compromise. You don't get all the ice time you want, or sometimes, even the position you want to play. You have to be a team player within the range of possibilities."[51] Her loyalty in precarious electoral circumstances stands in contrast to a floor crosser with a similar nickname. In the 1979 BC election, NDP candidate Al Passarell defeated a long-time incumbent (himself a past party switcher) by a single vote, earning him the moniker

"Landslide Al." In opposition, he fashioned a maverick image by occasionally breaking ranks, and eventually crossed the floor to the governing Social Credit Party to accomplish more.[52] What that would have meant for his career is unclear given that Passarell died before he could seek re-election with his new party. Some politicians value power over party; for others, power is incidental.

The length of time that a parliamentarian is in office is not necessarily a predictor of their partisanship[53] – as we will show, all sorts of things can erupt in their political career that causes their connection with a party to dissolve. Similarly, party affinity is found at all stages of a political career, from candidates who agree to run in a seemingly unwinnable riding through to seasoned parliamentarians who voluntarily resign from a safe seat to trigger a by-election for a new leader to seek election. Political veterans typically have the deepest attachment, as we would expect given their long association with their party. They mentor less-experienced colleagues about the importance of unity, and convey that once the caucus makes a decision, then all members must publicly support it.[54] They can chastise those who go against the grain, sometimes by demanding that a controversial colleague publicly apologize.[55]

Political parties that align around a core political philosophy attract and expect more conformity. Leaders who share those values seldom need to resort to coercive measures because a caucus with shared character traits and strong ideological alignment is naturally inclined to function as a cohesive unit.[56] Leaders who appear to compromise on these principles so that they can broaden their parties' bases of support do so at the risk of being called sell-outs or traitors to the cause.

Some parties are anchored in philosophical principles and thus have greater ideological stickiness than in a big-tent party that follows public opinion and bundles together political coalitions. In the New Democratic Party, supporting the leader, upholding the party's platform, reenforcing party policies endorsed at convention, or respecting caucus positions developed through rigorous internal debate is often a priority over advocating personal or constituents' interests.[57] For many New Democrats, deference is anchored in their experiences in labour unions where collective bargaining and strike action train workers in the need to demonstrate cohesion as employers try to weaken that resolve by pinpointing divisions.[58] The union motto "Teamwork in the leadership and solidarity in the ranks" inspires labour leaders but can be suffocating to some independent thinkers in the party.[59] A former NDP MP has vented that the party's acronym "stands for Non-Democratic Party. It's got its roots in unions and solidarity at all costs and you're either a team player or you're not, and if you're not 100 per cent a team player, you're evil."[60]

In populist parties with a grass-roots or libertarian bent, internal disagreement may be framed as evidence of free debate among members of caucus.[61] In the late twentieth century, the Reform Party of Canada's policy held that a parliamentarian must balance three overarching representation impulses:

1. the principles, policies, and platform of the [party] on which the MP was elected;

2. the views and interests of constituents in the MP's riding, in particular the consensus among constituents, if such a consensus can be determined; and

3. the MP's own knowledge, judgment, and conscience regarding the issues at hand.[62]

The tensions of finding equilibrium among these three representational imperatives proved to be a constant source of acrimony between Reform MPs and the leader's office.[63] Reformers who were elected by a slim margin were especially conflicted because they felt that their re-election hinged on their ability to advocate for their constituents.[64] In this paradigm, loyalty shifts from the party and its leader towards people in the parliamentarian's electoral district, particularly to local supporters. While party leaders occasionally champion the same free speech values as Reform once did,[65] the political havoc that follows frequently leads them to acknowledge the importance of caucus members being more restrained and measured.

Once in power, there is a special responsibility for the caucus to be publicly united. Because government-side backbenchers are widely perceived as government spokespersons, their criticism undermines a minister and confuses stakeholders, which compels a communications response from the government. Cohesion in a governing party caucus mimics the principle of collective ministerial responsibility. A former premier put it thusly to us: "You have a decision to make every day in politics: you support the decision of the larger group and the leader, or you're not part of that group anymore. Lots of times in cabinet, ministers do not agree. You either have to support the decision and live to influence the decision on another day, or else you have to leave."[66] Backbenchers can easily align with the leader by repeating key messages or taking cues from a designated spokesperson's remarks – and, if in doubt, by saying nothing. Unity of message is even more crucial when their party has negative momentum, lest the team break apart.

Partisan Teams

Political teams congeal as they work together to solve problems. Partisans strategize in small group settings, such as impromptu conversations in their offices, in parliamentary hallways, at events, and while travelling. As they derive support from one another, they forge social connections that can outlast their tenure in a legislature. "You build deep, lasting friendships when you go into battle against an opponent," one partisan told us.[67] The kinship combined with an adversarial outlook inhibits betrayal.

Partisan teams are filled with supporting players. Many parliamentarians are relegated to a superficial role, such as serving as props behind a spokesperson at a news conference, applauding with excessive enthusiasm.[68] In this sense, they are more like fans observing the spectacle of political theatre than active participants. Of course, organized sports is only one way to look at a team concept. In medicine, health care providers are dubbed health teams.[69] It is in the collective interest of all members of the medical community to be successful with a patient, which means working together, rooting out problems, and acknowledging mistakes.[70] Consequently, politicians with a background in healthcare can have a particularly difficult time adjusting to the combativeness of party politics. Conversely, hyper-partisans view themselves as part of warring tribes or factions – inflammatory language that does more harm than good for democratic discourse.[71] If they are silver-tongued or abrasive with opponents, it is because they are part of an in-group culture that is stoked by the "us versus them" attitude used to justify aggressive tactics and caustic language.

As we noted in chapter 1, the team culture equates a party with family. To some partisans, team is intimate: it refers to caucus solidarity and a close-knit group, whereas party encompasses the wider spectrum of party supporters and infrastructure.[72] Thinking about a caucus as a family tugs on a more profound sense of social identity, responsibility, and loyalty.[73] Family members inevitably disagree, and yet their innate bonds motivate them to reconcile and look out for each other. To former Vancouver MP Libby Davies, being "part of a team of New Democrats was like being in a big family, and as in any family, there are squabbles and siblings can become competitive and downright nasty, but they are also loving and will go to the wall for you."[74] When they retire, parliamentarians reminisce fondly about the friendships they forged through socializing, by talking about common interests and sharing information about their personal lives. "Boy, those were good times, because we were a family," they say.[75] The metaphor is used by higher-ups and devout partisans to maintain the social order that familial affinity instils and to paper over cracks in party solidarity.[76] For a subset of elected officials, party loyalty is truly a family matter when their relatives are or were parliamentarians.[77] Being a member of a caucus is also likened to a marriage in thàt most of the time two partners agree but sometimes they do not.[78] Meanwhile, party members' real families can be under duress – one study found that 85 per cent of Canadian MPs in 2013 had been or were divorced[79] – and for some partisans, their colleagues fill a gap in their personal lives. The language of team and family reinforces their dedication to a close-knit network of friends, allies, and colleagues united by a shared partisan identity and a collective pursuit of common goals.

Most team players are party loyalists. The depth of their attachment to the party, the security of their re-election, their personal ambitions, and their temperament all vary. Because so many of them are indiscernible, their detractors dismiss them as irrelevant backbenchers who behave as trained seals.[80] From our perspective, team loyalty among parliamentarians manifests as relationship-builders who work across party lines, hyper-partisans who incessantly chide opponents, and, nestled in between, inconspicuous backbenchers. We explain each of these in the following pages.

The Low-Profile Backbencher

For decades, the team framework has been readily accepted in Canadian party politics because of the compatibility of most parliamentarians to work together to achieve their goals. Rooted in the country's accommodative political culture, the dual principles of consensus and deference encourage elites to compromise within their partisan silos, prioritizing progress over the paralysis of internal division.[81] Most partisans accept that the parliamentary system is one of party control and grumble that it is taxing to follow the party line when it goes against their personal views.[82] They learn to embrace a political culture in which personal concessions are made for the greater good – essentially, "taking one for the team".[83] With experience, they realize that they can trade on their support to get what matters to them and to negotiate so that other members of the team benefit too.[84] They seldom, if ever, attract attention for making a show of deviating from the party line or critiquing the leader.

Most of a backbencher's work occurs without fanfare, provided they stay on brand. Some team players are extremely cautious about rocking the boat. They spend a lot of time listening in caucus and do not say much.[85] Worrying about how they are perceived by higher-ups affects their decisions, such as going to events out of concern that their attendance is being tracked, putting in extra shifts in the legislature to be present for votes when others are away, or rushing back to the capital while they are coping with personal loss.[86] "Be there for them whenever they want," is the attitude of some team players towards House leaders and party whips.[87] Gradually, they realize that partisanship is a gateway for building personal connections with individual partisans because it is people, not the party entity, who help them navigate problems and accomplish goals. A former Conservative MP explains the reciprocation of loyalty in party politics:

> There are lots of loyalties, individual loyalties within the caucuses, with the people. But if you think that being loyal, as I did, to the party is going to pay off in some way to you, [that] the party is just going to take care of you or something, forget it! The party is not going to take care of you. You might have someone in the party who really likes you and values you and feels that there's a debt of gratitude and will help you out. That might happen. But, without that, there's no party loyalty. It's a one-way street, was my experience.... Your colleagues who help you, if you're a loyal person, you help them back.[88]

In this sense, loyalty within a party caucus is a series of reciprocal exchanges among like-minded people. It involves developing trustworthy relationships, working together to leverage each other's talents, going to one another's events, and avoiding being labelled a self-serving opportunist.[89] This is especially true for members of the governing party. Chuck Strahl, a minister in the Harper government, counselled that backbenchers need to recognize the importance of teamwork. His advice is to "remember that the caucus and the cabinet are in the political fray with you, and they need to know you have their back – and they, yours. The team isn't the be-all and end-all, but it's important. And you will hang together, or you will hang separately."[90]

With time, low-profile backbenchers look for strategic and tactful opportunities to register disagreement in confidential settings without coming across as disloyal or disrespectful.[91] They can have pluck, but it takes a special skillset to get a message across that energizes the party and improves its reputation. They tell the whip and/or the leader in advance when they are unwilling to compromise on an issue and are thinking of voting differently than the rest of the caucus.[92] After making a point, they support the majority opinion. Surprising the leadership by going public with a complaint would be betrayal.

Whether their ambition is discrete, static, progressive, or even intra-institutional, for many backbenchers toeing the party line in the legislature becomes a normal thing to do. Vote instructions save them considerable time and effort and inoculate them from interest groups and lobbyists who try to persuade them how to vote. Some team players dutifully read from notes supplied by the leader's office or minister's office and speak *ad nauseam* to run out the clock,[93] and their members' statements are coordinated by the leader's office.[94] The centralization can eradicate motivation to perform even basic tasks: sometimes partisans vote with their party without really understanding the issue at hand or what is being proposed,[95] and some never utter a word in the House.[96] Others fancy the opportunity to be a party propagandist. In Question Period, members of the opposition can lob witty quips and fiery retorts as they apply a partisan slant to topical issues,[97] while those on the government benches can ask planted "friendly" questions that ministers know are coming.[98] On both sides, their heckling challenges partisan spin, addresses distortions or misinformation, and props up colleagues by chastising opponents.[99] Those who master the art of witty soundbites gain respect within their party, and might be tapped to assume greater responsibility.

Hyper-partisans

Loyal team players with political influence are granted more leeway to deviate from party messaging, including popular regional ministers, high-profile figures closely aligned with the party's ideological foundations, or a politician with personal ties to the leader.[100] A small number whom the leader trusts to use tough language and lob insults develop reputations as ardent partisans who contribute to a growing tone of incivility.[101] These faithful militants aggressively chastise and needle their adversaries. Some of them train their rhetoric outside the parliamentary arena on journalists, pundits, interest group leaders, and other critics.[102] Hyper-partisans who excel at dismantling their foes get zoomorphized by the media as "attack dogs" or "pit bulls" for their obstinate one-sidedness, skill at exploiting vulnerabilities, name-calling, and vitriol.[103] As in the United Kingdom[104] and United States,[105] their biting comments in the legislature and scrums go viral on social media, amplified by fervent members of the party's base. Their public image is often a caricature: they are portrayed as uncompromising ideologues who are less interested in the public good than they are celebrating the moral superiority of their party, ridiculing their rivals, and defending their position to farcical degrees. Their message track can be part of a coordinated de-branding strategy that critically weakens an opponent through a combination of communications tactics.[106] Their hard edge can allow the leader and others, whose image would be damaged by engaging in such rancour, to be at arms-length.

Leaders turn to nimble debaters and brutishness to help advance political dogma. A cadre of tenacious parliamentarians who are entrusted to advocate for party interests can be given licence to ruthlessly critique an opponent, particularly if they are astute at finding ways to fulfil the news media's need for titillating content.[107] Hyper-partisans vigorously criticize the government when they are in opposition and defend it when they are in power. Their volleys excite the caucus and a party's base, as well as the press gallery which is attracted to the saucy assertiveness, hyperbole, and fearless accusations. Those with a talent for political jousting can be accorded the label early in their political career. When Pierre Poilievre was a thirty-year-old parliamentary secretary to Prime Minister Harper, one media profile described the Conservative MP as "the government's attack dog" who was "toy terrier–like, constantly yipping and yapping at the opposition and never, ever wavering from his talking points."[108] Some of them channel this truculence with their colleagues, albeit in softer tones. In Newfoundland and Labrador, Member of the House of Assembly (MHA) Paul Lane, whose unusual career path is discussed in chapter 7, wrote browbeating messages to the caucus to urge them to participate in public opinion straw polls on local news websites.[109]

This uncompromising hardball style of politics coupled with a disinterest in diplomacy or collaboration tends to make hyper-partisans unsuitable for situations that call for working with members of a different party. Their hard-headedness has a function, but relationship-building across party lines is left to others. Hyper-partisans can take team competition to extremes, as some former MPs told the Samara Centre:

There were some people who were effective attack dogs in the House, but they became a lot less effective because they didn't know how to temper their attacks and use the scalpel instead of the bludgeon.... This is politics, not war. You may differ on the issues, but there's no reason to hate the person across the way.[110]

Our system has evolved to this really hyper-partisan system where you shut down [and] shut each other down. That hyper-partisan[ship] means you're on the other team. I can't agree with you because of that.[111]

I wasn't a hardhead or one of the pit bulls or attack dogs.... If you get a reputation of being a hard ass, [if] people don't trust you because as soon they turn their back on you, you're going to get partisan and stab them in the back, [then] you can't get anything done.[112]

That said, the persona of a political bully is exaggerated for theatrical effect, as part of the mediatization of politics that uses conflict to grab the attention of audiences. For instance, John Baird, a trusted point person for the Harper government, was frequently depicted in editorial cartoons as an enraged figure because of his animated yelling in the House of Commons. His bombastic freelancing contrasted with Conservative backbenchers who were portrayed as being on a short leash. Despite his depiction as an angry man, Baird was well-liked across all parties and, moreover, at the time, NDP leader Jack Layton, who had a friendly image, was far more negative in Question Period.[113] Other parliamentarians labelled by the media as attack dogs have a composed yet incisive demeanour, such as House leader Katrina Gould in the Justin Trudeau government.[114]

Certain senior political staff adopt hyper-partisan behaviour and a combative tone that conveys the leadership's expectation of unwavering loyalty while normalizing the treatment of opponents as enemies. The impact of their sharp rhetoric is bolstered by the leader's tacit approval, which amplifies their authority. Parliamentarians take notice when the leader's office discredits a colleague, whether through anonymous leaks or direct online character attacks. The media can depict these uncompromising backroom operators as staunch enforcers, whose fierce partisanship and unflinching loyalty to the leader have earned them a reputation for ostracizing party members perceived to have violated the unwritten code of absolute allegiance.[115] In the extreme, brusque politicos yell, swear, and threaten people beneath them in the organizational hierarchy. They have a narrow view of insubordination.[116]

The most volatile senior staffers drive unnerved caucus members to raise concerns with the media as unidentified sources, portraying the leader's staff as unhinged. This occurred with Premier Ford's first chief of staff who reportedly instilled a culture of fear by monitoring MPPs' applause for the premier, by belittling them in caucus meetings, challenging ministers in cabinet sessions, orchestrating staff firings, and controlling the appointments process.[117] Left unchecked, the berating can be too much for some backbenchers who lash out, leave the party, or do not run again. Equally, political staff can bear the brunt of abuse when things go badly, and their precarious employment means that many are on edge that they will be fired on a whim.[118] The inside of party politics can thus be a toxic soup. A former leader put it this way to us: "There's always manipulation going on. In politics you swim with sharks. It's not just the politicians, it's the people around them as well."[119] However, belligerent staff are rare and usually outstay their welcome,[120] particularly when they run up against strong-willed parliamentarians who balk at commands. The reality is that senior staffers are more likely to be relationship-builders, as are many parliamentarians.

Relationship-Builders

The false dichotomy of "us versus them" creates a vicious cycle whereby partisans become wary of appearing too friendly with members from opposing parties. In fact, many parliamentarians routinely advocate within and across party lines without breaking the bonds of partisanship. Tenacious politicians can specialize in an issue and persuade the caucus and the leadership that a course of action is necessary and will help the group, as opposed to serving to aggrandize their own personal status. They initiate and capitalize on research, they consult widely, and they build a coalition that impresses the leader.[121]

Whether through experience or audacity, some team players generate the political acumen to work across party lines. Given that so many partisans have deep emotional and intellectual connections to a partisan community, to the point that the party becomes embedded in their social fabric and individual identity, it can surprise them to find that they have a lot in common with members of other parties. Travelling together within their region, on parliamentary committee trips and especially on parliamentary junkets abroad, plays a substantial role in building cross-party friendships, as does participating in unofficial all-party groups that form to study or advocate a common interest.[122]

The more that partisans interact with parliamentarians in other parties, the more they discover that personality, demographics and shared interests rather than ideology or party identity are at the core of relationship-building in politics. Forging ties with likeable people in a different caucus can be a welcome surprise. Former Ontario MP Stella Ambler explains: "I'm as Conservative as they come. And I'm loyal to the party and I wouldn't want to do things that embarrass them.... But I also found that I could get along with other people too who believed completely different things than I did.... There were people on the opposite side of the House that I liked better than some of my own party members.... I'm not afraid of being partisan and wanting my party to win and wanting my party to form the government and so on. But you also have to be a reasonable human being."[123] Some opposition backbenchers shared that ministers can be receptive to their suggestions to modify policies and how cross-party collaboration can deliver results for constituents.[124]

Certain politicians excel at connecting with people from different political parties. The multi-party engagement of Peter Stoffer, a plain-speaking NDP MP in Nova Scotia from 1997 to 2015, was legion. For nearly two decades, he nurtured cross-party friendships by hosting an annual "all-party party," a social gathering for politicians and staff from across the political spectrum.[125] Part of Stoffer's allure was that his Parliament Hill office became a man cave: the walls and ceiling were covered with thousands of baseball caps, political buttons, and pins from across Canada; it had a pool table, a dartboard, a fridge stocked with refreshments, and a guestbook.[126] The office was a sanctuary for stressed-out ministers, backbenchers, and staff from all parties who wanted to have a chat.[127] In Ottawa, other cross-party social encounters include MPs playing soccer with parliamentary pages and softball with the press gallery.

Team players can trade on their relationships to build political alliances. Wrangling support for a private member's bill is the epitome of this sort of collegiality. The mechanism is an outlet where members have greater freedom to vote as they choose, even when the leader's office attempts to ensure the substance and outcome are uncontroversial or co-opts the process so that backbenchers contribute to advancing the party's agenda. An exemplary case of cross-party interactions leading to the passage of a PMB was the *Reform Act, 2014*. Initiated by Conservative MP Michael Chong, it amended the *Parliament of Canada Act* to stipulate that in their first caucus meeting after a general election, MPs must vote on whether to opt in to several elements for the duration of the Parliament that empowers them, not the leader, to determine caucus membership.[128] If so, the caucus has the ability to vote out their party's leader, which the Conservatives did with O'Toole following a disappointing result in the 2021 federal election. An MP can only be expelled or admitted if at least 20 per cent of the caucus submits to the chair a written request for a secret ballot vote, followed by a majority of the caucus voting in favour of expulsion. Caucuses other than Conservatives have been reluctant to opt in; doing so can lead to prolonged negative press when MPs deliberate whether to expel a troublemaker.[129] The *Reform Act, 2014* also made a symbolic change by amending the *Canada Elections Act* so that the leader's delegate signs nomination paperwork instead of the leader, though in practice the leader is still in control. These laws would not exist without the tenacity of a government-side MP who was determined to strengthen the foundations of Canada's democratic institutions. Chong nurtured the backing of a critical mass within his own caucus and opposition parties by listening to suggestions for friendly changes such that his bill eventually garnered cross-party support, including from Prime Minister Harper.[130]

Occasionally leaders are the ones who find common ground. Informal strategic alliances between parties allow caucus members to preserve their party identity while collaborating with another party on a temporary or issue-specific basis.[131] A more formal arrangement sees the leader of a minority government sign an agreement with another party leader to form a parliamentary alliance. A confidence and supply arrangement typically provides for regular cross-party meetings between the leaders and their staff, a mutual commitment to advance shared policy objectives, and an understanding that the opposition partner will support the government on budgetary and confidence votes in the legislature for a period of several years. This level of interparty cooperation falls short of the formal linkages provided in a coalition government, which integrates opposition members into the cabinet and can blur party lines (chapter 6). Several times, New Democrats have entered into a confidence and supply agreement, including propping up the Ontario Liberals in 1985 and securing the support of the BC Greens in 2017 to form a government.[132] The 2022 agreement between Justin Trudeau and Jagmeet Singh committed them to collaborate on shared policy goals, including quarterly meetings between the leaders, regular engagement between their house leaders and party whips, and an oversight group consisting of a select few staff members and politicians that met monthly.[133] The NDP caucus voted on the deal; the Liberal caucus was given two hours' notice of a virtual meeting where the prime minister outlined his reasons for signing it.[134] Liberal backbenchers were shocked by the announcement and some were upset that they were not consulted, yet as dutiful team players, they accepted it. The deal proved fruitful because it opened interparty lines of communication between staff and officeholders, which resulted in tangible policy outcomes, notably dental care for low-income Canadians.[135] When Singh called off the arrangement in 2024, partisan negativity between the leaders resurfaced.

Interparty cooperation like this is uncommon in party systems that have become more polarized and as partisan divides among parliamentarians have become starker. There is less cross-party fraternizing than in the past; indeed, some leaders discourage their caucus members from it.[136] Building relationships across the aisle by going for drinks with members of another party can be chastised – gossip about a social rendezvous and photographs of conviviality can end up online, and senior partisans worry that parliamentarians who discover shared interests and form personal connections are susceptible to political persuasion.[137] In some parties, being a good teammate can mean campaigning alongside candidates in a related party seeking election to a different legislature;[138] other times, loyalty can be tested if a provincial leader demands that their caucus stay away from, or even publicly berate, a federal counterpart from the same party lineage.[139] Such moments strain partisan identities and can be defining moments of loyalty.

Friction

Team players told us that there are lots of days that they get angry about an issue, an opponent, or a set of circumstances. Ministers, critics, party whips, caucus liaisons, and political staff might accord them the respect of listening to their concerns and help them understand that a decision has been made and cannot be surmounted. Those who are committed to the cause find ways to channel their negative energy into a constructive output. They pause, let the issue pass and move on.

Being a team player does not mean forgoing the drive to challenge authority when the need arises. Indeed, for a party and its leader to be successful it is imperative that parliamentarians bring their concerns forward. As former NDP MP Peggy Nash told us, "If loyalty means never being critical, that isn't helpful. Criticism is essential to seeing different points of view. If a party is getting into trouble, it's a duty of an individual to stand up for principle. But as much as you can, keep that debate internal. Understand that if you damage the leader, you are damaging the party."[140] Those who canvass their colleagues can find that other members of caucus support their point of view, and ultimately convince the leadership to change course. "I had MPs come up to me and say, 'You know, you're right. You're right,'" relayed a former member of Parliament to us,[141] and sometimes the leader's circle signals agreement too. "We didn't think about that. That was a good point. You know, we don't want to go off the rails here," a PMO staffer might say.[142] Most of the time, however, the party leadership holds firm.

Some team players are satisfied with the elasticity their leader accords them. "I mean, we've come out in the papers and the media with all kinds of criticism. You know, I voted against our own government on certain bills, I voted with opposition parties on certain bills. I've not once been slapped with any sort of constructive criticism," said a Liberal MP about being a member of Justin Trudeau's caucus.[143] But inevitably, even committed team players become deeply unhappy at times. They are unsettled by personality conflicts with colleagues, differences of opinion with leadership, impatience with the pace of success, being away from family, and other factors. Backbenchers can be dissatisfied with their role, especially if they are left out of cabinet, as a PEI MLA reflected: "[I was] being requested to hold the party line, vote on the party line, chair committees with never a thank you, nothing. I felt like a junkyard dog chained up in the corner.... They just wanted me to be docile. They needed me to work and to vote their way. It's hard to be in a situation where you're not wanted, but I'll be damned if I was going to quit over it."[144] Most of them rationalize that the best option is to carry on in an unsatisfactory situation, particularly those who are anxious about change and who fear being alone.[145] They weigh their sense of identity, and structural factors such as perceived alternatives, social pressures, and the costs of a break-up.[146] This is one of the reasons leaders and their agents sow the seeds of animosity towards their opponents: to lower the attractiveness of switching sides. It follows that team players will remain in a party caucus even if they are unhappy about it.

Many of the former MPs interviewed by the Samara Centre who fit the team player label reflected on moments of advocacy and defiance. Some were proud of their fleeting bravado, such as the MP who was the only one in a national caucus meeting to voice opposition to North American Treaty Organization bombings in Libya; the MP who provoked eye-rolls whenever he asked pointed questions in parliamentary committees about the cost of members' travel; and the former MP who once abstained from a committee vote.[147] Others were despondent about a conformist political system. If they voted against their own party's government, they felt like they were letting down their colleagues and they were sad that some of those colleagues refused to speak to with them as a result.[148] "What the heck are you doing? Your issue is now causing me problems!" is the kind of reaction that a lone agent can expect from other members of the caucus.[149]

In all caucuses, members feel disrespected when they are presented with a decision as though it is a *fait accompli* and consultation is perfunctory. In the governing party, backbenchers get flustered when policy decisions that affect their constituents are made without their knowledge or against their objections.[150] In Ottawa's national caucus meetings, ministers may deliver a 90-second summary of a bill without distributing any supporting materials. They answer a few questions before the caucus chair moves onto the next agenda item without a vote.[151] Backbenchers are then expected to support the bill as outlined on the vote sheet laid on their desk.[152] There is more opportunity for dialogue in opposition caucuses, as a former NDP MP explained to us: "I think people are more likely to defy a party line if there is not a fair opportunity to debate it internally. If there is a very open and full discussion in caucus and people democratically come to a decision, then of course most caucus members will feel some responsibility to uphold that decision. Whereas if the leader's office just imposes a decision, then most MPs might still go along with it for various reasons, but some who disagree might feel more of a need to speak out if they weren't able to do so internally."[153] Regardless of the extent of caucus dialogue, when the group goes in a different direction on an issue that cuts to the core of a politician's identity and personal conviction, that individual can feel isolated and disconnected. Most internalize and keep their angst within a closed circle, though some vent their frustrations as they try to make sense of whether they still belong.[154] Sometimes they ponder what it would be like if they were to switch sides. "I do think about it. I think about it a lot," one parliamentarian told us.[155] In a fit of pique, they sometimes privately pledge to leave a party *en masse*, but these threats rarely materialize.[156] The norm is to grin and bear it. "I'd rather stay and lose with integrity than hand over my integrity," a former MLA proclaimed to us.[157]

In all caucuses, there is more flexibility for defying the party leadership on a vote when a parliamentarian has been vocal about an issue for a long time.[158] Negotiating internally to work out frustrations is diametrically different than venting to the media – one action builds trust, the other damages or destroys it. According to a Conservative MP, feelings of purpose and accomplishment arise from periodically going against the grain by "being principled, standing by your core beliefs, doing your best to represent your riding and advance the issues you hear from your constituents" without undermining the party.[159] Occasionally, a backbencher informs the whip that they have grave concerns and cannot vote as instructed, which sets off internal back-and-forth to manage the potential discord.[160] Recalcitrant members may break ranks by voting against the party line to support an opponent's private members' bill, which is of relatively low consequence. For example, two Liberal MPs backed a Conservative's proposed legislation to prohibit protesters from concealing identities during riots; the gesture garnered little media attention, as the bill's passage was never in doubt.[161] If a member insists on taking a public stand on something other than a confidence vote, the leadership can be accommodating as long as the member works with the minister or critic on the framing, and publicly affirms support for the party and its leader. At times, obstreperous behaviour can result in an appointment as part of executive creep, allowing the leader to better manage and control individualist actions.[162]

In Canadian party politics, the typical way for a parliamentarian to express disagreement with their party on a bill or motion is to quietly step out and miss the vote. There are plenty of examples of this feigned indifference, including the MP who told a constituent that the process for expressing disapproval is to have conversations with the whip's office and then not vote,[163] and the former MNA who told us that in Quebec City you go for a stroll on the nearby Plains of Abraham,[164] although we note that Alberta MLAs are encouraged to remain in their seat so that their abstention can be recorded.[165] To make a respectful show of disapproval, a team player can issue a statement about being "disappointed" in a minister's decision while effusing praise for the legitimacy of the process.[166] A Liberal MP who voted in 2016 against a government bill that, if implemented, would contribute to a loss of skilled aircraft repair jobs in his riding walked this public relations tightrope: "I don't want to come off like a rebel, or a loose cannon or anything like that. I wanted to follow all the processes and procedures, certainly be respectful and to be supportive of the government. Because I am supportive of this government. I have no regrets about having become an MP in this government. But it felt good to have made this statement that my constituents came first."[167] Rebuffing the constraints of party loyalty without causing trouble can be therapeutic for parliamentarians who yearn for freedom that they incrementally relinquish, who feel strongly about an issue, and who want to show constituents that their interests are being advocated. Team players who have clout may be appeased by the leader through concessions or, in another instance of executive creep, a strategic special appointment.[168]

In contrast, the party leadership gets frustrated when partisans catch them off-guard with bursts of independence. Team players can challenge a minister during a parliamentary committee meeting,[169] call for an officer of the legislature to review a government decision,[170] or accuse the leadership of infringing on parliamentary privileges for blocking their ability to make a member's statement.[171] A parliamentarian who has employment alternatives, is financially independent, or is confident of re-election has a stronger basis to resist conformity pressures, to advocate for parliamentary ideals, or to champion bed-rock party principles.[172] Personality, ambition, stage of political career, and the parliamentarian's relationship with the leader are also factors. Friction can be episodic and principled, as exemplified by Scott Reid, a longtime Conservative MP who withheld unanimous consent to block the collective effort of party leaders seeking to have most MPs stay away from Parliament during the rushed passage of COVID-19 emergency bills, while physical distancing policies were in effect.[173] Low-profile party stalwarts whom a leader views as insubordinates – and therefore prone to acts of disloyalty, no matter how principled – are rarely entrusted with positions on the front benches.

In short, team players can occasionally stir things up. When their parliamentary careers come to an end, the prevailing sentiment among these party loyalists is that they did their best within a large, complex system that demands fidelity. In return, they gained opportunities, such as the chance to be elected, influence policy, secure resources for constituents, improve their community, form lifelong friendships, and earn personal recognition.

Summary

Most Canadian parliamentarians are team players who deftly avoid causing trouble for their party. Their partisan attachment is anchored in many of the same socio-psychological reasons why humans are loyal to organized groups, including that membership becomes part of their social identity and helps them achieve shared goals. Partisans have specific motivations to belong to a party that can be rooted in their upbringing and can result in them relinquishing their autonomy to party interests. Like other employees, their satisfaction and commitment to the organization vary, largely depending on their status and perception of available alternatives. Throughout their parliamentary career, they experience many situations where they must decide if they are willing to compromise in the hope that their colleagues will do so in return on another issue. The vast majority of Canadian parliamentarians stay in line – so much so that it is surprising when they defy their party leadership. Our focus now shifts to those who often do, beginning with the mavericks whose individualism clashes with norms of party loyalty in parliamentary caucuses, and who can embody authentic representation that their constituents appreciate and respect.

5 Party Mavericks

Michelle Rempel Garner has a reputation as a Conservative firebrand.[1] In 2011, as a rookie MP, her unscripted volleys in the House of Commons contrasted with the ministers who read answers from their iPads.[2] At the height of the #MeToo movement, she blogged that parliamentarians who speak up about sexual harassment would forego the possibility of promotion for being a troublemaker, whereas those who remained quiet would be rewarded by the leader's office for being reliable.[3] In 2020, she was one of the co-authors of the *Buffalo Declaration* manifesto that demanded the federal government drive back policies that disadvantage Alberta.[4] Yet Rempel Garner is also aware of the importance of party unity. She has talked openly about the damaging squabbles that beset conservative parties during the pandemic (chapter 6), and to avoid trouble she rushed off when confronted by a journalist seeking her opinion about the Conservative party's controversial policy on transgender women.[5]

If party discipline is so strict in Canada, and has evolved into message discipline, how is it that some partisans seem to get away with courting attention or making incendiary remarks without facing consequences? A shrinking number of parliamentarians adopt stances that appear to disregard the leader's office.[6] Party mavericks (in French they are called *franc-tireurs*) are free spirits who challenge group norms. Some are populists who channel support that both divides and transcends their party; others are malcontents who rouse internal conflict by being prickly and espousing righteous conviction.[7] Some even become boisterous cabinet ministers, whether because of their talents or large following, or because the leader wants to keep them in line using the levers of cabinet confidence and solidarity. All these recusants have an issue with authority, yet as devoted partisans, they complete their parliamentary career without ever changing party affiliation.

Their rendition of party loyalty may be peppered with agitation that distinguishes them from trouble-averse team players, but their presence is abating in a brand-centric marketplace that increasingly views constructive individualism as harmful dissent.

Mavericks: From Pop Culture to Politics

Mythology surrounds mavericks. In American popular culture and marketing, they are stereotypically white, male straight shooters who fight for freedom by overthrowing or ridiculing the establishment.[8] The term "maverick" traces its origins to the nineteenth century and Texas politician Samuel Maverick, who refused to brand his cows, claiming it was cruel. Locals suspected this was a clever tactic to claim any roaming unbranded cattle.[9] People began referring to unbranded calves and wandering yearlings as mavericks, and by the 1880s the label was applied to humans, used to describe someone as "individualistic, unorthodox, or independent-minded."[10] Its usage gained broader popularity in the mid-twentieth century, roughly coinciding with the American Western TV series *Maverick*, which featured nomadic gamblers with a moral compass travelling the frontier, playing poker, and winning fistfights.[11] Later, Maverick was the call sign of Tom Cruise's character in the *Top Gun* movies, about a charismatic, patriotic, and skilled American naval aviator who defies orders, wins dogfights, rallies his units behind him, and transforms from an outcast to a hero. Usage peaked in 2008 when US presidential candidate John McCain and his plain-speaking running mate Sarah Palin portrayed themselves as outsiders standing up for average Americans and as anti-establishment crusaders determined to reform both their party and Washington.[12]

The term's association with politics is now firmly entrenched, though the interpretation of maverick behaviour carries distinct connotations in Canada. To former Conservative MP Jay Hill, who went on to be interim leader of the Maverick Party of Canada, a political maverick "challenges the status quo and believes very strongly in forging ahead … [to] chart a new path."[13] Yet, whereas a white man is deemed a maverick and benefits from the positive connotations of rebelling, a woman or racialized politician might be labelled difficult and pay a price for being anti-collegial.[14] As a party leader from Saskatchewan put it after the caucus revolted against her brash style, "when women are strident, men are called tough. When women are called abrasive, men are called straight talkers."[15] For some members of traditionally under-represented groups, the very traits that make them authentic members of their community may be viewed with suspicion or disapproval beyond it.

For our purposes, a maverick is a parliamentarian who attracts considerable attention for repeatedly agitating against their own party without leaving it. The robust party discipline in Canada is such that even lesser-known backbenchers might earn the label of a maverick if they deviate from the party line in a vote or express their opinions forcefully.[16] Despite these occasional acts of independence, those rare outbursts still fit within the team player archetype, in our view. True mavericks need to sustain a media image of a provocateur to truly achieve the moniker. With the important caveat that politicians all have their own idiosyncrasies, in Canada many of these antagonizers are party stalwarts whose innate familiarity with the party's values emboldens them to speak off the cuff without fearing repercussions. Mavericks can be politically incorrect or question parliamentary tradition. Their outsized personalities are energized by the cut and thrust of political debate, realizing that by hurling accusations they can rankle authority figures.[17] They do not fear the leader, the caucus, journalists, or the social media mob the way that some of their colleagues do. Indeed, mavericks court attention. They have a knack for controversy and publicity and find that being edgy can capture a journalist's interest. They relish making the headlines by agitating opponents and pundits, and causing people to think. Party mavericks usually have a strong, deep-rooted attachment to their party, but sometimes they feel greater loyalty to their own convictions or to their followers, especially if they are at loggerheads with the leader or take a principled stand on a political agenda they do not support.[18] If they are constrained, they get bored or distraught and grow restless. A political party can only hold back a busy mind for so long.

Party mavericks have as much rope as a leader is willing to give them. They help the party when they float a policy idea, and the leadership can gauge the public reaction. Insurgents championing core party values and protecting the party from itself are far more likely to outlast the leader than are the troublemakers who prioritize their own point of view. Mavericks are a burning problem when they advocate a divisive issue that causes tempers to flare and drives a wedge within the caucus. Those who hold strong convictions on controversial topics but who are in the minority can feel the sting of party discipline and chafe under a gag order, particularly when they are baited by opponents who expose a rift in the party, drawing in the leader to settle the disquiet.[19]

Leaders and team players can hold very different opinions about these unconventional partisans. Mavericks become renowned for not having *la langue dans leur poche*, a French expression reserved for those who speak freely and honestly, and it can be thrilling for teammates when a skilled orator berates opponents or admonishes the government.[20] Conversely, it can be uncomfortable when a gutsy member tries to persuade everyone to support an offbeat course of action.[21] Some of them contribute to "wild swings" in party unity in division votes.[22] Whether a caucus admires an independent-minded member or dismisses them as a loose cannon, as we have seen, most Canadian parliamentarians are risk-adverse team players who prefer the stability of consensus and upholding predictable norms of how people act and think.[23] Many believe that a maverick should be a team player like them who avoids being the focus of a news story that contradicts their efforts to project a united front. Moreover, as we have explained, partisans who critique party policy or the leader can make life difficult for their colleagues who field accusations from their constituents for being a weak representative by comparison.[24]

Party mavericks can be idealists who identify strongly with a party, yet their views do not fit neatly into any political ideology and sometimes clash with the leader's. Compared with most politicians, they might have a rebellious background and/or be well-read deep thinkers.[25] These "ideological misfits" treat political parties as vehicles rather than clubs.[26] They can lack the political ambition to attain a higher position, other than perhaps that of leader, and instead forge a reputation as someone who refuses to be buttonholed into partisanship. For mavericks who come from a background of political advocacy and engagement in social movements, the ability to champion causes on a larger stage is exactly why they sought election.[27]

Outspoken parliamentarians who engage in intelligent policy analysis are not to be conflated with egocentric colleagues who have no filter, who have a short temper, and who speak flippantly without regard for the consequences. Mavericks can be arguers, doubters, and loners. They are strong-willed and diligent, though their colleagues might describe them as obstinate and narcissistic.[28] Leaders are cautious about offering these fomenters a prominent position; in any event, mavericks may reject such entreaties because they do not want to be controlled, even though their exclusion from circles of power can spur more independent-minded behaviour. Some get crankier as they are alienated from the group and are on a path to deserting or being expelled from the caucus (chapter 6). Others, however, become pillars of the party. Their outbursts can be truncated if they are consulted before a decision is made or if someone explains the rationale for a decision before it is announced.[29] With a bit of latitude, a charismatic politician who refuses to be a minion, is a good communicator, and is trusted by the public can be a political asset. Some go on to be exemplary frontbenchers.

Mavericks can defend a constituency that would otherwise lack a voice – what American political theorist Hannah Pitkin labels substantive representation.[30] Some vocal backbenchers push bound-aries as a broad geographic region's only representative in the caucus. So-called lone wolves can have a larger portfolio of responsibilities, such as a greater likelihood of a critic position, a bigger role in Ques-tion Period, and being the party's primary contact for stakeholder meetings in an area.[31] In other cases, mavericks can advocate the inter-ests of a marginalized community. Take former New Democrat Elijah Harper, for example. As the Manitoba legislature's only Indigenous member – and one of the only First Nations lawmakers in Canada at the time – the opposition MLA was thrust into the national spotlight during the late stages of debate over the Meech Lake constitutional accord, which required ratification by every provincial legislature. In 1990, all three Manitoba party leaders urged their caucuses to vote in favour of a motion to put the accord to an emergency debate. Cit-ing the fact that Indigenous Peoples had not been consulted on the new constitutional package, Harper simply said "no" while holding an eagle feather when the House was asked for the necessary unani-mous consent, after which the legislature adjourned without a vote.[32] The accord failed soon afterwards. The Oji-Cree politician was not expelled from the party for his momentous defiance and became an icon in Indigenous communities across Canada.

Since then, social media and the quest for brand consistency have altered what is considered rebellious and reduced the threshold for dis-loyalty. Nonconformity swiftly draws attention in political circles, and parliamentarians are tethered faster for less egregious acts. In the past, backbenchers could stake their position, build public support, and catch the party leadership by surprise. Leaders tolerated outrageous polemics and media stunts by iconoclasts who personified delegate and trustee models of representation. Perhaps none was as poignant as in 1998 when Bloc Québécois MP Stephan Tremblay symbolically brought his House of Commons chair to his riding rather than watch Parliament ignore his constituents' concerns.[33] As we have seen, leaders still sometimes choose to ignore such antics, but, unlike in the past, social media ensures that displays of excessive independence are quickly transmitted to party operatives, prompting a rapid response. As a result, if they want to stay in caucus, mavericks need to be well-researched, deliberate, and, above all, willing to back down when they have made their point.[34]

Mavericks of the Past and Present

There is a media market for unvarnished politicians, ranging from those who speak with authority based on their prior experiences to those who engage in attention-grabbing antics that lead to sanctions from the Speaker.[35] The prototype of a party maverick conjures someone whose disposition is the antithesis of a team player. In fact, mavericks who are loyal to the party – often more so than its leader – straddle working within party lines and eschewing them. Those who care about the team are unfettered by norms because they want the organization to succeed. They leverage the spotlight to advance a cause they are passionate about. When supported by facts and experience, and when they avoid personalizing critiques, their feisty quest for betterment benefits the party. It is individualists who have little regard for group interest. They rely on conviction rather than research, they rebuff party norms, and they provoke personality clashes. Those types of mavericks are usually on track to leave the caucus.

What constitutes maverick behaviour is highly circumstantial – identical actions by parliamentarians in different caucuses might be outrageous to one leader and ignored by another. Counting the number of mavericks across time is a fool's errand requiring a firm distinction between them and subtler pushback by team players from time to time. As well, standards of insolence evolve. A definitive measure might be wanting, but the party leadership makes it known that there is less leniency nowadays for maverick-type behaviour in party caucuses, and the colourful characters of yesteryear are vanishing.

Before internet-based communication, leaders' offices struggled to systematically coordinate message consistency across geographical expanses. As a result, party mavericks were more common and less constrained. Regional chieftains whose bluster caused problems for party bosses did so to the delight of their constituents, while others championed ideological causes. The exploits of parliamentarians in the late twentieth century who became household names for authentic representation and a gift of the gab seem implausible in today's milieu where political parties train recruits in the art of message discipline and scold, threaten, sanction, or expel nonconformists.

The first maverick in Canadian politics was possibly Nova Scotia MP Stewart Campbell, a member of the Anti-Confederation party who often voted with the Liberal-Conservative government, until 1868 when he became the first Canadian MP to cross the floor.[36] Party loyalty was a looser construct in that era; nevertheless, when Campbell returned to his riding, some constituents threw eggs at him.[37] A century later, a leading party maverick was Judy LaMarsh, the flamboyant and impatient Liberal MP who represented Niagara Falls from 1960 to 1968. In opposition, LaMarsh spoke her mind and levelled accusations, leading to her characterization as "outspoken, unstuffy, forthright, free-swinging."[38] As a minister, she sometimes ignored the prime minister's request to clam up,[39] which in her view cemented her image as a "quarrelsome, stubborn, heavy-handed fighter."[40] In an era when ministers crafted their own speeches, the government House leader once insisted that LaMarsh rehearse a speech with the full cabinet and make changes before delivering it in the House.[41] For a while, she was the only woman in the federal cabinet. LaMarsh encountered constant reminders of otherness, ranging from women not chairing parliamentary committees to gendered exclusion from a parliamentary barber shop.[42] Her maverick persona was intermingled with femininity that contributed to the allure of breaking stereotypes: "My clothes, my stockings, my wigs were a matter of public discussion.... My weight, my age, my home, my cooking, my hobbies, my friends, my tastes, my likes and dislikes, all became public property to a degree suffered by none of my colleagues, including the prime minister.... Cartoonists delighted in sketching me and my clothes and swelling girth.... For a while I talked freely on television and to the press, hoping that once my views were thoroughly known, I would be an object of curiosity no longer, but the publicity seemed to increase it."[43] When LaMarsh died, the self-described "snarky bitch" was remembered for being undiplomatic, tenacious, and, above all, interesting.[44]

John Reid, a congenial Liberal MP in northwestern Ontario from 1965 to 1984, was a different kind of maverick who revelled in debating policy and urging accountability. Reid was incensed at the growth of the PMO under Pierre Trudeau. The nonconformist was conscious of a "primeval loyalty" to parties and the "enormous internally generated discipline" among partisans.[45] He sometimes stood his ground against his own party's government, which contributed to his reputation for being nastier to ministers than the opposition and conveyed his belief in cross-partisan collaboration.[46] Reid's colleagues urged him to redirect the carping at opposition parties, but he believed that flustering higher-ups engendered respect from partisans of all stripes and, furthermore, he was alarmed that his fellow caucus members seemed more anxious about party unity than the leader's office was.[47] He withstood perceptions that the critiques went too far by making well-reasoned criticisms of policy without besmirching the prime minister, who sometimes welcomed the sagacious feedback.[48] However, following a brief stint in cabinet, Reid became a vocal critic of the leader who he felt should stand down.[49]

Svend Robinson is arguably Canada's most notorious party maverick. From 1979 to 2004, the NDP MP for Burnaby combined argumentation with attracting publicity in an era when politicians relied upon journalists to get their message out. His representational style was defined by ideological posturing, a disregard for authority, and an innate understanding that sharing real stories about the impact of public policy on people can transform abstract political debates into powerful opportunities to educate and win over skeptics.[50] Robinson's passionate and well-articulated left-wing convictions both pleased and frustrated leaders who were caught between inspiring the party faithful and trying to attract broader support. His exploits included heckling American president Ronald Reagan during an address to the House of Commons, petitioning the House to remove God from the Constitution, and opposing the adoption of the *Charter of Rights and Freedoms* because of its notwithstanding clause. Calling for the decriminalization of soliciting sex, advocating same-sex rights, criticizing China's human rights record, and supporting organized labour solidified his electoral and party base even as leaders demoted him from critic roles.[51] Being on the frontlines with logging protesters led to Robinson serving a fourteen-day prison sentence in 1994 while an MP, which set off public debate about the limits of civil disobedience.[52] That year, he was present at the physician-assisted death of right-to-die advocate Sue Rodriguez, whose cause he passionately supported, one that would not be legalized until decades later. By calling out the NDP leader for courting the business community he endeared himself to ideological hardliners on the political left but confounded moderates who wanted to improve the party's electoral salience by moving towards the political centre.[53] Part of the reason for such unconventional behaviour is that social activists become frustrated by esoteric processes that resist change and care more about those affected by political causes than about political parties.[54] Robinson's strong party and local ties helped his re-election, while his path-breaking disclosure that he is gay added to his authenticity. Like other mavericks who stay within a party's ranks, he was a shrewd media personality who got issues on the public agenda, and who never veered far enough from party values for a leader to expel him without upsetting party purists. Yet there was constant tension because leaders felt that he was indebted to them for managing the fallout from his activism.[55]

Mavericks like LaMarsh, Reid, and Robinson have been essential in promoting, critiquing, and defending policy. A long but dwindling list of parliamentarians have forged reputations for being blunt and causing offense, engaging in invidious behaviour that excites the media, supporters, and opponents alike. Their frankness has often compelled their leader to weigh in, whether to set the record straight, affirm that disciplinary action will be taken, or even to back up their colleague.

Over time, party leaders and their agents have worked to silence caucus members who make outlandish remarks or are baited into responding with fiery retorts. The 1990s marked the beginning of a copious decline in politicians speaking their minds, as a surge of unfiltered remarks from Reform MPs brought that party into disrepute. Once celebrated for supporting free speech and autonomous thinking, Reform became mired in a parade of inflammatory remarks, eventually leading the caucus to sign a formal agreement that they would not publicly contradict the leader or engage in mutual criticism.[56] The toxicity was so evidently damaging that political parties across Canada clamped down: the vetting of aspiring election candidates ramped up, sticking to message lines became the norm, and gradually troublemakers were silenced. Former Reform MP Darrell Stinson, known for his candidness, believes that the fear of saying the wrong thing has led to generation of tepid representatives who place party interests over the needs of constituents. "I think we need to quit being politically correct. Today, politicians are all afraid of the reporter," he has lamented.[57] While Canadian politics is better off for party leaders taking a hard line against prejudice and discrimination, Stinson is right that too many Canadian parliamentarians are now anodyne, to the detriment of democratic representation. "It's beyond me why backbenchers right now are not more assertive. Come on. You're in this to do something. Be assertive, speak out, and do it! And take your lumps," an MP from the 1980s grumbled to us.[58]

In an era of party message discipline, agitators must find ways to operate within the unwritten codes of caucus behaviour while making their voices heard. The thoughtful analysis of a Liberal MP in Toronto reflects a contemporary style of party maverick who treads carefully. Nathaniel Erskine-Smith, first elected in 2015, has an unconventional view that government-side backbenchers should be principled and hold the government to account on private members' bills and opposition day motions.[59] After his initial foray into PMBs was gutted by the government, he learned to collaborate with the Prime Minister's Office and the whip's office to refine his proposals, effectively paving the way for legislation to be introduced by a minister.[60] When he voted differently than the party line – which he did more frequently than any other MP in his cohort[61] – Erskine-Smith articulated his reasoning, was careful to say that he supports the prime minister, and situated what he called "respectful disagreement" within the context of free vote parameters set out in the Liberal election platform. This resulted in dissenting votes that were principled yet inconsequential to the outcome.[62] He also hosted a podcast, *Uncommons*, where he interviewed policy experts and politicians from different parties, and sometimes criticized his own party. Towards the end of his third term as an MP, his respectful advocacy had come at a personal cost of never being appointed to even a committee chair position, yet he achieved a strong second-place finish in the Ontario Liberal leadership race. His announcement in 2024 that he would not run again led to a turning point: Trudeau appeared on the podcast and made him a minister, a role that Erskine-Smith blogged put him in a good position to hold the government accountable. After his re-election, Prime Minister Carney dropped him from cabinet.[63]

In contrast to this "respectful" parliamentary advocacy, the dwindling number of mavericks who set off a political firestorm for intemperate remarks are given less and less rope. Cheryl Gallant, a veteran Conservative MP in the Ottawa Valley, has a long history of controversies that have provoked strong reactions from the political left. Since her initial election in 2000, Gallant has defended gun ownership, supported pro-life advocates and the military, warned about government overstepping on climate action and COVID-19 vaccines, and advocated for private property rights. Early in her parliamentary career, she equated abortion to terrorist beheadings, circulated a leaflet alleging Christianity is being persecuted, said that sexual orientation should not be included among hate crime protections, and mocked an MP for being gay.[64] She made the news for saying that Atlantic seafarers should not rely on the Coast Guard for help, for linking the Liberal leader with a Libyan dictator, for distributing an Easter fundraising email that featured the image of the corporal who was killed in the Parliament Hill shootings, and for posting a video that appeared to depict Justin Trudeau with a noose around his neck.[65] As well, Gallant has been accused of peddling right-wing conspiracy theories and was criticized for encouraging people to join anti-vaccine mandate protesters in downtown Ottawa after the government invoked the *Emergencies Act*.[66] The party's containment strategy has included keeping her away from all-candidate debates, requiring her to publicly apologize or openly declare support for party policy, getting her to take down social media posts, and urging her to ignore media requests.[67] Nevertheless, Gallant has been handily re-elected over and over as opponents run up against her image of authenticity and populism as a social conservative whose beliefs outrage urban progressives.[68] Multiple leaders have condemned her comments, yet she outlasted them all. Her political survival is a combination of local popularity, expressing political opinions that are shared by some of her party's core believers including in her riding, and falling in line when a leader does damage control. However, despite Gallant's extensive experience and strong local popularity, her unpredictability has caused each leader to bypass her for influential roles. Over time, as party message discipline has tightened, she has become more careful about expressing bold opinions in public.

We might expect less maverick behaviour in the provinces given that premiers exert more control over their governments and caucuses than prime ministers do.[69] In fact, as we show throughout the book, each provincial laboratory has personas who reflect local political dynamics. Laurie Blakeman was a boisterous Liberal MLA in Alberta from 1997 to 2015. At times her spirited advocacy exasperated members of her caucus. "I think there would be colleagues who would say I was difficult. There would be colleagues from across the floor that felt I was a terrorist," she told us.[70] "I think people really saw me as an attack dog, oppositional, all those unattractive adjectives that are applied to women who are forceful." Blakeman sustained a long parliamentary career with one party by working hard, forging relationships with ministers instead of calling them names, holding her nose when she disagreed with the caucus, and giving people a heads-up about what she planned to do. "You never blindside your caucus colleagues, because that's where they get really pissed off because they're made to look like a jerk in front of the media. So, never blindside them. Always tell them in advance what your concern is, offer a solution, and try and work it out with them in advance," she explains. In an attempt to unite centrist voters, in her final campaign she was nominated to represent three small parties but was ultimately permitted to have only one party's label on the ballot.[71] When her re-election bid was unsuccessful, the Liberal party cut her loose for diluting its brand. Most of the time, provincial mavericks like Blakeman champion causes in their own backyard. Occasionally they have a global outlook, as with the following case in Ontario.

Message Discipline as the New Normal

Party politics in Canada has evolved with the growth of social media, including how activists draw attention to political causes and how party leaders handle disruptive behaviour within their ranks. Consider forays into the thorny issue of Israel–Palestine relations, a topic that is especially divisive for left-wing parties.[72] The following vignettes about a New Democratic Party MP in 2002 and an Ontario NDP MPP in 2023 demonstrate how activism is influenced by communications technology. They also show that contemporary party leaders are far more determined to use crisis management to regulate these brand ambassadors.

One of the many publicity stunts that Svend Robinson orchestrated occurred when he was the NDP foreign affairs critic. After a series of

Palestinian suicide bombings, in March 2002 Israeli soldiers occupied the Ramallah compound of the chairman of the Palestine Liberation Organization and closed the city to foreigners. On 3 April, Robinson issued a news release announcing that he would travel to Israel and attempt to meet with him to express support because Israel was "guilty of state terrorism."[73] The maverick MP believed that being "on the front lines" was a more effective way to attract attention than delivering speeches in Parliament.[74] Four days later, he donned a flak jacket and, with television cameras in tow, he argued and tussled with Israeli soldiers guarding a checkpoint between Jerusalem and Ramallah, before being turned away.[75] The leader of the NDP, Alexa McDonough, backed Robinson's comments and agreed with generating public awareness about the Middle East crisis, but clarified that both sides were engaging in terrorism.[76] Robinson's junket was a top story across Canada, pundits deliberated its effectiveness, and it was a popular topic in newspapers' letters to the editor. On 10 April, MPs discussed the crisis in a special House of Commons debate that lasted until nearly three o'clock in the morning.[77] A week later, former Ontario NDP Premier Bob Rae penned a blistering op-ed in the *National Post* reasoning that Robinson, whom he labelled "a histrionic crank," had singlehandedly shifted party policy and so deemed the party no longer worthy of support.[78]

The denouncement from such a senior stalwart contributed to testy exchanges in a caucus meeting where NDP MPs clashed over whether Robinson should lose his critic position.[79] The party posted a statement from McDonough on its website clarifying its position of supporting a secure Israel and a Palestinian homeland[80] and the next day announced that the leader had assumed the Middle East portion of the party's foreign affairs critic role. In a news conference, Robinson vowed to continue his pro-Palestine crusade and accused Israel of a war crime.[81] His actions were consistent with an activist's impulse to rebel against state authority, to disrupt norms, and call attention to political concerns. He drew confidence from party ideologues, strong re-election results, and vigorous fundraising.[82] Conversely, the leader showed little inclination to crack down on freelancing or defiance. Robinson kept up his remaining critic duties and was re-nominated to run again, but withdrew due to an unrelated criminal incident.

Contrast this era of mainstream media activism with the landscape two decades later, where expressing opinions is easy on social media, and party leaders are more steadfast in demanding that caucus members act as team players whose communications align closely with the leader's messages. In 2023, Ontario NDP candidate Sarah Jama won a by-election in Hamilton Centre. She had pledged to bring "peaceful disruption" to the old guard in the party – her background in community activism included provocative speeches, marches, sit-ins, street art, and media stunts – and she became the first lower-income Black woman in a wheelchair at Queen's Park.[83] During the campaign, Jama apologized for her past social media posts criticizing Israel and promised to "speak out against antisemitism" if elected.[84] As with Robinson, the topic was a personal conviction as opposed to a constituency priority.[85] Unlike him, Jama was new to party politics and did not hold a critic post; furthermore, foreign affairs is not provincial jurisdiction. Nevertheless, the politics of the Middle East would define her brief stint with the Official Opposition and, ultimately, as an MPP.

On 7 October 2023, Hamas militants carried out attacks in Israel and took civilian hostages. The Israeli government declared war, initiated a blockade of the Gaza strip, and began airstrikes in Palestine. As the news spread rapidly through mainstream media and online platforms, Western leaders condemned the brutality by Hamas. Some differing perspectives emerged on the political left. On 10 October, Jama posted a statement on X (formerly Twitter) featuring the Ontario coat of arms and NDP orange. Her letter called for a ceasefire, condemned Israel's "apartheid" and "settler colonialism," and the post included the hashtag #FreePalestine.[86] She did not mention the Hamas terrorism.

Within hours, Jewish organizations and the Ontario Liberal leader posted calls for her removal from the caucus. The Ontario NDP leader, Marit Stiles, demanded that Jama delete the post. The rookie MPP did not comply. Premier Ford posted a statement on X accusing the backbencher of anti-Semitism and called for her resignation from the legislature. Jama posted a lukewarm apology, and Stiles issued a statement rationalizing that the MPP has Palestinian relatives and had recently joined the party in denouncing Hamas' terror attacks.[87] Jama's original post remained online, amassing nearly three million views.[88]

When the Ontario legislature reconvened on 16 October, the PCs moved that Jama be censured from speaking in the legislature until she retracted the statement on X and apologized to the House. She stayed out of public view, but defiantly pinned the post to give it a higher profile at the top of her page. On 19 October, through her lawyer, she accused Premier Ford of libel for harming her reputation; the NDP chief of staff circulated a memo reminding the caucus that their public statements must be pre-approved.[89] The next day, Jama posted on X that walk-ins to her constituency office were being paused due to staff safety concerns. When members returned on 23 October, Stiles issued the following statement announcing that Jama had been expelled from the caucus:

> In our caucus, there is room for different viewpoints, even dissenting ones. But that is based on the foundational principles of trust and working together as a team. Ms. Jama and I had reached an agreement to keep her in the NDP caucus, which included working together in good faith with no surprises. Our caucus and staff have made significant efforts to support her during an undoubtedly difficult time. Since then, she has undertaken a number of unilateral actions that have undermined our collective work and broken the trust of her colleagues. Some of Ms. Jama's actions have contributed to unsafe work environments for her staff. As such, with the support of our Ontario NDP MPPs, I have been left with no option but to remove Ms. Jama from our caucus.[90]

The statement mirrored language that party leaders across Canada use when they cut ties with a colleague. At its core was broken trust with an uncooperative team member who refused to abide by party message discipline. Some alleged the expulsion was racist.[91]

The Ontario NDP weathered thirteen days of upheaval as its leader grappled with a rogue member determined to take a public stand on a deeply contentious international issue. When the motion to censure was up for a vote, Jama broke her silence by reiterating to the legislature that she supported Palestinians against "Israeli apartheid," and posted those remarks on X.[92] The motion passed with PCs voting in favour, the NDP opposed, and Liberals abstaining. In a post-vote scrum, Stiles emphasized that Jama's unilateral actions had undermined the team[93] and explained that a parliamentarian who acts independently must sit as an Independent.[94] Jama emailed constituents to advise that the party had blocked her from accessing emails, calendars, and the constituent file database, and that she was setting up a new office, hiring staff, installing phone lines, and creating a website.[95]

Turmoil persisted. The media reported that one New Democrat MPP had threated to quit if Jama was not expelled,[96] and there were complaints that the caucus "got the shit kicked out of us for two weeks" due to the leader's inaction.[97] The deputy leader emphasized that the expulsion was due to broken trust and the need "to work as a team" because "politics is a team sport."[98] Several other NDP MPPs, including the caucus chair, explained that acting unilaterally and breaking commitments is a path to rescinding the privilege of being part of a political party. "Being a member of a team means working as a team," said one.[99] Said another, "A party caucus needs to work together, as a team."[100]

A third MPP reflected on how a caucus has difficult conversations and cannot function if a commitment to "teamwork and collaboration" is shattered.[101] Another MPP concluded that "we stand together as a team."[102] However, the only remaining Black member of the NDP caucus posted a thread on X accusing Stiles of misrepresenting that there had been caucus consultation about the expulsion and admonished the leader's use of "stereotypical tropes about Black people, especially Black women, who are perceived as difficult."[103] Members of the party's Guelph riding association wrote to Stiles to seek Jama's reinstatement to atone for the "white fragility" that motivated the ouster.[104]

In the wake of the expulsion, the attentive public skirmished on social media and news comment boards about the silencing of an elected official and potential racism. Columnists and Hamilton Centre's MP pointed to a problem of political parties recruiting election candidates from traditionally marginalized groups and then clamping down on diversity of thought when they are principled.[105] Three NDP riding associations, including Hamilton Centre, posted statements on X calling for a formal leadership review,[106] and the front of Stiles's Toronto constituency office was vandalized with red paint simulating blood. An online rally in solidarity with Jama attracted hundreds of people, including those who chastised the party's inability to accommodate activists and, according to some participants, a system of party discipline that treats Black women as uncontrollable.[107] In a year-end interview, Stiles stood her ground that a leader must prioritize team unity, saying that "as a political leader, it's on me to ensure that my team is strong and united and sometimes that means making very difficult decisions."[108] As time went on, Jama expressed a desire to return to the party and submitted a candidate vetting package to seek the local nomination.[109] The party rejected her application. Undeterred, she ran as an Independent in the 2025 Ontario election and finished fourth.

Comparing the Robinson and Jama case studies is instructive. Both succeeded with unconventional approaches to ignite public conversation about a cause they were passionate about. Arguably, the scale of discipline was exacted based on the degree of recalcitrance, length of tenure, and each leader's approach to leading a party of protest versus one interested in forming government, although it is difficult to ignore the racialized and gendered nature of how these two mavericks were treated, as well as the contrast in their knowledge about how political parties operate. These cases are a stark illustration that changes in political communication have forever altered how partisans behave, how other political actors pile on, and how there is a greater proclivity for leaders to manage a troublemaker by cancelling their association with the party. At the onset of the twenty-first century, leaders had a more laissez-faire attitude towards mavericks who got their party noticed. Today, a backbencher who takes a divisive stance can spark a torrent of demands for the leader to impose sanctions or even dismiss them, exemplifying the influence of cancel culture. The ability of parliamentarians to communicate through social media is a potential powder keg for blowing apart the message consistency that leaders try so hard to maintain, which motivates them to exact tough discipline on those who light the fuse.

Summary

Mavericks are becoming less common in mainstream Canadian political parties, but their democratic function is more important than ever. They may be irritable, even maddening, yet they play a vital role in a vibrant democracy by promoting robust policy discussions and expressing themselves with openness that engenders authenticity and trustworthiness. By challenging groupthink, they ensure that the political system is responsive, adaptable, and open to change. Their motivations vary, with some prioritizing their constituency's interests over party loyalty, some driven by deeply held beliefs and policy objectives, while others are keen for new leadership. A maverick's oversized personality requires careful management by the leader's office to balance party unity with a style of representation that can walk a fine line between helping and harming party interests. Party leaders have always struggled to manage caucus members who attract the sizeable following necessary to ward off threats of expulsion. They have less tolerance nowadays for parliamentarians in their flock who assert a different point of view, which can embolden free spirits to consider exiting the party of their own volition or can result in their expulsion from caucus. If and once they take this step, mavericks become party leavers, the subject of our next chapter.

6 Party Leavers

Initially, Brent Rathgeber was an exemplary team player. The Conservative MP was on time for House duties and filled in for people who were absent. But a drift set in as it became evident that there was no path to the front benches. He increasingly felt that sometimes party loyalty should be set aside in favour of his constituents' interests and his personal beliefs, and he grew convinced that thoughtful criticism from a government backbencher is an act of loyalty when better public policy results.[1] Rathgeber was on the outs with fellow Conservatives after he criticized a minister on his blog. In 2013, he left the caucus when his colleagues on a parliamentary committee watered down his private members' bill, upon which he alleged that the attitude of the "PMO and the whip's office is that caucus members should essentially be cheerleaders for the government and spread the government's message as opposed to being some sort of legislative check on executive power."[2] He sought freedom from that mindset by sitting as an Independent, and then defied his former party by withdrawing his support of his reworked bill before it could reach the committee stage, marking the first time in Canadian parliamentary history that an MP did so on their own bill.[3] Like so many other partisans who wind up as Independents, he was not re-elected.

We have seen that many partisans equate being a member of a parliamentary caucus to being part of a family. Most are content enough with their kinfolk to overlook some disagreements or personality differences; black sheep of the family may even endear themselves to their counterparts. In extreme cases, they may make huge personal sacrifices with little in return. When the relationship deteriorates enough, however, they consider alternatives. Some, like Rathgeber, decide to leave and therefore control both the timing and manner of their exit; others are abruptly expelled against their wishes and suffer reputational damage. Sometimes, parliamentarians who leave a party liken the decision to a divorce, citing irreconcilable differences and the need to choose between remaining unhappy or moving on.[4] But what are the circumstances that lead to a Canadian politician's announcement to leave a party's caucus and sit as an Independent? Organizational behaviour studies hold some clues about the internal dynamics of voluntary and involuntary departures from a parliamentary group. A key difference between turmoil in an ordinary workplace and tensions within a party caucus is that, in the latter, accusations, passions, and power struggles can play out in the public eye, amplifying the discord.

Relationship Breakdowns

There are many reasons why people in organized groups become dissatisfied, and why some of them leave. One prominent theory holds that conflict is endemic throughout a group's life cycle as members grow used to working with one another, and establish and revisit norms.[5] Group members who feel disrespected are likely to perceive a negative team identity and those who feel undervalued lose motivation to do things for the group.[6] Rejection of a nonconformist is fiercest by loyalists who derive personal fulfilment by admonishing a dissident in their ranks.[7] A target of shunning becomes gloomy, wounded, anxious, lonely, jealous, and/or annoyed, which contributes to further alienation.[8]

In workplaces, departures are either voluntary, whereby an employee initiates and controls the exit (e.g., resignation due to dissatisfaction, to facilitate moving to a competing firm, for family reasons), or involuntary, whereby the employer initiates and is in control (e.g., dismissal due to absenteeism, poor performance, reorganization).[9] There are signs when a worker has one foot out the door. They might withdraw by missing meetings, leaving early or being late, failing to complete tasks, calling in sick, and other acts of psychological detachment resulting in low output ("quiet quitting"), or perhaps they will opt for the conflict of causing crises by rebuffing organizational objectives and disrespecting leaders ("loud quitting").[10] Workers resign when they realize that their initial expectations of the role are incompatible with reality,[11] such as dissatisfaction with financial rewards, the mundanity of the job, immediate circumstances, or personal reasons.[12] They can be frustrated with management and the corporate culture, how new recruits are hired, their work going unrecognized, low pay, or a toxic workplace.[13] They can have impromptu reasons, such as friends leaving or interest in a fresh start,[14] or they might depart for a more homogenous organization that has common views.[15] At all levels, dissatisfied workers with a higher degree of loyalty are more likely to speak up in an attempt to resolve their cognitive dissonance, which can involve wielding the threat of exit, whereas those with weak attachments are more likely to quietly investigate alternatives and quit.[16] Loyalty is closely tied to whether someone tolerates dissatisfaction in an organization or seeks new opportunities.

Difficult workplaces can see higher levels of turnover. Workers can resign in response to passive aggressive treatment by an employer who does not value them. They quit when there is intense pressure to deliver, if they are bored due to a lack of responsibility, when they are excluded from decision-making, when a demanding supervisor reigns terror, or if they are bullied.[17] How the organization's leadership engages with members, such as how much influence employees have in decision-making, is a significant predictor of turnover as is clarity about roles – more so than the degree of group cohesion or opportunity for promotion.[18] For workers, a decision to leave can therefore be a positive act, particularly if they flee an unsatisfying job for a more suitable one.

Employers also experience ramifications. A departure is negative when a high performer exits, and it is positive when a weak worker is shed. A vacancy can create an opportunity to fill the position with a member of an under-represented group, and the organization and upper management benefit if a replacement infuses the workplace with positivity, skills, and energy.[19] The employer can recruit someone who is more loyal to the organization and its values, reinforcing the importance of fealty to the leadership team, and those left behind can profit if the exit creates more opportunities for upward mobility, alleviates workplace tensions, and motivates them to work harder.[20] Thus, shedding an employee can be a matter of addition by subtraction: turnover infuses organizations with new talent and possibly new ways of thinking, which contributes to improved performance.[21] That said, someone quitting disrupts normal operations. The employer suffers a loss of skillsets and institutional knowledge and needs to recruit and train a replacement. When a worker leaves for a rival organization, the employer potentially sheds clients and risks disclosure of competitive information. Mass employee turnover is particularly destabilizing because it weakens morale, softens productivity, and exposes the organization to reputational damage.

As in many other workplaces, parliamentarians experience growing discomfort in a caucus for all sorts of reasons. It comes as a shock when the leader's staff micromanage what they say and scold them for speaking to the media.[22] They can be dissatisfied with the leader, have a philosophical disagreement over policy, be frustrated with a lack of advancement or role, be irritated over powerlessness, be concerned about future success, and so forth. It can dawn on them that the team concept skews unidirectional: backbenchers are expected to be team players who give up far more autonomy than higher-ups do.[23] They gradually stray from the social side of politics, as Rathgeber did. "I was marginalizing myself, not only from the PMO and the whip's office, but also from my colleagues. And that was okay," he told us. "I wasn't ever really into the Ottawa social scene, I didn't play for the caucus hockey team, I rarely, rarely went out for dinner with any other MPs. I kind of kept to myself and came home every weekend. So being socially ostracized really didn't have that much effect on me, but I did know that it was happening."[24] Leaders recognize that the members of caucus who are on a path to leaving it do not hold positions of great responsibility, feel sidelined and isolated, and become loners who experience difficulties functioning with the group.[25] Lacking a connection to the team can forecast individualism.

For some parliamentarians, the call for party unity can feel like a straitjacket, yet they persist in challenging the status quo and championing ideas when the leadership would rather they be quiet. A former Alberta MLA told us about how he took it upon himself to promote the views of timid caucus colleagues, thereby putting him in the leadership's crosshairs, and how he became irritated at being told what to do by political staff: "I wasn't very happy with how things had become where we're listening to our back-room staff. People that were supposed to be working for us telling us what to do.... From day one I was the proverbial shit disturber. I'd always have lots of MLAs come to me with an issue that they didn't like that was going on in caucus or an agenda item that was going to happen in caucus and they wanted somebody to kind of lead it.... Our job was to represent our constituents and it's okay to have votes that aren't unanimous."[26] Discontent can seethe into daily interactions that aggravate interpersonal tensions, potentially escalating to noncompliance and standoffs. Some parliamentarians bite their tongue; some have a mercurial temperament. Those who resign or do not reoffer do so for reasons that include pension eligibility, thwarted ambition, change in leadership, dire electoral prospects, and a disconnect between their original aspirations to affect public policy decisions and the reality of being on the sidelines.[27] Others like the job but not their situation.

Partisans who were bypassed for a ministerial or shadow minister role are especially prone to feel excluded, alienated, and aggrieved, and to blame the leader.[28] Resentment builds if they do not get even small perks, such as being appointed to a preferred committee, and if they feel under-used. They might perceive the leader as unapproachable, unresponsive, and overly reliant on staffers for caucus management. The establishment can seem against them when the leader appears to direct ministers and staff to stand firm on a policy, despite the member's concerns. "We appreciate your passion for this issue. Please do not bring this up again. Nothing is changing. You're wasting your time," they say.[29]

From the party leadership's perspective, some members of caucus are individualistic and would rather be noticed than be right.[30] Attention feeds their craving for recognition. Or they might perceive individualists as failing to grasp the norms of party loyalty or understand their place in the organizational hierarchy. Partisans are frozen out if the leader holds a grudge or otherwise wants little to do with them. For example, a parliamentary secretary like former MP Celina Caesar-Chavannes who is not given meaningful work, who experiences poor lines of communication, and who feels the appointment was for tokenistic reasons can build simmering resentment,[31] while a backbencher can confirm suspicions of being shunned when constituents are the ones who tell them that the leader will be visiting the riding.[32] As we have established, a leader has an easier time isolating one troublemaker than managing several of them. Paranoia begins to take hold within the leadership circle when multiple individualists assert themselves, propelling fears of internal factions conspiring to sabotage caucus unity in an attempt to pressure the leader into resigning.

Unlike members of most other organizations, partisan politicians are expected to play a role in the selection of their own leader, which creates division as they split off into leadership camps. The absence of a permanent leader reduces the pressure around party message discipline; during a leadership race, some backbenchers are emboldened to speak out and share insider stories that would typically be off-limits.[33] A leadership contest and a change of leader are potent triggers for alienating some caucus members, particularly those who backed the wrong campaign. In particular, a failed leadership contestant can be corrosive to caucus unity, especially if the new leader pours salt in fresh wounds by excluding the loser from the front benches. Failed contestants absorb a rebuke of both ambition and ideology, and they and anyone who supported a rival candidate can resent the winner and never connect ideologically or personally with the new leader despite being given positions of responsibility.[34] While many caucus members opt to remain neutral during leadership reviews or races, that too can result in being left out of the new inner circle and forgoing opportunities for

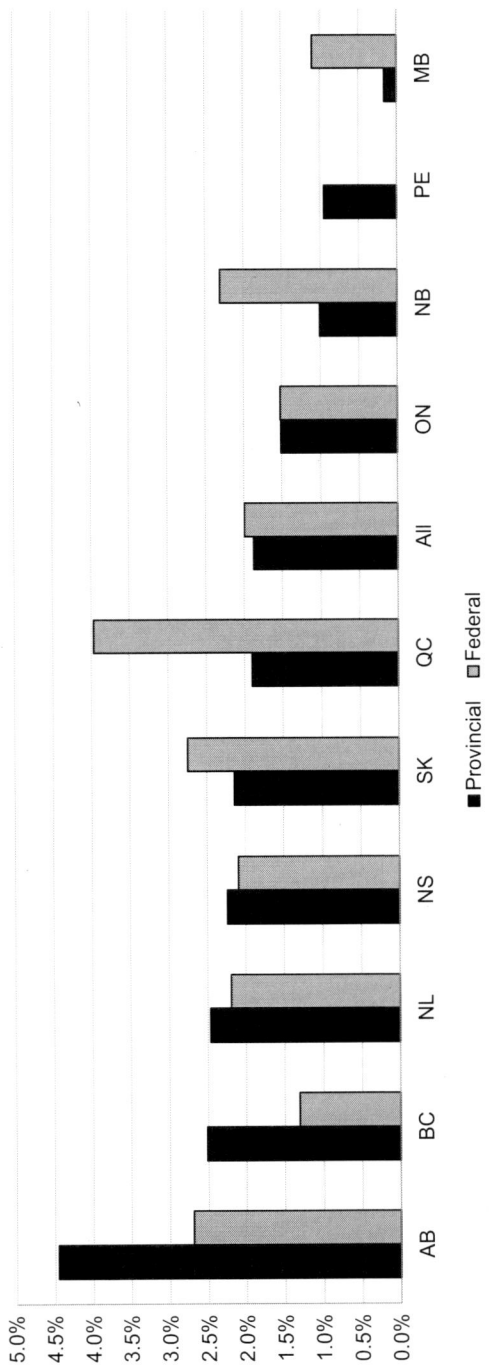

Figure 6.1. Departure Rates from Federal and Provincial Parties by Province, 1980–2021

Notes: The departure rate for each jurisdiction is calculated by dividing the total number of federal and provincial party defectors by the combined total of seats in each federal parliament and provincial legislature over the 1980 to 2021 period. "All" represents the total number of departures over the total number of seats across Canada.

progressive advancement. Conversely, a leadership change also offers a chance for redemption, as a previously banished caucus member may be welcomed back.[35]

As we will show, most caucus break-ups are permanent. Our analysis of party departures from 1980 to 2021 found that over three-quarters of the parliamentarians we identified who left a caucus did so voluntarily. Some of them surprised their colleagues, while others anticipated being expelled and chose to jump before being pushed. The remaining quarter were exiled by the party's leadership. During our study period, caucus departure rates varied considerably across Canada, with approximately 4 per cent of Alberta MLAs and Quebec MPs leaving, while Prince Edward Island experienced almost no caucus exits (figure 6.1), which reflects each region's constellation of political actors, parties, cultures, and leadership dynamics at a given time.[36]

Many parliamentarians who choose to leave a caucus lack deep roots in the party. In contrast with the team players who grew up in a partisan environment, we heard from some ex-partisans, including Caesar-Chavannes, that they had been new entrants into the world of partisan politics when they decided to run, and were politically naive.[37] Some of them were accidental candidates in that they never imagined that they would get involved in party politics and were motivated to stand for public office because they wanted to make a difference. People who are actively involved in their community or in local protests can field suggestions that they offer themselves for election, a proposition that they might not have seriously considered, and the norms of party politics are entirely new to them.[38] Their animosity towards a head of government or anger about a policy can incite them to join a party to effect change. For these politicians, the choice of party is more circumstantial than tribal, and is a means to an end.

Party Quitters

In chapter 1, we presented a typology of the different forms of loyalties within party politics. In the following pages, we will discuss the broad category of party leavers, focusing on the two main ways in which they depart: those who resign from a caucus and choose to sit as an Independent, in contrast with those who are expelled against their will. Partisans who remain in their party but effectively give up, tune out, and do not run again – whether through quiet quitting, loud quitting, or otherwise – are another type of quitter altogether. In addition, three types of extraordinary caucus desertions need not require a permanent change in party affiliation: mass resignations, splinter groups, and coalition governments.[39] Conversely, a party going defunct does compel change. All of these situations involve intra-party tensions that can have profound implications for governance and/or the party system.

Resigning to Sit as an Independent

The decision to leave a parliamentary caucus is typically preceded by many letdowns and quarrels. "It's a long burn," was how Rathgeber described it to us.[40] A dominant motive for voluntarily quitting is irreconcilable differences with the leader, which is a symptom of deeper frustrations about policy, office, and/or votes.

Dissonance flares up when a new leader takes charge, particularly if someone was inspired to join the party due to a previous leader's appeal, as with the MPs who gradually left the NDP after Layton died.[41] Some caucus members who cannot abide by a new leader leave right away, driven by factors such as ambition, a perceived lack of advancement opportunities,[42] and general alienation or philosophical disagreement. A notable example of this occurred in 1990, when two Liberal MPs announced they were quitting the party following Jean Chrétien's selection as the new Liberal leader.[43] It was such a hurtful act that when Chrétien was diagnosed with two nodules in his lung, he nicknamed them after the betrayers.[44] Other reasons for leaving after a new leader assumes command can surface, such as a parliamentarian who supported an unsuccessful leadership contender bolting out of concern that their renomination could be in jeopardy.[45] Following the initial exodus that often accompanies leadership change, additional caucus members gradually depart if disappointment and discomfort with a new leader sets in. Some avoid the stigma of abandoning their party by withdrawing from federal or provincial politics altogether.

Criticism of a leader or policy can be a harbinger of a political divorce.[46] Party leaders and their agents invest a lot of effort into trying to convince a malcontent about a course of action, to no avail.[47] Some parliamentarians signal for months that they are unhappy, and publicly muse that they are questioning their place in the party.[48] They complain that it has moved in a different direction and has left them behind; the most despondent talk about low morale and complete detachment.[49] Unique to Quebec, hardline separatists can grow exasperated with a leader who adopts a more cautious or measured approach to sovereignty.[50]

Some parliamentarians who feel estranged offer no clues that they are thinking about resigning to sit as an Independent. All sorts of things play on their mind, such as worrying that if they leave there will be a lower caucus budget and political staff will lose their jobs.[51] They are careful about who they confide in and avoid people who will tattle,[52] and they might draft a resignation letter impulsively but later choose not to submit it.[53] In one case, a Nova Scotia Liberal MLA baffled colleagues when he abruptly resigned after participating in a caucus retreat. The reported reasons came out later: he felt ostracized after withdrawing from the party's leadership race, for breaking party lines on a budget vote, and because his political beliefs were different than the new leader's.[54] Other partisans feel rejected when they lose a nomination race, have no obvious path to re-election, and thumb their nose at the leadership by quitting the caucus.[55]

Some party leavers go public with their motivations, and their allegations can pull on a thread that unravels deeper internal issues. In British Columbia, an MLA who quit the Liberal caucus alleged that Premier Gordon Campbell was authoritarian; the premier admitted swearing at her. The whip sought to discredit the backbencher by disclosing that she had been suspended for assaulting a fellow caucus member, but this led to a broader revelation that other members of the party's caucus had also been suspended for misdeeds.[56] Another BC case saw a Jewish MLA quit the NDP caucus a month after stepping down from cabinet over a flippant remark deemed Islamophobic. The *National Post* published her resignation letter, which admonished her colleagues for their silence in the face of rising anti-Semitism.[57] Premier David Eby was then under pressure to root out prejudices against Jews in his caucus and government.[58]

Ex-partisans often rationalize their exit as ideological disparity, policy disagreement, or frustration with election results. At the heart of the dispute is often their strained relationship with the leader. Upon leaving, they can vent that they were fed up with the leader's oppression, which is magnified when they feel disrespected, particularly after a demotion.[59] They can clap back against autocratic behaviour and stifled political debate by complaining that there is a lack of opportunity to offer policy input, that decisions are preordained, and that the political system itself is controlled.[60] Some allege that the caucus is afraid to speak up because of angry outbursts, bullying, and intimidation from the leader and/or the leader's staff.[61] Across the country, party leavers have accused their former leaders of creating an atmosphere of intimidation and for exerting excessive control over the caucus:

> Not only are there rarely free votes in the legislature, there are very few free votes in caucus. Virtually all legislation is created and developed by various unelected government appointees, with direction from the premier and a small cadre of ministers whose distinguishing attribute is unconditional allegiance to their leader.[62]

I don't agree with the conversations that the leader and I have had.... I was told to be quiet until the rest of caucus spoke and then if I wanted to share my opinion, I could share it then.[63]

I find his leadership to be autocratic, not democratic. In order to fight his image as a weak leader, he's trying to rule with an iron fist. The morale in the [party] caucus is less than good.... He's trying to impose his own views on the rest of the caucus, presumably on the advice of his political advisers, and we're expected to follow.[64]

Personality conflicts, animosity, disrespect, and grudges can be so potent that they overwhelm the pursuit of public policy, the seeking of office, or the securing of votes. As well, gender dynamics can play a role, with male leaders seemingly more inclined towards dictatorial leadership styles, prompting some women caucus members to feel compelled to withdraw.[65] There is relatively little that a parliamentarian with a grudge can do, and weakening the leader's power through a high-profile exit is a final option. The divide between a leader and a former caucus member can run so deep that they never speak again.[66]

Losing a member of caucus can be a quandary for the leader if the rejection is framed on political terms and gains momentum. An exit raises questions about a leader's competency and can be a warning sign of simmering dissent.[67] Retired partisans can pile on by criticizing how the party is being run, which presses the leader to take a gambit of digging in by disclosing a former colleague's perceived inadequacies or else conveying that the member would be welcomed back under certain conditions.[68] When a petulant colleague exits, it is a big relief, especially if they were suspected of leaking information from caucus meetings. In the view of a former premier, it is better to "get rid of the cancer" because politicians who put themselves ahead of the group cannot be trusted.[69]

Others resign to sit as an Independent without expressing qualms with the leader. A politician who has fulfilled their discrete ambition can leave the caucus without fanfare on a point of principle or campaign for a position in a different political arena.[70] To limit attention, a jilted leader might say little, provided the former colleague says little as well. "The member voluntarily removed himself from caucus. The member was not seeking re-election," was all the Harper PMO had to offer about an MP who quietly left the Conservative caucus to have freedom to extol his religious beliefs.[71] Partisans alleged to have committed serious ethical, moral, or legal breaches can minimize embarrassment for their party by leaving, which spares the leader the grief of deliberating what to do while the allegations are investigated.[72] Leaders can graciously accept the resignation, and even wish their former colleague well[73] or privately give them a hug.[74] As well, some parliamentarians leave over personal issues. The distress, fear, and panic of being rejected by others – even something as subtle as being on the receiving end of a critical remark – can cause some people to avoid exclusion by not forming social bonds.[75] Few people outside of politics would think of a politician as socially anxious or understand the toll of party politics on mental health.

It is a cliché for politicians to step away for family or medical reasons. Until at least the 1960s, resigning a seat involved so many formalities that it was difficult for MPs to do so on grounds other than accepting an appointment by the Crown.[76] Nowadays, citing personal issues is a socially and politically acceptable reason for quitting. For example, the leader of the BC Green Party framed his decision to sit as an Independent as necessary so that he could attend to some undisclosed family health matters.[77] Others reveal their personal battles only after they leave politics, such as Mumilaaq Qaqqaq who as MP for Nunavut dealt with so many constituents with dire needs that she was diagnosed with burnout, anxiety, and depression.[78] That said, a spiteful leader can cast doubt on a former colleague's fitness for office, contributing to speculation and fuelling rumours.[79]

Mass Resignations and Splinter Groups

When multiple employees resign, a "turnover contagion" can occur, increasing the likelihood that remaining workers will also choose to leave.[80] Likewise in party politics, a caucus exit can lead to other departures. Staggered exits – whether as part of a political calculation or happenstance – generate layers of news stories that blast the rejected leader's capabilities and invite speculation about whether the leader will step down.[81] In 1984, a cascade of PQ ministers and MNAs resigned when Premier René Lévesque shelved sovereignty in favour of a more conciliatory approach to federalism, which culminated in his resignation. Nearly three decades later, the premiership of Pauline Marois was dealt a critical blow when a procession of *péquistes* quit in protest over a bill to privatize a Quebec City amphitheatre.[82] The leader leaving creates an opening for the mass of displaced partisans to return.

A pack of dissidents can temporarily break away from their party and band together as a non-party parliamentary group that is itself subject to splintering and dissolving. An early example is the Ginger Group. In 1924, approximately eight Western MPs who opposed party structures left the Progressives – among them Agnes MacPhail, the first woman elected to the House of Commons – and were subsequently joined by some Labour MPs.[83] Two years after suffering election losses, the remaining Ginger Group members returned to the Progressives, and the dissident who was assigned the role of party whip pledged a light disciplinary touch.[84] Conversely, a splinter group can set the stage for the formation of a new party that runs election candidates. The genesis of the Bloc Québécois was a group of party leavers initially sitting together in the House as *Option Québec*.[85] Forming a parliamentary group can also be a pressure tactic to get a forsaken leader to step down. In 2018, seven MPs left the Bloc caucus to protest leader Martine Ouellet's domineering style and sat as the Groupe parlementaire québécois. They announced plans to form a new party and became known as Québec debout.[86] Some of them immediately rejoined the party after she resigned; others did so months later. In such scenarios, the task of persuading holdouts to return falls to an interim leader or else the next permanent leader.

A prominent case of a splinter group arose in 2001 after Canadian Alliance leader Stockwell Day failed to lead the party to an expected electoral breakthrough. A cabal of Alliance MPs demanded the ability to speak freely on issues of principle and called upon Day to resign as opposition leader following a series of controversies.[87] The rancour saw several senior critics relinquish their positions, which escalated into thirteen MPs being suspended from the Alliance caucus or resigning from it. After Day agreed to a leadership race, a dozen of them engaged in talks with the Progressive Conservative caucus to create a new parliamentary group, the Democratic Representative Caucus (DRC).[88] Deborah Grey was key to cementing its legitimacy. The party icon had been the Reform Party's first MP and had a knack for witticism that grabbed headlines. She resigned as deputy leader of the Alliance following Day's demands for unwavering loyalty, alleging that he had colourfully told the caucus that, as leader, if he were to murder his grandmother with an axe that it would be up to them to publicly say that granny deserved it.[89] The DRC fizzled away when most of its MPs returned to the Canadian Alliance under new leader Stephen Harper. The embattled Tories criticized their own leader, Joe Clark, which set the stage for a PC leadership contest to replace him and the parties merging into the Conservative Party of Canada.[90]

Coalition Governments

A coalition government brings some opposition members into the cabinet without the requirement to switch parties. In Canada, a national government coalition has formed just once, when a group of pro-conscription Liberal MPs engaged in extensive negotiations before joining the Conservatives, led by Prime Minister Robert Borden, to form a Union government during World War I.[91] A failed attempt in 2008 demonized the word "coalition" in the Canadian lexicon.[92] Public furore erupted during the so-called coalition crisis when the federal Liberals and New Democrats, who depended on the support of the Bloc Québécois, proposed a coalition to the governor general to replace the freshly re-elected Conservative government. The manoeuvre was portrayed by some as anti-democratic, with the news media paying considerable attention to the political strategy involved.[93]

In the provinces, war-time coalition governments formed in Manitoba and British Columbia in the 1940s. The only such post-war arrangement to date in Canada arose in Saskatchewan, with a cataclysmic result for the smaller party. In the 1999 provincial election, the governing New Democrats lost the popular vote yet won exactly half (twenty-nine) of the seats, with the other half distributed between the Saskatchewan Party (twenty-five) and the Liberals (four). The morning after the election, Premier Roy Romanow phoned the Liberal leader to say, "We've got a lot in common. Can we talk?"[94] Meetings at the Saskatoon cabinet office about shared policy objectives led to drafting a coalition agreement and unveiling what the premier described as a "joint coalition cabinet" with two Liberal ministers and a third appointed as Speaker, without switching parties.[95] The NDP caucus accepted the arrangement to avoid an early election and to advance their policy agenda.[96] Election results in the fourth Liberal seat were overturned, which the SaskParty would end up winning in a by-election, adding to turbulence in the Saskatchewan Liberal party.

The province's Liberal party executive was on board, but a growing number of rank-and-file members were unnerved that the party's MLAs, including the leader, had been co-opted by the NDP. When Romanow retired in 2001, one of the Liberal MLAs gave up being a minister, sat as an Independent Liberal, and advocated for a review of the Liberal leader, who was still in the cabinet.[97] The MLA cautioned that, as the smaller partner in the coalition government, the Liberals had been restricted from effectively conveying their own messaging.[98]

The NDP-Liberal coalition tenuously continued under Premier Lorne Calvert when the Speaker resigned from that role to become a minister. Liberal party members elected a new leader, who instructed the party's two remaining coalition MLAs to pick a side. The Liberal MLAs opted to remain in cabinet, sat as Independents, and (unsuccessfully) sought re-election as NDP candidates. One of them rationalized that by joining the New Democrats he had not crossed the floor because he was already part of the government.[99] The coalition episode marks the final time that a Liberal held a seat in the Saskatchewan legislature. The party never recovered, and in 2023 it rebranded as the Saskatchewan Progress Party.

Defunct Parties

Some partisans become political orphans when their party ceases to exist. When a party folds, parliamentarians who see value in being a member of a parliamentary group and who are interested in re-election are forced to pursue a new affiliation. An early case is the Anti-Confederates disbanding in 1869, resulting in over a dozen MPs looking for other parties to join in an era when partisan distinctions were "often blurred."[100] In 1982, the Alberta Social Credit leader quit amid financial woes, in-fighting, and fading popularity. The party executive announced that the once mighty Socreds would not field candidates in the next election. Two of the remaining Socred MLAs were re-elected as Independents. In the election after that, they were re-elected under the banner of a new party that they created, which dissolved after one of them crossed the floor to the PCs.[101] In 2024, history seemed to repeat itself when the leader of BC United, despite being the Official Opposition, announced that the party would not run candidates in that year's provincial election.

As well, ex-partisans can adopt a symbolic label in the legislature that communicates a whimsical affiliation with their former party. There are many cases of parliamentarians signifying a continued connection with an existing party, such as the Independent Liberal in Saskatchewan we just mentioned. But those parties still exist at the time. Where defunct parties are concerned, this includes the four BC Social Credit MLAs who sat as Independent Social Credit members,[102] the former NDP MP who symbolically resurrected the CCF moniker,[103] and the PC MPs who rejected the formation of the Conservative Party and sat as Independent Progressive Conservatives.[104]

Expelled Members

There is a delicate balance between constructive individualism, which encourages a party leader to reconsider decisions and challenges groupthink, and destructive individualism, which undermines party solidarity, harms reputations, and creates chaos. From 1980 to 2021, proven or alleged, thirty-seven Canadian parliamentarians were jettisoned from their party for gross misconduct or criminal behaviour. In order of prevalence, these included expulsions from federal or provincial caucuses due to financial impropriety by the politician (e.g., fraud, embezzlement); sexual misconduct (e.g., assault, harassment); other forms of illegal activity (e.g., fleeing the scene of an accident, obstruction of justice, public mischief); and concerning discrimination (e.g., anti-francophone sentiment, ableism, homophobia).

Some behaviours that result in caucus expulsion can be truly astonishing. In British Columbia, one parliamentarian repeatedly used MLA letterhead to advocate for his family's interests,[105] another provided a character reference for two convicted sex offenders,[106] and yet another wrote letters to newspaper editors under false names.[107] There was an Ontario MPP who struck a pedestrian with a minivan and falsely claimed her husband was the driver,[108] a Quebec MNA who used a security firm's credit card to pay for his gasoline,[109] and a PEI MLA who repeatedly used his legislature calling card to make phone calls to adult sex lines.[110] In Nova Scotia, an MLA was banished for invoking parliamentary privilege to avoid testifying in a criminal trial involving a party staffer with whom he allegedly had an extra-marital affair.[111] Additionally, Alberta MLAs were involved in renting out a publicly subsidized apartment on Airbnb[112] and removing ballots from a table at a nomination meeting.[113] Most of them are among the four-in-five expelled parliamentarians who finished their careers as Independents without joining another party. These types of expulsions are beyond the scope of our analysis because tests of loyalty are not at the forefront. We are interested in the limits of constructive individualism within a parliamentary party caucus, which can climax in the leader wanting to dismiss an argumentative partisan who is beyond salvation.[114]

Fireable Offenses

Organized groups expel individuals for three main reasons: failing to actively contribute, violating group norms of interpersonal behaviour, or possessing a repugnant personality.[115] In parliamentary parties, serious offences like allegations of sexual harassment or impaired driving can lead to immediate suspension or expulsion from caucus, but beyond these clear transgressions, much is left to interpretation.

In parliamentary circles, trustworthiness is a cornerstone of party loyalty, beginning with the sacred duty to protect the confidentiality of caucus discussions. When an aggrieved partisan leaks sensitive information to journalists or political opponents, it creates both unwanted publicity for the leader and suspicion within the caucus, causing members to become more guarded.[116] Disrespecting caucus confidentiality erodes trust and disrupts the group's ability to function cohesively – even routine meetings become problematic. Another cardinal sin in parliamentary politics is publicly criticizing senior personnel in the leader's office. For example, one Alberta MLA we interviewed aired his frustrations over the leader's insistence that all matters be discussed with the chief of staff, resulting in the MLA's expulsion from caucus.[117] Loyalty issues also arise when the leader's inner circle perceives a maverick as uncontrollable. Contrarians who relent after warnings and disciplinary actions, which can include a temporary suspension from caucus, can potentially be reintegrated if they demonstrate renewed compliance.[118]

Disagreeing with the party on a signature policy is another redline. A backbencher is being reckless if they acerbically criticize a central cog in their party's agenda, particularly if the resulting news coverage brings the leader's judgment into question or portrays the caucus as divided.[119] While voting against the government on a confidence matter is grounds for dismissal for a member of the governing caucus, there was once greater tolerance for open dissent in the lead-up to the vote. A well-known case occurred in 1990 when Brian Mulroney warned his caucus to stand firm against public outrage towards the government's plans to introduce a Goods and Services Tax (GST). Two Progressive Conservative MPs, David Kilgour and Alex Kindy, who had a reputation for criticizing their own government, were suspended from meetings of the Alberta regional caucus for railing against the proposed consumption tax, including delivering speeches denouncing it.[120] Kindy had remained even after siding with the Liberals and NDP in opposing unrelated tax measures.[121] The duo continued attending national caucus meetings, prompting other members to assert that they had eroded confidence in the government, made caucus meetings untenable, and failed to carry out legislative duties and represent their constituents effectively.[122] Nevertheless, the mavericks continued to sit as Tories, even after they voted with the opposition against the government's use of closure to halt debate on the GST proposal. It was only after they voted against the GST bill that the prime minister urged a caucus vote to expel them entirely.[123]

Increasingly, leaders and fellow partisans do what they can to avoid such standoffs, and try desperately to work things out with a divergent colleague to prevent a media circus and an action that will result in partisan divorce.[124] In 2007, several Conservative ministers and the party whip urged MP Bill Casey to reconsider his decision after he informed Prime Minister Harper and the finance minister that he would vote against the budget. His objection stemmed from a lack of adequate exemption for Nova Scotia's offshore oil revenues, which he argued would lead to claw-backs in equalization payments. The chief of staff walked him through ongoing negotiations with the premier and offered blunt advice: "If I were you, I wouldn't leave the caucus until I know what that looks like. Don't make a big decision while pieces are still moving on the chessboard."[125] On the day of the vote, senior Conservatives attempted to persuade Casey by locking him in a room to talk things through and even pulling him behind a curtain in the legislature.[126] It was to no avail; despite these efforts, he remained firm in his stance, and soon after casting his dissenting vote, the MP was expelled from the caucus. Other times, colleagues can see a pivotal vote as an opportunity to finally be rid of an individualist. In Nova Scotia, a backbencher who felt like a stranger in his own caucus declared that he would vote differently than his party on the budget. A caucus member close to the leader told him to "f*ck off," and two days later the MLA arrived at the legislative precinct to find his office furniture was gone.[127] This rigidity is why we urge leaders to consider a different approach to the confidence convention in all but exceptional circumstances (chapter 10).

Big philosophical debates that transcend jurisdictions, such as conscription of military recruits in World Wars I and II, constitutional reform, or federal-provincial finances, are a considerable source of caucus upheaval and exoduses.[128] From 2020 to 2023, the coronavirus (COVID-19) pandemic was a defining global event, provoking intense debates over health and safety, civil liberties, science, the economy, and policy responses. One outcome in Canada was a spate of caucus departures at peak moments of the public health emergency as leaders contended with broken trust and open defiance from parliamentarians who resented rules that struck a libertarian nerve.

Party leaders' touchiness with individualism during the pandemic stands in contrast with how their predecessors in the twentieth century accepted self-expression as a tenet of democratic representation. Government-side backbenchers were expelled from caucus for ignoring public health guidance to not leave the country,[129] for voting against a bill to temporarily expand the government's authority,[130] and for openly criticizing public health restrictions.[131] A Member of the National Assembly stepped aside from the CAQ caucus for three months after video surfaced of him breaking physical distancing rules while socializing at a brewery.[132] When a fourth wave of the pandemic emerged in 2021, Premier Ford declared that all members of the Ontario PC caucus must be vaccinated, which resulted in the removal of a veteran MPP who refused to comply[133] and another who resigned after misrepresenting her vaccination status.[134] Other partisans across Canada were demoted, such as the Liberal MP who disobeyed the government whip's instructions to avoid non-essential travel outside the country and so was stripped of a committee post,[135] and the Manitoba PC minister who was fired from cabinet for refusing to declare if he had been vaccinated.[136] In Alberta, an NDP MLA resigned from caucus while under RCMP investigation for hacking the provincial government's vaccination verification website in an alleged effort to expose its vulnerabilities.[137] Reaction to public protests against vaccine mandates also exposed divisions in some parties, with different results. While a PC MLA in Nova Scotia was banished for promoting a traffic blockade at the New Brunswick border,[138] an Alberta MLA remained in the UCP caucus after praising the Freedom Convoy movement and posing with law-breakers near the Coutts Port of Entry.[139] All told, thirteen politicians left provincial caucuses in 2021 alone, of whom nine were expelled. Michelle Rempel Garner blogged about the bedlam that beset conservative parties in Ottawa and Alberta, alleging "public meltdowns, nearly missed physical fights, coups, smear jobs, leaked recordings and confidential emails, lack of consensus on critical issues, caucus turfings, people harassed to the point where they resign roles ... heated exchanges to get basic concerns addressed, unjustified insularity in decision making, shunnings, exclusionary cliques, and more."[140] Such public candour from a sitting member of Parliament about internal party dynamics was possible because her party was undergoing in a leadership race at the time.

It is now widely understood that a member who contravenes the team principle, such as by flagrantly disagreeing with policy endorsed by the caucus, can no longer be part of the group.[141] Spats that lead to a party banishment turn on a basic principle: do not subvert the authority of the leader or the primacy of the party. Partisans who purge one of their own talk about the pride of being part of a team, of supporting a group, of learning from one another, and mutual respect.[142] In 2006, when Garth Turner was on the cusp of being expelled from the Conservative caucus for blogging critical comments about the Harper government and for being dismissive of his colleagues, fellow Ontario MPs lectured him. As Turner recalls it, the finance minister declared, "You owe a duty to everyone. To the team. The team comes first."[143] Backbenchers were more pointed: "We play as a team, or we lose as a team. We have no room for an independent thinker on our team," said one MP. Another added, "You have to be a team player. If you're not, then get out." Breaking the conditions of a behavioural agreement with the whip is another way that a troublemaker can affirm that they are not a team player.[144]

Party loyalty in Canada runs so deep that, for some partisans, opposing it is tantamount to political treason. Incumbents who lose the party nomination can be turfed from caucus for suggesting that they might run as an Independent,[145] and a party might swiftly eject from the fold one of their own in response to news reports that the individual is exploring a switch of parties.[146] Partisans will be shown the door if they donate to another party[147] or sign up to support another party's leadership candidates.[148] In parties joined at the hip nationally and provincially, a parliamentarian can be expelled for criticizing a core policy of their party's brethren in another jurisdiction. Case in point: the Bloc Québécois expelled one of their MPs because she refused to follow the party line about the secular charter proposed by their provincial counterpart, the Parti Québécois.[149]

Getting the Boot

There are three main ways for a leader to turf a problematic colleague: secure their agreement to voluntarily resign, follow a process of caucus consultation and hold an *in camera* vote to expel them, or unilaterally announce that the parliamentarian has been removed. The easiest route is someone jumping before they are pushed out,[150] or when they recognize that a newly installed leader takes a firm line on dalliances that an interim leader tolerated.[151] "Have you thought about resignation?" Stephen Harper said to a Canadian Alliance MP whose anti-LGBTQ2+ comments were dominating the news and who was called to the carpet in the leader's office. "These kinds of things are usually handled with a temporary resignation from caucus until things get worked out," added the House leader.[152] These private conversations, if successful, enable the party leadership to frame the departure and gives the troublemaker faint hope that reconciliation is possible.

Consulting the caucus validates a leader's desire to cut ties. In Ottawa, the smaller scale of a regional caucus or a special meeting allows more people to speak on a motion to expel one of their own before making a recommendation or announcement to the full caucus.[153] The leader's opinion carries considerable weight: the two GST rebels realized their time in the regional caucus was up when they were turned away from an Alberta caucus meeting attended by Prime Minister Mulroney.[154] Internal consultation about ending a parliamentarian's caucus membership is valued for its decentralized approach; however, the deliberations can prolong internal turmoil and fuel media frenzy, especially if details are leaked or, worse, livestreamed.[155] Some parties have rules requiring an internal vote prior to expelling a member. This includes a federal caucus that opts into *Reform Act, 2014* provisions that empower it alone to initiate and approve expulsion – a mechanism that allows MPs to threaten mavericks to tone down their rhetoric and get on side.[156] *In camera*, some team members disparage a troublemaker they believe should be banished to the distant back seats alongside other renegades,[157] while others may argue against expulsion on principle, even if they disapprove of what that person did.[158] To them, a parliamentarian must have freedom to speak and the onus is on the leadership to substantiate that party loyalty or a code of conduct has been breached. When a caucus vote is called, there can be unanimity, or there can be division, including abstentions. A rejected parliamentarian has no legal recourse: courts have ruled that it is up to legislatures and parties to govern their own affairs.[159]

A leader's unilateral decision to expel a parliamentarian affirms who is in charge at the price of upsetting those who loathe despotism. The caucus usually accepts a quick expulsion when someone crosses a well-known boundary, whether that is a galling transgression, or a series of actions deemed seditious. Caucus consultation can be superficial after the leader has informed a parliamentarian that they are out and asks that nothing be said until the caucus is informed,[160] or if, before a caucus vote is held, IT personnel are on standby to shut down the member's office computers and the Speaker's office reconfigures the House seating plan.[161] Backlash against the leader is possible if a party stalwart is expelled without sufficient justification.[162]

Partisans are removed for various acts of disloyalty, with breaking ranks on a major bill being a clear red line.[163] Such acts of defiance often represent the culmination of escalating tensions that the leadership deems intolerable, particularly when multiple warnings have been ignored.[164] A record of poor attendance in the legislature is a common complaint,[165] and absenteeism from representing constituents can be grounds for eviction.[166] Recurring episodes magnify each other, as with an opposition member repeatedly voting with the government and alleging that caucus discipline chokes off independence,[167] a parliamentarian pillorying the leader in a series of blog posts,[168] or a member of caucus who comments on internal power struggles.[169] Some actions leave a leader with little alternative. Allegations of inappropriate office behaviour can kindle a prolonged internal investigation, necessitate an ethics probe, or provoke an immediate decision to expel.[170] On politically explosive matters such as sexual harassment or violating election rules, the leadership group quickly distances itself from a miscreant, sometimes without revealing the reason.[171] Not taking action would result in unrelenting controversy and the possibility of constituents petitioning for their representative to be ousted.[172] There is disappointment and regret on both sides when the behaviour of a parliamentarian who is otherwise on good terms with the party corners the leader into dismissal.[173]

Formal notification is usually blunt. In 1996, Liberal MP John Nunziata registered a protest vote against the budget because his party had reneged on a promise to eliminate the GST and was notified of his dismissal via a fax sent to his home.[174] When Casey voted against the 2007 budget, the government whip told him, "You're no longer in our caucus. It's a vote of non-confidence in your own government and we cannot have people in our own caucus that express non-confidence."[175] One morning in 2019, Jody Wilson-Raybould had a curt meeting with the prime minister who coldly said she was being removed from the caucus and would no longer be a Liberal candidate, and who advised her to say nothing about it until he addressed the national caucus that evening.[176] In Alberta, an MLA was summoned to the leader's office to discuss caucus research funding, only to be informed that he was out of the caucus because he did not get along with others.[177] Leaders can deliver the bad news at inopportune moments, such as the PEI MLA who received the call while coaching a youth soccer team[178] or the NDP MP who was informed at midnight that an announcement would be made the next day about his removal.[179] Even expulsion after voting against the government's budget can come as a surprise if the member was naive about the severity of the repercussions.[180] Ex-partisans must cope with the emotional upheaval of being banished as they try to rationalize what just happened. "I have been loyal. I believe I have been a hard-working minister and MLA and have been part of the team. To be treated like this is reprehensible and just not acceptable," said a Manitoba New Democrat who was dismissed from caucus in 2014.[181]

Tensions are high when a missive is publicly released. The leader of the BC Liberals issued a terse statement upholding the culture of politics as "a team sport" when he announced in 2022 that, in light of "a pattern of behaviour" that undermined "principles of mutual respect and trust," a long-time MLA had been expelled for questioning on social media the science behind climate change.[182] A letter from New Brunswick Premier Blaine Higgs, expelling a former minister from caucus after accusations of autocratic leadership, illustrates the strategic use of communications to frame a caucus departure (figure 6.2).[183] This type of public volley serves to build a case against the ex-partisan by disclosing a series of alleged problematic actions. The vitriol of the expelled member can be every bit as nasty as those who leave voluntarily.[184]

News of a caucus exit can expose internal soap operas as allegations flow into the public domain. In Nova Scotia, a PC MLA was expelled after she refused to pave part of a gravel driveway at her constituency office to make it accessible to people with physical disabilities. She alleged harassment by the legislature's management commission that

October 14, 2022

Mr. Dominic Cardy
MLA – Fredericton West-Hanwell

Mr. Cardy,

This letter is to inform you that the Progressive Conservative caucus supported my recommendation to expel you. As a group we found your conduct and your actions, most notably, over the last few days to be inexcusable.

During the meeting you and I had on Thursday morning, I informed you of my deep concern over the lack of improvement in our education system, and I also informed you of my decision to remove you from Cabinet. I was surprised to then immediately receive your resignation letter. I believe the content of the letter is vindictive and misleading. It is unfortunate and hurtful that you chose to leave in this way.

That being said, I am going to move forward, doing the hard work our team was elected to do. I am focused on making improvements that benefit New Brunswick in critical areas like health and education.

It's time for us all to rise above and stay focused on the mission at hand.

Province before politics.

Blaine Higgs

Blaine M. Higgs
Premier

Figure 6.2. Letter Notifying MLA of Caucus Expulsion (2022)

Source: Higgs, "Letter."

directed her to use her constituency budget to pay for the asphalt. The leader cited those complaints as the "last straw" and likewise pointed to "a pattern of behaviour" that had prompted meetings to discuss how she managed her office, her lack of availability to constituents, and her apartment expenses.[185] In Saskatchewan, a Liberal MLA was banished because of his penchant for disrupting parliamentary proceedings with drawn out speeches.[186] Occasionally it is unclear whether a parliamentarian left a party voluntarily or involuntarily. In Ontario, MPP Jack MacLaren held on after journalists revealed that his website was adorned with praise from fake constituents and after he was told to stay away from the legislature for making sexist jokes.[187] He was finally dismissed from the PC caucus in 2017 when a video emerged of him implying that the party had a hidden agenda against French-language rights. One of his former caucus mates reacted by posting online, "Not a team player. Bye bye."[188] Hours after the expulsion, MacLaren posted that his campaign literature with the Trillium Party of Ontario was already printed and he told the media that he had been preparing to announce the switch along with an exodus of the PC party's electoral district association.[189] He placed a distant fifth in the ensuing election, which was handily won by the PC candidate.

Accusations of the leader being a bully who demeans caucus members are common when a backbencher is expelled.[190] In BC, an MLA who was dropped from cabinet for publicly criticizing the premier persisted with his diatribe in a media scrum. He levelled bitter condemnations of the leader as a temperamental bully, the cabinet as hapless, and the caucus as meek.[191] The remarks contributed to the MLA's expulsion from caucus. Few are as composed as Steven Fletcher, the Manitoba PC backbencher who was ousted for exuberant scrutiny of his party's own government, including filibustering two of its bills at committee.[192] "Caucus membership is not a right. Caucus membership is a privilege. It is extended by your colleagues to you," Fletcher reflected after his colleagues voted him out.[193]

Expulsion from caucus is a career-ending event for most partisans. Of the ninety-six politicians who were expelled from caucus between 1980 and 2021 and became Independents, only eleven managed to retain their seats without adopting a new party label.[194] Extreme cases involve censuring a member by preventing them from being recognized by the Speaker, as occurred with Sarah Jama, or attempts to suspend or even expel a parliamentarian from the legislature entirely, a tactic which has been most prevalent in Nova Scotia. A notorious episode saw that province's House of Assembly being recalled in 1986 to pass a bill banning MLAs convicted of a major crime from holding a seat within five years of a conviction. The legislation was prompted by a desire to disqualify MLA Billy Joe MacLean, who was dropped from the PC cabinet and caucus for inflating his expense claims. He was suspended from the legislature when the so-called "Billy Joe Bill" became law. However, a provincial court ruled the legislation unconstitutional, and voters returned MacLean to office in the ensuing by-election, this time as an Independent. Nearly three decades later, the Nova Scotia legislature was recalled to debate expelling an NDP MLA who pled guilty to fraud over falsified expense claims. The MLA, who defiantly sat as an Independent, blamed the assembly for deciding "the fate of representation in my community"[195] and asserted that it would be unfair to shut down his constituency office that employed a single mother.[196] He abruptly resigned before potentially being compelled to forfeit his pension plan contributions and severance.[197] A third case involved the Progressive Conservatives tabling a notice of motion in 2023 to ban MLA Elizabeth Smith-McCrossin from the chamber for alleging that a now-deceased political staffer had been coerced by that party to sign a non-disclosure agreement about sexual harassment. Smith-McCrossin, who had been a member of the PC caucus and was re-elected as an Independent, tabled an unsigned document that she said was the NDA. The Tories claimed that she had misled the House and moved that she not be permitted to take her seat until she retracted the allegations and apologized.[198] After she threatened legal action, the government held off calling for a debate on the motion but left it on the order paper, with the lingering threat that it could be resurrected.[199] The difficulty of suspending a parliamentarian from the legislature lies in the principle that voters, not political parties, fellow parliamentarians, or the courts, should serve as the final arbiters.

Expulsions sometimes occur even before a parliamentarian has been officially sworn in. Occasionally, a candidate causes a kerfuffle during an election campaign after the replacement deadline has passed, leaving their party with no choice but to have the candidate's name appear on the ballot as its official nominee.[200] In response, a leader can distance themselves by saying that individual, if elected, would not be permitted to sit with the party until certain actions are undertaken to demonstrate rehabilitation.[201] Alternatively, the leader can disavow the candidate altogether. When this happens, the shunning is swift and punishing. The candidate is immediately treated by the party as though they did something unforgivable – there is no presumption of innocence or due process in the waning days of an election campaign – and overnight their local campaign infrastructure evaporates.[202] If such a candidate is nevertheless elected, they sit as an Independent.

Life as an Independent

An intriguing consequence of heightened partisanship is the growing presence of Independents in Canadian legislatures compared to recent years. Since 1980, the number of sitting MPs and provincial politicians who left their parties during a parliamentary session increased at a rate that exceeds the total growth in the size of legislatures (figure 6.3). In 2021, about 2 per cent of all parliamentarians elected under a party banner finished their term either as an Independent or with another party, about four times as many as in 1980. Independent thinkers nowadays are less willing to remain in a party they cease to support. With social media, they can make their voices heard and rally supporters using technology once considered science fiction, giving them a real chance to get (re-)elected despite the odds. At the same time, party leaders have a shorter fuse with

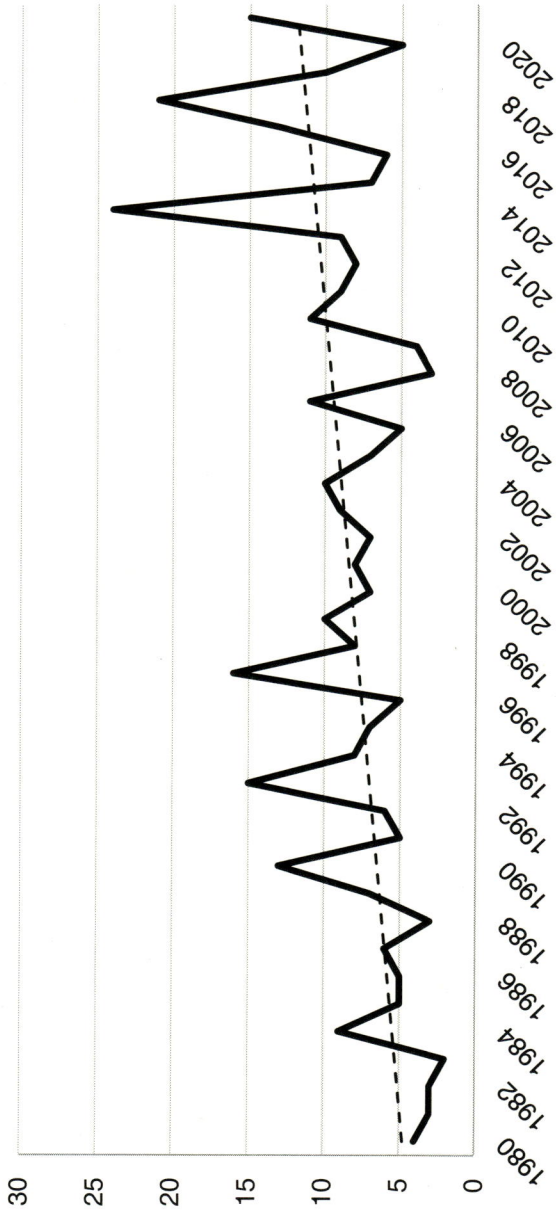

Figure 6.3. Elected Parliamentarians Who Left Their Parties by Year, Canada and Provinces, 1980–2021

Note: Includes both voluntary departures and expulsions.

Source: Authors' dataset.

subversives than in the past, and their crisis communications protocol now dictates that they swiftly cut ties with someone bringing the party brand into disrepute. Regardless of how they come to reject party politics, serving as a parliamentarian without a caucus is a fundamentally different experience. As one Quebec Independent put it, "C'est presque un nouveau job."[203]

There is a certain cachet to being an Independent in a political system widely seen as tainted by hyper-partisanship. The Independent label conjures a principled, liberated thinker who is unafraid to put constituents ahead of personal or party interests, and an underdog battling a dysfunctional, bloated system run by out-of-touch elites.[204] Democracy benefits when parliamentarians engage an alienated electorate, challenge the government, and counteract a collective mindset and turf protection that arises in organized groups.[205] Yet Independents battle twin constraints in a political system that over time has been co-opted by partisans to favour their own interests. This is where the theory that political parties operate as cartels has credence. First, the rules make it exceptionally difficult to be (re-)elected without being the nominated candidate of a reputable political party. Second, Canadian legislatures are structured around recognized political parties, which marginalizes Independents and often renders them invisible to the press gallery. Understandably, the perceived powerlessness of Independents, coupled with their isolation and re-election obstacles, makes the role an anathema to most partisans. Yet, despite these obstacles and the struggle to exert influence, the contributions of Independents can sometimes outweigh those of some party backbenchers.

Most parliamentarians who leave a parliamentary caucus serve out their term with little fanfare as they struggle to navigate political structures that revolve around parties. Most of them do not seek re-election. Of those that do run again, the vast majority lose. From 1980 to 2021, 164 Canadian parliamentarians who were elected with a party completed their term as an Independent. When the legislature was dissolved, the majority of them retired instead of running again. Facing long odds without party backing, many ex-partisans shy away from independent bids. Independents must have strong name recognition, deep personal connections within their community, and the ability to rally former partisans to support their campaign. They also require sufficient resources and the courage to stand alone. To succeed, a critical mass of constituents must be dissatisfied not only with political parties in general, but also with the party the Independent would otherwise align with. Leaving a party following a high-profile, principled dispute helps. Even then, former partisans running for re-election as

Table 6.1. Partisans and Independents Elected in General Elections, Canada and Provinces, 1980–2021

General Election	Partisans Elected	Independents Elected	% Seats Won by Party Candidates
Quebec	1,369	0	100%
Manitoba	626	0	100%
Saskatchewan	606	0	100%
New Brunswick	596	0	100%
Prince Edward Island	317	0	100%
Ontario	1,290	1	99.9%
Federal/Canada	3,994	8	99.8%
Alberta	832	2	99.8%
British Columbia	776	2	99.7%
Nova Scotia	622	3	99.5%
Newfoundland and Labrador	562	6	98.9%
Total	11,028	16	99.9%

Note: Federal and provincial elections held between 1 January 1980 and 31 December 2021. Does not include by-elections.

Independents have limited prospects, winning fewer than one-third of the elections they contest.

In Canadian federal and provincial elections held from 1980 to 2021, 99.9 per cent of seats were won by party candidates (table 6.1). Provincial contests in Quebec, Manitoba, Saskatchewan, New Brunswick, and PEI were the least hospitable: every single seat over that time span was won by a partisan. Newfoundland and Labrador is a recent outlier, where several expelled MHAs were re-elected as Independents in 2019 and 2021 on the strength of their popularity in small electoral districts and lack of public enthusiasm for the party leaders. Little wonder that some Independents incorporate party colours into their campaigns, such as by affixing stickers to their old signs.[206]

Over the course of that forty-one-year period, only two MPs and two provincial parliamentarians were elected as Independents without having first served in the legislature with a political party. Federally, in 1984, local Conservatives and Liberals recruited former Toronto-area mayor Tony Roman to run as an alternative to an unpopular PC incumbent amid a national surge in support for that party. In 2006, André Arthur, a talk-radio host in Quebec, was elected when the Conservative Party failed to field a candidate and quietly endorsed him. Provincially, Yvonne Jones was elected independently in Labrador in 1996 after losing the Liberal nomination contest, later rejoining the party. In British Columbia, former municipal councillor Vicki Huntington was elected in 2009 after the governing party took the unpopular step of transplanting an incumbent from another rid-ing into her district.[207] A fifth Independent, Ontario MPP Bobbi Ann Brady, was successful in 2022, just beyond the scope of our study period. These cases are anomalies – the candidacy of most Independents goes unnoticed and fails to make a dent in the party oligopoly.

Democracy can benefit from Independents pitching fresh ideas dur-ing election campaigns. Unaffiliated candidates can connect on a per-sonal level with electors through their authenticity, and they can say what they think instead of having to flip through a party platform to find messaging.[208] However, because Canadian parliamentary elec-tions turn around political parties and party leaders, Independents are usually treated by the media as quaint human interest stories at the start of the campaign. The news media struggle with how to accord them appropriate attention,[209] and they can be excluded from local all-candidates' debates.[210] Money is another challenge. The public disclo-sure of donors makes some hesitant to contribute to an Independent,[211] and in the federal arena it is only when the official campaign begins that Independents are eligible to access the list of electors or issue tax receipts for donations.[212] The barrier is so high that an Independent might feel compelled to fundraise for the next campaign soon after being elected.[213] Not having access to party resources is a further impediment to election. Independents are unable to avail of communications templates, policy platforms, voter contact databases, or party funds.[214] A partisan-turned-Independent often loses experienced campaign workers and volunteers who side with the party's new nominee. They can even have difficulty hiring local contractors given that many have party ties.[215]

In office, Independents find that being unaffiliated allows for a more authentic form of representation.[216] They speak more openly and fre-quently than many party backbenchers do, and they can raise perspec-tives that the other parties overlook or want to suppress. Unrestrained voices are important in a polarized milieu, as a former Independent MLA explained to us: "The whole question of polarity is a very big one. How do you inject new ideas? How do you stop the cloaking of the parties with this thick band of loyalty that is impervious? Do we have to infuse that with the voice of Independents? I think that's an important ques-tion that we'd better start thinking about."[217] In the right circumstances, an Independent can perform a meaningful parliamentary role. Indepen-dents can ask smart questions during Question Period. Some welcome the opportunity to build friendships across party lines,[218] and if they find allies in party caucuses, they can advance debate on issues of importance to them and their constituents.[219] As well, Independents have the proce-dural ability to deny the unanimous consent that is required when a party wants the legislature to vote on a motion without official notice, which is how Wilson-Raybould temporarily blocked a Bloc Québécois motion in 2021 that had all-party support to recognize Quebec as a nation.[220] Denying consent is potent in moments of urgency, or when parliamentarians want to adjourn early, which an Independent can leverage in exchange for speaking time or a policy commitment that will benefit their electoral district.[221] Their influence peaks when the governing party holds a slim minority of seats, and their vote has the power to obstruct or potentially bring down the government.

Independent parliamentarians interested in re-election feel a greater sense of urgency to work on behalf of their constituents. Freed from party constraints and obligations, they have more time and incentive to interact with their constituents directly, taking pride that their independence shifts accountability from party bosses to the voters themselves.[222] They can attract the attention of journalists and public servants who might not take heed of a government-side backbencher, and an Independent who is being courted by other political parties can collaborate on files and work across party lines to deliver results for their district.[223] While experiences vary, some of them delight in the agency to make their own decisions and sense that constituents value being heard and represented. Internet communications enable them to connect with like-minded supporters and even to build alliances across jurisdictions. The End the Lockdowns National Caucus that formed during the COVID-19 pandemic included several outspoken Independents across the country who had been removed from their party's caucus.[224] The impromptu alliance of federal, provincial, and municipal politicians who opposed public health orders was short-lived, yet it provided an improvised support network for members to uphold their values against perceived overreach.

The small number of parliamentarians elected on their own recognizance derive the satisfaction that many partisan backbenchers crave. As mentioned, Bobbi Ann Brady is one of the handful of people in modern times whose first election to a Canadian legislature was as an Independent. In 2022, the long-time constituency assistant to a rural Ontario PC MPP sought the party nomination when her boss did not reoffer. However, local party members endorsed someone backed by the premier. Undaunted, she put her name on the ballot in the general election. Voters rallied around her, including people who ordinarily supported other parties who spotted an opportunity for change in a safe Tory seat.[225] According to Brady, as an Independent there is no monopoly on a good idea, a philosophy that she believes suits her constituents given that they rejected party politics by electing her, and did so again in 2025. Brady explained to us why being elected without a party label is so empowering:

As an Independent, I'm not a brand ambassador, which gives me the freedom to be unique and fun. When a politician is a brand ambassador, they strip you of your unique qualities and quirky behaviours. You can't be individualistic. You have to be cookie cutter. As an Independent, I don't have to be cookie cutter. I don't have to be someone I'm not; I can be myself and real. An example that springs to mind is when I once opened the Norfolk County Fair, I was introduced as being "one of us." I love the fact that my constituents view me as "one of them." I relate to them. They relate to me. That's all because I haven't been stripped of my unique personality by a party.[226]

Parliamentarians who leave their party behind to sit as an Independent have an added sense of relief of being free from the banalities of partisanship. Several told us that they felt greater self-worth and accomplishment:

I loved being an Independent MP. I had questions that belonged to me, I could tackle any subject that I found important, I had my declarations in the chamber, I had bills that I piloted.... I represented my population without any constraints, without all the hassle or the petty politics of the caucus, I no longer had all that. Oh my God, it was fun.[227]

I would say the best time that I had in terms of feeling like I was productive and changing the world a little bit for the better was while I was an Independent.[228]

I love being an Independent. When you're an Independent, your team is your people, the people you represent.... If you're with the party, you're expected to be part of *that* team, and too often that team is not representing the people that elected you. So, I have a lot less conflict in my life. I'm able to go to the legislature and put forth bills and legislation and ask the questions in Question Period that actually matter to the people I represent.[229]

This said, Independents might exaggerate the benefits of non-affiliation, particularly amid a swell of excitement in the aftermath of leaving a party.[230] An upbeat attitude and a strong work ethic are essential to thrive in a party-dominated system. Electoral challenges, like limited campaign infrastructure, can turn into a competitive advantage if an Independent inspires active community involvement. Operating on a tight budget forces them to work hard to connect with fickle voters and build an online presence to project their authenticity.

The reality is that Independents are excluded from many aspects of parliamentary life. In the House of Commons, they have fewer opportunities to participate in debate, and they are ineligible for membership on a parliamentary committee, although they may attend public meetings.[231] They must put in considerable effort to ensure that they are seen and accessible, and they are unable to lean on party staff to conduct research about a wide array of topics that the Independent member knows little about.[232] There are various small frustrations that make life difficult, such as the lack of speaking time in the legislature to hit back when former colleagues mock them,[233] or the unfair lumping of Independents elected on their own merit alongside ex-partisans who still vote with their former party or who left amid controversy.[234] As one backbencher put it, sitting as an Independent "sounds great and righteous"; however, it can be difficult to accomplish much, especially in a majority-government scenario.[235] As well, life in the capital city can be lonely. One former Independent told us about being excluded from the party social scene and spending weekday evenings alone while in Ottawa.[236] Another talked about the pain of losing the warmth and reassurance of being a member of a political family.[237]

Sometimes an ex-partisan's desire to reconcile with a former party is not mutual. An Independent can twist in the wind waiting indefinitely for the leader to decide about readmission, as occurred with a former Liberal MP banished over allegations of siding with China.[238] During the hiatus, a leader can field demands from caucus members and the extra-parliamentary party to reinstate the transgressor.[239] Some ex-partisans search for a new caucus to join but cannot find a willing partner, especially if they were disavowed by their original party.[240] Other Independents, whom we call "two-steppers," do find receptive partners – an archetype we examine in chapter 7.

Summary

This chapter discussed parliamentarians who cease being a member of a party caucus. Some choose to exit because of dissatisfaction with the leader, ideological differences, foiled ambition, and strained relationships within the party. Others are kicked out for lack of contribution, public outbursts, personality conflicts, violation of group norms, gross misconduct, or illegal behaviour. Expulsions can have negative consequences for caucus morale and public perception, yet some situations leave leaders with little choice. Becoming an Independent brings opportunities to authentically represent constituents, albeit with the challenge of seeking a voice in the legislature and overcoming barriers to re-election. In sum, as with any workplace, in parliamentary circles there is turnover as unhappy people resign and as leaders fire incompatible or incompetent personnel. For many Independents, taking time to let the dust settle after leaving a party caucus is a reprieve before committing the ultimate disloyalty of joining another party, which is the focus of the next chapter.

7 Party Switchers

In 1990, Lucien Bouchard rocked Canadian politics when he protested the watering down of the Meech Lake constitutional accord by resigning from the Progressive Conservative cabinet and caucus to sit as an Independent. He then became leader of the Bloc Québécois, a coalition of Quebec nationalists and separatists whose popularity in the 1993 federal election contributed to the decimation of his former party and his instalment as leader of Her Majesty's Loyal Opposition. The *Ottawa Sun* dubbed him "Benedict Bouchard," evoking the eponym of Benedict Arnold, the famous traitor.[1] During the American Revolution, Arnold was a patriot who led military forays against the British. As battles raged in the 1770s, the fighting general's military accomplishments and a painful leg injury masked a burning ambition to become a wealthy member of the aristocracy.[2] In 1779, Arnold began corresponding with the British to see what they would offer if he were to defect. The next year, he was discovered planning to surrender a fort, at which point he switched to the British army and fought against his former colleagues. Ever since, Benedict Arnold's name is equated with disloyalty and betrayal, which rank among the worst political offenses a partisan can commit.

Switching political parties evokes treachery for a reason, and renegades do not change political allegiances lightly. They understand that joining a different party will make them a lightning rod for public discontent, that they will be vilified by their former colleagues, and that they will have an uneasy relationship as an interloper in their new caucus and with constituents. Which leads us to ask: under what circumstances do partisans change political teams in Canada? This chapter examines the mindset and actions involved with abandoning one party for another. It expands on our typology of party loyalty among parliamentarians by exploring the ways partisans become political traitors by crossing the floor, two-stepping, party hopping, and boomeranging, as well as through entrepreneurialism. Leaders who switch, mass defections, and party mergers are some of the other ways that partisans leap into new surroundings, plunging them into fast alliances with people they campaigned against.

Crossing the Floor and Two-Stepping

Social identity theory holds that people practise social mobility by leaving a group for another that they view more favourably.[3] In workplaces, employees evaluate their options when they are on the wrong side of a paradigm shift, such as when a new leader takes the organization in a different direction.[4] They assess whether their role continues to align with their expectations and self-image, and thoughts of quitting recede or solidify as they investigate alternatives. Unlike simply exiting a group or retiring from the field altogether, defecting to another organization involves the dual forces of push and pull: switchers must feel both pushed out of the group they are leaving and drawn to the one they are joining.[5] That appeal may be along social lines, with friends and close colleagues encouraging them to change sides.[6] Similar forces are at play in party politics.

We define party switching as the act of a parliamentarian changing their party affiliation while still holding a seat in that legislature, either through the sensationalism of going directly from one caucus to another (crossing the floor) or by taking a more circuitous route (which we call "two-stepping"). In the United States, the act of changing political parties is heavily influenced by a consortium of partisans trying to pull someone over to their side.[7] There, as in Canada, party affiliation is both deeply embedded as part of a legislator's identity and a strategic choice, and partisans are aware that framing their move as motivated by championing their constituents can mute allegations of self-interest.[8] Political ambition, re-election prospects, legislative influence, and support for the party's policy positions are considered the main variables in whether an American legislator is likely to stay in the fold or jump to another party.[9] In Canada, most parliamentarians who switch parties do so to resolve ideological dissonance by aligning with a group whose leader, values, and objectives are a better fit. Normally, then, a party switcher is attracted to a party that is ideologically compatible, with parties occupying the middle ground able to attract moderates from both the political left and right.[10] What truly motivates the decision may be deliberately concealed. However, changing parties is not always an antidote to their troubles. Indeed, new problems can emerge from joining another party, some unforeseen.

We identified eighty-two events of Canadian parliamentarians cross-ing the floor to another caucus in the same legislature without sitting as an Independent (table 7.1).[11] The betrayal puts wind in the sails of the welcoming party and demoralizes the abandoned caucus, with pivotal defections remaking power structures when they contribute to forcing out a leader, realigning the party system, or even determining who gov-erns.[12] A special concern of leaders is that a double-crosser might use strategic intelligence such as internal files, political tactics, knowledge about personnel, and caucus conversations against their former party. A leader whose tenure was cut short by floor crossing put it thusly to us: "It's all about power. If someone crosses the floor, and you're down in polls, and there's nervousness in caucus, it creates a sense that something is wrong. When people are bailing it can change the bal-ance of power. That's why party discipline and loyalty are important."[13] Opportunities and risks abound for both a caucus that welcomes a floor crosser and, especially, for floor crossers themselves. Leaving one party for another can go sideways in unpredictable ways. On the cusp of the 1979 federal election, a veteran Liberal MP was welcomed into the Pro-gressive Conservative caucus – only to be defeated in the ensuing PC nomination race by a twenty-two-year-old.[14] In particular, discussed below, the 2014 mass defection of Wildrose MLAs illustrates how floor crossing can have unintended consequences.

For many, crossing the floor is a smart political move that resolves personal misery as well as improving their policy, office, and vote cir-cumstances. In 2019, Jenica Atwin became the first Green elected to the House of Commons east of British Columbia, winning a tight three-way contest in Fredericton. As a Green MP, she voted more often with the NDP than with any other mainstream party[15] and felt isolated in Atlantic Canada, far away from the federal party structure.[16] After she quarrelled in 2021 on social media about the party's policy on Israel and Palestine, she vented to some colleagues about in-fighting and began looking for a way out. Atwin confided in her hockey coach, whom she knew to be politically connected and who acted as a "pathway" to phone calls and meetings with the Liberal government's regional minis-ter for New Brunswick, Dominic LeBlanc.[17] Over a span of three weeks, they discussed the friendships she had formed with some members of the Liberal caucus, and whether she could accomplish more on the government side. As she weighed options, Atwin endured sleepless-ness, stress, and worry, including about those who had helped get her elected against the odds. She examined her situation "from a thousand, million different angles,"[18] and concluded that she had "irreconcilable differences" with the Green Party's new leader, Annamie Paul.[19] Atwin told us that too many representational constraints had arisen with the change in party leadership:

> My issues within the federal Green Party began long before [leader] Anna-
> mie Paul, but under her leadership, I was unable to make autonomous deci-
> sions for important things like media communication, votes or be the voice
> for local issues. That was not okay with me. I was being silenced and had to
> move on. I wanted to leave so that she could stay and lead the party the way
> she wanted. I did tell them on a final caucus Zoom call after much tumult
> that unless something changed, I was walking away. There was a shrug – I
> shut my computer and never looked back at the Green Party of Canada.[20]

Thoughts of quitting the party were facilitated by a lack of the deep social identity attachments that course through so many partisans. Atwin rejected sitting as an Independent because, she told us, it is a role marked by inefficacy and solitude. She was keen to be part of a caucus: "I want a team. I'm a team player."[21] Thus she also pictured life with the NDP. "For me, it was always difficult to choose which party flag to fly over my head," she observed.[22]

Negotiations with the Liberals ensued. Atwin spoke with Prime Minister Trudeau and then Finance Minister Freeland over the phone, then informed LeBlanc of her decision, who promptly texted the prime minister. A news conference was scheduled to officially announce her shift in party loyalty. Atwin told journalists that she wanted to work in a more "supportive and collaborative" environment.[23] She stood by her anti-Israel remarks and stated that she planned on robust conversations in the Liberal caucus.[24] Yet within days of becoming a Liberal MP, she issued a statement that both Israelis and Palestinians suffer and back-tracked on her prior labelling of Israel's actions as an apartheid.[25] Atwin and her staff endured online misogyny and violent threats; she locked her X/Twitter account from public view. After a media hiatus, Atwin issued a statement on Facebook that she got involved in politics "to say things most people won't say," that sitting as an Independent would not have been in the best interests of her constituents, and that she was having vigorous policy discussions within the Liberal party's Atlantic caucus.[26] Two months after the switch, ministers had visited her riding seven times to make government funding announcements, compared with no such announcements previously.[27]

The brouhaha set off an internal power struggle between the Green Party's executive council and the leader, generating a stream of appallingly bad headlines. The negative publicity contributed to a spiral of declining monetary donations to the Greens, difficulty recruiting election candidates, dismal results in the 2021 federal election, allegations of racism and sexism, and, ultimately, Annamie Paul's resignation. For her part, Atwin was re-elected as a Liberal, and in 2023 was appointed as a parliamentary secretary. Two weeks after Hamas militants entered Israel and killed civilians that October, she was not among the twenty-three Liberal MPs, including six parliamentary secretaries, who defiantly signed an open letter urging the prime minister to call for a ceasefire between Israel and Hamas.[28] Behind the scenes, she sent personal emails to Trudeau, held private calls with the foreign affairs minister and her departmental officials, and participated in "tough conversations with colleagues in my new team," she told us.[29] As the conflict wore on, Atwin posted a letter on Instagram stating that Canada must both call for a ceasefire by Israel and reiterate demands for Hamas to release hostages.[30] The nuanced approach reflected political learning from her 2021 altercation that social media can attract toxic attention whereas personal conversations can be constructive.[31] Crossing the floor does not free a parliamentarian from obligations to abide by team culture, but it can prove to be a much better fit – while potentially setting off a chain of events that destroy the spurned leader's political career.

A longer, more guarded route to another party's caucus involves two-stepping. A two-step process occurs when a parliamentarian leaves a caucus to sit as an Independent and, after a period, joins a different caucus in that legislature. Alternatively, a two-stepper may forego the Independent route. Instead, they resign their seat, seek the nomination to run as a candidate with their new party, and are re-elected under its banner in the resulting by-election or in the next general election.

We identified sixty-five cases of Canadian parliamentarians following the two-step process from 1980 to 2021. At the federal level, men are more likely to two-step than to cross the floor directly; otherwise, among women and all provincial parliamentarians, floor crossing is the more common form of party switching (table 7.1). Federally, our party-defector database includes 21 MP floor crossers, 22 two-steppers, and 56 who were originally elected with a party, sat as an Independent, and did not join another caucus.[32] Provincially, we tallied 61 floor crossers, 43 two-steppers, and 146 ex-partisans who sat as an Independent without joining another party.

Almost all two-steppers serve as Independents before they join another caucus. A rare exception is Buckley Belanger, a standard setter who resigned as a Saskatchewan Liberal MLA in 1998, won a contested nomination with the New Democratic Party, and was re-elected in the resulting by-election with a resounding 94 per cent of the vote.[33] That outlier reflects the NDP's dual-stage policy whereby a parliamentarian must resign and be re-elected with the party in a by-election or,

Table 7.1. Floor Crossers, Two-Steppers, and Ex-Partisans in Canadian Parliamentary Legislatures, 1980–2021

Type	Federal (n = 99)		Provincial (n = 250)	
	Men	Women	Men	Women
Floor crossers (n = 82)	13	8	51	10
Two-steppers (n = 65)	19	3	37	6
Ex-partisans (n = 202)	43	13	125	21

Notes: Includes data for sixteen politicians leaving parties more than once.
"Ex-partisans" refers to parliamentarians elected with a party who left the party while in office, sat as an Independent, and did not join another party caucus.

more likely, to sit as an Independent and then seek re-election with the party in the next general election. By postponing the switch, the welcoming party and the switcher can ward off calls to resign that accompany changing parties while elected.[34] Maria Mourani is an example. Her evolving views on Quebec nationalism led to her departure from the Bloc Québécois in 2013, but she was extremely unhappy as an Independent, and was touched by a supportive phone call from NDP leader Tom Mulcair.[35] She settled on joining the party; however, she had to remain an Independent because its policy stipulated that only people elected as a New Democrat could be part of the caucus.[36] Mourani's re-election bid failed in the ensuing federal election and thus, according to parliamentary records, she never switched parties while an MP. (We classify her as a party leaver.)

There is far less public and partisan outrage when a parliamentarian takes the two-step route compared with crossing the floor. Those who become an Independent by choice can be initially lauded for rejecting partisanship and avoid the unpleasantries of a raging party machine determined to undercut them. This phased approach acknowledges public mistrust of opportunists who nullify what party their constituents supported in the previous election. An example is David Kilgour, who was first elected to the House of Commons as a Progressive Conservative MP in 1979. An outspoken champion of Western Canada, in 1987 he publicly threatened to cross the floor over his party's handling of appointments.[37] He was stripped of his parliamentary secretary role and banned from attending caucus meetings for nine months.[38] As we noted in chapter 6, three years later he was permanently expelled from the Progressive Conservative caucus for voting against the Mulroney government's plan to implement the GST. In 1991, he joined the Liberal Party after months of public negotiations while an Independent.[39] He remained in that caucus until 2005, when he resigned out of disagreement with several government policies, and once again sat as an Independent until his retirement the following year.[40]

The added legitimacy brought about by a pause in party affiliation, especially if constituents are consulted during the interlude, is one of the reasons why we suggest that legislatures codify a modified two-step process and do away with the practice of floor crossing altogether (chapter 10). When an Independent does join another party, they typically mention that they are following the wishes of constituents and cite the benefits of being part of a parliamentary group and/or government, including access to resources and a better perch to advocate for their district.[41] The news media might report an interesting angle about the Independent's path to another party, such as someone who is uncomfortable joining a merged party[42] or the relative of a former leader abandoning their party.[43]

Two-steppers can already know which party they are going to join. In 1998, the Alberta Liberals held an emergency caucus meeting to address policy differences between their leader and their treasury critic, Gene Zwozdesky. During the meeting, Zwozdesky declared that he would sit as an Independent.[44] Some Liberal MLAs publicly called for him to reconsider. They soured when it was revealed that two days beforehand their former colleague had met with PC Premier Ralph Klein on the pretext of discussing a trade mission, whereupon the premier broached the topic of crossing the floor. When the now-Independent MLA joined the PCs a month later, the government whip was adamant that incentives were neither requested nor offered.[45] The pause allowed Zwozdesky to knock on doors, which supported a frame that he joined the Tories because that's what his constituents wanted.[46]

Sometimes two-stepping lacks political acumen. In 1989, Richard Holden was elected in an English region of Montreal on the back of a protest vote to sit in the Quebec legislature as a member of the English-rights Equality Party that he co-founded, which opposed French language laws.[47] Within a couple of years, the MNA sat as an Independent following run-ins with party discipline. In 1992, the ardent federalist joined the separatist Parti Québécois in what may well be the most counter-intuitive case of party switching in Canadian history. Anglophones were appalled, calling Holden a "turncoat" and a "jerk," and dismissed his claim that he would be their voice in a francophone caucus.[48] He was soundly defeated in the next election.

Extraordinary Defections

Party switching is sometimes more than an isolated event. Several parliamentarians can be on the move simultaneously, political parties can dissolve, and some politicians bounce around. In the following pages, we summarize the varied ways that members of Canadian federal and provincial legislatures change their party affiliation while in office, beyond the norms of floor crossing or two-stepping. These unconventional defections predominantly involve white men, highlighting their disposition as well as their sizeable numbers and political ambition, especially in contrast to women and racialized politicians.[49]

Party Hoppers

Today's workers are more willing to change jobs multiple times, referred to by occupational scholars as job hoppers.[50] These individuals reject conventional career paths, like climbing the corporate ladder, and embrace searching for better opportunities without being tied down to one organization. Likewise, some parliamentarians shop around for better prospects, changing parties more than once. Occasionally a party defection is brief, with a switcher exiting a second caucus after only a short stay.[51] A parliamentarian in a failing party can be attracted to a small party gaining traction, only to hop to an established party.[52] An initial switch can make it easier for a peripatetic to change teams again because it becomes a more familiar process.

A prime example of a party hopper was MP Paul Hellyer, an influential defence minister in the 1960s, whose frequent party switching earned him a reputation as an eclectic, anti-establishment contrarian and a staunch individualist.[53] After leaving the Liberals to sit as an Independent, he briefly tried to form a new party before joining the Progressive Conservatives, with whom he was re-elected for one term. Years later, Hellyer failed in bids to be nominated as a Liberal candidate, and went on to establish the Canadian Action Party, finally achieving his leadership ambitions after earlier unsuccessful attempts to lead both the Liberal and PC parties. Unlike the cases that follow, much of Hellyer's party hopping took place after he left Parliament, and it involved not only joining established parties, but also founding new ones.

Party hoppers are usually brash men who reject what they perceive as the obsequiousness inherent in party loyalty. William Sveinson was elected as a Progressive Conservative to the Legislative Assembly of Saskatchewan in 1982. He crossed the floor to sit as a Liberal, was kicked out for being obstructionist and theatrical in the legislature, sat as an Independent, and then joined the Western Canada Concept

Party, becoming its first MLA.[54] One-term Quebec MP Robert Toupin similarly exited two caucuses and did so during a brief parliamentary career in the 1980s.[55] Toupin's political journey began as a Liberal staffer, followed by his election as a Progressive Conservative. After a localized policy dispute, he left to sit as an Independent, later joining the NDP. He then quit that caucus, accusing the party of harbouring communists, and ultimately failed in his re-election bid as an Independent. For Toupin, sitting as an Independent meant freeing himself from the threat of caucus expulsion, which party leaders brandish to enforce obedience.[56]

Party hopping is more viable in smaller places where constituency-focused representatives have strong personal support. Two Pauls stand out as political nomads whose constituents travelled with them. The first is Paul MacEwan, who served from 1970 to 2003 as a Nova Scotia MLA. His long tenure reflected a deep connection to constituents: he drafted letters for them, filled out forms, represented them at appeals, visited them at church, and hand-delivered bereavement cards.[57] He never really fit in with other partisans: in his riding, he would eagerly cheer up a hospitalized constituent, but in Halifax (the provincial capital) he did not socialize with parliamentarians; he spent hours racking up long-distance fees calling constituents from telephones in the legislature's lobby; and was generally excluded from the "club-like atmosphere" of the assembly.[58] In 1980, MacEwan was expelled from the NDP for – like Toupin – alleging that communists were running the party and for denouncing the authoritarianism of the party executive.[59] His exile was the climax of a prolonged process that is foreign in today's leader-centric parties that practise crisis communications: the extra-parliamentary executive spent weeks deliberating the allegations, formulated a series of accusations to be debated and litigated, and ultimately terminated his membership in the party itself (i.e., not just the caucus).[60] The ex-partisan exhibited uncharacteristic humility when he lobbied leadership contestants to readmit him.[61] He was re-elected as an Independent in 1981 and the following year became leader of the upstart Cape Breton Labour Party. In 1984, MacEwan was the only Labour candidate elected, the party folded, and he was re-elected as an Independent. He reportedly considered joining the governing PCs before becoming a Liberal in 1990.[62] MacEwan went on to serve as Speaker, House leader, and party whip. He built an impressive electoral record spanning multiple affiliations, reflecting his immense local popularity. However, his parliamentary career was rather solitary until he accepted the team culture of being part of a larger party caucus.

The second Paul is Newfoundland and Labrador's Paul Lane. As a PC MHA, Lane ensured that he was accessible to constituents even as he was building a reputation as Premier Kathy Dunderdale's attack dog who coordinated hard-hitting partisan swipes at opponents.[63] His frustrations with her leadership in 2014 climaxed during a massive winter power outage which led to him crossing to the Liberals – the catalyst for her resigning four days later. Lane went on to be re-elected as a Liberal, yet he was left out of cabinet, again, when the Liberals formed a government. In 2016, he declared that he would vote with the NDP on a non-binding resolution to protest an austerity budget, which led to the government House leader notifying him by email that the caucus had unanimously voted to expel him. Lane told us that in both parties he was appalled when the cabinet refused to make concessions on immensely unpopular decisions, and that nobody would listen to him: "I don't want to be dismissed and shoved into the back of the room when the people calling the shots are telling you the way it's going to be, and that you're going to support it, and defend it, even though you had no input or opportunity to do things better. All I wanted was an opportunity for meaningful input, not lip service. I wanted to be respected and treated as an equal. But that's not the way the system is set up."[64]

In 2019, Lane was re-elected as an Independent and pulled off the rare feat again in 2021 as one of three ex-partisans who did so in a legislature of just forty members. All of those MHAs were re-elected in electoral districts with fewer than eleven thousand eligible voters, suggesting that in smaller places an incumbent stands a chance against party machines. In Lane's experience, it is wiser to two-step because a floor crosser is accused of opportunism and of betraying voters by joining an arch-enemy.[65] For both Pauls, a relentless interest in constituency service, in forming personal relationships with voters, and in permanent campaigning contributed to their constituents developing bonds of loyalty to them, and the politicians to their constituents. The party was incidental.

Boomerang Partisans

Human resources scholarship refers to former workers who return to an organization as boomerang employees.[66] Most returners do so within two years of departing, having been disappointed in their new surroundings, lured back by a promotion, and/or missing their old colleagues.[67] In the same way, a small number of partisans are elected, join a different party, and return to their original party. This includes the party quitters who form a splinter group. Returning is not easy to do. As Winston Churchill, the British prime minister and a repeat party switcher, allegedly quipped, "Anyone can rat, but it takes a certain amount of ingenuity to re-rat."[68]

Boomerang partisans who leave a caucus and later return often have a personal animus with the leader. A prominent example is H.H. Stevens, the Conservative minister who in 1935 quit over a rift with Prime Minister R.B. Bennett.[69] He hastily formed the Reconstruction Party, was re-elected with that party, and then crossed back to the Conservatives when they were casting for a new leader. Another is Jean Lapierre, one of the Liberals who quit the party after Chrétien bested Martin for the leadership. He briefly sat as an Independent before becoming one of the founding MPs of the Bloc Québécois. After retiring from politics, he returned a decade later to serve in Martin's cabinet. Provincial legislatures also have their share of boomerangers. In British Columbia, a minister was thrown out of caucus for deriding Premier Campbell. When a leadership contest was underway to anoint a successor, the now-Independent MLA conceded that his personal attacks had gone too far, which laid the groundwork for Christy Clark inviting him to return.[70] For these politicians, the departure of a leader they disliked was essential for staging a comeback within their original party.

Some dalliances are short-lived. In 1992, the leader of the Nova Scotia Liberal party expelled a popular MLA for publicly advocating a leadership review. However, two days later, the MLA was readmitted after the leader, facing pressure from party members, agreed to the review.[71] Another quick about-face occurred in New Brunswick in 2006. There, a Progressive Conservative MLA who was passed over in a cabinet shuffle left to sit as an Independent. The assembly elected him as Speaker, but in a fortnight he rejoined the PCs, outraging the opposition.[72] There was also the Quebec MP who deserted the Mulroney PCs over the failure of the Meech Lake Accord, sat for seven months as an Independent, was a member of the Bloc for fifteen weeks, thought the better of it, and rejoined the PC caucus.[73] An intriguing case of boomeranging involved Labrador MHA Lela Evans, who left the PC caucus shortly after the 2021 provincial election, citing the party and its interim leader's lack of support for her efforts to advocate for her constituents.[74] Evans served as an Independent for a few months, joined the New Democrats for two years, and returned to the Tories under a new permanent leader – thereby becoming a two-stepper, a party hopper, a boomerang partisan, and a floor crosser, all before the next general election. Boomeranging can also occur after a member is re-elected as an Independent or with another party.[75]

Some parliamentarians depart caucus under a cloud, only to return humbled after an unwanted stint as an Independent. At times, they are invited back after being acquitted of criminal charges. Examples include the Ontario NDP MPP charged with assault after forcibly taking cigarettes away from his daughter,[76] and the Conservative MP who made a libertarian argument for refusing to take a breathalyser test.[77] In Alberta, an MLA arrested in a prostitution sting while travelling on government business accepted responsibility, repaid the government, and resigned from caucus. Premier Redford decried the affair as "disgusting," but under the next leader the caucus voted to bring the repentant MLA back.[78]

Leaders with a fragile hold on power have compelling reasons to welcome the return of a former colleague. After being cleared of criminal charges, a Nova Scotia MLA expressed gratitude for rejoining the PC caucus in 1992, stating "It's a loyalty that I certainly had no desire to completely sever."[79] In Newfoundland and Labrador, an MHA who left the Liberal caucus after making disparaging remarks about Indigenous Peoples was re-elected as an Independent. A year later, Premier Andrew Furey invited him back in.[80] Both cases involved governing parties whose majority government status was at risk.

The standards for rejoining a caucus reflect evolving public morals, ethics, and attitudes, as well as the party's ideology and, ultimately, the opinion of its leader. In 1996, two Reform Party MPs were suspended for four months for making vile homophobic remarks. Jan Brown, the lone Reformer to vocalize her disgust at the bigotry, was suspended for not being a team player.[81] She spent three days as an Independent-Reform MP before quitting the party to complete her term as an Independent, and failed to be re-elected under the Progressive Conservative banner. Flash forward to 2015. A freshly elected New Democrat in Alberta was suspended when homophobic posts were discovered on her social media accounts.[82] She apologized, was sworn in as an Independent MLA, followed the premier's request to work hard, and rejoined the caucus nearly a year later.[83] In 2024, an Alberta UCP MLA who had been expelled for transphobic remarks was readmitted after a caucus vote seventeen months later. In a news release, she cited personal growth and community involvement, offering a public apology in an online video.[84] For a party leader to consider a miscreant's return to caucus, the leader typically requires a combination of atonement, a sincere public apology, and full compliance with the conditions set by the party leadership for reacceptance.

The path to returning can have pitfalls, particularly if a leadership transition is underway. Consider Jean-Guy Carignan, who was elected to the House of Commons as a Liberal in 2000 without publicly disclosing that he was recently involved in a hit-and-run accident in Quebec. Criminal charges were laid on Election Day. The MP sat as an Independent during his sentence of one year of open custody, including four months of house arrest except to go to work.[85]

His status became a political football. Prime Minister Chrétien readmitted Carignan when the sentence was fulfilled, saying there was a clean slate, but Paul Martin declared that upon becoming leader he would reverse the decision, in line with the opinion of the party's Quebec caucus. Two days after Chrétien's commitment, the PMO announced that the MP had once again left the caucus, which it spun as a consequence for not disclosing that a curfew was still in effect and thus the criminal sentence was incomplete.[86] Return arrangements can clearly unravel: one MLA shared that, amid a media storm, a leadership contender assured him that stepping down from the caucus would be temporary. However, after assuming the leadership, the same individual supported another candidate for the nomination instead.[87]

Leaders who Switch Parties

On occasion, a leader switches parties, normally from a smaller party to a bigger one and potentially resulting in a seat at the cabinet table. Interactions between leaders can set the stage. In the mid-1990s, Gordon Wilson, the leader of the fading Progressive Democratic Alliance (PDA) of British Columbia, agreed to be the NDP premier's chief constitutional advisor. Within a few years the MLA joined the cabinet, disbanding his former party in the process.[88] In 2020, Kris Austin, the leader of the People's Alliance of New Brunswick, was part of an extraordinary multi-party cabinet advisory committee that participated in the provincial government's response to the COVID-19 pandemic.[89] Two years later, he crossed the floor to the Tories, as did his party's only other MLA.[90] Austin was appointed to cabinet six months later.

The leader of a languishing opposition party can crave the stability of a party that can better fulfil their ambition. In New Brunswick, NDP leader Dominic Cardy – who had failed to be elected in two by-elections and a general election – was exasperated with party militants who tussled with him over party dogma as an election loomed. He resigned the leadership, became a political staffer with the Progressive Conservatives, and went on to be a PC MLA and minister.[91] Cardy ended up having a public falling out with the Premier Higgs (figure 6.2) and sat as an Independent, during which time he simultaneously served as interim leader of a new federal party, Canadian Future. In Alberta, Raj Sherman became a PC MLA in 2008 and was appointed parliamentary assistant to the health minister. The caucus voted to suspend him after he pilloried the minister over hospital wait times and for sending an email to MLAs and doctors that criticized the premier's inaction.[92] A year later, Sherman became Liberal leader. In 2012 he was elected as a Liberal, but after the party fell to just a handful of seats, he resigned the leadership and did not seek re-election. Sherman returned to politics as a United Conservative Party candidate in 2023 and tried to become leader of that party; however, the prodigal partisan's comeback was unsuccessful. Even rarer is the leader of the Official Opposition joining the governing party, which we discuss next.

Mass Defections

Just as there can be large-scale resignations, there can also be widespread defections. Occasionally multiple parliamentarians cross the floor at the same time as a symptom of greater upheaval and realignment. In 1994, three British Columbia MLAs left the flagging Social Credit Party to join the neophyte BC Reform Party,[93] and in 2014 two Newfoundland and Labrador MHAs abandoned the fading NDP in favour of the ascending Liberals, both of which reverberated into the next provincial elections.[94] At least two provinces have witnessed romantic partners move in tango. A prominent case occurred in BC when a tryst between a Liberal MLA and Wilson – at the time the Liberal leader – was exposed, which led to them forming the PDA.[95] New Brunswick witnessed another such event when a married couple walked across the aisle together to join the governing Liberals.[96]

A contingent of parliamentarians crossing the floor can signal that a party system is reorganizing. The largest mass defection event in Canadian history occurred in December 2014 when nine Wildrose Party MLAs, including opposition leader Danielle Smith, went over to the Progressive Conservative party, which was enjoying uninterrupted rule over the Alberta government since 1971. Two other Wildrose MLAs had done so a month earlier, resulting in the PCs controlling a colossal seventy-two of eighty-seven seats. To our knowledge, this marks the only time that a leader of the Official Opposition has crossed the aisle to join the governing party in Canada without being part of a coalition government.

The move was prompted by ideological rifts within Wildrose. Entering the party in the Calgary Pride Parade was an initial fork in the road because some caucus members, including Smith, had a positive experience in the Edmonton parade while others were vehemently opposed to participating in LGBTQ2+ events.[97] Constituents of some MLAs who marched in Calgary received nasty robocalls sullying their representative's judgment. The fissure deepened when rank-and-file members voted down an anti-discrimination policy at a party convention. The failure to win some urban by-elections caused the factions to reflect on the party's direction, its election readiness, and its leadership. Some of the moderate conservatives mused about merging with the PCs, which led to a Wildrose MLA speaking with the premier's chief of staff, which broadened into a wider circle of conversations.[98] The two Wildrose MLAs crossed the floor. They voiced frustration that the party's grass roots were driving policy and stated that they believed that they would be more effective with the governing party.[99] Other members of the Wildrose caucus continued to evaluate their options.

Behind the scenes, discussions to merge the parties were underway, including Premier Jim Prentice chatting with some caucus members at a Wildrose MLA's home.[100] Initially, negotiators centred on identifying the most salient public policies, which branched into conversations about a mass exodus. The governing party had the upper hand in setting the terms. The Wildrose party membership would not be consulted, the floor crossers would have to seek the local PC nomination, and no cabinet positions would be tendered. Some Wildrose MLAs who supported exploratory talks about a potential merger told us that they were suddenly pressed to get on board when the leaders settled on floor crossing instead:

> When this idea was formed and presented to us, it was a merger, it wasn't a floor crossing.... We were under the understanding that the best policies of the Wildrose and the best policies of the Progressive Conservatives would be amalgamated and form one policy platform.... It happened too fast. Most of us that were involved in the Wildrose or our caucus members, we were all first-time MLAs. We didn't have the political background or the knowledge and the awareness of someone with a lot of political experience.[101]

> Well, [a merger] was the intent. I think those of us who genuinely felt that, and I know that I was one of them, this was us literally laying down the partisan sword and doing what we thought was best for the province. It was deeply impactful, personally on the back end of that, for the narrative to be so very different and so very direct in terms of looking at us as traitors and whatnot to the cause and destroyers of democracy.[102]

Within a couple of weeks, the leaders announced the mass switch. The premier framed the PC party as having a broad tent that could accommodate diverse conservative voices,[103] and the switchers cited a lack of perks as evidence that they had set their personal ambitions aside for the good of conservatism and the province.[104] No one forecasted the magnitude of the public wrath or its lasting impact on the 2015 general election. Within a year of the mass defection, the PC party's hegemony was over, thanks largely to vote-splitting with the Wildrose rump. The

Alberta NDP formed its first government, some of the floor crossers did not seek re-election, and the rest were defeated. Smith did not even win the PC nomination in her own riding. Despite the backlash, the floor crossers ultimately achieved their initial goal: by 2017, the two conservative parties merged to form the United Conservative Party. This paved the way for a remarkable comeback when Smith returned to politics, becoming UCP premier in 2022.

There are also mass defections that fail to launch. A former parliamentarian told us that when her party was floundering, she received the support of several caucus colleagues to approach another opposition party about brokering a mass defection.[105] Collectively they would have enough members to form the Official Opposition. However, her party lost a by-election and lost momentum. The overture failed without attracting any notice.

Party Rebranding and Mergers

To prevent a political party from becoming stagnant, leaders can reinvigorate the party's brand. New leaders pursue fresh slates of candidates, change up the front benches, adopt new policies and slogans, and tinker with the party's identity. These changes can be ephemeral, as when the Manitoba New Democrats revised their public name to "Today's NDP,"[106] or peskier, as when the Alberta New Democrats required candidates to drop the "P" in the acronym (to become the NDs) and adopted the colour purple in lieu of orange.[107] More ambitious rebranding that formally changes the party's name, its constitution, or ideological position is both aspirational and risky. A brand makeover can set off party dealignment and realignment as parliamentarians and electors evaluate how the revised entity aligns with their political values.[108] The BC Liberals, which had been in power consecutively from 2001 to 2017, sought to distance themselves from their increasingly unpopular federal namesake by adopting the name BC United in 2023. The rebranding was a colossal flop. Voter confusion contributed to lower public support, efforts to merge with the BC Conservative party failed, multiple MLAs left for the Conservatives, and donors withdrew funding.[109] As mentioned, just sixteen months after changing the name of this once-mighty party, the BC United leader suspended the party's election campaign and set about negotiating its incumbents running as Conservatives. A new splinter party, CentreBC, emerged from the wreckage.

Upheaval is unavoidable when two political parties merge in a bid to improve their electoral prospects.[110] In the corporate sector, when organizations merge there is an immediate exodus of senior executives, with others leaving in the ensuing years.[111] A party merger similarly brings along a mass of team players and gradually sheds people who no longer fit, through expulsion, desertion, and defection.[112] Conversely, some former supporters return, sometimes with positive results, as with Danielle Smith. One successful merger of political parties occurred in Quebec in 2012 when the Action démocratique du Québec folded into the emerging Coalition Avenir Québec. The party's MNAs joined the CAQ, which attracted several other MNAs, including some party leavers and party switchers. In 2018, the CAQ formed government, shattering Quebec's traditional party system in the process.[113] Alternatively, there can be a marriage of relative equals when two parties fuse under a new name, as occurred with the creation of the Conservative Party of Canada some years before.

The formation of the Conservative Party is a pivotal case of party loyalties being tested. The 1990s saw the Progressive Conservative and Reform parties compete for a narrow voter pool, driven by a growing desire to "unite the right" and offer a single conservative alternative to the Liberal dominance that had emerged. Many Reformers had flexible loyalties given that their party had a short history and it was a champion of constituency populism over party supremacy. Conversely, the PC Party's roots dated to the nineteenth century, it had formed many federal and provincial governments, and it was embedded in its supporters' identity. When overtures to merge went nowhere, Reformers supported the rebranding of their party into the Canadian Alliance in 2000. Driven by a shared desire to put the Liberals out of office, most MPs on both sides went along in 2003 when their leaders announced plans to merge the parties.[114] A small number felt that the extinction of their party meant they now had a choice to make.

Some ideological orphans found refuge in the more centrist Liberal Party, including PC MP Scott Brison and Alliance MP Keith Martin. Both had failed in past leadership bids, and neither was prepared to challenge Stephen Harper, who was the front-runner, to lead the new entity. For Brison, thoughts of leaving crystalized after Harper promised him a front-bench role while asserting that courting the religious right would be essential for the new party to form a government.[115] Feelings of political homelessness led to chats with a senior Liberal staffer and a conversation with Liberal leader Paul Martin who was days away from being appointed prime minister. At a news conference announcing that he was crossing the floor, Brison stated that the party he had identified with throughout his life no longer existed,[116] and Martin declared his intention to seek guidance from his new recruit on how to attract other progressives who were concerned about the Conservative Party's stance on social issues.[117] The following month, Keith Martin, originally elected with Reform, acted on that shared concern after reflecting on Harper's plans for the direction of the new party.[118] He felt that the rightward turn on social issues ran counter to his personal values as a physician, yet he was a strong believer that constituents should have the final say about which party a parliamentarian sits with. The back-bencher gave Harper and the whip a heads-up before a press confer-ence to announce his intent to sit as an Independent for the remainder of the Parliament, which led to pleas from colleagues not to go.[119] Both men were re-elected as Liberals in 2004 and in subsequent federal elec-tions. As these examples illustrate, party rebranding and mergers have a ripple effect on parliamentary careers. So does forming a new party, discussed next.

New Parties and Party Entrepreneurs

Creating a new political party is a natural move when a parliamen-tarian has strong views with no outlet.[120] Audacious egocentrics take the initiative to establish and lead a party, craft policy, fundraise, and recruit election candidates. It is a daunting undertaking. The single member plurality (SMP) electoral system can pose an immense obsta-cle to getting anyone elected, and the difficulty of persuading donors to contribute can be so overwhelming that a party entrepreneur may question the wisdom of their venture.[121] Typically, new party ventures sputter unless they are backed by parliamentarians from at least two different established parties.

Lucien Bouchard – the Benedict Arnold of Canadian politics – was arguably the most successful party entrepreneur of his generation. In May 1990, the proposed Meech Lake constitutional accord was faltering, and with it the enshrinement of Quebec as a distinct society. A trickle of MPs, including some who gave up salary for being a minister or parliamentary secretary, most prominently Bouchard, quit the Progres-sive Conservatives to sit as Independents when the Mulroney govern-ment contemplated recommendations to dilute the agreement. Within days of the accord's failure that June, three PC MPs and a Liberal joined Bouchard's splinter group.[122] They were driven by principles concern-ing Quebec's place in Canada, rather than by animosity towards the prime minister, as one of them, Louis Plamondon, explained to us: "I wasn't arguing with the boss. On the contrary, it pained me to leave Mr. Mulroney because he had worked very hard to try to reconcile Quebec and Canada and by leaving I knew that it would harm Mr. Mulroney and help Mr. Chrétien who was the Meech Lake murderer....

[But] I was incapable of staying there because I no longer believed that reconciliation with Quebec was possible.... So, it was a question of principle.... It was quite simply that I would not have been able to swallow snakes."[123] Another was attracted to the new venture because as a member of the governing party's caucus he was "muzzled" from voicing his opposition to the government's plans.[124] The coalition of Quebec nationalists set the stage for constituting the Bloc Québécois in 1991. Over the years, the party has endured its share of leavers and switchers, including over disagreement about holding a third referendum,[125] divergence on secession negotiations[126] and dealignment resulting from the waning federalist-separatist axis.[127] Bouchard himself left, to become Parti Québécois premier.

Another notable instance of parliamentarians walking away from multiple parties to establish a new one occurred in 1997 when four Liberal MLAs and four Progressive Conservative MLAs joined forces under the Saskatchewan Party banner, creating a unified alternative to the governing New Democrats. As one of them put it, they put their "political necks on the line" to do so.[128] The SaskParty spent a decade as the Official Opposition before repositioning itself closer to the political centre, a strategic move that contributed to it forming government and achieving repeated re-election victories. More commonly, new parties receive a temporary boost when a sitting parliamentarian becomes their first recruit through floor crossing or two-stepping, as occurred with the Alberta Alliance Party in 2004 and the Freedom Conservative Party of Alberta in 2018, respectively. Legacy parties that have floundered can restore their relevance in this way, as seen with the BC Conservatives in 2023, who attracted MLA John Rustad and went on to become the official opposition.

Most party entrepreneurs fail miserably at the ballot box, even in their own seat. In the early 1980s, former Saskatchewan PC leader Dick Collver left to form the Unionist Party, while in Manitoba several NDP MLAs resurrected the Progressive Party, but the new ventures failed to catch on. In 2014, Jean-François Larose was one of two Quebec MPs who left their parties to form Forces et Démocratie (Strength in Democracy). "Leaving a political party is a nasty job. It exhausted me. I was already exhausted, and it tired me out even more," he told the Samara Centre.[129] He obtained just 135 votes (0.2 per cent of the vote) under the new party's banner in the ensuing election.

New parties can be a revenge mechanism or a vanity vehicle for one or more isolated yet ambitious politicians. A notable leaver-turned-entrepreneur is Jean-Martin Aussant. The hardline separatist called out Premier Marois for not actively promoting separatism, and in 2011 he was one of four Parti Québécois MNAs to leave when she did not consult the caucus about a commitment to construct a new amphitheatre in Quebec City.[130] Initially, he sat as an Independent, then registered Option Nationale, which he led. The party appealed to disappointed *péquistes* and younger voters, and attracted considerable media attention, including for its use of social media in the 2012 Quebec election campaign.[131] Nevertheless, none of Option Nationale's candidates were elected. Aussant returned years later to his former party but was unable to get elected. A more successful party entrepreneur is Maxime Bernier, who narrowly lost the 2017 Conservative Party leadership race, got in public skirmishes by making provocative remarks, and left the party before he was kicked out. He filled an ideological gap on the political right by founding the People's Party of Canada, but was not re-elected. In the 2021 federal election, the party obtained twice as many votes as the Green Party, although it failed to win any seats. Its surge during the campaign, driven by populists and libertarians angered by pandemic lockdowns, faded by 2025, when it won less than 1 per cent of the vote.

In Canada, it is rare for women parliamentarians to take the lead in founding political parties. In 1993, BC MLA Judi Tyabji co-founded the Progressive Democratic Alliance, but did not become its leader.[132] Martine Ouellet, a former Parti Québécois MLA and Bloc Québécois leader, returned to provincial politics to create Climat Québec. She and her party received less than 1 per cent of the vote in the 2022 Quebec election. Another example is Nadine Wilson, who left the SaskParty caucus in 2021 following a dispute over her COVID-19 vaccine status and subsequently founded the Saskatchewan United Party.[133] She later passed the leadership to a man, and none of the party's candidates were elected in the ensuing provincial election. To our knowledge, no women who have left a national party's caucus have gone on to establish a federal political party.[134]

We note that attempting to ignite a political movement can be viewed as an alternative to establishing a new political party. In 2019, MNA Catherine Fournier – who, at just twenty-four years old, became the youngest woman ever elected to the Quebec legislature – resigned from the Parti Québécois caucus. She condemned the partisanship fracturing the separatist movement, declared the PQ a spent force, and advocated for citizen assemblies as a means to rally public support for Quebec sovereignty. Her aspirations to devise a political coalition were articulated in a manifesto that rejected the traditional role of political parties and called on separatists to advance their cause within a non-partisan society.[135] However, she resigned her seat upon becoming Longueil's mayor, and the Projet Ambition Québec movement lost momentum.

Multilevel Party Switchers

Our research has focused on parliamentarians' loyalties within one legislature and political arena. However, we must also acknowledge the dynamics of politicians switching between federal and provincial parties. Such moves offer distinct advantages, such as the ability to gauge public and media reactions to a potential move through a trial balloon, whereas crossing the floor in a legislative assembly requires secrecy to control the narrative (chapter 8).[136] We exclude these cross-jurisdictional cases from our party defector database because the switch occurs outside the context of the same legislature. Nevertheless, multilevel party switching is a sufficiently common occurrence in Canada that it warrants comment.

Drifting between affiliated parties leverages many advantages when partisans treat one another as part of the same team or political family. In Quebec, switching between the Parti Québécois and the Bloc Québécois – such as Yves-François Blanchet, who transitioned from MNA to Bloc leader, or Bouchard, who moved from Bloc leader to PQ premier – is often seen as a demonstration of continued loyalty. A comparable situation arises when a federal party lacks an official provincial counterpart, as is the case in Saskatchewan, where the SaskParty is the ideological counterpart of the federal Conservatives. In contrast, most would agree that Ujjal Dosanjh and Bob Rae, the former NDP premiers of British Columbia and Ontario, respectively, disavowed the New Democrats when they became Liberal MPs.

Multilevel switches can attract considerable attention. One notable instance involved Ontario Liberal operatives allegedly offering inducements to an NDP MP to persuade him to run as a Liberal in a 2015 provincial by-election, leading to a protracted legal saga.[137] Jean Charest stands out as one of Canada's most prominent multilevel switchers. Initially elected as a Progressive Conservative MP, he served in the Mulroney cabinet and became the party's leader following its devastating defeat in the 1993 federal election. Five years later, Charest transitioned to provincial politics, taking the helm of the Quebec Liberal Party and serving as premier for nearly a decade. He returned to public life in 2022 by placing second in the federal Conservative Party's leadership race. These different parties were connected: at the time, Quebec federalists united under the provincial Liberal banner, and the federal Conservatives are an evolution of the defunct PC Party. In this light, Charest is less of a party hopper than a political chameleon who was ideologically consistent despite shifting party colours. In his experience, parliamentarians who leave parties feel excluded and seek greater opportunities to contribute elsewhere. He told us that "caucus politics are tribal. It's tribal in the noble sense of the word. In politics, we're part of a tribe. Abandoning the tribe, separating from it, denouncing it is an important event ... someone who leaves is usually not someone who holds a position of great responsibility in the caucus. It's very often a person who at the outset feels sidelined, isolated ... [and] ends up concluding that their future lies elsewhere."[138] Conversely, with low-profile switchers there is barely any record of a changed multilevel party allegiance. For example, in 2016 the media reported that former NDP MP Rathika Sitsabaiesan wanted to be a candidate with the Ontario Liberal Party, however little was published about her failing to win the nomination.[139]

Intra-party movement is more complicated when there is interparty strife. In 2005, MHA Fabian Manning was expelled from the Newfoundland and Labrador PC caucus over a policy dispute, and he was elected as a Conservative MP the following year.[140] Although the Conservative Party lacks formal ties to provincial parties, Manning faced intense criticism and suffered an electoral setback when his former leader, Progressive Conservative Premier Danny Williams, launched an "anything but Conservative" campaign against the federal party's candidates in the 2008 federal election. Other times, a politician can bounce around ideologically similar political parties. For example, soon after being defeated in his bid to be re-elected as a Conservative MP, in 2016 Steven Fletcher was elected as a Progressive Conservative MLA in Manitoba, was expelled from the caucus, sat as an Independent, became leader of the libertarian and short-lived Manitoba Party, and was unsuccessful as a People's Party candidate in the 2019 federal election.

Summary

This chapter has established that there are many possible pathways when a parliamentarian's party loyalty is severed. Most party switchers are two-steppers who become an Independent before joining a different party, or else they cross the floor directly to another caucus. A small number follow a more complicated route as they hop from one party to another and another, or they boomerang back to their original party. There are also entrepreneurs who leave their party and create another one, and despondent leaders who switch parties. Occasional bouts of mass defections and parties merging result in political realignment. In sum, a variety of party switching scenarios can both result from and have far-reaching consequences for party system dynamics, with most defections involving an intense journey to get to the other side. In the next chapter, we discuss the interconnected personal, ideological, and strategic factors that influence these decisions by examining the behind-the-scenes aspects of changing party loyalties.

8 Switching Sides

Tensions grew between Stephen Harper and Belinda Stronach after he prevailed in the Conservative Party of Canada's 2004 leadership race. A series of party-inflicted humiliations accumulated for the runner-up and former corporate CEO: she was denied a prominent role at a party convention; she was warned at a regional caucus meeting to fall in line with the leader; her speaking time in the national caucus meeting was clipped; and she was excluded from TV ads that featured star MPs.[1] Harper and Stronach had some serious disagreements, including a fiery exchange in his office after she went off-message in a news story. "If I wanted to knife you in the back, I could've done that hundreds of times, but I want to remain a team player," Stronach reportedly told her former opponent.[2] After that blow-up, Harper suspected that she might leave the caucus, and quietly verified that her electoral district association remained loyal to the party and that money in its bank accounts had not been moved.[3] With a whipped vote against the 2005 budget looming, Stronach abandoned the Conservative Party to become a Liberal cabinet minister, a treacherous action for such a high-profile partisan whose vote stood to make the difference between the Liberal minority government falling or carrying on.

Floor crossers like Belinda Stronach, two-steppers, party hoppers, and others have many intersecting reasons for leaving one party for another. In this chapter, we present the anatomy of trading party loyalties. We delve into the motivations and dynamics behind party departures and switches, shedding light on the intricate steps involved in back-room negotiations. Why do politicians abandon one party for another? What is unseen in the lead-up to a politician agreeing to change sides? In broad strokes, we show that the motivations behind party switching involve frustrations with party leadership stemming from ideological disagreements over policy direction, a drive for power, and/or electoral ambitions.

Motivations for Leaving and Changing Parties

Why do politicians cross the floor? They want more than to get to the other side. Leaving one caucus for another sets off conversation about a parliamentarian's motives, ranging from a principled act to speculation about a secret deal. As mentioned in chapter 1, the policy/office/votes model suggests that politicians are motivated by pursuing specific courses of action (policy), acquiring and maintaining power (office), or seeking electoral support (votes).[4] This rational choice approach supposes that they are self-interested actors who strive to maximize the influence, benefits, and security of being a legislator.[5] This includes their progressive ambition to improve their political career. As well, politicians act in non-rational and non-ideological ways: they are driven by ego, they get into personality conflicts, they run afoul of party conventions of behaviour – all of which can lead to a caucus exit. At a point in time, some of them see little difference between two parties, which increases the importance of other considerations including leadership.[6] Spite is a motive, such as when a retiring parliamentarian sticks it to a leader by switching parties without any intent of seeking re-election.[7] Many insist that their primary loyalty is to constituents. Socialization also plays a role: a switcher might have historical connections to the welcoming party or its leader, such as family or business connections, volunteering as a youth, or having been a party worker.[8] Meanwhile, the pursuit of good policy can be connected to re-election, or vice versa. This said, the policy/office/votes model is useful for understanding how and why parliamentarians reconsider their party affiliation, which in Canada is interconnected with the party leader's role in all three.

In our party defector database, we categorized each of the 349 party departures (those who left and those who switched) from 1980 to 2021 as being motivated by policy, office, or vote-seeking, as well as public-oriented, value-driven, gross misconduct, and a general "other" category. These are not mutually exclusive categories: each departure event could be coded as having more than one motive. To inform our coding, we drew on all available information, including the reported perspective of the leaver, their colleagues, leaders, and outside observers, with particular emphasis on how parliamentarians themselves framed the move. For expulsions, we considered the party leadership's intentions along similar lines, such as preventing the loss of popularity or seats, removing a minister from cabinet and caucus, or resolving a policy dispute. However, the true motives may be elusive, perhaps even to the politicians themselves, some of whom are no longer living.

The conventional vote-, office-, policy-seeking model explains some of these drivers. Figure 8.1 depicts the breakdown of those three specific

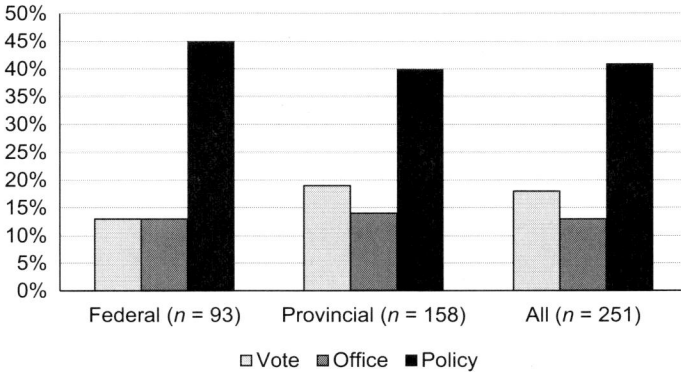

Figure 8.1. Policy, Office, and Vote-Based Motivations for Caucus Exits, 1980–2021

Source: Authors' dataset.

types of motivations in Canada during our study period. We found that just over 40 per cent of party leavers were driven by policy differences, while ambitions for higher office were a factor in about 13 per cent of caucus exits, and vote-seeking motivations played a role in about 18 per cent of departures. The distribution was similar at the federal and provincial levels. Among these three traditional explanations for parliamentarian behaviour found in the literature, policy-seeking was the dominant frame in every jurisdiction, suggesting most party departures by Canadian parliamentarians are less out of career ambition and more out of personal conviction over issues.

However, many caucus departures did not entail any of the policy/office/votes motivations. In Canada, disagreements with leadership and personal reasons are often involved in politicians' calculations, and we found that they are more common than conflicts over policy, office, or votes. According to our analysis, over two-thirds of party departures involved a broader form of values conflict between parliamentarians and their leaders. While other analyses may have lumped deeper ideological differences of opinion between parliamentarians and leaders under the category of policy-seeking behaviour, our narrower coding approach found that most departures were not driven by disputes over a specific policy issue, such as a party's position on health care funding or how to address climate change. Rather, the conflict surrounded much broader philosophical principles about the general orientation of the party or competing visions about the definition of the public good.

More parliamentarians left their caucus not because they lost an internal policy debate, but because they fundamentally disagreed with the values espoused by the party and its leadership. The vote-, office-, and policy-seeking model also fails to account for the parliamentarians who resigned or were expelled for a host of personal transgressions or scandals (chapter 6). All of this invites a re-thinking of how political scientists measure the motivations of partisan actors.

Throughout the book we discuss the many tensions between leaders and party values that lead to caucus departures. Turning our attention to the policy/office/votes model, of those three specific motives it is unsurprising that Canadian parliamentarians place significant importance on party policy, as for many it was the driving force behind their decision to seek elected office with a party.[9] Consequently, it is also a reason that many leave. Those elected to the House of Commons who entered politics hoping to influence policy are roughly twice as likely to voluntarily exit the job (i.e., resign before the next election or not seek re-election) than are partisans who were socialized into a political party or those who are motivated to help constituents.[10] As noted, policy discord was a primary motivation behind a caucus departure in just over one-third of the cases that we examined.

Convincing leaders and others about a policy direction is a core responsibility of a legislator. So is making a "policy sacrifice," whereby members of a parliamentary caucus feel compelled to back a policy that greatly differs from their public commitments or personal beliefs.[11] Ideological dissonance flares up when their opinions are shirked by internal processes, when a new leader introduces a novel agenda, or when there is profound disagreement on an issue. People with specialized expertise or interests can be especially zealous about certain policies, such as a francophone concerned about cuts to French-language services[12] or a physician who is disillusioned with the state of the health care system.[13] Other policy disagreements are grounded in personal beliefs, such as the minister who left the party over the government's plan to transfer civil servants to rural areas.[14] As well, a parliamentarian may cite a policy disagreement as the reason for switching affiliations, even though it is widely suspected that ambitions for office and votes are the real driving factors.[15]

A governing party can use policy to lure an opponent to their side and, equally, a parliamentarian can bargain their party affiliation to extract a policy commitment from the government. In 1979, Peter Ittinuar was elected as an NDP MP for Nunatsiaq, becoming Canada's first Inuk MP. During intergovernmental negotiations to reform the Canadian constitution, he garnered national attention by insisting that Indigenous rights be enshrined.[16] He mingled with senior Liberals on parliamentary trips and became convinced that he would make more progress advocating for Indigenous self-government as a member of the governing party.[17] In 1982, Ittinuar crossed to the Liberals moments after the minister of Indian and northern affairs announced a forum that would lead to the creation of Nunavut. Looking back, Ittinuar is convinced that the Nunavut Constitutional Forum happened only because he switched parties.[18]

Achieving a policy goal can convince some party switchers that they made the right move. For others, policy is not enough, especially if they are disillusioned with the political system. The creation of a constitutional forum pulled Ittinuar towards the Liberals, but he did not feel at home in the party or, for that matter, in Ottawa. The switching brought isolation and "a very hot fire of ambition and backstabbing" after he argued with Liberals who demanded that he be a team player and who took issue with his newsletter informing constituents that the switch was "an experiment."[19] Wearing a helmet adorned with "Eskimo" while riding a motorcycle around Ottawa added to his maverick image.[20] Security guards sometimes mistook him for a tourist,[21] and his Indigeneity made him feel like a political outsider in an adversarial system. At the time, Ittinuar said, "sometimes I feel like an intruder.... I feel as if I'm criticizing everyone in this place because they're all the same colour.... It would be lovely to have another Eskimo MP up here whom I could confide in and who would also understand the psychological hardship of being alone up here ethnically."[22] That solitude and lack of party attachment led to more switching. Convinced that the Liberals would not support his nomination because he was dealing with criminal charges regarding his travel expenses, Ittinuar sought re-election as an Independent, but was unsuccessful.[23] He was acquitted. In 1993, the NDP leader refused to accept his nomination by the local riding association,[24] and in 2008 his legal troubles again became topical when he was a Green candidate.[25] Thus, policy drove this party hopper's first foray into changing his party identity, and repeat switching was made easier by the absence of strong bonds to the party system itself. Ittinuar believes that Canadian partisans fail to understand that the loyalty of some Indigenous Peoples is foremost to their homeland.[26]

As we saw with Sarah Jama, activists who enter party politics to change public policy learn that the political culture demands that they abide by norms of teamwork and loyalty. Backbenchers usually have more leeway in opposition than in the governing party to advocate for policy change because less is at stake if an opposition member speaks out and votes independently on select issues.[27] Hinrich Bitter-Suermann is an example. A liver transplant surgeon, he became incensed by the Nova Scotia Liberal government's spending cuts in health care. He was inspired by PC opposition leader John Hamm, also a physician, to run as a candidate in the 1998 provincial election on a platform of health care advocacy. As a rookie Tory MLA, he received permission to vote against the Liberal minority government's budget to express displeasure with its health care management, even though all other PC MLAs were required to support it to prevent a snap election.[28] Soon afterwards, Bitter-Suermann quit the party out of disillusionment that it was propping up a Liberal government that he was determined to bring down. After a short stint as an Independent, he joined the New Democratic Party because of shared values, the appeal of getting more speaking time in the legislature, and to avoid the futility of being unaffiliated in an election campaign.[29] His multiple bids for re-election were unsuccessful, as was his candidacy to become NDP leader. Bitter-Suermann is among a small number of Canadian parliamentarians to transition from one end of the party spectrum to the other. This was possible due to his lack of partisan roots, the ideological similarities within the party system, and his shared concern with both opposition parties that the government was mismanaging the health care system.

Yet even when politicians express concern about public policy and their chances of re-election, some of them are chiefly focused on securing resources and advancing their rank. The ambition that fuels a political ego can be formidable, a senior staffer explained to us. "In general, when a floor crossing is explained to the public, there is always some sort of narrative," we were told. "Something like, 'My old party didn't represent my values, my new party does, I wasn't comfortable with how things were going with my former crew.' But in my experience the real reason is ambition, and that would feed cynicism. People don't care about whether the leader wasn't giving you enough space to make a meaningful contribution, or that staff in the leader's office made it apparent that you would never be appointed to cabinet."[30]

Progressive ambition is indeed a key driver behind certain Canadian parliamentarians abandoning loyalty to their party. As mentioned, about 13 per cent of those who changed parties did so with a desire to be part of a government and access the benefits of office, notably public goods such as patronage appointments that reward friends and allies, and pork-barrel politics that allocate funds to local projects in their electoral district or government contracts to supporters. Some high-flyers on the opposition benches are wary of being a rising star without a clear path forward,[31] and some seek the recognition that comes with a powerful position in government, particularly that of a cabinet minister.[32] We suspect that far more parliamentarians leave for office reasons than the public record suggests. Few are as forthcoming as the Manitoba MLA who, upon resigning from the NDP caucus in 1982 after being passed over for cabinet, stated to journalists, "I've known for months that if I was not offered a post in cabinet, I would resign."[33]

Isolating forms of ambition is difficult because party switchers do not want to admit to their opportunism. In our interviews, a former leader told us that dissatisfied partisans sometimes want to explore what status position they might receive and are no longer interested when the conversation turns to policy.[34] One party stalwart was adamant that pension status and proximity to retirement are key factors in determining party loyalty,[35] and indeed Canadian MPs on the cusp of qualifying for a defined benefit pension are 11 per cent more likely to seek re-election than their counterparts.[36] As well, proximity to power is tantalizing. Party switchers who leave an opposition caucus often rationalize to journalists that being close to the government will enable them to do more for their constituents:

> This way I will be able to sit at the table where the decisions will be made. I'll be able to have input into the policy. I'll be able to say from the inside what I've been saying from the outside.[37]

> To be in a government is a crucial instrument to making change.[38]

> [In opposition] I was doing a lot of shouting and bawling through the media, but I was getting little attention.[39]

> For my constituents, I think I can do the best from the inside making the decisions around the table with the governing party.[40]

Claims of doing more for constituents as a member of the governing party must be placed in proper context alongside complaints from many government-side backbenchers about their lack of agency.[41] Nevertheless, it is instructive that nearly all cases of party switching concern backbenchers; ministers simply do not resign from cabinet to join an opposition caucus. Between 1980 and 2021, one-fifth of parliamentarians who left their party caucus transitioned to a governing party. The remainder either carried on as Independents (about two-thirds) or aligned with an opposition party (one in nine). Among all leavers, a majority vacated a party on the opposition benches, while under half defected from a governing party.

A member of the opposition who is keen to secure a prominent position can time a switch for maximum leverage. The crass opportunism of joining the governing party when a geographic or other vacancy arises in cabinet that needs to be filled can pay off,[42] as can switching sides when a minority government needs support for its legislative agenda, or when the party affiliation of the Speaker can determine who forms government. In this sense, cabinet positions are not the only prize worth

switching parties for. In the 1979 New Brunswick election, the governing PCs won two more seats than the opposition Liberals. To solidify
a majority, the premier visited the home of a former Liberal leadership
contestant to persuade the MLA to serve as Speaker, to which the MLA
agreed.[43] Premier Romanow did the same when convincing a Liberal
member to serve as Speaker during his stint at the helm of Saskatchewan's coalition government. As well, in 2017 the BC NDP leader's ability to convince a Liberal MLA to become Speaker dealt a fatal blow to
the Liberals' attempt to hold on to government.[44] In all three cases, the
Speaker was expelled from or left their party's caucus.

Moving from one opposition party to another is attractive if it transforms a disregarded, obscure, or exiled politician into a power broker.
Being elevated to party leader can entice some to switch, as with the
interim leader of the withering BC Social Credit Party leaving to lead
the upstart provincial Reform Party, although he eventually left to sit
as an Independent.[45] A parliamentarian can be celebrated for making
political history by becoming a party's first elected official, the first in
a geographic region, or its first in decades. A transgressor from another
party can be treated as a saviour by a party desperate to have its first
elected representative, which accords the party legitimacy and profile,
as well as access to special advantages such as the leaders' debates in the
next election.[46] A backbencher can play kingmaker if the switch enables
a caucus to reach the threshold for official party status in the legislature,
rendering it eligible for a greater role in legislative debate and additional resources.[47] Other times, a politician in a small party can be motivated to join a larger party to help prevent another party from forming
government,[48] or their experience in a dishevelled opposition can be so
awful that joining a fledgling party is preferred.[49] As well, an ambitious
politician can want to get out of the shadow of a powerful regional colleague who is blocking their ascent into an influential role.

For some politicians, vote-getting is essential for their career survival
and to realize their ambitions. Those who are anxious about getting re-
elected are particularly attracted to vote-seeking activities, and those
focused on influencing policy and holding a government office need
to belong to a team that maximizes votes and wins the most seats.[50]
Partisans keep a close eye on public opinion polls and may deduce that
going from one caucus to another in search of votes is a fool's errand.
While their constituents might enjoy being represented by someone
who occasionally kicks off against the party, far fewer approve of a
party switcher.[51] Many parliamentarians are also aware of the electoral risks of migrating to another caucus: party incumbents enjoy a
sizeable vote advantage over their opponents,[52] and, according to our
data, Canadian parliamentarians who switch parties have less than a

50 per cent chance of being re-elected, even though this figure includes many who switched to improve their electoral prospects.[53]

Earlier, we observed that fewer than one-fifth of party defectors were primarily motivated by electoral considerations when deciding to join a new caucus. That said, vote maximizers who change parties may obscure that their decision was an act of electoral self-preservation. Instead, they offer dignified explanations, such as that they wanted to avoid splitting the federalist vote that would put a separatist in office,[54] or that they disagreed with the leader about government austerity.[55] Jenica Atwin's stated reasons for crossing the floor – disagreements over policy, a desire for government resources, incompatibility with the party leader, and experiencing solitude in a small party – are valid and evoke some sympathy. In contrast, if she had publicly cited that her prospects of re-election with the Liberal Party were much better than with the Green Party, her motives would be viewed as opportunist, unprincipled, and selfish. News reports documenting instances of parliamentarians forsaking their party loyalty are the most reliable means for cataloging politicians' motives across Canada over the past four decades. However, re-election and ambition for office are likely under-represented as primary motivations in these accounts.

Nevertheless, sometimes it is obvious that getting re-elected is at the forefront of a party switcher's move. A parliamentarian who flipped a seat in another party's stronghold, or whose thin margin of victory seems unsustainable, can openly muse about the electoral ramifications of their party affiliation.[56] Dismal public support and a dour local mood can stir doubts of remaining with an unpopular party, as can constituents urging a switch when a politician interacts with them on the doorsteps.[57] "It really started when people in my own district started approaching me asking questions about whether the party was going anywhere," reflected one party switcher in a 1996 *Maclean's* story.[58] A poor performance in a recent general election or a suite of by-election losses soften confidence in the party. In Nova Scotia, an interim leader toured the province to learn from partisans what went wrong in the last election, which contributed to her decision to switch parties once a permanent leader was in place.[59]

Incumbents who are not renominated and want to carry on are forced to look for alternatives. Conflicting narratives are proffered for changing parties as an election approaches, as with the Bloc Québécois MP who joined the Liberal Party claiming to be inspired by Martin becoming leader, which prompted his former colleagues to allege that his renomination was in peril due to a policy dispute with the local EDA.[60] Every decade or so, some partisans are left out when redistribution causes their electoral district to morph or even vanish, prompting them to scramble.[61] The effects of redistribution were abundant in 1999 when the Ontario legislature shrank by twenty-seven seats, resulting in a mass of incumbents competing against each other. Liberal MPP Annamarie Castrilli lost an intense nomination race in an amalgamated electoral district. Despite the loss, she vowed to work tirelessly to support the party and its candidate, even though senior Liberal officials had backed the victor.[62] Castrilli ultimately set aside her fearmongering about the Tories and their leader when she became the PC nominee in another district just hours before a provincial election was called.[63] During the campaign, protesters called her a turncoat and a hypocrite, and she was not re-elected.[64]

Preparing to Switch Party Loyalties

There are many variables at play when a parliamentarian engages in private negotiations with high-ranking political actors about joining a party's caucus. Game theory outlines the degrees of risk that individuals and groups are willing to entertain; the skill, experience, and ambition of negotiators and participants; and the power advantages and payoffs.[65] Bargaining involves multiple rounds of exchanges, including offers, demands, concessions, and trade-offs. Some politicians exploit their positional advantages; others are cautious, inexperienced negotiators with little bargaining position who make less ambitious proposals. In the United States, emissaries lay the groundwork for a conversation with the leader who offers inducements, notably committee assignments.[66] The entreaties are hidden from public view due to the backlash that would result from exposing such exchanges, particularly when outreach fails or involves inducements.[67] We know little about this in Canada.

Our findings are organized around a four-stage negotiation process for sitting parliamentarians elected with one party who consider joining another party's caucus (i.e., floor crossers and two-steppers). The stages – discussion, bargaining, agreement, and framing – are not necessarily linear or unidirectional. In some cases, a partisan experiences a series of letdowns in their caucus and brokering a secret deal to join another is an extensive undertaking. For others, a move happens quickly after a clash with the leader, inability to support a disagreeable policy, or change brought by party realignment. All voluntary departures, however, begin with a parliamentarian recognizing that they are dissatisfied in a party, combined with their leader perceiving a personnel problem or another leader identifying a political opportunity.

Stage 1: Discussion

As we have established, a voluntary departure from a political party to become an Independent is generally less contentious than being expelled from a caucus. Similarly, two-stepping tends to be less controversial than crossing the floor. Whatever the circumstances, trading party loyalties involves profound self-reflection and information-gathering by a partisan who is unhappy for all sorts of reasons that we have summarized. Ruminations about becoming a member of an opponent's team is gut-wrenching and involves "agonizing soul searching," especially if it means rejecting lifelong attachments to the party they were elected with.[68] Few party switchers describe a speedy decision without hesitation.[69] They need to wrestle with the consequences of a new political identity and be certain that they have exhausted all possibilities to change their circumstances from within. Confronted with the choice of enduring a caucus they feel detached from under a leader they no longer respect, or the isolation of being an Independent, many vexed partisans think about leaving politics entirely.

The first step for a parliamentarian considering a change of party loyalties is to consider ways to resolve their dissatisfaction. Members of other parties are on the lookout to woo someone they consider an asset and, as an election approaches, they can delay calling candidate nominations to keep options open.[70] They pay attention to parliamentarians who seem to be an ideological mismatch in a caucus, such as a fiscal hawk in a left-wing party or a progressive-minded politician in a right-wing party. They monitor ministerial and critic portfolios and seating arrangements in the House. A backbencher who supported a losing leadership candidate[71] or a politician in a swing district are prime targets for recruitment.[72] Likewise, a partisan who openly criticizes a leader or party orthodoxy, or one with a stellar reputation, is highly susceptible to being poached.

Politicians and senior staff who catch wind of rumours of someone potentially being persuaded to join their cause deliberate whether to initiate contact. Strategic conversations unfold about how to capitalize on an opponent's distress, as a former minister told us: "Who should reach out? What should we say? Is there an alignment with our party? Do we want them? Those are the types of conversations. When the House is sitting, you make observations about a pissing match between people. Maybe there's a wedge you can play. Can you use your House strategy to splinter the other group to your advantage? Can that play outside of the House? You need to capitalize on gamesmanship."[73]

Partisans make small talk with a downcast parliamentarian and plant the idea that a different caucus holds the promise of happiness. In the House, they jest that an Independent wearing party colours should join their caucus, or they heckle that someone should cross the floor. In the Saskatchewan legislature, ministers occasionally called upon Buckley Belanger to come over to the government side. "In the Assembly, you get the odd comment from a cabinet minister: 'What are you doing over there, Buckley? You're one of us.' Those little comments are very effective," he told us. "You'd be sitting there within the Liberal caucus, and people would yell across: 'Buckley, come on. Come to your senses. Join us. You're part of us.'"[74] Parliamentarians chat and commiserate with members of other parties at stakeholder events, at committees, on media panels, and while travelling. Leaders of small parties talk with their Independent seatmates. As they build trusting relationships, it is natural to offer a supportive shoulder, allowing their parliamentary colleague to vent. "I noticed you had a bit of a pained expression when you had to speak on this particular issue and that sure seems tough. How's that going for you?" they say.[75]

A chance encounter away from the legislature can set forth discussions. After Hazen Argue placed second for the NDP leadership at its founding convention, he happened upon a Liberal in a barbershop and voiced his frustrations about organized labour, which set the stage for a discussion with a senior Liberal MP about crossing the floor.[76] We were told of another parliamentarian who bumped into a party stalwart at a social event and initiated a phone call a week later to discuss options.[77] Airports have been the scene for travelling to a different party. In Newfoundland and Labrador, a new Liberal leader who came upon a PC MHA in the St. John's airport sparked interest by saying it was too bad that they would be opposing each other,[78] and at the Vancouver airport David Emerson informed the Conservative campaign co-chair of his interest in remaining in cabinet following the Liberals' election defeat, which set in motion an accelerated courtship process.[79]

Overtures can be direct: "You know, we should go for coffee and talk about the future," partisans say.[80] Inviting a parliamentarian to socialize at a pub, a restaurant, or someone's home takes things further. Alternatively, the parliamentarian might be the one to initiate a meeting. In provinces without sharp polarization, it is uncontroversial for politicians in different parties to go for coffee together, especially if they are both in opposition,[81] or for an Independent to show up at a party's Christmas social.[82] The cross-party banter can lead to putting the question to them. For example, a Liberal backbencher who was critical of his own government fielded feelers from a Conservative MP who asked, "Have you considered joining us?" and who suggested that it might be "more comfortable" in the Conservative caucus.[83] Advances also occur the moment that news breaks that someone with similar values has quit a caucus.[84] In addition, senior political staff try to make friends with someone who is discontented. "I couldn't believe that your leader did this. Doesn't your leader recognize that you're an expert in this field and that it's an issue in your riding? God, it must be tough in your caucus now," they say.[85] Mischief like this can stir loyalty doubts. Public pressure is another lever. In Ontario, prominent Liberals released an open letter urging the Ontario Green Party leader to run for leadership of their party, but he was unpersuaded.[86] These dalliances are partly why leaders are touchy about interparty relations, and why the leader's staff and party whip are tasked with shoring up loyalty in their own caucus.

Politicians are impervious to such cross-party chatter until they begin to think that their situation needs to change. Paul Lane's letdown about being compelled to toe the line on an unpopular government bill deepened at a caucus retreat where his concerns were dismissed. Afterwards, he vented to his wife: "I just can't take it anymore. Nothing is going to change; nobody wants to listen. I've got to get out of here, somehow I got to get outta here."[87] Spouses and close family members are a common sounding board, including for negotiators. In Belinda Stronach's case, it was her own staffer who put the question to her by saying, "You've got to be questioning whether you're in the right home."[88] Rarely do politicians internalize everything and act without counsel from people they trust.

Two-way dialogue arises when a parliamentarian is ready to explore alternatives and another party is willing to entertain the move. At some point, the parliamentarian or an agent reaches out to a partisan on the other side, be it a former or current politician, a staffer, or a member of a riding association who offers advice and acts as an intermediary by contacting someone close to the leader. Those who know and trust a high-ranking party stalwart go to them. It was David Peterson, the former Ontario Liberal premier, who informed Prime Minister Martin's chief of staff that Stronach might be persuaded to cross the floor.[89] Equally, a provincial parliamentarian can seek counsel from federal colleagues.[90] Some of the most compelling emissaries are former party switchers with a well of experience about such a rare yet pivotal event.[91] Conversely, if someone is thought to be kicking tires and would not be a big catch, a junior partisan is designated to go on a reconnaissance mission. Interactions with a leader's surrogates involve trust-building and exchanging information. If the conversations go well, a senior staffer will arrange a conversation between the leader and the potential recruit so that they can size each other up.[92] At that point, it is about forming a human, emotional connection with one another. In other cases, the leader of a small party is directly involved from the outset.[93]

Parliamentarians who initiate or entertain conversations about joining a caucus gamble that they can keep the discussions quiet. Political circles are small, and people gossip. If details leak, they are in danger of having a deal annulled or, worse, rejected by both parties. Senior political staff worry when they hear whispers that a caucus member was spotted with someone on the other side and can be proactive to root out a potential traitor. We were told a story about a journalist who shared a rumour of an impending floor crossing with a party's press secretary, who then passed it along to a senior staffer. In response, the leader's staff sprang into action, mobilizing personnel to gather and exchange intelligence. They divvied up making phone calls to caucus members and their staff to pinpoint which MP was about to jump. They operated on the basis that a committed partisan promptly returns a call from the leader's office, whereas it is a warning sign if someone is unreachable. The ensuing conversations seemed innocuous but were in fact surveillance. "Hi there. Just checking in to see how you are doing. I like the committee work you're doing. How are things in your riding?" a staffer would say to someone deemed a flight risk.[94]

Some Independents make a public show of surveying constituents about whether to (re)join a party and, if so, which one.[95] Publicizing that constituents are being consulted via a newsletter inviting feedback or through a public opinion survey raises awareness that the Independent is considering a move, demonstrates an interest in constituents' views, and helps legitimize the eventual announcement. Unlike a member of a caucus, an Independent can negotiate through the media. Someone desperate to join a caucus can go public with their interest,[96] whereas a bigger catch can voice demands for meaningful opportunities to participate in policy-making and to advocate for constituents.[97] The public negotiating can be ignored by a party leader, and the dalliance ends when it becomes clear that a political marriage is not viable.

There are countless failed attempts to broker a party switch. After Chuck Cadman was re-elected as an Independent in 2004, MPs approached him in parliamentary hallways to persuade him to join their caucus, and some enterprising Conservative officials allegedly offered the terminally ill MP a life insurance policy to secure his vote against a budget bill, which he rejected.[98] We were told about an intervention where staff in an opposition party were worried that a back-bencher who was dealing with difficult personal circumstances was in an emotional state and susceptible to crossing the floor.[99] A senior staffer invited the MP to lunch, during which it became clear that the governing party's staff had been cultivating a rapport with the back-bencher and that he was on the verge of accepting an invitation to accompany the prime minister on an international trip. Flattered by the opportunity, he was too politically naive to recognize that accepting would strain relationships within his own party and potentially lead to severing party ties altogether. In the staffer's estimation, it was a case of someone who was naive about being courted and about the boundaries of party loyalty. In another case, a political staffer told us about a meeting with an MLA from an opposing party who vented over a beer, rationalized that switching parties would hurt too many people, and decided not to run again.[100]

Stage 2: Bargaining

Once lines of communication are open, bargaining follows. Some parliamentarians negotiate from a position of strength; others are simply looking for an escape route. Conversations take place privately around kitchen tables and in living rooms, as well as through phone calls, video calls, and office meetings. People in different political camps get to know each other by talking about their philosophical views and their opinions about the direction of the country or their province. Sometimes bargaining goes no further when it becomes axiomatic that a potential recruit is uncommitted, such as if they express qualms with the party's platform or have unrealistic expectations of rewards. The leader's sentries must consider the goodness of fit. "It's one thing to have mavericks elected under your party ticket. It's another to introduce mavericks into your caucus, who weren't elected on your team, and then can be disruptive and/or leave at an inappropriate time, causing the government all kinds of angst," a former chief of staff disclosed to us.[101]

Political staff and party emissaries play a crucial role in negotiations in all but the smallest parties.[102] In large parties, senior staff deal directly with a high-profile recruit whereas with smaller catches they can outsource the conversation to a lower-ranking staffer.[103] At this stage, the leader of a major party and especially one who heads a government is wary of getting involved, and works through intermediaries. "As the leader, you don't touch this yourself. You have other people do it. It's more than deniability: you don't want to embarrass yourself," David Peterson, the former Ontario Liberal premier, told us.[104] Provincial leaders have fewer layers of staff and are so accessible that they might host conversations in the privacy of their home. Everyone must be on the alert that what is said could end up in the public domain and that the negotiations could even be a political trap. A former leader explains: "You have to be careful in negotiations. You can't just be buddy-buddy. You have to be totally professional in dealing with that person, and you can't give them anything that they could use against you afterwards. That person is there for their own reasons.

They are not there to make you feel good."[105] Peterson explained that the forays can feel like a spy swap: "If you're negotiating these sorts of things, you must have the confidence of both sides. Things could go wrong. It's so politically sensitive; if it gets out, it will ruin a whole pile of careers."[106]

The brokers facilitating a potential caucus entry recognize that an Independent or someone who does not have deep roots in a party is far more pliable than a long-standing partisan. They attempt to persuade their recruit by pointing out how many friends await in the new caucus and by stereotyping the other party.[107] Privately, they and the leader are guarded about the person's motives, and they are wary of offering inducements. They want to attract someone who is inspired to join their cause, as opposed to a climber trying to move up the ranks. Some parliamentarians immediately disarm notions that they are seeking an appointment or the promise of one,[108] and lesser-knowns might need only to talk with the whip because there is nothing to negotiate.[109] When a mass switch is on the table, parliamentarians who leave the bargaining to others can be disappointed or unhappy with the result.[110]

At some point, a formal encounter occurs with the leader of the interested party, which might be preceded by a meeting with staff. Only a small group can know. A circle of trust is crucial, as everyone involved is concerned about potential leaks. The leader's office is a common venue, but the leader's home holds greater appeal due to its ability to foster certitude and camaraderie in a private, comfortable environment, away from eavesdroppers and onlookers. Such spaces are ideal for creating a meeting of the minds, as demonstrated when Alberta PC MLA Sandra Jansen met with NDP Premier Rachel Notley – a meeting Jansen described to us as remarkably uplifting:

> So, a meeting was booked for me and the premier. It was supposed to be thirty minutes. I brought my policy binder.... I spent two hours with Rachel, and we went over the entire binder. I just sat there, and what went through my head was: "I want to work for this woman." And after that it became fairly simple. She was intelligent. She was funny. She assured me that her tent is big enough for me. I said to her, "I'm going to consider myself a Progressive Conservative in an NDP caucus." And she said, "That's fine with me. My tent is big enough for you." She was excited, and I was excited, because for the first time somebody was looking at my policy books and paying attention! Which was wonderful. And so that's when I made my decision.[111]

Bargaining continues if the parliamentarian is indecisive or assessing options, if they are keen to discuss policy minutiae, and if they make repeated demands. Persuasion involves the leader's agent(s) emphasizing the upsides, such as working with a likeable leader and opportunities to make a difference; acknowledging the drawbacks, such as betraying relationships, being publicly disparaged, and the impacts on office staff; and discussing intangibles, such as family considerations.[112] Pay raises are usually not on the table because most Canadian legislatures have parliamentarians' salaries fixed in statute. Given that remuneration is affiliation-blind, and not role-blind, politicians who want a pay raise need to negotiate a higher-status position with a stipend.

A welcoming party wants to attract a parliamentarian who does not require an inducement. Astute leaders recognize that militants in their party will be outraged if a turncoat jumps the promotion queue ahead of them, and that negative headlines will accompany the perception that a leader dangled public goods for partisan reasons, which could trigger bad press and perhaps even an ethics or police investigation. In Ontario, criminal charges were filed against a staffer concerning her allusions to a patronage appointment being available should an aspiring nominee agree to step aside, in order to make way for a switcher to be the party's candidate.[113] The case was thrown out, but the reputational damage was considerable.

A principle of no special treatment inoculates everyone from recriminations, and leaves open the potential for the leader to promote a party switcher after demonstrating loyalty as a caucus member, at which point the media furore will have died down and colleagues with progressive ambition are less likely to feel disrespected. Consequently, leaders and their agents typically only allude to a plum appointment someday and use vague turns of phrase that could be interpreted as an offer, though they did not make one. They say, "Come be a member of our caucus, and over time if it works out you might be able to move up,"[114] or that the parliamentarian can "look forward to achieving a responsible position."[115] Likewise, senior political staff are cautious about offering rewards. "There's not a lot of truth about promising inducements. There can be wink-wink, nudge-nudge stuff," a senior staffer told us.[116] Another staffer explained the wording nuances that emphasize aspiration: "It isn't, 'If you cross the floor, I will make you a cabinet minister.' It is: 'Would you like to be a cabinet minister?'"[117]

To really test a recruit's commitment to the team, a leader can inform a switcher that it will be up to them to win the local nomination with their new party and/or that it will be a caucus decision to invite the member into their ranks. Internal consultations are paramount if a leader is concerned that accepting someone who campaigned against the party and was a thorn in its side will wreck group harmony.

Indeed, existing members of the caucus can threaten to quit if they hear rumours about a former adversary potentially joining their side.[118] The switcher's motives make a difference: partisans may be more open to accepting an opponent who seeks to join the team for ideological or policy reasons than one motivated by revenge against a spurned leader or a desire to secure a higher status.[119]

To close the deal, staff hone in on providing emotional support with questions such as, "How do you feel about this?" and "How can I make you feel better about this?" and "What are your feelings?"[120] The leader's circle gets antsy if negotiations drag on, and the leader might seek assurances that an agreement is in sight. "Are you still considering doing this? What do you need to know from us about running for our party?" staff ask.[121] Equally, the welcoming party might have second thoughts. The leader and top advisors weigh the politics of the move. "What values will we express to the public? Will we be perceived as doing this as a partisan thing? Is it reflective of a policy set that we want the public to highlight? Is the notion of one more for us and one less for you a reason in itself?" a staffer explained to us.[122]

Sometimes the bargaining collapses. A senior staffer told us of efforts to recruit the former leader of another party.[123] There was an ideological alignment, but ultimately that politician decided that it was too difficult to walk away from a lifetime of friendships and did not want to be excluded from backyard barbeques or given the cold shoulder at cocktail receptions. Another staffer recalled how after meeting with an MP, he advised Prime Minister Chrétien to reject the potential floor crosser due to a lack of shared political values that would be a bad fit in the caucus.[124] We were also told about an opposition MP who wanted a plum position, but the proposition was dismissed by the PMO as too controversial.[125] Bargaining across the aisle can fall apart over an assortment of policy, office, and vote reasons, and more.

The transcript of negotiations about a notorious aborted floor crossing shows how a first minister's representatives dangle incentives while ensuring the leader will be protected by plausible deniability. In 2005, a Vancouver businessman reportedly informed a Liberal minister that two Conservative MPs – a married couple in the area – were open to crossing the floor in exchange for appointments to cabinet, the Senate, or the United Nations.[126] Conservative MP Gurmant Grewal secretly audio-recorded the negotiations, during which the minister emphasized the importance of refuting allegations of a back-room deal: "Nobody will make you totally blunt promises, because that is not done in politics, usually. [But] cabinet right away may be possible.... You have to be able to say that 'I did not make a deal.' That's very important. That's why these kind of deals are not made in that fashion.... They require a certain degree of deniability."[127] The minister urged Grewal to speak with Prime Minister Martin and the chief of staff: "Cabinet can be arranged right away.... I talked to the PM moments ago. He said he is going to Regina right now and he said he will be happy to talk to you over the phone tonight or in person if you want to move. I think you should have a thorough conversation with [the PM's chief of staff].... It's just like talking to the PM.... I suggest you meet with the prime minister this evening, shake hands with him and talk to him."[128] However, Martin's chief of staff explained to Grewal that a patronage appointment was not feasible due to the public outrage following Stronach's floor crossing. The staffer dangled the possibility of one later, contingent on both MPs crossing together. In a tight minority government, controlling the seats was crucial to its survival, and a joint move would allow the PMO to frame the switch as one motivated by principle:

> CHIEF OF STAFF: Two votes from the Conservative side of the ledger can make a difference. And a significant difference. One doesn't and two do. And I think, as you may have seen the prime minister say, he said, 'I'm not offering and I'm making no offers.' And I think that is a narrative we have to stick to.... [But] we understand that those people who take risks ought to be rewarded for the risks they take.... It is better for us and frankly for someone like you to get that reward [in the summer].... We [can] come to an agreement based on something is going to happen.... The first question people will ask you is, 'Well, what were you promised, anything? Did you ask for something?' I think we want the answer to all those questions to be 'No,' then we can be honest about that, right? So that we can be able to say, actually that can be a better position for you to say, that you will be principled.... Obviously if someone [switches parties] out of conviction and courage like you are, the person plays an elevated role.

Ultimately the MPs stayed put. The ethics commissioner interviewed the prime minister, who said that he had instructed his minister to make no promises.[129] The commissioner ruled that Grewal acted inappropriately by either bargaining his vote for an inducement or attempting to entrap a minister.[130] It is impossible to know how often these types of confidential negotiations fail.

Stage 3: Agreement

When bargaining is successful, a verbal agreement for a parliamentarian to join a parliamentary caucus is reached once interests align with those of the leader of the party they want to join. Typically, the normal candidate vetting process is bypassed, and any deal is tentative until it is publicly announced. Some parties require caucus consultation, a formality that leaders might welcome because they want assurance that their recruit will be accepted by the group.[131]

The public nature of parliamentary careers lays bare whether an understanding was reached that someone will be immediately given a status role. A cabinet appointment is the most visible, disruptive, and controversial type of preferment if a parliamentarian walks right into the party and straight into a minister's office; much less so if a cabinet position is assigned down the line during what appears to be a routine shuffle. Being offered a lower-tier role, such as parliamentary secretary, can suggest potential for advancement without the leader making any firm commitment. Some rewards are covert, such as a pledge by the leader's office to support the candidate's pursuit of the party nomination. Other inducements are more granular. In the Ontario case that went to trial, staff in the switcher's constituency office received party money to offset lost income.[132] Generally speaking, bigger catches extract the best terms.

On occasion a party switcher is immediately thrust into a big job, particularly if they have a high profile and their departure can critically weaken an opponent. As mentioned, Gordon Wilson effectively folded the PDA when he joined the BC NDP cabinet.[133] To secure that position, the star MLA exploited the desperation of the governing party. Initially, Premier Glen Clark only offered support to get Wilson re-elected as an NDP candidate in exchange for crossing the floor. Wilson countered with a demand to be in cabinet; furthermore, he wanted to be minister of Aboriginal Affairs to participate in treaty negotiations with the Nisga'a Nation.[134] After a few days, the premier agreed on the condition that Wilson seek re-election as a New Democrat. The agreement caused internal problems because the existing minister had to be shuffled to make room for a floor crosser who opposed socialist thinking. In Ottawa, Peterson told Martin's chief of staff that Stronach would not be "coming across to sit as a backbencher"[135] because she was attracted to the policy influence of being a minister.[136] They discussed her filling a cabinet position that had been temporarily integrated into another minister's portfolio, as well as being added to a powerful cabinet committee. When her list of demands grew, the chief of staff ceased negotiating until he could talk with Stronach in person. A close circle of Liberal staffers was giddy that flipping her to their side would save the government from defeat on a tight budget vote. Stronach had dinner at 24 Sussex Drive, where she shared her frustrations about the Conservative Party with the prime minister and two PMO staffers.[137] Discussions about the offer of a cabinet post included confirming that the former Liberal

MP in her riding was willing to stand down as the party's nominee so that Stronach could run as a Liberal.[138] After high-level discussions like these are worked out, staff are tasked with sorting out logistics, such as which parliamentary office the switcher will relocate to and how the switch will be publicly announced.

Stage 4: Framing

A maxim of political communications is to define a situation before others can. That is why surprise is so pivotal when a parliamentarian joins a party's caucus, especially in cases of floor crossing. Keeping the decision secret is essential to control the frame: if a party discovers that one of their own is about to switch, the narrative can be changed by going public with news that the parliamentarian was expelled,[139] or a peeved parliamentarian can quit to pre-empt being thrown out.[140] Moreover, journalists who hear rumours can pester a potential switcher for weeks,[141] and if news leaks of an announcement the switcher will be inundated with a phalanx of phone calls, emails, and texts. Furthermore, the parliamentarian will be pressed to fess up to colleagues and the leader that trust has been irreparably broken by their decision to negotiate a move to an opposing party. Yet, even amid rumours, the element of surprise can hobble an opponent. In 2000, PC leader Joe Clark was on track to win a by-election to re-enter the House. To blunt the former PM's momentum, on polling day the Chrétien Liberals leaked that two PC MPs would be crossing the floor to their side. Clark was forced to address the rumoured rejection in his victory speech, which foiled his party's plans to project an image of a winner on the upswing.[142]

Participants involved in negotiating a change of affiliation are on tenterhooks until the big reveal. A caucus member who is planning an exit often plays along in meetings, social events, media interviews, and conversations before going public, and can get a colleague to cover their House duty responsibilities.[143] Those who do not seek revenge can go quietly by informing the leader's office, the caucus, and/or their EDA, and the Speaker's office, but speculation mounts if a journalist spies a member's office being cleared out.[144] Politicos who deny that anything is afoot can destroy trust with journalists.[145]

In the lead-up to going public with a decision to quit a caucus or join a new team, most switchers have sleepless nights and are in an emotional state. Some have second thoughts and ask to postpone an announcement; interlocutors work overtime to reassure their nervous recruit.[146] A departure is imminent when a parliamentarian dodges phone calls, has curt interactions with colleagues, or misses a cabinet meeting.[147] Some snubbed leaders field warnings from a member of caucus or an EDA president that a switch is imminent,[148] but many leaders are caught off guard, and can find out moments before the media does.[149] In the past, a leader might receive a couriered letter an hour before a parliamentarian holds a news conference,[150] although then as now some switchers extend the courtesy of a personal meeting or phone call.[151] A leader is blindsided if their colleague had been outwardly loyal up to the end and was refuting rumours of a possible departure. Partisans place such strong faith in the code of party message discipline that a colleague's betrayal of it feels especially devastating.

A lot is riding on the public announcement. Calling a news conference, only to have the recruit back out, would be a disaster. Staff are both convivial and nervous in the moments leading up the big reveal. The leader's circle wants everything to run like clockwork, so they monitor the parliamentarian's movements, which can include sending a car to pick up the recruit and assigning an escort to ensure that everything goes to plan.[152] Behind the scenes, if engaged to do so, employees in the legislature hastily reconfigure seating arrangements in consultation with the House leader or whip, which in some chambers includes moving chairs around. When a change of office location is required, the leader's staff might offer to help with packing and moving. The cusp of the agreement being formalized is when the leader and the recruit walk together to a news conference where, ideally, waiting journalists have no idea why they have been summoned. The visual of a grinning leader alongside a new caucus member from another party can deliver powerful optics; decades after her switch, many still recall the image of Stronach shaking hands with PM Martin. Of course, there are other ways to announce a change in party affiliation, with statements posted on social media becoming common.[153]

Most floor crossers do not literally walk to the other side in the legislative chamber when announcing their change in party loyalties, and those who do so might not be captured by the legislature's cameras.[154] That is what made video of Toronto-area Liberal MP Leona Alleslev crossing the floor in 2018 all the more striking. She rose in the House of Commons, declared that as a member of the governing party she was unable to openly challenge the government about its leftward ideological turn, and asserted that her "oath is to country, not party, and my sacred obligation is to serve my constituents."[155] Alleslev left her seat, briefly approached the Speaker's chair, and walked over to sit with the Official Opposition as Conservative MPs cheered her on. The announcement was undoubtedly designed to generate public attention, and it oozed parliamentary tradition compared with assembling journalists for an announcement. Alleslev was likely in for a shock afterwards: in other cases, when a parliamentarian has announced in the legislature that they are changing their party affiliation, they have discovered upon returning to their office that staff have already removed the contents and changed the locks,[156] and that access to funds in the local riding association's bank account has been restricted.[157]

When news of the defection breaks, political rhetoric erupts as partisans jockey to control the political narrative. As we have seen, the receiving party characterizes the move as evidence of its openness and momentum, and it is *pro forma* for party switchers to heap praise on the leader of the party they are joining. As turbulence envelopes the spurned party, rejected partisans channel their anger by making nasty accusations about their former colleague. We devote the next chapter to a fuller discussion of the framing of these events.

Summary

In this chapter, we unpacked the reasons that motivate partisans to leave their team and join another one, and we explained what happens away from public view in the lead-up to a politician agreeing to switch parties. Some are drawn by the promise of better re-election prospects; some, a potential spot in cabinet, the Speakership, or even the leadership of a party; some by the chance to pursue meaningful policy change or to avoid policies that conflict with their own values. Many are frustrated with their party's leader. We organized the private negotiations between a would-be switcher and representatives of another party into four stages of discussion, bargaining, agreement, and framing. These are not watertight compartments: within these steps there are multidirectional interactions between the defector, the party leader, and intermediaries. Nevertheless, no matter their personal motives or the procedure leading to their new adventure, party switchers soon discover that the framing is beyond their control. The parties involved jockey to portray the change in loyalties, often misrepresenting the events and actions that prompted the change, which is amplified by punditry and news slants. We now turn to examining the aftermath.

9 Aftermath of Defecting

Party disloyalty can have nasty consequences. In the 2015 Alberta election, Sandra Jansen was one of just nine Progressive Conservative candidates elected, and the only woman in that caucus. She subsequently withdrew from seeking the party leadership and, as we have seen, crossed the floor to the arch-rival New Democrats after an inspiring conversation with Rachel Notley. The NDP's newest backbencher received a standing ovation in the legislature when she read aloud some of the misogynistic messages directed at her and Premier Notley on social media. Jansen opened a member's statement as follows: "'What a traitorous bitch.' 'You both are a disgrace to Alberta, lying bitches.' 'Now you have two blonde bimbos in that party that are clueless.' 'Another useless tit goes NDP.' 'Dead meat.' 'Sandra should stay in the kitchen where she belongs.' 'Fly with the crows [and] get shot.' 'Dumb broad. A good place for her to be is with the rest of the queers.'"[1] Jansen was temporarily assigned a security detail to ensure her personal safety,[2] but widespread criticism over the cost of the protection officer led her to cancel the arrangement after just a few days.[3] Although she was appointed to cabinet a year later, the blowback from crossing the floor factored heavily in her decision not to seek re-election.

Given the deep-rooted party loyalties in Canada, it is no surprise that many voters feel betrayed when their elected representative unilaterally switches parties between elections, and that rejected partisans pile on criticism to make a perceived traitor's life miserable. While each situation is unique, there are some themes, including that most exits are the climax of long-brewing discontent, and that the full saga is seldom captured in headlines and soundbites. How does the news media frame party departures and switches? What are the implications of shunning a political party, being expelled from one, or switching parties while still in office? In this chapter, we examine how interparty movement is framed in media discourses, and we summarize the benefits and costs of trading party jerseys while in office.

Media Frames of Party Switching

Discussed throughout this book, the news media and party operatives share a symbiotic relationship, continually adapting to each other's behaviour through the process of mediatization.[4] Naturally, politicians and their handlers were far more reliant on the mainstream media to disseminate information in 1980 than they were in 2021 or today. Yet, even in the era of ubiquitous internet communication, mediated interactions remain a powerful force in influencing the behaviour of political actors.[5] For their part, journalists rely on political actors for information and reactions, as part of a reciprocal yet inherently adversarial relationship.

News outlets tend to present themselves as neutral entities. In fact, even the most skilled journalists operate under institutional constraints and external pressures, whether from the relentless competition for audience attention and advertising revenue, or from limited resources that hamper in-depth investigative reporting and encourage reliance on repackaged information. Whatever the reasons, politicians are cautious that the construction of political news is selective and involves finger-pointing that skews negative, creating a distorted reality.[6] As mentioned in chapter 2, politics is framed as a game or a war, and vocabulary is metaphorized to create attractive news.[7] It follows that journalists are drawn to caucus exits and entries, which are fraught with conflict and treachery, and which expose the warts of democracy. A party departure is a form of political scandal: there is a transgression, an element of secrecy, the disapproval of actions by non-participants, a public denunciation, and, finally, the condemnation of the action that causes reputational damage.[8] Reporting focuses on the individual actors involved – their ideas, their characters, their personal lives – which is part of the personalization of news that causes journalists to attribute partisan behaviour to individual choices and not necessarily to party or system dynamics.[9]

News headlines about parliamentarians pushing the limits of party loyalty can be straightforward, such as "Ontario Liberal MP to Sit as Independent."[10] But more often, media biases result in interpretations of what is newsworthy and how political information ought to be framed. Some headlines paint an ex-partisan in a positive light, such as "The Forging of Jane Philpott's Moral Will,"[11] or present a leader in a triumphant manner, such as "Chrétien Reels in Another Defector."[12] Caucus defections are often portrayed as treasonous, a veiled comparison to conditions on war-time battlefields.[13] Headlines refer to betrayal, caucus turmoil, shady deal-making, and party switchers who benefit from government largesse.[14] Audiences are informed that angry constituents want their representative to resign, and that aggrieved parliamentarians believe that the system turns them into party lackeys who must put up with autocratic leadership. Leaders can bear the brunt as being the ones whose personal failings caused them to lose a caucus member. They are said to be "irate" or "flabbergasted" that someone departed voluntarily,[15] the caucus can be seen as damaged by a departure,[16] and the party's electoral fortunes are said to be harmed.[17] Sensationalism arises when partisans unleash their criticisms on a former colleague, captured in headlines that depict them as "slamming" and "blasting" a deserter, labelling them as "a traitor" and someone who "wasn't a team player."[18] There are also instances of politicians blaming the media for their troubles, and leaders refusing to disclose their reasons for showing someone the door.[19] Sometimes spurned partisans even sue their former party.[20]

Analyzing media frames of party defections requires a close examination of competing narratives. Among the angles put forward are the parties' official lines versus what a party leaver says. For instance, in 2018, the premier of Prince Edward Island alleged that a persistently dissatisfied MLA left the caucus because his preferred candidate for the local EDA presidency had been defeated. However, the MLA contended that his departure was due to being overlooked for a cabinet position and not yet being re-nominated to run for his seat.[21] In another case, news that NDP MP Glenn Thibeault was about to switch to the Ontario Liberals was leaked to a *Toronto Star* reporter who held off filing the story so that the Liberals could provide exclusive details.[22] The story ended up featuring a statement from Thibeault that we assume was written by a Liberal staffer because it praised the premier and, oddly, her ministerial mandate letters.[23] Afterwards, in a media interview, the MP indicated that the move was predicated by a fractured relationship with his own party's leader.[24] Thus, in the frame advanced by the leader's office in the welcoming party, we have a switcher who was attracted to a dynamic, policy-oriented leader; in the switcher's frame, he was seeking refuge from a leader he did not like. Both things could be true, but the party he was joining wanted to emphasize the pull whereas the parliamentarian was feeling a push. Meanwhile, opponents levelled counter-frames that the MP was putting career interests above the needs of constituents and that he was an opportunist drawn to power.[25] What is not reported in these stories is just as pertinent. The media's focus on defectors and leaders leaves little room for the leader's agents – in particular, emissaries like the chief of staff – or constituents, let alone space for civic education about the representational efficacy of backbenchers who are expected to abide by party message discipline.

To examine the media narratives around party switching, as stated in chapter 1, we used a case study and discourse analysis that involved collecting, coding, and analysing 2,850 media stories about partisans in Canadian legislatures becoming Independents or crossing the floor from 1980 to 2021. Our news stories database shows that defections are melodramatic and personalized events, and that the tango between leavers and leaders becomes the key explaining factor at the centre of both the media's and the politicians' narratives. We identified three main storylines about how defections are framed: tales of leadership, tales of political ambition, and tales of loyalty to voters. The frames feature protagonists and antagonists, interpretations of the reasons why the politician left, appraisal of ethical dimensions, and, more broadly, discussions about the democratic effects of abandoning one's party.

The first media storyline concerns power dynamics between the party leader(s) and leaver(s). Few desertions are reported without some reference to a party leader, even when parliamentarians exit their parties over disgraceful acts, illegalities, or health issues. In the media stories we analysed, some leaders were presented as inspiring charmers whose alluring leadership style attracts new people; other leaders were framed as assertive, autocratic, or unable to be admired. In this narrative, parliamentarians like Thibeault reportedly leave because the leader treats them poorly and is a divisive figure, and they are attracted to another leader who is inspiring. When Eve Adams crossed the floor from the Conservatives to the Liberals in 2015, the Ontario MP vilified Prime Minister Harper and exalted the benevolence of Justin Trudeau by saying that she was seeking "a kind, generous, and strong leadership that champions a shared vision for how to make Canada work for everyone. I want to work with someone who inspires, not fear mongers and bullies."[26] Conversely, when David Emerson crossed after having just been re-elected as a Liberal, he declared that his conversations with Harper had led him to conclude that the new prime minister was sincere and had "noble objectives."[27] In such frames, the leader is at the crux of the leaver's decision, with the loss of a seat interpreted as a sign of weak leadership and the gain of a caucus member viewed as evidence of strong leadership.

A parliamentarian's desire for the party leader to involve them in decision-making is apparent in many news stories about party switching.[28]

A leader's openness brings partisans together and inspires them, whereas parliamentarians dissociate and think about leaving if they feel alienated by a leader and the leader's acolytes. Alienation is apparent in complaints that their party had transformed under a new leader who did not value them and who engendered feelings of fear instead of fondness,[29] about someone who did not listen, and perceptions that power is concentrated in the leader's circle.[30] Allegations of an authoritarian style are common in these stories. In 2011, a Parti Québécois stalwart emphasized that she was fed up with "the outrageous authority of [leader Pauline Marois], who is obsessed with power. The atmosphere has become unbreathable."[31] Other MNAs echoed the complaints when leaving the party.[32] In 2018, a Bloc Québécois MP who joined a splinter group alleged about leader Martine Ouellet that "it is always confrontation; she wanted submission."[33] Themes of bullying likewise emerged during Alison Redford's short tenure as PC premier of Alberta. A backbencher who quit caucus claimed that she was "just really not a nice lady.... I cannot work for an individual who treats people poorly" and alleged "intimidation and bullying.... Fits of rage, temper tantrums."[34] These anecdotes are in line with research by Canadian political scientist Sylvia Bashevkin and others that partisans, particularly men, are less tolerant of a domineering style by women leaders, whom they expect to be supportive, collaborative, and focused on teamwork.[35] We note that more recently a white male Manitoba MLA who was removed from the NDP caucus accused Premier Wab Kinew, an Indigenous man, of being "a dysfunctional and toxic leader.... Wab's a bully and when he cannot convince people to do things, he needs to pressure them, bully them, demean them."[36] Perceptions of authoritarianism is only part of the story. Venting about being disrespected is natural when a parliamentarian finally exits a caucus. Leaving and switching empower a parliamentarian to transform exclusion into inclusion by turning the tables on rejection, and to replace sentiments of being on the periphery of power with positive feelings of being part of a welcoming family.[37]

The second dominant frame of party defections is a tale of progressive ambition, where a parliamentarian leaves to improve their chances of being re-elected and/or to climb the career ladder. In Canada, media stories treat ambition as a personality defect, whereby ex-partisans are the antithesis of team players for being egotistical by putting influence and their political career before party loyalty. Critics deride defectors as selfish opportunists lured by power, prestige, and perks, or motivated to get re-elected at any cost.[38] The sharpest barbs are reserved for those who change teams. Floor crossers are denounced for being cowards[39] and toxic personalities[40] for putting

self-interest first, for betraying constituents' wishes,[41] and for prioritizing their own future over that of their abandoned party.[42] Politicians try to dissociate themselves from the ambition narrative, and
minimize the frame of being conniving. "I resigned, first of all, because
I did not want to make any more compromises. It is not really by
opportunism," responded a PC MP when asked why she was joining
the Bloc.[43] Likewise, a New Democrat MP defended herself when she
crossed over to the Tories by acknowledging that "some will describe
my move as opportunistic" and then spun the switch of loyalties as
opening doors to one day being part of a governing party.[44] Accusations of being self-interested and calculating are far less common for
a parliamentarian who two-steps as an Independent compared with
those who cross the floor.

Spurned leaders and hyper-partisans propogate the character assas-
sinations. They might initiate or echo appraisals of a former colleague
as unprincipled and opportunistic, and whose career aspirations overwhelm political values.[45] Leaders have labelled a switcher's motives as
"ambition, ego, temporary insanity,"[46] and have mocked their former
colleague as an unscrupulous carpet-bagger.[47] The extra-parliamentary
party sometimes joins in with further repudiations, such as issuing a
communiqué alleging that the switcher was casting around for reasons to quit.[48] The welcoming party's leader is also open to critique,
including from pundits, such as when Trudeau was chided for praising
Adams' "commitment to public service" and her political values even
though the Conservatives had rejected her for engaging in renomination shenanigans.[49] Finding out about a departure from the media can
bewilder a snubbed leader, who is portrayed as a dud for complaining about being blindsided, about betrayal, and about outreach efforts
being rebuffed.[50]

The third tale in media stories about party switching is one of loyalty to constituents. In our analysis of party departures from 1980 to
2021, about one-in-four media reports made some mention of prioritizing the public ahead of personal ambition or differences with party
leadership. Presenting oneself as a dedicated delegate of constituents
frames the decision to exit a party as lucid and rational, and effuses the
primacy of loyalty to democratic principles over partisanship.[51] A common sentiment is that of a back-bench MP who switched sides: "I'm
hoping people appreciate [that joining the Conservatives] gives me a
better voice than I can have with the Liberals."[52] Parliamentarians who
join the government benches often frame the move as an opportunity to
effect change from within. One of the Wildrose MLAs who participated
in the mass defection event explained that he was seeking opportunity

for his electoral district. "For my constituents, I think I can do the best from the inside making the decisions around the table with the governing party," he reasoned.[53]

The constituent-first narrative is cloaked in ethical representation. The delegate loyalty frame emphasizes public service and introspection, and a path of rectitude that prioritizes people over party.[54] Party switchers can position their decision as serving a higher democratic purpose, claiming that they have little regard for their own re-election or inducements from their new leader, who can then speak to their integrity.[55] Journalists and commentators adopt an empathetic tone when a change in party affiliation seems principled and selfless given that it will jeopardize votes and likely harm the politician's career.[56] In these stories, constituents are seen to benefit when ambition is cast aside, and they are at the centre of the story instead of partisans, parties, or leaders. Switching parties is presented as noble and even rational, unlike narratives that attribute the advantages of defecting solely to the party switcher.

Benefits of Desertion or Defection

There are many benefits of deserting a party or defecting to an opponent. For some, leaving a caucus is a superb decision that leads to fruitful relationships and realizes their career ambitions. Even if the political pay-off turns out to be disappointing – such as a backbencher with dashed hopes of being appointed to cabinet or a floor crosser losing a nomination race or being defeated in the next general election – for many switchers, it was the right move to escape the unhappiness of being in a group that became a poor fit.

The rewards enjoyed by a parliamentarian who joins the caucus of a different party are summarized in box 9.1. The excitement of a move is invigorating, including a burst of media attention and receiving messages of support from strangers. Aside from resolving the distress of wanting out, there can be additional advantages if we believe the trope that politicians make shady deals in party back rooms. As we have seen, while Canada has experienced instances of politicians benefiting from inducements to cross the floor, it is far more typical for party switchers to prove their trustworthiness and dedication before being considered for a coveted position on the front benches. Tom Osborne is a prime example. After the veteran MHA was dropped from the PC cabinet following a post-election shuffle in 2007 and failed in his bid to become Speaker of the Newfoundland and Labrador legislature, he chose to sit as an Independent. Osborne consulted his constituents about his

Box 9.1. Benefits of Party Desertion and/or Defection

Benefits for Parliamentarian

- a new political "family"
- ability to alleviate personal angst and frustrations
- better ideological fit
- burst of media attention
- congratulatory messages
- image of integrity and constituents-first
- improved rapport with the leader
- increased personal satisfaction
- new relationships
- opportunity to advocate a particular policy
- positive effects on political identity
- possibility of improved re-election prospects
- potential for higher status role/influence
- retribution against leader of exited party

Benefits for Deserted Party

- fortification of caucus unity
- opportunity to free up personnel from managing trouble
- protection of brand reputation
- reduction of disruption and negative energy

Benefits for Welcoming Party

- addition of a seat
- chance to gain foothold in new constituency
- competitive intelligence
- damage to an opponent's reputation
- image of public appeal and momentum
- opportunity to turn a foe into an ally
- potential to frame the leader positively

political future, eventually joining the opposition Liberals and winning re-election with ease. Explaining his decision at the time, he emphasized the advantages of caucus membership, stating it provided "the resources of the party, the team aspect, you're much better able to represent the district you serve."[57] When the Liberals came to power in 2015, he was elected Speaker and returned to cabinet two years later.

When he retired in 2024, with twenty-eight years of service, he was the province's longest-serving MHA – and then became a Liberal MP. Few party switchers have such a record of longevity, and almost all of them confront a high bar of proving their loyalty before being considered for an influential appointment. In this sense, party switching is a double-edged sword, because the act of betraying a party and constituents to join a rival party establishes that a switcher is disloyal and raises doubts about whether they can be a team player.

We have shown that most Canadian party switchers have a policy-oriented or electoral motivation that is entangled in a failing relationship with the leader and the leading voices in the caucus, and that leaders are often reluctant to offer anything at all. We have also established that switchers claim to need more latitude to advocate for their constituents, that the party they were elected with has changed, or that there is more capacity to advance a policy agenda on the government-side of the House. Switching parties relieves the stress and misery of having to support a leader and/or parliamentary group from which the parliamentarian has become ideologically estranged. A move can resolve dissatisfaction with the leader's surrogates who – to varying degrees – micromanaged their public speaking, constrained the ability to advocate for a preferred policy, controlled committee assignments, and excluded them from media opportunities, parliamentary trips, and political meetings.

The welcoming party and its leader arguably have the most to gain from receiving a switcher and picking up a seat from an opponent. The ability to control admission to a political club means they can attempt to poach star performers from the other side, deliberate the circumstances and implications of admitting a former adversary, and reject advances from troublemakers. Prominent switches can influence the perceived credibility and election prospects of a party and its leader, particularly if a high-profile move generates momentum for other partisans to switch too.[58] The welcoming party can roll out the red carpet at a media announcement where the leader positions the switch as a triumph for a party on the upswing and as evidence of problems with the rejected leader. Switchers can have a relatively seamless transition if their new colleagues are friendly and if members of their EDA follow along with them. Jansen told us that she was overwhelmed by how supportive members of her new political family were: "[NDP MLAs] were dropping notes off. I was in the premier's office for hours. They all took me out for dinner that night and we went to an Italian restaurant, and they were like a big family around the table. I get emotional thinking about how wonderful they were. It was overwhelming. My office was moved very quickly.... And every day colleagues would show up unannounced to escort me to the legislature. It was just wonderful."[59]

The dominant media frame can be uplifting. As we have seen, a parliamentarian who exits over a policy dispute can be portrayed as ethical and selfless, even as an exemplar, if they are perceived as standing up for their constituents, taking a hard line on an honourable cause, and/or sacrificing career prospects for the betterment of others. A principled move can lead to laudatory headlines characterizing the parliamentarian as a "political hero,"[60] while their new leader exalts the recruit's experience, policy expertise, and dedication to constituents.[61] If a switcher is held in high regard, acclaim comes from local supporters of the deserted party, especially if they have reservations about that party's direction.[62] Occasionally, a political move can be heart-wrenching. News coverage of an opposition MLA who crossed the floor directly into the Nova Scotia cabinet to become the minister of community services featured his experience of overcoming abandonment by his biological parents as a child, growing up in foster homes, and sleeping on the streets as a teenager.[63] The promotion seemed like a natural fit and made for an inspiring story; even the rejected leader responded positively. This uplifting move shared a common theme with others over the decades: departing parliamentarians can avoid partisan retaliation and negative media framing if they speak favourably about the leader and the party they just abandoned.[64]

Media stories gloss over the potential benefits a shunned caucus can gain from a departure. Provided the exit is contained to a single individual, caucus morale can actually improve, especially if it involves the removal of a curmudgeon with designs on discrediting the leader or sowing discord within the group. The party can reallocate staff time and other resources away from handling the troublesome parliamentarian and can refocus on advancing a legislative agenda or building support among voters. This only goes so far: shedding malcontents becomes perilous if the defection bug spreads.

A party leaver or switcher who goes on to lose in their re-election bid may assert they have no regrets, arguing that feigning support for a leader they oppose and campaigning with their former party would have been unbearable. Alberta MP Jack Horner lost to Clark in the 1976 Progressive Conservative leadership race.[65] For seven months, he publicly undermined the party's new leader and sometimes sided with the Liberals. When Clark refused to back him for the party nomination against another PC MP in a redistricted riding, Horner crossed the floor into the Liberal cabinet; however, he was thumped in the ensuing election. Years later, he reflected that it seemed to be a good career move at the time.[66] Jane Philpott, the former minister who, alongside Wilson-Raybould, was expelled from the Liberal caucus during the SNC-Lavalin affair in 2019, lost her re-election bid as an Independent. She has reconciled that the sudden end of her political career can inspire other parliamentarians to speak their minds and stick to their principles.[67] Party switchers usually express confidence that their change in party destiny was the right choice. As one put it to us, "I'm confident in the decision I made. I don't think I could have made a different decision,"[68] and Jansen believes that crossing the floor "was one of the best decisions of my career."[69] Yet many of them surely harbour misgivings due to the considerable costs of betraying party loyalty, discussed next.

Costs of Desertion or Defection

Abandoning one organization for another creates havoc with human relationships. In workplaces, employees who switch jobs sustain stress and upheaval, lose seniority, and experience a brief honeymoon before reality settles in.[70] The disavowal of shared goals, past experiences, and norms can hurt their former colleagues, who experience feelings of rejection[71] and whose morale is weakened.[72] A departure has deep resonance in a close-knit group that endures humiliation, which can give rise to hatred, to the point of inflicting psychological harm.[73] A group reacts more harshly when one of their own defects to a competing organization than to a deserter who simply leaves;[74] some members perceive shades of treason, which is extreme given the historical view that treason is "the highest of all crimes."[75] Consequently, upper management must contain the negative repercussions on workplace cohesion and brace for other workers willing to depart.[76] At the same time, members of the organization that welcomes a defector can have feelings of resentment and suspicion, with some of them keeping their distance from a potential double-agent. It follows that partisans have a fierce reaction to parliamentarians who betray their cause and bring ignominy upon the group.

The psychological grip of party loyalty becomes evident when partisans feel betrayed by one of their own. In party politics, the repercussions of desertion or defection are considerable (box 9.2) and reflect the risks involved in vote-, office-, and policy-seeking behaviour. The reputational damage of being portrayed as deceitful and losing voters' trust translates into hostility and contempt. As David Peterson cautioned us, "Don't switch parties! Unless there is some principle. There's a lot of unhappiness and heartbreak."[77]

Box 9.2. Costs of Party Desertion and/or Defection

Costs for Parliamentarian

- alienation of friends and allies
- backlash and public criticism
- destruction of professional relationships
- difficulty in winning the party nomination and re-election
- loss of trust among constituents and other parliamentarians
- need to develop new support base
- potential loss of upward mobility
- reputational effects (e.g., disloyal, opportunist, flip-flopper)
- resetting of political identity
- shedding of local campaign workers
- struggle bridging ideological divides
- ties to previous party's voting record
- upset staunch supporters and donors

Costs for Deserted Party

- exposure of internal secrets
- internal fighting
- loss of a seat
- negative news coverage
- portrayal as a loser
- potential to motivate more departures
- weakening of morale

Costs for Welcoming Party

- displacement of local nominee
- disruption of caucus cohesion
- exasperated donors and local party members
- feelings of infiltration
- increased competition for limited roles
- need to accommodate a diverging ideology
- negative news coverage
- potential to inherit a troublemaker
- unsettled or angry caucus members

In the following pages, we discuss the personal, social, reputational, and political costs of leaving one political party for another. There is the practical side of changing jobs, such as lack of familiarity with the new organization's customs and workplace culture, and not knowing who people are. There is the added dimension of needing to build trust with suspicious colleagues, most of whom until recently were adversaries, both within a caucus and an electoral district association. There are also the opinions of constituents to manage and a need to court their vote. A political staffer who has negotiated some prominent switches summarizes the hazards: "Don't underestimate how hard it's going to be to change parties! Some people are going to be upset, some will hate you, some people will feel totally betrayed. Members of the party you are joining won't necessarily trust you; you might feel lonely out of the gate. The media castigations of being a turncoat and selfish will follow."[78] For some individuals, the consequences of joining a different parliamentary caucus can be severe, and their treatment as an outcast within their new party can be so disheartening that they may regret not completing their term as an Independent.[79] While every politician who turns their back on a political party encounters unique circumstances, common repercussions include disparagement, damaged relationships, and potential setbacks to their career.

Political parties can go to great lengths to make a deserter's life miserable. As we have shown, a partisan who brushes aside party loyalty must brace for a cascade of media stories, partisan salvos, and efforts to frame the narrative, especially if they criticize the leader and the party on the way out. The broadsides signal to other parliamentarians that if a departure harms the group, it may lead to internecine conflict. Party switchers receive hateful mail and phone messages, are the target of scathing posts on social media, and are at the centre of harsh news coverage that creates "a big stew of venom," as one party leaver put it to us.[80]

The dressing down of an ex-partisan can be harsh. The rejected party tries to paint the defector as a weak link whose departure will make the team stronger.[81] Spurned colleagues use ambition-framing to chastise the switcher as an opportunist seeking more money[82] or who was upset at not being in the limelight,[83] and depict them as a selfish turncoat whose move contributes to political cynicism.[84] Switchers are dismissed as self-interested actors[85] who, it is prophesized, will pay a price at the ballot box for turning their backs on local supporters who want retribution.[86] Accusations of inappropriate behaviour are levelled, such as the departed member who allegedly violated privacy rules by taking data about constituents who did not consent to their information being shared with a different political party.[87]

In the legislature, erstwhile allies often heckle, boo, taunt, and ridicule their former associate.[88] The character and judgment of the switcher can be impugned. They are dismissed as a substandard representative who is coping with personal problems[89] or financial difficulties,[90] who had poor attendance at caucus meetings,[91] and who either rarely said anything in caucus[92] or was belligerent.[93] Sometimes a tit-for-tat arises. In Manitoba, a PC MLA was expelled for levelling allegations of tyranny against Premier Gary Filmon. Party officials retorted that he was resentful at being passed over for cabinet and that executives on his riding association were threatening to quit over his substandard work.[94] The premier added that the MLA was "erratic" and had "trouble getting along with people," and that his removal would help with caucus unity.[95] Other debates in the legislature involve discussion about how party switching fuels perceptions of politicians as self-serving.[96]

Special cases generate their own condemnation, such as the married couple who crossed together from the New Brunswick PC caucus and were labelled political spies for allegedly leaking information to the governing Liberals.[97] Hypocrisy flows when a former switcher expresses disgust at the integrity of a new switcher[98] or when someone who previously denounced party switching goes on to do it themselves.[99] Cries of insincerity also ensue when the spurned party releases emails and audio showing that a floor crosser had been effusing praise on senior officeholders in the party not long before admonishing it.[100]

Juvenile antics reinforce the party's team spirit in the face of rejection, such as mailing party propaganda to their former colleague's home[101] or a staffer sending flowers to another party's staffer as a satirical thank you for taking a troublemaker off their hands.[102] Pettiness and ostracization can fester: decades after the CCF's final leader crossed the floor from the New Democratic Party to the Liberal Party, his portrait was absent from a montage of the party's leaders in the House of Commons.[103] Occasionally, the aggrieved party takes aggressive action. In 2013, the NDP launched robocalls and advertising to pressure their former colleague, who had joined the Bloc Québécois, to resign from his seat and seek re-election with his new party in a by-election.[104] In another case, upon the election of Pierre Poilievre as leader in 2022, a Conservative MP who left to sit as an Independent was downcast when party members in his riding received a text message from his former party accusing him of abandoning the team and urging constituents to phone his office to demand his resignation. The MP alleged intimidation, decried how party discipline breeds cynicism in politics, and eventually announced that he would not seek re-election.[105]

Sexism can erupt when party loyalty is shattered. Women politicians are subject to harsher media coverage generally, including misogynistic innuendos and direct assaults on their fidelity that exploit societal views on sexuality.[106] For example, *Le Devoir* reported that an unnamed source alleged that an MNA who switched parties was so uncontrollable that her husband had to be persuaded to get her to calm down and work as part of a team.[107] In particular, the aforementioned misogyny that Sandra Jansen encountered online echoed the mass media vitriol that Belinda Stronach endured in 2005. The frames questioning Stronach's integrity and credibility, along with punditry about how her move would stoke cynicism about politics, were by far the most intense of any of the cases we examined. Conservatives were fed message lines that she had been a no-show at parliamentary committee meetings and that she was trying to get out of paying her leadership campaign debt.[108] Pundits discussed how she had left her romantic partner, Peter MacKay, the Conservatives' deputy leader, who had sympathized in private yet was loyal to the leader in public. After the news broke, MacKay allegedly compared her to a disloyal dog.[109] Male callers to talk-radio shows labelled her a "political harlot" and the "Benedict Arnold of Canadian politics,"[110] while a prominent female columnist tagged her as a "treacherous wench" and a "political whore."[111] A *Journal de Montréal* cartoon depicted Stronach as a sex worker.[112] She received death threats, and security guards were assigned to her children at school.[113] Some male politicians levelled brutal insults. "She sort of defined herself as something of a dipstick, an attractive one, but still a dipstick, with what she's done here today. She is, at the end of the day, going to paint herself as something of a joke," said one.[114] "Some people prostitute themselves for different costs or different prices. She sold out for a cabinet position," said another.[115] "What it is to me is a little rich girl who is basically whoring herself out to the Liberals," added a third.[116] Stephen Harper chided, "I've never really noticed complexity to be Belinda's strong point."[117] During her re-election campaign, Stronach rued the derogatory comments and the celebrity sensationalism of breaking up with MacKay, not just with a party.[118] She was re-elected as a Liberal with an impressive increase in share of vote; however, Conservatives formed the government, and she did not re-offer.

We determined that the Stronach and Jansen cases are outliers, with the former involving "tabloid-like" treatment of a political celebrity.[119] One Quebec MP claimed that nobody mentioned her own changed affiliation when she attended community events on the weekend after her announcement,[120] and another told us that her switch was warmly received.[121] Lela Evans, the boomerang partisan in Labrador, sidestepped party backlash by visiting the NDP leader's home to inform him of her departure. At a news conference to announce her return, she expressed admiration for him while standing next to the PC leader, stating that her decision was motivated solely by a desire to better advocate for constituents facing an indifferent Liberal government.[122] On X, which has limited editorial filtering, comments reacting to news stories about Evans rejoining the PC caucus levelled the usual allegations – an opportunist, unscrupulous, a waffler, a phoney – but we did not observe anything overtly sexist or homophobic.[123] In any case, when male floor crossers face verbal harassment, their gender is not the focus of the conversation.

The public criticism results in reputational harm that extends to personal relationships. When a parliamentarian shuns one party for another, they can become a *persona non grata* within much of their established network. The partisans they abandon can be deeply wounded. Former colleagues feel that a switcher is egotistical and arrogant,[124] and some of them leave private messages to express sadness, incomprehension, and anger.[125] Relationships with many people a switcher respects, including long-time friends and even family members, are permanently altered, if not destroyed.[126] In the capital city, some of a switcher's former partisan allies refuse to speak with them. Some pretend not to see them and turn their backs or cross the street to avoid them;[127] their spouse might get snubbed in social situations.[128] Even a two-stepper whose move does not attract fanfare feels the sting, we were told: "It's such a traumatic event professionally. There's a lot of pain and suffering that goes with it on a personal level, because these are friends you've had for years. Colleagues you've worked with. You're going to lose those. And you will find also at the constituency level, some people will be very angry at you. You have to be prepared for that."[129]

In their electoral district, it can be hard on a switcher to be alienated from local partisans who delivered flyers for them, who put away chairs at the end of an event, and who pounded in lawn signs. A switcher can feel guilt for abandoning supporters and for not giving members of their electoral district association the courtesy of a heads-up to blunt the surprise. Friendships are soured, even severed, including ones that predate the switcher's entry into political life. Provided they were left out of the bargaining, members of the spurned EDA experience feelings of shock, disbelief, and betrayal when someone they helped get elected becomes a partisan traitor,[130] and they can speak harshly about the parliamentarian's representative style.[131] We were told about a former campaign worker who spat on a party switcher at a public event and threatened to punch him,[132] and about how donors feel duped and have

no recourse to obtain a refund. On the receiving side, rank-and-file partisans are dubious that an ex-partisan can be trusted to change loyalties
and values.[133] They are irked that they will be expected to support a
rival they worked against in the previous campaign and can scold the
leader for accepting a former opponent.[134] Some party loyalists find it
difficult to support a turncoat who will potentially wrest the nomination away from a committed party member. From the capital city, party
operatives can work the phones to shore up the hurt feelings of local
partisans who campaigned against the switcher.[135]

Constituents have polarized reactions to news that their representative has traded one party hat for another. Some of them approve or are
ambivalent, while enraged partisans let loose on talk-radio shows where
they disparage the "fence-jumper" as a "little quisling guttersnipe,"
and worse.[136] A party switcher told us about attending social gatherings
where constituents were overheard whispering their displeasure about
the decision.[137] Another recalled that his mother-in-law felt the wrath
of parishioners at her church and that his lawn signs were vandalized
with swastikas.[138] Lisa Raitt, the Conservative who unseated two-stepper
Garth Turner, got an earful from voters who felt he disrespected their
vote.[139] A Wildrose floor crosser summarizes the views that he fielded
from the public: "I had people come into my office and tear a strip off
me. As a public servant it was my job to listen to them and to hear what
they had to say. Some of it wasn't pleasant. And I had other ones come
in and calling me and texting me and saying, 'You did the right thing. I
understand why you did it.' So, depending on the mindset of the people,
some of them felt betrayed."[140] In this context, frustrated constituents can
extend well beyond the parliamentarian's electoral boundaries to constitute people whom they stand for or share characteristics with – what Pitkin, the political theorist, calls symbolic or descriptive representation.[141]
When Elenore Sturko defected to the BC Conservatives, she sparked
bewilderment in the LGBTQ2+ community nationwide, given her advocacy for LGBTQ2+ rights, past criticism of the party's social conservatism, and the perceived hypocrisy of her move.[142]

Several elections later, people remain angry at a party switcher, some
of whom refuse to talk to the betrayer. When the politician's parliamentary career is over, it can be difficult to find work because they
are tainted. Long after exiting politics, party leavers can field apologies from former caucus colleagues who concede that at the time they
were unable to talk or socialize with them.[143] Years later, switchers can
caution others against changing parties because of the personal hard-
ships and broken friendships.[144] As well, a switcher can look back on
the hypocrisy of some of their fiercest critics who themselves went on

to change parties.[145] Most tempers cool down with time. Some relationships are repaired and new friendships emerge; however, one of the most painful aspects for an elected official who changes party affiliation in Canada is their sadness about friendships that are lost forever.

A party switcher may be disappointed that the move does not translate into fulfilling their career ambitions. Apart from star recruits, the special treatment that they envision drains away when they are installed in the back benches and must navigate getting nominated to stand for re-election, or if they anticipated that their new party would form government but never does. Then there are the electoral repercussions. In a riding where a newly joined party is dormant, a party switcher needs to assemble a campaign team, fundraise, and identify supporters. If the EDA is active, the switcher will need to get them onside. Either way, challenging interactions with voters lie ahead, and securing re-election can be tough.

Canadian MPs who switch political parties have historically paid an electoral price of approximately 5 per cent, though in recent years the vote penalty has bordered on 20 per cent.[146] Members of Parliament who are pushed out of their party lose the most votes, followed by those who switch for electoral reasons, and least of all those who leave an opposition party to take a government appointment.[147] Our analysis of federal and provincial departures from 1980 to 2021 finds that a majority of parliamentarians who left their party did not survive into the next assembly. During that time frame, two-thirds of party leavers went on to contest the next general election, which is lower than the four-fifths of all incumbents who typically do so.[148] Of the parliamentarians who sought re-election under a different party banner, two-thirds failed, and of the former partisans who ran as Independents, nearly three-quarters failed. In contrast, the winning percentage among all incumbents in Canadian federal elections is 77 per cent,[149] suggesting that being a team player is a good re-election strategy. A former floor crosser cautions, "It's not something I would wish upon anyone.... There's this public perception that if you do it automatically, you're rewarded with influence and power. And in this case, it was anything but.... [Yet] I'll be accused of being a floor crosser who is greedy and doing it for power and all of these things and there is none of that. I'm sure that there are some who have their individual agreements that are worked out. But that certainly was not my experience. Make sure that you're prepared for this to be the last term that you serve."[150] Nevertheless, some party switchers go on to have a long parliamentary career and forge an influential political legacy. For them, there is no looking back.

Summary

As demonstrated in this chapter, a parliamentarian leaving or defecting from their party is often treated as scandalous event that attracts a lot of attention, regardless of whether the decision to sever ties was their own or imposed upon them. We showed that the media's interest tends to be driven by the dramatic aspects of events, overlooking behind-the-scenes actors and the discontent leading up to a departure. In the media maelstrom that ensues, three key narratives emerge: a tale of power politics between the leader and the leaver, a tale of political ambition and opportunism, and a tale of loyalty to constituents. Party leaders, team players, and leavers draw on these storylines to preserve their public image or augment their reputation, and journalists quote participants who emphasize the problematic aspects of the switch.[151] This framing and counter-framing is endemic to party departures given that news consumers are attracted to negative information about politics and political actors.[152]

We also summarized the costs and benefits of shunning a political party while still in office. Given the very public and nasty nature of most party defections – plus the steep personal, social, and political risks involved – it is little wonder most of Canada's partisans stay loyal or else retire from politics altogether rather than gamble on changing parties. As we have shown, some contexts are more conducive than others when it comes to taking that ultimate step, but everyone who leaves a party loses friends.

10 Empowering Team Members

In the twenty-first century, adherence to the party line by parliamentarians goes beyond whipped votes in the legislative chamber to include comments and actions in the broader public sphere. Compared to their predecessors, Canadian parliamentarians are much less original, as they are under greater pressure to align with their party's priorities, which are largely set by the leader's inner circle. To play the political game, they are conditioned to show unwavering loyalty to the team by echoing party messages, praising the leader, and attacking opponents. The ubiquity of party loyalty is a glaring flaw of Canada's parliamentary democracy. In this concluding chapter, we summarize our findings and propose measures to ease the stranglehold of political parties on backbenchers so that they may better serve their constituents, work across party lines, and ensure that leaders and senior officeholders are held accountable.

Party Games

Why are most Canadian parliamentarians so firmly aligned with their political party? This was the main research question flowing throughout our investigation, which originally set out to study politicians who abandon one political party for another. We employed a comprehensive research strategy to gather data on the clandestine aspects of parliamentary party dynamics, focusing on how leaders seek assurances of group loyalty and examining the repercussions when a parliamentarian deviates from group norms. We reviewed literature in social psychology, organizational behaviour, and political science. We created a party defector database of 349 party exit events involving 333 MPs and provincial legislators from 1980 to 2021; developed a news stories database of 2,850 media reports of party switching episodes that were coded to identify themes; synthesized information from 3,300 news stories into 333 briefing notes about parliamentarians; administered 90 in-depth interviews with politicians and political staff across Canada; and utilized supplementary sources of qualitative secondary data, including the coding of transcripts from 91 exit interviews with retiring MPs conducted by the Samara Centre for Democracy and a review of a dozen long-form interviews with party switchers administered by the Library of Parliament's Oral History Project. We organized Canadian parliamentarians along a spectrum of party loyalty: team players, party mavericks, party leavers (quitters and expelled members), and party switchers (which encompasses floor crossers and two-steppers, as well as party hoppers, boomerang partisans, party entrepreneurs, and others).

We now have a richer understanding of the forces that drive party (dis)unity, which both animate and encumber representation. We have shown that advancements in communication technologies have accentuated a web of interconnected dynamics that intensify party loyalty among Canadian parliamentarians. As a result, they are concerned about being perceived as out-of-sync with their leader and fellow caucus members, which drives them to adhere to messaging guidelines set by the leader's office. This mindset limits their capacity to publicly advocate for their constituents, discourages them from voicing constructive criticism of policies and leadership, and contributes to divisive political discourse. Scholars of Canadian politics should treat party discipline (which focuses on incentives to ensure unified voting on bills) and candidate discipline (which involves preventing election candidates from freelancing) as components of the broader concept of party message discipline (which involves partisans repeating strategic messages across all platforms at all times).

Our research was informed by several theoretical frameworks. Broadly speaking, we have contributed further evidence in the canon of literature about the socio-psychological effects of groups on individual members, particularly when they form an attachment to a group that is styled as a team or family that infuses their personal identity. Within political science, we have shown ways that the parliamentary workplace bears similarities to other occupational settings of employer–employee relations, and have bolstered the analogy of political parties as franchisors who contract politicians as franchisees.[1] We have greater clarity about the institutional, political, social, and technological pressures that condition party unity, and we have added perspectives about the consequences of political parties behaving as cartels that exploit rules and resources to augment their power, about caucus cohesion being stronger when there is greater homogeneity among its members, and about political parties striving to mimic the discipline of successful counterparts.[2] We illustrated the representational tensions that arise when serving as a trustee charged with making decisions on behalf of constituents, as a delegate who acts on constituents' wishes, as a politico who must balance between local demands and the broader public good, or as a loyal partisan who prioritizes party interests. We showed that policy issues usually outweigh the allure of office or votes when Canadian parliamentarians switch political parties, and that their pursuit of these ambitions is influenced by the reward and coercive powers wielded by the leader and their staff. As party loyalty diminishes, personality conflicts can erupt into the public arena, leading to intense arguments and open accusations.

Throughout this book, we have profiled the struggles of a selection of politicians who have shouldered the weight of a political system designed to be confrontational and which splits them into teams. Their stories shed light on the darker corners of internal party politics and the fluctuating allegiances within them. These experiences reveal an increasingly divided political landscape where party loyalties are more pronounced than ever, largely attributable to considerable shifts in communication technologies. That said, each incident of party disloyalty has multiple perspectives. We have underscored the necessity of examining each case thoroughly to establish available facts, as borne out by the competing accounts about why and when former MP Pauline Jewett left the Liberal Party, and the need to examine the details of numerous complex cases to arrive at generalizations.

Our analysis of 349 cases of party exiting events in Canada reveals some key themes. Regional political parties, with their narrower ideological or geographical focus, encounter unique challenges that contribute to higher rates of factional disputes and defections. Some politicians leave their parties strategically, either to seize new opportunities, advance their careers, or align with shifting political dynamics. Strict party discipline often acts as a catalyst for defections, particularly when dissenting members feel stifled, with numerous party leavers citing a strong desire to better represent their constituents, while political activists who are relatively new to party politics can struggle to adapt to the rigid team culture. Furthermore, personal scandals – ranging from financial mismanagement and moral lapses to even criminal charges – are frequently intensified by broader political contexts and media scrutiny, leading to high-profile departures that warn others that their caucus or even party membership can be revoked.

Our main contribution to knowledge is to push forward awareness that party loyalty among Canadian parliamentarians is infused by message discipline. Branding, repetition of succinct information, and communications coordination strengthened as social media emerged and then flourished during the tenures of Prime Ministers Stephen Harper and Justin Trudeau. We began the book with the alarm of first-time candidate Noah Richler, who begrudgingly performed the role of a party cheerleader during the 2015 Canadian federal election campaign. To former Quebec MNA Claire Samson, backbenchers are so stage-managed that they have turned into decorative greenery. Her concern reflects a sobering reality that most Canadian parliamentarians are team players who accept the franchising bargain: that in return for being elected as a party candidate, they feel duty-bound to act on requests from the party leadership where possible, which involves toeing the line not just on parliamentary votes but in what is said both publicly and privately. Women, Indigenous Peoples, racialized people, and other individuals can have a rough time working within the biases that arise within this unwritten team code of behaviour largely developed by white men, as former MP Jody Wilson-Raybould and former MNA Catherine Dorion experienced. Yet others embrace the team lifestyle. Dedicated partisans like former deputy prime minister Anne McLellan have deep roots in a political party that predate their adulthood and prepare them to seamlessly navigate the party game. Most team players in Canadian politics are loyal party soldiers who avoid trouble, comply with requests, focus on constituency casework, and repeat party messages. Some become hyper-partisans who unleash harsh insults in the legislature and draw comparisons to attack dogs or pit bulls, seemingly intent on harming their opponents. Similarly, the leader's staff can contribute to this hostile dynamic, ratcheting up polarization.

To team players, it is entirely reasonable for caucus members to present a unified public front to prevent media chaos and internal discord, which can inhibit the advancement of the shared political agenda they campaigned on and can weaken their re-election prospects. To them, being a caucus person is highly advantageous, and loyalty is so integral to their partisan identity that they equate the party's interests with their own. However, politics becomes increasingly polarized as the party leadership demands stricter in-group conformity to messaging while encouraging out-group animosity. At its extreme, this leads to a belief system where caucus members are expected to abide by the will of a dominant leader and their inner circle, the sidelining of independent thinkers, and the use of manipulative tactics to assert control.

In contrast to the conventional image of a parliamentarian as a congenial team player, certain steadfast partisans distinguish themselves through unorthodox behaviour, challenging group norms and refusing to conform to the expectations of a loyal party acolyte. The authenticity of committed team players can be admired by constituents, as exemplified by MLA Ron MacKinley in Prince Edward Island, who, with his cigar-chomping demeanour, defied party directives without crossing a line. MP Michelle Rempel Garner and former Alberta MLA Laurie Blakeman carved reputations for brazenly expressing their opinions within the boundaries of party values, while parliamentary purists like MP Nathaniel Erskine-Smith are methodical in their dissent. The behaviour of these mavericks is relatively tame when contrasted with the outspokenness of their counterparts in the pre–social media era, such as former MPs Judy LaMarsh and John Reid. A close comparison is long-time MP Cheryl Gallant, whose early twenty-first-century bluster faded as party message discipline ramped up. In today's brand-focused political climate, there is much less acceptance of provocative strategies once embraced by political agitators. On the surface, backbenchers' online advocacy may seem more subdued than the bold media stunts of the past. However, the intensity of their defiance is amplified by stringent norms of party loyalty, leading to much harsher consequences. This is exemplified by the contrasting treatment of New Democrats Svend Robinson and Sarah Jama, Sarah Jama, who expressed support for Palestine in 2002 and 2023, respectively – showing how a single social media post can derail a parliamentary career.

Agreeable parliamentarians can become disruptive when there are insufficient policy, office, or vote incentives to control them. Sometimes they emerge largely unscathed after challenging the party line, as with MP Ken McDonald who calmly channelled his constituents' concerns about the carbon tax. However, resentful partisans can become a serious problem if left unmanaged, with a classic case being Manitoba MLA Jim Walding who participated in bringing down his own party's government. Caucus management is thus an important part of a party leader's job. Some leaders go out of their way to talk with backbenchers, such as Prime Minister Brian Mulroney, former BC Premier Christy Clark, former NDP leader Jack Layton, and Alberta Premier Danielle Smith. Others take harsh measures to tamp down caucus dissent. Leaders can themselves feel the sting of party unrest, as Prime Ministers Jean Chrétien and Justin Trudeau, Canadian Alliance leader Stockwell Day, and Alberta Premiers Alison Redford and Jason Kenney found out.

Partisans who are unhappy and isolated can end up leaving the caucus. Some, such as former MP Brent Rathgeber, exit before their disobedience gets them expelled. Independents can relish the freedom from party control. Ontario MPP Bobbi Ann Brady, one of the handful of first-time candidates elected on her own name in modern times, flourishes in the freedom to express herself – and to be interesting. In her view, "A party takes away your ability to be an individual, to be unique, to be dynamic, to be interesting. They want you as boring as possible. I don't believe that I'm boring, and my constituents don't think I'm boring either.... As an Independent the thing that I love the most is that my creativity and my personality aren't stifled by a brand."[3] Parliamentarians who cannot abide by the ideological direction of a party can pursue their own agenda as Independents, as MNA Catherine Fournier attempted, however strategies and tactics that work in political movements do not always translate effectively into parliamentary politics. Some go further by creating their own party, as seen with MP Lucien Bouchard or MNA Jean-Martin Aussant, but such acts of party entrepreneurship are uncommon among women and virtually unexplored by racialized politicians. Most ex-partisans who go their own way struggle to get re-elected.

Changing party affiliation typically involves one of two pathways. A parliamentarian who switches sides either crosses the floor directly from one caucus to another (as with MPs Leona Alleslev and Jenica Atwin) or two-steps, which normally involves sitting as an Independent and then going over to another party (as with MP Louis Plamadon) or, more unusually, resigning and getting re-elected in a by-election (as with Saskatchewan MLA Buckley Belanger). Occasionally, multiple people switch, epitomized by the Wildrose mass floor crossing. There are politicians, such as MPs Keith Martin and Scott Brison, who change parties when theirs ceases to exist after it merges and/or dissolves. Occasionally, someone hops between parties and independence, as with Nova Scotia MLA Paul MacEwan and Newfoundland and Labrador MHA Paul Lane. Leaders sometimes change parties too, such as BC's Gordon Wilson, New Brunswick's Dominic Cardy, and Alberta's Raj Sherman. There are boomerang partisans who leave and then return to their original party. Reunification can occur after a relatively brief sojourn or after many years away, as with Lela Evans of Labrador and Jean Lapierre of Quebec, respectively. There are also partisans who switch party families as they move between federal and provincial politics, among them Jean Charest, Ujjal Dosanjh, Steven Fletcher, Bob Rae, and Glenn Thibeault.

We organized the multi-stage process of joining a rival political party into four phases: discussion, bargaining, agreement, and framing. Politicians who change parties can be motivated to achieve policy goals or exert policy influence, as with MP Peter Ittinuar and Nova Scotia MLA Hinrich Bitter-Suermann. They might be attracted to the power of government office, especially if they are struggling in an opposition party. There are also vote reasons for switching, such as MPP Annamarie Castrilli running for another party after she was unable to get renominated when her riding fell victim to redistribution. A deal is reached when there is a meeting of the minds, as there was between Alberta MLA Sandra Jansen and Premier Rachel Notley. Leaders are wary of promising anything to convince someone to cross, though sometimes incentives are indeed dangled by emissaries, most prominently with MPs Gurmant Grewal, Belinda Stronach, and David Emerson during a fractious period of minority government.

The outcomes of changing one's party allegiance can be both beneficial and unsettling for a parliamentarian. They can either succeed or fall short in achieving their policy objectives, accomplishing their goal of sitting in a government office, or securing more votes. At the forefront is a media tsunami, particularly if floor crossing is chosen over two-stepping, if a high-profile politician joins a rival party they worked against, if a cabinet position is involved, and/or if the move is seen to have political consequences for a party leader. Those who take a principled stand can be personified as noble underdogs battling a broken political system and are celebrated for sacrificing their career for the greater good. Other nonconformists are vilified as selfish and irrational ideologues who disrespect how parliamentary politics works and betray partisan supporters. Switchers such as MP Eve Adams draw sharp contrasts between two leaders; other switchers are framed as ambitious or as putting constituents first. Stronach and Jansen were high-profile floor crossers who experienced severe misogyny. Conversely, when a troublemaker is evicted from the caucus the news coverage is likely to focus on their transgressions. Ultimately, loyalty in parliamentary politics is so intertwined with some partisans' identity and worldview that a parliamentarian who betrays the group can anticipate fractured, if not permanently severed, relationships with supporters, constituents, and friends. For some, this outcome was an unavoidable consequence of escaping the misery of being in a caucus where they felt isolated under the leadership of someone they felt disconnected from or, even worse, someone they despised.

Party Dynamics

Party politics in Ottawa and the provinces are constantly changing. Our study period began at a time when Canada's party systems were more aligned than we see today. Three parties won seats in the 1980 federal election and for the most part the same cast of parties existed in the provinces, except for Quebec. That year, the Progressive Conservatives became the Official Opposition at the federal level with 32.5 per cent of the vote – a shade lower than the 32.6 per cent that the Liberals received in 2021, which enabled them to form a minority government following an election that sent MPs from five parties to Ottawa. In 1980, leading experts declared that Canada consisted of ten distinct political "worlds" (one for each province),[4] yet from a party perspective the similarities among them were greater than any time since. By the end of 2021, provincial governments were being run by political parties bearing one of six distinct names, marking a doubling in number from four decades earlier. Nationally and in most provinces, political parties have become more doctrinaire than the pliable brokerage organizations that came before them.[5] A clear manifestation of this shift is the entrenched team culture within party caucuses, where political success is perceived to depend on strategically delineating differences from opponents and maintaining a strong commitment to message discipline.

With each election, Canada's legislatures welcome a growing number of parliamentarians who are less inclined to challenge party orthodoxy. This trend of elected representatives deferring to the party leadership runs counter to the foundational principles of democracy, which were never intended to operate this way. Canada's Westminster model of government was originally designed to encourage the open exchange of ideas in public forums, free from fear of suppression or reprisal. It ought to foster innovation and adaptability by allowing people with competing interests to contribute to the political process, which will lead to policies that reflect a broad consensus and the evolving needs of the populace, thereby limiting concentrated power. To the extent that partisanship supports this sort of pluralism, it does so through political parties articulating distinct viewpoints in the public sphere, with caucus members pressed to speak with a unified voice. This process funnels contestation through party structures, as not all perspectives are reflected in party rhetoric or policy. Consequently, the extent to which internal party democracy supports inclusivity and constructive dissent among caucus members plays a pivotal role in shaping the overall vitality of the political system.

However, backbenchers, and even senior ministers, are up against concentrated power. Party leaders can initiate and steer policy-making, and they have access to far more information and resources than other caucus members do. They are the chief spokespersons of the party, and their words carry weight inside and outside the legislature. They and their associates control a range of rewards and can impose punishments to both incentivize and enforce discipline. Deference to the leader is both natural and commanded, and criticism or dissent often subsides when the leader or the leader's representatives are present, which stifles disagreement and individuality in favour of the united front and brand consistency that are necessary for a parliamentary group to achieve its objectives. The leader's staff are so embedded in coordinating and managing affairs that one might assume it was always this way, yet their indispensability and presence has grown alongside changes in political communications.

Centralized power has its limits, and backbenchers often possess more clout than they realize. Leaders who disregard their caucus endanger democratic discourse and public displays of unity; they can lose control over their agenda, which can cost them their job. Parliamentarians who cultivate a public persona of authenticity – when constituents view them as genuine, sincere, and true to themselves – become personalities in their own right whose opinions are accorded more attention. In a sea of indistinguishable politicians, media-savvy and sharp-witted parliamentarians who are seemingly unafraid to speak their mind stand out, even if it means challenging the wisdom of party messaging. Yet, mavericks and team players usually have less influence when acting alone compared to when they unite within a caucus. Individual backbenchers can effect change when they thoroughly research an issue, advocate within party boundaries, and convince their colleagues to support them.[6] If enough backbenchers oppose the government's agenda, they can keep the cabinet in line rather than vice versa, and apply pressure on the leader to reverse course or even to resign. Mobilizing colleagues behind the scenes, away from both media scrutiny and opponents' knowledge, projects an image of unity that promotes stability. Conversely, when too much unfolds in public, the resulting instability can impair the party's reputation and paralyse a government. This is why limits to caucus dissent are necessary, particularly when disagreement jeopardizes the core functioning and legitimacy of the democratic system. But the constraints of party message discipline go too far, and too few parliamentarians practise the respectful disagreement that is essential for a healthy and vibrant democracy.

Whereas party enforcers used to focus their policing on members' voting in the legislature, they now effuse communications symmetry from the point of candidate recruitment, followed by campaign training that instils a central directive that candidates must not be a distraction. Party leaders and their agents now know far more about prospective candidates before approving their nomination, leading to pronounced selection bias and ideological alignment. The rejection of people whose actions or attitudes, now or in the past, conflict with party values and good judgment has cleaned up politics. But it has come at a cost of empowering party officials to cast aside applicants who are prone to challenge their authority, which lays the groundwork for fewer conflicting pressures in a caucus and greater homogeneity. Once elected, parliamentarians are guided by approved messages, and off-the-cuff remarks may prompt the leader's office to implement crisis communications measures, such as issuing a written statement that the member misspoke and is, for the time being, unavailable for further comment.[7] Backbenchers absorb these lessons, and typically modify their behaviour to align with the archetype of being a team player, appearing to lack authenticity and individuality.

In these ways, the sectarianism of hyper-partisanship is antithetical to liberal democracy, the principle of pluralism, and the concept of responsible government. When party loyalty flexes its might, parliamentarians must prioritize party positions, thereby limiting the diversity of viewpoints expressed in election campaigns, legislative debates, decision-making processes, and public discourse in general. The resulting homogenization of perspectives undermines pluralism, which thrives on the open competition of ideas and the representation of varied interests within the political arena. Without a pluralistic framework that integrates diverse opinions into the political sphere, and with excessive message discipline that suppresses dissenting views, there is a risk of divisive "us" versus "them" factionalism whereby compromise and consensus-building are replaced by conflict and zero-sum competition.[8] A thriving democracy requires politicians who are not penalized for challenging groupthink.

Returning to the Roots of Representation

In the opening chapter, we identified representational roles played by parliamentarians. As Edmund Burke once described, they are expected to be trustees of the broader public good who make decisions for the betterment of all of society; at times, this may mean defending the interests of the polity against the opinions of their constituents.[9] At other times, parliamentarians are expected to serve as delegates who represent the interests of those who voted for them and the broader constituency from which they were elected. These roles are frequently in tension, requiring elected officials to trade off between local and societal priorities. Reinterpretations of Burke's dichotomy suggest that many parliamentarians navigate multiple roles, playing the part of a politico who adopts trustee and delegate roles as necessary.[10] Balancing these roles encourages a more collaborative and less adversarial approach to politics, where compromise and consensus-building are valued over party loyalty and division. This can lead to more stable and inclusive policies that reflect a wider range of views and interests, reducing party polarization in the process. Bumping aside these functions is that of the loyal partisan who prioritizes the party.[11] Partisanship can be an important counterweight to elitism and parochialism, while also incentivizing parliamentarians to engage with constituents, such as by requiring those interested in renomination to actively communicate, knock on doors, place phone calls, and recruit donors. Unfortunately, in Canada both the trustee and delegate functions have been subsumed to the whims of partisanship and, increasingly, to the imperatives of hyper-partisanship, with many parliamentarians being asked to deprioritize raising awareness of local concerns and to abandon cross-party consensus. In the following pages we outline some reasonable avenues for reform, summarized in box 10.1.

Box 10.1. Areas for Reform

1. Create an arms-length, multipartisan training program for rookie parliamentarians.
2. Tinker with the formal rules of procedure in legislatures to reduce the power of parliamentary parties.
3. Curtail the flagrant use of the confidence convention.
4. Formalize rules for caucus meetings, including an in-camera session without political staff.
5. Prohibit floor crossing and formalize two-stepping.
6. Prevent political parties from withholding constituent files from a former caucus member.
7. Change election rules and Standing Orders to be more inclusive of Independents.

Empower Rookie Parliamentarians

One of the most important ways to empower parliamentarians is to educate them at the outset on how to be effective representatives, even while working within the constraints of caucus membership and party message discipline. At present, most parliamentarian orientation training takes place in the weeks following an election during a frenzied time when rookies are inundated with information and tasks.[12] Nonpartisan employees of the legislature typically convene a series of presentations to introduce new parliamentarians to the procedural rules of the assembly, ethics and human resource guidelines, and legal responsibilities.[13] Parliamentarians receive organization charts and procedure manuals. They get answers to basic workplace questions, such as where to pick up their office keys. Most of the political onboarding is done informally within caucus, however, giving the party leader and their closest advisors immense control over the socialization of new parliamentarians. This includes all-important norms around representation.[14] The leadership and party veterans use this opportunity to impress the importance of unity and reinforce the cardinal rule that maintaining a consistent message in public forums is essential.

Knowing the formal and informal rules of the legislature is a good way for backbenchers to get the upper hand. Parliamentarians who have difficulty sorting out the norms of team culture or who get upset with their limited role can struggle mightily in a party caucus and the legislature. Only those with a keen interest in procedure devote ample time to mastering parliamentary rules, and typically only those who have the security of re-election or who have the option to pivot to another career feel that they can afford to be dogmatic about it.[15] As well, an ability to work with all members regardless of partisanship is essential to advancing policy, especially if that involves reforming a legislature's rules of procedure, often known as the Standing Orders. Gaining knowledge of the system is particularly vital for members of under-represented groups in elected assemblies to level the playing field, assert their expertise and insights, and enable equitable participation.

We believe that new parliamentarians across Canada would benefit from participating in a specialized, multipartisan training program, designed and delivered by former parliamentarians. This program would offer a deeper understanding of parliamentary and political practices, while also contextualizing partisanship as but one representative function. A centre for parliamentary democracy could bring together rookie parliamentarians to learn about their roles in the broader

Westminster system and how partisanship can both bolster and hinder them in pursuit of the public good. They could study the procedures of their respective legislatures, which would empower them to effectively advance or oppose policy initiatives, and potentially inspire them to spearhead efforts aimed at reducing the preferential treatment given to recognized political parties. Exercises could be designed to foster respectful critique, neuter attack-dog politics and online vitriol, and forge intra- and interparty relationships. Closed-door sessions could offer forums for discussing work-life balance and managing toxicity. This programming could build on existing infrastructure, including onboarding and continuous education through the Inter-Parliamentary Union, the House of Commons Administration, and the Parliamentary Centre, and infuse a Canadian-centred focus that complements the international curriculum of McGill University's programming in parliamentary governance for MPs and the global programming offered by the Commonwealth Parliamentary Association.[16]

Empower Backbenchers

The extent to which backbenchers should have a more meaningful role in governance depends on one's perspective of parliamentary sovereignty.[17] While it is essential for party leaders to exert influence over their parliamentary caucus, the equilibrium has shifted disproportionately, especially within governing parties. Empowering parliamentarians to represent their constituents means relaxing many of the procedural rules of the legislature that contribute to centralized power. In Ottawa, a periodic window for MPs to talk about revising the Standing Orders is built-in. Standing Order 51(1) stipulates that somewhere between the sixtieth and ninetieth sitting day of a Parliament, a priority order of the day will be to discuss the operations of the House and its committees.[18] Michael Chong, the MP behind the *Reform Act, 2014*, used the opportunity in 2022 to call for changes to provide backbenchers with more say.[19] He advocated for a return to the historical practice where the Speaker decides which MPs are recognized to speak, thereby doing away with the lists provided by party whips and house leaders. He recommended that the Board of Internal Economy – the powerful body responsible for overseeing the House of Commons' operations – be made up of backbenchers elected by secret ballot instead of parliamentarians nominated by the party leadership. In provincial legislatures, many of these and the *Reform Act, 2014* provisions could be adopted to enhance the delegate function of parliamentarians. Where applicable, this includes amending election laws and practices so that someone other than the leader, such as the presidents of electoral district associations, is responsible for approving party candidates. As well, the procedural rules of each legislature could be changed so that internal votes are held about caucus membership procedures.

Parliamentarians need institutional support to serve as trustees of the public good. At present, party whips award most parliamentary committee assignments. Enabling parliamentarians to select committee membership by secret ballot might result in a better alignment of experience and skill around the table in designated committees. The revised process would tone down the government's efforts to push its agenda forward with minimal scrutiny and would open committees up to parliamentarians who were elected as Independents. Chong is a proponent of related changes. As part of his 2022 reform proposal, he advocated for allocating committee chairs to parties in proportion to their share of seats in the legislature, instead of restricting chairperson roles to the two largest parties. He also proposed dividing the time for discussing routine motions in committees equally among its members, which would give members of smaller parties and Independents more opportunity to participate.[20]

Another way to empower the back benches is to limit the ability of party leaders and whips to manipulate the confidence convention to bully everyone into line. Current interpretations of the convention provide no leeway for dissent on important legislation, including massive omnibus bills, and in minority government situations this dynamic can result in brinksmanship and polarization. An obvious solution is to permit more free votes. More specifically, one set of solutions involves introducing a practice that if the government loses a vote on a major policy initiative, it can continue to govern unless it is defeated on an immediate and clearly worded motion of non-confidence. This idea was advocated by the Reform Party in the 1990s[21] and resurrected by New Democrat MP Daniel Blaikie in 2023.[22] Allowing parliamentarians the flexibility to reject individual bills without triggering the fall of the government, as practised in the nineteenth century, would have far-reaching effects, such as curbing the government's ability to advance omnibus bills that bypass focused policy debates. Additionally, providing members with an unambiguous question about whether they want the legislature to be dissolved would alleviate equating opposition to a government bill with support for an immediate general election. This approach would also resolve questions about whether certain votes constitute matters of confidence by, for instance, eliminating confusion over whether the defeat of a procedural motion can lead to the government's collapse.[23]

Another substantive way for backbenchers to reclaim some represen-tational agency is for them to take the initiative to limit the encroach-ment of political staff. Our research highlighted the formidable role that the leader's senior staff play in maintaining caucus harmony and discipline. Their work is essential in a fast-paced, multilayered political environment. However, the power of political staff – many of whom are considerably younger than the parliamentarians they advise – is a source of friction, particularly when they act as agents of the gov-ernment, overshadowing elected members of the legislature. Addition-ally, there are perceptions (whether accurate or not) that the leader's staff brandishes influence over policy decisions and the trajectory of political careers.[24] A practical and symbolic way to mitigate that del-egated influence is for caucus meeting agendas to include an *in camera* component whereby all staff must exit, allowing parliamentarians to have time alone with the party leader. As well, a leader can be urged to convene special meetings without any staff present. More broadly, we see value in institutionalizing caucus meetings with formal rules and procedures that establish some accountability for how caucus chairs run them.[25]

Formalize Two-Stepping

Some politicians are not cut out to be a caucus person due to their per-sonality and a mismatch of political values, which can endanger caucus harmony and the party's brand image. Equally, some parties and their leaders are inhospitable or are the wrong vehicle to satisfy a parliamen-tarian's ambitions. For these reasons and more, it can be necessary for a parliamentarian to leave a party, which can lead to them crossing the floor directly into another caucus or taking a more labyrinthine route into one.

When a parliamentarian changes their party affiliation, there can be calls to address perceived opportunism and a blatant disregard for the will of voters. A 2018 Angus Reid public opinion survey found that Canadians were evenly divided on whether to allow or ban crossing the floor, and whether a party switcher should have to sit as an Independent until the next election or should be obliged to resign and recontest the seat.[26] The resignation principle reinforces the primacy of political parties, while elevating the notion that voters should have the final say. Until 1931, legislation prevented a prime minister from poaching a member of Parliament to join the cabinet without the MP first resigning and being re-elected in a by-election so that constituents could be the final arbiter. The requirement, a long-standing feature of parliamentary supremacy, was similarly abolished by provincial legislatures.[27] In this tradition, some Canadian partisans – particularly New Democrats – have called upon parliamentarians seeking to change caucuses to first sit as an Independent, secure the nomination to run as their party's candidate, and be elected with their new party in a general election, or alternatively, resign and pursue re-election in a by-election.[28] For them, membership in a parliamentary caucus should be reserved for those who were elected under the party's banner. In Manitoba, an NDP government introduced a ban on floor crossing in 2006, requiring any MLA who left a caucus to serve the remainder of their term as an Independent. The legislation was challenged in court and found to be constitutional, though it was repealed by a PC government in 2017.[29] Unlike two-step processes that occur between elections, these election-focused approaches strengthen the power of party leaders by removing one of the few mechanisms available to caucus members to limit that power, as party discipline becomes even more rigid when members feel that they cannot flee.[30] These feelings of powerlessness to leave a caucus must be understood within the context of parliamentary rules, which are heavily biased against independence.

A less arduous two-step path to joining another caucus is for a parliamentarian to sit as an Independent and take some time to consult constituents before affiliating with a new party. We have shown that the two-step process is more politically astute and democratically acceptable than floor crossing, offering caucus members a vital check on the authority of a party leader. We believe that procedural rules in Canadian legislatures should require that a parliamentarian sit as an Independent for a minimum period before they can be permitted to join another caucus and, by extension, to cross the floor into cabinet. This would establish a cooling-off period, lessen cross-party salvos, ensure a measure of empowering constituents, and diminish the leader's reward power.

Relatedly, it is troubling that political parties can restrict a former caucus member's access to electronic records that contain important information about their constituents. In some cases, parliamentarians and their constituency office staff have been locked out of casework files and emails after leaving a party.[31] Additionally, they may lose access to local campaign data, including details about donors, supporters who have taken campaign signs, and volunteer lists.[32] The central issue is ownership of the data collected and stored about electors, and whether individuals who provide their information to a local party representative give informed consent for that information to become the exclusive property of the party. This control over local data grants political parties additional power over parliamentarians, which can damage an elected official's ability to effectively serve constituents and pursue re-election. Clear rules are needed to guarantee that parliamentarians retain access to constituent files upon leaving a party.

Empower Independents

We recognize the profound advantages that political parties bring to organizing legislatures and elections, along with the value of teamwork among like-minded parliamentarians and the benefits of upholding a cohesive party brand. We also understand that critics contend that Independents are counterproductive to effective representation, to the formation of governments, and to the efficiency of legislatures. These are among the reasons political parties have adopted cartel-like strategies to create election and parliamentary rules that are heavily stacked against Independents: to safeguard the stability, efficiency, and dominance of party rule. However, political parties should not monopolize representation, and being an Independent need not be an aberration. Every legislature could benefit from a few diligent Independents who have the freedom to voice perspectives that partisans will not and who have a fighting chance at re-election.

Independents face an uphill battle. They lack the resources and staff that members of a party with official status have, they have limited influence as solitary actors, they can feel isolated, and the media and voters can view them as ineffective and inconsequential. To make matters worse, governments restrict when Independents can fundraise (even as incumbents) and whether they can serve on parliamentary committees, which makes it much harder for Independents to get (re-)elected, and to serve as delegates and trustees. We see no compelling justification for subjecting incumbents to different election finance rules based on their lack of party affiliation, nor do we believe that Independents should be excluded from membership on parliamentary committees, where such practices exist. As party message discipline intensifies, ensuring that Independents have a fairer chance of (re-)election and the opportunity to play meaningful roles in legislative affairs become increasingly important to upholding the principles of parliamentary democracy.

A symbolic start would be to use distinct terminology to differentiate those elected on their own recognizance from partisans who depart a caucus, sometimes for unethical behaviour. We do not believe that parliamentarians elected with a political party should be accorded the esteemed status of Independent unless they are elected as one. Instead, we believe that legislatures should refer to parliamentarians who exit a party as "Unaffiliated" and that they should reserve the title of "Independent" for those who defy the odds to get elected without a party affiliation. Variations of this terminology are already in use on some election ballots.[33] This small yet mighty change would boost the status and prestige of true Independents in Canadian legislatures, such as Vicki Huntington, Paul Lane, and Bobbi Ann Brady (who suggested this to us). In addition, where possible, elected Independents should be seated separately from ex-partisans who become Unaffiliated members. An Independent's pride of being elected on their own name is degraded when partisans see them sitting among sex offenders and other transgressors.[34] This proposed distinction would truly matter if Independents were afforded more equitable opportunities within legislatures and elections, both of which are structured around political parties, to the detriment of a healthy democracy.

Conclusion

In this book, we have explored the complex interplay of the many variables that transform Canadian parliamentarians into loyal partisans. While the tendency to present a unified front is not a new phenomenon, constraints on their actions and communications, both inside and outside the legislature, have tightened. These pressures have contributed to the perception of political parties and their leaders as uncompromising rivals who demand obedience from their parliamentary caucuses. As we illustrate, Canadian party politics has left little room for an "I" in "team."

We have sought to address a stubborn mystery about Canadian politics: why is party allegiance so primal for so many Canadian parliamentarians? They are loyal to their party because of a mix of institutional, political, social, and technological forces. As we summarized in table 1.1, institutional factors that condition their behaviour include leader-focused systems, legal frameworks, governance structures, and party rules. Then there is a layer of political elements, including leadership and ambition, vote-getting and branding, networks and unity, and policy positioning. Add to that the considerable social elements, including their socio-economic class and world view, group dynamics, relationships, and shared identity and belonging. Finally, technological developments – an area that we argue has added considerable conformity pressures in the twenty-first century – include media and messaging, public opinion research and data mining, and digital communications. Each parliamentarian has a unique story about how they ended up in party politics, but all of them form bonds of loyalty to their party based on some combination of these forces. This in turn reflects their willingness to embrace the conformity demands of party affiliation, and turn against those who resist it.

For parliamentarians of all types and stripes, we contend that party discipline now extends beyond the legislature to encompass message discipline because political parties possess the technology to coordinate their communications and the motivation to do so. In a digital age filled with a cacophony of platforms, channels, and voices, there is a pressing desire for party representatives to consistently repeat key messages so that the public hears them. This is important not only for strategic marketing and branding purposes, but also for the practicality of reaching audiences, presenting clear choices, and minimizing the risk of crisis communication. For most parliamentarians, acting as a local stand-in for the leader and amplifying party messages on social media means relinquishing part of their own identity, which is vitally important for establishing a personal bond with constituents. Without this authenticity, parliamentarians become more dependent on the party for their own career prospects and influence, and less independent as an autonomous voice within the democratic process.

Parliamentarians who disrupt norms of party loyalty manage to remain in the party provided they embody its values, have a strong following, and are prepared to submit to the leader's supremacy. When team players agitate, they do so respectfully which can involve working with the chief of staff or party whip to issue a thoughtful public statement that affirms support for the leader. When party mavericks cause a ruckus, their actions can either generate useful publicity and the leader's begrudging admiration, or else they can stir controversy and the leader's ire. There is also strength in numbers: if enough team players disagree with the leadership it will have to take notice and it will be unable to level the same tools used to control individual renegades. Leaders disregard their caucuses at their own peril.

At times, unrest leads to an irreparable split and a switch in party allegiance. Some initially sit as an Independent before crossing the floor to another caucus, which we call two-stepping. For those who make the leap, initial conversations with close advisors about potentially changing party allegiances escalate into reaching out to a trusted representative of another party. This progression leads to negotiations and, if successful, culminates in a handshake agreement. The leader's staff then sort out how to spin the story. Amid the ensuing back-and-forth, it can be difficult to discern the true motives behind the defection or expulsion. We have shown that attitudes towards the leader are important, with the caveat that many public interest rationales might be post hoc justifications for why politicians behave the way that they do. Claiming to selflessly prioritize constituents or a policy is highly respected, whereas impressions of selfish opportunism or sour grapes tend to invite criticism, leading to overrepresentation of the former motives and suppression of the latter.

Party loyalty is reinforced when a parliamentarian rejects the caucus: the spurned party activates latent partisanship to launch a fiery attack, energizing group identity and signalling the cost of disloyalty. Those who choose to leave often contend with a barrage of negativity, including from distraught constituents and irate former colleagues. Some of them liken the break-up to divorce. Some go on to have successful political careers, but the majority face harsher fates, either retiring or losing their bid to keep their seat. Few manage to be re-elected as Independents, a role often seen as a political dead end, yet one that holds the potential to revitalize Canadian parliamentary democracy.

The emphasis on communication strategies and tactics aimed at solidifying partisanship among Canadian parliamentarians shows no indication of abating. In fact, it is likely to intensify as more loyalists self-select into the system and as advancements in communications technology ranging from database marketing to artificial intelligence further contribute to polarization. Party message discipline and hyper-partisanship constitute wicked problems that defy traditional problem-solving or straightforward solutions. We anticipate that Canada's political parties, especially those holding large numbers of seats in the legislature, will continue to promote entrenched positions and lose interest in finding common ground with opponents, edging Canada closer to the deep polarization seen in the United States. The individual agency of backbenchers, and even ministers, will further erode as their public profiles dwindle and decision-making power consolidates within the leader's office.

Our research has exposed many overlooked realities of life as an elected official in a Canadian parliamentary party. Like other hidden worlds, it reveals that much remains unknown about the inner workings of Canadian party politics, from cultural norms and individual behaviour to institutional reform and structural party power. The findings open new avenues for inquiry. What would it take for Canadian politicians to resist the prevailing norm of adopting the identity of a team player who puts the party and its leader first? How can parliamentarians project authenticity and independent thinking without forfeiting the benefits of party loyalty? How can society stop treating even modest acts of independence or dissent as abnormal? What would enable sitting parliamentarians to speak out about partisanship while still seeking re-election, rather than waiting until retirement? How can hyper-partisan rhetoric that casts opponents as enemies – and undermines the consensus-building essential to pluralistic democracy – be challenged?

These are just some of the many questions left unanswered. Others include the following: What meaningful roles can backbenchers in large caucuses play in formulating and evaluating policy? How can partisanship be reduced on parliamentary committees? What measures could counter the growing centralization of power in party leaders and their senior staff? What rules are needed to limit the unintended consequences of branding, candidate vetting, and party database management? What reforms would create space for parliamentarians to openly disagree with their party? And how do we curb the ability of political parties to act as cartels that design rules and monopolize resources to the disadvantage of Independents and internal dissenters alike? These and many other questions need to be put to parliamentarians and other political actors in government, legislatures, and extra-parliamentary parties. Future research can build on our interdisciplinary approach, which combines political science with insights from workplace studies, organizational behaviour, social psychology, marketing, and communications.

A challenging question emerging from this research is how to stall or reverse the trend of party message discipline and the diminishing ability of parliamentarians to prioritize constituent interests over agendas set by the leadership. We believe that ultimately it is up to backbenchers – especially those in the governing party – to rise above institutional, political, social, and technological pressures and take action to steer Canada away from the dangers of blind, unwavering party loyalty, moving instead towards a more responsive, inclusive, and representative democracy. Whether they assume them or not, parliamentarians must navigate multiple representational roles, balancing trustee, delegate, and partisan functions, though partisanship has increasingly overshadowed independent decision-making. We have recommended several reforms to restore this balance, including multipartisan training for rookies, changes to legislative procedures to reduce party dominance, and constraints on the confidence convention. Empowering backbenchers requires allowing more free votes, reforming committee selection processes, and limiting the influence of political staff. Floor crossing remains contentious, with proposals for mandatory cooling-off periods to ensure accountability to constituents rather than party leaders. Independents face institutional barriers that need to be removed, including restrictions on fundraising and committee participation. Addressing these challenges could enhance democratic representation by strengthening individual parliamentary agency.

Change is essential to address rising hyper-partisanship, centralizing party control, and the evolving norms of representation that are reshaping political life in Canada. These trends have intensified along with advances in communications technology, with profound implications – not only for governance but also for the very nature of democratic accountability and public trust. Citizens and voters must demand responsiveness, transparency, and substantive debate from the people they elect. Back-bench politicians must understand that there is room for meaningful engagement, advocacy, and representation. Party leaders and their staff must take action to resolve the frustrations felt by many caucus members in a system that treats them as franchisees and brand ambassadors instead of people who can make a meaningful contribution if given the chance. Being aware of these constraints and opportunities is the first step towards finding ways for parliamentarians to have more flexibility to exercise independent judgment within the boundaries of party structures.

True teamwork is not about blind obedience or unquestioning loyalty; it is about collaboration, open debate, and a shared sense of purpose. For Canadian political parties and their leaders to truly serve democracy, they must create space for independent voices within their teams.

Appendix 1: Interview Recruitment and Script

Recruitment

We used purposive and convenience sampling methods when determining who to approach for an interview. Our initial objective was to interview a wide variety of Canadian politicians who had left or switched political parties since 1980. This task was made more challenging by the limited number of parliamentarians who had switched parties, compounded by factors such as poor health, deaths, a lack of publicly available contact information, and refusals due to the sensitivity of the topic. As interviews were completed, we ceased contacting male switchers in Ontario due to an overabundance of them, and contacted a modicum of political leaders and political staff as their important roles became apparent. Another supplementary round of interviews encompassed conversations with team players, party mavericks, and Independents, as well as specific individuals whose career arcs we were following in the news.

To recruit interview participants, we compiled contact information through online searches and by reaching out to legislative librarians, political party offices, and partisans we already knew. From 2018 to 2020, we extended invitations by email, social media, and/or telephone. Additionally, in January 2020, the Canadian Association of Former Parliamentarians assisted by mailing letters to twenty former MPs on our behalf. We ceased attempts to connect after four attempts over a period of months, and limited initiating new requests upon the declaration by the World Health Organization (WHO) in March 2020 that the COVID-19 virus was a global pandemic. That unexpected interruption led to some rescheduling and cancellations. We resumed with some specialized interview requests after the WHO declared the pandemic to be over in May 2023.

Our interview request included some project information, a consent form, and an interview script, along with an interviewer biography and, if applicable, a briefing note timeline that summarized key events, actors, and quotes that we gleaned from news reports about a party-switching episode. That briefing note provided the politician with an opportunity to set the record straight, demonstrated our intellectual curiosity and preparedness, served as a memory recall device during the interviews, and enabled us to engage in more meaningful discussions beyond simply revisiting publicly available information. The interview acceptance rate was approximately 50 per cent among those who left a party and among party leaders and senior staff, with higher rates of acceptance among retired politicians than sitting ones. Those who turned us down did not want to divulge private information. Some were concerned about the legal implications of revealing cabinet confidences or discussions about inducements; others said they were writing their memoirs. Acceptance was approximately 90 per cent among the partisans we subsequently contacted from 2023 to 2024 to discuss specialized content in a less formal manner. All told, we completed seventy-two interviews in English and eighteen in French.

The conversations ranged from twenty to ninety minutes in duration. Most were administered by telephone, with some taking place in person. A methodological shift took place: interviews conducted pre-pandemic were either by telephone or in person, while those conducted post-pandemic prioritized Teams or Zoom, reflecting the new norm of video conferencing. Subject to participant consent, we audio-recorded and transcribed most interviews, which we manually reviewed multiple times to flesh out concepts, verify understandings, and add evidence that bolstered the formal coding of Samara Centre MP exit interview transcripts. We assured participants that information would be attributed to them only with their written consent. Some requested that their comments be anonymous. These protocols were approved by research ethics boards at Memorial University of Newfoundland, the University of Alberta, and Université du Québec à Trois-Rivières.

Interview Script

We created three distinct versions of the interview script, tailored to parliamentarians, party leaders, and political staff. Below is an abridged interview guide provided to parliamentarians. Subsequent interviews were unstructured, usually to explore a particular knowledge gap.

1. Suppose you were to pick up a book about diehard partisans, party mavericks, Independents and party switchers in Canada. What do you think should be in the book?
2. When and why did you first get involved in party politics?
3. Why did you pick the party that you did when you first ran for elected office?
4. To what extent are you personally comfortable with the trade-offs of being a partisan?
5. How does a partisan reconcile personal beliefs when they differ from the party line?
6. Can you help me understand why some partisans sometimes publicly defy the party line?
7. Can you tell me about a time that you got in a heated disagreement within your party?
8. Can you explain why some parliamentarians who have outbursts and/or defy the party whip manage to stay in their party? Why do leaders tolerate these party mavericks?
9. If applicable: What is appealing about being an Independent? About sitting in another party's caucus?
10. If applicable: What is off-putting about being an Independent? About sitting in another party's caucus?
11. What considerations are involved when deciding to leave a caucus?
12. If applicable: Take me back to the days or even hours before you left your caucus. What questions were you asking yourself? Who did you confide in? What were you feeling?
13. Please walk me through any hidden processes or stages that we haven't covered about leaving a caucus and/or joining another caucus.
14. How were you treated after leaving your caucus? (e.g., by partisans, the media, locally)
15. What would surprise people the most about becoming an Independent or switching parties? What are the biggest misconceptions?
16. What would you recommend to a partisan who is unhappy in their caucus?
17. Is there anything you thought we would cover today, but didn't?

Appendix 2: List of Interviews

Albas, Dan. Conservative MP for Central Okanagan—Similkameen—Nicola, British Columbia. 17 January 2024.

Atwin, Jenica. Liberal MP and former Green MP for Fredericton, New Brunswick. 22 February 2024.

Aussant, Jean-Martin. Former PQ, Independent, and Option Nationale MNA for Nicolet-Yamaska, Quebec. 21 October 2019.

Beaudoin, Louise. Former PQ and Independent MNA for Rosemount, Quebec. 29 June 2020.

Belanger, Buckley. Former Liberal and NDP MLA for Athabasca, Saskatchewan. 23 August 2019.

Bennett, Jim. Former chief of staff to BC Social Credit leader Grace McCarthy. 6 August 2020.

Bernard, Karla. Green MLA for Charlottetown-Victoria Park, Prince Edward Island. 11 March 2024.

Blakeman, Laurie. Former Liberal MLA for Edmonton Centre, Alberta. 14 August 2020.

Bitter-Suermann, Hinrich. Former PC and NDP MLA for Chester—St. Margaret's, Nova Scotia. 1 October 2019.

Boutilier, Guy. Former PC and Independent MLA for Fort McMurray-Wood Buffalo. Alberta. 8 August 2019.

Brady, Bobbi Ann. Independent MPP for Haldimand-Norfolk, Ontario. 15 December 2023.

Brison, Scott. Former PC and Liberal MP for King's-Hants, Nova Scotia. 13 December 2019.

Brodie, Ian. Former chief of staff to Conservative Prime Minister Harper. 18 September 2019.

Brown, Mike. Former director of communications to Manitoba PC Premier Pallister. 8 July 2020.

Byrne, Jenni. Former deputy chief of staff to Conservative Prime Minister Harper. 27 May 2020.

Caesar-Chavannes, Celina. Former Liberal and Independent MP for Whitby, Ontario. 3 March 2020.

Cardy, Dominic. PC MLA for Fredericton West-Hanwell and former NDP leader, New Brunswick. 30 October 2019.

Carter, Stephen. Former Alberta PC leadership campaign manager. 17 August 2020.

Charbonneau, Jean-Pierre. Former PQ MNA for Verchères, Quebec. 1 June 2020.

Charest, Jean. Former leader of the PC Party of Canada and MP for Sherbrooke, and former Liberal premier and MLA for Sherbrooke, Quebec. 26 February 2019.

Chong, Michael. Conservative MP for Wellington—Halton Hills, Ontario. 25 January 2024.

Clark, Greg. Former leader of the Alberta Party and former MLA for Calgary-Elbow, Alberta. 10 August 2020.

Curzi, Pierre. Former PQ and Independent MNA for Borduas, Quebec. 17 July 2020.

Davis, Paul. PC MHA for Topsail-Paradise and former premier of Newfoundland & Labrador. 15 August 2018.

Donovan, Ian. Former Wildrose and PC MLA for Little Bow, Alberta. 13 August 2019.

Downe, Percy. Senator and former chief of staff to Prime Minister Jean Chrétien. 10 August 2020.

Duceppe, Gilles. Former leader of the Bloc Québécois and MP for Laurier—Sainte-Marie, Quebec. 22 January 2020.

Dunderdale, Kathy. Former PC premier and former MLA for Virginia Waters, Newfoundland & Labrador. 21 January 2020.

Fildebrandt, Derek. Former Wildrose, UCP, and Independent MLA for Strathmore Brooks, and former leader of the Freedom Conservative Party, Alberta. 22 August 2019.

Fournier, Catherine. Former PQ and Independent MNA for Marie-Victorin, Quebec. 13 November 2019.

Fraser, Rick. Former PC, UCP, and Independent MLA for Calgary-South East, Alberta. 7 August 2019.

Gill, Prab. Former PC and Independent MLA for Calgary-Greenway, Alberta. 11 August 2020.

Godin, Rosemary. Former NDP MLA for Sackville—Beaver Bank and former Liberal candidate in Dartmouth North, Nova Scotia. 5 March 2020.

Goodale, Ralph. Former Liberal MP for Regina—Wascana, Saskatchewan. 6 September 2023.

Harel, Louise. Former PQ MLA for Hochelaga-Maisonneuve, Quebec. 10 June 2020.

Harvey, André. Former PC, Independent, and Liberal MP for Chicoutimi, Quebec. 25 February 2020.

Herle, David. Former Liberal Party of Canada election campaign co-chair and former Ontario Liberal campaign co-chair. 6 October 2020.

Herron, John. Former PC MP and former Liberal candidate for Fundy—Royal, New Brunswick. 16 October 2019.

Hyer, Bruce. Former NDP and Green MP for Thunder Bay—Superior North, Ontario. 4 December 2019.

Jama, Sarah. Independent and former NDP MPP for Hamilton Centre, Ontario. 8 February 2024.

Jansen, Sandra. Former NDP and PC MLA for Calgary-North West, Alberta. 29 August 2019.

Kennedy-Glans, Donna. Former PC and Independent MLA for Calgary-Varsity, Alberta. 6 August 2020.

Lane, Paul. Independent MHA and former PC and Liberal MHA for Mount Pearl—Southlands, Newfoundland & Labrador. 16 August 2019.

MacEachern, Greg. Former executive assistant to Liberal Minister Belinda Stronach. 29 January 2024.

Mark, Inky. Former PC, Reform, Canadian Alliance, Independent, and Conservative MP for Dauphin-Swan River-Marquette, Manitoba. 11 August 2020.

Martin, Keith. Former Reform, Canadian Alliance, Independent, and Liberal MP for Esquimalt-Juan de Fuca, British Columbia. 5 August 2020.

Martin, Paul. Former Liberal Prime Minister of Canada and former MP for LaSalle—Émard, Quebec. 9 December 2019.

Mattia, Marie Della. Former NDP of Canada election campaign co-chair and provincial NDP strategist. 19 June 2020.

McGrath, Anne. National director of the NDP of Canada and former principal secretary to Alberta NDP Premier Rachel Notley. 26 May 2020.

McLellan, Anne. Former Liberal MP for Edmonton Centre, Alberta. 5 December 2023.

Melenchuk, Jim. Former leader of the Saskatchewan Liberal Party and Liberal, Independent, and NDP MLA for Saskatoon Northwest, Saskatchewan. 27 August 2020.

Michael, Lorraine. Former MHA for Signal Hill—Quidi Vidi and former leader of the NDP of Newfoundland & Labrador. 27 November 2018.

Mourani, Maria. Former Bloc Québécois and Independent MP and NDP candidate for Ahuntsic, Quebec. 4 March 2020.

Mulcair, Tom. Former New Democratic Party of Canada leader and MP for Outremont, and former Liberal MLA for Chomedey, Quebec. 8 November 2023.

Murphy, Tim. Former chief of staff to Liberal Prime Minister Martin. 18 December 2019.

Name withheld. Former Wildrose and PC MLA, Alberta. 26 August 2019.

Nash, Peggy. Former NDP MP for Parkdale—High Park, Ontario. 12 January 2024.

Nunziata, John. Former Liberal and Independent MP for York South—Weston, Ontario. 25 February 2020.

Paillé, Daniel. Former leader of the Bloc Québécois and MP for Hochelaga, and former PQ MNA for Prévost, Quebec. 2 and 5 March 2020.

Paquette, Gilbert. Former PQ and Independent MNA for Rosemont, Quebec. 15 June 2020.

Parrish, Carolyn. Former Liberal and Independent MP for Missisauga—Erindale, Ontario. 9 March 2020.

Pedersen, Blake. Former Wildrose and PC MLA for Medicine Hat, Alberta. 19 November 2019.

Peterson, David. Former Liberal premier and MPP for London Centre, Ontario. 15 October 2019.

Philpott, Jane. Former Liberal and Independent MP for Markham—Stouffville, Ontario. 6 February 2020.

Pimblett, Jim. Former executive assistant to Liberal Prime Minister Martin. 23 February 2020.

Plamondon, Louis. Bloc Québécois MP for Bécancour-Nicolet-Saurel and former PC MP, Quebec. 25 October 2020.

Price, David. Former PC and Liberal MP for Compton-Stanstead, Quebec. 29 October 2019.

Raitt, Lisa. Former Conservative MP for Milton, Ontario. 20 October 2020.

Rathgeber, Brent. Former Conservative and Independent MP for Edmonton-St. Albert, Alberta and former PC MLA for Edmonton Calder, Alberta. 11 August 2020.

Ratthé, Daniel. Former PQ, Independent and CAQ MNA for Blainville, Quebec. 24 October 2019.

Robinson, Svend. Former NDP MP for Burnaby—Douglas, British Columbia. 16 August 2018.

Romanow, Roy. Former NDP premier of Saskatchewan and former MLA for Saskatoon Riversdale, Saskatchewan. 10 August 2020.

Simms, Scott. Former Liberal MP for Coast of Bays—Central—Notre Dame, Newfoundland and Labrador. 16 January 2024.

Smith-McCrossin, Elizabeth. Independent MLA and former PC MLA for Cumberland North, Nova Scotia. 5 January 2024.

St-Denis, Lise. Former NDP and Liberal MP for Saint-Maurice-Champlain, Quebec. 18 October 2019.

Stelmach, Ed. Former PC premier and former MLA for Vegreville-Viking, Alberta. 10 August 2020.

St-Jacques, Diane. Former PC and Liberal MP for Shefford, Quebec. 22 October 2019.

Swann, David. Former leader of the Alberta Liberal Party and former MLA for Calgary-Mountain View, Alberta. 10 August 2020.

Taylor, Dave. Former Liberal, Independent and Alberta Party MLA for Calgary-Currie, Alberta. 21 August 2019.

Tremblay, Benoit. Former PC, Independent, and Bloc Québécois MP for Rosemont, Quebec. 3 December 2019.

Tyabji, Judi. Former Liberal and Progressive Democratic Alliance MLA for Okanagan East, British Columbia. 2 August 2019.

Vaugeois, Denis. Former PQ MNA for Trois-Rivières, Quebec. 16 June 2020.

Vuong, Kevin. Independent MP and former Liberal candidate for Spadina—Fort York, Ontario. 5 January 2024.

Waddell, Ian. Former NDP MP for Port Moody-Coquitlam and former NDP MLA for Vancouver-Fraserview, British Columbia. 21 August 2020.

Weir, Erin. Former NDP and Independent MP for Regina-Lewvan, Saskatchewan. 14 August 2020.

Wilson, Jeff. Former Wildrose and PC MLA for Calgary-Shaw, Alberta. 20 August 2020.

Wilson, Gordon. Former Liberal, Progressive Democratic Alliance, and NDP MLA for Powell River-Sunshine Coast and former leader of the Liberal and PDA parties, British Columbia. 15 August 2019.

Wiseman, Ross. Former Liberal and PC MHA for Trinity North, Newfoundland & Labrador. 15 August 2018.

Wright, Nigel. Former chief of staff to Conservative Prime Minister Harper. 1 February 2024.

Young, Steve. Former PC MLA for Edmonton-Riverview, Alberta. 6 August 2020.

Notes

Preface: The Persistence of Party Loyalty

1 Canadian Press, "Corrective to Story."
2 Robbins-Kanter and Mattan, "Recruiting Brand Ambassadors."
3 We thank Mr. Erskine-Smith for joining a panel discussion about this book at George Brown College in June 2025. Among his reflections was a thought-provoking question for parliamentarians: "Who is your team: your riding association, or the wider party?"
4 Rana, "PMO Staffers."
5 Davies, "Statement."
6 Aiello, "Mark Carney Says."
7 Depner, "John Rustad Accuses."

1. Party Loyalty in Canada

1 Richler, *The Candidate*, 34.
2 Richler, *The Candidate*, 38.
3 Richler, *The Candidate*, 56. Relatedly, see chapter 5 in Wagner, *The Candidacy Calculation*.
4 Quoted in Richler, *The Candidate*, 232 and 235.
5 Robbins-Kanter, "Canadian Parties in the Constituencies."
6 Lewis et al., "Cabinet Solidarity"; Koop et al., *Representation in Action*; Robbins-Kanter, "Undisciplined Constituency"; Yates, "National-Local Messaging."
7 Carty, "Politics of Tecumseh Corners."
8 Given the scope of work and limited provincial scholarship, in this book we judiciously use federal and provincial terminology interchangeably, while recognizing that phenomena in one legislature might not always apply to others.
9 Close et al., "Party Organisation and Party-Delegate Style."
10 Maher, *The Prince*, 143.
11 Cross et al., *The Political Party in Canada*.
12 For more on team cohesion, see Sullivan and Feltz, "The Relationship between Intrateam."

13 Cotterill, *Team Psychology in Sports*.
14 Scammell, "Populism and Political Marketing."
15 Carty, "Politics of Tecumseh Corners," 727; Godbout and Høyland, "Unity in Diversity?"
16 Kam, *Party Discipline*, 3. See also Godbout, *Lost on Division*.
17 Marland, *Brand Command*; Marland, *Whipped*.
18 Wesley, *Big Worlds*; Wesley and Buckley, "Provincial Party Systems."
19 Holt, "What Explains Party Unity?"
20 For a review, see Ladewig, "Conditional Party Government."
21 Lebo et al., "Strategic Party Government," 464.
22 González et al., "Theory on Party Discipline."
23 Lebo et al., "Strategic Party Government."
24 Young, "Party, State and Political Competition."
25 Benzie, Ferguson and Rushow, "Ford Fears Disgruntled."
26 Michels, *Political Parties*; Husted et al., "Political Parties"; Diefenbach, "Why Michels' 'Iron Law of Oligarchy,'" 556.
27 Gert, "Loyalty and Morality," 18–19.
28 Asmussen and Ramey, "When Loyalty is Tested."
29 González et al., "Theory on Party Discipline."
30 Wamble et al., "We Are One."
31 Marland, *Whipped*, 193 and 331.
32 Lalancette et al., *What's Trending?*
33 Brodie, *At the Centre of Government*, 146.
34 Lim, "Failed NDP Leadership Candidate."
35 Dyer, "Liberal MP Majid Jowhari."
36 Dinshaw, "McNeil Mocked on Social Media."
37 Woo, "B.C. Deputy Green."
38 Aiello, "Liberal MP Sahota"; Marland, *Whipped*, chap. 5.
39 Dyer, "Key Liberal MP Rips Government." The full headline referred to the government's policy on the Israel-Hamas war. See also Rana and Lapointe, "Oliphant's Leaked Private Conversation."
40 Angus Reid Institute, "Pointless Parliament?"
41 For example, see Dyck, "Federal and Provincial Parties."
42 Franks, *The Parliament of Canada*, 22; Godbout, *Lost on Division*.
43 Pelletier et al., "The Structures of Canadian Political Parties," 281–5.
44 Courtney, "Canadian Prime Minister."
45 For example, Duffy, *Fights of Our Lives*, 267.
46 Bélanger and Stephenson, "Parties and Partisans."
47 Johnston and Sharman, "Introduction."
48 Bakvis, *Regional Ministers*.
49 For example, Thomas, "The Role of National Party Caucuses."
50 Monopoli, "Government and News Media."
51 Taras, *Digital Mosaic*.
52 Marland et al., *Permanent Campaigning*.
53 Marland, *Brand Command*, 191–3.
54 Pendakur and Sarna, "Mr Speaker"; Stewart et al., "Barbarians at the Gate?"
55 Flanagan, *Winning Power*, 71–2, and Marland and Giasson, "The Evolution of Brokerage Politics." But see Bennett and Gordon, "Political Micro-targeting."
56 Marland, "Communications Coordination."
57 For example, see Morden and Anderson, "Don't Blame 'the People'"; Scammell, "Populism and Political Marketing"; Stewart, *How Not to be a Politician*, 215.

58 For example, see Lalancette et al., *What's Trending?*; Marland et al., *Permanent Campaigning*; Merkley, "Ideological and Partisan Bias"; Pennycook et al., "Beliefs about COVID-19."
59 Grenier, "Bill Who?"; Levitz, "Who's That Guy?"; Marland, *Whipped*, 64–71; Marland et al., "Scripted Messengers"; Pollara Strategic Insights, "Awareness of Political Leaders."
60 Gidengil et al., "COVID-19 and Support for Executive."
61 See, in part, Black, "Racial Diversity."
62 Marland, *Whipped*, 322–5; Petit-Vouriot et al., *2019 Democracy 360*, 27–32.
63 Rusbult and Zembrodt, "Responses to Dissatisfaction."
64 Yoshinaka, *Crossing the Aisle*.
65 For example, Bélanger and Stephenson, "Parties and Partisans"; Campbell et al., *The American Voter*; Everitt et al., "Patterns of Party Identification"; Gidengil et al., *Dominance and Decline*; Gidengil, "Voting Behaviour"; Jenson, "Party Loyalty"; Merkley, "Ideological and Partisan Bias."
66 Everitt et al., "Patterns of Party Identification"; Jenson, "Party Loyalty."
67 Bélanger and Nadeau, "Political Trust and the Vote."
68 Gidengil et al., *Dominance and Decline*, 13–18.
69 Bittner, "Effects of Information and Social Cleavages."
70 Cochrane, *Left and Right*.
71 Wiseman, "Ideological Competition"; Cross et al., *The Political Party in Canada*, 39–47.
72 Kevins and Soroka, "Growing Apart?" See also Ozbudun, *Party Cohesion*, 350–4.
73 Bélanger and Stephenson, "Parties and Partisans."
74 Cross et al., *The Political Party in Canada*, 124–7.
75 Carty, "Has Brokerage Politics Ended?"
76 Schwartz and Tatalovich, *Rise and Fall of Moral Conflicts*, 140–9.
77 Cuddy, "When Does Partisanship Become Excessive?"
78 Hankins, "Hyperpartisanship."
79 Kehoe, *Empire and Emancipation*; Lipset, *Continental Divide*.
80 Chief Electoral Officer of Canada, *History of the Vote in Canada*; Levine, *Scrum Wars*; Nolan, "Political Communication Methods."
81 Ward, "Early Use of Radio for Political Communication."
82 Ibbitson, *The Duel*.
83 Whyte, "The Face that Sank a Thousand Tories."
84 Ibbitson, "Here's the Story."
85 Schumpeter, *Capitalism, Socialism, and Democracy*.
86 Waldrop, "Modeling the Power of Polarization."
87 Merkley, "Mass Polarization in Canada."
88 Dassonneville, *Voters Under Pressure*; Kevins and Soroka, "Growing Apart?"
89 Caruana et al., "The Power of the Dark Side."
90 Graves, "Polarization, Populism, and Evolving Public."
91 Angus Reid Institute, "Missing Political Middle."
92 Wesley et al., "Polarization in Alberta."
93 However, as Gidengil, "Voting Behaviour in Canada" notes, research about partisanship as part of social identity is lacking.
94 Tasker, "Speaker Kicks Poilievre Out."
95 Lederman, "Conservative MPs Display."
96 Bosc, "The Commons Then and Now."
97 Whyte, "Modelling Parliamentary Interruptions."

98   Havrot, "Throne Speech Debate."
99   National Post, "Trudeau's Hyper Partisanship."
100 Starke, "The Rise of Partisanship."
101 Huo and Malloy, "Extreme Partisanship is Infecting Committees."
102 Orhan, "Affective Polarization and Democratic Backsliding."
103 Raney and Collier, Gender-Based Violence.
104 Damoff, "Statement."
105 Bellefontaine, "UCP Accused of Curbing Debate."
106 Kleinfeld, "Polarization, Democracy, and Political Violence."
107 Morgan and Pulignano, "Solidarity at Work."
108 Garner and Letki, "Party Structure"; Godbout, Lost on Division; Kam, "Parliamentary Behaviour."
109 Morton, "Party Switchers"; Sevi et al., "Legislative Party Switching."
110 Weber et al., "An Election Too Far."
111 Malloy, "High Discipline"; Malloy, Paradox of Parliament; McGrane, The New NDP; Thomas, "The Role of National Party Caucuses."
112 Rehmert, "Party Membership."
113 Godbout, Lost on Division.
114 Kam, "Parliamentary Behaviour."
115 Johnston and Sharman, "Introduction," 5.
116 Marland, Whipped.
117 Figure 2.2 in Marland, Whipped, 51; Sorbara, Let 'Em Howl, 162–3.
118 Sorbara, Let 'Em Howl, 130.
119 Heard, "A Vote of Confidence?," 397–9. See also Desserud, "Confidence Convention"; Forsey, "Government Defeats."
120 Godbout, Lost on Division, 145; Kam, Party Discipline, 52–3.
121 Sieberer, "Party Unity," 161. See also Godbout, Lost on Division.
122 Data kindly provided by Jean-François Godbout.
123 Thomas et al., "House Inspection," 13–14.
124 The most recent source we could locate is Massicotte, "Cohésion et dissidence."
125 Chartash et al., "When the Team's Jersey."
126 Godbout, Lost on Division, 72; Marland, Whipped; Platt, "Second Liberal MP."
127 Parliament of Canada, "Recorded Votes."
128 Godbout, Lost on Division, 83. See also Curry and Thompson, "Conservative MPs Break"; Grenier, "Liberal Backbenchers."
129 Godbout, Lost on Division, 118.
130 Godbout, Lost on Division, 189.
131 Globe and Mail, "Raps Method."
132 Aiken, The Backbencher, 132.
133 Marland, Whipped, chap. 5.
134 Clark, "Ethics Commissioner"; Office of the Ethics Commissioner of Canada, Harper-Emerson Inquiry.
135 MLAs in Nunavut and Northwest Territories are elected as Independents, meet as a group to set priorities, and select a premier. For more on consensus government, see White, "Traditional Aboriginal Values."
136 Eulau et al., "Role of the Representative," 750.
137 Converse and Pierce, Political Representation in France, 14.
138 Bøggild, "Politicians as Party Hacks."
139 Müller and Strøm, "Hard Choices." See also Marland, Whipped, 91.
140 Downs, An Economic Theory of Democracy.

141 Kam, *Party Discipline*, 15.
142 Schlesginger, *Ambition and Politics*; Herrick and Moore, "Political Ambition's Effect." See also Yoshinaka, *Crossing the Aisle*.
143 For example, see John Cummins, former Conservative MP in British Columbia, Samara Centre interview.
144 Wagner, "Motivations for Federal Candidacy."
145 As indicated by incentives among party members; see Young and Cross, "Incentives to Membership."
146 Koop et al., *Representation in Action*.
147 Kennedy and Oved, "Why these MPs aren't Speaking?"
148 Baumeister and Leary, "Anxiety and Social Exclusion."
149 Leary, "Interpersonal Rejection," 4.
150 For example, see Asch, "Effects of Group Pressure."
151 Brown and Pehrson, "Group Formation," 40.
152 Thomas, "The Role of National Party Caucuses," 84–5.
153 Copps, "PM had No Choice."
154 For example, see Steele, *What I Learned About Politics*, 33.
155 Quoted in Bazzo, "Pas de chicane."
156 Quoted in Benzie, "How Doug Ford."
157 Walker, "Liberals Reluctantly Accept."
158 For example, Brodie, *At the Centre of Government*, 179; Malloy, "High Discipline"; Sevi et al., "Legislative Party Switching," 692.
159 For example, Nova Scotia MLA Paul MacEwan (profiled in chapter 7) insisted he was born in PEI when in fact he was from New York. See Stewart, *Politics on the Edge*, 5.
160 Garner and Letki, "Party Structure," 469.
161 Francis, *Ottawa Boy*, 162.
162 Tolley, *Framed*, 216.
163 Esselment and Marland, "Want to Interview a Politician?"
164 Macdonald, "Liberals Sunny."
165 Weber et al., "An Election Too Far."
166 Hom et al., *Employer Retention and Turnover*, 7.
167 Kulik et al., "Can We Still be Friends?"
168 For example, Canadian Press, "Irate N.S. Premier"; CBC News, "Kim Craitor," CBC News, "Ontario PC."
169 For example, see Argue, "Senator Hazen Argue," 28, and Shackleton, *Tommy Douglas*, 258. See also Dowd, "Few are the Politicians"; Grey, *Never Retreat*, 204; Turner, *Sheeple*, 65.
170 As with not disclosing allegations by the (alleged) request of a complainant in an Ontario case. See Stone, "Doug Ford Confirms."
171 For example, Fraser, "Is Diefenbaker Running?"
172 Kerby, "Ministerial Careers."
173 Jewett, "Pauline Jewett," 13.
174 Mackie, "Jewett Switches," says 1966; McKenzie, *Pauline Jewett*, 73, says 1967.
175 McKenzie, *Pauline Jewett*, chap. 4 and 5.
176 Mackie, "Jewett Switches"; Russell, "Former Liberal." See also Jewett, "Pauline Jewett," 42.
177 Bain, "Jewett's Decision"; Jewett, "Pauline Jewett," 41.
178 McKenzie, *Pauline Jewett*, 86.
179 Belshaw, *Canadian History*; Feminist Institute of Social Transformation, "Biography"; Wright, "Trudeaumania."

180 Agnew and Vanderdrift, "Commitment Processes," 440. See also Sanders, "Former Tory MLA."
181 Snagovsky and Kerby, "Electoral Consequences."
182 Parliament of Canada, "Parliamentarians." The lack of cohesive parliamentary career records in some provinces and limited inclusion of local news outlets in media databases raises the possibility that the provincial numbers may be under-represented.
183 Search terms included the following: break ranks, controversy, defy, discipline, dissent, independent, maverick, offside, outspoken, party line, protest, rebel, resign*, party, caucus, MLA, MP, MHA, MPP, MNA, switch*, quit*, cross*, leav*, expel*, oust*, kick* out, toss*, and join*. Corresponding French-language terms were also searched.
184 The limitations of online news databases are examined in Milligan, "Illusionary Order."
185 Two of these interviews were also used for Marland, *Whipped*.
186 Details are available upon request from the authors.
187 Creswell, *Qualitative Inquiry*.
188 de Clercy and Marland, "Party Discipline," 35.
189 Entman, "Toward the Clarification," 52.
190 O'Neil, "Emerson Hails," A13; Wells, *Right Side Up*, 251; Wells, *The Longer I'm Prime Minister*, 17–18.
191 Lawrence and Rose, *Hillary Clinton's Race*.
192 Yoshinaka, *Crossing the Aisle*, 16.

2. Party Message Discipline

1 Recounted in Turner, *Sheeple*, 121.
2 Underhill, "National Political Parties," 369.
3 Underhill, "National Political Parties." See also Franks, *Parliament of Canada*, 21; Thomas, "The Role of National Party Caucuses," 81.
4 Forsey, "Government Defeats"; Heard, "A Vote of Confidence?" See also Desserud, "Confidence Convention."
5 Brancati, "Winning Alone," 648.
6 Thomas, "The Role of National Party Caucuses," 81–2.
7 Ames, "Organization of Political Parties."
8 For example, Quinn, "Third National Convention."
9 Godbout, *Lost on Division*, 197–9.
10 Strong-Boag, *Liberal-Labour Lady*, 117.
11 Morton, *The Progressive Party*.
12 Wiseman, *Partisan Odysseys*.
13 This was known as a "recall" letter. See Morton, *The Progressive Party*, 120–1.
14 For example, Irwin, "Progressive Party's Split," 1.
15 Carty, "Politics of Tecumseh Corners."
16 Godbout, *Lost on Division*, 242.
17 Ozbudun, *Party Cohesion*, 323.
18 Courtney, "Political Parties in Parliament," 34.
19 Godbout, *Lost on Division*, 76 and 187.
20 Godbout, *Lost on Division*, 190.
21 Godbout, *Lost on Division*, chap. 8.
22 Godbout, *Lost on Division*, 191.
23 Blidook, *Constituency Influence*, 31–6; Godbout, *Lost on Division*, 59.

24 Godbout, *Lost on Division*, 242.

25 Marland, *Whipped*, 223, 389–90.

26 Newman, "Dilemma of a Maverick."

27 Thorburn, "Parliament and Policy-Making."

28 Courtney, "Political Parties in Parliament," 34.

29 Courtney, "Political Parties in Parliament," 37.

30 Robertson, "Parliamentary Recognition."

31 Young, "The System," 7.

32 For a provincial example see Chevrette, "Government Member." See also Marland, *Whipped*, 195–6.

33 Blumler and Kavanagh, "The Third Age."

34 Marland, *Whipped*, 224.

35 Courtney, "Political Parties in Parliament," 51.

36 Sevi, "The Incumbency Advantage."

37 Information is courtesy legislative librarians in those provinces, who supplied us with Hansard and Elections Act records; see also Edmonton Bulletin, "Alberta Voting Age." In other provinces, parties choose to require that the leader to sign nomination papers when it is not required by law.

38 Sozzi, "Rebels in Parliament," 341.

39 John Roberts, Liberal MP for Ontario, quoted in CBC, "The Noblest of Callings."

40 McGrath, *Report of the Special Committee*, 2. See also Landes, "Special Committee."

41 McGrath, *Report of the Special Committee*, 15–16.

42 Globe and Mail, "The Independent MP," A6.

43 Docherty, "Could the Rebels Find a Cause?," 285–7.

44 Lecomte, "Party Discipline."

45 Blidook, *Constituency Influence*; Godbout, *Lost on Division*, 9 and 145.

46 "Poltext."

47 Esselment, "Designing Campaign Platforms."

48 Quoted in Canadian Press, "Chrétien Expects."

49 Wesley and Nauta, "Party Platform Builders." The leader's circle itself was constrained by growing forces of globalization, horizontal integration of government departments, and public demands for consultation (Flynn, "Rethinking Policy Capacity").

50 Carty, Cross and Young, *Rebuilding Canadian Party Politics*; Wolinetz, "Beyond the Catch-All Party."

51 Quoted in Loriggio, "Ford Aims to Woo."

52 Dhanraj, "Suspended MPP."

53 Kulp, "Randy Hillier."

54 CBC News, "Hillier Expelled."

55 Adams, "Ford Defends Decision"; Artuso, "Premier Ford Ejects MPP."

56 Quoted in Rushowy, "Doug Ford Removes MPP."

57 For example, Strömbäck and Van Aelst, "Political Parties Adapt."

58 Gerrits et al., "Political Battlefield."

59 For example, Stefanovich, "Atlantic Liberal MPs."

60 For example, Boutilier, "Conservatives Clamp Down."

61 Cappella and Jamieson, *Spiral of Cynicism*.

62 Public Policy Forum, *Mind the Gaps*.

63 Scott Simms interview.

64 Johnston, "Affective Polarization"; Kevins and Soroka, "Growing Apart?"; Merkley, "Polarization Eh?"

65 Wilson-Raybould, *Indian in the Cabinet*, 288.

66 O'Toole, "Resignation of Member."
67 Ling, *Far and Widening*, 19–20; Raj, "MPs Are Acting Out."
68 Tumilty, "It's a Content Studio."
69 Raj, "MPs Are Acting Out."
70 Wagner, "Tolerating the Trolls?"
71 Dubois and McKelvey, "Political Bots."
72 For example, Zimonjic, "Embassy Takes Down."
73 Gwyn, "Ad-Men," 121–3.
74 Adams, "Canadian Polling Industry"; Turcotte and Grenier, "Pollsters."
75 Patten, "Databases."
76 Adams, "Canadian Polling Industry"; Delacourt, *Shopping for Votes*, 122–4, 265–72.
77 Marland and Mathews, "Friend, Can You Chip in $3?"
78 Bulow, "The Use of CRM."
79 Boutilier, "Poilievre Meeting."
80 Elections Canada, "50th Anniversary."
81 Marland and Giasson, "The Evolution of Brokerage Politics."
82 Esselment, "Market Orientation," 131–2; Marland, *Whipped*, chap. 7.
83 Parliamentarian 13 interview.
84 Delacourt, "Liberals Are Nervous."
85 Coombs and Holladay, "The Paracrisis."
86 Koerber, "Crisis Communication," 315.
87 Canadian Press, "Tory MP Michelle Ferreri."
88 Tom Mulcair interview.
89 Gaber, "Government by Spin."
90 For example, Marland, *Brand Command*; Wesley and Moyes, "Selling Social Democracy"; Wood, "Brands."
91 Nan and Faber, "Advertising Theory"; Popkin, *Reasoning Voter*.
92 Pechmann and Stewart, "Advertising Repetition."
93 Chaudhuri and Holbrook, "Chain of Effects."
94 Kornberger, *Brand Society*, xii.
95 For example, Chen and Tseng, "Customer-Based Airline Brand."
96 Copeland, "Consumers' Buying Habits."
97 Albertson, "Dog-Whistle Politics"; Thomas and Sabin, "Candidate Messaging."
98 Liberal Party of Canada, "Visual Identity Guidelines," 8.
99 Liberal Party of Canada, "Visual Identity Guidelines," 1.
100 For example, Press Progress, "BC Liberal Riding President."
101 LeBrun, "Save the Children Convoy."
102 Fendick, "Thornhill Back to Save Tories"; Crone, "Ferguson Acquitted."
103 For example, Boutilier, "Conservative MP Derek Sloan."
104 CBC News, "Kim Craitor"; Ferguson, "NDP Kicks Out MPP"; Stone, "Doug Ford Confirms."
105 For example, McSheffrey, "Nova Scotia Liberal Riding Association."
106 French, "Shandro's Appointment."
107 Junker, "Justice Minister Kacee Madu."
108 Fiorina, "Culture War?"
109 Gallagher and Jones, "Conservative MP Under Fire."
110 For example, Yakabuski, "Quebec Liberal MP Learns."
111 Smith, "Liberal MP George Chahal."
112 CBC News, "Bruce County Mayor."
113 For example, Cheadle, "Liberals Demand MP."

114 Eneas, "Sask. Party Leader."
115 For example, Wood, "Wall to Address Resignation."
116 Packer et al., "Loyal Deviance."
117 For example, Tremblay, "Do Female MPs"; Trimble et al., *Stalled*; Wagner, *The Candidacy Calculation*.
118 Parliamentarian 1 interview.
119 MacLaren, *Invisible Power*, 109.
120 Pilote and Montreuil, "Cracking the (Unwritten)."
121 Catherine Dorion interview. Translated by the authors.
122 Dorion, *Les têtes brûlés*.
123 Joël Godin, Conservative MP in Quebec, quoted in Smith, "Parliament's Stuffy Men's." Also Larry Miller, Conservative MP in Ontario, quoted in MacCharles et al., "They're Over the Hill."
124 Thomas and Bittner, *Mothers and Others*.
125 Catherine McKenna, former Liberal MP in Ontario, Samara Centre interview.
126 Rusbult et al., "Exit, Voice, and Neglect."
127 Rodriguez et al., "Managing the Next Generation."
128 For example, Caesar-Chavannes, *Can You Hear Me Now?*; Qaqqaq, "MP Mumilaaq Qaqqaq."
129 Wilson-Raybould, *Indian in the Cabinet*, 57.
130 Wilson-Raybould, *Indian in the Cabinet*, 287.
131 Jean-François Larose, former NDP MP in Quebec, Samara Centre interview.
132 Esselment and Lilleker, "Marketing Authenticity."
133 Newman, "Psychology of Authenticity"; Newman and Smith, "Kinds of Authenticity."
134 Luebke, "Political Authenticity."
135 For example, Foot, "The Ronnie Show," A3.
136 Hinrich Bitter-Suermann interview.
137 MacPhail and Hogg, *Ron MacKinley*; Walker, "PEI's Maverick."
138 Scott Simms interview.
139 Angus Reid Institute, "Trust in Government"; Environics Institute, "Confidence"; "Trusting Federal"; Wesley and Ribeiro, "The Public."
140 Monopoli, "Government and News Media."
141 Morrice, "Backbenchers' Backyards."
142 Campbell et al., "Legislator Dissent."
143 Campbell et al., "Legislator Dissent."
144 Caesar-Chavannes, *Can You Hear Me Now?*, 6.
145 Lanoue and Bowler, "Picking the Winners."
146 Sevi et al., "Reassessing Local Candidate"; Stevens et al., "Local Candidate Effects."
147 Lanoue and Bowler, "Picking the Winners."
148 Roy and Alcantara, "Candidate Effect."
149 Justice and Lanoue, "Strategic and Sincere Voting."
150 Kendall and Rekkas, "Incumbency Advantages; Sevi, "The Incumbency Advantage."
151 Marland, *Whipped*, 278.
152 Parliamentarian 15 interview.
153 Malloy, *Paradox of Parliament*, 93.
154 Pruysers and Blais, "Narcissistic Women."
155 Blais et al., "Why Do They Run?"
156 Wagner, *The Candidacy Calculation*.

157 Donna Kennedy-Glans interview.
158 Jim Melenchuk interview.
159 Pruysers and Blais, "Narcissistic Women."
160 Tolley, "Who You Know."
161 Everitt et al., "Pathway to Office."
162 Levesque, "Searching for Persons."
163 Ozbudun, *Party Cohesion*, 337–9; Sieberer, "Party Unity."
164 Bryden, "Liberals Ease."
165 Docherty, *Mr. Smith Goes to Ottawa*, 61–2; Franks, *Parliament of Canada*, 100; Sayers, *Parties*, chap. 4.
166 Jeffrey, *Divided Loyalties*, 226–8.
167 Marland, "Vetting of Election Candidates," 578–9.
168 Trottier, "Scandal Mining"; Sarkonak, "Revenge of Caylan Ford."
169 Berkelaar and Buzzanell, "Cybervetting."
170 For example, Lazenby, "B.C. Conservative."
171 Marland and DeCillia, "Reputation and Brand Management."
172 Esselment and Bondy, "Local Nominations"; Hutchins, "Candidate Get Green Light?"; Thompson, "Mounting a Local Campaign," 200.
173 Political Staffer 6 interview.
174 Canada, National Security and Intelligence Committee, *Special Report*.
175 Maher, "Conservative Party Fight."
176 Howlett and Giovannetti, "Brown Vetting Process"; Maher, "Conservative Party Fight."
177 Marlene Jennings quoted in Leblanc, "Trudeau Approved Blocking."
178 Political Staffer 2 interview.
179 Political Staffer 1 interview.
180 Mitchell, "Ejected Hamilton MPP."
181 Esselment and Bondy, "Local Nominations"; Loat and MacMillan, "*Tragedy in the Commons*," 43–56; Thomas and Morden, "Party Favours."
182 MacCharles, "Toronto Conservatives."
183 For example, Cross, "Members of Parliament," 12.
184 Rana, "Upcoming Montreal Byelection," 1.
185 Carty, "Politics of Tecumseh Corners."
186 Simms, "The Independents."
187 Cross et al., "Money Talks."
188 Kam, "Parliamentary Behaviour."
189 Kenney, "Memorandum to UCP."
190 Political staffer 7 interview.
191 Jeffrey, *Divided Loyalties*, 234; Sayers, *Parties*, 92.
192 Cross, "Members of Parliament," 14.
193 For example, Canadian Press, "Jean-Francois Delisle Backs Off."
194 Marland, *Brand Command*; Wesley and Moyes, "Selling Social Democracy."
195 Lalancette et al., "Personalization of Local Candidates."
196 Robbins-Kanter, "Undisciplined Constituency"; Yates, "National-Local Messaging"; Robbins-Kanter, "Canadian Parties in the Constituencies."
197 Cross et al., "Money Talks."
198 Munroe and Munroe, "Local Data-Driven Campaigning."
199 Katz, "Problem of Candidate Selection," 280–2.
200 In their orientation, British MPs are informed that politics is a team sport, and that teamwork is essential for the government to deliver on its election promises (Stewart, *How Not to be a Politician*, 53).

201 MacCharles et al., "They're Over the Hill"; Horwood, "Like Getting Thrown."
202 Smith-McCrossin, "The Independents." Also Smith-McCrossin interview; Canadian Parliamentary Review, "Independents: Roundtable."
203 Stefanovich et al., "NDP Members Call."
204 For example, Patel et al., "I'm Disappointed.'"
205 Parliamentarian 1 interview.
206 For more details, see Marleau and Montpetit, *House of Commons Procedure*.
207 Cappella and Jamieson, *Spiral of Cynicism*; Marland, *Whipped*, 80–1.
208 For example, DeRosa, "Melanie Mark Will Resign"; Qaqqaq, "MP Mumilaaq Qaqqaq."
209 Docherty, *Mr. Smith Goes to Ottawa*, 36–59; Pow, "Amateurs versus Professionals."
210 Pasieka, "Felt Like I was Grieving."
211 Docherty, *Mr. Smith Goes to Ottawa*, 53.
212 Kyle Seeback, former Conservative MP in Ontario, Samara Centre interview.
213 Koop et al., *Representation in Action*.
214 Penner, "Private Member," 22.
215 For example, Qaqqaq, "MP Mumilaaq Qaqqaq."
216 Dyer, "Key Liberal MP Rips Government"; Rana and Lapointe, "Oliphant's Leaked Private Conversation."
217 Crandall and Roy, "Party Fundraisers."
218 Marland, *Whipped*, 154.
219 Ali, "Sarah Jama"; Guelph Mercury, "Ex-Tory MP Cries Foul"; Marland, *Whipped*, 153–5.
220 Milliken, *Selected Decisions*, 120.
221 Woodbury, "Liberals Allege."
222 Marland, *Whipped*, 64–71; Marland and Wagner, "Scripted Messengers"; Robbins-Kanter and Mattan, "Recruiting Brand Ambassadors."
223 Marland, *Whipped*, chap. 8; Plante, "Spoiler Alert"; Smith, "Liberal MPs to Blitz"; Thomas et al., "House Inspection," 20.
224 For example, Marland, *Whipped*, 113.
225 For example, Fung, "Not Worth the Cost."
226 Marland, "Communications Coordination."
227 Grenier, "Bill Who?"; Marland, *Brand Command*, 172; Taber, "Tories Scramble."
228 Muhammed Fiaz, SaskParty MLA, quoted in Leader-Post, "Toe the Leader's Line."
229 Tumilty, "Conservatives Fast-Tracked."
230 Taylor, "Conservative MPs Told."
231 Boutilier, "Poilievre's Office."
232 Walsh, "Conservatives Tell MPs."
233 Potestio, "Kamloops MP Won't Offer."
234 Potestio, "Caputo Cancels Kamloops."
235 Quoted in Noel, "Poilievre's Office."
236 Lilley, "It's Official."
237 Catherine McKenna, Liberal Minister of Environment and Climate Change, quoted in Goldstein, "Screeched-In McKenna."
238 Coflin, "Pierre Trudeau Misquoted."
239 Pollara Strategic Insights, "Awareness of Political Leaders." See also Grenier, "Bill Who?"
240 Levitz, "Who's That Guy?"

241 Marland, *Brand Command,* chap. 6; Wesley and Murray, "To Market or Demarket?"
242 Lloyd, "2005 General Election."
243 Daniele et al., "Abandon Ship?"

3. Caucus Management

1 Quoted in Grafstein, *A Leader*, 296.
2 Shaw and Zussman, *Matter of Confidence*, 100–1.
3 Flanagan, *Winning Power*; Jeffrey, *Divided Loyalties*, 52; Kam, *Party Discipline*, 66.
4 Hogg, "Social Identity Theory."
5 Raven and French, "Legitimate Power."
6 For an overview of types of control, see Rennstam, "Object-Control."
7 Bittner, "Effects of Information and Social Cleavages."
8 Pruysers and Cross, "Negative' Personalization."
9 For example, Blais and Boyer, "Impact of Televised Debates."
10 Helms, "Democratic Political Leadership"; Whitaker, "Virtual Political Parties."
11 Davies and Mian, "Reputation of Party Leader."
12 Mendelsohn, "Media's Persuasive Effects."
13 For example, Duffy, *Fights of Our Lives*.
14 CBC News, "Winnipeg's Ben Carr."
15 Axworthy, "Of Secretaries to Princes," 257–8.
16 Savoie, *Governing from the Centre*.
17 Whitaker, *Government Party*; Wesley and Maksymetz, "Regional Campaign Directors."
18 For example, Taber, "Martin Faces Backlash."
19 O'Malley, "Power of Prime Ministers."
20 de Clercy, "Communications as the Workhorse."
21 Quoted in CBC News, "Peter Mansbridge's Interview."
22 Rana, "PM Instructs Cabinet."
23 Wright Allen, "Trudeau PMO Tightening."
24 Ie, "Ministerial Mandate Letters."
25 Lalancette and Raynauld, "Power of Political Image."
26 Burke, "Liberal MP Backtracks."
27 Bryden, "Liberals Embrace Trudeau's." Relatedly, see de Clercy, "Communications as the Workhorse."
28 Axworthy, "Of Secretaries to Princes"; Lees-Marshment, *Human Resource*; Marland, *Whipped*.
29 Feldman and Brandstater, "Speed of Parliament." See also Brodie, *At the Centre of Government*.
30 Sean Casey, Liberal MP for Charlottetown, quoted in Stefanovich, "Spooked by Polls."
31 Party leader 6 interview.
32 Sorbara, *Let 'Em Howl*, 89 and 91.
33 Lees-Marshment, *Human Resource*.
34 Exempt staff, partisan advisers, political advisers, ministerial advisers, political staff, and special advisers are among the terms used in government (Craft, "Conceptualizing Policy Work," 135–6).
35 Sorbara, *Let 'Em Howl*, 161–2. See also Stewart, *How Not to be a Politician*, 315.

36 Westall, "Ottawa's Ministering."
37 Parliamentarian 13 interview.
38 Sorbara, *Let 'Em Howl*, 33.
39 Hustedt et al., "Ministerial Advisers," 300.
40 Privy Council Office, "Open and Accountable Government."
41 Robson, "Spending on Political Staffers," 676.
42 Political Staffer 4 interview.
43 Political Staffer 1 interview. See also Marland, *Brand Command*, 218–19.
44 Marland, *Whipped*, 181–8. See also Wilson-Raybould, *Indian in the Cabinet*, 115.
45 Simms, "The Independents." See also Canadian Parliamentary Review, "Independents: Roundtable."
46 Wayne Easter, former MP for PEI, quoted in Neatby, "Former P.E.I. MP."
47 Rana, "Some Backbench Liberal MPs."
48 Rana, "Some Backbench Liberal MPs."
49 Marland et al., *Permanent Campaigning.*
50 Robson, "Spending on Political Staffers."
51 Mallory, "The Minister's Office Staff."
52 Esselment and Wilson, "Campaigning from the Centre," 226. See also Burgess, "Swelling of Feds' Communications"; Robson, "Spending on Political Staffers," 677.
53 Based on a 2023 review by the authors of PMO staff data in the Government Electronic Directory Services listings.
54 Sorbara, *Let 'Em Howl*, 113.
55 Craft, *Backrooms and Beyond*; Dutil and Constantinou, "Office of Premier of Ontario."
56 Statistics Canada, "Smartphone Personal Use."
57 Statistics Canada, "Household Internet Use."
58 Eaves, "BlackBerry Campaign."
59 Marland, "Branding of a Prime Minister."
60 Callan and D'Mello, "Senior Ford Government."
61 Crawley, "Doug Ford's Push."
62 However, in the 1960s some executive assistants in the Lester Pearson government became celebrity activists who scrummed with reporters (Benoit, "Ministerial Staff," 152).
63 Martin, "Jean Pelletier."
64 Sibley, "Spotlight on Ray Novak."
65 Saunders, "Leaders, Advisors," 2122–23; Marland, *Whipped*, chap. 8; Warmington, "Prime Minister's Staffer."
66 Furey, "You'd Think Sooner or Later."
67 Warmington, "Prime Minister's Staffer."
68 Proudfoot, "What You Get."
69 Rusnell, "The Bully Who Haunts."
70 Rusnell, "Alberta Premier Jason Kenney."
71 Zare, "Deviance as Inauthenticity," 152.
72 Wellen and Neale, "Deviance, Self-Typicality."
73 Mannetti et al., "Group Reaction to Defection," 448.
74 Abrams et al., "Maintenance of Entitativity"; Eidelman and Biernat, "Derogating Black Sheep."
75 Packer and Chasteen, "Loyal Deviance," 15.
76 Lévesque, "Said Exactly what a Lot of Us Think."
77 Gary Doer, former Premier of Manitoba, Canada West Foundation webinar.

78 Sorbara, *Let 'Em Howl*, 130.
79 Paul Lane interview.
80 Unidentified Liberal MP quoted in Raj, "Liberal MPs Say." See also Stewart, *How Not to be a Politician*, 135.
81 Kam, *Party Discipline*, 3.
82 Ed Stelmach, former Premier of Alberta, Canada West Foundation webinar.
83 McGregor and Maher, "Tories Delay Election Bill."
84 Burns, "Backbench Reaction."
85 Marland, *Whipped*, 160–1; Wilson, "Minister's Caucus."
86 White, *Cabinets and First Ministers*, 177–9.
87 Dosser, "MLAs Pleased."
88 Ed Stelmach, former Premier of Alberta, Canada West Foundation webinar.
89 Jean Charest interview. Gilles Duceppe interview.
90 Parliamentarian 2 interview.
91 Inky Mark interview.
92 Christy Clark, former premier of British Columbia, Canada West Foundation webinar.
93 Marland, *Whipped*, 84–7 and 183–5.
94 Louis Plamondon interview.
95 Jean Charest interview. Translated by the authors.
96 Nycole Turmel, former NDP MP in Quebec, Samara Centre interview. Translated by the authors.
97 Rathika Sitsabaiesan, former NDP MP in Ontario, Samara Centre interview.
98 Marie-Claude Morin, former NDP MP in Quebec, Samara Centre interview. Translated by the authors.
99 Peter Stoffer, former NDP MP in Nova Scotia, Samara Centre interview.
100 Markusoff, "A Matter of Time."
101 David Swann interview.
102 Lysane Blanchette-Lamothe, former NDP MP in Quebec, Samara Centre interview.
103 Marland, *Whipped*, 88.
104 Aiello, "Trudeau Adds New."
105 Raj, "Trudeau is Ignoring Them."
106 Rana and Cnockaert, "Hybrid House Sittings."
107 These efforts can refer to opportunities in the extra-parliamentary party. See Müller and Strøm, "Hard Choices," 17.
108 Claessen, "Accruing Career Capital."
109 Marland, *Whipped*, 198.
110 Political Staffer 7 interview.
111 Political Staffer 6 interview.
112 Crowe, "Web of Authority." See also Marland, *Whipped*.
113 Holt, "What Explains Party Unity?," 295.
114 Godbout, *Lost on Division*, 118.
115 Lane, "Navigating Party Discipline."
116 Brent Rathgeber, former Conservative MP in Alberta, Samara Centre interview.
117 Quoted in Stewart, *How Not to be a Politician*, 390.
118 MacCharles et al., "They're Over the Hill"; Political Staffer 4 interview.
119 Louise Harel interview. Translated by the authors.
120 Matheson, *The Prime Minister*, 70.
121 Panetta, "Tory Rumblings." See also Turner, *Sheeple*, 76.

122 Kerby and Snagovsky, "Not All Experience."
123 Thomas and Lewis, "Executive Creep."
124 For example, DeRosa, "Critics Say David Eby."
125 Brodie, *At the Centre of Government*, 136–7.
126 Buffam, "All NDP MLAs"; Gorman, "N.S. Premier Announces."
127 Ron Cannan, former Conservative MP in British Columbia, Samara Centre interview.
128 Political Staffer 4 interview.
129 Thomas et al., "House Inspection," 19.
130 Sieberer, "Party Unity," 164–5.
131 Bosc and Gagnon, *House of Commons Procedure*; Marland, *Whipped*; Smith, "Standing Committee System."
132 Marland, *Whipped*, 236.
133 Yoshinaka, *Crossing the Aisle*.
134 Patel et al., "I'm Disappointed."
135 Jay Hill, former Conservative MP in British Columbia, Samara Centre interview.
136 For example, Laroche, "Houston Government."
137 de Clercy, "Communications as the Workhorse"; Marland, *Whipped*, 196–8.
138 Regan, "Special Meeting."
139 Levy, "Canadian Participation."
140 For example, Canadian Press, "Green Party Rift."
141 Kennedy Stewart, former NDP MP in British Columbia, Samara Centre interview.
142 Djaouida Sellah, former NDP MP in Quebec, Samara Centre interview. Translated by the authors.
143 Dwyer, *Interpersonal Relationships*, 73.
144 Parliamentarian 5 interview. For examples of vote sheets, see Marland, *Whipped*, 248–9.
145 For example, Ovenden, "Manning Lays Down."
146 Penner, "Private Member," 24.
147 Stewart, *Just One Vote*, chap. 6.
148 Abrams et al., "Maintenance of Entitativity," 268 and 277.
149 Cleary, "Navigating Party Discipline"; Robert-Falcon Ouellette, former Liberal MP in Manitoba, Samara Centre interview.
150 For example, Smyth, "Recliners and Decliners," A5.
151 Jean-François Larose, former NDP MP in Quebec, Samara Centre interview. Translated by the authors.
152 Raj, "Justin Trudeau."
153 Buckley Belanger interview.
154 Canadian Press, "MP says Mark Warawa"; Raj, "Liberals Don't Want"; Wingrove, "It's Gone too Far"; Tumilty et al., "Threatened with 'Consequences.'"
155 Political Staffer 3 interview.
156 Andeweg and Thomassen, "Pathways to Party Unity."
157 Brennan, "Priest MPP Quits"; Lofaro and Greig, "Anglade's Leadership"; Stone, "NDP Leader Jagmeet Singh."
158 Rana, "MPs were 'Very, Very Tough.'"
159 Patel et al., "I'm Disappointed."
160 Party leader 4 interview.
161 For example, Bovens et al., "Political Death and Survival."
162 For example, Marland, *Whipped*, 294.

163 For example, Gerson, "PC Associate Minister."
164 Wingrove, "It's Gone too Far."
165 Hopper, "Liberal Backbenchers Are Revolting"; Rana, "Grit MP McDonald."
166 For example, Jerrers, "MacLean Calls Surprise Vote."
167 Cooke, "MP Ken McDonald."
168 Bailey, "Liberal Caucus Meets."
169 For example, van Praet, "MPs Expressing Opposition."
170 Kam, *Party Discipline*, 2.
171 Bulowski, "Liberals Face Inside Pressure"; French, "Sixteen Government MLAs."
172 Vienneau, "Battle for Gun Control."
173 Gunn, "Nova Scotia Senator's Bill."
174 Tasker, "Liberal Backbenchers Defy."
175 Stefanovich, "Supreme Court of Canada Upholds."
176 Stone, "MP Who Set Off"; Wherry, "Liberal Backbenchers Rise."
177 Bauch, "Putting Down."
178 Glenn, *Very Canadian Coup*.
179 CBC News, "Premier Greg Selinger."
180 Dykstra, "There Goes Another."
181 Boothby, "Says He will Boot"; Cryderman and Keller, "MLAs Who Joined."
182 Joannou, "Alberta Speaker Apologizes."
183 Naylor, "UCP Caucus Debating."
184 Thomson, "Kenney's Outspoken UCP."
185 Bennett, "Alberta Premier's Caucus."
186 Rusnell and Russell, "Inside the Kenney Government's System of Secrecy."
187 Simpson, *Friendly Dictatorship*.

4. Team Players

1 Quoted in Lachance, "La députée a quitté." Translated by the authors.
2 Richer, "La députée de la CAQ."
3 Authier, "Right-of-Centre Voters"; Dubreuil, "Claire Samson."
4 Quoted in Dubreuil, "Claire Samson."
5 Feldman and Groves, "Legislatures in Evolution," 7.
6 Van Vugt and Hart, "Social Identity as Social Glue."
7 De Lamater et al., *Social Psychology*, 440–1.
8 Brown and Pehrson, "Group Formation," 32.
9 Abrams and Hogg, "Introduction to the Social Identity," 4.
10 Hildreth et al., "Blind Loyalty?"
11 Longley and Hazan, "On the Uneasy, Delicate," 4–5.
12 Redmond, "Voluntary Ceding of Control."
13 Abrams and Hogg, *Social Identifications,* 82; De Lamater et al., *Social Psychology,* 442.
14 Brown and Pehrson, "Group Formation," 37–8.
15 Abrams and Hogg, "Introduction to the Social Identity," 2.
16 Berlet, "Trump, Sado-Populism."
17 Zdaniuk and Levine, "Group Loyalty."
18 Berry et al., "Double-Edged Sword."
19 Dovidio et al., "Intergroup Relations," 329–30.
20 Abrams and Hogg, *Social Identifications*.
21 Hamilton, *Federalist Papers*.
22 Swann et al., "Identity Fusion."

23 Ignatieff, "Enemies vs. Adversaries."
24 Ghosh et al., "Who Stays with You?" 288–9.
25 Cole and Bruch, "Organizational Identity," 600.
26 Hom et al., *Employer Retention*, 56–8.
27 Ghosh et al., "Who Stays with You?" 290.
28 Kumar and Mishra, "Subordinate-Superior Upward Communication."
29 March and Simon, *Organizations*.
30 de Lange et al., "Should I Stay or Should I Go?"
31 Cole and Bruch, "Organizational Identity," 599–600.
32 Mitchell et al., "Why People Stay."
33 Buchko et al., "Why Do Good Employees Stay."
34 Agnew and Vanderdrift, "Commitment Processes," 437–48.
35 Ozbudun, *Party Cohesion*, 339–42.
36 Duverger, *Political Parties*.
37 Owens, "Explaining Party Cohesion."
38 For example, Campbell et al., *The American Voter.*
39 Cross and Young, "Contours of Political Party."
40 van Zoonen, "Imagining the Fan Democracy."
41 Duverger, *Political Parties*, 110–14.
42 Mai and Wenzelburger, "Loyal Activists?" See also Hazan, "Does Cohesion Equal Discipline?" 6; Rehmert, "Party Membership."
43 Bélanger and Stephenson, "Parties and Partisans"; Everitt et al., "Patterns of Party Identification"; Gidengil, "Voting Behaviour"; Gidengil et al., *Dominance and Decline.*
44 For example, Sheppard, "Secrets of a Trailblazer," 19–20.
45 Carolyn Parrish interview.
46 Cross, *Political Parties*, 24.
47 Cross and Young, "Contours of Political Party"; Petit-Vouriot et al., *2019 Democracy 360*, 24.
48 Cross and Young, "Contours of Political Party."
49 Cross, Pruysers and Currie-Wood, *The Political Party in Canada*, 113–14.
50 Morrice, "Backbenchers' Backyards."
51 Anne McLellan interview.
52 Canadian Press, "Maverick MLA Killed." See also Canadian Press, "Bill will Restrict Location."
53 Godbout, *Lost on Division*, 118.
54 Peter Kent, former Conservative MP in Ontario, Samara Centre interview.
55 Boutilier, "Conservative MP Derek Sloan."
56 Curry and Thompson, "Conservative MPs Break."
57 McGrane, *The New NDP*, 119–20.
58 Morgan and Pulignano, "Solidarity at Work"; Peggy Nash interview.
59 Barnard, *American Vanguard*, chap. 7. Also Peggy Nash interview.
60 Bruce Hyer, former NDP MP in Ontario, Samara Centre interview.
61 Laycock, "Reforming Canadian Democracy?"
62 Reform Party of Canada, *Blue Book,* 38.
63 Ovenden, "Manning Lays Down."
64 Keith Martin, former Reform MP in British Columbia, Samara Centre interview.
65 Lazenby, "John Rustad Vows."
66 Party leader 5 interview.
67 Political Staffer 4 interview.
68 Delacourt, "His Poll Numbers."

69 Ontario, "Health Teams."
70 Philpott, "Navigating Party Discipline."
71 Ignatieff, "Enemies vs. Adversaries."
72 Dan Albas interview.
73 Close, "Parliamentary Party Loyalty."
74 Davies, *Outside In*, 120.
75 Ed Stelmach interview.
76 Wherry, "Behind Closed Doors."
77 Rivard et al., "Political Dynasties."
78 Jeffrey, "Powlowski Not Deterred."
79 Smyth, "Divorce Rates So High."
80 Nunziata, "John Nunziata."
81 Lipset, *Continental Divide*.
82 For example, Antle, "Political Blood."
83 Strahl, "Advice to My Son."
84 Vomiero, "Ministers Gone Rogue."
85 Ève Peclet, former NDP MP in Quebec, Samara Centre interview.
86 Kyle Seeback, former Conservative MP in Ontario, Samara Centre interview.
87 Lynne Yelich, former Conservative MP in Saskatchewan, Samara Centre interview.
88 Terence Young, former Conservative MP in Ontario, Samara Centre interview.
89 Adam Vaughan, former Liberal MP in Ontario, Samara Centre interview.
90 Strahl, "Advice to My Son."
91 Stephen Owen, former Liberal MP in British Columbia, Samara Centre interview.
92 Jinny Sims, former NDP MP in British Columbia, Samara Centre interview. Also Marland, *Whipped*, 250–1.
93 Cousins, "Opposition Parties Frustrated."
94 Blidook, "Changing Use of Standing Order."
95 Boucher, "L'effet Westminster"; Paul Lane interview.
96 Kennedy and Oved, "Why these MPs Aren't Speaking?"
97 Penner et al., "Legislative Priorities."
98 Marland, *Whipped*, 230.
99 Grisdale et al., "Cheering or Jeering?"
100 Geddes, "How Do They Get Away with It?"
101 Ramzy, "Mean and Nasty."
102 For example, Ivison, "Flaherty the Pragmatist"; Stone, "Tory Pit Bull."
103 The Canadian Parliamentary Press Gallery reportedly had an Attack Dog of the Year award (Boesveld, "Question Period Rife"). See also McCutcheon and Mark, *Dog Whistles*, 2–3.
104 Dickson et al., "Meet Westminster's Attack Dogs."
105 Rathje et al., "Out-Group Animosity."
106 Marland, *Brand Command*, 190–200.
107 Bryan, *28 Seconds*.
108 Taber, "10 Most Irritating Politicians."
109 See sources in Kerby and Marland, "Media Management."
110 Monte Solberg, former Conservative MP in Alberta, Samara Centre interview.
111 Cheryl Hardcastle, former NDP MP in Ontario, Samara Centre interview.
112 Rick Casson, former Conservative MP in Alberta, Samara Centre interview.
113 Butler, "Two Faces of John Baird"; Boesveld, "Question Period Rife."
114 Djuric, "Karina Gould Has Redefined."
115 Radwanski, "Harper's Enforcer."

116 Benoit, "Ministerial Staff," 180; Marland, *Brand Command*, 205–6.
117 Radwanski, "Meet Dean French."
118 Political Staffer 8 interview.
119 Party leader 3 interview.
120 For example, Stone and Mahoney, "Ontario Premier Doug Ford's Chief."
121 Marland, *Whipped*, 325–40.
122 Marland, *Whipped*, 82 and 197.
123 Stella Ambler, former Conservative MP in Ontario, Samara Centre interview.
124 For example, Keith Martin interview.
125 MacLeod, "What a Night." The event began as a response to political parties having their own Christmas parties and grew into a well-attended fundraiser.
126 Starr, "Defeated MP."
127 Jeffreys, "Meet the Chillest Man."
128 Canada, *Reform Act, 2014*. See also Marland, Whipped, 17–18; Morden et al., "Assessing the Reform Act."
129 As with the banishment of Conservative MPs Maxime Bernier in 2018 and Derek Sloan in 2020.
130 Ditchburn, "Michael Chong's Friendlier Reform."
131 Godbout and Cochrane, "Minority Governments in Canada."
132 We note that in 2021 the Yukon Liberal government signed a confidence and supply agreement with the Yukon NDP that was renewed in 2023.
133 Prime Minister of Canada, "Delivering for Canadians."
134 Rana, "No Difference Left."
135 Wherry, "The Liberals and NDP."
136 See, in part, Stewart, *Politics on the Edge*, 224.
137 Bruce Hyer, former Green MP in Ontario, Samara Centre interview.
138 Esselment, "Fighting Elections."
139 For example, Murphy, "Danny Boy."
140 Peggy Nash interview.
141 Ian Waddell interview.
142 Percy Downe interview.
143 Heath MacDonald, Liberal MP in Prince Edward Island, quoted in Neatby, "Former P.E.I. MP."
144 Bush Dumville, Liberal MLA in Prince Edward Island, quoted in Wright, "Dumville Breaks His Silence."
145 George et al., "Remaining in Unhappy Relationships."
146 Dwyer, *Interpersonal Relationships*, 71–2.
147 See Samara Centre interviews with Jean-François Larose, former NDP MP in Quebec; John Weston, former Conservative MP in British Columbia; and Kyle Seeback, former Conservative MP in Ontario.
148 Robert-Falcon Ouellette, former Liberal MP in Manitoba, Samara Centre interview.
149 Parliamentarian 9 interview.
150 Mitchell, "Bob Bratina Says He will Not."
151 Brent Rathgeber interview.
152 Wilson-Raybould, *Indian in the Cabinet*, 287.
153 Erin Weir interview.
154 For example, Van Dyk, "Liberal MP Housefather."
155 Parliamentarian 16 interview.
156 Paul Lane interview.
157 Parliamentarian 15 interview.

158 Aiken, *The Backbencher*, 126.
159 Michael Cooper, Conservative MP in Alberta, quoted in Horwood, "Like Getting Thrown," 17.
160 Marland, *Whipped*, 250–1.
161 While the media did pick up on the bill (Payton, "Mask Ban Bill Passes"), there was no mention of the fact that Liberal MPs Mark Eyking and Rodger Cruzner supported the legislation.
162 Thomas and Lewis, "Executive Creep."
163 Platt, "Second Liberal MP."
164 Parliamentarian 11 interview.
165 Alberta, "Standing Orders, Order 32(5)."
166 For example, Northern Pen, "Bonavista-Burin-Trinity MP."
167 Doug Eyolfson, Liberal MP in Manitoba, quoted in Wherry, "MP Doug Eyolfson Breaks."
168 For example, Major, "Anthony Housefather to Stay."
169 Canadian Press, "Liberal MP Confronts Minister."
170 Mitchell, "MP Bob Bratina Asking."
171 Hall, "Abortion Politics."
172 Tavits, "Making of Mavericks."
173 Marland, *Whipped*, 337–8.

5. Party Mavericks

1   For example, Woolf, "Conservative MPs Furious."
2   Taber, "Confident Rookie MP."
3   Rempel Garner, "Liberal Silence."
4   Rempel Garner et al., *The Buffalo Declaration*, 12.
5   Nash, "Lantsman Calls Poilievre's."
6   For example, O'Neil, "Liberal MP Don Bell."
7   Kilgour, "David Kilgour, MP," 47.
8   Dempsey, "Increasing Technology Divide."
9   Safire, "Maverick Ticket."
10 Cresswell, "Maverick."
11 Results of a Google Ngram search of historical word use, March 2023.
12 For example, Busby, "Republican Mavericks."
13 Quoted in Dryden, "Seeking Broader Appeal."
14 For example, Rabson, "Wilson-Raybould Entered."
15 Lynda Haverstock, Liberal MLA in Saskatchewan, quoted in Roberts, "Liberal Leader Quits."
16 For example, Kyle Seeback, former Conservative MP in Ontario, Samara Centre interview.
17 For example, Howard, "Rookie MP Rankles Tory."
18 Longley and Hazan, "On the Uneasy," 5–7.
19 For example, Warick, "MP Trost Questions."
20 For example, Foot, "The Ronnie Show."
21 Howard, "Rookie MP Rankles."
22 Kam, *Party Discipline*, 46.
23 Cowen, "Effective Organizational Maverick."
24 For example, Stokes Sullivan, "MHA Disciplined."
25 For example, Newman, "Dilemma of a Maverick."
26 Yoshinaka, *Crossing the Aisle*, 60.

27 For example, Peacock, "She is Very Clear."
28 Aiken, *The Backbencher*, 127.
29 Political Staffer 7 interview.
30 Pitkin, *Concept of Representation*.
31 Chen, "Lone Wolf MPs."
32 Hawkes and Devine, "Meech Lake."
33 Bryden, "Have Chair."
34 Lévesque, "Said Exactly what a Lot of Us Think."
35 Harris, "Speaker Gives Tory MP."
36 Minsky, "Brief History of Floor Crossing."
37 MacLean, "Campbell, Stewart."
38 Kritzwiser, "MP Who Shuns."
39 Globe and Mail, "PM Ignored by LaMarsh."
40 LaMarsh, *Memoirs of a Bird*, 99.
41 LaMarsh, *Memoirs of a Bird*, 86.
42 LaMarsh, *Memoirs of a Bird*, 287–8.
43 LaMarsh, *Memoirs of a Bird*, 303.
44 Globe and Mail, "Judy LaMarch."
45 Quoted in Reid, "Honourable John Reid," 14–15.
46 Reid, "Evidence."
47 Reid, "Honourable John Reid," 37.
48 For example, Reid, "Honourable John Reid," 11.
49 Montgomery, "He'll Disclose."
50 Truelove, *Svend Robinson*, 95 and 213.
51 Rayside, *On the Fringe*, 179.
52 Truelove, *Svend Robinson*, 157–60.
53 Greenspon and Sallot, "Pragmatic McDonough."
54 Rayside, *On the Fringe,* 179–80.
55 Truelove, *Sven Robinson*, 116.
56 Ovenden, "Manning Lays Down." See also Marland, *Brand Command*, 168–9.
57 Charlebois, "Former MP Breaks Silence."
58 Ian Waddell interview.
59 Nathaniel Erskine-Smith, Liberal MP in Ontario, quoted in Raj, "Trudeau's Pledge."
60 Wherry, "Liberal Backbencher."
61 Thomson, "Liberal MP Nathaniel Erskine-Smith."
62 Erskine-Smith, "Yes"; Thomson, "Liberal MP Nathaniel Erskine-Smith."
63 Erskine-Smith, "Taking On a New Challenge."
64 Elliot, "Alliance MP Gallant"; Panetta, "Harper Won't Discuss"; The Record, "Sexual Orientation"; Turner, *Sheeple*, 62.
65 Arnprior Chronicle-Guide, "Cheryl Gallant Escapes."; National Post, "MP in Hot Water"; Paulsen, "Gallant in Hot Water"; Rabson, "Hipster Air Flies."
66 Laucius, "Gallant's Media Posts."
67 For example, Blewett, "Gallant Attends Riding"; Dyson, "Candidate Cheryl Gallant."
68 Coates, "Power of Authenticity."
69 White, *Cabinets and First Ministers*.
70 Laurie Blakeman interview.
71 Mertz, "MLA Laurie Blakeman."
72 For example, DeRosa, "Selina Robinson Resigns"; Heppell, "British Labour Party"; National Post, "You Broke My Heart."

73 Canadian Press Newswire, "New Democrat MP"; Curry, "MPs Plan Trip."
74 Trickey, "MP Shows Support."
75 Calgary Herald, "Bush Demands Israel."
76 Brown, "NDP Accuses Israel"; Curry, "MPs Plan Trip"; Dunfield, "Canada Lacks Leadership." See also Truelove, *Svend Robinson*, 230.
77 Brown, "NDP Accuses Israel."
78 Rae, "Parting Company." See also Truelove, *Svend Robinson*, 231.
79 Bryden, "Svend Robinson." Also Svend Robinson interview.
80 Fong, "Rae Leaves NDP."
81 O'Neil, "Israel 'Appears' Guilty."
82 Svend Robinson interview.
83 Quoted in Hristova, "Activist Sarah Jama." See also Hristova, "Sarah Jama Elected."
84 Ferguson, "Jama Has 'Doubled Down'"; Hristova, "Sarah Jama Elected."
85 About 1 per cent of the residents of Hamilton Centre identified as Jewish or Arab, evenly divided. See Statistics Canada, "Census Profile. 2021."
86 Jama, "Call for an Immediate Cease Fire."
87 Callan, "Hamas-Israel Comments Controversy."
88 As of mid-October 2023.
89 Ferguson and Rushowy, "Jama Has 'Doubled Down.'"
90 Stiles, "My Statement."
91 Maynard et al., "Black Feminists."
92 Jama, "Thirteen Days Ago."
93 Quoted in Lilley, "Scrum with Marit Stiles."
94 Quoted in Ferguson and Rushowy, "Jama Ejected from NDP."
95 Ali, "Jama Says She Can"; Beattie, "Hamilton MPP."
96 Ferguson and Rushowy, "Jama's Removal Divides."
97 Unidentified MPP quoted in Ferguson and Rushowy, "Jama Ejected from NDP."
98 Doly Begum, NDP MPP in Ontario, quoted in Ferguson and Rushowy, "Jama's Removal Divides."
99 Jeff Burch, NDP MPP in Ontario, quoted in Ali, "Hundreds Gather."
100 Peggy Sattler, NDP MPP in Ontario, quoted in Ali, "Hundreds Gather."
101 Wayne Gates, NDP MPP in Ontario, quoted in Forsyth, "MPPs Support Leader's."
102 Jennie Stevens, NDP MPP in Ontario, quoted in Forsyth, "MPPs Support Leader's."
103 Ferguson and Rushowy, "Jama's Removal Divides."
104 Passifiume, "NDP Candidate Backs."
105 DeClerq, "Jama's Removal"; Selley, "It's Up to Voters."
106 DeClerq, "Jama's Removal."
107 Ali, "Hundreds Gather."
108 Quoted in Callan and D'Mello, "Marit Stiles Reflects."
109 Brown and Carreño Rosas, "MPP Sarah Jama."

6. Party Leavers

1 Rathgeber, *Irresponsible Government*, 82. See also Samara Centre interview.
2 Quoted in CBC News, "Rathgeber Refuses."
3 Wherry, "Brent Rathgeber."

4 CBC News, "Lela Evans"; Dave Taylor interview; House of Assembly, "Proceedings."
5 Bonebright, "40 Years of Storming."
6 Ellemers et al., " Feeling Included and Valued."
7 Leary, "Responses to Social Exclusion"; Leary, "Interpersonal Rejection," 5; Levine and Marques, "Norm Violators."
8 Leary, "Interpersonal Rejection," 4.
9 Ghosh et al., "Who Stays with You?," 290; Hom et al., *Employer Retention and Turnover,* 3–8.
10 Hom et al., *Employer Retention and Turnover,* 8–9 and 65; Formica and Sfodera, "Great Resignation."
11 Hom et al., *Employer Retention and Turnover,* 53.
12 Ghosh et al. "Who Stays with You?" 290.
13 Abbasi and Hollman, "Turnover."
14 Hartman and Yrle, "The Hobo Phenomenon."
15 Jackson et al., "Some Differences."
16 Hirschman, *Exit, Voice, and Loyalty,* 78.
17 Buchko et al., "Why Do Good Employees Stay?" 730.
18 Hom et al., *Employer Retention and Turnover,* 54–6.
19 Hom et al., *Employer Retention and Turnover,* 25.
20 Hom et al., *Employer Retention and Turnover,* 18–23.
21 Hom et al., *Employer Retention and Turnover,* 36–7.
22 Wright, "Dumville Breaks His Silence." Also Smith-McCrossin interview.
23 Parliamentarian 8 interview.
24 Brent Rathgeber interview.
25 Jean Charest interview.
26 Ian Donovan interview.
27 Kerby and Blidook, "It's Not You, It's Me."
28 For example, Richer, "Benjamin menace de quitter." Also, Party Leader 3 interview.
29 Lane, "Navigating Party Discipline."
30 Political Staffer 6 interview.
31 Caesar-Chavannes, *Can You Hear Me Now?* Also Celina Caeser-Chavannes interview.
32 CBC News, "Perry Trimper Says He Felt."
33 Marland, *Whipped,* 338; Rempel Garner, "I Just Made a Big Decision."
34 As with Léon Balcer, PC MP in Quebec (1949–65), who was one of a number of Quebec MPs who had a frosty relationship with John Diefenbaker (Balcer, "Léon Balcer Interviewed").
35 Theodore, "Clark Welcomes MLA Blair Lekstrom."
36 For more on provincial political worlds, see Elkins and Simeon, *Small Worlds;* Wesley, *Big Worlds.*
37 Celina Caeser-Chavannes interview.
38 Hinrich Bitter-Suermann interview.
39 We do not count such cases in our database of party exit events.
40 Brent Rathgeber interview.
41 For example, Mas, "Hyer Joins Green Party"; Radio-Canada, "NPD perd un autre député."
42 For example, Hunter, "Last Reform MLA."

43 Ross, "Chrétien Advises." See also Young, "Deux autres defections."
44 Martin, "Jean Pelletier."
45 Cleary, "Wiseman's Walk."
46 For example, Canadian Press, "Amanda Simard, Ontario PC."
47 Party Leader 1 interview.
48 CBC News, "Ontario Liberal MP"; Van Dyk, "Liberal MP Housefather."
49 Cohen, "Yurko, Frustrated."
50 Macpherson, "Hardliner Quits PQ."
51 Catherine Dorion interview.
52 Martin, *Hell or High Water*, 93.
53 "The Independents." See also Canadian Parliamentary Review, "Independents: Roundtable."
54 Smith, "MacKinnon, Liberals."
55 Hunter, "Warnke's Move from Liberals."
56 Beatty, "Brenzinger Not First"; Smyth, "I Got to My Car."
57 National Post, "You Broke My Heart."
58 Quoted in DeRosa, "Selina Robinson Resigns."
59 For example, Bennett, "Lloyd Snelgrove."
60 For example, Marland, *Whipped*, 66–7.
61 For example, Schneider, "MLA Len Webber."
62 Rob Anderson, Wildrose MLA in Alberta, quoted in Köhler, "Dysfunction' Drives."
63 Chuck Porter, Independent MLA in Nova Scotia, quoted in CBC News, "Chuck Porter Leaves."
64 Gilles Roch, Liberal MLA in Manitoba, quoted in York, "MLA quits Tories."
65 Smyth, "Toying with Our Time."
66 Balcer, "Léon Balcer Interviewed," 41.
67 For example, Helm, "Leadership Scrutinized."
68 Lofaro and Greig, "Anglade's Leadership."
69 Ed Stelmach interview.
70 Blouin and Cabrera, "Pablo Rodriguez."
71 Chase, "B.C. MP Quits."
72 For example, Canadian Press, "Dean Del Mastro Resigns."
73 For example, CBC News, "Facing Impaired Driving."
74 Fife, "Hunter Tootoo's Messy."
75 Baumeister and Tice, "Anxiety and Social Exclusion," 172.
76 Mallory, "Vacation of Seats."
77 Zussman, "MLA Andrew Weaver."
78 Qaqqaq, "MP Mumilaaq Qaqqaq."
79 Lecavalier, "Legault réagit au depart."
80 Felps et al., "Turnover Contagion."
81 Buzzetti and Cornellier, "Parti progressiste-conservateur"; Canadian Press, "We're Not a Zebra Party"; Jannard, "Mulroney perd trois"; Young, "Deux autres Defections."
82 Postmedia News, "Fourth PQ Member."
83 Keenleyside, "Canadian Election of 1925."
84 Mears, "Western Members."
85 Jannard, "Mulroney perd trois."
86 Canadian Press, "Crise au Bloc."
87 MacCharles, "Rebel MPs' Return." See also Grey, *Never Retreat*, chaps. 19–20; Kam, *Party Discipline*, 10.

88 For example, Bellavance, "Come to the PC Party"; Spencer, *Sacrificed?*
89 Grey, *Never Retreat*, 192–94; Johnsrude, "Alliance 'Matriarch."
90 Fife, "Clark Faces Criticism"; Marland and Flanagan, "Opposition to Government."
91 Ford, "Some Notes."
92 Topp, *Almost Gave the Tories*. See also Malloy, *Paradox of Parliament*, 30–1.
93 Miljan, "Television Frames."
94 Jim Melenchuk interview.
95 Maclean's, "Prairie Storm"; Woods, "Legislative Reports."
96 Party Leader 6 interview.
97 Canadian Press, "Sask. Liberals Vote."
98 "Hillson to Sit as Independent Liberal."
99 Perkins, "Former Liberals Join."
100 Godbout and Høyland. "Emergence of Parties," 784.
101 Canadian Press, "Socred Faithful." The three MLAs were Ray Speaker, Fred Mandeville, and Walter Buck.
102 Kieran et al., "Socreds in Turmoil."
103 Marotta, "Weir Declares Himself."
104 Yourk, "Herron to Run."
105 Smyth, "You'd be Mad."
106 Hunter, "Two Rights Groups."
107 CBC News, "B.C. MLA Paul Reitsma Resigns."
108 Rupert, "Guilty MPP Kicked Out."
109 CBC News, "Tony Tomassi."
110 "Politician Quits over Sex Line Calls."
111 CBC News, "Andrew Younger."
112 Graney, "Finance Critic."
113 Bellefontaine, "MLA Prab Gill."
114 Yoshinaka, *Crossing the Aisle*, 188.
115 Baumeister and Tice, "Anxiety and Social Exclusion," 168–9.
116 Ovenden, "Maverick Tories," G1; Yoshinaka, *Crossing the Aisle*, 189.
117 Canadian Press, "MLA Kicked Out."
118 "Renegade Grit Welcomed Back"; CBC News, "Dr. Jim Parrott Rejoins."
119 For example, Jang, "Liberals Turf MLA."
120 Ovenden, "Maverick Tories."
121 Ovenden, "Kindy joins Grits."
122 Ovenden, "Maverick Tories."
123 Kilgour, "David Kilgour," 16; Mulroney, *Memoirs*, 756–7.
124 Marland, *Whipped*, chap. 10.
125 Ian Brodie interview.
126 Galloway, "Tory MP Kicked Out"; Moose Jaw Times Herald, "Political Hero."
127 Hinrich Bitter-Suermann interview.
128 For example David Mitchell, Liberal MLA in British Columbia, who broke ranks with his party over the Charlottetown Accord in 1992 (Clark and Hauka, "Liberal Caucus Toasts") or Jim Hodder, Liberal and PC MHA in Newfoundland and Labrador, who switched parties in 1985 over an offshore oil agreement (Roche, "Newfoundland Oil").
129 Ramsay, "Kenney Removes MLA."
130 Canadian Press, "MPP Booted from PC."
131 Davidson, "MPP Kicked Out of PC."
132 Plante, "Opposition Criticizes CAQ."

133 CBC News, "Wilson-Raybould Quashes."
134 Canadian Press, "MPP Resigns from Tory." A Saskatchewan Party MLA resigned from caucus in September 2021 for misrepresenting her vaccination status as well.
135 Woolf, "Liberal MP Censured."
136 Dacey, "Premier Boots Ron Schuler."
137 Gibson, "Thomas Dang Hopes."
138 Cooke, "MLA Who Promoted."
139 Tran, "UCP MLA Slammed."
140 Rempel Garner, "I Just Made a Big Decision."
141 CBC News, "Alta. MLA Kicked." See also Stiles, "My Statement."
142 Canadian Press, "Tories Dump Steven Fletcher."
143 Quoted in Turner, *Sheeple*, 67. For an opposing view, see Brodie, *At the Centre of Government*, 146.
144 Smyth, "You'd be Mad." See also Marland, *Whipped*.
145 Smith, "Disgruntled Boudreau."
146 Canadian Press, "NDP Removes MP."
147 As with Claire Samson, Coalition Avenir Québec MNA in 2021 (Authier, "Right-of-Centre Voters").
148 CBC News, "Liberals Expel Doug Young."
149 Buzzetti, "Mourani a voulu partir."
150 For example, CBC News, "Chuck Porter Leaves."
151 CBC News, "MP Khan Leaves."
152 Spencer, *Sacrificed?*, 75.
153 Turner, *Sheeple*, 58–7.
154 Kilgour, "David Kilgour," 16.
155 Dryden, "2 MLAs Out."
156 Levitz, "Garner Doubles Down."
157 Maher, *The Prince*, 165.
158 Spencer, *Sacrificed?*, 105–8; Turner, *Sheeple*, 77.
159 Canadian Press, "Simard Leaving PCs"; Globe and Mail, "Reform MP Sues." See also Spencer, *Sacrificed*.
160 Wilson-Raybould, *Indian in the Cabinet*, 253.
161 Kilgour, "David Kilgour," 17; Turner, *Sheeple*, 78 and 167–8.
162 Lofaro and Greig, "Anglade's Leadership."
163 Rabson, "Rocan Turfed from Caucus."
164 See Marland, *Whipped*, chap. 10.
165 For example, Ovenden, "Maverick Tories."
166 Dawson, "Kenney Kicks Pat Rehn Out."
167 Nowlan, "Patrick Nowlan," 18.
168 CBC News, "Alta. MLA kicked." See also Turner, *Sheeple*.
169 Wright, "Olive Crane."
170 For example, Ferguson, "Jama Ejected."
171 For example, Crawford, "'I Felt I had No Choice.'"
172 For example, Canadian Press, "Facing the 'Hooligans.'"
173 Adams, "Ford Defends Decision."
174 John Nunziata interview.
175 Jay Hill, Conservative Government Whip, quoted in O'Neill, "Tory MP Expelled." Relatedly, see Copps, "PM had No Choice."
176 Wilson-Raybould, *Indian in the Cabinet*, 253.

177 Cryderman, "Leader Dumps MLA."
178 Wright, "Olive Crane."
179 Erin Weir interview.
180 Galloway, "MP Kicked Out."
181 Christine Melnick, NDP MLA in Manitoba, quoted in Lambert, "Ousted Minister."
182 Kevin Falcon, B.C. Liberal Leader, quoted in Kurjata, "Liberal MLA Removed."
183 Higgs, "Letter to MLA."
184 Froese, "MLA Mark Wasyliw."
185 Tim Houston, leader of the PC Party of Nova Scotia, quoted in Tutton, "N.S. Tory Booted."
186 Canadian Press, "Grits Turf Maverick."
187 Canadian Press, "Grits Turf Maverick."
188 Reevely, "Conservatives Need to Crush."
189 CBC News, "MacLaren Expelled."
190 Froese, "MLA Mark Wasyliw."
191 Bill Bennett, Liberal MLA in British Columbia, quoted in CBC News, "B.C. Premier 'Abusive.'"
192 Canadian Press, "Tories Dump Steven Fletcher."
193 Quoted in Pursaga, "Fletcher Kicked Out."
194 Nineteen chose not to run again and nineteen lost their bids for re-election. As of mid-2025, another six Independents had yet to face the prospect of a general election since being expelled from caucus. The remainder either rejoined their parties or joined another caucus.
195 Trevor Zinck, Independent MLA in Nova Scotia, quoted in CBC News, "Zinck Held On."
196 Quoted in Doucette, "Trevor Zinck Resigns."
197 Doucette, "Trevor Zinck Resigns."
198 MacFarlane, "Resolution No. 598."
199 Cooke, "N.S. Tories Abandon"; Elizabeth Smith-McCrossin interview. See also Cooke, "MLA Who Promoted."
200 For example, Burke, "Expelled Liberal."
201 For example, Franklin, "She has a Lot of Work."
202 Parliamentarian 17 interview.
203 Youri Chassin, Independent MNA in Quebec, quoted in Lévesque, "Devenir independent."
204 For more on Independent MPs in Britain, see Cowley and Stuart, "There Was a Doctor."
205 "The Independents"; Brancati, "Winning Alone," 648–9; Canadian Parliamentary Review, "Independents: Roundtable."
206 John Nunziata interview.
207 Huntington, "Defining the Role."
208 Wilson-Raybould, *Indian in the Cabinet*, 275.
209 Wilson-Raybould, *Indian in the Cabinet*, 275–6.
210 Borcsok, "No One Cares."
211 Joannou, "Independent B.C. Election Candidates."
212 Small and Philpott, "The Independent Candidate," 202.
213 Clark, "MPP Brady Launches."
214 Small and Philpott, "The Independent Candidate," 201.

215 Wilson-Raybould, *Indian in the Cabinet*, 275.
216 For example, Hays, "Kimball Quits."
217 Donna Marie Kennedy-Glans interview.
218 Postmedia News, "Life After the Party."
219 Wherry, "Last Decent Man," 16–17.
220 Canadian Press, "Wilson-Raybould Quashes."
221 Canada, *House of Commons Debates*.
222 For example, CBC News, "Perry Trimper Says He Felt"; Fitzpatrick, "Bruce Hyer Quits"; Thomas, "Gesell Runs."
223 Louise Beaudoin interview.
224 Shuttleworth, "Integrity Commissioner."
225 Antonacci, "I won't Cross."
226 Bobbi Ann Brady interview.
227 Parliamentarian 12 interview.
228 David Taylor interview.
229 "The Independents." Also Elizabeth Smith-McCrossin interview.
230 For example, King, "James Lunney Quits"; Canadian Press, "NDP MPP Leaves."
231 O'Malley, "Process Nerd."
232 CBC News, "Osborne Quits"; CBC News, "Perry Trimper Says He Felt"; Huntington, "Defining the Role," 3.
233 Hinrich Bitter-Suermann interview.
234 Bobbi Ann Brady interview.
235 Jenica Atwin, Liberal MP in New Brunswick, quoted in Karadeglija, "Defection."
236 Carolyn Parrish interview.
237 Parliamentarian 11 interview.
238 For example, Tunney and Cochrane, "LeBlanc Says."
239 Markusoff, "Lacombe-Ponoka MLA."
240 Taylor, "Independent Toronto MP."

7. Party Switchers

 1 Wilson, *Benedict Arnold*, xiv.
 2 Philbrick, "Arnold Turned Traitor."
 3 Dovidio et al., "Intergroup Relations," 327.
 4 Hom et al., *Employer Retention and Turnover*, 102–7 and 302–3.
 5 Aho, "Out of Hate."
 6 Burt, "Contingent Value."
 7 Yoshinaka, *Crossing the Aisle*, chap. 9.
 8 Yoshinaka, *Crossing the Aisle*, 17 and 224.
 9 Yoshinaka, *Crossing the Aisle*, chap. 3.
10 For example, Canadian Press, "We're Not a Zebra Party."
11 Among the more granular forms of party switching that fall outside of our catchment foci include parliamentarians who seek election in another jurisdiction, a partisan endorsing a candidate with another party, or a defeated parliamentarian being hired as a political staffer with a different party. CBC News, "MLA on Welfare"; Leon, "Ex-Tory MP."
12 Yoshinaka, *Crossing the Aisle*, 14. See also CBC News, "Lane Crosses."
13 Party Leader 3 interview.
14 Globe and Mail, "Stewart Beaten."

15 Moss and Al-Mehdar, "Atwin Voted."
16 Jenica Atwin interview.
17 Quoted in Huras, "Behind-the-Scenes."
18 Quoted in Poitras, "Atwin Defends."
19 Quoted in Aiello, "Liberals Approached Me." Also Cochrane, "Atwin Crossing"; Huras, "Behind-the-Scenes."
20 Jenica Atwin interview.
21 Quoted in Poitras, "Atwin Defends."
22 Quoted in Cochrane, "Green MP."
23 Quoted in Cochrane, "Green MP."
24 Gilmore, "Green Party MP."
25 Walsh and Bailey, "Former Green Party."
26 Atwin, "Please Read."
27 Brown, "Atwin Switches."
28 Walsh and Chase, "Rift in Liberal."
29 Jenica Atwin interview.
30 Atwin, "Letter to Prime Minister."
31 Jenica Atwin interview.
32 Our database places Bill Casey in the ex-partisan group. After the Conservative MP was dismissed from the caucus in 2007, he won re-election as an Independent but resigned the seat in 2009. He returned to Parliament as a Liberal in 2015; however, he did not change parties while in office.
33 Wyatt, "Second-Most Lopsided."
34 For example, CBC News, "Taylor Becomes."
35 Maria Mourani interview.
36 Buzzetti, "Mourani a voulu partir"; Postmedia News, "Mourani Joins NDP;" Maria Mourani interview.
37 Poirier, "Disillusioned."
38 Cleroux, "Maverick Tory."
39 Howard, "Ex-Tory MP."
40 CBC News, "Kilgour Quits."
41 CBC News, "Osborne Joins."
42 Yourk, "Herron to Run."
43 Canadian Press, "Grit MPP."
44 Arnold, "MLA Quits."
45 Gibson, "Alberta Grit Joins."
46 Gibson, "Alberta Grit Joins."
47 Gray, "Richard Holden."
48 Maser, "Westmount Fumes."
49 Holman and Schneider, "Gender, Race."
50 Judge and Watanabe, "Is the Past prologue?"; Steenackers and Guerry, "Job-Hopping."
51 For example, Bailey, "Conservatives' Sole MLA."
52 Hogben, "New Liberal MLA."
53 Freeman, "Maverick Politician Paul Hellyer."
54 "Saskatchewan Grits Turf Maverick MLA."
55 CBC News, "Crossing the Floor."
56 Cohn, "NDP MP Quits."
57 Saltwire Network, "MacEwan Dies."
58 Stewart, *Politics on the Edge*, 3, 45 and 225.
59 Surette, "New Democrats Appeared," 8.

60 Stewart, *Politics on the Edge*, chap. 8.
61 Stewart, *Politics on the Edge*, 199.
62 Canadian Press, "Tried to Switch."
63 CBC News, "Lane Crosses"; Paul Lane interview.
64 Paul Lane interview.
65 Paul Lane interview.
66 Shipp et al., "Gone Today."
67 Visier, *Boomerang Employees*.
68 Langworth, *Churchill's Wit*, 75.
69 Wilbur, "H.H. Stevens."
70 Fowlie, "Bennett on Campbell."
71 Fendick, "MacLean OK's Leadership Review."
72 CBC News, "Malley Denies."
73 Lortie, "Verdun quitte le Bloc."
74 CBC News, "Lela Evans"; Howard, "MHA for Torngat Mountains."
75 Although studying the territories is beyond our remit, we note that Yukon Party MLA John Edzerza sat as an Independent to protest the withdrawal of funding to build a school. He was later re-elected with the opposition NDP, became an Independent over his frustration with the party's instability, and rejoined the Yukon Party in 2009 to stave off the government being toppled in a no-confidence vote (CBC News, "Edzerza Rejoins").
76 Josey, "Durham MPP Back in Caucus."
77 Wingrove, "MP Rejoins Tories."
78 Alberta PC Premier Alison Redford quoted in CBC News, "Del Mastro Resigns."
79 Rollie Thornhill, PC MLA in Nova Scotia, quoted in Waterloo Region Record, "Ex-Cabinet Minister Rejoins."
80 Ward, "Independent MHA."
81 Came, "A Credible Effort." See also Grey, *Never Retreat*, 148–49.
82 CBC News, "Drever Suspended."
83 Howell, "Drevor Returns."
84 Black, "Jennifer Johnson Joins UCP Caucus."
85 O'Neill, "Liberal MP Quits."
86 Laghi, "MP resigns."
87 Derek Fildebrandt interview.
88 Nanaimo Daily News, "Wilson Flips."
89 Marland, *Whipped*, 175–6.
90 Sturgeon and Cooke, "People's Alliance."
91 Daily Gleaner, "Cardy Joins Tories."
92 Quoted in CBC News, "Alta. MLA Kicked."
93 Cernetig, "Three Socred MLAs."
94 CBC News, "Dale Kirby and Christopher Mitchelmore."
95 Hunter, "High-Stakes Gamble."
96 Morris, "Couple quit Tories."
97 Jeff Wilson interview.
98 Giovannetti, "Alberta MLA Defections."
99 Bellefontaine, "Wildrose MLAs."
100 Jeff Wilson interview.
101 Parliamentarian 14 interview.
102 Jeff Wilson interview.
103 CBC News, "9 Wildrose MLAs."

104 Anderson, "I Chose to Cross."
105 Laurie Blakeman interview. Also Stephen Carter interview.
106 Wesley and Moyes, "Selling Social Democracy," 82.
107 Canadian Press, "N.B. Member Defects."
108 DeRosa, "Banman Defects."
109 Canadian Press, "Elenore Sturko's Defection"; Little and Zussman, "Conservatives Keep Up"; MacLeod, "Another BC United."
110 Marland and Flanagan, "Brand New Party"; "Opposition to Government."
111 Krug et al., "Top Management."
112 Marland and Flanagan, "Opposition to Government"; Ovenden, "Manning Lays Down."
113 Radio-Canada, "Fusion CAQ-ADQ."
114 Grey, *Never Retreat*, chap. 16; Marland and Flanagan, "Brand New Party."
115 Scott Brison interview. Also see Martin, *Harperland*, 244.
116 CBC News, "MacKay Slams Brison."
117 Campbell, "Martin's Prize."
118 Keith Martin interview.
119 Keith Martin interview.
120 For example, La Vertu, "B.C. Ex-Minister."
121 Gordon Wilson interview.
122 Jannard, "Mulroney perd trois."
123 Louis Plamondon interview.
124 Ferguson, "Chartrand also Quits."
125 For example, Moalla, "Charette Part."
126 Reuters, "Canadian Opposition."
127 Robitaille, "La CAQ aidera."
128 Rod Gantefoer, SaskParty MLA, quoted in Todd, "Throwback."
129 Jean-François Larose, former NDP MP in Quebec, Samara Centre interview. Translated by the authors.
130 Vermot-Desroches, "Aussant Quitte."
131 Giasson et al., "Social Media Transforming."
132 Palmer, "Gordon, Judi."
133 Simes, "Day 1."
134 We note the creation of the Feminist Party of Canada by non-parliamentarians in 1979. See Zaborsky, "Feminist Politics."
135 Bourgault-Côté, "Fournier en mission."
136 For example, Rana, "Aldag in Talks."
137 Sorbara, *Let 'Em Howl*.
138 Jean Charest interview.
139 For example, Shah, "Ex-NDP MP."
140 CBC News, "Manning Ejected from Tory Caucus."

8. Switching Sides

1 Martin, *Belinda*, 180–1.
2 Quoted in Martin, *Belinda*, 178.
3 Staffers 1 and 4 interviews.
4 Strøm and Mueller, *Policy, Office or Votes?*
5 Russell, "Parliamentary Party Cohesion."
6 Buckley Belanger interview.
7 CTV News, "Harper Makes It Official."

8 For example, Clark and Mickleburgh, "Alliance MP Blasted."
9 Edmonton Journal, "City MLA Quits"; Hatter, "Cocky protégé Rises"; LeClair, "Hale Crosses."
10 Kerby and Blidook, "It's Not You, It's Me."
11 Müller and Strøm, "Hard Choices," 7.
12 CBC News, "Simard Leaving PCs."
13 For example, Braid and D'Aliesio, "Raj Sherman"; Kimber, "Bitter Pill."
14 Canadian Press, "Saskatchewan Minister."
15 Benson, "Political Stripes of Convenience."
16 Bell, "Nunavut's Own."
17 Sallot, "No Cabinet Promise."
18 Quoted in Rodon, Teach an Eskimo, 149–50.
19 Quoted in Montgomery, "Ittinuar Faces."
20 Sallot, "No Cabinet Promise."
21 Sallot, "No Cabinet Promise."
22 Quoted in Montgomery, "Ittinuar Faces."
23 Canadian Press, "MP Sees Betrayal."
24 Bell, "Nunavut's Own."
25 Curry and Chase, "Candidate Controversy."
26 Bell, "Nunavut's Own."
27 Kilgour, "David Kilgour," 22.
28 Quoted in Kimber, "Bitter Pill."
29 Halifax Chronicle-Herald, "Tory Defector"; Hinrich Bitter-Suermann interview.
30 Political Staffer 4 interview.
31 Canadian Press, "N.B. Member Defects."
32 Müller and Strøm, "Hard Choices," 6.
33 Henry Carroll, NDP MLA in Manitoba, quoted in Fitzgerald, "Carroll Cities Snub for Resignation."
34 Lorraine Michael interview.
35 Parliamentarian 6 interview.
36 Burzo et al., "Legislative Pensions."
37 Bridget Pastoor, PC MLA in Alberta, quoted in CBC News, "Lethbridge MLA."
38 Rick Laliberte, Liberal MP in Saskatchewan, quoted in CBC News, "NDP MP Defects."
39 Garfield Warren, PC MHA in Newfoundland & Labrador, quoted in Yaffe, "Garfield Warren."
40 Ian Donovan, PC MLA in Alberta, quoted in Bennett, "Two Wildrose Members."
41 For example, Kleiss, "Towle."
42 As with David Ramsay, Liberal MPP in Ontario; see Canadian Press, "Rae is 'Flabbergasted.'" A prominent example is federal Minister David Emerson in 2006.
43 Poitras, "Guns, Revenge."
44 Palmer, "Coleman Accuses Speaker."
45 Hunter, "Reform MLA Quits." We note that discussions over a couple of years between Yukon NDP MLA Dennis Fentie and some Liberal ministers led to the offer of a cabinet post to join the government side. Instead, in 2002 he crossed the floor to the conservative-leaning Yukon Party, became leader,

and went on to lead the third-place party to an election victory that same year (Tobin, "Liberals Beckoned"; "Fentie Deserts NDP").

46 CBC News, "Green Party Announces."
47 DeRosa, "Banman Defects."
48 Adams, "Chrétien Reels."
49 As with Dave Taylor, Calgary-Currie MLA, who joined the Alberta Party (CBC News, "Taylor Becomes").
50 Müller and Strøm, "Hard Choices," 8–9.
51 McAndrews et al., "How Citizens Judge."
52 Kendall and Rekkas, "Incumbency Advantages."
53 We tallied 101 federal and provincial parliamentarians who contested consecutive elections under different party banners from 1980 to 2021; of them, fifty-two lost their re-election bids and forty-nine won. An additional twenty-three party switchers chose not to seek re-election. These figures do not include politicians whose parties changed because of rebranding or mergers.
54 Young, "Deux autres Defections."
55 Gold, "Langevin Crosses."
56 Cleary, "No Faith in Grimes."
57 For example, Little and Zussman, "Conservatives Keep Up."
58 Rick Woodford, Liberal MHA in Newfoundland & Labrador, quoted in MacIsac, "Rhetoric on the Rock." See also Buzzetti and Cornellier, "Parti progressiste-conservateur."
59 Malloy, "Casey Crosses."
60 Le Devoir, "Bloc perd un premier."
61 For example, Turchansky, "Backbencher Quits."
62 Ruimy, "Kwinter Wins," A6.
63 Southam Newspapers, "Liberal MPP Defects."
64 CBC News, "Harris Turns Up."
65 Bottom et al., "Negotiating a Coalition."
66 Yoshinaka, *Crossing the Aisle*, 185.
67 Yoshinaka, *Crossing the Aisle*, 27–8.
68 Rod Fox, PC MLA in Alberta, quoted in Fox, "Open Letter." Also Parliamentarian 8 interview.
69 Yaffe, "Garfield Warren."
70 Little and Zussman, "Conservatives Keep Up."
71 Parliamentarian 8 interview.
72 For example, Yoshinaka, *Crossing the Aisle*, 185.
73 Parliamentarian 8 interview.
74 Buckley Belanger interview.
75 Greg Clark interview.
76 Argue, "Senator Hazen Argue."
77 David Peterson interview.
78 Sullivan, "Rick Woodford."
79 O'Neil, "Emerson Hails"; Wells, *Right Side Up*, 251; Wells, *The Longer I'm Prime Minister*, 17–18.
80 Brent Rathgeber interview.
81 Dominic Cardy interview.
82 Party Leader 5 interview.

83 Don Bell, Liberal MP in British Columbia, quoted in O'Neil, "Don Bell Not Joining."
84 Lorraine Michael interview; Political Staffer 6 interview.
85 Political Staffer 6 interview.
86 Benzie, "Veteran Ontario Liberals."
87 Lane, "Navigating Party Discipline." Also Paul Lane interview.
88 Quoted in Martin, *Belinda*, 182.
89 Martin, 183–90. Also David Peterson interview.
90 Jeff Wilson interview.
91 Yoshinaka, *Crossing the Aisle*, 196–8.
92 CBC News, "Lane Crosses"; Sorbara, *Let 'Em Howl*, 142.
93 Parliamentarian 7 interview.
94 Political Staffer 6 interview.
95 For example, Canadian Press, "Inky Mark Polls Riding"; CBC News, "Osborne Joins."
96 Taylor, "Independent Toronto MP."
97 Quoted in Cooke, "Independent MHA."
98 Rana, "Cadman Says"; Zytaruk, *Like a Rock*.
99 Political Staffer 6 interview.
100 Greg MacEachern interview.
101 Percy Downe interview.
102 For example, Sorbara, *Let 'Em Howl*.
103 Political Staffer 6 interview.
104 David Peterson interview.
105 Party Leader 4 interview.
106 David Peterson interview.
107 Political Staffer 2 interview.
108 Lane, "Navigating Party Discipline."
109 Ian Brodie interview.
110 Blake Pedersen interview.
111 Sandra Jansen interview.
112 Sorbara, *Let 'Em Howl*, 143 and 192.
113 Sorbara, *Let 'Em Howl*.
114 Political Staffer 9 interview. See also Sorbara, *Let 'Em Howl*, 142.
115 Pearson, *Mike*, 96.
116 Political Staffer 6 interview.
117 Political Staffer 4 interview.
118 Stewart, *Politics on the Edge*, 203.
119 Walker, "Liberals Reluctantly Accept."
120 Herle, "The Insiders."
121 Canadian Press, "Sorbara Charged."
122 Political Staffer 9 interview.
123 Political Staffer 2 interview.
124 Percy Downe interview.
125 Political Staffer 4 interview.
126 Shapiro, *Grewal-Dosanjh Inquiry*.
127 Quoted in Blatchford, "Quiet Nods."
128 Quoted in National Post, "Grewal Questions."
129 Shapiro, *Grewal-Dosanjh Inquiry*.
130 Shapiro, *Grewal-Dosanjh Inquiry*.
131 Party Leader 4 interview.

132 Sorbara, *Let 'Em Howl*, 147 and 170; White, "Sudbury Byelection."
133 Hunter, "High-Stakes Gamble."
134 Gordon Wilson interview.
135 Martin, *Belinda*, 188.
136 Trevisan, "Stronach on Switching."
137 Canadian Press, "Stronach Jumps"; Globe and Mail, "Martin's Statement";
     Martin, *Belinda*, 193; Martin, *Hell or High Water,* 430–1.
138 Globe and Mail, "Martin's Statement"; Martin, *Belinda,* 191.
139 Benzie, "MPP Jack MacLaren."
140 Trevor, "Anglin Splits."
141 Parliamentarian 10 interview.
142 CBC News, "Clark Wins."
143 Inky Mark interview.
144 Canadian Press, "Third B.C. United."
145 Thomson, "Lying Politicians."
146 Martin, *Belinda*, 194–5.
147 Canadian Press, "Grit MPP"; Lortie, "Verdun quitte le Bloc."
148 For example, Cunningham, "Grits Planning."
149 CBC News, "Casey Crosses."
150 Gold, "Grit Crosses."
151 Howard, "MHA for Torngat Mountains."
152 Political Staffer 6 interview.
153 CBC News, "Trimper to Run."
154 Trueman, "TV Missed Switch."
155 Alleslev, "Government Orders." See also Alleslev, "MP Leona Alleslev."
156 Shaw and Zussman, *Matter of Confidence*, 33.
157 Lévesque, "Defecting Quebec."

9. **Aftermath of Defecting**

1 Jansen, "Members' Statements."
2 Gibson, "Jansen Given Security."
3 Sandra Jansen interview.
4 Baugut, "From Interactions"; Strömbäck and Van Aelst, "Why Political Parties
   Adapt?"
5 de Vreese, "Mediatization of News"; Lemarier-Saulnier, "Définitions du
   cadrage."
6 Beharrell et al., *More Bad News.*
7 Lalancette et al., "Playing Along."
8 Thompson, *Political Scandal*, 420–1.
9 For example, Langer, *Personalization of Politics;* van Zoonen, "Imagining the Fan."
10 CBC News, "Ontario Liberal MP."
11 Harris, "Forging of Jane Philpott's."
12 Adams, "Chrétien Reels."
13 Canadian Press, "Socred Faithful." See also Jeff Wilson interview.
14 Blatchford, "Quiet Nods"; Brown, "Jenica Atwin Switches"; Köhler,
   "Dysfunction' Drives."
15 Canadian Press, "Irate N.S. Premier"; Canadian Press, "Rae is
   'Flabbergasted'"; Cleary, "No Faith in Grimes"; Jannard, "Mulroney perd
   trois."
16 Canadian Press, "Crise au Bloc"; Hébert, "Crise au PQ."

17 Hays, "Kimball Quits."
18 Canadian Press, "Tories Dump Steven Fletcher"; CBC News, "MacKay Slams Brison"; Clark and Mickleburgh, "Alliance MP Blasted"; Harding, "Stronach a Traitor."
19 Crawford, "I Felt I had No Choice."
20 Globe and Mail, "Reform MP Sues."
21 Wright, "Dumville Breaks His Silence."
22 Sorbara, Let 'Em Howl, 150.
23 Quoted in Benzie, "NDP MP Defects."
24 CBC News, "Sudbury MP."
25 CBC News, "NDP's Glenn Thibeault."
26 Bryden, "Spurned Tory MP." See also Maher, The Prince, 49.
27 O'Neil, "Emerson Hails."
28 Lalancette et al., "Retourner sa veste."
29 Mas, "Hyer Joins Green Party"; Radio-Canada, "NPD perd un autre."
30 Pierre Michel Auger, Liberal MNA in Quebec, quoted in Chouinard and Beauchemin, "L'ADQ est le parti." Translated from French by the authors.
31 Lisette Lapointe, Parti Québécois MNA, quoted in Hébert, "Crise au PQ." Translated by authors.
32 Such as MNAs Jean-Martin Aussant and Pierre Curzi.
33 Gabriel Ste-Marie, Bloc Québécois MP, quoted in Brouillette, "Ste-Marie quitte."
34 Len Webber, PC MLA in Alberta, quoted in CBC News, "Len Webber Quits."
35 Bashevkin, Women, Power, Politics.
36 Mark Wasyliw, Independent MLA in Manitoba, quoted in Froese, "MLA Mark Wasyliw."
37 Walker, "New Democratic MPP"; "Liberals Reluctantly Accept."
38 For example, CTV News, "Tory MLAs Cross."
39 Lévesque, "Bloc perd un premier."
40 Hunter, "High-Stakes Gamble."
41 For example, McMartin, "Emerson: The Power."
42 CBC News, "MacKay Slams Brison." See also Martin, Belinda, 207.
43 Pierrette Venne, PC MP in Quebec, quoted in Lapointe, "Conservateurs reprochent."
44 Angela Vautour, NDP MP in New Brunswick, quoted in Fraser, "NDP Left Reeling."
45 For example, Gold, "Langevin Crosses"; Stevenson, "Defection Trips Up."
46 George Little, leader of the Nova Scotia NDP, quoted in Canadian Press, "N.B. Member Defects."
47 Brennan, "Cullen Finds Home."
48 Radio-Canada, "NPD perd un autre."
49 Quoted in Minsky, "Adams Joins Liberals." See also Maher, The Prince, 49.
50 For example, Canadian Press, "Rae is 'Flabbergasted.'"
51 For example, Bailey, "Wilson Rejoins."
52 John Bryden, Conservative MP in Ontario, quoted in Puxley, "Bryden Joins."
53 Ian Donovan, PC MLA in Alberta, quoted in Bellefontaine, "Wildrose MLAs."
54 For example, Canadian Press, "Liberals Lose"; Lacombe Express, "Rod Fox Crosses."
55 Bellefontaine, "Wildrose MLAs."
56 Rowe, Is That You Bill?, 5.
57 Quoted in CBC News, "Osborne Joins." See also CBC News, "Osborne Quits."
58 Desposato, "Parties for Rent?," 64.

59 Sandra Jansen interview.
60 Moose Jaw Times Herald, "Political Hero."
61 For example, CBC News, "Casey Crosses"; Globe and Mail, "Martin's Statement"; Gold, "Langevin Crosses."
62 For example, Daily News, "Defection to the Liberal."
63 For example, Cooke, "Brendan Maguire Dumps N.S."
64 Doucette, "Nova Scotia Liberal Brendan Maguire"; Greenaway, "Tory MP Defects"; Malloy, "Casey Crosses."
65 Simpson, Discipline of Power, 52 and 79–80.
66 Horner, My Own Brand, 183.
67 Harris, "Forging of Jane Philpott."
68 Donna Marie Kennedy-Glans interview.
69 Quoted in Calgary Herald, "NDP Loses Fifth."
70 Hom et al., Employer Retention and Turnover, 18–20.
71 Mowday et al., Employee-Organization Linkages.
72 Methot et al., "Network Architecture."
73 O'Neill, "Liberal MP Quits."
74 Travaglino et al., "How Groups React."
75 Campbell, "Case of Louis Riel," 9.
76 Hom et al., Employer Retention and Turnover, 22–3.
77 Party Leader 2 interview.
78 Political Staffer 9 interview.
79 Hinrich Bitter-Suermann interview.
80 Celina Caesar-Chavannes interview.
81 CBC News, "Osborne Quits."
82 For example, CBC News, "Blaney Says Tory."
83 Tanner, "New Democrats See Gain."
84 Barron, "Taylor Turning Tory"; Benzie, "NDP MP Defects."
85 CBC News, "MacKay Slams Brison."
86 Canadian Press, "Rae is 'Flabbergasted.'"
87 Lazenby, "Battle between Conservatives."
88 Canadian Press, "Newfoundland's Newest."
89 Shaw and Zussman, A Matter of Confidence, 32.
90 Roche, "Newfoundland Oil"; Yaffe, "Garfield Warren."
91 Halifax Chronicle-Herald, "Tory Defector."
92 Stephens, "Ontario MPP Crosses."
93 Lethbridge Herald, "Liberals."
94 Ferguson, "Manitoba Tory Defects."
95 Manitoba PC Premier Gary Filmon, quoted in York, "MLA Quits Tories."
96 Legislative Assembly of Manitoba, "Debates and Proceedings."
97 CBC News, "Stiles, MacAlpine-Stiles."
98 Roche, "Newfoundland Oil."
99 For example, Payton, "NDP Target Claude Patry."
100 Cochrane, "Floor-Crossing MP."
101 Ian Brodie interview.
102 Maher, The Prince, 49.
103 Argue, "Senator Hazen Argue."
104 Bellavance, "NPD veut forcer"; Payton, "NDP Target Claude Patry."
105 Lévesque, "Defecting Quebec."
106 Goodyear-Grant, Gendered News, 59.
107 Buzzetti, "Mourani a voulu partir."

108 Canadian Press, "Stronach Jumps"; The Hill Times, "Shortly After Stronach's."
109 CBC News, "Stronach Demands MacKay". See also Martin, *Belinda.*
110 Harding, "Stronach a Traitor."
111 Blatchford, "Who You Calling?"
112 Martin, *Belinda,* 227–8.
113 Martin, *Belinda,* 200.
114 Bob Runciman, PC MPP in Ontario, quoted in Weber, "Stronach Deserves Apology." See also Martin, *Belinda,* 227; Turner, *Sheeple,* 22.
115 Maurice Vellacott, Conservative MP in Saskatchewan, quoted in Canadian Press, "Western Tories Livid." See also Turner, *Sheeple,* 23.
116 Tony Abbott, PC MLA in Alberta, quoted in Harding, "Stronach a Traitor." See also Turner, *Sheeple,* 23.
117 Quoted in Weber, "Stronach Deserves Apology." See also Martin, *Belinda,* 200; Turner, *Sheeple,* 23.
118 Trevisan, "Stronach on Switching."
119 Trimble and Everitt, "Stronach and the Gender," 66.
120 Plante, "Ça été difficile."
121 Parliamentarian 10 interview.
122 Howard, "MHA for Torngat Mountains."
123 A search of posts on X was conducted in the aftermath of Evans crossing the floor on 16 July 2024.
124 Parliamentarian 15 interview.
125 Vermot-Desroches, "Aussant quitte."
126 For example, Argue, "Senator Hazen Argue," 41; Plante, "Ça été difficile."
127 Aiken, *The Backbencher,* 133–4.
128 Kilgour, "David Kilgour," 19. For an overview of political and social sanctions, see Marland, *Whipped,* chap. 10.
129 Keith Martin interview.
130 Clark and Mickleburgh, "Alliance MP Blasted."
131 Beatty, "Brenzinger Not First."
132 Bruce Hyer interview.
133 For example, Canadian Press, "Liberal MPP Appalled."
134 Laghi, "Alliance Defector's Riding."
135 Political Staffer 4 interview.
136 Quoted in Clark and Mickleburgh, "Alliance MP Blasted."
137 Parliamentarian 8 interview.
138 Hinrich Bitter-Suermann interview.
139 Lisa Raitt interview.
140 Parliamentarian 14 interview.
141 Pitkin, *Concept of Representation.*
142 Canadian Press, "Elenore Sturko's Defection."
143 Brent Rathgeber interview.
144 CBC News, "Former Timiskaming MPP."
145 Parliamentarian 10 interview.
146 Snagovsky and Kerby, "Electoral Consequences," 438; Sevi et al., "Legislative Party Switching," 679. American party switchers also lose votes (Yoshinaka, *Crossing the Aisle,* 8 and 140).
147 Snagovsky and Kerby, "Electoral Consequences," 438.
148 Kendall and Rekkas, "Incumbency Advantages," 1572.

149 Kendall and Rekkas, "Incumbency Advantages," 1572.
150 Parliamentarian 10 interview.
151 Thompson, *Political Scandal*.
152 Soroka, "Issue Attributes."

10. Empowering Team Members

1 Carty, "Politics of Tecumseh Corners."
2 For example, Young, "Party, State, and Political Competition."
3 Brady, "The Independents." See also Canadian Parliamentary Review, "Independents: Roundtable."
4 Elkins and Simeon, *Small Worlds.*
5 Wesley and Buckley, "Provincial Party Systems."
6 Marland, *Whipped*, chap. 12
7 For example, Robertson, "Liberal MP Decries."
8 On factionalism and political parties, see Boucek, "Rethinking Factionalism."
9 Judge, "Representation in Westminster," 14.
10 Eulau et al., "Role of the Representative," 750.
11 Converse and Pierce, *Political Representation in France,* 14.
12 Coghill, "Learning."
13 Albaidhani and Laperrière-Macoux, "Building capabilities"; Smith, "Rookie MPs in Ottawa."
14 Cockram, "A Process."
15 Docherty, "Canadian Political Career."
16 Relatedly, see Thomas, "Developing Better Political Leaders."
17 Landes, "Special Committee."
18 House of Commons, "Standing Orders."
19 Chong, "Government Orders."
20 Chong, "Government Orders."
21 Manning, "Obstacles."
22 Aiello, "NDP MP Wants."
23 Desserud, "Confidence Convention," 8.
24 For example, Benoit, "Ministerial Staff"; Lees-Marshment, *Human Resource*; Mallory, "Casey Crosses."
25 In South Africa, for example, caucus rules are approved by the extra-parliamentary party; see McGee, "Parties and Government," 21.
26 Angus Reid Institute, "Crossing the Floor."
27 Provincial legislatures abolished the practice between 1926 to 1941. See Isaacs, "Missing Premier," 40.
28 For example, Canadian Press, "Tories, NDP call"; Dewing, "Changes."
29 Roziere, "Reconsidering Bill 4."
30 Freeman, "Floor Crossing's"; Trevisan, "Stronach on switching."
31 Ali, "Jama Says She Can"; Beattie, "Hamilton MPP"; Kelly, "Coralee Oates"; Marland, *Whipped*, 155.
32 Kelly, "Coralee Oates."
33 Section 66(1)(a)(v) of the *Canada Elections Act*.
34 Maher, *The Prince*, 165.

References

Abbasi, Sami, and Kenneth Hollman. "Turnover: The Real Bottomline." *Public Personnel Management* 29, no. 3 (September 2000): 333–42. https://doi .org/10.1177/009102600002900303.

Abrams, Dominic, and Michael A. Hogg. "An Introduction to the Social Identity Approach." In *Social Identity Theory: Constructive and Critical Advances*, edited by Dominic Abrams and Michael A. Hogg. Harvester-Wheatsheaf, 1990.

– *Social Identifications: A Social Psychology of Intergroup Relations and Group Processes*. Taylor & Francis/Routledge, 1990. https://doi.org/10.4324 /9780203135457.

Abrams, Dominic, José M. Marques, Georgine Randsley de Moura, Paul Hutchison, and Nicola J. Brown. "The Maintenance of Entitativity: A Subjective Group Dynamics Approach." In *The Psychology of Group Perception*, edited by Vincent Yzerbyt, Charles M. Judd, and Olivier Corneille. Psychology Press, 2004.

Adams, Blair. "Ford Defends Decision to Kick Karahalios Out of PC Caucus." *City News Kitchener*, 22 July 2020. https://kitchener.citynews.ca/2020/07/22/ford -defends-decision-to-kick-karahalios-out-of-pc-caucus-2583647/.

Adams, Christopher. "The Canadian Polling Industry, Government Procurement, Changing Methods, and Party Polling in the 2000s." Paper presented to the Canadian Political Science Association annual conference, York University, Toronto. 31 May 2023.

Adams, Paul. "Chrétien Reels in Another Defector." *Globe and Mail*, 28 September 2000. https://www.theglobeandmail.com/news/national/chretien-reels -in-another-defector/article1042665.

Agnew, Christopher R., and Laura E. Vanderdrift. "Commitment Processes in Personal Relationships." In *The Cambridge Handbook of Personal Relationships*, edited by Anita L. Vangelisti and Daniel Perlman. Cambridge University Press, 2018.

Aho, James A. "Out of Hate: A Sociology of Defection from Neo-Nazism." *Current Research on Peace and Violence* 11, no. 4 (December 1988): 159–68.

Aiello, Rachel. "Liberal MP Sahota Contradicts PM, Foreign Minister on Reason for Russians' Expulsion." *CTV News*, 8 April 2018. https://www.ctvnews.ca /politics/liberal-mp-sahota-contradicts-pm-foreign-minister-on-reason-for -russians-expulsion-1.3875105.

– "Liberals Approached Me to Cross the Floor, Issues with Green Leader 'Irreconcilable': Atwin." *CTV News*, 13 June 2021. https://www.ctvnews

.ca/politics/liberals-approached-me-to-cross-the-floor-issues-with-green
-leader-irreconcilable-atwin-1.5467087.

– "Mark Carney Says He's Not Chasing Floor-Crossers from Any Party." *CTV News*, 14 May 2023. https://www.ctvnews.ca/politics/article/we-have-a-clear-mandate-carney-says-hes-not-chasing-floor-crossers-from-any-party.

– "NDP MP Wants 'Democratic Controls' on the Prime Minister's Powers." *CTV News*, 15 May 2023. https://www.ctvnews.ca/politics/ndp-mp-wants
-democratic-controls-on-the-prime-minister-s-powers-1.6399198.

– "Trudeau Adds New Caucus-PMO Liaison." *CTV News*, 22 March 2019. https://www.ctvnews.ca/politics/trudeau-adds-new-caucus-pmo-liaison-1.4347960.

Aiken, Gordon. *The Backbencher: Trials and Tribulations of a Member of Parliament.* McClelland and Stewart, 1974.

Albaidhani, Ismail, and Guillaume LaPerrière-Marcoux. "Building Capabilities for the Future – Keeping Up with Change." *Canadian Parliamentary Review* 45, no. 1 (Spring 2022): 15–22.

Alberta. Standing Orders of the Legislative Assembly of Alberta, Order 32(5), 2024. https://www.assembly.ab.ca/docs/default-source/reference/assembly
-documents/standingorders.pdf.

Albertson, Bethany. "Dog-whistle Politics: Multivocal Communication and Religious Appeals." *Political Behavior* 37, no. 1 (March 2015): 3–26. https://doi.org/10.1007/s11109-013-9265-x.

Ali, Rukhsar. "Hundreds Gather in Support of Hamilton MPP Sarah Jama in Virtual Rally." *Global News*, 28 October 2023. https://globalnews.ca/news/10054868/rally-support-sarah-jama-ontario-ndp.

– "Sarah Jama Says She Can Still 'Advocate' for Riding Despite Being Removed from Ontario NDP." *Global News*, 26 October 2023. https://globalnews.ca/news/10050778/sarah-jama-outsider-ndp-ontario-hamilton.

Alleslev, Leona. "Government Orders – Privilege." Canada. Parliament. House of Commons. *Edited Hansard* 148(319). 42nd Parliament, 1st session, 17 September 2018.

– "MP Leona Alleslev: Why I Crossed the Floor to the Conservatives." *National Post*, 24 September 2018. https://nationalpost.com/news/politics/exclusive-mp-leona-alleslev-why-i-crossed-the-floor-to-the-conservatives.

Ames, Herbert B. "The Organization of Political Parties in Canada." *Proceedings of the American Political Science Association* 8 (1911): 181–8. https://doi.org/10.2307/3038406.

Anderson, Rob. "Anderson: Why I Chose to Cross the Floor." *Calgary Herald*, 1 June 2020. https://calgaryherald.com/opinion/columnists/anderson
-why-i-chose-to-cross-the-floor.

Andeweg, Rudy B., and Jacques Thomassen. "Pathways to Party Unity: Sanctions, Loyalty, Homogeneity and Division of Labour in the Dutch Parliament." *Party Politics* 17, no. 5 (September 2010): 655–72. https://doi.org/10.1177/1354068810377188.

Angus Reid Institute. "Crossing the Floor: Canadians Weigh in on Elected Members Who Quit Their Parties between Elections." *Angus Reid Institute*, 11 December 2018. https://angusreid.org/floor-crossing.

– "Missing Political Middle." *Angus Reid Institute*, 12 September 2024. https://angusreid.org/canada-centrism-extremism-political-spectrum-left-wing
-right-wing-poilievre-trudeau.

– "Pointless Parliament? Disenchanted Canadians Describe Debates in House of Commons as 'posturing', 'useless.'" *Angus Reid Institute*, 2 November 2023. https://angusreid.org/house-of-commons-decorum-debate.

– "Trust in Government: Canadians Wary of Politicians and Their Intentions." *Angus Reid Institute*, 24 June 2019. https://angusreid.org/views-of-politicians.

Antle, Rob. "Political Blood Still Astir: Warren." *The Express*, 26 January 1994.

Antonacci, J.P. "I Won't Cross the Floor, Says Haldimand-Norfolk's Independent MPP." *Hamilton Spectator*, 9 August 2022. https://www.thespec.com/news /hamilton-region/i-won-t-cross-the-floor-says-haldimand-norfolk-s -independent-mpp/article_d9d4ac7b-ce33-58ba-9cff-00ade286c1ef.html.

Argue, Hazen. "Senator Hazen Argue His Memories of Prime Minister Pearson and the Pearson Government in an Interview with Peter Stursberg." Oral History Project, Library of Parliament, National Archives of Canada, 7 December 1976.

Arnold, Tom. "MLA Quits Liberals over Policy Dispute." *Edmonton Journal*, 18 July 1998.

Arnprior Chronicle-Guide. "Cheryl Gallant Escapes Conservative Leader's Wrath on Campaign Trail." *Arnprior Chronicle-Guide*, 1 September 2021. https://www .insideottawavalley.com/news-story/10468102-cheryl-gallant-escapes -conservative-leader-s-wrath-on-campaign-trail.

Artuso, Antonella. "Premier Ford Ejects MPP Roman Baber after Speaking Out against Lockdown." *Toronto Sun*, 15 January 2021. https://torontosun .com/news/provincial/premier-ford-ejects-mpp-roman-baber-who -spoke-out-against-lockdown.

Asch, Solomon E. "Effects of Group Pressure Upon the Modification and Distortion of Judgments." In *Groups, Leadership and Men: Research in Human Relations*, edited by Harold Guetzkow. Carnegie Press, 1951.

Asmussen, Nicole, and Adam Ramey. "When Loyalty Is Tested: Do Party Leaders Use Committee Assignments as Rewards?" *Congress & The Presidency* 45, no. 1 (2018): 41–65. https://doi.org/10.1080/07343469.2017.1418764.

Atwin, Jenica. "Letter to Prime Minister Trudeau and Minister Mélanie Joly." Instagram (post), 9 November 2023. https://www.instagram.com/jenicaatwin.

– "Please Read the Following Statement." Facebook (post), 24 June 2021. https:// www.facebook.com/JenicaAtwinFredericton/photos/a.688677771489066 /1454638848226284.

Authier, Philip. "Right-of-Centre Voters Will Get Voice in Legislature, Duhaime Says." *Montreal Gazette*, 18 June 2021. https://www.montrealgazette.com/news /provincial-news/article95210.html.

Axworthy, Thomas S. "Of Secretaries to Princes." *Canadian Public Administration* 31, no. 2 (July 1988): 247–64. https://doi.org/10.1111/j.1754-7121.1988.tb01316.x.

Bailey, Ian. "B.C. Conservatives' Sole MLA Quits, Citing Difficulties with Leader Cummins." *Globe and Mail*, 22 September 2012. https://www.theglobeandmail .com/news/british-columbia/bc-conservatives-sole-mla-quits-citing-difficulties -with-leader-cummins/article4561462.

– "Gordon Wilson Rejoins Liberal Camp, Backing Clark." *Globe and Mail*, 5 May 2013. https://www.theglobeandmail.com/news/british-columbia /gordon-wilson-rejoins-liberal-camp-backing-clark/article11729209.

– "Liberal Caucus Meets in Ottawa as MP Backs Away from Leadership Review Comments." *Globe and Mail*, 25 January 2024. https://www.theglobeandmail .com/politics/article-politics-briefing-liberal-caucus-meets-in-ottawa-as-mp -backs-away-from.

Bain, George. "Miss Jewett's Decision." *Globe and Mail*, 13 April 1972.

Balcer, Léon. "Léon Balcer Interviewed by Peter Stursberg." Oral History Project, Library of Parliament, National Archives of Canada, 31 January 1972.

Bakvis, Herman. *Regional Ministers: Power and Influence in the Canadian Cabinet.* University of Toronto Press, 1991.

Barnard, John. *American Vanguard: The United Auto Workers during the Reuther Years, 1935–1970.* Wayne State University Press, 2004.

Barron, Tracy. "Taylor Turning Tory for Next Election." *The Western Star,* 23 December 2000.

Bashevkin, Sylvia. *Women, Power, Politics: The Hidden Story of Canada's Unfinished Democracy.* Oxford University Press, 2009.

Bauch, Hubert. "Putting Down the Putsch." *The Gazette,* 30 April 1988.

Baugut, Paul. "From Interactions to the Mediatization of Politics: How the Relationships between Journalists and Political Actors Explain Media Influences on Political Processes and the Presentation of Politics." *Journalism Studies* 20, no. 16 (2019): 2366–85. https://doi.org/10.1080/1461670X.2019.1598886.

Baumeister, Roy F., and Mark R. Leary. "The Need to Belong: Desire for Interpersonal Attachments as a Fundamental Human Motivation." *Psychological Bulletin* 117, no. 3 (May 1995): 497–529. https://doi.org/10.1037//0033-2909.117.3.497.

Baumeister, Roy F., and Dianne M. Tice. "Point-Counterpoints: Anxiety and Social Exclusion." *Journal of Social and Clinical Psychology* 9, no. 2 (June 1990): 165–95. https://doi.org/10.1521/jscp.1990.9.2.165.

Bazzo, Marie-France. "Pas de chicane dans ma cabane." *La Presse,* 25 October 2022. https://plus.lapresse.ca/screens/600f24c4-b880-4cb7-a2ec-a85b0110b800__7C___0.html.

Beattie, Samantha. "Hamilton MPP Sarah Jama Says She's 'Committed' to Constituents, as NDP Decision to Remove Her Sparks Outcry." *CBC News,* 25 October 2023. https://www.cbc.ca/news/canada/hamilton/jama-hamilton-centre-constituents-1.7007265.

Beatty, Jim. "Brenzinger Not First MLA to Be Suspended." *The Vancouver Sun,* 10 March 2004.

Beharrell, Peter, Howard Davis, John Eldridge, et al. *More Bad News.* Glasgow University Media Group. Taylor and Francis, 2009. https://doi.org/10.4324/9780203092637.

Bélanger, Éric, and Richard Nadeau. "Political Trust and the Vote in Multiparty Elections: The Canadian Case." *European Journal of Political Research* 44, no. 1 (January 2005): 121–46. https://doi.org/10.1111/j.1475-6765.2005.00221.x.

Bélanger, Éric, and Laura B. Stephenson. "Parties and Partisans: The Influence of Ideology and Brokerage on the Durability of Partisanship in Canada." In *Voting Behaviour in Canada,* edited by Cameron D. Anderson and Laura B. Stephenson. UBC Press, 2010. https://doi.org/10.59962/9780774817851-008.

Bell, Jim. "Nunavut's Own Floor-crosser Sympathizes with Belinda Stronach." *Nunatsiaq News,* 27 May 2005. https://nunatsiaq.com/stories/article/nunavuts_own_floor-crosser_sympathizes_with_belinda_stronach.

Bellavance, Joel-Denis. "Le NPD veut forcer Claude Patry à démissonner." *La Presse,* 5 March 2013. https://www.lapresse.ca/actualites/politique/politique-canadienne/201303/05/01-4627820-le-npd-veut-forcer-claude-patry-a-demissonner.php.

– "'They Have to Come to the PC Party': Elsie Wayne Speaks Out." *National Post,* 18 August 2001.

Bellefontaine, Michelle. "MLA Prab Gill Improperly Removed Ballots at Calgary UCP Meeting, Investigator Finds." *CBC News,* 5 December 2018. https://www.cbc.ca/news/canada/edmonton/prab-gill-report-ballots-calgary-ucp-meeting-1.4934290.

– "UCP Accused of Curbing Debate on Contentious Bills as Spring Legislative Session Winds Down." *CBC News*, 28 May 2024. https://www.cbc.ca/news/canada/edmonton/ucp-accused-of-curbing-debate-on-contentious-bills-as-spring-legislative-session-winds-down-1.7217757.

– "Wildrose MLAs Kerry Towle and Ian Donovan Cross Floor to Tories." *CBC News*, 24 November 2014. https://www.cbc.ca/news/canada/edmonton/wildrose-mlas-kerry-towle-and-ian-donovan-cross-floor-to-tories-1.2847378.

Belshaw, John Douglas. *Canadian History: Post-Confederation*. 2nd ed. BC Open Textbook Project, 2020. https://opentextbc.ca/postconfederation2e/.

Bennett, Colin J., and Jesse Gordon. "Understanding the 'Micro' in Political Micro-targeting: An Analysis of Facebook Digital Advertising in the 2019 Federal Canadian Election." *Canadian Journal of Communication* 46, no. 3 (September 2021): 431–59. https://doi.org/10.22230/cjc.2021v46n3a3815.

Bennett, Dean. "Alberta Premier's Caucus Foe Calls Him Soft on Ottawa, Gets Verbal Slap in Return." *Globe and Mail*, 5 May 2022. https://www.theglobeandmail.com/canada/article-alberta-premiers-caucus-foe-calls-him-soft-on-ottawa-gets-verbal-slap.

– "Lloyd Snelgrove, Former Alberta Treasurer, Leaves Caucus after Critical Remarks." *Global News*, 27 January 2012. https://globalnews.ca/news/204572/lloyd-snelgrove-former-alberta-treasurer-leaves-caucus-after-critical-remarks.

– "Two Wildrose Members Crossing the Floor to Join Tories." *Globe and Mail*, 24 November 2014. https://www.theglobeandmail.com/news/alberta/two-wildrose-members-crossing-the-floor-to-join-tories-sources-say/article21733277.

Benoit, Liane E. "Ministerial Staff: The Life and Times of Parliament's Statutory Orphans." In *Commission of Inquiry into the Sponsorship Program and Advertising Activities, Restoring Accountability: Research Studies Volume 1 – Parliament, Ministers and Deputy Ministers*. Public Works and Government Services Canada, 2006.

Benson, Bob. "Political Stripes of Convenience." *The Telegram*, 26 October 1997, 10.

Benzie, Robert. "How Doug Ford Schooled His Rivals in the Milton Byelection." *Toronto Star*, 3 May 2024. https://www.thestar.com/politics/provincial/how-doug-ford-schooled-his-rivals-in-the-milton-byelection/article_8a1293aa-0953-11ef-ad5f-231f5791319c.html.

– "MPP Jack MacLaren out of Tory Caucus after Comments about French Language Rights." *Toronto Star*, 28 May 2017. https://www.thestar.com/politics/provincial/mpp-jack-maclaren-out-of-tory-caucus-after-comments-about-french-language-rights/article_e9c7c11a-32f5-58f8-96b6-15ecf644903a.html.

– "NDP MP Defects to Run for Wynne's Liberals in Sudbury Byelection." *Toronto Star*, 16 December 2014. https://www.thestar.com/news/canada/ndp-mp-defects-to-run-for-wynne-s-liberals-in-sudbury-byelection/article_0669211a-3005-5b80-8041-1834abc9a9fc.html.

– "Veteran Ontario Liberals Want Green MPP Mike Schreiner to Be Their Leader." *Toronto Star*, 28 January 2023. https://www.thestar.com/politics/provincial/veteran-ontario-liberals-want-green-mpp-mike-schreiner-to-be-their-leader/article_dbbfc12c-42ef-5b70-afb9-51dec4e1ea5a.html.

Benzie, Robert, Rob Ferguson, and Kristin Rushowy. "Ford Fears Disgruntled Tory MPPs Might Defect to Liberals, Source Says." *Toronto Star*, 23 November 2018. https://www.thestar.com/politics/provincial/ford-fears-disgruntled-tory-mpps-might-defect-to-liberals-source-says/article_7c5b43d4-12ce-5a1c-a7cc-05e5fe87cf07.html.

Berkelaar, Brenda L., and Patrice M. Buzzanell. "Cybervetting, Person–environment Fit, and Personnel Selection: Employers' Surveillance and Sensemaking of Job Applicants' Online Information." *Journal of Applied Communication Research* 42, no. 4 (2014): 456–76. https://doi.org/10.1080/00909882.2014.954595.

Berlet, Chip. "Trump, Sado-populism, Alt-right, and Apocalyptic Neofascism." In *Trumping Democracy: From Reagan to the Alt-Right*, edited by Chip Berlet. Routledge, 2019. https://doi.org/10.4324/9781315438412.

Berry, Zachariah, Neil A. Lewis Jr., and Walter J. Sowden. "The Double-Edged Sword of Loyalty." *Current Directions in Psychological Science* 30, no. 4 (August 2021): 321–6. https://doi.org/10.1177/09637214211010759.

Bittner, Amanda. "The Effects of Information and Social Cleavages: Explaining Issue Attitudes and Vote Choice in Canada." *Canadian Journal of Political Science* 40, no. 4 (December 2007): 935–68. https://www.jstor.org/stable/25166179.

– "Leaders Always Mattered: The Persistence of Personality in Canadian Elections." *Electoral Studies* 54 (August 2018): 297–302. https://doi.org/10.1016/j.electstud.2018.04.013.

Black, Jerome H. "Racial Diversity and the 2021 Federal Election: Visible Minority Candidates and MPs." *Canadian Parliamentary Review* 45, no. 2 (Summer 2022): 19–25.

Black, Matthew. "Jennifer Johnson Joins UCP Caucus after Being Banned for Transphobic Remarks." *Edmonton Journal*, 9 October 2024. https://edmontonjournal.com/news/politics/jennifer-johnson-alberta-ucp-caucus.

Black Press Media Staff. "Rod Fox Crosses Over to Join Tories." *Lacombe Express*, 25 December 2014. https://www.lacombeexpress.com/news/rod-fox-crosses-over-to-join-tories.

Blais, André, and M. Martin Boyer. "Assessing the Impact of Televised Debates: The Case of the 1988 Canadian Election." *British Journal of Political Science* 26, no. 2 (April 1996): 143–64. https://doi.org/10.1017/S0007123400000405.

Blais, Julie, Scott Pruysers, and Philip G. Chen. "Why Do They Run? The Psychological Underpinnings of Political Ambition." *Canadian Journal of Political Science* 52, no. 4 (December 2019): 761–79. https://doi.org/10.1017/S0008423918001075.

Blatchford, Christie. "Quiet Nods and Welcoming Winks." *Globe and Mail*, 1 June 2005. https://www.theglobeandmail.com/news/national/quiet-nods-and-welcoming-winks/article736634.

– "Who You Calling 'Sexist,' Buster?" *Globe and Mail*, 21 May 2005. https://www.theglobeandmail.com/opinion/who-you-calling-sexist-buster/article1119536.

Blewett, Taylor. "Cheryl Gallant Attends Riding Event Where Criticism Is Not Allowed, Skips Other Debates." *Pembroke Observer*, 19 October 2019. https://www.pembrokeobserver.com/news/local-news/cheryl-gallant-attends-riding-event-where-criticism-is-not-allowed-skips-other-debates.

Blidook, Kelly. "The Changing Use of Standing Order 31 Statements." *Canadian Parliamentary Review* 36, no. 4 (Winter 2013): 25–9.

– *Constituency Influence in Parliament: Countering the Centre.* UBC Press, 2012. https://doi.org/10.59962/9780774821582.

Blouin, Louis, and Holly Cabrera. "Pablo Rodriguez to Sit as Independent While Seeking Quebec Liberal Leadership." *CBC News*, 16 September 2024. https://www.cbc.ca/news/politics/rodriguez-announcement-resignation-1.7327794.

Blumler, Jay G., and Dennis Kavanagh. "The Third Age of Political Communication: Influences and Features." *Political Communication* 16, no. 3 (1999): 209–30. https://doi.org/10.1080/105846099198596.

Boesveld, Sarah. "Question Period Rife with Rudeness, Layton Most Negative, New Index Finds." *National Post*, 31 May 2011. https://nationalpost.com/news/canada/question-period-rife-with-rudeness-layton-most-negative-new-index-finds.

Bøggild, Troels. "Politicians as Party Hacks: Party Loyalty and Public Distrust in Politicians." *The Journal of Politics* 82, no. 4 (October 2020): 1516–29. https://doi.org/10.1086/708681.

Bonebright, Denise. "40 Years of Storming: A Historical Review of Tuckman's Model of Small Group Development." *Human Resource Development International* 13, no. 1 (2010): 111–20. https://doi.org/10.1080/13678861003589099.

Boothby, Lauren. "Kenney Says He Will Boot UCP MLAs from Caucus If They Break COVID-19 Rules or Encourage Others to Do So." *Edmonton Journal*, 8 April 2021. https://edmontonjournal.com/news/kenney-ucp-mlas-caucus-covid-break-rules.

Borcsok, Thomas. "No One Cares about a Political Candidate without a Party." *Ottawa Citizen*, 8 June 2022. https://ottawacitizen.com/opinion/borcsok-no-one-cares-about-a-political-candidate-without-a-party.

Bosc, Marc. "The Commons Then and Now: Decorum." *Canadian Parliamentary Review* 10, no. 3 (Autumn 1987): 33–4.

Bosc, Marc, and André Gagnon, eds. *House of Commons Procedure and Practice*. 3rd ed., 2017. https://www.ourcommons.ca/About/ProcedureAndPractice3rdEdition/ch_20_1-e.html.

Bottom, William P., James Holloway, Scott McClurg, and Gary J. Miller. "Negotiating a Coalition: Risk, Quota Shaving, and Learning to Bargain." *The Journal of Conflict Resolution* 44, no. 2 (April 2000): 147–69. https://doi.org/10.1177/0022002700044002001.

Boucek, Françoise. "Rethinking Factionalism: Typologies, Intra-party Dynamics and Three Faces of Factionalism." *Party Politics* 15, no. 4 (July 2009): 455–85. https://doi.org/10.1177/1354068809334553.

Boucher, Maxime. "L'effet Westminster: les cibles et les stratégies de lobbying dans le système parlementaire canadien." *Canadian Journal of Political Science* 48, no. 4 (December 2016): 839–61. https://doi.org/10.1017/S0008423916000019.

Bourgault-Côté, Guillaume. "Catherine Fournier en mission pour rassembler les souverainistes." *Le Devoir*, 17 November 2020. https://www.ledevoir.com/politique/quebec/589826/l-apres-pq-de-catherine-fournier.

Boutilier, Alex. "Conservative MP Derek Sloan Refuses to Apologize for Asking If Chief Health Officer Worked 'for China.'" *Toronto Star*, 29 April 2020. https://www.thestar.com/politics/federal/conservative-mp-derek-sloan-refuses-to-apologize-for-asking-if-chief-health-officer-worked-for/article_b5d41e6f-8af0-541d-a694-68082a251863.html.

– "Conservatives Clamp Down on Governing Body's Dealings with Reporters, Social Media Posts." *Global News*, 4 April 2022. https://globalnews.ca/news/8734574/conservatives-clamp-down-reporters-social-media-posts.

– "Poilievre Meeting with Each Conservative MP Ahead of October Shadow Cabinet Decisions." *Global News*, 23 September 2022. https://globalnews.ca/news/9152040/poilievre-meeting-mps-shadow-cabinet-october.

– "Poilievre's Office Asks Tory MPs to 'Not Talk to Media' on 'Gender Ideology' Protests." *Global News*, 20 September 2023. https://globalnews.ca/news /9974879/ottawa-protests-pierre-poilievre.

Bovens, Mark, Gijs Jan Brandsma, and Dick Thesingh. "Political Death and Survival in the Netherlands: Explaining Resignations of Individual Cabinet Members 1946–2010." *Acta Polit* 50, no. 2 (April 2015): 127–50. https://doi .org/10.1057/ap.2014.1.

Brabazon, Honor, and Kirsten Kozolanka. "Neoliberalism, Authoritarianism-Populism, and the 'Photo-op Democracy' of the Publicity State: Changes to Legislative and Parliamentary Norms by the Harper Government." *Canadian Journal of Political Science* 51, no. 2 (June 2018): 253–77. https://doi.org/10.1017 /S0008423917001020.

Braid, Don, and Renata D'Aliesio. "Raj Sherman, Tory MLA and Physician, Assails Ailing Medical System." *Edmonton Journal*, 18 November 2010. https:// edmontonjournal.com/news/raj-sherman-tory-mla-and-physician-assails -ailing-medical-system/wcm/b45ee3fd-089c-4329-9caf-38fc6d0c8ce6.

Brancati, Dawn. "Winning Alone: The Electoral Fate of Independent Candidates Worldwide." *The Journal of Politics* 70, no. 30 (July 2008): 648–62. https://doi .org/10.1017/S0022381608080675.

Brennan, Richard. "Booted from the Liberals, Cullen Finds Home with NDP." *The Standard*, 24 November 1998.

– "Priest MPP Quits NDP Caucus." *The Windsor Star*, 29 April 1993.

Brodie, Ian. *At the Centre of Government: The Prime Minister and the Limits on Political Power.* McGill-Queen's University Press, 2018. https://doi .org/10.1515/9780773553774.

Brouillette, Élise. "Gabriel Ste-Marie quitte le Bloc." *L'Action*, 28 February 2018. https://www.laction.com/article/2018/02/28/gabriel-ste-marie-quitte-le-bloc -quebecois.

Brown, Desmond, and Aura Carreño Rosas. "MPP Sarah Jama Says She's 'Hopeful' to Return to Ontario NDP after Submitting Vetting Package." *CBC News*, 10 January 2025. https://www.cbc.ca/news/canada/hamilton/sarah -jama-ndp-return-1.7425220.

Brown, Jim. "NDP Accuses Israel of State Terrorism as Middle East Debate Boils in Ottawa." *The Canadian Press*, 10 April 2002.

Brown, Rupert, and Samuel Pehrson. "Group Formation and Other Elementary Group Processes." *Group Processes: Dynamics Within and between Groups.* John Wiley & Sons, 2019. https://doi.org/10.1002/9781118719244.

Brown, Silas. "Jenica Atwin Switches from Greens to Liberals, Riding Funding Announcements Go from 0 to 7." *Global News*, 9 August 2021. https:// globalnews.ca/news/8092149/jenica-atwin-floor-crossing.

Bryant, Michael. *28 Seconds: A True Story of Addiction, Tragedy, and Hope.* Viking, 2012.

Bryden, Joan. "Have Chair, Will Travel." *Kingston Whig – Standard*, 21 April 1998.

– "Liberals Ease Candidate Nomination Rules in Case of Snap Election." *Global News*, 9 October 2020. https://globalnews.ca/news/7389883 /liberals-candidate-nomination-rules.

– "Liberals Embrace Trudeau's Plan to Transform Party into Open Movement." *CTV News*, 28 May 2016. https://www.ctvnews.ca/politics/liberals-embrace -trudeau-s-plan-to-transform-party-into-open-movement-1.2921238.

– "Spurned Tory MP Eve Adams Crosses Floor to Join Liberals." *The Record*, 9 February 2015. https://www.therecord.com/news/canada/spurned

-tory-mp-eve-adams-crosses-floor-to-join-liberals/article_499e28ef-86a7
-5197-a538-ab7264ae9925.html.

– "Svend Robinson Came under Intense Criticism Wednesday." *CanWest News*, 17 April 2002.

Buchko, Aaron A., Caleb Buscher, and Kathleen J. Buchko. "Why Do Good Employees Stay in Bad Organizations?" *Business Horizons* 60, no. 5 (September–October 2017): 729–39. https://doi.org/10.1016/j.bushor.2017.06.001.

Buffam, Robert. "All NDP MLAs Receive a New Title, and All but One Get a Raise." *CTV News*, 19 November 2024. https://bc.ctvnews.ca /all-ndp-mlas-receive-a-new-title-and-all-but-one-get-a-raise-1.7116349.

Bulow, George M. "The Use of CRM in Political Fund-Raising." *Journal of Political Marketing* 2, no. 2 (2003): 105–9.

Bulowski, Natasha. "Liberals Face Inside Pressure to Announce Oil and Gas Cap." *National Observer*, 24 November 2023. https://www.nationalobserver .com/2023/11/24/news/liberals-face-inside-pressure-oil-and-gas-cap.

Burgess, Mark. "Swelling of Feds' Communications Staff Reflects Growing 'Public Relations State': Experts." *The Hill Times*, 11 August 2014.

Burke, Ashley. "Expelled Liberal Candidate Says He'll Sit as an Independent as Angry Voters Call for Byelection." *CBC News*, 22 September 2021. https:// www.cbc.ca/news/politics/undecided-races-2021-federal-election -1.6185685.

– "Liberal MP Backtracks after Voicing Support for Resolution Critics Call a Threat to Press Freedom." *CBC News*, 10 May 2023. https://www.cbc.ca /news/politics/liberal-mps-defend-parts-of-controversial-party-policy-to -combat-disinformation-1.6838810.

Burns, John. "Backbench Reaction to New-format Caucus 98 Per Cent Positive." *Globe and Mail*, 17 September 1969.

Burt, Ronald S. "The Contingent Value of Social Capital." *Administrative Science Quarterly* 42, no. 2 (June 1997): 339–65. https://doi.org/10.2307/2393923.

Burzo, Stefano, Bert Kramer, Daniel Irwin, and Christopher Kam. "Legislative Pensions and Re-election Seeking: Evidence from Canadian Legislatures." *Legislative Studies Quarterly* 49, no. 2 (May 2024): 383–409. https://doi .org/10.1111/lsq.12424.

Busby, Robert. "Republican Mavericks: The Anti-Obama Impulse in the 2008 Election." In *Barack Obama and the Myth of a Post-Racial America*, edited by Mark Ledwidge, Kevern Verney, and Inderjeet Parmar. Routledge, 2013. https://doi .org/10.4324/9780203067796.

Butler, Don. "The Two Faces of John Baird: Attack-dog or Mr. Congeniality." *Ottawa Citizen*, 3 February 2015. https://ottawacitizen.com/news/politics /the-two-faces-of-john-baird-attack-dog-or-mr-congeniality.

Buzzetti, Hélène. "Mourani a voulu partir, dit Daniel Paillé." *Le Devoir*, 14 September 2013. https://www.ledevoir.com/politique/canada/387497 /mourani-a-voulu-partir-dit-daniel-paille.

Buzzetti, Hélène, and Manon Cornellier. "Parti progressiste-conservateur : Clark perd un troisième député." *Le Devoir*, 26 April 2000.

Caesar-Chavannes, Celina. *Can You Hear Me Now?* Random House Canada, 2021.

Calgary Herald. "Bush Demands Israel Withdrawal 'Now.'" 7 April 2002.

– "NDP Loses Fifth Calgary Candidate as MLA Sandra Jansen Says She Won't Seek Re-election." 21 January 2019. https://calgaryherald.com/news /local-news/infrastructure-minister-calgary-mla-sandra-jansen-wont -seek-re-election.

Callan, Isaac. "MPP Involved in Hamas-Israel Comments Controversy to Remain Part of Ontario NDP." *Global News*, 11 October 2023. https://globalnews.ca/news/10018386/sarah-jama-israel-hamas-comments-ndp-caucus.

Callan, Isaac, and Colin D'Mello. "Ontario NDP Leader Marit Stiles Reflects on 2023: Greenbelt and Internal Governance." *Global News*, 28 December 2023. https://globalnews.ca/news/10191820/marit-stiles-ontario-ndp-2023-year-end.

– "Senior Ford Government Cabinet Ministers Barely Using Work Phones, Docs Show." *Global News*, 14 November 2023. https://globalnews.ca/news/10026091/senior-ford-government-cabinet-ministers-work-phones.

Came, Barry. "'A Credible Effort.'" *Maclean's*, 20 May 1996. https://archive.org/details/Macleans-Magazine-1996-05-20/page/n11/mode/2up.

Campbell, Alexander. "The Case of Louis Riel, Convicted of Treason, and Executed Therefor." Memorandum. Maclean, Roger & Co., 1885.

Campbell, Angus, Philip E. Converse, Warren E. Miller, and Donald E. Stokes. *The American Voter*. John Wiley & Sons, 1960.

Campbell, Clark. "Martin's Prize Catch." *Globe and Mail*, 11 December 2003. https://www.theglobeandmail.com/news/national/martins-prize-catch/article18439670/.

Campbell, Ian, and Abbas Rana. "Only Pushback from Members Will Drive Party Leadership to Loosen Grip on Nominations, Say Campaign Veterans." *The Hill Times*, 6 September 2024. https://www.hilltimes.com/story/2024/09/06/only-pushback-from-members-will-drive-party-leadership-to-loosen-grip-on-nominations-say-campaign-veterans/433421.

Campbell, Rosie, Philip Cowley, Nick Vivyan, and Markus Wagner. "Legislator Dissent as a Valence Signal." *British Journal of Political Science* 49, no. 1 (January 2016): 105–28. https://doi.org/10.1017/S0007123416000223.

Canada. *House of Commons Debates*, 17 June 2008 (Ms. Louise Thibault, Ind.). https://www.ourcommons.ca/documentviewer/en/39-2/house/sitting-114/hansard.

– *Open and Accountable Government*. Privy Council Office, 2015. https://www.pm.gc.ca/sites/pm/files/inline-files/oag_2015_english.pdf.

– "Prime Minister's Office." Government Electronic Directory Services. 30 August 2023. https://www.geds-sage.gc.ca/en/GEDS.

– *Reform Act, 2014*. Statutes of Canada, 2015, c 37. https://laws-lois.justice.gc.ca/PDF/2015_37.pdf.

Canada, National Security and Intelligence Committee of Parliamentarians. *Special Report on Foreign Interference in Canada's Democratic Processes and Institutions*. 1st. sess., 44th Parliament. Committee Special Report, 2024. https://www.nsicop-cpsnr.ca/reports/rp-2024-06-03/special-report-foreign-interference.pdf.

Canadian Parliamentary Review. "The Independents: A Roundtable Discussion with Independent and Independently-Minded Parliamentarians." *Canadian Parliamentary Review* 46, no. 2 (Summer 2024): 11–17.

Canadian Press. "Alberta MLA Kicked Out of Tory Caucus Over Health Spending Spat." *CBC News*, 8 July 2009. https://www.cbc.ca/news/canada/edmonton/alberta-mla-kicked-out-of-tory-caucus-over-health-spending-spat-1.784788.

– "Amanda Simard, Ontario PC MPP, Speaks Out against Doug Ford Government's French Services Cuts." *Global News*, 22 November 2018. https://globalnews.ca/news/4687810/amanda-simard-doug-ford-government-french-services-cuts.

- "Bill Will Restrict Location of Doctors." *Lethbridge Herald*, 24 May 1985.
- "Cambridge MPP Booted from PC Caucus after Voting against Pandemic Emergency Powers Bill." *Global News*, 21 July 2020. https://globalnews.ca /news/7202960/belinda-karahalios-kicked-out-ontario-pc-caucus.
- "Chrétien Expects Liberal MPs to be Onside for Contentious Votes." *Waterloo Region Record*, 25 November 1994.
- "Conservative MP Says Mark Warawa and 'Rogue' Backbenchers Must 'Suffer the Consequences' for Anti-abortion Stance." *National Post*, 27 March 2013. https:// nationalpost.com/news/politics/conservative-mp-says-mark-warawa-and-rogue -backbenchers-must-suffer-the-consequences-for-anti-abortion-stance.
- "Corrective to Story about Mark Carney Ending the Carbon Price." *Toronto Star*, 17 March 2025. https://www.thestar.com/news/corrective-to-story-about-mark- carney-ending-the-carbon-price/article_729ed533-99e4-59c4-b733-fe308112d714. html.
- "Crise au Bloc québécois : les sept dissidents songent à fonder un nouveau parti." *Radio-Canada*, 1 May 2018. https://ici.radio-canada.ca/nouvelle/1098380 /crise-bloc-quebecois-sept-deputes-dissidents-tournent-la-page.
- "Dean Del Mastro Resigns His Seat in House of Commons before Vote to Suspend Him." *National Post*, 5 November 2014. https://nationalpost.com /news/politics/dean-del-mastro-resigns-his-seat-in-house-of-commons -after-hes-found-guilty-of-violating-canada-elections-act.
- "Elenore Sturko's Defection to BC Conservatives Confuses, Disappoints LGBTQ+ Advocates." *Toronto Star*, 4 June 2024. https://www.thestar .com/news/canada/british-columbia/elenore-sturkos-defection-to -bc-conservatives-confuses-disappoints-lgbtq-advocates/article_a79a38e2 -e98b-51c2-a895-1c828939aec2.html.
- "Facing the 'Hooligans' Bhaduria Discussion Erupts in Shouting Match." *Waterloo Region Record*, 28 February 1994.
- "Former Floor-Crossing Law Not a Violation of Rights." *Global News*, 20 June 2018. https://globalnews.ca/news/4285126/former-floor-crossing-law -not-a-violation-of-rights-manitoba-judge-after-fletcher-lawsuit.
- "Green Party Rift over Israeli-Palestine Conflict Widens as MPs Break from Leader." *Globe and Mail*, 1 June 2021. https://www.theglobeandmail.com /canada/article-green-party-rift-over-israeli-palestinian-conflict-widens -as-mps-break.
- "Grit MPP, Brother of Ex-premier Peterson, Turns Tory." *The Standard*, 30 March 2007.
- "Irate N.S. Premier Ejects Maverick from Caucus." *Toronto Star*, 25 October 1986.
- "Liberal MP Confronts Minister over New Watchdog to Oversee Canadian Companies Abroad." *CBC News*, 24 March 2021. https://www.cbc.ca/news /politics/mckay-ng-ombudsperson-responsible-enterprise-1.5961607.
- "Liberal MPP Appalled by Tory Defector's Plan to Run for Federal Grits." *CTV News*, 10 February 2015. https://toronto.ctvnews.ca/liberal-mpp-appalled -by-tory-defector-s-plan-to-run-for-federal-grits-1.2229920.
- "Liberal Pat Sorbara Charged with Bribing Glenn Thibeault to Defect from NDP." *CBC News*, 2 November 2016. https://www.cbc.ca/news/canada /sudbury/thibeault-sorbara-bribery-charges-1.3832863.
- "Manitoba MP Inky Mark Polls Riding to Decide If He Should Jump to Tories." *Winnipeg Free Press*, 3 July 2002.
- "Manitoba Tories Dump Steven Fletcher from Caucus Saying He Wasn't a Team Player." *National Post*, 30 June 2017. https://nationalpost.com/pmn

/news-pmn/canada-news-pmn/manitoba-premier-comments-on-reports
-mla-steven-fletcher-dumped-from-caucus.

– "Maverick MLA Killed in Plane Crash." *Ottawa Citizen*, 29 September 1986.

– "MP Sees Betrayal by Liberals." *Globe and Mail*, 26 July 1984.

– "MPP Resigns from Tory Caucus, Disputing She Misrepresented COVID-19
Vaccination Status." *Globe and Mail*, 22 October 2021. https://www
.theglobeandmail.com/canada/article-mpp-resigns-from-tory-caucus
-disputing-that-she-misrepresented.

– "NDP Candidate Jean-Francois Delisle Backs Off Proposal to Reopen Constitution."
CBC News, 19 September 2015. http://www.cbc.ca/news/politics
/canada-election-2015-ndp-candidate-backs-off-constitution-1.3235458.

– "NDP Removes MP as Candidate Who Was in Discussions with Another
Party." *CTV News*, 16 August 2019. https://www.ctvnews.ca/politics
/ndp-removes-mp-as-candidate-who-was-in-discussions-with-another
-party-1.4553192.

– "NDP Sees Its Foothold Slip as N.B. Member Defects." *Globe and Mail*,
10 September 1985.

– "Newfoundland Liberals Lose MNA to the Tories." *Globe and Mail*,
9 February 1985.

– "Newfoundland's Newest Liberal Heckled by Tory ex-colleagues." *Globe and
Mail*, 14 March 1984.

– "Ontario NDP MPP Leaves Caucus to Sit as Independent after Losing
Nomination Contest." *Global News*, 22 April 2022. https://globalnews.ca
/news/8779034/kevin-yarde-mpp-independent-ontario-election.

– "Rae Is 'Flabbergasted' as New Democrat Crosses Floor to Join Peterson's
Liberals." *Toronto Star*, 6 October 1986.

– "Sask. Liberals Vote to Hold Leadership Convention." *Moose Jaw Times Herald*,
5 March 2001.

– "Saskatchewan Grits Turf Maverick MLA." *Calgary Herald*, 21 December 1984.

– "Saskatchewan Minister Quits over Job Transfers." *Globe and Mail*, 18 June 1991.

– "Socred Faithful Hope to Defeat Defectors." *Calgary Herald*, 7 October 1982.

– "Stronach Jumps Ship." *Peterborough Examiner*, 18 May 2005.

– "Third B.C. United MLA Set to Go to B.C.'s Conservatives." *Vancouver
Sun*, 29 July 2024. https://vancouversun.com/news/third-b-c-united
-mla-set-to-go-to-b-c-s-conservatives.

– "Tories, NDP Call for Ban on Politicians Crossing the Floor." *Cape Breton Post*,
19 April 2007.

– "Tory MP Michelle Ferreri Deletes Post That Claimed Cost of Living
Is Driving Parents to Traffic Kids." *Globe and Mail*, 21 August 2014.
https://www.theglobeandmail.com/canada/article-tory-mp-michelle
-ferreri-deletes-post-that-claimed-cost-of-living-is.

– "Tried to Switch." *Montreal Gazette*, 11 December 1986.

– "'We're Not a Zebra Party,' Newfoundland Grit Leader Says of Latest Additions."
CTV News, 4 February 2014. https://www.ctvnews.ca/politics/we-re-not-a
-zebra-party-newfoundland-grit-leader-says-of-latest-additions-1.1669771.

– "Western Tories Livid." *Chronicle Herald*, 18 May 2005.

– "Wilson-Raybould Quashes Hopes to Unanimously Pass Bloc Motion on
Quebec Nationhood, Constitutional Change." *National Post*, 26 May 2021.
https://nationalpost.com/news/politics/singh-says-quebecs-proposed
-constitutional-change-important-but-symbolic.

Canadian Press NewsWire. "New Democrat MP Svend Robinson Hopes to Meet Besieged Arafat." *Canadian Press NewsWire*, 3 April 2002.

Cappella, Joseph N., and Kathleen Hall Jamieson. *Spiral of Cynicism: The Press and the Public Good*. Oxford University Press, 1997. https://doi.org/10.1093/oso/9780195090635.001.0001.

Carroll, Glenn R., and Dennis Ray Wheaton. "The Organizational Construction of Authenticity: An Examination of Contemporary Food and Dining in the US." *Research in Organizational Behavior* 29 (2009): 255–82. https://doi.org/10.1016/j.riob.2009.06.003.

Carty, R. Kenneth. "Has Brokerage Politics Ended? Canadian Parties in the New Century." In *Parties, Elections, and the Future of Canadian Politics*, edited by Amanda Bittner and Royce Koop. UBC Press, 2013. https://doi.org/10.59962/9780774824101-004.

– "The Politics of Tecumseh Corners: Canadian Political Parties as Franchise Organizations." *Canadian Journal of Political Science* 35, no. 4 (December 2002): 723–45. https://doi.org/10.1017/S0008423902778402.

Carty, R. Kenneth, William Cross, and Lisa Young. *Rebuilding Canadian Party Politics*. UBC Press, 2000.

Caruana, Nicholas J., R. Michael McGregor, and Laura B. Stephenson. "The Power of the Dark Side: Negative Partisanship and Political Behaviour in Canada." *Canadian Journal of Political Science* 48, no. 4 (December 2015): 771–89. https://doi.org/10.1017/S0008423914000882.

CBC News. "9 Wildrose MLAs, Including Danielle Smith, Cross to Alberta Tories." *CBC News*, 17 December 2014. https://www.cbc.ca/news/canada/edmonton/9-wildrose-mlas-including-danielle-smith-cross-to-alberta-tories-1.2876412.

– "Alberta MP David Kilgour Quits the Liberal Party." *CBC News*, 13 April 2005. https://www.cbc.ca/news/canada/alberta-mp-david-kilgour-quits-the-liberal-party-1.532010.

– "Alta. MLA Kicked from Caucus over ER Remarks." *CBC News*, 22 November 2010. https://www.cbc.ca/news/canada/edmonton/alta-mla-kicked-from-caucus-over-er-remarks-1.920592.

– "Andrew Younger Says He Never Refused to Testify in Assault Case." *CBC News*, 5 November 2015. https://www.cbc.ca/news/canada/nova-scotia/tara-gault-andrew-younger-trial-1.3305103.

– "B.C. MLA Paul Reitsma Resigns." *CBC News*, 6 December 1999. https://www.cbc.ca/news/canada/b-c-mla-paul-reitsma-resigns-1.164439.

– "B.C. NDP Leader Kicks Out Cariboo MLA." *CBC News*, 7 October 2010. https://www.cbc.ca/news/canada/british-columbia/b-c-ndp-leader-kicks-out-cariboo-mla-1.888961.

– "B.C. Premier 'Abusive,' Says Fired Minister." *CBC News*, 17 November 2010. https://www.cbc.ca/news/canada/british-columbia/b-c-premier-abusive-says-fired-minister-1.898564.

– "Blaney Says Tory Crossed the Floor over Money." *CBC News*, 18 April 2007. https://www.cbc.ca/news/canada/new-brunswick/blaney-says-tory-crossed-the-floor-over-money-1.685419.

– "Bruce County Mayor Who Resigned Apologizes for 'Ignorant, Insensitive' Comments about First Nation." *CBC News*, 30 August 2023. https://www.cbc.ca/news/canada/london/garry-michi-south-bruce-mayor-resignation-apology-1.6952654.

- "Calgary MLA Len Webber Quits Tory Caucus to Protest Premier." *CBC News*, 13 March 2014. https://www.cbc.ca/news/canada/calgary/calgary-mla -len-webber-quits-tory-caucus-to-protest-premier-1.2570893.
- "Chuck Porter Leaves PC Caucus, Cites Leadership as a Factor." *CBC News*, 13 June 2014. https://www.cbc.ca/news/canada/nova-scotia/chuck-porter -leaves-pc-caucus-cites-leadership-as-a-factor-1.2674567.
- "Clark Wins Kings-Hants Byelection." *CBC News*, 12 September 2000. https:// www.cbc.ca/news/canada/clark-wins-kings-hants-byelection-1.207476.
- "Crossing the Floor." *CBC News*, 27 June 2007. https://www.cbc.ca/news2 /background/cdngovernment/crossing.html.
- "Dale Kirby and Christopher Mitchelmore Join Liberals." *CBC News*, 4 February 2014. https://www.cbc.ca/news/canada/newfoundland-labrador /dale-kirby-and-christopher-mitchelmore-join-liberals-1.2522282.
- "Deborah Drever Suspended from NDP Caucus." *CBC News*, 22 May 2015. https://www.cbc.ca/news/canada/calgary/deborah-drever-suspended -from-ndp-caucus-1.3084083.
- "Derek Fildebrandt Acclaimed as Freedom Conservative Party Leader." *CBC News*, 21 October 2018. https://www.cbc.ca/news/canada/edmonton /freedom-alberta-party-fildebrandt-acclaimed-1.4872293.
- "Dr. Jim Parrott Rejoins Progressive Conservative Caucus." *CBC News*, 30 April 2014. https://www.cbc.ca/news/canada/new-brunswick /dr-jim-parrott-rejoins-progressive-conservative-caucus-1.2627005.
- "Edzerza Rejoins Yukon Party." *CBC News*, 22 October 2009. https://www .cbc.ca/news/canada/north/edzerza-rejoins-yukon-party-1.841336.
- "Facing Impaired Driving Charge, Hugh MacKay Resigns from Liberal Caucus." *CBC News*, 23 February 2020. https://www.cbc.ca/news/canada /nova-scotia/high-mackay-resigns-liberal-caucus-1.5473144.
- "Former MLA on Welfare after Election Loss." *CBC News*, 24 April 2000. https://www.cbc.ca/news/canada/former-mla-on-welfare-after -election-loss-1.218845.
- "Former Timiskaming MPP and Liberal Cabinet Minister David Ramsay Dies." *CBC News*, 30 July 2020. https://www.cbc.ca/news/canada/sudbury /david-ramsay-timiskaming-mpp-obituary-1.5668478.
- "Fort McMurray Tories Question Boutilier's Removal." *CBC News*, 20 July 2009. https://www.cbc.ca/news/canada/edmonton/fort-mcmurray-tories-question -boutilier-s-removal-1.856653.
- "Full Text of Peter Mansbridge's Interview with Justin Trudeau." *CBC News*, 8 September 2015. http://www.cbc.ca/news/politics/canada-election-2015 -justin-trudeau-interview-peter-mansbridge-full-transcript-1.3219779.
- "Green Party Announces Its First Member of Parliament." *CBC News*, 30 August 2008. https://www.cbc.ca/news/canada/green-party -announces-its-first-member-of-parliament-1.697339.
- "Harris Turns Up to Support Former Liberal on His Team." *CBC News*, 31 May 1999. https://www.cbc.ca/news/canada/harris-turns-up-to -support-former-liberal-on-his-team-1.173074.
- "Kim Craitor, Ex-Liberal MPP, Resigned Over Sexual Harassment Allegations, Premier Says." *CBC News*, 6 May 2016. https://www.cbc.ca/news/canada /toronto/premier-sexual-harassment-case-1.3571104.
- "Lela Evans, MHA for Labrador's Torngat Mountains District, Leaving PC Party." *CBC News*, 25 October 2021. https://www.cbc.ca/news/canada /newfoundland-labrador/lela-evans-leaving-pc-party-1.6223802.

– "Lethbridge MLA Crosses Floor to Join Tories." *CBC News*, 21 November 2011. https://www.cbc.ca/news/canada/edmonton/lethbridge-mla-crosses-floor-to -join-tories-1.981329.
– "Liberals Expel Doug Young for Ties to Alliance." *CBC News*, 2 May 2000. https://www.cbc.ca/news/canada/liberals-expel-doug-young-for-ties-to -alliance-1.247167.
– "MacKay Slams Brison for Joining Liberals." *CBC News*, 10 December 2003. https://www.cbc.ca/news/canada/mackay-slams-brison-for-joining -liberals-1.371668.
– "Malley Denies Allegations of Blackmail." *CBC News*, 22 February 2006. https:// www.cbc.ca/news/canada/new-brunswick/malley-denies-allegations-of -blackmail-1.613885.
– "Manning Ejected from Tory Caucus." *CBC News*, 5 May 2005. https:// www.cbc.ca/news/canada/newfoundland-labrador/manning-ejected-from -tory-caucus-1.536704.
– "MP Rathgeber Refuses to Be 'Cheerleader' and Quits Tory Caucus." *CBC News*, 6 June 2013. https://www.cbc.ca/news/canada/edmonton /mp-rathgeber-refuses-to-be-cheerleader-and-quits-tory-caucus-1.1330541.
– "MPP Amanda Simard Leaving PCs, Will Sit as Independent." *CBC News*, 29 November 2018. https://www.cbc.ca/news/canada/ottawa/amanda-simard -mpp-progressive-conservative-1.4925179.
– "NDP MP Defects to Liberal Party." *CBC News*, 28 September 2000. https://www.cbc.ca/amp/1.205152.
– "NDP's Glenn Thibeault 'Proud' to Defect to Ontario Liberals." *CBC News*, 16 December 2014. https://www.cbc.ca/news/canada /sudbury/ndp-s-glenn-thibeault-proud-to-defect-to-ontario-liberals -1.2874576.
– "Ontario Liberal MP to Sit as Independent." *CBC News*, 6 June 2005. https://www.cbc.ca/news/canada/ontario-liberal-mp-to-sit-as-independent -1.525779.
– "Ontario MP Khan Leaves Liberals to Join Tories." *CBC News*, 5 January 2007. https://www.cbc.ca/news/canada/ontario-mp-khan-leaves-liberals -to-join-tories-1.633168.
– "Ontario MPP Rick Nicholls Booted from PC Caucus after Refusing to Take COVID-19 Vaccine." *CBC News*, 19 August 2021. https://www.cbc.ca/news /canada/toronto/rick-nicholls-mpp-vaccine-1.6146791.
– "Ontario PC Party Removes Kitchener-Conestoga MPP Michael Harris from Caucus." *CBC News*, 9 April 2018. https://www.cbc.ca/news/canada/ kitchener-waterloo/sarah-michael-harris-pc-kitchener-conestoga-election-1.4611090.
– "Osborne Quits Tories, Cites Dunderdale Leadership." *CBC News*, 13 September 2012. https://www.cbc.ca/news/canada/newfoundland -labrador/osborne-quits-tories-cites-dunderdale-leadership-1.1135226.
– "Ottawa-area MPP Jack MacLaren Expelled from PC Caucus." *CBC News*, 28 May 2017. https://www.cbc.ca/news/canada/ottawa/jack-maclaren -removed-pc-caucus-1.4134959.
– "Paul Lane Crosses Floor to Liberals, Blames Kathy Dunderdale." *CBC News*, 20 January 2014. https://www.cbc.ca/news/canada/newfoundland-labrador /paul-lane-crosses-floor-to-liberals-blames-kathy-dunderdale-1.2503211.
– "Perry Trimper Says He Felt 'Increasingly Isolated,' Excluded from Liberal Caucus." *CBC News*, 16 November 2020. https://www.cbc.ca/news/canada /newfoundland-labrador/perry-trimper-indepdendent-reaction-1.5803992.

– "Perry Trimper to Run as Independent in Next Election, Resigns from Liberal Caucus." *CBC News*, 10 November 2020. https://www.cbc.ca/news/canada /newfoundland-labrador/perry-trimper-independent-election-1.5797130.
– "Premier Greg Selinger Replaces 5 Cabinet Ministers in Government Revolt." *CBC News*, 3 November 2014. https://www.cbc.ca/news/canada /manitoba/premier-greg-selinger-replaces-5-cabinet-ministers-in -government-revolt-1.2822132.
– "Randy Hillier Expelled from Ontario PC Caucus." *CBC News*, 15 March 2019. https://www.cbc.ca/news/canada/ottawa/hillier-expelled -opc-caucus-1.5058281.
– "Stiles, MacAlpine-Stiles Deny Spying Allegations." *CBC News*, 18 April 2007. https://www.cbc.ca/news/canada/new-brunswick /stiles-macalpine-stiles-deny-spying-allegations-1.689360.
– "Stronach Demands MacKay Apologize for Alleged 'Dog' Comment." *CBC News*, 20 October 2006. https://www.cbc.ca/news/canada /stronach-demands-mackay-apologize-for-alleged-dog-comment-1.599061.
– "Sudbury MP Glenn Thibeault 'Invigorated' by Move to Ontario Liberals." *CBC News*, 17 December 2014. https://www.cbc.ca/news/canada/sudbury /sudbury-mp-glenn-thibeault-invigorated-by-move-to-ontario-liberals -1.2875951.
– "Taylor becomes Alberta Party's First MLA." *CBC News*, 24 January 2011. https://www.cbc.ca/news/canada/calgary/taylor-becomes-alberta-party-s -first-mla-1.1022875.
– "The Noblest of Callings ... the Vilest of Trades. Potterton Film Productions." Library and Archives Canada, WO#51249, 1971.
– "Tom Osborne Joins Liberals." *CBC News*, 29 August 2013. https://www .cbc.ca/news/canada/newfoundland-labrador/tom-osborne-joins-liberals -1.1354801.
– "Tony Tomassi, ex-Quebec Liberal MNA, Will Plead Guilty to Fraud." *CBC News*, 20 May 2014. https://www.cbc.ca/news/canada/montreal /tony-tomassi-ex-quebec-liberal-mna-will-plead-guilty-to-fraud-1.2648281.
– "Tory MLA Casey Crosses Floor." *CBC News*, 10 January 2011. https://www .cbc.ca/news/canada/nova-scotia/tory-mla-casey-crosses-floor-1.997275.
– "Trevor Zinck Held on to MLA Seat Until Bitter End." *CBC News*, 19 June 2013. https://www.cbc.ca/news/canada/nova-scotia/trevor-zinck-held-on-to-mla -seat-until-bitter-end-1.1397453.
– "Winnipeg's Ben Carr Becomes 1st Manitoba Liberal MP to Call for Trudeau to Step Down as Party Leader." *CBC News*, 3 January 2025. https://www.cbc.ca/news/canada/manitoba/ben-carr-liberal-mp -justin-trudeau-step-down-1.7423047.
Cernetig, Miro. "Three Socred MLAs Snub B.C. Liberals, Join Reform Party." *Globe and Mail*, 15 March 1994. https://link.gale.com/apps/doc /A163779034/AONE?u=anon~db0f236c&sid=sitemap&xid=7f9d688e.
Charlebois, Brienna. "Former MP Breaks Silence, Comments on Politics Today." *Vernon Morning Star*, 9 March 2019. https://www.vernonmorningstar.com /community/former-mp-breaks-silence-comments-on-politics-today-3293007.
Chartash, David, Nicholas J. Caruana, Markus Dickinson, and Laura B. Stephenson. "When the Team's Jersey is What Matters: Network Analysis of Party Cohesion and Structure in the Canadian House of

Commons." *Party Politics* 26, no. 5 (September 2020): 555–69. https://doi
.org/10.1177/1354068818795196.

Chase, Stevens. "B.C. MP Quits Conservatives to Defend Views on
Evolution." *Globe and Mail*, 1 April 2015. https://www.theglobeandmail
.com/news/politics/bc-mp-quits-conservatives-says-his-christian
-worldview-was-suppressed/article23709160.

Chaudhuri, Arjun, and Morris B. Holbrook. "The Chain of Effects from Brand
Trust and Brand Affect to Brand Performance: The Role of Brand Loyalty."
Journal of Marketing 65, no. 2 (April 2001): 81–93. https://doi.org/10.1509
/jmkg.65.2.81.18255.

Cheadle, Bruce. "Liberals Demand MP John Williamson Be Expelled from Tory
Caucus over Remarks." *CTV News*, 11 March 2015. https://atlantic.ctvnews.ca
/liberals-demand-mp-john-williamson-be-expelled-from-tory-caucus-over
-remarks-1.2274526.

Chen, Alice. "Lone Wolf MPs Break Down What It's Like to Be a Region's Solitary
Voice." *The Hill Times*, 14 April 2021. https://www.hilltimes.com/story/2021
/04/14/lone-wolf-mps-break-down-what-its-like-to-be-a-regions-solitary
-party-voice/229241/.

Chen, Ching-Fu, and Wen-Shiang Tseng. "Exploring Customer-Based Airline
Brand Equity: Evidence from Taiwan." *Transportation Journal* 49, no. 1 (Winter
2010): 24–34. https://doi.org/10.5325/transportationj.49.1.0024.

Chevrette, Guy. "The Government Member: His Relations with Caucus and
Cabinet." *Canadian Parliamentary Review* 4, no. 1 (Spring 1981): 5–8.

Chief Electoral Officer of Canada. *A History of the Vote in Canada*. 2nd ed. Elections
Canada, 2007.

Chong, Michael. "Government Orders – Standing Orders and Procedure of the
House of Commons." Canada. Parliament. House of Commons. *Edited Hansard*
080, 44th Parliament, 1st session, 2 June 2022.

Chouinard, Tommy, and Malorie Beauchemin. "L'ADQ est le parti d'un seul
homme." *La Presse*, 24 October 2008. https://www.lapresse.ca/actualites
/politique/politique-quebecoise/200810/24/01-32402-ladq-est-le-parti-dun
-seul-homme.php.

Claessen, Clint. "Accruing Career Capital: How Party Leaders with More Political
Experience Survive Longer." *Party Politics* 30, no. 4 (July 2024): 719–35. https://
doi.org/10.1177/13540688231170381.

Clark, Campbell. "Ethics Commissioner Clears PM, Emerson." *Globe and Mail*,
21 March 2006. https://www.theglobeandmail.com/news/national
/ethics-commissioner-clears-pm-emerson/article18158874.

Clark, Campbell, and Rod Mickleburgh. "Alliance MP Blasted for Crossing to
Liberals." *Globe and Mail*, 28 January 2002. https://www.theglobeandmail.com
/news/national/alliance-mp-blasted-for-crossing-to-liberals/article25290898.

Clark, Gordon, and Don Hauka. "Liberal Caucus Toasts Exit of Maverick MLA."
The Province, 8 December 1992.

Clark, Kaitlyn. "MPP Brady Launches Fundraising Campaign toward 2026
Election." *The Haldimand Press*, 6 April 2023. https://haldimandpress.com
/mpp-brady-launches-fundraising-campaign-toward-2026-election.

Cleary, Ryan. "Navigating Party Discipline." Panel Event, Bruneau Centre for
Research, Memorial University, St. John's. 6 February 2020.

– "No Faith in Grimes, Says MHA." *The Western Star*, 7 September 2001.

– "Wiseman's Walk across the Floor Seems Strange to Critics." *The Western Star*, 8 September 2001.

Cleroux, Richard. "Maverick Tory Is Fired as Minister's Secretary." *Globe and Mail*, 8 April 1987.

Close, Caroline. "Parliamentary Party Loyalty and Party Family: The Missing Link?" *Party Politics* 24, no. 2 (March 2018): 209–19. https://doi.org/10.1177/1354068816655562.

Close, Caroline, Thomas Legein, and Conor Little. "Party Organisation and the Party-Delegate Style of Representation." *Party Politics* 30, no. 2 (March 2024): 247–59. https://doi.org/10.1177/13540688221122332.

Coalition Avenir Québec. "Votre équipe." 23 August 2023. https://coalitionavenirquebec.org/fr/votre-equipe.

Coates, Mike. "The Power of Authenticity." *National Post*, 20 July 2018. https://nationalpost.com/opinion/the-power-of-authenticity-i-took-on-tory-populist-mp-cheryl-gallant-and-got-squashed.

Cochrane, Christopher. *Left and Right: The Small World of Political Ideas*. McGill-Queen's University Press, 2015. https://doi.org/10.1515/9780773597440.

Cochrane, David. "Floor-Crossing MP Praised Trudeau Government in Weeks before Departure." *CBC News*, 18 September 2018. https://www.cbc.ca/news/politics/leona-alleslev-floor-crossing-1.4828822.

– "Green MP Jenica Atwin Crossing the Floor to Join the Liberals." *CBC News*, 10 June 2021. https://www.cbc.ca/news/politics/jenica-atwin-joining-the-liberals-1.6060501.

Cockram, Louise. "A Process, Not Just an Event: MP Orientation and Representational Style and Focus in Canada and the UK." PhD Diss., Carleton University, 2023.

Coflin, Jim. "Pierre Trudeau Misquoted." *Toronto Star*, 29 September 2016. https://www.thestar.com/opinion/letters-to-the-editor/pierre-trudeau-misquoted/article_79f3814c-5470-5138-8276-7f6b8831be23.html.

Coghill, Ken. "Learning to Be Learned." In *Parliamentarians' Professional Development: The Need for Reform*, edited by Colleen Lewis and Ken Coghill. Springer, 2016. https://doi.org/10.1007/978-3-319-24181-4_5.

Cohen, Andrew. "Conservative MP William Yurko, Frustrated and Isolated in his … " *United Press International*, 29 January 1982. https://www.upi.com/Archives/1982/01/29/Conservative-MP-William-Yurko-frustrated-and-isolated-in-his/5923381128400.

Cohn, Martin. "Lone Quebec NDP MP Quits Party after Bitter Dispute with Broadbent." *Toronto Star*, 27 October 1987. https://www.newspapers.com/article/the-toronto-star-lone-quebec-ndp-mp-quit/143457057/.

Cole, Michael S., and Heike Bruch. "Organizational Identity Strength, Identification, and Commitment and Their Relationships to Turnover Intention: Does Organizational Hierarchy Matter?" *Journal of Organizational Behaviour* 27, no. 5 (August 2006): 585–605. https://doi.org/10.1002/job.378.

Conservative Party of Canada. "After 8 Years of Trudeau." X (post), 13 September 2023a. https://x.com/CPC_HQ/status/1702066897502527932.

– "Welcome to the Team!" *The Conservative Party of Canada*, accessed 13 September 2023b. https://www.conservative.ca/welcome.

Converse, Philip E., and Roy Pierce. *Political Representation in France*. Harvard University Press, 1986. https://doi.org/10.4159/harvard.9780674187887.

Cooke, Alex. "Brendan Maguire Dumps N.S. Liberals as MLA, Joins Progressive Conservatives." *Global News*, 22 February 2024. https://globalnews.ca/news/10310309/brendan-maguire-joins-progressive-conservatives.

– "MLA Who Promoted Nova Scotia Border Protest Booted from Tories Caucus." *Global News*, 24 June 2021. https://globalnews.ca/news/7977126/smith-mccrossin-booted-from-caucus.

– "N.S. Tories Abandon Threat to Remove MLA over NDA Debate." *Global News*, 6 April 2023. https://globalnews.ca/news/9606539/ns-tories-elizabeth-smith-mccrossin-nda.

Cooke, Ryan. "Independent MHA Paul Lane Says All 3 Parties Have Asked Him about Next Election." *CBC News*, 13 November 2018. https://www.cbc.ca/news/canada/newfoundland-labrador/paul-lane-party-selection-1.4902496.

– "MP Ken McDonald Walks Back His Claim That Liberals Need a Leadership Review." *CBC News*, 25 January 2024. https://www.cbc.ca/news/canada/newfoundland-labrador/ken-mcdonald-about-face-trudeau-leadership-review-1.7094270.

Coombs, W. Timothy, and J. Sherry Holladay. "The Paracrisis: The Challenges Created by Publicly Managing Crisis Prevention." *Public Relations Review* 38, no. 3 (September 2012): 408–15. https://doi.org/10.1016/j.pubrev.2012.04.004.

Copeland, Melvin T. "Relation of Consumers' Buying Habits to Marketing Methods." *Harvard Business Review* 1, no. 3 (April 1923): 282–9.

Copps, Sheila. "PM had No Choice but to Turf Anti-budget MP." *Toronto Sun*, 10 June 2007.

Cotterill, Stewart. *Team Psychology in Sports: Theory and Practice*. Routledge, 2013. https://doi.org/10.4324/9780203131428.

Courtney, John C. "Has the Canadian Prime Minister become 'Presidentialized?'" *Presidential Studies Quarterly* 14, no. 2 (April 1984): 238–41.

– "Recognition of Canadian Political Parties in Parliament and in Law." *Canadian Journal of Political Science* 9, no. 1 (March 1978): 33–60. https://doi.org/10.1017/S0008423900038750.

Cousins, Ben. "Opposition Parties Frustrated after Debate Regarding Trudeau's Top Aide Abruptly Cancelled." *CTV News*, 3 May 2021. https://www.ctvnews.ca/politics/opposition-parties-frustrated-after-debate-regarding-trudeau-s-top-aide-abruptly-cancelled-1.5412034.

Cowen, Scott. "How to Be an Effective Organizational Maverick." *Knowledge at Wharton* (blog). 12 September 2019. https://knowledge.wharton.upenn.edu/article/effective-mavericks-in-business.

Cowley, Philip, and Mark Stuart. "There Was a Doctor, a Journalist and Two Welshmen: The Voting Behaviour of Independent MPs in the United Kingdom House of Commons, 1997–2007." *Parliamentary Affairs* 62, no. 1 (January 2009): 19–31. https://doi.org/10.1093/pa/gsn033.

Cox, G.W., and M.D. McCubbins. *Setting the Agenda: Responsible Party Government in the U.S. House of Representatives*. Cambridge University Press, 2005. https://doi.org/10.1017/CBO9780511791123.

Craft, Jonathan. *Backrooms and Beyond: Partisan Advisers and the Politics of Policy Work in Canada*. University of Toronto Press, 2016. https://doi.org/10.3138/9781442617636.

– "Conceptualizing the Policy Work of Partisan Advisers." *Policy Sciences* 48, no. 2 (June 2015): 135–58. https://doi.org/10.1007/s11077-015-9212-2.

Crandall, Erin, and Michael Roy. "Party Fundraisers." In *Inside the Campaign: Managing Elections in Canada*, edited by Alex Marland and Thierry Giasson. UBC Press, 2020. https://doi.org/10.59962/9780774864688-011.

Crawford, Emma. "'I Felt I Had No Choice': Premier Eby Remains Vague on Ousting of MLA Adam Walker." *CityNews*, 18 September 2023. https://vancouver.citynews.ca/2023/09/18/bc-premier-adam-walker-mla-ouster.

Crawley, Mike. "Doug Ford's Push for 'Efficiencies' Includes Scrapping Landlines at Queen's Park." *CBC News*, 4 October 2018. https://www.cbc.ca/news/canada/toronto/doug-ford-government-vic-fedeli-landline-phones-1.4849290.

Creswell, John W. *Qualitative Inquiry and Research Design: Choosing among Five Traditions*. Sage, 1998.

Cresswell, Julia. "Maverick." In *Oxford Dictionary of Word Origins*, 3rd ed. Oxford University Press, 2021. https://doi.org/10.1093/acref/9780198868750.001.0001.

Crone, Greg. "Ferguson Acquitted, Invited Back into New Democrat Fold." *The Ottawa Citizen*, 15 June 1994.

Cross, William. "Members of Parliament, Voters, and Democracy in the Canadian House of Commons." *Parliamentary Perspectives*, Canadian Study of Parliament Group, October 2000. http://cspg-gcep.ca/pdf/Bill_Cross-e.pdf.

– *Political Parties*. UBC Press, 2004.

Cross, William P., Rob Currie-Wood, and Scott Pruysers. "Money Talks: Decentralized Personalism and the Sources of Campaign Funding." *Political Geography* 82 (October 2020): 102242. https://doi.org/10.1016/j.polgeo.2020.102242.

Cross, William, and Lisa Young. "The Contours of Political Party Membership in Canada." *Party Politics* 10, no. 4 (July 2004): 427–44. https://doi.org/10.1177/1354068804043907.

Cross, William P., Scott Pruysers, and Rob Currie-Wood. *The Political Party in Canada*. University of Toronto Press, 2022. https://doi.org/10.59962/9780774868259.

Crowe, Edward. "The Web of Authority: Party Loyalty and Social Control in the British House of Commons." *Legislative Studies Quarterly* 11, no. 2 (May 1986): 161–85.

Cryderman, Kelly. "Liberal Leader Dumps MLA from Caucus." *Calgary Herald*, 21 November 2006.

Cryderman, Kelly, and James Keller. "Alberta MLAs Who Joined Anti-lockdown Group to Remain in Caucus, Jason Kenney Says." *Globe and Mail*, 10 February 2021. https://www.theglobeandmail.com/canada/alberta/article-alberta-mlas-who-joined-anti-lockdown-group-to-remain-in-caucus-jason.

CTV News. "Harper Makes It Official: Comuzzi Joins Tory Fold." *CTV News*, 26 June 2007. https://www.ctvnews.ca/harper-makes-it-official-comuzzi-joins-tory-fold-1.246514.

– "Tory MLAs Cross the Floor to Join Wildrose Alliance." *CTV News*, 5 January 2010. https://edmonton.ctvnews.ca/tory-mlas-cross-the-floor-to-join-wildrose-alliance-1.470428.

Cuddy, Andrew. "When Does Partisanship become Excessive?" *Representation* 54, no. 3 (2018): 261–77. https://doi.org/10.1080/00344893.2018.1525420.

Cunningham, Jim. "Grits Planning 'Outreach.'" *Calgary Herald*, 7 April 1994.

Curry, Bill. "Canadian MPs Plan Trip to Middle East." *The Hill Times*, 8 April 2002. https://www.hilltimes.com/story/2002/04/08/canadian-mps-plan-trip-to-middle-east-mps-want-to-observe-human-rights-violations-happening-on-both-side/225519/.

Curry, Bill, and Steven Chase. "Candidate Controversy Continues for Nearly Every Party." *Globe and Mail*, 25 September 2008. https://www

.theglobeandmail.com/news/politics/candidate-controversy
-continues-for-nearly-every-party/article20388105.

Curry, Bill, and Stuart A. Thompson. "Conservative MPs Break Ranks More Often
Than Opposition." *Globe and Mail*, 3 February 2013. https://www
.theglobeandmail.com/news/politics/conservative-mps-break-ranks-more
-often-than-opposition/article8156279.

Dacey, Elisha. "Manitoba Premier Boots Ron Schuler from Cabinet, Reg Helwer
New Infrastructure Minister." *Global News*, 30 December 2021. https://
globalnews.ca/news/8481205/manitoba-ron-schuler-reg-howler-cabinet.

Daily Gleaner. "Former NDP Leader Dominic Cardy Joins Tories to Help Blaine
Higgs become Premier." *Daily Gleaner*, 28 January 2017.

Daily News. "Defection to the Liberal Party Draws Mixed Reaction." *Daily News*,
11 January 2011.

Damoff, Pam. "Statement." Facebook (post), 1 May 2024. https://www
.facebook.com/PamDamoff/posts/865264915408222.

Daniele, Gianmarco, Sergio Galletta, and Benny Geys. "Abandon Ship?
Party Brands and Politicians' Responses to a Political Scandal." *Journal
of Public Economics* 184 (April 2021): 104172. https://doi.org/10.1016/j.jpubeco
.2020.104172.

Dassonneville, Ruth. *Voters under Pressure: Group-Based Cross-Pressure and
Electoral Volatility*. Oxford University Press, 2023. https://doi.org/10.1093/oso
/9780192894137.001.0001.

Davidson, Sean. "Ontario MPP Kicked Out of PC Caucus for Calling Lockdown
'Deadlier Than COVID.'" *CTV News*, 15 January 2021. https://toronto.ctvnews
.ca/ontario-mpp-kicked-out-of-pc-caucus-for-calling
-lockdown-deadlier-than-covid-1.5268225.

Davies, Don. "Statement by NDP Leader Don Davies." News release, 18 June 2025.
https://www.ndp.ca/news/statement-ndp-leader-don-davies.

Davies, Gary, and Takir Mian. "The Reputation of the Party Leader and of the
Party Being Led." *European Journal of Marketing* 44, nos. 3/4 (2010): 331–50.
https://doi.org/10.1108/03090561011020453.

Davies, Libby. *Outside In: A Political Memoir*. Between the Lines, 2019.

Dawson, Tyler. "Premier Jason Kenney Kicks Pat Rehn out of Alberta UCP Caucus
after Vacation, Complaints." *National Post*, 14 January 2021. https://nationalpost
.com/news/politics/cp-newsalert-kenney-kicks-pat-rehn-out
-of-ucp-caucus-after-municipal-complaints.

de Clercy, Cristine. "Communications as the Workhorse of Governmental Politics:
The Liberal Party Leader and the Liberal Caucus." In *Political Elites in Canada:
Power and Influence in Instantaneous Times*, edited by Alex Marland, Thierry
Giasson, and Andrea Lawlor. UBC Press, 2018. https://doi.org/10.59962
/9780774837958-012.

de Clercy, Cristine, and Alex Marland. "Party Discipline in Canada: Former
Members of Parliament Speak Up." In *Legislatures in Evolution*, edited by Charles
Feldman, Geneviève Tellier, and David Groves. University of Ottawa Press,
2022. https://doi.org/10.2307/j.ctv33p9zx6.6.

De Gieter, Sara, Rein De Cooman, Joeri Hofmans, Roland Pepermans, and
Marc Jegers. "Pay-Level Satisfaction and Psychological Reward Satisfaction
as Mediators of the Organizational Justice–Turnover Intention Relationship."
International Studies of Management and Organization 42, no. 1 (2012): 50–67.
https://doi.org/10.2753/IMO0020-8825420103.

Delacourt, Susan. *Shopping for Votes*. Mandeira Park, BC: Douglas and McIntyre, 2013.

De Lamater, John D., Daniel J. Myers, and Jessica L. Collett. *Social Psychology*. 8th ed. Routledge, 2018. https://doi.org/10.4324/9780429493096.

de Lange, Annet H., Hans De Witte, and Guy Notelaers. "Should I Stay or Should I Go? Examining Longitudinal Relations among Job Resources and Work Engagement for Stayers versus Movers." *Work & Stress* 22, no. 3 (2008): 201–23. https://doi.org/10.1080/02678370802390132.

de Vreese, Claes. "Mediatization of News: The Role of Journalistic Framing." In *Mediatization of Politics*, edited by Frank Esser and Jesper Strömbäck. Palgrave Macmillan, 2014. https://doi.org/10.1057/9781137275844_8.

DeClerq, Katherine. "Sarah Jama's Removal from Ontario NDP Prompts Calls for Leader's Resignation." *CTV News*, 26 October 2023. https://toronto.ctvnews.ca/sarah-jama-s-removal-from-ontario-ndp-prompts-calls-for-leader-s-resignation-and-review-1.6618490.

Delacourt, Susan. "His Poll Numbers Are Plunging." *Toronto Star*, 17 September 2023. https://www.thestar.com/politics/political-opinion/his-poll-numbers-are-plunging-his-mps-are-griping-but-justin-trudeau-isn-t-changing/article_1a532531-460c-5f81-9529-596160b90a67.html.

– "Sometimes When Liberals Are Nervous, They Have Good Reason to Be." *Toronto Star*, 26 August 2021. https://www.thestar.com/politics/political-opinion/sometimes-when-liberals-are-nervous-they-have-good-reason-to-be/article_dcf508b7-78de-5f64-b4c3-a1ab2454a8a4.html.

Dempsey, Sarah E. "The Increasing Technology Divide: Persistent Portrayals of Maverick Masculinity in US Marketing." *Feminist Media Studies* 9, no. 1 (2009): 37–55. https://doi.org/10.1080/14680770802619482.

Depner, Wolfgang. "John Rustad Accuses Former B.C. Conservative MLAs of Blackmail." *Vancouver Sun*, 16 June 2025. https://vancouversun.com/news/john-rusted-bc-conservative-mla-blackmail-accusations.

DeRosa, Katie. "Critics Say David Eby Setting Up Parallel 'Cabinet' as He Centralizes Power in His Office." *Vancouver Sun*, 26 January 2023. https://vancouversun.com/news/local-news/lisa-helps-appointed-housing-advisor-bc-government.

– "Melanie Mark Will Resign as MLA, Saying B.C. Legislature Felt Like a 'Torture Chamber.'" *Vancouver Sun*, 22 February 2023. https://vancouversun.com/news/politics/melanie-mark-resigns-criticizes-legislature-torture-chamber.

– "MLA's Defection to B.C. Conservatives Could Spell Trouble for B.C. United Party." *Vancouver Sun*, 13 September 2023. https://vancouversun.com/news/politics/bc-united-bruce-banman-joins-conservatives.

– "Selina Robinson Resigns from B.C. NDP Caucus, Citing Antisemitism within Party." *Vancouver Sun*, 6 March 2014. https://vancouversun.com/news/local-news/breaking-selina-robinson-resigns-from-b-c-ndp-caucus-citing-antisemitism-within-ndp/wcm/66c094b6-7578-4de2-ab37-50eea4e1c4c6/amp.

Desposato, Scott W. "Parties for Rent? Ambition, Ideology, and Party Switching in Brazil's Chamber of Deputies." *American Journal of Political Science* 50, no. 1 (January 2006): 62–80. https://doi.org/10.1111/j.1540-5907.2006.00170.x.

Desserud, Donald. "The Confidence Convention under the Canadian Parliamentary System." *Parliamentary Perspectives*, no. 7. Canadian Study of

Parliament Group, 2006. https://cspg-gcep.ca/pdf/Parliamentary
_Perspectives_7_2006-e.pdf.

Dewing, Michael. "Changes in a Parliamentarian's Party Affiliation." Library of
Parliament, 20 October 2016, publication no. 2016–101-E. https://publications
.gc.ca/site/eng/9.831737/publication.html.

Dhanraj, Travis. "Suspended MPP Randy Hillier Hits Back at Doug Ford
Government in Letter, Cites 'Childish Grievances.'" *Global News*, 12 March 2019.
https://globalnews.ca/news/5048818/randy-hillier-suspension-letter.

Dickson, Annabelle, Esther Webber, and Andrew McDonald. "Meet
Westminster's Attack Dogs." *Politico*. 11 August 2023. https://www.politico
.eu/article/westminster-uk-general-election-2024-political-attack-dogs.

Diefenbach, Thomas. "Why Michels' 'Iron Law of Oligarchy' Is Not an
Iron Law – and How Democratic Organisations Can Stay 'Oligarchy
-free.'" *Organization Studies* 40, no. 4 (April 2019): 545–62. https://doi
.org/10.1177/0170840617751007.

Dinshaw, Fram. "McNeil Mocked on Social Media for Early Campaign Ad Typo."
Chronicle Herald, 28 April 2017.

Ditchburn, Jennifer. "Michael Chong's Friendlier Reform Bill Gets PM
Stamp of Approval." *CBC News*, 17 September 2014. https://www.cbc.ca
/news/politics/michael-chong-s-friendlier-reform-bill-gets-pm-stamp-of
-approval-1.2769589.

Djuric, Mickey. "Karina Gould Has Redefined What It Means to Be a PM's
Chief Attack Dog." *The Gazette*, 4 January 2024. https://montrealgazette
.com/news/national/karina-gould-has-redefined-what-it-means-to
-be-a-pms-chief-attack-dog.

Docherty, David C. "The Canadian Political Career Structure: From Stability to
Free Agency." *Regional and Federal Studies* 21, no. 2 (2011): 185–203. https://doi
.org/10.1080/13597566.2011.530018.

– "Could the Rebels Find a Cause? House of Commons Reform in the Chrétien
Era." *Review of Constitutional Studies* 9, no. 1 (2004): 283–302.

– *Mr. Smith Goes to Ottawa: Life in the House of Commons*. UBC Press, 1997.

Dorion, Catherine. *Les têtes brûlés: carnets d'espoir punk*. Lux Éditeur, 2023.

Dosser, Travis. "MLAs Pleased with Smith's Leadership." *Sherwood Park News*,
27 October 2022. https://www.sherwoodparknews.com/news/local-news
/mlas-pleased-with-smiths-leadership.

Doucette, Keith. "Nova Scotia Liberal Brendan Maguire Crosses the Floor to Join
Tory Cabinet." *Toronto Star*, 22 February 2024. https://www.thestar.com/news
/canada/nova-scotia/nova-scotia-liberal-brendan-maguire-crosses-floor-to
-join-tory-cabinet/article_72ecd840-f7b1-541b-b5ae-73b3dbd83a71.html.

– "Trevor Zinck Resigns after Legislature Recalled to Consider Removal." *CTV
News*, 19 June 2013. https://atlantic.ctvnews.ca/trevor-zinck-resigns
-after-legislature-recalled-to-consider-removal-1.1332049.

Dovidio, John F., Samuel L. Gaertner, and Erin L. Thomas. "Intergroup Relations."
In *Group Processes*, edited by John M. Levine. Taylor and Francis Group, 2012.
https://doi.org/10.4324/9780203869673.

Dowd, Eric. "Few Are the Politicians Who Quit the Game because of Principles."
Welland Tribune, 1 February 2000.

Downs, Anthony. *An Economic Theory of Democracy*. Harper & Bros., 1957.

Dryden, Joel. "Seeking Broader Appeal, Separatist Wexit Canada Party
Changes Its Name to the Maverick Party." *CBC News*, 17 September 2020.

https://www.cbc.ca/news/canada/calgary/jay-hill-wexit-top-gun-maverick
-party-calgary-canada-1.5728875.

– "The UCP Booted 2 MLAs Out of Caucus." *CBC News*, 16 May 2021.
https://www.cbc.ca/news/canada/calgary/jason-kenney-drew-barnes
-kathleen-petty-alberta-ucp-1.6028379.

Dubois, Elizabeth, and Fenwick McKelvey. "Political Bots: Disrupting Canada's
Democracy." *Canadian Journal of Communication* 44, no. 2 (2019): 27–33. https://
doi.org/10.22230/cjc.2019v44n2a3511.

Dubreuil, Emilie. "Claire Samson et les plantes vertes." *Radio-Canada*,
11 June 2022. https://ici.radio-canada.ca/nouvelle/1890203/claire-samson
-plantes-vertes-deputee.

Duffy, John. *Fights of Our Lives: Elections, Leadership and the Making of Canada*.
HarperCollins, 2002.

Dunfield, Allison. "Canada Lacks Leadership on Mideast, Opposition Says." *Globe
and Mail*, 8 April 2002.

Dutil, Patrice, and Peter P. Constantinou. "The Office of Premier of Ontario,
1945–2010: Who Really Advises?" *Canadian Parliamentary Review* 36, no. 1
(Spring 2013): 43–50.

Duverger, Maurice. *Political Parties*. John Wiley & Sons, 1963.

Dwyer, Diana. *Interpersonal Relationships*. Routledge, 2000. https://doi
.org/10.4324/9780203135556.

Dyck, Rand. "Relations Between Federal and Provincial Parties." In *Canadian
Parties in Transition*, 2nd ed., edited by A. Brian Tanguay and Alain-G. Gagnon.
Nelson Canada, 1996.

Dyer, Evan. "Key Liberal MP Rips His Government's Policy on Gaza war in
Private Call with Constituent." *CBC News*, 15 February 2024. https://www
.cbc.ca/news/politics/rob-oliphant-gaza-israel-joly-hamas-unrwa-1.7115468.

– "Liberal MP Majid Jowhari's Iran Tweets Roil His Heavily Iran Riding." *CBC
News*, 4 January 2018. https://www.cbc.ca/news/politics/majid-jowhari-iran
-tweet-1.4473817.

Dykstra, Matt. "There Goes another One." *Edmonton Sun*, 18 March 2014.

Dyson, Dylan. "Conservative Candidate Cheryl Gallant Nowhere to Be Found
during Campaign in Renfrew-Nipissing-Pembroke." *CTV News*, 1 September
2021. https://ottawa.ctvnews.ca/conservative-candidate-cheryl-gallant
-nowhere-to-be-found-during-campaign-in-renfrew-nipissing-pembroke
-1.5570234.

Eaves, Sutton. "The BlackBerry Campaign." *Ottawa Citizen*, 23 June 2004.

Edmonton Bulletin. "Plan to Lower Alberta Voting Age from 21 to 19 Years."
Alberta Legislature Library Scrapbook Hansard Collection, 2 March 1944.

Edmonton Journal. "City MLA Quits Liberal Caucus." *Edmonton Journal*,
16 November 1999.

Eidelman, Scott, and Monica Biernat. "Derogating Black Sheep: Individual or
Group Protection?" *Journal of Experimental Social Psychology* 39, no. 6 (November
2003): 602–9. https://doi.org/10.1016/S0022-1031(03)00042-8.

Elections Canada. "50th Anniversary of Canada's Federal Political Financing
Regime." 14 August 2024. https://www.elections.ca/content.aspx?section
=vot&dir=bkg&document=anni&lang=e.

Elkins, David J., and Richard Simeon. *Small Worlds: Provinces and Parties in
Canadian Political Life*. Methuen Publications, 1980.

Ellemers, Naomi, Ed Sleebos, Daan Stam, and Dick de Gilder. "Feeling Included
and Valued: How Perceived Respect Affects Positive Team Identity and

Willingness to Invest in the Team." *British Journal of Management* 24, no. 1 (March 2013): 21–37. https://doi.org/10.1111/j.1467-8551.2011.00784.x.

Elliott, Louise. "Alliance MP Gallant Apologizes for Anti-gay Remark in Commons." *Canadian Press NewsWire*, 15 April 2002.

Eneas, Bryan. "Sask. Party Leader Scott Moe Discloses Previously Unknown Impaired Driving Charge." *CBC News*, 7 October 2020. https://www.cbc.ca /news/canada/saskatchewan/party-leader-discloses-previously-unknown -impaired-driving-charge-1.5753789.

Entman, Robert. "Toward the Clarification of a Fractured Paradigm." *Journal of Communication* 43, no. 4 (December 1993): 51–8. https://doi.org/10.1111 /j.1460-2466.1993.tb01304.x.

Environics Institute. *Confidence in Democracy and the Political System: An Update on Trends in Public Opinion in Canada*. Environics Institute for Survey Research, 2019. https://www.environicsinstitute.org/docs/default-source /default-document-library/ab-democracy-report-revised-sept11_209. pdf?sfvrsn=bda257b6_0.

– *Trusting Federal and Provincial Government Decision-making on Key Issues*. Environics Institute for Survey Research, 2024. https://www .environicsinstitute.org/docs/default-source/default-document-library/read -the-report01b48002-19d8-4f24-8201-74f2bc2c30b5.pdf?sfvrsn=637c3e9f_1.

Erskine-Smith, Nathaniel. "Should Dissident Liberals Stay in Caucus? Yes.'" *Toronto Star*, 26 March 2019. https://www.thestar.com/opinion /contributors/the-big-debate/should-dissident-liberals-stay-in-caucus-yes /article_035006b1-cfff-5e46-844e-8a8f63517810.html.

– "Taking On a New Challenge." *Uncommons Feed* (blog). 21 December 2024. https://www.uncommons.ca/p/taking-on-a-new-challenge.

Esselment, Anna Lennox. "Designing Campaign Platforms." In *The Informed Citizens' Guide to Elections: Electioneering Based on the Rule of Law*, edited by Gregory Tardi and Richard Balasko. Carswell, 2015.

– "Fighting Elections: Cross-level Political Party Integration in Ontario." *Canadian Journal of Political Science* 43, no. 4 (December 2010): 871–92. https://doi .org/10.1017/S0008423910000727.

– "Market Orientation in a Minority Government: The Challenges of Product Delivery." In *Political Marketing in Canada*, edited by Alex Marland, Thierry Giasson, and Jennifer Lees-Marshment. UBC Press, 2012. https://doi .org/10.59962/9780774822305-011.

Esselment, Anna Lennox, and Matthew Bondy. "Local Nominations." In *Inside the Local Campaign: Constituency Elections in Canada*, edited by Alex Marland and Thierry Giasson. UBC Press, 2022.

Esselment, Anna Lennox, and Darren Lilleker. "Marketing Authenticity." In *Political Marketing in a Canadian Election*, edited by Alex Marland, Thierry Giasson, and Elizabeth Dubois. UBC Press, forthcoming.

Esselment, Anna Lennox, and Alex Marland. "Want to Interview a Politician? Ways to Prepare for Digital Vetting by Political Staffers." *PS: Political Science and Politics* 52, no. 4 (October 2019): 696–700. https://doi.org/10.1017/S1049096519000921.

Esselment, Anna Lennox, and Paul Wilson. "Campaigning from the Centre." In *Permanent Campaigning in Canada*, edited by Alex Marland, Thierry Giasson, and Anna Lennox Esselment. UBC Press, 2017. https://doi.org/10.59962 /9780774834506-016.

Eulau, Heinz, John C. Wahlke, William Buchanan, and Leroy C. Ferguson. "The Role of the Representative: Some Empirical Observations on the Theory of

Edmund Burke." *American Political Science Review* 53, no. 3 (September 1959): 742–56. https://doi.org/10.2307/1951941.

Everitt, Joanna, Elisabeth Gidengil, Patrick Fournier, and Neil Nevitte. "Patterns of Party Identification in Canada." In *Election*, edited by Heather MacIvor. Emond Montgomery, 2009.

Everitt, Joanna, Manon Tremblay, and Angelia Wagner. "Pathway to Office: The Eligibility, Recruitment, Selection, and Election of LGBT Candidates." In *Queering Representation: LGBTQ People and Electoral Politics in Canada*, edited by Manon Tremblay. UBC Press, 2019. https://doi.org/10.59962/9780774861830-013.

"Ex-Cabinet Minister Rejoins N.S. Tory Fold." *Waterloo Region Record*, 9 January 1992, A10.

Feldman, Charles, and David Groves. "Legislatures in Evolution." In *Legislatures in Evolution*, edited by Charles Feldman, Geneviève Tellier, and David Groves. University of Ottawa Press, 2022. https://doi.org/10.2307/j.ctv33p9zx6.

Feldman, Charlie, and Zachery Brandstater. "Governing at the Speed of Parliament: Legislative Duration in Recent Parliamentary Sessions." Mulroney Papers in Public Policy and Governance Review Essay No. 2. September 2023. https://www.mulroneyinstitute.ca/sites/mulroney/files/2023-09/FELDMAN%20BRANDSTATER%20MPPG%20RE%20N2_web.pdf.

Felps, Will, Terence R. Mitchell, David R. Hekman, Thomas W. Lee, Brooks C. Holtom, and Wendy S. Harman. "Turnover Contagion: How Coworkers' Job Embeddedness and Coworkers' Job Search Behaviors Influence Quitting." *Academy of Management Journal* 52, no. 3 (June 2009): 545–61. https://doi.org/10.5465/amj.2009.41331075.

Feminist Institute of Social Transformation. "Biography of Pauline Jewett." The Pauline Jewett Institute, Carleton University. 26 September 2023. https://carleton.ca/fist/about-us/pauline-jewett-bio.

Fendick, Reg. "MacLean OK's Leadership Review Liberal Leader Restores Brown after 2-Day Exile." *The Daily News* (Halifax), 28 February 1992.

– "Thornhill back to save Tories from defeat Return restores House majority." *The Daily News* (Halifax), 9 January 1992.

Ferguson, Derek. "Manitoba Tory Defects to Liberals." *Toronto Star*, 9 September 1988.

– "Quebec MP Chartrand Also Quits over Meech." *Toronto Star*, 23 May 1990.

Ferguson, Rob. "Antisemitism Charges Upend Ontario Byelection Race in NDP Stronghold." *Toronto Star*, 12 March 2023. https://www.thestar.com/politics/provincial/antisemitism-charges-upend-ontario-byelection-race-in-ndp-stronghold/article_bb40dfa7-b48b-5a04-9b5d-ca7a4c164e56.html.

– "NDP Kicks Out MPP after Misconduct Investigation." *Toronto Star*, 15 August 2023. https://www.thestar.com/politics/provincial/ndp-kicks-out-mpp-after-misconduct-investigation/article_77b59ac1-6aac-5f22-bf43-4af3d3eb1336.html.

Ferguson, Rob, and Kristin Rushowy. "MPP Sarah Jama's Removal Divides the NDP." *Toronto Star*, 25 October 2023. https://www.thestar.com/politics/provincial/mpp-sarah-jama-s-removal-divides-the-ndp/article_a86ae195-2c72-5280-a342-803b7a678575.html.

– "NDP MPP Sarah Jama Has 'Doubled Down' on Controversial Mideast Post, Doug Ford's Tories Charge." *Toronto Star*, 18 October 2023. https://www.thestar.com/politics/provincial/ndp-mpp-sarah-jama-has-doubled-down-on-controversial-mideast-post-doug-ford-s-tories/article_9b10dd2f-bdda-5466-8e4c-73b45101c582.html.

– "Sarah Jama Ejected from NDP Caucus over Israel-Hamas Comments." *Toronto Star*, 23 October 2023. https://www.thestar.com/politics/provincial /sarah-jama-ejected-from-ndp-caucus-over-israel-hamas-comments -this-was-undermining-our-work/article_9e4c7831-8847-517e-bb1b -4df634b22648.html.

Fife, Robert. "Clark Faces Criticism as CA Rebels Go Home." *National Post*, 11 April 2002.

– "Hunter Tootoo's Messy Love Triangle Helped Spur Resignation from Cabinet." *Globe and Mail*, 12 September 2016. https://www.theglobeandmail .com/news/politics/hunter-tootoos-messy-love-triangle-helped-spur -resignation-from-cabinet/article31822441.

Fiorina, Morris P. *Culture War? The Myth of a Polarized America*. Pearson Longman, 2006.

Fitzgerald, Mary Ann. "Carroll Cites Snub for Resignation." *Winnipeg Free Press*, 21 August 1982.

Fitzpatrick, Meagan. "Bruce Hyer Quits NDP Caucus to Sit as an Independent." *CBC News*, 24 April 2012. https://www.cbc.ca/news/politics/bruce-hyer-quits -ndp-caucus-to-sit-as-an-independent-1.1170157.

Flanagan, Thomas. *Winning Power: Canadian Campaigning in the Twenty-first Century*. McGill-Queen's University Press, 2014. https://doi.org/10.1515/9780773590366.

Fletcher, Luke, Kerstin Alfes, and Dilys Robinson. "The Relationship between Perceived Training and Development and Employee Retention: The Mediating Role of Work Attitudes." *International Journal of Human Resource Management* 29, no. 18 (2018): 2701–28. https://doi.org/10.1080/09585192.2016.1262888.

Flynn, Greg. "Rethinking Policy Capacity in Canada: The Role of Parties and Election Platforms in Government Policy-Making." *Canadian Public Administration* 54, no. 2 (June 2011): 235–53. https://doi.org/10.1111 /j.1754-7121.2011.00172.x.

Fong, Petti. "Bob Rae Leaves NDP over Party's Stance on Israel." *The Vancouver Sun*, 17 April 2002.

Foot, Richard. "'The Ronnie Show' Keeps Tories on Toes." *National Post*, 21 May 2002.

Ford, Arthur. "Some Notes on the Formation of the Union Government in 1917." *The Canadian Historical Review* 19, no. 4 (Winter 1938): 357–64. https://doi.org /10.3138/chr-019-04-01.

Formica, Sandro, and Fabiola Sfodera. "The Great Resignation and Quiet Quitting Paradigm Shifts: An Overview of Current Situation and Future Research Directions." *Journal of Hospitality Marketing & Management* 31, no. 8 (2022): 899–907. https://doi.org/10.1080/19368623.2022.2136601.

Forsey, Eugene. "Government Defeats in the House of Commons, 1867–73." *Canadian Journal of Economics and Political Science* 29, no. 3 (August 1963): 364–7. https://doi.org/10.2307/139221.

Forsyth, Paul. "Niagara NDP MPPs Support Leader's Removal of Sarah Jama from Caucus." *Niagara This Week*, 1 November 2023. https://www.niagarathisweek .com/news/niagara-ndp-mpps-support-leaders-removal-of-sarah-jama-from -caucus/article_d120d82b-2140-5424-b215-b46863822089.html.

Fowlie, Jonathan. "Bennett on Campbell Criticisms: 'I Went Too Far.'" *Vancouver Sun*, 14 February 2011. https://vancouversun.com/news/staff-blogs/bennett -on-campbell-criticisms-i-went-too-far.

Fox, Rod. "An Open Letter to Constituents." *Lacombe Globe*, 23 December 2014.

Fraenkel, Jon. "Party-Hopping Laws in the Southern Hemisphere." *Political Science* 64, no. 2 (2012): 106–20. https://doi.org/10.1177/0032318712466758.

Francis, Lloyd. *Ottawa Boy: An Autobiography*. General Store Publishing, 2000.

Franklin, Michael. "'She Has a Lot of Work to Do': Smith Suggests Door Still Open for Controversial UCP Candidate." *CTV News*, 20 May 2023. https://calgary.ctvnews.ca/she-has-a-lot-of-work-to-do-smith-suggests-door-still-open-for-controversial-ucp-candidate-1.6406195.

Franks, C.E.S. *The Parliament of Canada*. University of Toronto Press, 1987. https://doi.org/10.3138/9781442678262.

Fraser, Blair. "Is Diefenbaker Running a One-man Government?" *Maclean's*, 14 March 1959. https://archive.org/details/Macleans-Magazine-1959-03-14/page/n7/mode/2up.

Fraser, Graham. "NDP Left Reeling as MP Joins Tories." *Globe and Mail*, 28 September 1999.

Freeman, Aaron. "Floor Crossing's Delicate Balance." *The Hill Times*, 8 May 2006. https://www.hilltimes.com/story/2006/05/08/floor-crossings-delicate-balance-may-be-a-chill-now-but-history-shows-floor-crossing-is-almost-inevitable/238305/.

Freeman, Alan. "Maverick Politician Paul Hellyer Was Ween as a Possible Candidate for PM." *Globe and Mail*, 8 September 2021. https://www.theglobeandmail.com/canada/article-maverick-politician-paul-hellyer-was-seen-as-a-possible-candidate-for/.

French, Janet. "Shandro's Appointment as Justice Minister Puts Law Society in Awkward Position, Law Professors Say." *CBC News*, 2 March 2022. https://www.cbc.ca/news/canada/edmonton/tyler-shandro-justice-minister-law-society-hearing-1.6369196.

– "Sixteen Government MLAs Speak Out against Latest Alberta Public Health Restrictions." *CBC News*, 7 April 2021. https://www.cbc.ca/news/canada/edmonton/alberta-mlas-public-health-restrictions-1.5978864.

Froese, Ian. "MLA Mark Wasyliw Removed Immediately from NDP Caucus, Claims Premier Kinew Is a 'Bully.'" *CBC News*, 16 September 2024. https://www.cbc.ca/news/canada/manitoba/mark-wasyliw-removed-ndp-caucus-1.7324640.

Fung, Nathan. "'Not Worth the Cost,' 'Axe the Tax,' and 'After Eight Long Years': Repetition of Phrases in the House May Be Annoying, but Also 'How Political Marketing Works,' Say Experts." *Hill Times*, 20 November 2023.

Furey, Anthony. "You'd Think Sooner or Later, Trudeau's Going to Have to Cut Gerald Butts Loose." *Ottawa Sun*, 23 March 2018. https://torontosun.com/opinion/columnists/furey-youd-think-sooner-or-later-trudeaus-going-to-have-to-cut-gerald-butts-loose.

Gaber, Ivor. "Government by Spin: An Analysis of the Process." *Media Culture & Society* 22, no. 4 (July 2000): 507–18. https://doi.org/10.1177/016344300022004008.

Gallagher, Kevin, and Alexandra Mae Jones. "Conservative MP Under Fire for Tweet with Anti-Semitic Undertones." *CTV News*, 30 August 2020. https://www.ctvnews.ca/canada/conservative-mp-under-fire-for-tweet-with-anti-semitic-undertones-1.5085645.

Galloway, Gloria. "Tory MP Kicked Out of Caucus Over Budget Vote." *Globe and Mail*, 6 June 2007. https://www.theglobeandmail.com/news/national/tory-mp-kicked-out-of-caucus-over-budget-vote/article686850/.

Garner, Christopher, and Natalia Letki. "Party Structure and Backbench Dissent in the Canadian and British Parliaments." *Canadian Journal of Political Science* 38, no. 2 (June 2005): 463–82. https://doi.org/10.1017/S0008423905040461.

Geddes, John. "How Do They Get Away with It?" *Maclean's*, 10 December 2010. https://macleans.ca/news/canada/how-do-they-get-away-with-it/.

George, Tiffany, Joshua Hart, and W. Steven Rholes. "Remaining in Unhappy Relationships: The Roles of Attachment Anxiety and Fear of Change." *Journal of Social and Personal Relationships* 37, no. 5 (May 2020): 1626–33. https://doi .org/10.1177/0265407520904156.

Gerrits, Bailey, Linda Trimble, Angelia Wagner, Daisy Raphael, and Shannon Sampert. "Political Battlefield: Aggressive Metaphors, Gender, and Power in News Coverage of Canadian Party Leadership Contests." *Feminist Media Studies* 17, no. 6 (2017): 1088–103. https://doi.org/10.1080/14680777.2017.1315734.

Gerson, Jen. "Alberta PC Associate Minister Donna Kennedy-Glans Quits in Another Blow to Alison Redford's Already Shaky Leadership." *National Post*, 17 March 2014. https://nationalpost.com/news/politics/alberta-pc-associate -minister-donna-kennedy-glans-quits-in-another-blow-to-alison-redfords -already-shaky-leadership.

Gert, Bernard. "Loyalty and Morality." *Nomos* 54 (2013): 3–21.

Ghosh, Piyali, Rachita Satyawadi, Jagdamba Prasad Joshi, and Mohd Shadman. "Who Stays with You? Factors Predicting Employees' Intention to Stay." *International Journal of Organizational Analysis* 21, no. 3 (2013): 288–312. https:// doi.org/10.1108/IJOA-Sep-2011-0511.

Giasson, Thierry, Gildas Le Bars, and Philippe Dubois. "Is Social Media Transforming Canadian Electioneering? Hybridity and Online Partisan Strategies in the 2012 Quebec Election." *Canadian Journal of Political Science* 52, no. 2 (June 2019): 323–41. https://doi.org/10.1017/S0008423918000902.

Gibson, Caley. "Alberta MLA Sandra Jansen Given Security Detail after Threats." *Global News*, 23 November 2016. https://globalnews.ca/news/3084612 /alberta-mla-sandra-jansen-given-security-detail-after-threats.

– "Thomas Dang Hopes to Rejoin NDP Caucus Following RCMP Investigation." *Global News*, 16 June 2022. https://globalnews.ca/news/8926582/alberta-mla -thomas-dang-rcmp-investigation.

Gibson, Will. "Alberta Grit Joins Governing Tories." *Canadian Press Newswire*, 13 August 1998.

Gidengil, Elisabeth. "Voting Behaviour in Canada: The State of the Discipline." *Canadian Journal of Political Science* 55, no. 4 (December 2022): 916–38. https:// doi.org/10.1017/S0008423922000531.

Gidengil, Elisabeth, Neil Nevitte, André Blais, Joanna Everitt, and Patrick Fournier. *Dominance and Decline: Making Sense of Recent Canadian Elections*. University of Toronto Press, 2012. https://doi.org/10.3138/9781442603905.

Gidengil, Elisabeth, Dietlind Stolle, and Olivier Bergeron-Boutin. "COVID-19 and Support for Executive Aggrandizement." *Canadian Journal of Political Science* 55, no. 2 (June 2022): 342–72. https://doi.org/10.1017/S0008423922000117.

Gilmore, Rachel. "Green Party MP Jenica Atwin Crossing the Floor to Join the Liberal Party." *Global News*, 10 June 2021. https://globalnews.ca/news/7938064 /green-party-mp-jenica-atwin-crossing-the-floor-to-join-the-liberal-party.

Giovannetti, Justin. "Alberta MLA Defections Were Negotiated Over a Month, Prentice Says." *Globe and Mail*, 19 December 2014. http://www.theglobeandmail .com/news/alberta/alberta-mla-defections-were-negotiated-over-a-month -prentice-says/article22156198.

Glenn, Ted. *A Very Canadian Coup: The Rise and Demise of Prime Minister Mackenzie Bowell, 1894–1896*. Dundurn Press, 2022.

Globe and Mail. "Alberta NDP Unveils New Logo." *Globe and Mail*, 22 October 1985.

– "Former Reform MP Sues Manning, Five Other Party Members." *Globe and Mail*, 20 February 2004. https://www.theglobeandmail.com/news/national/former -reform-mp-sues-manning-five-other-party-members/article1128275.

– "The Independent MP." *Globe and Mail*, 12 October 1985.

– "Judy LaMarch." *Globe and Mail*, 28 October 1980.

– "Martin's Statement About Stronach." *Globe and Mail*, 17 May 2005.

– "Parliament Must Reform Itself." *Globe and Mail*, 5 December 1947.

– "PM Ignored by LaMarsh on Pensions." *Globe and Mail*, 17 September 1963.

– "Raps Method of Parliament." *Globe and Mail*, 28 October 1942.

– "Stewart Beaten for Nomination by Woman, 22." *Globe and Mail*, 2 April 1979. https://www.theglobeandmail.com/news/national/martins-statement -about-stronach/article20422182.

Godbout, Jean-François. *Lost on Division: Party Unity in the Canadian Parliament*. University of Toronto Press, 2020. https://doi.org/10.3138/9781487535421.

Godbout, Jean-François, and Bjørn Høyland. "The Emergence of Parties in the Canadian House of Commons (1867–1908)." *Canadian Journal of Political Science* 46, no. 4 (December 2013): 773–97. https://doi.org/10.1017 /S0008423913000632.

– "Legislative Voting in the Canadian Parliament." *Canadian Journal of Political Science* 44, no. 2 (June 2011): 367–88. https://doi.org/10.1017/ S0008423911000175.

– "Unity in Diversity? The Development of Political Parties in the Parliament of Canada, 1867–2011." *British Journal of Political Science* 47, no. 3 (July 2017): 545–69. https://doi.org/10.1017/S0007123415000368.

Godbout, Jean-François, and Christopher Cochrane. "Minority Governments in Canada: Stability through Voting Alliances." In *Minority Governments in Comparative Perspective*, edited by Bonnie N. Field and Shane Martin. Oxford University Press, 2022. https://doi.org/10.1093/oso/9780192871657.003.0008.

Gold, Marta. "Grit Crosses Floor to Join Tories." *Medicine Hat News*, 10 December 1994.

– "Langevin Crosses to Tory Fold." *Edmonton Journal*, 26 April 1995.

Goldstein, Lorrie. "Screeched-In McKenna Commits a Classic Political Gaffe." *Toronto Sun*, 27 May 2019. https://torontosun.com/opinion/columnists /goldstein-screeched-in-mckenna-commits-a-classic-political-gaffe.

González, Paula, Francesca Passarelli, and M. Socorro Puy. "A Theory on Party Discipline and Vote Switching by Legislators." *European Journal of Political Economy* 66 (January 2021): 101960. https://doi.org/10.1016/j .ejpoleco.2020.101960.

Goodyear-Grant, Elizabeth. *Gendered News: Media Coverage and Electoral Politics in Canada*. UBC Press, 2013. https://doi.org/10.59962/9780774826259.

Gorman, Michael. "N.S. Premier Announces Ministerial Assistant Roles." *CBC News*, 19 December 2024. https://www.cbc.ca/news/canada/nova-scotia /premier-tim-houston-ministerial-assistants-1.7415133.

Grafstein, Jerry S. *A Leader Must Be a Leader*. Mosaic Press, 2019.

Graney, Emma. "Finance Critic Derek Fildebrandt Rents Downtown Digs on Airbnb While Claiming Housing Allowance." *Edmonton Journal*, 10 August 2017. https://edmontonjournal.com/news/politics/finance-critic-derek-fildebrandt -rents-downtown-digs-on-airbnb-while-claiming-housing-allowance.

Graves, Frank. "Polarization, Populism, and Evolving Public Outlook on Canada and the World." EKOS Research Associates. Presentation to Canadian Global Affairs Institute, 17 January 2023. https://www.ekospolitics.com/wp-content/uploads/presentation20230117.pdf.

Gray, John. "Richard Holden, Lawyer and Politician 1931–2005." *Globe and Mail*, 23 September 2005.

Greenaway, Norma. "Tory MP Defects to Liberals." *Calgary Herald*, 14 August 1999.

Greenspon, Edward, and Jeff Sallot. "Pragmatic McDonough Nudges NDP to Centre." *Globe and Mail*, 21 September 1998.

Grenier, Éric. "Bill Who? Canadians Might Not Know the Finance Minister's Name, but They Know What They Think of Him." *CBC News*, 23 November 2017. https://www.cbc.ca/news/politics/grenier-ministers-polls-1.4410596.

– "Liberal Backbenchers, Tory Leadership Hopefuls Among Parliament's Biggest Dissenters." *CBC News*, 21 February 2017. https://www.cbc.ca/news/politics/grenier-party-line-voting-1.3984516.

Grey, Deborah. *Never Retreat, Never Explain, Never Apologize: My Life, My Politics.* Key Porter Books, 2004.

Griffeth, Rodger W., Peter W. Hom, and Stefan Gaertner. "A Meta-Analysis of Antecedents and Correlates of Employee Turnover: Update, Moderator Tests, and Research Implications for the Next Millennium." *Journal of Management* 26, no. 3 (June 2000): 463–88. https://doi.org/10.1177/014920630002600305.

Grisdale, Mackenzie, Kendall Anderson, Laura Anthony, and Jane Hilderman. "Cheering or Jeering? Members of Parliament Open Up About Civility in the House of Commons." *The Samara Centre for Democracy*, 15 January 2016. https://www.samaracentre.ca/articles/cheering-or-jeering.

Guelph Mercury. "Ex-Tory MP Cries Foul." *Guelph Mercury*, 7 June 2007.

Gunn, Andrea. "Nova Scotia Senator's Bill Under Fire." *Halifax Chronicle-Herald*, 20 February 2017.

Gwyn, Richard. "Ad-Men and Scientists Run This Election." In *Party Politics in Canada*, 2nd ed., edited by Hugh G. Thorburn. Prentice-Hall, 1967.

Halifax Chronicle-Herald. "Tory Defector May Join NDP." *The Guardian*, 28 October 1998.

Hall, Chris. "Abortion Politics Masquerading as Free Speech." *CBC News*, 28 March 2013. https://www.cbc.ca/news/politics/chris-hall-abortion-politics-masquerading-as-free-speech-1.1315364.

Hamilton, Alexander. *The Federalist Papers, No. 10*. The New American Library, 1787 (1961). https://doi.org/10.4159/harvard.9780674332133.

Hankins, James. "Hyperpartisanship." *Claremont Review of Books*, Winter 2020. https://claremontreviewofbooks.com/hyperpartisanship.

Harding, Katherine. "Stronach a Traitor, Westerners Say." *Globe and Mail*, 18 May 2005. https://www.theglobeandmail.com/news/national/stronach-a-traitor-westerners-say/article18227383.

Harris, Kathleen. "Speaker Gives Tory MP the Boot from House for Heckling." *CBC News*, 30 November 2017. https://www.cbc.ca/news/politics/speaker-expels-tory-mp-heckling-1.4427036.

Harris, Michael. "The Forging of Jane Philpott's Moral Will." *The Tyee*, 5 July 2019. https://thetyee.ca/News/2019/07/05/Forging-Jane-Philpott-Moral-Will.

Hartman, Sandra, and Augusta Yrle. "Can the Hobo Phenomenon Help Explain Voluntary Turnover?" *International Journal of Contemporary*

Hospitality Management 8, no. 4 (1996): 11–16. https://doi.org/10.1108 /09596119610119930.

Hatter, David. "Peckford's Cocky Protégé Rises to the Top." *Financial Post*, 14 March 1989.

Havrot, Ed. "Throne Speech Debate." Ontario. Legislative Assembly of Ontario. 29th Parliament, 5th Session, 26 March 1975.

Hawkes, David C., and Marina Devine. "Meech Lake and Elijah Harper: Native-State Relations in the 1990s." In *How Ottawa Spends, 1991–1992: The Politics of Fragmentation*, edited by Frances Abele. Carleton University Press, 1991. https:// doi.org/10.1515/9780773591219-003.

Hays, Peter. "Kimball Quits, Putting Tories in Peril." *The Daily News*, 6 January 1993.

Hazan, Reuven Y. "Does Cohesion Equal Discipline? Towards a Conceptual Delineation." *Journal of Legislative Studies* 9, no. 4 (2003): 1–11. https://doi.org /10.1080/1357233042000306227.

Heard, Andrew. "Just What Is a Vote of Confidence? The Curious Case of May 10, 2005." *Canadian Journal of Political Science* 40, no. 2 (June 2007): 395–416. https:// doi.org/10.1017/S000842390707014X.

Hébert, Michel. "Crise au PQ." *Journal de Québec*, 6 June 2011. https://www .journaldequebec.com/2011/06/06/crise-au-pq.

Helm, Richard. "Leadership Scrutinized after Liberals Lose MLA." *Edmonton Journal*, 7 April 1994.

Helms, Ludger. "Democratic Political Leadership in the New Media Age: A Farewell to Excellence?" *British Journal of Politics* 14, no. 4 (November 2012): 651–70. https://doi.org/10.1111/j.1467-856X.2011.00495.x.

Heppell, Timothy. "The British Labour Party and the Antisemitism Crisis: Jeremy Corbyn and Image Repair Theory." *British Journal of Politics and International Relations* 23, no. 4 (November 2021): 645–62. https://doi.org/10.1177 /13691481211015920.

Herle, David. "The Insiders." *CBC The National*, 25 February 2014.

Herrick, Rebekah, and Michael K. Moore. "Political Ambition's Effect on Legislative Behavior: Schlesinger's Typology Reconsidered and Revised." *Journal of Politics* 55, no. 3 (August 1993): 765–76. h ttps://doi.org/10.2307 /2132000.

Higgs, Blaine M. "Letter to MLA Dominic Cardy." X (post), 14 October 2022. https://x.com/poitrasCBC/status/1581004821695692803.

Hildreth, John Angus D., Francesca Gino, and Max Bazerman. "Blind Loyalty? When Group Loyalty Makes Us See Evil or Engage in It." *Organizational Behavior and Human Decision Processes* 132 (January 2015): 16–36. https://doi.org/10.1016 /j.obhdp.2015.10.001.

The Hill Times. "Shortly after Stronach's Presser, the Conservative 'Talking Points' Come Out." *Hill Times*, 23 May 2005. https://www.hilltimes.com /2005/05/23/shortly-after-stronachs-presser-the-conservative-talking -points-come-out/5202.

"Hillson to sit as independent Liberal." *The Times Herald* (Moose Jaw), 2 February 2001.

Hirschman, Albert O. *Exit, Voice, and Loyalty: Responses to Decline in Firms, Organizations and States*. Harvard University Press, 1970. https://archive.org /details/exitvoiceloyalty0000hirs/page/n5/mode/2up.

Hobson, Brittany. "Manitoba NDP Caucus Chair Says Turfed Backbencher Was Disrespectful, Deceitful." *Toronto Star*, 18 September 2024. https://www.thestar .com/news/canada/manitoba/manitoba-ndp-caucus-chair -says-turfed-backbencher-was-disrespectful-deceitful/article_a13bdd4f -285d-5f06-b8f0-97cb5a9238bc.html.

Hogben, David. "New Liberal MLA Expects Major Role." *The Vancouver Sun*, 8 October 1997.

Hogg, Michael A. "A Social Identity Theory of Leadership." *Personality and Social Psychology Review* 5, no. 3 (August 2001): 184–200. https://doi .org/10.1207/S15327957PSPR0503_1.

Holman, Mirya R., and Monica C. Schneider. "Gender, Race, and Political Ambition: How Intersectionality and Frames Influence Interest in Political Office." *Politics, Groups, and Identities* 6, no. 2 (2018): 264–80. https://doi.org /10.1080/21565503.2016.1208105.

Holt, Jacob. "What Explains Party Unity? A Test of Competing Theories." *Party Politics* 29, no. 2 (March 2023): 294–305. https://doi.org/10.1177 /13540688211064601.

Hom, Peter W., David G. Allen, and Rodger W. Griffeth. *Employer Retention and Turnover: Why Employees Stay or Leave*. 1st ed. Routledge, 2020. https://doi .org/10.4324/9781315145587-1.

Hopper, Tristin. "Why Liberal backbenchers Are Revolting over the Carbon Tax." *National Post*, 6 October 2023. https://nationalpost.com/news/canada/liberal -backbenchers-revolt-carbon-tax.

Horner, Jack. *My Own Brand*. Hurtig, 1980. https://openlibrary.org/books /OL3816105M/My_own_brand.

Horwood, Matt. "'It's Like Getting Thrown into the Deep End of the Pool': Rookie MPs Navigate New House Waters." *The Hill Times*, 18 October 2021. https://www.hilltimes.com/story/2021/10/14/its-like-getting-thrown -into-the-deep-end-of-the-pool-rookie-mps-navigate-new-house- waters/229689/.

House of Assembly. "Proceedings." *Newfoundland and Labrador* XLIX, no. 22 (21 November 2019): 1052–118.

House of Commons. "Standing Orders of the House of Commons, Consolidated Version." Consolidated version as of 18 September 2023. https://www .ourcommons.ca/procedure/standing-orders/index-e.html.

Howard, Bailey. "MHA for Torngat Mountains Lela Evans Rejoins PC Party." *NTV News*, 16 July 2024. https://ntv.ca/mha-for-torngat-mountains-lela -evans-rejoins-pc-party.

Howard, Ross. "Ex-Tory MP Kilgour Plans to Join Liberals." *Globe and Mail*, 29 September 1990.

– "Rookie MP Rankles Tory Heavyweights." *Globe and Mail*, 4 April 1985.

Howell, Trevor. "Calgary MLA Deborah Drevor Returns to NDP Caucus." *Calgary Herald*, 8 January 2016. https://calgaryherald.com/news/politics /brian-mason-deborah-drever-to-make-announcement-in-calgary.

Howlett, Karen, and Justin Giovannetti. "Brown Vetting Process 'Manipulated,' Ontario PC Committee Member Says." *Globe and Mail*, 22 February 2018. https://www.theglobeandmail.com/news/politics/ caroline-mulroney-urges-patrick-brown-to-quit-ontario-pc-leadership-race/ article38063657.

Hristova, Bobby. "Disability Activist Sarah Jama to Seek Nomination as Ontario NDP Candidate for Hamilton Centre." *CBC News*, 26 July 2022. https://www.cbc.ca/news/canada/hamilton/hamilton-centre-mpp-ndp-candidate-1.6532314.

– "NDP's Sarah Jama Elected as Next MPP for Hamilton Centre." *CBC News*, 16 March 2023. https://www.cbc.ca/news/canada/hamilton/byelection-hamilton-centre-results-1.6781562.

Hunter, Jennifer. "A High-Stakes Gamble." *Maclean's*, 1 March 1999. https://archive.org/details/Macleans-Magazine-1999-03-01/page/n9/mode/2up.

Hunter, Justine. "Last Reform MLA Quits Party." *Vancouver Sun*, 29 November 1997.

– "Two Rights Groups Condemn MLA: Liberal Tanner Offered Character References for Two Child-Sex Offenders." *Vancouver Sun*, 2 December 1992, A1.

– "Warnke's Move from Liberals Stuns Campbell, Cheers NDP." *Vancouver Sun*, 29 April 1996, A1.

Huntington, Vicki. "Defining the Role of an Independent Member." *Canadian Parliamentary Review* 35, no. 1 (Spring 2012): 2–5.

Huo, Cynthia, and Jonathan Malloy. "Extreme Partisanship Is Infecting Committees, and We Should Be Worried." *Policy Options*, 20 March 2023. https://policyoptions.irpp.org/magazines/march-2023/house-committees-extreme-partisanship.

Huras, Adam. "The Behind-the-Scenes Story of How Atwin Became a Liberal." *Telegraph Journal*, 14 June 2021.

Husted, Emil, Mona Moufahim, and Martin Fredriksson. "Political Parties and Organization Studies: The Party as a Critical Case of Organizing." *Organization Studies* 43, no. 8 (August 2022): 1327–41. https://doi.org/10.1177/01708406211010979.

Hustedt, Thurid, Kristoffer Kolltveit, and Heidi Houlberg Salomonsen. "Ministerial Advisers in Executive Government: Out from the Dark and into the Limelight." *Public Administration* 95, no. 2 (June 2017): 299–311. https://doi.org/10.1111/padm.12329.

Hutchins, Aaron. "How Did That Candidate Get the Green Light?" *MacLean's*, 19 September 2015. https://www.macleans.ca/politics/ottawa/how-did-that-candidate-get-the-green-light.

Ibbitson, John. *The Duel: Diefenbaker, Pearson and the Making of Modern Canada.* Signal, 2023.

– "Here's the Story behind the Story." *Globe and Mail*, 12 January 2006. https://www.theglobeandmail.com/news/world/heres-the-story-behind-the-story/article727205/.

Ie, Kenny William. "Ministerial Mandate Letters and Co-ordination in the Canadian Executive." *Canadian Journal of Political Science* 56, no. 4 (December 2023): 811–31. https://doi.org/10.1017/S0008423923000598.

Ignatieff, Michael. "Enemies vs. Adversaries." *The New York Times*, 13 October 2013. https://www.nytimes.com/2013/10/17/opinion/enemies-vs-adversaries.html.

"The Independents." Panel event, Churchill Society for the Advancement of Parliamentary Democracy, 18 January 2024. Posted 26 February 2024, by The Churchill Society. YouTube, 1:16:11. https://www.youtube.com/watch?v=qp0FI_U_BPI.

Irwin, W.A. "Progressive Party's Split May Mean Liberal Gain." *The Globe*, 5 May 1925.

Isaacs, Victor. "The Case of the Missing Premier – A Strange Parliamentary Practice." *Australian Parliamentary Review* 20, no. 1 (March 2005): 34–53. https://www.aspg.org.au/wp-content/uploads/2017/09/03-Isaacs.pdf.

Ivison, John. "Flaherty the Pragmatist Wins Out Over Pitbull." *National Post*, 3 March 2011. https://nationalpost.com/full-comment/john-ivison-flaherty-the-pragmatist-wins-out-over-pitbull.

Jackson, Susan E., Joan F. Brett, Valerie I. Sessa, Dawn M. Cooper, Johan A. Julin, and Karl Peyronnin. "Some Differences Make a Difference: Individual Dissimilarity and Group Heterogeneity as Correlates of Recruitment, Promotions, and Turnover." *Journal of Applied Psychology* 76, no. 5 (October 1991): 675–89. https://doi.org/10.1037/0021-9010.76.5.675.

Jama, Sarah. "A Call for an Immediate Cease Fire." X (post), 10 October 2023. https://x.com/SarahJama_/status/1711808190889746854.

– "Thirteen Days Ago." X (post), 23 October 2023. https://x.com/SarahJama_/status/1716473167722504563.

Jang, Brent. "B.C. Liberals Turf MLA Over Hydro Allegations." *Globe and Mail*, 20 November 2002.

Jannard, Maurice. "Mulroney perd trois autres députés." *La Presse*, 27 June 1990. https://collections.banq.qc.ca/ark:/52327/2169410.

Jansen, Sandra. "Members' Statements." Alberta. Legislative Assembly. *Alberta Hansard* 50. 29th Legislature, 2nd session, 22 November 2016.

Jeffrey, Brooke. *Divided Loyalties: The Liberal Party of Canada, 1984–2008*. University of Toronto Press, 2010. https://doi.org/10.3138/9781442660182.

Jeffrey, Kevin. "Powlowski Not Deterred by Trudeau Cabinet Shuffle." *Fort Frances Times*, 1 August 2023. https://fftimes.com/news/district-news/powlowski-not-deterred-by-trudeau-cabinet-shuffle.

Jeffreys, Jenn. "Meet the Chillest Man in Canadian Politics." *Vice*, 3 November 2015. https://www.vice.com/en/article/bnpkm5/drinking-with-peter-stoffer-the-last-regular-guy-on-parliament-hill.

Jenson, Jane. "Party Loyalty in Canada: The Question of Party Identification." *Canadian Journal of Political Science* 8, no. 4 (December 1975): 543–53. https://doi.org/10.1017/S000842390004628X.

Jerrers, Alan. "MacLean Calls Surprise Vote on N.S. Liberal Leadership." *Montreal Gazette*, 28 February 1992.

Jewett, Pauline. "Pauline Jewett Her Memories of Prime Minister Pearson and the Pearson Government in an Interview with Peter Stursberg." Oral History Project, Library of Parliament, National Archives of Canada, 15 May 1976.

Joannou, Ashley. "Alberta Speaker Apologizes for 'Crossing a Line' after Signing Letter Opposing Government Pandemic Health Restrictions." *Edmonton Journal*, 21 April 2021. https://edmontonjournal.com/news/politics/alberta-speaker-apologizes-for-crossing-a-line-after-signing-letter-opposing-government-pandemic-health-restrictions.

– "Independent B.C. Election Candidates See Opportunity in Shifting Political Landscape." *Globe and Mail*, 13 October 2024. https://www.theglobeandmail.com/canada/british-columbia/article-independent-bc-election-candidates-see-opportunity-in-shifting.

Johnsrude, Larry. "Alliance 'Matriarch' Returns to the Family." *Edmonton Journal*, 11 April 2002.

Johnston, Richard. "Affective Polarization in the Canadian Party System, 1988–2021." *Canadian Journal of Political Science* 56, no. 2 (June 2023): 372–95. https://doi.org/10.1017/S0008423923000112.

Johnston, Richard, and Campbell Sharman. "Introduction." In *Parties and Party Systems: Structure and Context*, edited by Richard Johnston and Campbell Sharman. UBC Press, 2015. https://doi.org/10.59962/9780774829571-003.

Josey, Stan. "Durham MPP Back in Caucus after Tug-of-War Case Dismissed." *Toronto Star*, 17 March 1994.

Judge, David. "Representation in Westminster in the 1990s: The Ghost of Edmund Burke." *The Journal of Legislative Studies* 5, no. 1 (1999): 12–34. https://doi.org/10.1080/13572339908420581.

Judge, Timothy A., and Shinichiro Watanabe. "Is the Past Prologue? A Test of Ghiselli's Hobo Syndrome." *Journal of Management* 21, no. 2 (April 1995): 211–29. https://doi.org/10.1016/0149-2063(95)90056-X.

Junker, Anna. "Justice Minister Kacee Madu to 'Step Back from Ministerial Duties' after Calling Edmonton Police Chief Over Distracted Driving Ticket." *Edmonton Journal*, 18 January 2022. https://edmontonjournal.com/news/politics/ndp-calls-for-justice-minister-kaycee-madu-to-resign-after-reports-he-called-edmonton-police-chief-over-distracted-driving-ticket.

Justice, J.W., and David J. Lanoue. "Strategic and Sincere Voting in a One-Sided Election: The Canadian Federal Election of 1997." *Social Science Quarterly* 86, no. 1 (March 2005): 129–46. https://doi.org/10.1111/j.0038-4941.2005.00294.x.

Kam, Christopher J. "Do Ideological Preferences Explain Parliamentary Behaviour? Evidence from Great Britain and Canada." *The Journal of Legislative Studies* 7, no. 4 (2001): 89–126. https://doi.org/10.1080/714003894.

– *Party Discipline and Parliamentary Politics*. Cambridge University Press, 2009.

Karadeglija, Anja. "Liberal Candidate's Defection from Greens in June Brings Baggage in Fredericton Riding." *National Post*, 14 September 2021. https://nationalpost.com/news/politics/election-2021/liberal-candidates-defection-from-greens-in-june-brings-baggage-in-fredericton-riding.

Katz, Richard S. "The Problem of Candidate Selection and Models of Party Democracy." *Party Politics* 7, no. 3 (May 2001): 277–96. https://doi.org/10.1177/1354068801007003002.

Keenleyside, Hugh L. "The Canadian Election of 1925." *Current History (1916–1940)* 23, no. 4 (January 1926): 508–11. https://doi.org/10.1525/curh.1926.23.4.508.

Kehoe, S. Karly. *Empire and Emancipation: Scottish and Irish Catholics at the Atlantic Fringe, 1780–1850*. University of Toronto Press, 2022. https://doi.org/10.3138/9781487541095.

Kelly, Austin. "Coralee Oakes Working with Constituents, Isn't Ready to Make Campaign Decision." *The Williams Lake Tribune*, 9 September 2024. https://www.wltribune.com/home/coralee-oakes-working-with-constituents-isnt-ready-to-make-campaign-decision-7526906.

Kendall, Chad, and Marie Rekkas. "Incumbency Advantages in the Canadian Parliament." *The Canadian Journal of Economics* 45, no. 4 (November 2012): 1560–85. https://doi.org/10.1111/j.1540-5982.2012.01739.x.

Kennedy, Brendan, and Marco Chown Oved. "Why These MPs Aren't Speaking During Question Period." *Toronto Star*, 20 June 2018. https://www.thestar.com/news/canada/why-these-mps-aren-t-speaking-during-question-period/article_b8369485-0a58-5774-a1da-e9682b35d004.html.

Kenney, Jason. "July 27, 2018 Memorandum to UCP Nomination Contestants." Internal party memo, 2018.

Kerby, Matthew. "Canada: Ministerial Careers." In *The Selection of Ministers Around the World*, edited by Keith Dowding and Patrick Dumont. Routledge, 2014. https://doi.org/10.4324/9781315757865.

Kerby, Matthew, and Kelly Blidook. "It's Not You, It's Me: Determinants of Voluntary Legislative Turnover in Canada." *Legislative Studies Quarterly* 36, no. 4 (November 2011): 621–43. https://doi.org/10.1111/j.1939-9162.2011.00029.x.

Kerby, Matthew, and Alex Marland. "Media Management in a Small Polity: Political Elites' Synchronized Calls to Regional Talk Radio and Attempted Manipulation of Public Opinion Polls." *Political Communication* 32, no. 3 (2015): 356–76. https://doi.org/10.1080/10584609.2014.947449.

Kerby, Matthew, and Feodor Snagovsky. "Not All Experience Is Created Equal: MP Career Typologies and Ministerial Appointments in the Canadian House of Commons, 1968–2015." *Government & Opposition* 56, no. 2 (April 2021): 326–44. https://doi.org/10.1017/gov.2019.29.

Kevins, Anthony, and Stuart N. Soroka. "Growing Apart? Partisan Sorting in Canada, 1992–2015." *Canadian Journal of Political Science* 51, no. 1 (March 2018): 103–33. https://doi.org/10.1017/S0008423917000713.

Kieran, Brian, Barbara McLintock, Don Hauka, and Keith Schaefer. "Socreds in Turmoil: Shock as Four MLAs Desert Caucus." *The Province* (Vancouver), 4 October 1989, 4.

Kilgour, David. "David Kilgour, MP." Oral History Project, Library of Parliament, National Archives of Canada, February 1995.

Kimber, Stephen. "Bitter Pill." *The Daily News*, 19 October 1998.

King, Robin Levinson. "MP James Lunney Quits Conservative Caucus Over Perceived Threats to His Religious Beliefs." *Toronto Star*, 31 March 2015. https://www.thestar.com/news/canada/mp-james-lunney-quits -conservative-caucus-over-perceived-threats-to-his-religious-beliefs /article_bacf5a91-05dc-5822-8fa2-896c905a2b1b.html.

Kleinfeld, Rachel. "Polarization, Democracy, and Political Violence in the United States: What the Research Says." *Carnegie Endowment for International Peace*, 5 September 2023. https://carnegieendowment.org/research/2023/09 /polarization-democracy-and-political-violence-in-the-united-states-what -the-research-says.

Kleiss, Karen. "Towle, a Fierce Advocate for Vulnerable Albertans, Decamps to Tories." *Edmonton Journal*, 24 November 2014. https://edmontonjournal.com /news/local-news/towle-a-fierce-advocate-for-vulnerable-albertans-decamps -to-tories.

Koerber, Duncan. "Crisis Communication Response and Political Communities: The Unusual Case of Toronto Mayor Rob Ford." *Canadian Journal of Communication* 39, no. 3 (September 2014): 311–31. https://doi.org/10.22230 /cjc.2014v39n3a2766.

Köhler, Nicholas. "'Dysfunction' Drives Two Across the Floor." *MacLean's*, 4 January 2010. https://www.macleans.ca/news/canada/dysfunction-drives -two-across-the-floor.

Koop, Royce. *Grassroots Liberals: Organizing for Local and National Politics.* UBC Press, 2010. https://doi.org/10.59962/9780774820998.

Koop, Royce, Heather Bastedo, and Kelly Blidook. *Representation in Action: Canadian MPs in the Constituencies.* UBC Press, 2018. https://doi.org/10.59962 /9780774836999.

Kornberger, Martin. *Brand Society: How Brands Transform Management and Lifestyle.* Cambridge University Press, 2010. https://doi.org/10.1017/CBO9780511802881.

Kritzwiser, Kay. "The MP Who Shuns Back Seats." *Globe and Mail,* 7 January 1961.

Krug, Jeffrey A., Peter Wright, and Mark Kroll. "Top Management Turnover Following Mergers and Acquisitions: Solid Research to Date but Much Still to Be Learned." *Academy of Management Perspectives* 28, no. 2 (May 2014): 147–63. https://doi.org/10.5465/amp.2011.0091.

Kulik, Carol, Belinda Rae, Shruti R. Sardeshmukh, and Sanjeewa Perera. "Can We Still Be Friends? The Role of Exit Conversations in Facilitating Post-Exit Relationships." *Human Resource Management* 54, no. 6 (November /December 2015): 893–912. https://doi.org/10.1002/hrm.21642.

Kulp, Ashley. "Randy Hillier Permanently Expelled from PC Caucus." *The Perth Courier,* 15 March 2019. https://www.insideottawavalley.com/news /randy-hillier-permanently-expelled-from-pc-caucus/article_541ecfe3 -af38-5206-8adc-121cf8fe6f54.html.

Kumar, Kunal Kamal, and Sushanta Kumar Mishra. "Subordinate-Superior Upward Communication: Power, Politics, and Political Skill." *Human Resource Management* 56, no. 6 (November/December 2017): 1015–37. https://doi.org/ 10.1002/hrm.21814.

Kurjata, Andrew. "Longtime B.C. Liberal MLA Removed from Caucus After Questioning Climate Change Science." *CBC News,* 18 August 2022. https://www. cbc.ca/news/canada/british-columbia/john-rustad-removed-caucus-1.6555527.

Lachance, Nicolas. "La députée a quitté la cérémonie avant la fin." *Le Journal de Québec,* 18 October 2018. https://www.journaldequebec.com/2018/10/18 /la-deputee-a-quitte-la-ceremonie-avant-la-fin-claire-samson-exclue-et-decue.

Ladewig, Jeffrey W. "Conditional Party Government and the Homogeneity of Constituent Interests." *Journal of Politics* 67, no. 4 (November 2005): 1006–29. https://doi.org/10.1111/j.1468-2508.2005.00348.x.

Laghi, Brian. "Alliance Defector's Riding Seeks Resignation." *Globe and Mail,* 2 February 2002. https://www.theglobeandmail.com/news/national /alliance-defectors-riding-seeks-resignation/article4130844.

– "MP Resigns for Second Time." *Globe and Mail,* 10 October 2003.

Lalancette, Mireille, Catherine Lemarier-Saulnier, and Alex Drouin. "Playing Along New Rules: Personalized Politics in a 24/7 Mediated World." In *Political Communication in Canada: Meet the Press and Tweet the Rest,* edited by Alex Marland, Thierry Giasson, and Tamara Small. UBC Press, 2014. https://doi .org/10.59962/9780774827782-011.

Lalancette, Mireille, Jared Wesley, and Alex Marland. "Retourner sa veste au Québec : une étude des défections transpartisanes politiques de 1980 à 2018." *Canadian Journal of Political Science* 56, no. 1 (March 2023): 162–83. https://doi .org/10.1017/S0008423923000021.

Lalancette, Mireille, and Vincent Raynauld. "The Hyper-Masculine Campaign: Party Leader Brand Image, Heteronormativity and the 2021 Canadian Federal Election." In *Political Marketing in the 2021 Canadian Federal Election,* edited by Jamie Gillies, Vincent Raynauld, and André Turcotte. Palgrave Macmillan, 2023. https://doi.org/10.1007/978-3-031-34404-6_4.

– "The Power of Political Image: Justin Trudeau, Instagram, and Celebrity Politics." *American Behavioral Scientist* 63, no. 7 (June 2019): 888–924. https://doi.org/10.1177/0002764217744838.

Lalancette, Mireille, Vincent Raynauld, and Anthony Ozorai. "Personalization of Local Candidates." In *Inside the Local Campaign: Constituency Elections in Canada*, edited by Alex Marland and Thierry Giasson. UBC Press, 2022.

Lalancette, Mireille, Vincent Raynauld, and Erin Crandall, eds. *What's Trending in Canadian Politics? Understanding Transformations in Power, Media, and the Public Sphere*. UBC Press, 2019. https://doi.org/10.59962/9780774861175.

LaMarsh, Judy. *Memoirs of a Bird in a Gilded Cage*. McClelland and Stewart, 1969. https://search.worldcat.org/title/memoirs-of-a-bird-in-a-gilded-cage/oclc/25050.

Lambert, Steve. 2014. "Ousted Minister Says She Was Told to Take Blame." *Global News*, 4 February 2014. https://globalnews.ca/news/1126009/ousted-minister-says-she-was-told-to-take-blame.

Landes, Ron. "Report of the Special Committee on Reform of the House of Commons." *Canadian Parliamentary Review* 8, no. 3 (Autumn 1985): 43–4.

Lane, Paul. "Navigating Party Discipline." Panel event, Bruneau Centre for Research, Memorial University, St. John's. 6 February 2020.

Langer, Anna-Inès. *The Personalization of Politics in the UK: Mediated Leadership from Attlee to Cameron*. Manchester University Press, 2012.

Langworth, Richard M. *Churchill's Wit: The Definitive Collection*. Ebury Press, 2009.

Lanoue, David J., and Shaun Bowler. "Picking the Winners: Perceptions of Party Viability and Their Impact on Voting Behavior." *Social Science Quarterly* 79, no. 2 (June 1998): 361–77. https://www.jstor.org/stable/42863794.

Lapointe, Josée. "Les conservateurs reprochent à la députée Venne sa décision prématurée." *La Presse*, 13 August 1991.

Laroche, Jean. "Houston Government Tightening Its Grip on Legislative Committee Work." *CBC News*, 18 January 2024. https://www.cbc.ca/news/canada/nova-scotia/nova-scotia-legislature-committees-house-of-assembly-1.7085392.

Laucius, Joanne. "MP Gallant's Media Posts Provoke Divisive Atmosphere, Constituents Say." *Ottawa Citizen*, 25 February 2022. https://ottawacitizen.com/news/local-news/some-constituents-furious-with-mp-cheryl-gallant-suggesting-they-attend-downtown-protest.

La Vertu, Charles. "B.C. Ex-Minister Considers Starting New Political Party." *Winnipeg Free Press*, 6 December 1984.

Lawrence, Regina G., and Melody Rose. *Hillary Clinton's Race for the White House: Gender Politics and the Media on the Campaign Trail*. Lynne Rienner, 2010. https://doi.org/10.1515/9781685856830.

Laycock, David. "Reforming Canadian Democracy? Institutions and Ideology in the Reform Party Project." *Canadian Journal of Political Science* 27, no. 2 (June 1994): 213–47. https://doi.org/10.1017/S0008423900017340.

Lazenby, Alec. "Battle Between Conservatives and NDP Narrows as Teresa Wat Defects from B.C. United." *Vancouver Sun*, 30 July 2024. https://vancouversun.com/news/bc-election-2024-teresa-wat-defects.

– "B.C. Conservative Constituency Executive Resigns as Controversy Swirls Over Party's Nomination Process." *Vancouver Sun*, 21 August 2024. https://vancouversun.com/news/conservative-vernon-lumby-constituency-association-resigns-amid-plans-to-override-nomination-process.

– "John Rustad Vows to 'Do Politics Differently' after Caucus Tensions Boil Over." *Vancouver Sun*, 12 December 2024. https://vancouversun.com/news/john-rustad-politics-differently-caucus-tensions-boil-over.

Leary, Mark R. "Responses to Social Exclusion: Social Anxiety, Jealousy, Loneliness, Depression, and Low Self-Esteem." *Journal of Social and Clinical Psychology* 9, no. 2 (June 1990): 221–9. https://doi.org/10.1521/jscp.1990.9.2.221.
– "Toward a Conceptualization of Interpersonal Rejection." In *Interpersonal Rejection*, edited by Mark R. Leary. Oxford University Press, 2001. https://psycnet.apa.org/record/2001-06667-001.
Leader-Post, Regina. "'Toe the Leader's Line': NDP Says Audio Shows Dissent among Sask. Party Members." 21 October 2024. https://leaderpost.com/news/toe-the-leaders-line-ndp-says-audio-shows-dissent-among-sask-party-members.
Leblanc, Daniel. "Trudeau Approved Blocking of Candidate from Liberal MP Race." *Globe and Mail*, 13 March 2017. https://www.theglobeandmail.com/news/national/trudeau-approved-blocking-of-montreal-candidate-from-liberal-mp-race/article34278156/.
Lebo, Matthew J., Adam J. McGlynn, and Gregory Koger. "Strategic Party Government: Party Influence in Congress, 1789–2000." *American Journal of Political Science* 51, no. 3 (July 2007): 464–81. https://doi.org/10.1111/j.1540-5907.2007.00262.x.
LeBrun, Luke. "'Save the Children Convoy' Says Conservative MP Invited Them into House of Commons as 'VIP' Guests." *Press Progress*, 18 October 2023. https://pressprogress.ca/save-the-children-convoy-says-conservative-mp-invited-them-into-house-of-commons-as-vip-guests.
Lecavalier, Charles. "Legault réagit au départ de Sylvie Roy." *Le Journal de Montréal*, 27 August 2015.
LeClair, Shannon. "Hale Crosses to PC Side." *Strathmore Times*, 23 December 2014. https://strathmoretimes.com/2014/hale-crosses-to-pc-side.
Lecomte, Lucie. "Party Discipline and Free Votes." Library of Parliament, 2018. https://publications.gc.ca/collections/collection_2019/bdp-lop/eb/YM32-5-2018-26-eng.pdf.
Lederman, Marsha. "Conservative MPs Display Statesmanlike Behaviour – Not!" *Globe and Mail*, 11 April 2024. https://www.theglobeandmail.com/opinion/article-conservative-mps-display-statesmanlike-behaviour-not.
Le Devoir. "Le Bloc perd un premier député aux mains des libéraux." 3 December 2003. https://www.ledevoir.com/politique/canada/42048/le-bloc-perd-un-premier-depute-aux-mains-des-liberaux.
Lees-Marshment, Jennifer. *The Human Resource Management of Political Staffers: Insights from Prime Ministers' Advisers and Reformers*. Routledge, 2023. https://doi.org/10.4324/9781032636429.
Legislative Assembly of Manitoba. "Debates and Proceedings." 7 April 1999. https://www.gov.mb.ca/legislature/hansard/36th_5th/vol_002/h002_1.html.
Lemarier-Saulnier, Catherine. "Cadrer les définitions du cadrage : une recension multidisciplinaire des approches du cadrage médiatique." *Canadian Journal of Communication* 41, no. 1 (February 2016): 65–73. https://doi.org/10.22230/cjc.2016v41n1a3010.
Leon, Calvi. "Ex-Tory MP 'Burns Bridge' by Backing Rival Liberal in Byelection." *London Free Press*, 3 May 2023. https://lfpress.com/news/local-news/former-tory-mp-burns-bridge-by-backing-rival-liberal-in-byelection-expert.
Lethbridge Herald. "Liberals." *Lethbridge Herald*, 13 April 2010.
Lévesque, Catherine. "Conservatives Apologize after Texts Sent to Members Attacking Defecting Quebec MP Alain Rayes." *National Post*, 14 September 2022.

https://nationalpost.com/news/politics/wave-of-text-messages-sent
-to-conservative-members-to-ask-mp-alain-rayes-to-resign-as-mp.
– "'Said Exactly What a Lot of Us Think': Liberal MP Reacts to Joël Lightbound's
Accusation of Divisive Tactics." *National Post*, 9 February 2022. https://
nationalpost.com/news/politics/its-not-good-timing-liberals
-downplay-mp-joel-lightbounds-accusation-of-divisive-tactics.
Lévesque, Fanny. "Devenir indépendant, 'c'est presque un nouveau job.'"
La Presse, 4 January 2025. https://www.lapresse.ca/actualites/politique/les
-hauts-et-les-bas-des-independants/2025-01-04/devenir-independant-c-est
-presque-un-nouveau-job.php.
Lévesque, Kathleen. "Le Bloc perd un premier député aux mains des libéraux."
Le Devoir, 3 December 2003. https://www.ledevoir.com/politique
/canada/42048/le-bloc-perd-un-premier-depute-aux-mains-des-liberaux.
Levesque, Mario. "Searching for Persons with Disabilities in Canadian Provincial
Office." *Canadian Journal of Disability Studies* 5, no. 1 (March 2016): 73–106.
https://doi.org/10.15353/cjds.v5i1.250.
Levine, Allan. *Scrum Wars: The Prime Ministers and the Media.* Dundurn
Press, 1996.
Levine, John M., and José M. Marques. "Norm Violators as Threats and
Opportunities: The Many Faces of Deviance in Groups." *Group Processes &
Intergroup Relations* 19, no. 5 (September 2016): 545–52. https://doi.org/10.1177
/1368430216657415.
Levitz, Stephanie. "Conservative MP Michelle Rempel Garner Doubles Down
After Star Reveals Push to Eject Her for Criticizing Colleagues." *Toronto Star*,
24 June 2022. https://www.thestar.com/politics/federal/conservative
-mp-michelle-rempel-garner-doubles-down-after-star-reveals-push-to
-eject-her-for/article_0ff1a94d-d335-524e-a3a6-a7e3138855f5.html.
– "Who's That Guy? Pierre Poilievre May Not Be Recognizable to Some
Canadians, but a Lot of Them Still Want to Vote for Him." *Toronto Star*, 12 July
2024. https://www.thestar.com/politics/federal/whos-that-guy-pierre-poilievre
-may-not-be-recognizable-to-some-canadians-but-a-lot/article_1134c6d6-3f01
-11ef-ad45-0fa85920abba.html.
Levy, Gary. "Canadian Participation in Parliamentary Associations." *Canadian
Journal of Political Science* 7, no. 2 (June 1974): 352–7. https://doi.org/10.1017
/S0008423900038397.
Lewis, J.P., Mireille Lalancette, and Vincent Raynauld. "Cabinet Solidarity in an
Age of Social Media: A Case Study of Twitter Use by MP Carolyn Bennett."
In *What's Trending in Canadian Politics? Understanding Transformations in Power,
Media, and the Public Sphere.* UBC Press, 2019. https://doi.org/10.59962
/9780774861175-013.
Liberal Party of Canada. "Team Trudeau Training." 23 August 2023. https://
liberal.ca/training.
– *Visual Identity Guidelines.* Liberal Party of Canada, April 2016. https://liberal
.ca/legacy-uploads/wp-content/uploads/2016/06/LPC-Visual-Identity
-Guidelines.pdf.
Lilley, Brian. "It's Official, @theJagmeetSingh Is Leaving His Coalition
Deal." X (post), 4 September 2024. https://x.com/brianlilley/status
/1831372662939189557.
– "Scrum with Marit Stiles." X (post), 23 October 2023. https://x.com/brianlilley
/status/1716508370876637510.

Lim, Jolson. "Failed NDP Leadership Candidate Angus Tweets, Then Deletes, Criticism of Party Under New Leader Singh." *The Hill Times*, 24 January 2018. https://www.hilltimes.com/2018/01/24/failed-ndp-leadership-candidate -angus-tweets-deletes-criticism-party-new-leader-singh/132162.

Ling, Justin. "Far and Widening: The Rise of Polarization in Canada." *Public Policy Forum*. August 2023. https://ppforum.ca/wp-content/uploads/2023/08 /TheRiseOfPolarizationInCanada-PPF-AUG2023-EN2.pdf.

Lipset, Seymour Martin. *Continental Divide: The Values and Institutions of the United States and Canada*. Routledge, 1990. https://www.routledge.com/Continental -Divide-The-Values-and-Institutions-of-the-United-States-and-Canada /Lipset/p/book/9780415903851.

Little, Simon, and Richard Zussman. "Can BC Conservatives Keep Up Momentum After Welcoming Defections?" *Global News*, 4 June 2024. https://globalnews.ca /news/10544731/bc-conservative-united-defections-election.

Lloyd, Jenny. "The 2005 General Election and the Emergence of the 'Negative Brand.'" In *The Marketing of Political Parties: Political Marketing at the 2005 British General Election*, edited by Darren G. Lilleker, Nigel A. Jackson, and Richard Scullion. Manchester University Press, 2006.

Loat, Alison, and Michael MacMillan. *Tragedy in the Commons: Former Members of Parliament Speak Out About Canada's Failing Democracy*. Random House Canada, 2014. https://www.penguinrandomhouse.ca/books/217230/tragedy-in-the -commons-by-alison-loat-and-michael-macmillan/9780307361318.

Lofaro, Joe, and Kelly Greig. "Anglade's Leadership on the Line After MNA Booted from Caucus." *CTV News Montreal*, 31 October 2022. https://montreal.ctvnews.ca /anglade-s-leadership-on-the-line-after-mna-booted-from-caucus -political-analysts-1.6132545.

Longley, Lawrence D., and Reuven Y. Hazan. "On the Uneasy, Delicate, Yet Necessary Relationships Between Parliamentary Members and Leaders." In *The Uneasy Relationships Between Parliamentary Members and Leaders*. Frank Cass, 2000. https://doi.org/10.1080/13572339908420597.

Loriggio, Paola. "Ford Aims to Woo Social Conservatives." *The Hamilton Spectator*, 7 March 2018.

Lortie, Marie-Claude. "Le député de Verdun quitte le Bloc et veut rentrer au bercail conservateur." *La Presse*, 10 April 1991.

Luebke, Simon M. "Political Authenticity: Conceptualization of a Popular Term." *The International Journal of Press/Politics* 26, no. 3 (July 2021): 635–53. https://doi .org/10.1177/1940161220948013.

MacCharles, Tondra. "Rebel MPs' Return Risks Party Status." *Hamilton Spectator*, 7 September 2001.

– "Toronto Conservatives Accuse Federal Party of 'Undemocratic' Meddling in Nomination of Karen Stintz." *Toronto Star*, 13 February 2024. https://www .thestar.com/politics/federal/toronto-conservatives-accuse-federal-party-of -undemocratic-meddling-in-nomination-of-karen-stintz/article_41c12f9e -ca97-11ee-b053-bfe1144ebe4b.html.

MacCharles, Tondra, Alex Ballingall, and Alex Boutilier. "They're Over the Hill (Or Are They?)." *Toronto Star*, 23 June 2019. https://www.thestar.com/politics /federal/they-re-over-the-hill-or-are-they-retiring-mps-talk-candidly-about -what-they/article_26bea509-9e1d-5ea9-8ced-149aa3458801.html.

Macdonald, Neil. "Liberals Sunny on the Surface, Much Fudgier Underneath." *CBC News*, 25 February 2016. http://www.cbc.ca/news/politics/liberals -sunny-surface-macdonald-1.3462885.

MacFarlane, Karla. "Resolution No. 598." Nova Scotia. House of Assembly. *Hansard* 23–68. Assembly 64, Session 1, 3 April 2023. https://nslegislature .ca/legislative-business/hansard-debates/assembly-64-session-1/house _23apr03#HPage5482.

MacIssac, Merle. "Rhetoric on the Rock." *Maclean's*, 12 February 1996. https:// archive.org/details/Macleans-Magazine-1996-02-12/page/n17/mode/2up.

Mackie, Victor. "Jewett Switches to NDP." *Winnipeg Free Press*, 11 April 1972.

MacLaren, Sherrill. *Invisible Power: The Women Who Run Canada*. Seal Books, 1992.

MacLean, R.A. "Campbell, Stewart." *Dictionary of Canadian Biography* 11. University of Toronto/Université Laval, 2003. http://www.biographi.ca/en/bio /campbell_stewart_11E.html.

Maclean's. "Canada Notes: Prairie Storm." *Maclean's*, 11 October 1999. https:// archive.org/details/Macleans-Magazine-1999-10-11/page/n21/mode/2up.

MacLeod, Andrew. "Another BC United MLA Defects to Rustad's Conservatives." *The Tyee*, 31 May 2024. https://thetyee.ca/News/2024/05/31/Another-BC-United -Defection-Lorne-Doerkson-Rustad-Conservatives.

MacLeod, Harris. "What a Night: NDP Stoffer's Salty All-Party Party and Swishy Chateau Politics and the Pen." *Hill Times*, 9 March 2009. https://www.hilltimes .com/2009/03/09/what-a-night-ndp-stoffers-salty-all-party -party-and-swishy-chateau-politics-and-the-pen/11496.

MacPhail, Sam, and Bill Hogg. *Ron MacKinley: No One's Fool. Stories of a PEI Politician*. Independently published, 2022.

Macpherson, Don. "Hardliner Quits PQ, Others Decide to Stay until Election." *Montreal Gazette*, 29 January 1985, A1.

Maher, Stephen. "Inside the Explosive Conservative Party Fight Over Rick Dykstra." *Maclean's*, 2 February 2018. https://www.macleans.ca/politics /ottawa/inside-the-explosive-conservative-party-fight-over-rick-dykstra.

– *The Prince: The Turbulent Reign of Justin Trudeau*. Simon & Schuster, 2024.

Mai, Philipp, and Georg Wenzelburger. "Loyal Activists? Party Socialization and Dissenting Voting Behaviour in Parliament." *Legislative Studies Quarterly* 49, no. 1 (February 2024): 131–60. https://doi.org/10.1111/lsq.12416.

Major, Darren. "MP Anthony Housefather to Stay on with Liberals After Period of 'Serious Reflection.'" *CBC News*, 5 April 2024. https://www.cbc.ca/news /politics/anthony-housefather-staying-with-liberals-1.7165299.

Mallory, J.R. "The Minister's Office Staff: An Unreformed Part of the Public Service." *Canadian Public Administration* 10, no. 1 (March 1967): 1–146. https://doi .org/10.1111/j.1754-7121.1967.tb00962.x.

– "Vacation of Seats in the House of Commons: The Problem of Burnaby-Coquitlam." *Canadian Journal of Economics and Political Science* 30, no. 1 (February 1964): 125–30. https://doi.org/10.2307/139176.

Malloy, Jason. "Casey Crosses the Floor." *The Daily News*, 11 January 2011.

Malloy, Jonathan. "High Discipline, Low Cohesion? The Uncertain Patterns of Canadian Parliamentary Party Groups." *Journal of Legislative Studies* 9, no. 4 (June 2002): 116–29. https://doi.org/10.1080/1357233042000306290.

– *The Paradox of Parliament*. University of Toronto Press, 2023.

Mannetti, Lucia, John M. Levine, Antonio Pierro, and Arie W. Kruglanski. "Group Reaction to Defection: The Impact of Shared Reality." *Social Cognition* 28, no. 3 (2010): 447–64. https://doi.org/10.1521/soco.2010.28.3.447.

Manning, Preston. "Obstacles and Opportunities for Parliamentary Reform." *Canadian Parliamentary Review* 17, no. 2 (Summer 1994): 2–5.

March, James G., and Herbert A. Simon. *Organizations*. Wiley, 1958.

Markusoff, Jason. "Lacombe-Ponoka MLA Who Made Derogatory Remarks about Trans Students Could Return to UCP Caucus." *CBC News*, 6 September 2024. https://www.cbc.ca/news/canada/calgary/jennifer-johnson-trans-debates-1.7316338.

– "A Matter of Time: Danielle Smith Is Putting in the Hours to Prevent UCP Unrest." *CBC News*, 14 December 2023. https://www.cbc.ca/news/canada/calgary/alberta-danielle-smith-putting-in-the-hours-1.7058358.

Marland, Alex. *Brand Command: Canadian Politics and Democracy in the Age of Message Control.* UBC Press, 2016. https://doi.org/10.59962/9780774832052.

– "The Branding of a Prime Minister: Digital Information Subsidies and the Image Management of Stephen Harper." In *Political Communication in Canada: Meet the Press and Tweet the Rest,* edited by Alex Marland, Thierry Giasson, and Tamara A. Small. UBC Press, 2014. https://doi.org/10.59962/9780774827782.

– "Communications Coordination by a Parliamentary Caucus Research Bureau: MPs Parroting Government Messages on Twitter." Canadian Study of Parliament Group, 2022. https://cspg-gcep.ca/pdf/mallory-2021-marland-f.pdf.

– "Vetting of Election Candidates by Political Parties: Centralization of Candidate Selection in Canada." *American Review of Canadian Studies* 51, no. 4 (2022): 573–91. https://doi.org/10.1080/02722011.2021.1986558.

– *Whipped: Party Discipline in Canada.* UBC Press, 2020. https://doi.org/10.59962/9780774864985.

Marland, Alex, and Brooks DeCillia. "Reputation and Brand Management by Political Parties: Vetting of Election Candidates in Canada." *Journal of Nonprofit & Public Sector Marketing* 32, no. 4 (2020): 342–63. https://doi.org/10.1080/10495142.2020.1798857.

Marland, Alex, and Tom Flanagan. "Brand New Party: Political Branding and the Conservative Party of Canada." *Canadian Journal of Political Science* 46, no. 4 (December 2013): 951–72. https://doi.org/10.1017/S0008423913001108.

– "From Opposition to Government: Party Merger as a Step on the Road to Power." *Parliamentary Affairs* 68, no. 2 (April 2015): 272–90. https://doi.org/10.1093/pa/gst015.

Marland, Alex, and Thierry Giasson. "The Evolution of Brokerage Politics to Political Marketing in Canada." In *Canadian Parties in Transition: Recent Evolution and New Paths for Research,* 5th ed., edited by Alain-G. Gagnon and Brian Tanguay. University of Toronto Press, 2024.

Marland, Alex, Thierry Giasson, and Anna Lennox Esselment, eds. *Permanent Campaigning in Canada.* UBC Press, 2017. https://doi.org/10.59962/9780774834506.

Marland, Alex, and Maria Mathews. "Friend, Can You Chip in $3? Canadian Political Parties, Perpetual Fundraising and Relationship Marketing." In *Permanent Campaigning in Canada,* edited by Alex Marland, Thierry Giasson, and Anna Lennox Esselment. UBC Press, 2017. https://doi.org/10.59962/9780774834506.

Marland, Alex, and Angelia Wagner. "Scripted Messengers: How Party Discipline and Branding Turn Election Candidates and Legislators into Brand Ambassadors." *Journal of Political Marketing* 19, nos. 1–2 (2020): 54–73. https://doi.org/10.1080/15377857.2019.1658022.

Marleau, Robert, and Camille Montpetit. *House of Commons Procedure and Practice.* House of Commons, 2000. https://www.ourcommons.ca/marleaumontpetit/DocumentViewer.aspx.

Marotta, Stefanie. "Erin Weir Declares Himself a Member of the CCF – A Party That No Longer Exists." *CBC News*, 11 May 2018. https://www.cbc.ca/news/politics/weir-new-party-ccf-1.4659853.

Martin, Don. *Belinda: The Political and Private Life of Belinda Stronach*. Key Porter Books, 2006.

Martin, Lawrence. *Harperland: The Politics of Control*. Viking Canada, 2010.

Martin, Paul. *Hell or High Water: My Life In and Out of Politics*. McClelland and Stewart, 2008.

Martin, Sandra. "Jean Pelletier, 73." *Globe and Mail*, 10 January 2009. https://www.theglobeandmail.com/news/national/jean-pelletier-73/article20439763.

Mas, Susana. "Thunder Bay MP Bruce Hyer Joins Green Party, Doubles Caucus." *CBC News*, 13 December 2013. https://www.cbc.ca/news/politics/thunder-bay-mp-bruce-hyer-joins-green-party-doubles-caucus-1.2462983.

Maser, Peter. "Westmount Fumes as Its MNA Bolts to PQ." *The Windsor Star*, 12 August 1992.

Massicotte, Louis. "Cohésion et dissidence à l'Assemblée nationale du Québec depuis 1867." *Canadian Journal of Political Science* 22, no. 3 (September 1989): 505–21. https://doi.org/10.1017/S0008423900010921.

Matheson, W.A. *The Prime Minister and the Cabinet*. Methuen, 1976.

Maynard, Robyn, Nisrin Elamin, and Alissa Trotz. "Black Feminists in Defence of Sarah Jama and Palestinian Human Rights." *Toronto Star*, 23 October 2023. https://www.thestar.com/opinion/contributors/black-feminists-in-defence-of-sarah-jama-and-palestinian-human-rights/article_1de90080-c685-5891-ba4d-87412bc23591.html.

McAndrews, John R., Feodor Snagovsky, and Paul E. J. Thomas. "How Citizens Judge Extreme Legislative Dissent: Experimental Evidence from Canada on Party Switching." *Parliamentary Affairs* 73, no. 2 (April 2020): 323–41. https://doi.org/10.1093/pa/gsy050.

McCormick, John P. *Against Politics as Technology: Carl Schmitt's Critique of Liberalism*. Cambridge University Press, 1996. https://doi.org/10.1017/CBO9780511608988.

McCutcheon, Chuck, and David Mark. *Dog Whistles, Walk-Backs and Washington Handshakes: Decoding the Jargon, Slang, and Bluster of American Political Speech*. ForeEdge, 2014. https://doi.org/10.2307/j.ctv1xx9j2s.

McDougall, Stephen. "Bachand Won't Be Part of New Conservative Party." *Record*, 9 December 2003.

McGee, David. "Parties and Government." In *Parliamentary Practice in New Zealand*, 4th ed., edited by Mary Harris and David Wilson. Oratia Books, 2017. https://www.parliament.nz/en/visit-and-learn/how-parliament-works/parliamentary-practice-in-new-zealand-archive/parliamentary-practice-in-new-zealand-2017/.

McGrane, David. *The New NDP: Moderation, Modernization, and Political Marketing*. UBC Press, 2019. https://doi.org/10.59962/9780774860475.

McGrath, James A. *Report of the Special Committee on Reform of the House of Commons*. Queen's Printer for Canada, 1985.

McGregor, Glen, and Stephen Maher. "Tories Delay Election Bill at Last Minute." *The Ottawa Citizen*, 18 April 2013. https://www.pressreader.com/canada/ottawa-citizen/20130418/281586648081167.

McKenzie, Judith. *Pauline Jewett: A Passion for Canada*. McGill-Queen's University Press, 1999. https://doi.org/10.1515/9780773567641.

McMartin, Will. "Emerson: The Power and the Tory." *The Tyee,* 9 February 2006. https://thetyee.ca/Views/2006/02/09/EmersonPower.

McSheffrey, Elizabeth. "Nova Scotia Liberal Riding Association Members Resign, Hugh MacKay to Make Statement Next Week." *Global News,* 28 February 2020. https://globalnews.ca/news/6609635/liberal-riding-members-resign-hugh-mackay.

Mears, F. "Western Members Bury the Hatchet and Appoint Whip." *Globe and Mail,* 6 January 1926.

Mendelsohn, Matthew. "The Media's Persuasive Effects: The Priming of Leadership in the 1988 Canadian Election." *Canadian Journal of Political Science* 27, no. 1 (March 1994): 81–97. https://doi.org/10.1017/S0008423900006223.

Merkley, Eric. "Ideological and Partisan Bias in the Canadian Public." *Canadian Journal of Political Science* 54, no. 2 (June 2021): 267–91. https://doi.org/10.1017/S0008423921000147.

– "Mass Polarization in Canada: What's Causing It? Why Should We Care?" Canadian Commission on Democratic Expression. McGill University, May 2023. https://www.mediatechdemocracy.com/all-work/mass-polarization-in-canada-whats-causing-it-why-should-we-care.

– "Polarization Eh? Ideological Divergence and Partisan Sorting in the Canadian Mass Public." *Public Opinion Quarterly* 86, no. 4 (Winter 2022): 932–43. https://doi.org/10.1093/poq/nfac047.

Mertz, Emily. "Alberta MLA Laurie Blakeman Nominated by Three Parties." *Global News,* 13 March 2015. https://globalnews.ca/news/1881299/alberta-mla-laurie-blakeman-nominated-by-three-parties.

Methot, Jessica R., Emily H. Rosado-Solomon, and David G. Allen. "The Network Architecture of Human Capital: A Relational Identity Perspective." *Academy of Management Review* 43, no. 4 (October 2018): 723–48. https://doi.org/10.5465/amr.2016.0338.

Michels, Robert. *Political Parties: A Sociological Study of the Oligarchical Tendencies of Modern Democracy.* Hearst's International Library, 1915.

Miljan, Lydia. "Television Frames of the 2008 Liberal and New Democrat Accord." *Canadian Journal of Communication* 36, no. 4 (2011): 559–78. https://doi.org/10.22230/cjc.2011v36n4a2446.

Milligan, Ian. "Illusionary Order: Online Databases, Optical Character Recognition, and Canadian History, 1997–2010." *The Canadian Historical Review* 94, no. 4 (2013): 540–69. https://doi.org/10.3138/chr.694.

Milliken, Peter. *Selected Decisions of Speaker Peter Milliken.* Clerk of the House of Commons, 2013.

Minsky, Amy. "A Brief History of Floor Crossing in Ottawa." *Global News,* 9 February 2015. https://globalnews.ca/news/1820421/a-brief-history-of-floor-crossing-in-ottawa.

– "Ontario MP Eve Adams Joins Liberals, Calls Tories 'Fear-Mongers and Bullies.'" *Global News,* 9 February 2015. https://globalnews.ca/news/1819453/ontario-mp-eve-adams-crosses-floor-to-liberals.

Mitchell, Don. "Ejected Hamilton MPP Miller Says He Has Evidence of No Wrongdoing Amid NDP Facebook Probe." *Global News,* 27 April 2022. https://globalnews.ca/news/8791554/hamilton-mpp-miller-evidence-no-wrongdoing.

– "Hamilton-Area MP Bob Bratina Asking for Parliamentary Review of $3.4B LRT Funding." *Global News,* 15 June 2021. https://globalnews.ca/news/7950023/bratina-parliamentary-review-hamilton-lrt.

– "Hamilton-Area MP Bob Bratina Says He Will Not Be Running for Re-Election." *Global News*, 17 May 2021. https://globalnews.ca/news/7868097/hamilton-mp-bratina-not-seeking-reelection.

Mitchell, Terence R., Brooks C. Holtom, Thomas W. Lee, Chris J. Sablynski, and Miriam Erez. "Why People Stay: Using Job Embeddedness to Predict Voluntary Turnover." *Academy of Management Journal* 44, no. 6 (December 2001): 1102–21. https://journals.aom.org/doi/10.5465/3069391.

Moalla, Taïeb. "Benoit Charette part à son tour." *Le Journal de Québec*, 22 June 2011. https://www.journaldequebec.com/2011/06/22/benoit-charette-part-a-son-tour.

Monopoli, Michael. "Millions of Canadians Lack Trust in Government and News Media." *Abacus Data*, 8 June 2022. https://abacusdata.ca/trust-and-disinformation-in-canada.

Montgomery, Charlotte. "He'll Disclose His Plans Soon, Testy PM Tells Liberal Caucus." *Globe and Mail*, 23 February 1984.

– "Ittinuar Faces Bleak Political Future." *Globe and Mail*, 21 November 1983.

Moose Jaw Times Herald. "A Political Hero Is Born." *Moose Jaw Times Herald*, 7 June 2007.

Morden, Michael, and Kendall Anderson. "Don't Blame 'the People': The Rise of Elite-Led Populism in Canada." *The Samara Centre for Democracy*, 7 May 2019. https://www.samaracentre.ca/articles/dont-blame-the-people.

Morden, Michael, Paul E. J. Thomas, and Adelina Petit-Vouriot. "Assessing the Reform Act as a Tool of Parliamentary Reform: One Step Forward, One Step Back." *Canadian Parliamentary Review* 43, no. 2 (Summer 2020): 10–17.

Morgan, Glenn, and Valeria Puilgnano. "Solidarity at Work: Concepts, Levels and Challenges." *Work, Employment and Society* 34, no. 1 (February 2020): 18–34. https://doi.org/10.1177/0950017019866626.

Morrice, Mike. "Backbenchers' Backyards: Green MP Mike Morrice." *CBC News: The House* (audio recording), 2 September 2023. https://www.cbc.ca/radio/thehouse/the-house-backbenchers-backyards-1.6948755.

Morris, Chris. "Couple Quit Tories to Cross Floor in N.B. House." *Globe and Mail*, 17 April 2007. https://www.theglobeandmail.com/news/national/couple-quit-tories-to-cross-floor-in-nb-house/article20396227.

Morton, Desmond. "A Note on Party Switchers." *Canadian Parliamentary Review* 29, no. 2 (Summer 2006): 4–8.

Morton, W.L. *The Progressive Party in Canada*. University of Toronto Press, 1950. https://doi.org/10.3138/9781487578077.

Moss, Neil, and Zainab Al-Mehdar. "Jenica Atwin Voted with Liberals 60 Percent of the Time as a Green MP." *The Hill Times*, 23 June 2021.

Mowday, Richard T., Lyman W. Porter, and Richard M. Steers. *Employee-Organization Linkages*. Academic Press, 1982. https://doi.org/10.1016/B978-0-12-509370-5.50005-8.

Müller, Wolfgang C., and Kaare Strøm. "Political Parties and Hard Choices." In *Policy, Office, or Votes? How Political Parties in Western Europe Make Hard Decisions*, edited by Wolfgang C. Müller and Kaare Strøm. Cambridge University Press, 1999. https://doi.org/10.1017/CBO9780511625695.

Mulroney, Brian. *Memoirs, 1939–1993*. McClelland and Stewart, 2007.

Munroe, Kaija Belfry, and H.D. Munroe. "Local Data-Driven Campaigning." In *Inside the Local Campaign: Constituency Elections in Canada*, edited by Alex Marland and Thierry Giasson, UBC Press, 2022.

Murphy, Rex. "Danny Boy Has Gone too Far." *Globe and Mail*, 12 September 2008. https://www.theglobeandmail.com/news/politics/danny-boy-has-gone-too-far/article20387369.

Nan, Xiaoli, and Ronald J. Faber. "Advertising Theory: Reconceptualizing the Building Blocks." *Marketing Theory* 4, nos. 1–2 (June 2004): 7–30. https://doi.org/10.1177/1470593104044085.

Nanaimo Daily News. "Wilson Flips to NDP." *Nanaimo Daily News*, 30 January 1999.

Nash, Chelsea. "Lantsman Calls Poilievre's Remarks on Trans Women 'the Position of the Conservative Party.'" *Hill Times*, 29 February 2024. https://www.hilltimes.com/story/2024/02/29/lantsman-calls-poilievres-comments-on-trans-women-the-position-of-the-conservative-party/413442/.

National Post. "The Grewal Questions." *National Post*, 4 June 2005.

– "MP in Hot Water on Cold-Water Rescue." *National Post*, 1 February 2011. https://www.pressreader.com/canada/national-post-latest-edition/20110211/281694021256639.

– "Trudeau's Hyper Partisanship Undermines Democracy." *National Post*, 17 March 2023. https://nationalpost.com/opinion/np-view-trudeau-the-partisan.

– "'You Broke My Heart': Read Selina Robinson's Resignation Letter to the B.C. NDP Caucus." *National Post*, 6 March 2024. https://nationalpost.com/news/politics/full-text-selina-robinson-resignation-letter-to-bc-ndp-caucus.

Naylor, Dave. "UCP Caucus Debating Expelling Barnes and Loewen." *Western Standard*, 13 May 2021. https://www.westernstandard.news/news/ws-exclusive-ucp-caucus-debating-expelling-barnes-and-loewen/article_3c84db67-ca05-513f-ab95-ac15b4aca67c.html.

Neatby, Stu. "Former P.E.I. MP Says Trudeau Avoided Hearing 'Hard Truths' from Caucus." *The Guardian*, 7 January 2025. https://www.saltwire.com/prince-edward-island/former-p-e-i-mp-says-trudeau-leadership-didnt-allow-hard-truths-from-caucus.

New Democratic Party of Canada. "Team Jagmeet – Équipe Jagmeet." Facebook Group, 23 August 2023. https://www.facebook.com/groups/teamjagmeet.

Newman, George E. "The Psychology of Authenticity." *Review of General Psychology* 23, no. 1 (March 2019): 8–18. https://doi.org/10.1037/gpr0000158.

Newman, George E., and Rosanna K. Smith. "Kinds of Authenticity." *Philosophy Compass* 11, no. 10 (October 2016): 609–18. https://doi.org/10.1111/phc3.12343.

Newman, Peter C. "Dilemma of a Maverick Politician: Too Many Ideas to Be a Success." *Maclean's*, 6 May 1961. https://archive.org/details/Macleans-Magazine-1961-05-06/page/n13/mode/2up.

Noel, Christian. "Poilievre's Office Maintains Tight Control over What Conservative MPs Say and Do." *CBC News*, 20 November 2024. https://www.cbc.ca/news/politics/poilievre-iron-fist-caucus-discipline-1.7387552.

Nolan, Michael. "Political Communication Methods in Canadian Federal Election Campaign 1987–1925." *Canadian Journal of Communication* 7, no. 4 (1981): 28–46. https://doi.org/10.22230/cjc.1981v7n4a260.

Northern Pen. "Bonavista-Burin-Trinity MP Disappointed with Fisheries Minister's Decision on Arctic Surf Clams." *Northern Pen*, 23 February 2018. https://www.saltwire.com/atlantic-canada/news/local/bonavista-burin-trinity-mp-disappointed-with-fisheries-ministers-decision-on-arctic-surf-clams-188587.

Nowlan, Patrick. "Patrick Nowlan." Oral History Project, Library of Parliament, National Archives of Canada, February and March 1987.

Nunziata, John. "John Nunziata." In *A Call to Account*, edited by Criss Hajek. Breakout Educational Network, 2003.

Office of the Ethics Commissioner of Canada. *The Harper-Emerson Inquiry.* Parliament of Canada, 2006. https://ciec-ccie.parl.gc.ca/en/publications /Documents/InvestigationReports/The%20Harper-Emerson%20Inquiry%20 (March%202006).pdf.

O'Malley, Eoin. "The Power of Prime Ministers: Results of an Expert Survey." *International Political Science Review* 28, no. 1 (January 2007): 7–27. https://doi .org/10.1177/0192512107070398.

O'Malley, Kady. "Process Nerd: What Can (and Can't) Bernier Do as an Independent MP?" *iPolitics*, 24 September 2018. https://ipolitics.ca/2018/09/24/process-nerd -what-can-and-cant-bernier-do-as-an-independent-mp.

O'Neil, Peter. "Emerson Hails New Party." *Montreal Gazette*, 7 February 2006.

– "Israel 'Appears' Guilty of War Crime: Robinson." *Vancouver Sun*, 19 April 2002.

– "Liberal MP Don Bell Not Joining Tories." *Vancouver Sun*, 14 April 2005.

O'Neill, Juliet. "Liberal MP Quits Caucus." *The Windsor Star*, 15 December 2001.

– "Veteran Tory MP Expelled from Caucus." *Calgary Herald*, 6 June 2007.

Ontario. "Ontario Health Teams." Government of Ontario. Published 30 May 2023; last updated 13 September 2024. https://www.ontario.ca/page/ontario-health -teams.

Open Parliament. "Vote #212 on March 8, 2017." *Open Parliament*, 2017. https:// openparliament.ca/votes/42-1/212.

Orhan, Yunus Emre. "The Relationship Between Affective Polarization and Democratic Backsliding: Comparative Evidence." *Democratization* 29, no. 4 (2022): 714–35. https://doi.org/10.1080/13510347.2021.2008912.

O'Toole, Erin. "Resignation of Member." Canada. Parliament. House of Commons. *Edited Hansard* 151 (211). 44th Parliament, 1st session, 12 June 2023.

Ovenden, Norm. "Kindy Joins Grits, NDP to Blast PC Fiscal Mess." *Edmonton Journal*, 11 October 1989.

– "Manning Lays Down Law on Discipline." *Edmonton Journal*, 20 September 1999.

– "Maverick Tories Inching Closer to Political Exile." *Edmonton Journal*, 7 April 1990.

Owens, John E. "Explaining Party Cohesion and Discipline in Democratic Legislatures: Purposiveness and Contexts." *Journal of Legislative Studies* 9, no. 4 (2003): 12–40. https://doi.org/10.1080/1357233042000306236.

Ozbudun, Ergun. *Party Cohesion in Western Democracies: A Causal Analysis.* Sage, 1970.

Packer, Dominic J., and Alison L. Chasteen. "Loyal Deviance: Testing the Normative Conflict Model of Dissent in Social Groups." *Personality and Social Psychology Bulletin* 36, no. 1 (January 2010): 5–18. https://doi.org/10.1177 /0146167209350628.

Packer, Dominic J., Christopher T. H. Miners, and Nick D. Ungson. "Benefiting from Diversity: How Groups' Coordinating Mechanisms Affect Leadership Opportunities for Marginalized Individuals." *Journal of Social Issues* 74, no. 1 (March 2018): 56–74. https://doi.org/10.1111/josi.12256.

Palmer, Vaughn. "Coleman Accuses Speaker Plecas of Betraying Liberal colleagues." *Vancouver Sun*, 9 September 2017. https://vancouversun.com /opinion/columnists/vaughn-palmer-coleman-accuses-speaker-plecas-of -betraying-liberal-colleagues.

– "Gordon, Judi & the Bellingham Blues." *Vancouver Sun*, 10 December 1993.

Panetta, Alexander. "Harper Won't Discuss MP's Remark about Persecution of Christians." *Brantford Expositor*, 18 March 2005.

– "Tory Rumblings: Some MPs in the New Government Want to Revive Legislation against Switching Parties." *The Hamilton Spectator*, 8 February 2006.

Parliament of Canada. "Parliamentarians." *Parlinfo*, n.d. Accessed 1 January 2025. https://lop.parl.ca/sites/ParlInfo/default/en_CA/People/parliamentarians.

– "Recorded Votes in the House of Commons, 1957 to Date." Library of Parliament, n.d. Accessed 1 January 2025. https://lop.parl.ca/sites/ParlInfo /default/en_CA/Parliament/recordedVotes.

Pasieka, Clara. "'I Felt Like I Was Grieving': Former MPs on Life After Election Defeat." *Global News*, 26 October 2019. https://globalnews.ca/news/6086551 /election-defeat-mps-grieving.

Passafiume, Alessia. "Tories Hold Lead Over Liberals, Canadians Report Limited Trust in Institutions: Poll." *Toronto Star*, 1 November 2023. https://www.thestar .com/politics/tories-hold-lead-over-liberals-canadians-report-limited-trust-in -institutions-poll/article_4b3062e8-f1f3-5a58-bc2a-2cda5f39fb9f.html.

Passifiume, Bryan. "Federal NDP Candidate Backs Accusation 'White Fragility' behind Caucus Ejection of MPP Sarah Jama." *National Post*, 25 January 2024. https://nationalpost.com/news/federal-ndp-candidate-backs-claim-white -fragility-behind-caucus-ejection-of-mpp-sarah-jama.

Patel, Raisa, Alex Ballingall, and Stephanie Levitz. "'I'm Disappointed': On the Liberal Back Benches, There's Grumbling about Justin Trudeau's Cabinet Shuffle." *Toronto Star*, 29 July 2023. https://www.thestar.com/politics/federal/i-m-disappointed-on-the-liberal-back-benches-there-s-grumbling-bout-justin-trudeau-s/article_e219e07e-f938-5265-a10c-90f4abbcb483.html.

Patten, Steve. "Databases, Microtargeting, and the Permanent Campaign: A Threat to Democracy?" In *Permanent Campaigning in Canada*, edited by Alex Marland, Thierry Giasson, and Anna Lennox Esselment. UBC Press, 2017. https://doi.org/10.59962/9780774834506-007.

Paulsen, Ryan. "Gallant in Hot Water." *Pembroke Observer*, 10 March 2016.

Payton, Laura. "Mask Ban Bill Passes House of Commons Vote." *CBC News*, 31 October 2012. https://www.cbc.ca/news/politics/mask-ban-bill-passes -house-of-commons-vote-1.1202553.

– "NDP Target Claude Patry with Robocalls After Defection." *CBC News*, 5 March 2013. https://www.cbc.ca/news/politics/ndp-target-claude-patry -with-robocalls-after-defection-1.1360914.

Peacock, Paige. "'She Is Very Clear About Why She Is There': Rookie MP Gazan Putting Her 'Movement' Stamp on First Year in House." *The Hill Times*, 21 December 2020. https://www.hilltimes.com/2020/12/21 /she-is-very-clear-about-why-she-is-there-rookie-mp-gazan-putting-her -movement-stamp-on-first-year-in-house/276710.

Pearson, Lester B. *Mike: The Memoirs of the Rt. Hon. Lester B. Pearson*. University of Toronto Press, 2015. https://doi.org/10.3138/9781442668638.

Pechmann, Cornelia, and David W. Stewart. "Advertising Repetition: A Critical Review of Wearin and Wearout." *Current Issues and Research in Advertising* 11, nos. 1–2 (1988): 285–329. https://doi.org/10.1080/01633392.1988.10504936.

Pelletier, Réjean, François Bundock, and Michel Sarra-Bournet. "The Structures of Canadian Political Parties: How They Operate." In *Canadian Political Parties: Leaders, Candidates and Organization*, edited by Herman Bakvis, Vol. 13 of the Royal Commission on Electoral Reform and Party Financing. Dundurn Press, 1991.

Pendakur, Ravi, and Sabrina Sarna. "Mr Speaker: The Changing Nature of Parliamentary Debates on Immigration in Canada." *Canadian Review of Sociology* 60, no. 4 (November 2023): 616–45. https://doi.org/10.1111/cars.12450.

Penner, Erin, Kelly Blidook, and Stuart Soroka. "Legislative Priorities and Public Opinion: Representation of Partisan Agendas in the Canadian House of Commons." *Journal of European Public Policy* 13, no. 7 (2006): 1006–20. https://doi.org/10.1080/1350176060023979.

Penner, Keith. "Parliament and the Private Member." *Canadian Parliamentary Review* 14, no. 2 (Summer 1991): 22–4.

Pennycook, Gordon, Jonathon McPhetres, Bence Bago, and David G. Rand. "Beliefs about COVID-19 in Canada, the United Kingdom, and the United States: A Novel Test of Political Polarization and Motivated Reasoning." *Personality and Social Psychology Bulletin* 48, no. 5 (May 2022): 750–65. https://doi .org/10.1177/01461672211023652.

Perkins, Tara. "Former Liberals Join Sask. NDP." *Globe and Mail*, 3 September 2003. https://www.theglobeandmail.com/news/national/former-liberals-join-sask-ndp /article20451017.

Perlin, George C. *The Tory Syndrome: Leadership Politics in the Progressive Conservative Party.* McGill-Queen's University Press, 1980. https://doi.org /10.1515/9780773593619.

Petit-Vouriot, Adelina, Michael Morden, and Kendall Anderson. *2019 Democracy 360: The Third Report Card on How Canadians Communicate, Participate, and Lead in Politics.* Samara Centre for Democracy, 2019.

Philbrick, Nathaniel. "Why Benedict Arnold Turned Traitor against the American Revolution." *Smithsonian Magazine*, May 2016. https://www.smithsonianmag .com/history/benedict-arnold-turned-traitor-american-revolution-180958786.

Philpott, Jane. "Navigating Party Discipline." Panel Event, Bruneau Centre for Research, Memorial University, St. John's. 6 February 2020.

Pilote, Anne-Marie, and Arnaud Montreuil. "Cracking the (Unwritten) Dress Codes." *Toronto Star*, 24 November 2019. https://www.pressreader.com /canada/toronto-star/20191124/281805695775844.

Pitkin, Hanna. *The Concept of Representation.* University of California Press, 1967.

Plante, Caroline. "Opposition Criticizes CAQ for Allowing Denis Tardif to Rejoin Caucus." *Montreal Gazette*, 14 April 2021. https://www.montreal gazette.com/news/provincial-news/article97477.html.

– "Spoiler Alert: Legault Government Inadvertently Sends Talking Points to Media." *Montreal Gazette*, 8 November 2023. https://montrealgazette.com/news/local-news /spoiler-alert-legault-government-inadvertently-sends-talking-points-to-media.

Plante, Richard. "Ça été difficile émotivement." *La voix de l'est*, 29 January 2000.

Platt, Brian. "Second Liberal MP Denounces Summer Jobs Abortion-Rights Clause, Says It Misrepresents the Charter." *National Post*, 2 April 2018. https:// nationalpost.com/news/politics/second-liberal-mp-denounces -summer-jobs-attestation-says-it-misrepresents-the-charter.

Poirier, Patricia. "Disillusioned by Mulroney Record, Tory MP Threatens to Quit Party." *Globe and Mail*, 6 April 1987.

Poitras, Jacques. "Atwin Defends Defection During Mostly Cordial Virtual Town Hall." *CBC News*, 22 July 2021. https://www.cbc.ca/news/canada/new -brunswick/jenica-atwin-green-party-fredericton-1.6112102.

– "Guns, Revenge and Floor-Crossing." *CBC News*, 6 July 2018. https://www .cbc.ca/news/canada/new-brunswick/bob-mccready-richard-hatfield-1978 -election-house-speaker-1.4735195.

"Politician Quits Over Sex Line Calls." *Toronto Star*, 22 August 1995, A12.

Pollara Strategic Insights. "Canadians' Awareness of Political Leaders." September, 2023. https://www.pollara.com/wp-content/uploads/2023/09/Pollara-Awareness-of-Politicians-Sept-2023.pdf.

"Poltext." Centre for Public Policy Analysis, Laval University, 2023. https://www.poltext.org.

Popkin, Samuel L. *The Reasoning Voter: Communication and Persuasion in Presidential Campaigns.* University of Chicago Press, 1991. https://doi.org/10.7208/chicago/9780226772875.001.0001.

Postmedia News. "Fourth PQ Member Quits Over Quebec Arena." *National Post*, 7 June 2011. https://nationalpost.com/news/canada/canadian-politics/fourth-pq-member-quits-over-quebec-arena.

– "Life After the Party: Independent MPs Free to Vote as They Please After Leaving World of 'Tribal' and Partisan Politics." *National Post*, 30 December 2013. https://nationalpost.com/news/politics/life-after-the-party-independent-mps-free-to-vote-as-they-please-after-leaving-world-of-tribal-partisan-politics.

– "Maria Mourani Joins NDP a Year after She Was Booted from Bloc Quebecois for Opposing Charter of Values." *National Post*, 19 November 2014. https://nationalpost.com/news/politics/maria-mourani-joins-ndp-more-than-a-year-after-she-was-booted-from-bloc-quebecois-for-opposing-the-charter-of-values.

Potestio, Michael. "Caputo Cancels Kamloops News Conference After Tory MPs Muzzled by Poilievre on Alberta Policy." *Castanet Kamloops*, 2 February 2024. https://www.castanetkamloops.net/news/Kamloops/470508/Caputo-cancels-Kamloops-news-conference-after-Tory-MPs-muzzled-by-Poilievre-on-Alberta-policy.

– "Kamloops MP Won't Offer Opinion on Party's Transgender Policy." *Kamloops This Week*, 12 September 2023. https://archive.kamloopsthisweek.com/2023/09/12/kamloops-mp-wont-offer-opinion-on-partys-transgender-policy/.

Pow, James T. "Amateurs Versus Professionals: Explaining the Political (In)Experience of Canadian Members of Parliament." *Parliamentary Affairs* 71, no. 3 (July 2018): 633–55. https://doi.org/10.1093/pa/gsx082.

Press Progress. "BC Liberal Riding President Resigns after Anti-LGBTQ Facebook Rants Come to Light." 10 August 2020. https://pressprogress.ca/bc-liberal-riding-president-resigns-after-anti-lgbtq-facebook-rants-come-to-light.

Prime Minister of Canada. "Delivering for Canadians Now." News release. 22 March 2022. https://www.pm.gc.ca/en/news/news-releases/2022/03/22/delivering-canadians-now.

Proudfoot, Shannon. "What You Get When Politics Becomes about Picking Fights." *Globe and Mail*, 18 January 2025. https://www.theglobeandmail.com/politics/opinion/article-what-you-get-when-politics-is-about-finding-a-face-to-punch.

Pruysers, Scott, and Julie Blais. "Narcissistic Women and Cash-Strapped Men: Who Can Be Encouraged to Consider Running for Political Office, and Who Should Do the Encouraging?" *Political Research Quarterly* 72, no. 1 (March 2019): 229–42. https://doi.org/10.1177/1065912918786040.

Pruysers, Scott, and William Cross. "'Negative' Personalization: Party Leaders and Party Strategy." *Canadian Journal of Political Science* 49, no. 3 (September 2016): 539–58. https://doi.org/10.1017/S0008423916000779.

Public Policy Forum. *Mind the Gaps: Quantifying the Decline of News Coverage in Canada*. Public Policy Forum, 2018. https://ppforum.ca/wp-content/uploads/2018/09/MindTheGaps-QuantifyingTheDeclineOfNewsCoverageInCanada-PPF-SEPT2018.pdf.

Pursaga, Joyanne. 2017. "Fletcher Kicked Out of Progressive Conservative Caucus." *Winnipeg Sun*, 30 June 2017. https://winnipegsun.com/2017/06/30/fletcher-kicked-out-of-progressive-conservative-caucus.

Puxley, Chinta. "Bryden Joins Former Foes." *Hamilton Spectator*, 26 February 2004.

Qaqqaq, Mumilaaq. "MP Mumilaaq Qaqqaq on Burnout and Taking on Canada's Broken Promises." *Refinery29*, 11 February 2021. https://www.refinery29.com/en-ca/2021/02/10252815/mp-mumilaaq-qaqqaq-burnout-anxiety.

Quinn, Herbert F. "The Third National Convention of the Liberal Party." *Canadian Journal of Economics and Political Science* 17, no. 2 (May 1951): 228–33. https://doi.org/10.2307/137784.

Rabson, Mia. "Hipster Air Flies Unfriendly Skies." *Winnipeg Free Press*, 4 April 2011. https://www.winnipegfreepress.com/local/2011/04/04/hipster-air-flies-unfriendly-skies.

– "Rocan Turfed from Caucus." *Winnipeg Free Press*, 19 April 2007.

– "Wilson-Raybould Entered Federal Politics Hoping to Be a Bridge Builder." *CTV News*, 9 February 2019. https://www.ctvnews.ca/politics/wilson-raybould-entered-federal-politics-hoping-to-be-a-bridge-builder-1.4289856.

Radio-Canada. "La fusion CAQ-ADQ entérinée par les membres de l'ADQ." *Radio-Canada*, 22 January 2012. https://ici.radio-canada.ca/nouvelle/546967/caq-adq-fusion-resultat-vote.

– "Le NPD perd un autre député au Québec." *Radio-Canada*, 20 August 2014. https://ici.radio-canada.ca/nouvelle/680981/depart-sana-hassainia-npd-quebec.

Radwanski, Adam. "Harper's Enforcer: Meet Jenni Byrne, the Most Powerful Woman in Ottawa." *Globe and Mail*, 29 May 2015. https://www.theglobeandmail.com/news/politics/meet-the-woman-driving-harpers-re-election-campaign/article24699535.

– "Meet Dean French, the Political Unknown Who Has Become an Omnipresent Force in Ford's Government." *Globe and Mail*, 16 November 2018. https://www.theglobeandmail.com/canada/article-meet-dean-french-the-political-unknown-who-has-become-an-omnipresent.

Rae, Bob. "Parting Company with the NDP." *National Post*, 16 April 2002.

Raj, Althia. "Justin Trudeau Draws in Mark Carney as Liberal MPs Gather to Consider the Coming Election." *Toronto Star*, 6 September 2024. https://www.thestar.com/politics/political-opinion/justin-trudeau-draws-in-mark-carney-as-liberal-mps-gather-to-consider-the-coming-election/article_57ffc2b2-6c80-11ef-8dff-637b7dd97719.html.

– "Liberal MPs Say Justin Trudeau Is Ignoring Them." *Toronto Star*, 30 October 2021. https://www.thestar.com/politics/political-opinion/liberal-mps-say-justin-trudeau-is-ignoring-them-the-pm-should-pay-attention/article_ddd5ba57-dcf2-5da5-8033-425877370bde.html.

– "Liberals Don't Want to Talk About Scott Simms' Punishment for Breaking Ranks." *Huffington Post Canada*, 20 April 2018. https://www.huffingtonpost.ca/2018/04/20/scott-simms-liberals-convention-halifax_a_23416456.

– "MPs Are Acting Out for One Reason – and It's the Ugly Truth Few Want to Talk About." *Toronto Star*, 30 November 2023. https://www.thestar.com

/politics/political-opinion/mps-are-acting-out-for-one-reason-and-it-s-the
-ugly-truth-few-want/article_1dfc7091-7099-5db1-8ef9-0cc07657762c.html.
– "Trudeau's Pledge of Freer Votes Embraced by Independent-Minded Liberals."
Huffington Post Canada, 28 July 2016. https://www.huffpost.com/archive/ca
/entry/nathaniel-erskine-smith-trudeau-freer-votes_n_11239876.
Ramsay, Caley. "Premier Jason Kenney Removes MLA Pat Rehn from UCP
Caucus." *Global News*, 14 January 2021. https://globalnews.ca/news/7575882
/alberta-mla-pat-rehn-removed-ucp-caucus.
Ramzy, Mark. "'Mean and Nasty – and Personal': Here's How MPs Took Insults to a
New Low in 2023." *Toronto Star*, 29 December 2023. https://www.thestar
.com/politics/federal/mean-and-nasty-and-personal-heres-how-mps-took
-insults-to-a-new-low-in/article_9df21a0e-99e0-11ee-b77a-e3f7048a53e4.html.
Rana, Abbas. "B.C. Liberal MP Aldag in Talks with Provincial NDP to Run in the
Fall Election." *The Hill Times*, 5 February 2024. https://www.hilltimes
.com/story/2024/02/05/b-c-liberal-mp-aldag-in-talks-with-b-c-ndp-to-run
-provincially-in-the-fall-election/410472.
– "Cadman Says He Would Return to Tories, Under Two Conditions." *The
Hill Times*, 25 October 2004. https://www.hilltimes.com/2004/10/25
/cadman-says-he-would-return-to-tories-under-two-conditions/4202.
– "Liberal MP McDonald Says He's Rebuffed Conservatives' Overtures Three
Times, but Won't Rule Out Crossing the Floor or Sitting as an Independent."
The Hill Times, 4 December 2023. https://www.hilltimes.com/story/2023/12/04/
grit-mp-mcdonald-has-rebuffed-tory-overtures-three-times-but-wont-rule-out-
crossing-the-floor-or-sitting-as-an-independent/404875.
– "Liberal MPs Were 'Very, Very Tough' and Gave 'Straight Goods' to Trudeau
at Caucus Meeting in London, Ont." *The Hill Times*, 25 September 2023. https://
www.hilltimes.com/story/2023/09/25/liberal-mps-were-very-very-tough
-and-gave-straight-goods-to-trudeau-at-caucus-meeting-in-london-ont
/397856/.
– "'No Difference Left Between the Liberals and the NDP' After Confidence and
Supply Agreement, Say Some Liberal MPs." *The Hill Times*, 14 November 2022.
https://www.hilltimes.com/story/2022/03/28/no-difference-left-between
-the-liberals-and-the-ndp-after-confidence-and-supply-agreement-say-some
-liberal-mps/230083.
– "PM Instructs Cabinet to Attend All Caucus Meetings, Tells Grit Caucus Any
Communications from Butts, Telford Should Be Considered as Coming from
Him." *The Hill Times*, 7 December 2015. https://www.hilltimes.com/story
/2015/12/07/pm-instructs-cabinet-to-attend-all-caucus-meetings-tells-grit
-caucus-any-communications-from-butts-telford-should-be-considered-as
-coming-from-him/252038/.
– "PMO Staffers No Longer Allowed Inside National Liberal Caucus Meetings,
say Liberal MPs." *The Hill Times*, 5 June 2025. https://www.hilltimes.com/
story/2025/06/09/pmo-staffers-no-longer-permitted-to-attend-national-liberal-
caucus-meetings-say-liberal-mps/463091.
– "Some Backbench Liberal MPs 'Livid' with Trudeau's Cabinet Shuffle, Say PMO
'Couldn't Have Done a Better Job at Undermining Caucus Morale.'" *The Hill
Times*, 7 August 2023. https://www.hilltimes.com/story/2023/08/07
/im-so-pissed-off-some-backbench-liberal-mps-livid-with-trudeaus-cabinet
-shuffle-saying-pmo-couldnt-have-done-a-better-job-at-undermining
-caucus-mor/394422.

– "Upcoming Montreal Byelection Will Be 'a Pretty Important Stay-or-Go Indicator' for PM Trudeau, Say Political Insiders and MPs." *The Hill Times*, 10 July 2024. https://www.hilltimes.com/story/2024/07/10/the-upcoming -montreal-byelection-will-be-a-pretty-important-stay-or-go-indicator-for -pm-trudeau-say-political-insiders-and-mps/427765/.

Rana, Abbas, and Jesse Cnockaert. "Hybrid House Sittings Will Further Boost PMO and Opposition Leaders' Control Over Backbench MPs, Says Former Grit Cabinet Minister Easter." *The Hill Times*, 19 June 2023. https://www.hilltimes .com/story/2023/06/19/permanent-hybrid-sittings-will-further-boost-the -pmo-and-opposition-leaders-control-over-backbench-mps-says-former -liberal-mp-easter/390510/.

Rana, Abbas, and Mike Lapointe. "Oliphant's Leaked Private Conversation Could Have a 'Chilling Effect' on MP-Constituent Relationships, Say Some Liberal MPs." *The Hill Times*, 26 February 2024. https://www.hilltimes.com /story/2024/02/26/oliphants-leaked-private-conversation-with-a-constituent -to-have-a-chilling-effect-on-mp-constituent-relationships-say -some-liberal-mps/412760/ .

Raney, Tracey, and Cheryl N. Collier, eds. *Gender-Based Violence in Canadian Politics in the #MeToo Era*. University of Toronto Press, 2024. https://utppublishing.com/ doi/book/10.3138/9781487540029.

Rathgeber, Brent. *Irresponsible Government: The Decline of Parliamentary Democracy in Canada*. Dundurn Press, 2014.

Rathje, Steve, Jay J. Van Bave, and Sander van der Linden. "Out-Group Animosity Drives Engagement on Social Media." *Psychological and Cognitive Sciences* 118, no. 26 (2023): 1–9. https://doi.org/10.1073/pnas.2024292118.

Raven, Bertram H., and John R.P. French. "Legitimate Power, Coercive Power, and Observability in Social Influence." *Sociometry* 21, no. 2 (June 1958): 83–97. https://doi.org/10.2307/2785895.

Rayside, David. *On the Fringe: Gays and Lesbians in Politics*. Cornell University Press, 1998. https://doi.org/10.7591/9781501729638.

The Record. "Sexual Orientation Shouldn't Be Included [in] Hate Law." *The Record*, 7 June 2004.

Redmond, William. "Voluntary Ceding of Control: Why Do People Join?" *Journal of Economic Issues* 42, no. 3 (2016): 695–707. https://doi.org/10.1080/00213624.2008 .11507174.

Reevely, David. "Why the Progressive Conservatives Need to Crush Jack MacLaren Now." *Ottawa Citizen*, 30 May 2017. https://ottawacitizen.com /news/local-news/reevely-why-the-progressive-conservatives-need-to -crush-jack-maclaren-now.

Reform Party of Canada. *Blue Book: 1996–1997 Principles & Policies of the Reform Party of Canada*. Reform Party of Canada, 1996.

Regan, Geoff. "Special Meeting of the Canadian NATO Parliamentary Association." 6 November 2018. Selected Decisions of Speaker Geoff Regan. Clerk of the House of Commons, 2022.

Rehmert, Jochen. "Party Membership, Pre-Parliamentary Socialization and Party Cohesion." *Party Politics* 28, no. 6 (November 2022): 1081–93. https://doi .org/10.1177/13540688211039088.

Reid, John. "Evidence – Standing Committee on Natural Resources and Government Operations." Canada. Parliament. House of Commons. *Edited Hansard* 36(1). 36th Parliament, 4 June 1998.

– "The Honourable John Reid in an Interview with Tom Earle." Oral History Project, Library of Parliament, National Archives of Canada, 1 April 1986.

Rempel Garner, Michelle. "I Just Made a Big Decision." Blog post, 23 June 2022. https://michellerempelgarner.substack.com/p/i-just-made-a-big-decision.

– "Liberal Silence on MP's Alleged #metoo Misdeeds Is Troubling." *National Post*, 26 June 2020. https://nationalpost.com/opinion/michelle-rempel-garner-liberal -silence-on-mps-alleged-metoo-misdeeds-is-troubling.

Rempel Garner, Michelle, Blake Richards, Glen Motz, and Arnold Viersen. "The Buffalo Declaration." 20 February 2020. https://buffalodeclaration.com/the -buffalo-declaration.

"Renegade Grit Welcomed Back." *The Times and Transcript* (Moncton), 30 January 1998.

Rennstam, Jens. "Object-Control: A Study of Technologically Dense Knowledge Work." *Organizational Studies* 33, no. 8 (August 2012): 1071–90. https://doi .org/10.1177/0170840612453527.

Reuters. "Canadian Opposition MP Defects to Quebec Separatists." *Reuters*, 28 February 2013. https://www.reuters.com/article/canada-us-canada-politics -separatists-idCABRE91R18X20130228.

Richer, Jocelyne. "La députée de la CAQ Claire Samson songe à démissionner." *La Presse*, 25 October 2018. https://www.lapresse.ca/actualites/politique /politique-quebecoise/201810/25/01-5201741-la-deputee-de-la-caq-claire -samson-songe-a-demissionner.php.

– "Le député Frantz Benjamin menace de quitter le caucus." *La Presse*, 14 November 2022. https://www.lapresse.ca/actualites/politique/2022-11-14 /parti-liberal-du-quebec/le-depute-frantz-benjamin-menace-de-quitter-le -caucus.php.

Richler, Noah. *The Candidate: Fear and Loathing on the Campaign Trail*. Doubleday Canada, 2016.

Rivard, Alex B., Jean-François Godbout, and Marc André Bodet. "Political Dynasties in Canada." *Government & Opposition* 60, no. 2 (April 2025): 456–76. https://doi.org/10.1017/gov.2024.11.

Robbins-Kanter, Jacob. "Canadian Parties in the Constituencies." In *Canadian Parties in Transition*, 5th ed., edited by Alain-G. Gagnon and A. Brian Tanguay. Toronto: University of Toronto Press, 2024.

– "Undisciplined Constituency Campaign Behaviour in Canadian Federal Elections." *Canadian Journal of Political Science* 55, no. 2 (June 2022): 444–66. https://doi.org/10.1017/S0008423922000282.

Robbins-Kanter, Jacob, and Andrew Mattan. "Recruiting Brand Ambassadors through Candidate Selection." In *Political Marketing in a Canadian Election*, edited by Alex Marland, Thierry Giasson, and Elizabeth Dubois. UBC Press, forthcoming.

Roberts, David. "Bitter Liberal Leader Quits." *Globe and Mail*, 13 November 1995.

Robertson, Dylan. "Liberal MP Decries 'Political Games' over Criticism of Conservatives on Ukraine." *CBC News*, 21 March 2024. https://www.cbc.ca /news/politics/oliphant-political-games-ukraine-1.7151205.

Robertson, James R. "Political Parties and Parliamentary Recognition." Library of Parliament, 1996. https://publications.gc.ca/Collection-R/LoPBdP/BP/bp243 -e.htm.

Robitaille, Antoine. "La CAQ aidera la souveraineté, croit Rebello." *Le Devoir*, 10 January 2012. https://www.ledevoir.com/politique/quebec/339939 /la-caq-aidera-la-souverainete-croit-rebello.

Robson, Jennifer. "Spending on Political Staffers and the Revealed Preferences of Cabinet: Examining a New Data Source on Federal Political Staff in Canada." *Canadian Journal of Political Science* 48, no. 3 (September 2015): 675–97. https://doi.org/10.1017/S0008423915000529.

Roche, Pat. "Newfoundland Oil Deal Converts Grit to a Tory." *Globe and Mail*, 21 February 1985.

Rodon, Thierry, ed. *Teach an Eskimo How to Read … Conversations with Peter Freuchen Ittinuar*. Nunavut Arctic College, 2008.

Rodriguez, Michael, Stefanie Boyer, David Fleming, and Scott Cohen. "Managing the Next Generation of Sales, Gen Z/Millennial Cusp: An Exploration of Grit, Entrepreneurship, and Loyalty." *Journal of Business-to-Business Marketing* 26, no. 1 (2019): 43–55. https://doi.org/10.1080/1051712X.2019.1565136.

Ross, Howard. "Chrétien Advises Two-Year Constitutional Hiatus." *Globe and Mail*, 25 June 1990.

Rowe, William. *Is That You Bill?* Jesperson Press, 1989.

Roy, Jason, and Christopher Alcantara. "The Candidate Effect: Does the Local Candidate Matter?" *Journal of Elections, Public Opinion and Parties* 25, no. 2 (2015): 195–214. https://doi.org/10.1080/17457289.2014.925461.

Roziere, Brendan. "Reconsidering Bill 4 – *The Legislative Assembly Amendment Act (Member Changing Parties)*: Finding a Balanced Approach to Floor Crossing in Manitoba." *Manitoba Law Journal* 42, no. 1 (2019): 73–104. https://doi.org/10.29173/mlj1138.

Ruimy, Joel. "Kwinter Wins Riding Nomination." *Toronto Star*, 8 March 1999.

Rupert, Jake. "Guilty MPP Kicked Out of Caucus After Lie to Police: Claudette Boyer, Husband, Not Honest About Van Accident." *Ottawa Citizen*, 27 March 2001.

Rusbult, Caryl E., and Isabella M. Zembrodt. "Responses to Dissatisfaction in Romantic Involvements: A Multidimensional Scaling Analysis." *Journal of Experimental Psychology* 19, no. 3 (May 1983): 274–93. https://doi.org/10.1016/0022-1031(83)90042-2.

Rusbult, Caryl E., Isabella M. Zembrodt, and Lawanna K. Gunn. "Exit, Voice, and Neglect: Responses to Dissatisfaction in Romantic Involvements." *Journal of Personality and Social Psychology* 43, no. 6 (December 1982): 1230–42. https://doi.org/10.1037//0022-3514.43.6.1230.

Rushowy, Kristin. "Doug Ford Removes MPP Goldie Ghamari from Caucus after She Met with British Far-Right Figure." *Toronto Star*, 28 June 2024. https://www.thestar.com/politics/provincial/doug-ford-removes-mpp-goldie-ghamari-from-caucus-after-she-met-with-british-far-right/article_ff7892ee-3553-11ef-9ccf-e38438079e05.html.

Rusnell, Charles. "Alberta Premier Jason Kenney Denies Call for Health Minister's Resignation Over Bullying Allegations." *CBC News*, 27 March 2023. https://www.cbc.ca/news/canada/edmonton/alberta-premier-jason-kenney-denies-call-for-health-minister-s-resignation-over-bullying-allegations-1.5512897.

– "The Bully Who Haunts Alberta's Election." *The Tyee*, 17 May 2023. https://thetyee.ca/News/2023/05/17/Bully-Haunting-Alberta-Election.

Rusnell, Charles, and Jennie Russell. "Inside the Kenney Government's System of Secrecy." *The Tyee*, 9 May 2022. https://thetyee.ca/News/2022/05/09/Inside-Kenney-Government-System-Secrecy.

Russell, George. "Former Liberal MP Jewett Joins NDP Ranks." *Globe and Mail*, 12 April 1972.

Russell, Meg. "Parliamentary Party Cohesion: Some Explanations from Psychology." *Party Politics* 20, no. 5 (September 2014): 712–23. https://doi.org /10.1177/1354068812453367.

Safire, William. "The Maverick Ticket." *The New York Times*, 6 September 2008. https://www.nytimes.com/2008/09/07/opinion/07safire.html.

Sallot, Jeff. "No Cabinet Promise, Colorful NDP Defector Says." *Globe and Mail*, 27 November 1982.

Saltwire Network. "Cape Breton Political Icon MacEwan Dies." *The Chronicle-Herald*, 4 May 2017.

Sanders, Carol. "Former Tory MLA Sues over Information Request." *The Free Press*, 28 December 2022. https://www.winnipegfreepress.com /breakingnews/2022/12/28/former-tory-mla-sues-over-information-request.

Sarkonak, Jamie. "The Revenge of Caylan Ford after Hit Job Ended Her Political Career." *National Post*, 10 April 2023. https://nationalpost.com/opinion /jamie-sarkonak-the-revenge-of-caylan-ford-after-hit-job-ended-her-political -career.

"Saskatchewan Grits Turf Maverick MLA." *Calgary Herald*, 21 December 1984, A6.

Saunders, Elizabeth N. "Leaders, Advisors, and the Political Origins of Elite Support for War." *Journal of Conflict Resolution* 62, no. 10 (November 2018): 2118–49. https://doi.org/10.1177/0022002718785670.

Savoie, Donald. *Governing From the Centre: The Concentration of Power in Canadian Politics*. University of Toronto Press, 1999. https://doi.org/10.3138 /9781442675445.

Sayers, Anthony M. *Parties, Candidates, and Constituency Campaigns in Canadian Elections*. UBC Press, 1999.

Scammell, Margaret. "Populism and Political Marketing: Is the Discipline Still Relevant?" *International Journal of Market Research* 67, nos. 2–3 (March/May 2025): 242–60. https://doi.org/10.1177/14707853241309765.

Schlesinger, Joseph A. *Ambition and Politics: Political Careers in the United States*. Rand McNally, 1966.

Schneider, Katie. "Alberta MLA Len Webber Leaves Tory Caucus to Sit as Independent." *Edmonton Sun*, 13 March 2014. https://edmontonsun .com/2014/03/13/alberta-mla-len-webber-leaves-tory-caucus-to-sit-as -independent/wcm/90ddd876-df39-400b-8e01-d2022191cb5e.

Schumpeter, Joseph A. *Capitalism, Socialism, and Democracy*. Harper & Row, 1962.

Schwartz, Mildred, and Raymond Tatalovich. *The Rise and Fall of Moral Conflicts in the United States and Canada*. University of Toronto Press, 2018. https://doi .org/10.3138/9781442625044.

Scotti, Adam. "Prime Minister Justin Trudeau: A Photographic Year in Review." *Medium* (photo blog), 20 December 2020. https://cdnadamscotti.medium.com /https-medium-com-adamscotti-2020review-f79cf106104e.

Selley, Chris. "It's Up to Voters to Discipline Sarah Jama, Not the Ontario Legislature." *National Post*, 25 October 2023. https://nationalpost.com/opinion/chris-selley -up-to-voters-discipline-sarah-jama-not-ontario-legislature.

Sevi, Semra. "The Incumbency Advantage in Canadian Elections." *Canadian Journal of Political Science* 58, no. 2 (June 2025): 394–407. https://doi.org/10.1017 /S0008423925000058.

Sevi, Semra, Marco Mendoza Aviña, and André Blais. "Reassessing Local Candidate Effects." *Canadian Journal of Political Science* 55, no. 2 (June 2022): 480–5. https://doi.org/10.1017/S000842392200004X.

Sevi, Semra, Antoine Yoshinaka, and André Blais. "Legislative Party Switching and the Changing Nature of the Canadian Party System, 1867–2015." *Canadian Journal of Political Science* 51, no. 3 (September 2018): 665–95. https://doi.org/10.1017/S0008423918000203.

Shackleton, Doris F. *Tommy Douglas.* McClelland and Stewart, 1975.

Shah, Maryam. "Ex-NDP MP Wants to Run for Provincial Liberals." *Toronto Sun,* 23 April 2016. https://torontosun.com/2016/04/23/ex-ndp-mp-wants-to-run-for-provincial-liberals.

Shapiro, Bernard J. *The Grewal-Dosanjh Inquiry.* Office of the Ethics Commissioner, 2006. https://ciec-ccie.parl.gc.ca/en/investigations-enquetes/Pages/GrewalDosanjhInquiry.aspx.

Shaw, Rob, and Richard Zussman. *A Matter of Confidence: The Inside Story of the Political Battle for BC.* Heritage House, 2018.

Sheppard, Sarah Jane. "Secrets of a Trailblazer." *Newfoundland Herald,* 3 November 2013.

Shipp, Abbie J., Stacie Furst-Holloway, T. Brad Harris, and Benson Rosen. "Gone Today but Here Tomorrow: Extending the Unfolding Model of Turnover to Consider Boomerang Employees." *Personnel Psychology* 67, no. 2 (Summer 2014): 421–62. https://doi.org/10.1111/peps.12039.

Shuttleworth, Joanne. "Integrity Commissioner: VanLeeuwen Did Not Contravene Code of Conduct When He Joined the End the Lockdowns Caucus." *Wellington Advertiser,* 26 August 2021. https://www.wellingtonadvertiser.com/integrity-commissioner-vanleeuwen-did-not-contravene-code-of-conduct-when-he-joined-the-end-the-lockdowns-caucus-last-year.

Sibley, Robert. "Spotlight on Ray Novak, PMO Chief Who Lived above Harper's Garage." *Ottawa Citizen,* 18 August 2015. https://ottawacitizen.com/news/politics/spotlight-on-ray-novak-pmo-chief-who-lived-above-harpers-garage.

Sieberer, Ulrich. "Party Unity in Parliamentary Democracies: A Comparative Analysis." *The Journal of Legislative Studies* 12, no. 2 (2006): 150–78. https://doi.org/10.1080/13572330600739413.

Simes, Jeremy. "Day 1 as Saskatchewan United Party Leader, Nadine Wilson Asks about Vaccine Injuries." *Regina Leader-Post,* 1 December 2022. https://leaderpost.com/news/saskatchewan/saskatchewan-united-party-becomes-official-nadine-wilson-named-leader.

Simpson, Jeffrey. *Discipline of Power: The Conservative Interlude and the Liberal Restoration.* University of Toronto Press, 1996.

– *The Friendly Dictatorship.* McClelland and Stewart, 2001.

Small, Tamara A., and Jane Philpott. "The Independent Candidate." In *Inside the Campaign: Managing Elections in Canada,* edited by Alex Marland and Thierry Giasson. UBC Press, 2020. https://doi.org/10.59962/9780774864688-018.

Smith, Alison. *The Standing Committee System and How Members of Parliament View Its Work.* Institute on Governance, 2011. https://www.files.ethz.ch/isn/126489/The%20Standing%20Committee%20System.pdf.

Smith, Amy. "Disgruntled Boudreau Resigns from Grit caucus." *Halifax Herald,* 3 April 2003.

– "MacKinnon, Liberals Part Ways." *Chronicle Herald,* 2 April 2005.

Smith, Joanna. "Liberal MPs to Blitz Home Ridings in Campaign to Spread Accomplishments." *Toronto Star,* 12 November 2017. https://www.thestar.com/news/canada/liberal-mps-to-blitz-home-ridings-in-campaign-to-spread-accomplishments/article_485c8139-49ca-55be-b2df-7df729caf531.html.

– "Rookie MPs in Ottawa for a Crash Course on Being a Parliamentarian." *CBC News*, 29 October 2019. https://www.cbc.ca/news/politics/mp-federal-election-2019-orientation-1.5340239.

Smith, Madeline. "Liberal MP George Chahal Doesn't Make Cabinet, Despite Expectations." *Calgary Herald*, 26 October 2021. https://calgaryherald.com/news/politics/liberal-mp-george-chahal-doesnt-make-cabinet-despite-expectations.

Smith, Marie-Danielle. "The Pandemic Puts Parliament's Stuffy Men's Dress Code to the Test." *Maclean's*, 15 April 2021. https://macleans.ca/politics/the-pandemic-puts-parliaments-stuffy-mens-dress-code-to-the-test.

Smyth, David. "Maybe You'd Be Mad, Too." *The Province*, 12 January 2001.

Smyth, Julie. "Recliners and Decliners in the Seats of Power: Where MPs Sit Important." *National Post*, 4 April 2006.

– "Why Are Divorce Rates So High for MPs?" *Maclean's*, 30 October 2013. https://macleans.ca/news/canada/why-are-divorce-rates-so-high-for-mps.

Smyth, Michael. "'I Got to My Car … Then the Tears Started.'" *The Province*, 21 March 2004.

– "They're Out to Get Me, Says Dalton." *The Province*, 18 January 2001.

– "Toying with Our Time and Money." *The Province*, 11 July 1997.

Snagovsky, Feodor, and Matthew Kerby. "The Electoral Consequences of Party Switching in Canada: 1945–2011." *Canadian Journal of Political Science* 51, no. 2 (June 2018): 425–45. https://doi.org/10.1017/S0008423917001445.

Sorbara, Pat. *Let 'Em Howl: Lessons from a Life in Backroom Politics*. Nightwood Editions, 2019.

Soroka, Stuart. "Issue Attributes and Agenda Setting by Media, the Public, and Policymakers in Canada." *International Journal of Public Opinion Research* 14, no. 3 (September 2002): 264–85. https://doi.org/10.1093/ijpor/14.3.264.

Southam Newspapers. "Liberal MPP Defects to Tories." *The Standard*, 6 May 1999.

Sozzi, Fabio. "Rebels in Parliament: The Effects of Candidate Selection Methods on Legislative Behaviours." *Parliamentary Affairs* 76, no. 2 (April 2023): 341–59. https://doi.org/10.1093/pa/gsab056.

Spencer, Larry D. *Sacrificed? Truth or Politics*. KayteeBella Productions, 2006.

Starke, Richard. "The Rise of Partisanship and How It Paralyses Parliaments." *Canadian Parliamentary Review* 41, no. 2 (Summer 2018): 2–7.

Starr, Katharine. "Defeated MP Peter Stoffer Packs Up Eccentric Parliament Hill Office after 18 Years." *CBC News*, 27 October 2015. https://www.cbc.ca/news/politics/ex-mp-peter-stoffer-reflects-on-parliament-hill-career-1.3290996.

Statistics Canada. "Census Profile. 2021 Census of Population." Statistics Canada Catalogue no. 98–316-X2021001. 29 March 2023. https://www12.statcan.gc.ca/census-recensement/2021/dp-pd/prof/index.cfm?Lang=E.

– "Household Internet Use Survey." *The Daily* (newsletter), 8 July 2004. http://www.statcan.gc.ca/daily-quotidien/040708/dq040708a-eng.htm.

– "Smartphone Personal Use and Selected Smartphone Habits by Gender and Age Group." 22 June 2021. https://www150.statcan.gc.ca/t1/tbl1/en/tv.action?pid=2210014301.

Steele, Graham. *What I Learned About Politics: Inside the Rise – and Collapse – of Nova Scotia's NDP Government*. Nimbus, 2014.

Steenackers, Kelly, and Marie-Anne Guerry. "Determinants of Job-Hopping: An Empirical Study in Belgium." *International Journal of Manpower* 37, no. 3 (2016): 494–510. https://doi.org/10.1108/IJM-09-2014-0184.

Stefanovich, Olivia. "Atlantic Liberal MPs Press Trudeau for Rural Carbon Tax Carve-out." *CBC News*, 15 September 2023. https://www.cbc.ca/news /politics/liberal-atlantic-mps-pitches-carbon-tax-rural-carve-out-1.6966939.

– "Spooked by Polls, Liberal MPs Hope Trudeau Hears Their Concerns as Caucus Gathers." *CBC News*, 12 September 2023. https://www.cbc.ca/news/politics /liberal-caucus-retreat-london-mps-concerns-1.6963135.

– "Supreme Court of Canada Upholds Genetic Non-discrimination Law." *CBC News*, 10 July 2020. https://www.cbc.ca/news/politics /stefanovich-supreme-court-of-canada-genetic-information-1.5643245.

Stefanovich, Olivia, Christina Romualdo, and David Thurton. "Some NDP Members Call on Party to Stop Clawing Back Campaign Rebate Cash." *CBC News*, 10 April 2021. https://www.cbc.ca/news/politics/federal-ndp-finances -elections-canada-rebates-decision-1.5979926.

Stephens, Robert. "Ontario MPP Crosses Floor to Join Tories." *Globe and Mail*, 23 May 1984.

Stevens, Benjamin Allen, Md Mujahedul Islam, Roosmarijn de Geus, Jonah Goldberg, John R. McAndrews, Alex Mierke-Zatwarnicki, Peter John Loewen, and Daniel Rubenson. "Local Candidate Effects in Canadian Elections." *Canadian Journal of Political Science* 52, no. 1 (March 2019): 83–96. https://doi .org/10.1017/S0008423918000367.

Stevenson, Mark. "Defection Trips Up Liberals." *Ottawa Citizen*, 6 May 1999.

Stewart, David K., and Ronald K. Carty. "Many Political Worlds? Provincial Parties and Party Systems." In *Provinces: Canadian Provincial Politics*, 2nd ed., edited by Christopher Dunn. Broadview, 2006.

Stewart, David K., and Anthony Sayers. "Barbarians at the Gate? Conservative Identifiers and the Myths of Brokerage Politics." In *Parties and Party Systems: Structure and Context*, edited by Richard Johnston and Campbell Sharman. UBC Press, 2015. https://doi.org/10.59962/9780774829571-006.

Stewart, Ian. *Just One Vote: From Jim Walding's Nomination to Constitutional Defeat.* University of Manitoba Press, 2009. https://doi.org/10.1515/9780887553325.

– *Politics on the Edge: The Remarkable Career of Paul MacEwan*. CBU Press, 2022.

Stewart, Rory. *How Not to be a Politician*. Penguin Press, 2023.

Stiles, Marit. "My Statement from This Morning." X (post), 23 October 2023. https://twitter.com/MaritStiles/status/1716481751227208190 (post has since been deleted.)

Stokes Sullivan, Deana. "MHA Disciplined for Crab Comments." *The Telegram*, 8 February 2005.

Stone, Laura. "Conservative MP Who Set Off Backbench Revolt Finally Set to Speak about Abortion." *Global News*, 7 May 2013. https://globalnews.ca /news/540917/conservative-mp-who-set-off-backbench-revolt-finally-set -to-speak-about-abortion.

– "Doug Ford Confirms Former Minister Jim Wilson Resigned over Sexual-misconduct Allegations." *Globe and Mail*, 7 November 2018. https:// www.theglobeandmail.com/politics/article-doug-ford-admits-former -minster-jim-wilson-resigned-over-sexual.

– "NDP Leader Jagmeet Singh Backs Down from Decision to Punish MP after Outcry from Caucus." *Globe and Mail*, 28 March 2018. https://www .theglobeandmail.com/politics/article-ndp-mp-criticizes-leader-singhs -punishment-of-fellow-new-democrat.

– "Tory Pit Bull Poilievre Looks for 'Vulnerability' in Attacks on Morneau." *Globe and Mail*, 17 November 2017. https://www.theglobeandmail.com/news

/politics/tory-pit-bull-poilievre-looks-for-vulnerability-in-attacks-on-morneau
/article37023077.

Stone, Laura, and Jill Mahoney. "Ontario Premier Doug Ford's Chief of Staff
Resigns Amid Appointment Controversy." *Globe and Mail*, 21 June 2019. https://
www.theglobeandmail.com/politics/article-premier-ford-revokes-two-new
-appointments-after-personal-ties-to-chief.

Strahl, Chuck. "Advice to My Son, the New MP." *Globe and Mail*, 2 June 2011.
https://www.theglobeandmail.com/opinion/advice-to-my-son-the-new
-mp/article581820.

Strøm, Kaare, and Wolfgang Mueller. *Policy, Office or Votes? How Political Parties in
Western Europe Make Hard Decisions*. Cambridge University Press, 1999.

Strömbäck, Jesper, and Peter Van Aelst. "Why Political Parties Adapt to the
Media: Exploring the Fourth Dimension of Mediatization." *The International
Communication Gazette* 75, no. 4 (June 2013): 341–58. https://doi.org/10.1177
/1748048513482266.

Strong-Boag, Veronica. *A Liberal-Labour Lady: The Times and Life of Mary Ellen Spear
Smith*. UBC Press, 2021. https://doi.org/10.59962/9780774867269.

Sturgeon, Nathalie, and Alex Cooke. "People's Alliance Leader Kris Austin Steps
Down, Joins N.B. Progressive Conservatives." *Global News*, 30 March 2022.
https://globalnews.ca/news/8721876/kris-austin-steps-down-progressive
-conservatives.

Sullivan, J.M. "Rick Woodford, Politician 1947–2006." *Globe and Mail*, 23 May 2006.

Sullivan, Philip J., and Deborah L. Feltz. "The Relationship Between Intrateam
Conflict and Cohesion Within Hockey Teams." *Small Group Research* 32, no. 3
(June 2001): 342–55. https://doi.org/10.1177/104649640103200304.

Surette, Ralph. "The New Democrats Appeared to Be Winning Friends Until
Their Internal Problems Got the Best of Them." *Globe and Mail*, 13 September
1980.

Swann, William B., Jr., Ángel Gómez, D. Conor Seyle, J. Francisco Morales, and
Carmen Huici. "Identity Fusion: The Interplay of Personal and Social Identities
in Extreme Group Behavior." *Journal of Personality and Social Psychology* 96, no. 5
(May 2009): 995–1011. https://doi.org/10.1037/a0013668.

Taber, Jane. "The 10 Most Irritating Politicians of 2009." *Globe and Mail*,
17 December 2009. http://www.theglobeandmail.com/news/politics
/ottawa-notebook/the-10-most-irritating-politicians-of-2009/article794098.

– "Confident Rookie MP One of a New Breed of Tory Women." *Globe and Mail*,
9 December 2011. https://www.theglobeandmail.com/news/politics
/ottawa-notebook/confident-rookie-mp-one-of-a-new-breed-of-tory
-women/article619942.

– "Martin Faces Backlash over PMO Powers." *Globe and Mail*, 25 August
2004. https://www.theglobeandmail.com/news/national/martin-faces
-backlash-over-pmo-powers/article4123999/.

– "Praising 'High Standard' of Conduct, Joe Clark Backs Scott Brison." *Globe and Mail*,
26 April 2011. https://www.theglobeandmail.com/news/politics/ottawa
-notebook/praising-high-standard-of-conduct-joe-clark-backs-scott-brison
/article613820.

– "Tories Scramble after MP Brags of Denying Funding to Family-planning
Group." *Globe and Mail*, 22 April 2011. https://www.theglobeandmail
.com/news/politics/tories-scramble-after-mp-brags-of-denying-funding
-to-family-planning-group/article577331/

Tanner, Adrienne. "New Democrats See Gain in Grit's Jump." *Medicine Hat News,*
   12 December 1994.
Taras, David. *Digital Mosaic: Media, Power, and Identity in Canada.* University of
   Toronto Press, 2015.
Tasker, John Paul. "Liberal Backbenchers Defy Cabinet Wishes and Vote to Enact
   Genetic Discrimination Law." *CBC News,* 8 March 2017. https://www
   .cbc.ca/news/politics/genetic-testing-bill-vote-wednesday-1.4015863.
– "Speaker Kicks Poilievre Out of the Commons after He Calls PM a 'Wacko' in
   Tense Question Period Exchange." *CBC News,* 30 April 2024. https://www.cbc
   .ca/news/politics/poilievre-trudeau-whacko-1.7189600.
Tavits, Margit. "The Making of Mavericks: Local Loyalties and Party Defection."
   Comparative Political Studies 42, no. 6 (June 2009): 793–815. https://doi.org
   /10.1177/0010414008329900.
Taylor, Stephanie. "Conservative MPs Told Not to Talk to Media, Post about
   'Parental Rights' Protests." *Toronto Star,* 20 September 2023. https://www
   .thestar.com/politics/conservative-mps-told-not-to-talk-to-media-post-about
   -parental-rights-protests/article_a2372aa5-2031-540b-b556-8fd9e848ff24.html.
– "Independent Toronto MP Kevin Vuong Asks Poilievre to Let Him Join
   Conservative Caucus." *Global News,* 24 May 2024. https://globalnews.ca
   /news/10522975/toronto-mp-kevin-vuong-asks-to-join-conservative-caucus.
Theodore, Terri. "Clark Welcomes MLA Blair Lekstrom Back to Caucus." *Daily
   Bulletin* (Kimberley, BC), 3 March 2011, 2.
Thomas, Don. "Gesell Runs as Independent after Losing Tory Nomination."
   Edmonton Journal, 27 May 1993.
Thomas, Melanee, and Amanda Bittner, eds. *Mothers and Others: The Role of
   Parenthood in Politics.* UBC Press, 2018. https://doi.org/10.59962/9780774834605.
Thomas, Paul E.J., and J.P. Lewis. "Executive Creep in Canadian Provincial
   Legislatures." *Canadian Journal of Political Science* 52, no. 2 (June 2019):
   363–83. https://doi.org/10.1017/S0008423918000781.
Thomas, Paul E.J., and Michael Morden. *Party Favours: How Federal Election
   Candidates Are Chosen.* The *Samara Centre for Democracy,* 2019. https://www
   .samaracentre.ca/articles/party-favours.
Thomas, Paul E.J., Adelina Petit-Vouriot, and Michael Morden. "House Inspection:
   A Retrospective of the 42nd Parliament." *The Samara Centre for Democracy,*
   20 January 2020. https://www.samaracentre.ca/articles/house-inspection.
Thomas, Paul E.J., and Jerald Sabin. "Candidate Messaging on Religious Issues in
   the 2016–17 Conservative Party of Canada Leadership Race." *Canadian Journal
   of Political Science* 52, no. 4 (December 2019): 801–23. https://doi.org/10.1017
   /S0008423919000246.
Thomas, Paul G. "Developing Better Political Leaders." *Canadian Parliamentary
   Review* 32, no. 3 (2009): 2–4.
– "The Role of National Party Caucuses." In *Party Government and Regional
   Representation in Canada,* edited by Peter Aucoin. University of Toronto Press,
   1985.
Thompson, Allan. "Mounting a Local Campaign." In *The Canadian Federal
   Election of 2015,* edited by Jon H. Pammett and Christopher Dornan. Dundurn
   Press, 2016.
Thompson, John B. *Political Scandal: Power and Disability in the Media Age.* Polity,
   2001.
Thomson, Graham. "What Will Jason Kenney's Outspoken UCP Caucus
   Mutineers Do Should He Win the Leadership Vote?" *CBC News,* 5 May 2022.

https://www.cbc.ca/news/canada/edmonton/what-will-jason-kenney
-s-outspoken-ucp-caucus-mutineers-do-should-he-win-the-leadership
-vote-1.6441858.

Thomson, Stuart. "Liberal MP Nathaniel Erskine-Smith: Free-spirited Maverick
or Savvy Political Operator?" *National Post*, 23 August 2019. https://nationalpost
.com/news/politics/liberal-mp-nathaniel-erskine
-smith-free-spirited-maverick-or-savvy-political-operator.

– "Truth: Political Leaders Lie because It Can Be Good for Their Careers."
National Post, 21 March 2024. https://nationalpost.com/feature/truths-about
-why-politicians-lie.

Thorburn, Hugh G. "Parliament and Policy-Making: The Case of the Trans-
Canada Gas Pipeline." *Canadian Journal of Economics and Political Science* 23, no. 4
(February 1957): 516–31. https://doi.org/10.2307/139017.

Tobin, Chuck. "Fentie Deserts NDP in Mid-session." *Whitehorse Star*, 7 May 2002.

– "Liberals Beckoned Fentie to Cabinet." *Whitehorse Star*, 2 May 2002.

Todd, Peggy. "Throwback: Saskatchewan Party Formed." *SaskToday*,
13 August 2017. https://www.sasktoday.ca/north/local-news/throwback
-saskatchewan-party-formed-gantefoer-considers-running-for-leader-4110378.

Tolley, Erin. *Framed: Media and the Coverage of Race in Canadian Politics*. UBC Press,
2015. https://doi.org/10.59962/9780774831253.

– "Who You Know: Local Party Presidents and Minority Candidate Emergence."
Electoral Studies 58 (April 2019): 70–9. https://doi.org/10.1016/j.electstud
.2019.02.007.

Topp, Brian. *How We Almost Gave the Tories the Boot: The Inside Story Behind the
Coalition*. Lorimer, 2010.

Tran, Paula. "UCP MLA Slammed for Participating in 'Illegal' Anti-mandate
Protest in Southern Alberta." *Global News*, 31 January 2022. https://globalnews
.ca/news/8583191/ucp-mla-grant-hunter-truck-protest-criticism.

Travaglino, Giovanni A., Dominic Abrams, Georgina Randsley de Moura, José M.
Marques, and Isabel R. Pinto. "How Groups React to Disloyalty in the Context
of Intergroup Competition: Evaluations of Group Deserters and Defectors."
Journal of Experimental Social Psychology 54 (September 2014): 178–87. https://doi
.org/10.1016/j.jesp.2014.05.006.

Tremblay, Manon. "Do Female MPs Substantively Represent Women? A Study of
Legislative Behaviour in Canada's 35th Parliament." *Canadian Journal of Political
Science* 31, no. 3 (September 1998): 435–65. https://doi.org/10.1017
/S0008423900009082.

Trevisan, Matthew. "Belinda Stronach on Switching Parties, Women in Politics
& What Will Happen If the Liberals Win … or Lose." *The Queen's Journal*,
13 January 2006. https://www.queensjournal.ca/belinda-stronach
-on-switching-parties-women-in-politics-and-what-will-happen-if-the
-liberals-win-or-lose/.

Trevor, Robb. "MLA Joe Anglin Splits from Wildrose Party." *Edmonton Sun*,
3 November 2014.

Trickey, Mike. "NDP MP Shows Support for Arafat." *Calgary Herald*, 4 April 2002.

Trimble, Linda, Jane Arscott, and Manon Tremblay, eds. *Stalled: The Representation
of Women in Canadian Government*. UBC Press, 2013. https://doi.org/10.59962
/9780774825221.

Trimble, Linda, and Joanna Everitt. "Belinda Stronach and the Gender Politics of Celebrity." In *Mediating Canadian Politics*, edited by Shannon Sampert and Linda Trimble. Pearson, 2010.

Trottier, Daniel. "Scandal Mining: Political Nobodies and Remediated Visibility." *Media Culture & Society* 40, no. 6 (September 2018): 893–908. https://doi.org /10.1177/0163443717734408.

Truelove, Graeme. *Svend Robinson: A Life in Politics*. New Star Books, 2013.

Trueman, Mary. "TV Missed Switch of MP by Design, Speaker Declares." *Globe and Mail*, 9 March 1979.

Tumilty, Ryan. "Conservatives Fast-Tracked Conversion Therapy Bill to Avoid a Fight They Would Surely Lose." *National Post*, 6 December 2021. https://nationalpost.com/news/politics/conservatives-fast-tracked -conversion-therapy-to-avoid-a-fight-they-would-surely-lose.

– "'It's a Content Studio': Inside the Rule-Bending, Highly-Scripted Strategies to Make a Splash in Question Period." *National Post*, 29 January 2024. https:// nationalpost.com/news/politics/its-a-content-studio-inside-the-rule-bending -highly-scripted-strategies-to-make-a-splash-in-question-period.

Tumilty, Ryan, Raisa Patel, and Alex Ballingall. 2024. "Liberal MP Says He Was Threatened with 'Consequences' for Opposing $250 Cheque Proposal." *Toronto Star*, 27 November 2024. https://www.thestar.com/politics/federal/liberal -mp-says-he-was-threatened-with-consequences-for-opposing-250-cheque -proposal/article_69f3cfa6-acde-11ef-807c-ebe72ea32b06.html.

Tunney, Catharine, and David Cochrane. "LeBlanc Says He'll Meet with Han Dong Soon to Discuss His Future with the Liberal Party." *CBC News*, 7 September 2023. https://www.cbc.ca/news/politics/lebalnc-han-dong -return-1.6959898.

Turchansky, Lorraine. "Alberta Backbencher Quits Tories, Citing Klein Sabotage of Harper Campaign." *Canadian Press*, 29 June 2004.

Turcotte, André, and Éric Grenier. "Pollsters." In *Inside the Campaign: Managing Elections in Canada*, edited by Alex Marland and Thierry Giasson. UBC Press, 2020. https://doi.org/10.59962/9780774864688-010.

Turner, Garth. *Sheeple: Caucus Confidential in Stephen Harper's Ottawa*. Key Porter Books, 2009.

Tutton, Michael. "N.S. Tory Booted over Accessibility of Office, 'Pattern of Behaviour.'" *CTV News*, 24 June 2019. https://atlantic.ctvnews.ca/n-s-tory -booted-over-accessibility-of-office-pattern-of-behaviour-1.4480150.

Underhill, Frank H. "The Development of National Political Parties in Canada." *The Canadian Historical Review* 16, no. 4 (Winter 1935): 367–87. https://doi.org /10.3138/chr-016-04-01.

Van Dyk, Spencer. "Liberal MP Housefather Not Ruling Out Crossing the Floor to the Conservatives." *CTV News*, 20 March 2024. https://www.ctvnews.ca /politics/liberal-mp-housefather-not-ruling-out-crossing-the-floor-to-the -conservatives-1.6815741.

Van Praet, Nicolas. "Liberal MPs Expressing Opposition to Proposed Melford Port in Nova Scotia." *Globe and Mail*, 17 July 2023. https://www .theglobeandmail.com/business/article-liberal-mps-expressing-opposition -to-proposed-melford-port-in-nova.

Van Vugt, Mark, and Claire M. Hart. "Social Identity as Social Glue: The Origins of Group Loyalty." *Journal of Personality and Social Psychology* 86, no. 4 (April 2004): 585–98. https://doi.org/10.1037/0022-3514.86.4.585.

van Zoonen, Liesbet. "Imagining the Fan Democracy." *European Journal of Communication* 19, no. 1 (March 2004): 39–52. https://doi.org/10.1177/0267323104040693.

Vermot-Desroches, Paule. "Jean-Martin Aussant quitte le PQ." *Le Nouvelliste*, 8 June 2011.

Vienneau, David. "Battle for Gun Control May Not Be Finished." *Toronto Star*, 17 June 1995.

Visier. *Boomerang Employees Make a Comeback: A Data-Based Approach to Hiring Top Talent*. Visier Insights Report, 2023. https://www.visier.com/lp/boomerang-employees.

Vomiero, Jessica. "'Ministers Gone Rogue.'" *Global News*, 5 March 2019. https://globalnews.ca/news/5024813/snc-lavalin-wilson-raybould-inexperience.

Wagner, Angelia. *The Candidacy Calculation: Challenges to Running for Elected Office in Canada*. University of Toronto Press, 2025.

– "Motivations for Federal Candidacy." In *Inside the Local Campaign: Constituency Elections in Canada*, edited by Alex Marland and Thierry Giasson. UBC Press, 2022.

– "Tolerating the Trolls? Gendered Perceptions of Online Harassment of Politicians in Canada." *Feminist Media Studies* 22, no. 1 (2022): 32–47. https://doi.org/10.1080/14680777.2020.1749691.

Waldrop, M. Mitchell. "Modeling the Power of Polarization." *PNAS* 118, no. 37 (14 September 2021): 1–5. https://doi.org/10.1073/pnas.2114484118.

Walker, Andy. "PEI's Maverick MLA, Ronnie MacKinley, Calling It Quits." *Winnipeg's Business*, 16 February 2015. https://winnipegsbusiness.troymedia.com/politicslaw/peis-maverick-mla-ronnie-mackinley-calling-quits (article has been removed).

Walker, William. "Liberals Reluctantly Accept New Democrat Defector." *Toronto Star*, 14 January 1987.

– "New Democratic MPP Wants to Join Liberals." *Toronto Star*, 18 December 1986.

Walsh, Marieke. "Conservatives Tell MPs Not to Comment on Alberta Transgender Policies, Prioritize Parental Rights, Internal E-mail Shows." *Globe and Mail*, 1 February 2024. https://www.theglobeandmail.com/politics/article-conservatives-tell-mps-not-to-comment-on-alberta-transgender-policies.

Walsh, Marieke, and Ian Bailey. "Former Green Party MP Jenica Atwin Changes Position on Israel to Align with Liberals." *Globe and Mail*, 14 June 2021. https://www.theglobeandmail.com/politics/article-former-green-party-mp-jenica-atwin-changes-position-on-israel-to-align.

Walsh, Marieke, and Steven Chase. "Rift in Liberal Party Grows as Nearly Two Dozen MPs Call for Ceasefire, PM Acknowledges Divisions." *Globe and Mail*, 20 October 2023. https://www.theglobeandmail.com/politics/article-trudeau-acknowledges-divisions-in-caucus-wont-repeat-canadian-envoys.

Wamble, Julian J., Chryl N. Laird, Corrine M. McConnaughy, and Ismail K. White. "We Are One: The Social Maintenance of Black Democratic Party Loyalty." *Journal of Politics* 84, no. 2 (April 2022): 682–97. https://doi.org/10.1086/716300.

Ward, Ian. "The Early Use of Radio for Political Communication in Australia and Canada: John Henry Austral, Mr. Sage and the Man from Mars." *Australian Journal of Politics and History* 45, no. 3 (September 1999): 311–29. https://doi.org/10.1111/1467-8497.00067.

Ward, Nick. "Independent MHA Perry Trimper Rejoins Liberal Caucus." *CBC News*, 12 September 2022. https://www.cbc.ca/news/canada/newfoundland-labrador/perry-trimper-liberal-party-1.6580018.

Warick, Jason. "Tory MP Trost Questions 'Ironclad' Party Discipline." *Saskatoon StarPhoenix*, 31 January 2012.

Warmington, Joe. "Prime Minister's Staffer Calls People Names but Gets Apology." *Toronto Sun*, 29 January 2024. https://torontosun.com/news/local-news/warmington-prime-ministers-staffer-calls-people-names-but-gets-apology.

Weber, Anthony, Marc André Bodet, François Gélineau, and André Blais. "An Election Too Far: Why Do MPs Leave Politics Before an Election?" *Party Politics* 30, no. 3 (May 2024): 493–504. https://doi.org/10.1177/13540688231159864.

Weber, Terry. "Stronach Deserves Apology, MPs Say." *Globe and Mail*, 18 May 2005. https://www.theglobeandmail.com/news/national/stronach-deserves-apology-mps-say/article1119024.

Wellen, Jackie M., and Matthew Neale. "Deviance, Self-typicality, and Group Cohesion: The Corrosive Effects of the Bad Apples on the Barrell." *Small Group Research* 37, no. 2 (April 2006): 165–86. https://doi.org/10.1177/1046496406286420.

Wells, Paul. *The Longer I'm Prime Minister: Stephen Harper and Canada, 2006–*. Random House Canada, 2013.

– *Right Side Up: The Fall of Paul Martin and the Rise of Stephen Harper's New Conservatism*. McClelland and Stewart, 2006.

Wesley, Jared J., ed. *Big Worlds: Politics and Elections in the Canadian Provinces and Territories*. University of Toronto Press, 2015.

Wesley, Jared J., and Clare Buckley. "Canadian Provincial Party Systems: An Analytical Typology." *American Review of Canadian Studies* 51, no. 2 (2021): 213–36. https://doi.org/10.1080/02722011.2021.1923249.

Wesley, Jared J., and Richard Maksymetz. "Regional Campaign Directors." In *Inside the Local Campaign: Constituency Elections in Canada*, edited by Alex Marland and Thierry Giasson. UBC Press, 2022.

Wesley, Jared J., and Mike Moyes. "Selling Social Democracy: Branding the Political Left in Canada." In *Political Communication in Canada: Meet the Press and Tweet the Rest*, edited by Alex Marland, Thierry Giasson, and Tamara A. Small. UBC Press, 2014. https://doi.org/10.59962/9780774827782-007.

Wesley, Jared J., and Kyle Murray. "To Market or Demarket? Public-Sector Branding of Cannabis in Canada." *Administration & Society* 53, no. 7 (August 2021): 1078–105. https://doi.org/10.1177/0095399721991129.

Wesley, Jared J., and Renze Nauta. "Party Platform Builders." In *Inside the Campaign: Managing Elections in Canada*, edited by Alex Marland and Thierry Giasson. UBC Press, 2020. https://doi.org/10.59962/9780774864688-012.

Wesley, Jared J., and Savannah Ribeiro. "The Public, the Pandemic, and the Public Service: The Case of Alberta." *Canadian Public Administration* 67, no. 1 (March 2024): 24–39. https://doi.org/10.1111/capa.12551.

Wesley, Jared J., Evan Walker, and Hannah Diner. "Polarization in Alberta." Paper presented at the Annual Meeting of the Prairie Political Science Association. Banff, AB. 20 September 2024.

Westall, Stanley. "Ottawa's Ministering Aides." *Globe and Mail*, 13 February 1965.

Wherry, Aaron. "Behind Closed Doors, Liberal MPs Have 'Robust' Discussion about Government's Challenges." *CBC News*, 13 September 2023. https://www.cbc.ca/news/politics/liberal-caucus-trudeau-london-1.6966145.

– "Brent Rathgeber Kills What Used to Be His Bill." *Maclean's*, 27 February 2014. https://macleans.ca/politics/ottawa/brent-rathgeber-kills-what-used-to-be-his-bill.

– "The Last Decent Man in Ottawa: MP Glen Pearson Is a Rarity: A Quiet, Respectful Politician." *Maclean's*, 12 May 2008. https://archive.org/details/Macleans-Magazine-2008-05-12/page/n9/mode/2up.

- "A Liberal Backbencher with an Independent Streak Is Eyeing a New Challenge – Party Leadership." *CBC News*, 24 February 2023. https://www.cbc.ca/news/politics/erskine-smith-ontario-liberal-analysis-wherry-1.6756380.
- "Liberal MP Doug Eyolfson Breaks Ranks with Party on Air Canada Bill." *CBC News*, 18 April 2016. https://www.cbc.ca/news/politics/wherry-eyolfson-vote-1.3556033.
- "The Liberals and NDP Are Learning to Work Together. Is That a Model for the Future?" *CBC News*, 9 April 2023. https://www.cbc.ca/news/politics/liberal-ndp-agreement-wherry-analysis-1.6804401.
- "What Happens When Liberal Backbenchers Rise Up: Aaron Wherry." *CBC News*, 11 March 2017. https://www.cbc.ca/news/politics/wherry-liberals-backbenchers-1.4017210.
Whitaker, Reg. *The Government Party: Organizing and Financing the Liberal Party of Canada 1930–58*. University of Toronto Press, 1967.
- "Virtual Political Parties and the Decline of Democracy." *Policy Options*, 1 June 2001. https://policyoptions.irpp.org/magazines/political-dissent/virtual-political-parties-and-the-decline-of-democracy/.
White, Erik. "Sudbury Byelection Trial: New Taped Conversation Details Liberal in-fighting." *CBC News*, 7 September 2017. https://www.cbc.ca/news/canada/sudbury/sudbury-byelection-bribery-trial-day-1-1.4278938.
White, Graham. *Cabinets and First Ministers*. UBC Press, 2005.
- "Traditional Aboriginal Values in a Westminster Parliament: The Legislative Assembly of Nunavut." *The Journal of Legislative Studies* 12, no. 1 (2006): 8–31. https://doi.org/10.1080/13572330500483930a.
Whyte, Kenneth. "The Face That Sank a Thousand Tories." *Saturday Night*, February 1994.
Whyte, Tanya. "Oh, oh! Modelling Parliamentary Interruptions in Canada, 1926–2015." Paper presented at the Canadian Political Science Association annual conference, Ryerson University, Toronto. 30 May–1 June 2017.
Wilbur, J.R.H. "H.H. Stevens and R.B. Bennett, 1930-34." *Canadian Historical Review* 43, no. 1 (March 1962): 1–16.
Wilson, Barry K. *Benedict Arnold: A Traitor in Our Midst*. McGill-Queen's University Press, 2001. https://doi.org/10.1515/9780773568976.
Wilson, R. Paul. "The Inter-executive Activity of Ministerial Policy Advisors in the Government of Canada." In *How Ottawa Spends 2016–2017: The Trudeau Liberals in Power*, edited by G. Bruce Doern and Christopher Stoney. Carleton University, 2016.
- "Minister's Caucus Advisory Committees under the Harper Government." *Canadian Public Administration* 58, no. 2 (June 2015): 227–48. https://doi.org/10.1111/capa.12112.
Wilson-Raybould, Jody. *Indian in the Cabinet: Speaking Truth to Power*. HarperCollins, 2021.
- "Submission to the House of Commons Standing Committee on Justice and Human Rights." *House of Commons*, 26 March 2019.
Wingrove, Josh. "Edmonton MP Rejoins Tories, Mulls Run for Mayor After Winning Breathalyzer Case." *Globe and Mail*, 7 June 2013. https://www.theglobeandmail.com/news/politics/edmonton-mp-mulls-run-for-mayor-after-winning-breathalyzer-case/article12414467.
- "'It's Gone Too Far': Conservative MP on Harper's Backbench Control." *Globe and Mail*, 12 April 2013. https://www.theglobeandmail.com/news/politics/globe-politics-insider/its-gone-too-far-conservative-mp-on-harpers-backbench-control/article11150792.

Wiseman, Nelson. "Ideological Competition in the Canadian Party System." In *Canadian Parties in Transition*, 4th ed., edited by A. Brian Tanguay and Alain-G. Gagnon. University of Toronto Press, 2017.

– *Partisan Odysseys: Canada's Political Parties*. University of Toronto Press, 2020. https://doi.org/10.3138/9781487536947.

Wolinetz, Steven B. "Beyond the Catch-all Party: Approaches to the Study of Parties and Party Organization in Contemporary Democracies." In *The Future of Political Parties*, edited by Juan Linz, Jose Ramon Montero, and Richard Gunther. Oxford University Press, 2002. https://doi.org/10.1093/0199246742.003.0006.

Woo, Andrea. "B.C. Deputy Green Leader Removed over Social Media 'Like.'" *Globe and Mail*, 9 November 2023. https://www.theglobeandmail.com/canada/article-bc-deputy-green-leader-removed-over-social-media-like.

Wood, James. "Wall to Address Resignation of LeClerc from Sask. Party Today." *Moose Jaw Times Herald*, 19 April 2010.

Wood, Lisa. "Brands and Brand Equity: Definition and Management." *Management Decision* 38, no. 9 (2000): 662–9. https://doi.org/10.1108/00251740010379100.

Woodbury, Richard. "Liberals Allege Former MLA who Switched to PCs Committed Privacy Breach." *CBC News*, 24 October 2024. https://www.cbc.ca/news/canada/nova-scotia/liberals-allege-former-mla-who-switched-to-pcs-committed-privacy-breach-1.7362033.

Woods, Margaret A. "Legislative Reports: Saskatchewan." *Canadian Parliamentary Review* 22, no. 4 (Winter 1999): 31–2.

Woolf, Marie. "Conservative MPs Furious after E-mails Show Federal Officials Worked on Ways Not to Answer Their Questions." *Globe and Mail*, 20 June 2023. https://www.theglobeandmail.com/politics/article-opposition-mps-questions-public-servants.

– "Liberal MP Censured for Travelling Outside of Canada Despite Advisory." *Global News*, 22 December 2021. https://globalnews.ca/news/8469783/yves-robillard-non-essential-travel.

Wright, Robert. "Trudeaumania, How It Began." *Toronto Star*, 17 September 2016.

Wright, Theresa. "Bush Dumville Breaks His Silence on Decision to Leave the Liberal Caucus." *The Guardian*, 7 February 2018. https://www.saltwire.com/prince-edward-island/news/exclusive-bush-dumville-breaks-his-silence-on-decision-to-leave-the-liberal-caucus-183949.

– "MLA Bush Dumville Resigns from Liberal Caucus to Sit as Independent." *The Guardian*, 31 January 2018. https://www.saltwire.com/prince-edward-island/news/update-mla-bush-dumville-resigns-from-liberal-caucus-to-sit-as-independent-182184.

– "Olive Crane Kicked Out of PC Caucus." *The Guardian*, 4 October 2013.

Wright Allen, Samantha. "Trudeau PMO Tightening Control over Ministerial Staffing." *The Hill Times*, 25 October 2017, 1.

Wyatt, Mark. "Second-Most Lopsided Victory in Provincial History." *Saskatoon StarPhoenix*, 27 October 1998.

– "Goohsen on His Own While Charges Pending." *Saskatoon StarPhoenix*, 13 August 1997.

Yaffe, Barbara. "Garfield Warren: Labrador's New Cabinet Minister." *The Sunday Express*, 17 March 1988.

Yakabuski, Konrad. "A Quebec Liberal MP Learns the Hard Way to Stand Up for French." *Globe and Mail*, 20 November 2020. https://www.theglobeandmail.com/opinion/article-a-quebec-liberal-mp-learns-the-hard-way-to-stand-up-for-french.

Yates, Stéphanie. "National-Local Messaging." In *Inside the Local Campaign: Constituency Elections in Canada,* edited by Alex Marland and Thierry Giasson. UBC Press, 2022.

York, Geoffrey. "MLA Quits Tories in Manitoba, Says Filmon Is Using Iron Fist." *Globe and Mail,* 9 September 1988.

Yoshinaka, Antoine. *Crossing the Aisle: Party Switching by U.S. Legislators in the Postwar Era.* Cambridge University Press, 2016. https://doi.org/10.1017/CBO9781316336281.

Young, Huguette. "Deux autres defections au PC." *L'Acadie Nouvelle,* 13 September 2000.

Young, Lisa. "Party, State and Political Competition in Canada: The Cartel Model Reconsidered." *Canadian Journal of Political Science* 31, no. 2 (June 1998): 339–58. https://doi.org/10.1017/S000842390001982X.

Young, Lisa, and William Cross. "Incentives to Membership in Canadian Political Parties." *Political Research Quarterly* 55, no. 3 (September 2002): 547–69. https://doi.org/10.1177/106591290205500303.

Young, Scott. "The System and Givens' Struggle for a Place in the Parliamentary Sun." *Globe and Mail,* 9 June 1969.

Yourk, Darren. "Herron to run for Liberals." *Globe and Mail,* 6 February 2004. https://www.theglobeandmail.com/news/national/herron-to-run-for-liberals/article1127201.

Zaborsky, Dorothy. "Feminist Politics: The Feminist Party of Canada." *Women's Studies International Forum* 10, no. 6 (1987): 613–21. https://doi.org/10.1016/0277-5395(87)90075-6.

Zare, Mortaza. "Deviance as Inauthenticity: An Ontological Perspective." *Philosophy of Management* 15, no. 2 (June 2016): 151–9. https://doi.org/10.1007/s40926-016-0034-x.

Zdaniuk, Bozena, and John M. Levine. "Group Loyalty: Impact of Members' Identification and Contributions." *Journal of Experimental Social Psychology* 37, no. 6 (November 2001): 502–9. https://doi.org/10.1006/jesp.2000.1474.

Zimonjic, Peter. "Embassy Takes down AI-Generated Canada Day Social Media Post." *CBC News,* 2 July 2024. https://www.cbc.ca/news/politics/washington-social-media-post-ai-generated-1.7252048.

Zussman, Richard. "MLA Andrew Weaver Quitting Green Caucus Due to Family Health Issues." *Global News,* 15 January 2020. https://globalnews.ca/news/6413516/mla-andrew-weaver-quitting-green-caucus-due-to-family-health-issues.

Zytaruk, Tom. *Like a Rock: The Chuck Cadman Story.* Harbour, 2008.

Index